CHURCH HISTORY

VOLUME ONE

From Christ to the Pre-Reformation

textbook*plus*⁺

Equipping Instructors and Students with
FREE RESOURCES for Core Zondervan Textbooks

Available Resources for Church History, Volume One

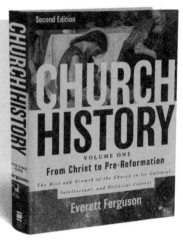

Instructor Resources

- Instructor's manual
- Presentation slides
- Chapter quizzes
- Midterm and final exams
- Sample syllabus
- Image/map library

Student Resources

- Quizzes
- Flashcards
- Exam study guides

*How To Access Resources

- Go to www.TextbookPlus.Zondervan.com
- Click "Register Now" button and complete registration process
- Find books using search field or "Browse Our Textbooks" feature
- Click "Instructor Resources" or "Student Resources" tab once you get to book page to access resources

www.TextbookPlus.Zondervan.com

Second Edition

CHURCH HISTORY

VOLUME ONE

From Christ to the Pre-Reformation

*The Rise and Growth of the Church
in Its Cultural, Intellectual, and Political Context*

Everett Ferguson

 ZONDERVAN®

We want to hear from you. Please send your comments about this
book to us in care of zreview@zondervan.com. Thank you.

ZONDERVAN

Church History, Volume One: From Christ to the Pre-Reformation

Copyright © 2005, 2013 by Everett Ferguson

This title is also available as a Zondervan ebook.
Visit www.zondervan.com/ebooks.

Requests for information should be addressed to:

Zondervan, *Grand Rapids, Michigan 49530*

Library of Congress Cataloging-in-Publication Data

Ferguson, Everett, 1933 –
    Church history : the rise and growth of the church in its cultural, intellectual, and political
    context / Everett Ferguson. — 2 [edition].
        volumes cm
        ISBN 978-0-310-51656-9 (v.1: hardcover) 1. Church history — Textbooks.   I. Title.
    BR145.3.F47 2013
    270 — dc23   2013017556

Cover design: Tobias' Outerwear for Books
Cover photos: Superstock; Steven Weinberg/Getty Images
Interior design: Tracey Walker
Interior composition: Greg Johnson/Textbook Perfect

Printed in the United States of America

13 14 15 16 17 18 19 20 /DCI/ 22 21 20 19 18 17 16 15 14 13 12 11 10 9 8 7 6 5 4 3 2 1

To the students who will use this textbook.
May they enter into the adventure of the life of the church
as they extend its history into the days ahead.

About the Author

Everett Ferguson (PhD. Harvard) is professor emeritus of Bible and distinguished scholar-in-residence at Abilene Christian University in Abilene, Texas, where he taught church history and Greek. He is the author of numerous works, including *Backgrounds of Early Christianity, Early Christians Speak, Inheriting Wisdom: Readings for Today from Ancient Christian Writers,* and *Baptism in the Early Church: History, Theology, and Liturgy in the First Five Centuries*, and is the editor of the two-volume *Encyclopedia of Early Christianity.*

Contents in Brief

Contents

Maps, Charts, and Illustrations

ILLUSTRATIONS

Preface

PERSPECTIVES ON CHURCH HISTORY

Church history is the study of the history of God's people in Christ, a theological claim, or, speaking more neutrally, of those who have wanted to be God's people in Christ. It is a mixed people, and the story is a mixed story. This comes as no surprise, of course. Just as the biblical record of the people of God is the story of a mixed people with great acts of faith and great failures in sin and unfaithfulness, so is the history of the people who have made up the church through the ages.

The contemporary student may find relative degrees of faithfulness and unfaithfulness in all areas of the church's life: doctrine, public worship, prayer and devotion, evangelism and missions, quality of fellowship and caring, and Christian living (morality and benevolence).

The study of church history may help one to pass judgment on what is perceived to be unfaithfulness in any area with sympathy and humility and a resolution to learn from the mistakes of the past; and it may teach one to rejoice in expressions of faithfulness with gratitude and a desire to imitate.

History necessarily entails some attention to names, external events, and the sequence of development, but the student should look beyond these things to the religious life of the people involved and grasp the perspective that this is the story of people.

Those who profess to dislike history may as well profess to dislike people. What they really mean is that they dislike the externals, the framework of information. Such details are necessary to the telling of the story, but the real story itself is the people who were involved. And they were a very human people, in spite of the theological affirmation of being a redeemed people.

The author writes from the perspective that church history is the story of the greatest community the world has known and the greatest movement in world history. It is a human story of a divinely called people who wanted to live by a divine revelation. These are people who have struggled with the meaning of the greatest event in history, the coming of the Son of God.

As a participant in the heritage of Western church history, the author necessarily gives more attention to the history of Christianity in the West. But as committed to the wholeness of Christian history, I have tried to give adequate attention to other expressions of Christianity. So, although the primary narrative thread for the period covered will be western Europe, especially the British Isles, the global and ecumenical environment of the twenty-first century requires coverage of Africa, eastern Europe, and Asia.

Nothing is more relevant for understanding the present than the history of the past experiences of those who sought to follow Jesus Christ. Out of the conviction that the proper way to approach contemporary problems is historically, the author of this textbook hopes to bring a historical consciousness to its readers.

> I ask therefore that one think rather of the intention of the writer than of his work, of the sense of the words rather than the rude speech, of truth rather than beauty, of the exercise of the affections rather than the erudition of the intellect.
>
> Bonaventura, *The Mind's Road to God*, Prologue 5.1

The Setting for the Story's Beginning

Three concentric circles of influence circumscribed the world in which early Christianity began. From the outside moving in, these influences were the Roman, the Greek, and the Jewish. The pattern of growth in the early church was the reverse, from the Jewish, to the Greek, to the Roman worlds. Unlike the mathematical image, however, these worlds were not sharply differentiated from each other, and the boundaries were quite porous.

Nevertheless, the classification of influences is helpful in grasping the environment in which the early church began. Moreover, these influences remained formative for much of subsequent Christian history.

I. THE ROMAN WORLD

Luke sets the story of Jesus and the early church firmly within Roman history, noting Jesus' birth under the emperor Augustus, his ministry under Tiberius, and mentioning the Roman governors and other officials with whom Jesus and later Paul had encounters (Luke 2:1–2; 3:1; Acts 13:7; 18:12; 24:27). Rome provided the larger governmental, military, and legal context of early Christianity.

At the birth of Jesus, Rome had recently completed the transition from the Republic to the imperial Principate under Augustus (27 BC–AD 14). Not long before that, the Roman general Pompey had conquered Palestine in 63 BC, and thereafter Rome ruled the Jewish homeland, alternating various administrative arrangements through which it exercised its will: legates based in Syria; client kings like Herod the Great, during whose rule Jesus was born; and governors like Pontius Pilate, under whom Jesus was crucified.

Emperor Augustus, portrayed as a god (Archaeological Museum, Thessalonica, Greece).

The organization of the empire seems to have provided a pattern for the eventual development of the church's hierarchy, and procedures in the senate at Rome and at city councils influenced the conduct of church synods.

The army—the legions made up of Roman citizens and the auxiliaries composed of native peoples—was a constant presence on the frontiers and in provinces where disturbances were frequent. Among the peacetime duties of soldiers were the building of roads and securing safety of travel; Christian travelers, whether for business or religious purposes, used these roads and carried the Christian message with them.

Roman law is one of Rome's enduring legacies to the Western world. When charges were brought against Christians, Roman magistrates and Roman law decided their cases. The imperial cult (the giving of divine honors to the emperor and his family), often allied with the local civic cults, provided an overarching religious cement to political unity and loyalty. The imperial court ceremonials, themselves borrowed from earlier eastern monarchs, continued under later Christian emperors.

Latin not only was the official language of government, but also became the common language in the western provinces; from the second century and after, Christianity in those regions expressed its message in Latin.

Emperor Tiberius, from Paestum (Archaeological Museum, Madrid).

II. THE GREEK WORLD

Greek influences were predominant in language, education, literature, and philosophy at the beginning of Christianity. For the early disciples, the Greek language and culture were more significant than the Latin, and they remained so for the eastern Mediterranean area under the Byzantine empire (even though Latin remained its official language of government for centuries). Since the conquests of Alexander the Great in the fourth century BC, the Greek language, coinage, culture, philosophy, and religion had permeated the regions from Greece around the eastern coast of the Mediterranean to Libya. Education was based on Homer and the Greek classics.

The Greek cultural influences were felt in Rome and regions to the west, even among those who did not speak Greek. Greek was the language of the church in Rome, it seems, until the middle of the third century. Christian writers employed the Greek language exclusively, it appears, until the late second century, when some works in Latin and Syriac are known. Greek (and then Latin) rhetoric provided the standards for how letters were written, speeches constructed, and arguments conducted.

The great philosophical systems of Plato and Aristotle had been largely replaced in the Hellenistic age by philosophies more directed to practical and moral interests, principally Stoicism and Epicureanism, but interest in Aristotle and especially Plato revived in the early Christian centuries. As Christian theology developed from the affirmations of the gospel and the early moral and doctrinal instruction, Greek philosophy provided the vocabulary, ethical assumptions, thought world, and intellectual options with which Christian thinkers worked.

Unidentified Greek philosopher of the second century AD (Delphi Museum, Greece).

The traditional civic cults continued to be important centers of local pride, and traditional religious attitudes and practices continued to be nourished by the educational curriculum that centered on Homer. Initiations into mystery religions, visits to oracles and healing shrines, acceptance of fate, belief in astrology, and the practice of magic gained new strength during the first two centuries of the Christian era.

The social lives of people were guided by a combination of Roman legal and Greek societal norms. Thus in matters as varied as customs at dinner parties, at weddings, and at funerals, Christians lived within the framework of existing ways of doing things. Laws of marriage and of inheritance and established distinctions of social classes provided the framework for family life and social relations.

Pre-existing mentalities shaped religious attitudes. Funerary customs continued to be observed by Christians, although now within a new frame of reference. Many of the features of Greco-Roman religion became incorporated into Christianity as the gospel spread into the pagan population.

III. THE JEWISH WORLD

Jesus was born of Jewish parents, "the son of David, the son of Abraham" (Matthew 1:1), and all his first disciples were Jewish. Jesus was born in Bethlehem and grew up in Nazareth; most of his ministry was in Galilee, and he was crucified in Jerusalem—all places in modern Israel and the adjoining Palestinian territories.

This was a Jewish world that, like the rest of the Near East, had felt the influence of Hellenistic culture and, by the first century, an overlay of Roman rule. A large Jewish population remained in Mesopotamia from the time of the Babylonian captivity (sixth century BC), and many Jews lived in the western Diaspora where Greek (and farther west, Roman) cultural influences were even stronger than in the homeland.

After the conquests of Alexander the Great, Jews in Palestine had lived under the rule of the Ptolemies (Egypt) and then the Seleucids (Syria). A religious and nationalistic revolt initially led by Judas Maccabee successfully brought a century of independence under the Hasmonean dynasty (164–163 BC) that continued to inspire Jewish religious and political aspirations after the Jewish homeland came under Roman oversight.

Three unsuccessful revolts—in AD 66–73 put down by Vespasian and Titus, resulting in the destruction of the temple; in 115–17 in the Diaspora communities of northeast Africa and Cyprus; and in 132–35, the Bar Kokhba revolt, under Hadrian—ended Jewish prospects of an independent homeland until modern times. By the end of these revolts, the early Christian movement was well under way.

Synagogue in Herod the Great's fortress of Herodion.

During Jesus' ministry in Galilee his principal religious opposition came from the Pharisees over the interpretation of the Law of Moses applied to matters of daily life. At Jerusalem the opposition came from the Sadducees, the leading priests and ruling aristocrats who controlled the temple and matters related to it. The Dead Sea Scrolls have fueled speculation that possibly Jesus and, with more plausibility, John the Baptist had contact with the Essenes or a group like them at Qumran.

Early Christian preaching, as recorded in Acts, typically began in the Jewish synagogues of the Diaspora and drew a following from a small number of Jews and a larger number of Gentiles who were either affiliated with the Jewish community or attracted to it in varying degrees.

Judaism, therefore, provided the immediate religious context for Christianity. The Jewish Scriptures were the Bible of the early church, especially in their Greek translation, the Septuagint or Old Greek, a translation that had its beginning in the third century BC.

The God of the Jews was the God of the early Christians, and the central affirmations of the early church—Jesus as the Messiah, his resurrection from the dead, a new age of the forgiveness of sins, and the gift of the Holy Spirit—took their meaning from Jewish hopes, based on the interpretation of the scriptural Prophets and stimulated by the later apocalyptic literature of the Jews.

The story of early Christianity is the story of how a religious movement that began as a "sect" within Judaism successfully made the transition to the larger Greco-Roman world and eventually in the fourth century gained recognition as the religion of the Roman Empire.

Could anything be more improbable than that a religion following a man born of an unwed mother among a widely despised people in an out-of-the-way part of the world—a man then crucified by the ruling authorities on a charge of treason—should become the official religion of the Roman world, the formative influence on Western civilization, and a significant influence in other parts of the world?

That is the story to be told in the following pages.

FOR FURTHER STUDY

Ferguson, Everett. *Backgrounds of Early Christianity*. 3rd ed. Grand Rapids: Eerdmans, 2003.

Green, Joel B., and Lee Martin McDonald. *The World of the New Testament: Cultural, Social, and Historical Contexts*. Grand Rapids: Baker, 2013.

2

Jesus and the Beginnings of the Church

I. THE MINISTRY OF JESUS

Jesus was born, according to the modern calendar, about 4 BC or earlier, while Herod the Great, by the will of Rome, was the king of Judea. After an apparently normal Jewish youth that was largely uneventful, he reached a turning point in his life, when, "about thirty years old" (Luke 3:23), he was baptized by John the Baptist in the Jordan River. Accompanying his baptism Jesus received a divine affirmation of his unique relationship to God as his much-loved Son.

Soon after, John was imprisoned and Jesus took up John's preaching, announcing that "The kingdom of God has come near. Repent and believe the good news!" (Mark 1:15). There ensued a ministry of preaching, teaching, and healing; and Jesus gathered a close circle of twelve disciples, who spent their time with him and on occasion were sent out in extension of his ministry. Jesus' miracles of healing and his expelling of demons made people aware of a powerful presence among them. His distinctive style of teaching—announcing the meaning of God's rule and will through intriguing parables based on his own immediate authority, not through the reciting of past interpretations—drew attention to an impressive personality that stirred various reactions.

"Love your enemies, do good to those who hate you, bless those who curse you, pray for those who mistreat you" (Luke 6:27–28).

Jesus' ministry gathered a popular following and aroused hopes that God's mighty intervention in the history of his people was imminent, hopes that many persons understood in terms of throwing off Roman rule and bringing an end to economic and political oppression.

One of the reactions to Jesus was the confession, first voiced by the leader of the Twelve, Peter, that "You are the Messiah" (Mark 8:29), the eagerly awaited "anointed of the Lord" who would bring deliverance to the Jewish people. It was a confession welcomed by many, doubted by others, and feared by still others in positions of power. Jesus' popularity provoked jealousy and opposition from some Pharisees and a range of sentiments from uneasiness to profound disturbance among the political leaders.

Implicit in the title "Messiah" was a claim to kingship. On this charge the Jewish leaders in Jerusalem secured the sentence of death against Jesus from the Roman governor Pilate, who ordered his crucifixion, a punishment applied to the worst criminals and those considered politically dangerous. After his crucifixion, the hopes of Jesus' disciples, even those closest to him, were crushed.

Then the unexpected happened. When women went to the tomb on Sunday morning to perform the burial anointing that the rapid falling of the Sabbath day had prevented after his death, they found the tomb empty. An angel reported: "He is not here; he is risen, just as he said" (Matthew 28:6). These women, and then other disciples, reported appearances of Jesus. The small company of the disciples, dispersed and dispirited, had their disappointments transformed into joy.

The resurrection was God's vindication of Jesus. It confirmed that his death was not simply the death of another good man but had atoning significance. Those two affirmations—the atoning death of Jesus and his resurrection from the dead (1 Corinthians 15:3–5)—became the pillars of the Christian faith.

The resurrected Jesus commissioned his disciples to wait in Jerusalem for the coming of the Holy Spirit, and then to proclaim his message to all.

"For what I received I passed on to you as of first importance: that Christ died for our sins according to the Scriptures, that he was buried, that he was raised on the third day according to the Scriptures" (1 Corinthians 15:3–4).

Mosaic of Christ teaching with his apostles, in the chapel of San Aquilino in the basilica of San Lorenzo, Milan, Italy (late fourth century).

II. THE CHURCH IN JERUSALEM AND JAMES

The appearances of the resurrected Jesus brought the disciples together again and confirmed their faith in him. The experience of the coming of the Holy Spirit, recorded in Acts 2, launched the church as a distinct entity on a mission of proclaiming Jesus as "both Lord and Messiah" (Acts 2:36).

There was initially no radical break with Jewish institutions. The early Jerusalem church frequented the temple and observed Jewish customs. It constituted a "synagogue" with some distinctive rites and beliefs, but there were other such groups in the broad spectrum of Judaism.

Core Jewish beliefs remained at the basis of the faith of the early disciples: the one God who had revealed himself in the Hebrew Scriptures, this God as the creator and sustainer of the universe, a chosen people called into covenant relationship with God, and a hope for end-time blessings.

To those core beliefs there was now added the conviction that the Jesus who had been rejected by the Jewish leadership and crucified by the Roman authorities was the promised deliverer through whom the end-time blessings were beginning to be realized, notably the forgiveness of sins and gift of the Holy Spirit.

This new conviction—guaranteed to the disciples by their faith in Jesus' resurrection from the dead—along with the rapid growth of the new community, drawing members from those who had earlier followed Jesus and from those impressed with the lifestyle and wonders manifest in his movement, soon brought the disciples into conflict with the Jerusalem authorities.

The church early drew adherents from strict Law-observant Jews, from faithful Jews who were not so strict in keeping the Law, from Gentile proselytes, and from those more Hellenized in their attitudes. Internal tension soon manifested itself between those designated by the culturally descriptive terms Hebrews (Hebraic Jews) and Hellenists (Grecian Jews).

Broadly speaking, we may identify three groups in the Jerusalem church: the followers of Jesus from his Galilaean ministry, led by Peter and the Twelve; Judaean converts, who came to look for leadership to James, brother of Jesus and also known as "James the Just"; and those from the Greek Diaspora and others in Jerusalem sympathetic to them, of whom Stephen became the spokesman.

These early disciples represented three different attitudes toward the Law, attitudes that did not exactly correspond to the three groupings: interpret the Law broadly in terms of its main emphases (a view that was congenial to the later use of typology), keep all the Law (the converted Pharisees), and preference for the tabernacle in the wilderness and the universalist strain in the Old Testament in opposition to the temple (represented by Stephen).

All three views contributed something to Paul's more sophisticated interpretation of the Law—employing typology, taking the Law seriously but not always literally, and developing the universalism implicit in some of the Prophets.

With the scattering of the Hellenists following the execution of Stephen and then the killing of the apostle James, brother of John, and the imprisonment of Peter by king Herod Agrippa I, increasingly James, brother of Jesus, came to prominent leadership in the Jerusalem church. His rise to prominence would have been quite unexpected during Jesus' ministry, but an appearance of the resurrected Jesus changed him from disbelief to devoted advocate. His family ties with Jesus and his acceptance of him as Lord gave James a personal authority.

Along with the elders, James provided leadership when the Twelve moved to other fields of activity. This arrangement provided a model for the second-century church's organization of a bishop assisted by elders in each city. The one document in the New Testament ascribed to James, the letter bearing his name, shows the influence of the practical wisdom literature of Judaism as refracted through the teachings of Jesus.

James's execution by Jewish leaders in AD 62, of which there are differing accounts in the Jewish historian Josephus, in Hegesippus (preserved by the church historian Eusebius), and the *Second Apocalypse of James* (from the Nag Hammadi library), left the most conservative Jewish Christians without a respected and moderate leader. Jewish Christianity continued to look back to him as their ideal and representative.

The conversion of Saul of Tarsus, a promising rabbinic student in Jerusalem, brought a dynamic new impulse into the Christian movement. His conversion carried with it a commission from the risen Jesus to be an apostle to the nations. He reached an agreement with Peter and the leaders in Jerusalem that his call to go to the Gentiles corresponded to Peter's mission to the circumcised (Galatians 2:7–9). An opening had already been made to the Gentiles by the Hellenists scattered from Jerusalem (Acts 11:20) and sanctioned by the experience of Peter in Caesarea (Acts 10–11).

The most significant controversy in the early church concerned the terms of acceptance of Gentiles into the Christian community: Must they come as full proselytes, receiving circumcision and an obligation to follow the Law, or was faith in Jesus and baptism sufficient to bring them under the covenant? Paul became the protagonist for a Law-free gospel for the Gentiles; some elements in the Jerusalem church insisted

> "Religion that God our Father accepts as pure and faultless is this: to look after orphans and widows in their distress and to keep oneself from being polluted by the world" (James 1:27).

on the necessity of circumcision; Peter and James, each from their own perspectives, tried to mediate (Acts 15).

The departure from Jerusalem of other elements left the more religiously and culturally conservative Jews as the predominant element in the Jerusalem church. The Hellenizers found a center in Antioch of Syria.

III. THE CHURCH IN ANTIOCH

The church began in Antioch when believers from Jerusalem were scattered because of the persecution arising from the preaching of Stephen. These more Hellenized Christians brought the message of Jesus to Greeks, so that it was in Antioch that the new name "Christians" (Acts 11:26) came into use to designate this new people that included both Jews and Gentiles and was beginning to be distinguished as being neither.

The dropping of the requirement of circumcision did not resolve, indeed intensified, the question of table fellowship between Jewish and Gentile believers. The question came to a head at Antioch, where Paul's insistence on not binding Jewish food laws on Gentile believers, in contrast to Peter and Barnabas's willingness to compromise (Galatians 2:11–14), made that city the center from which the Gentile mission of the church spread.

Under the initiative of the Spirit, Paul and Barnabas went forth from Antioch on journeys to spread the gospel of Jesus. Their mission took them to the synagogues of Diaspora Jews in the Greek cities of Cyprus and Asia Minor, preaching first to Jews and then to Gentile adherents of Judaism who were associated in varying ways with the synagogues.

Although Paul continued to look to Jerusalem as the mother church, he found in Antioch a more congenial base of operations for his subsequent missionary travels.

IV. PAUL

Paul has sometimes been called the "second founder" of Christianity, a title of which he would not have approved. He looms large in the story of early Christianity because of the prominence Luke gives him in the Acts of the Apostles and the number of his letters in the canon of the New Testament. Paul was spiritually a Jew, legally a Roman, and

Christ as the Good Shepherd, the most popular image of Jesus in the earliest Christian art, from the Catacomb of San Callisto, Rome (third century?).

intellectually a Greek—three trump cards for a missionary in the first century.

Paul was the apostle to the Gentiles par excellence, so much so that the church became predominantly Gentile by the end of the first century. Paul's formative influence on the churches he founded, and on those begun or nurtured by his associates, gave him an undeniable significance in early church history, even though the place of the Twelve as the original witnesses to Jesus' life and ministry was not forgotten.

Paul understood his apostolic calling in a missionary sense and the extent of his travels is truly astounding. He carried the gospel of Jesus across Asia Minor, through Greece, and eventually—although as a prisoner—to Rome itself. Later reports said he fulfilled his intention to go to Spain, thus traversing the breadth of the Mediterranean Sea.

In his travels, Paul first approached Jews in their synagogues and then worked among Gentile sympathizers who were contacted through the synagogues. Because Paul's gospel did not require Gentiles to observe the Law of Moses, these believers soon found it impossible to remain within the established Jewish communities, so Paul formed them into new communities with their own characteristics. Seldom working alone, Paul took associates with him on his travels, some of whom he left to continue work with the new believers. Through them and other messengers and by letter he maintained contact with the Christian communities.

> "For we maintain that a person is justified by faith apart from the works of the law" (Paul, Romans 3:28).

Paul's championing of his mission to the Gentiles involved him as a key participant in the major issue in the church of his time—defining the terms of acceptance of Gentiles into the Christian Israel. Paul's literary contributions to that struggle are principally his letters to the churches of Galatia, where Judaizers (whether local or from the outside) insisted on Gentile acceptance of circumcision, and to the church in Rome, where Paul sought to unify its Christian groups in acceptance of his program of mission work.

The argument of the Judaizers in Galatia, as of the conservative Jewish Christians in Jerusalem, was that in order to enter into the covenant promises of God one must be incorporated into the people of Abraham and receive with him the covenant sign of circumcision.

Paul's reply was that the basis of Abraham's acceptance by God was his faith ("Abram believed the LORD, and he credited it to him as righteousness," Genesis 15:6) before he received the seal of circumcision. Therefore, Paul argued, those who share the same faith as Abraham

A modern Greek painting of the apostle Paul.

Jesus and the Beginnings of the Church

Peter being persuaded by the disciples to leave Rome, met Jesus, who was coming into the city. He asked him, "Lord, where are you going (*quo vadis*)?" On the reply, "To Rome, to be crucified again," a chastened Peter returned to the city to face his own death (*Acts of Peter* 35).

receive righteousness in the same way and become the nations blessed in him without the necessity of the sign of circumcision.

Paul's pastoral sensitivity and ability to draw on both Hebrew Scriptures and Greek moral philosophy in the instruction of his converts are seen in his letters, especially to the Greek churches in Thessalonica, Corinth, and Philippi. His letters were circulated among the Christian congregations and became the basis of guidance for a distinctive Christian lifestyle.

Extra-canonical sources relate Paul's execution by beheading in Rome under the emperor Nero in the mid-sixties. His death in Rome linked him in the church's memory with Peter—the common experience of the martyrdom of the apostle to the uncircumcision and the apostle to the circumcision in the same city served as a symbol of the unity of the faith.

V. THE CHURCH IN ROME AND PETER

Visitors from Rome, both Jews and proselytes, are reported to have been present at Jerusalem on the first Pentecost after the resurrection of Jesus (Acts 2:10), and some of them may have carried the faith in Jesus back to Rome.

Whatever the origins, there was already a large number of Christians, composed of both Jews and Gentiles, in Rome when Paul wrote his major letter to the Romans in the mid-to-late fifties. Drawn from a cosmopolitan background, the church was Greek-speaking.

A later tradition reported by Eusebius assigned Peter a twenty-five-year episcopate in Rome, which would put his arrival there in the early forties. The silence of both Acts and Romans argues that Peter's arrival in Rome must be placed later than that.

It is impossible to trace Peter's journeys after his departure from Jerusalem, but his presence in Antioch is attested by Paul, a ministry in parts of Asia Minor is implied by 1 Peter, and the presence of a "Peter party" in Corinth suggests his activity there at some point.

Second-century sources offer strong evidence for the presence of both Paul and Peter in Rome and their martyrdom there, and the reference to the church in "Babylon" in 1 Peter 5:13 is probably to be taken as a veiled reference to Rome as the place from which this Petrine letter was written.

Clement of Rome (ca. 96) and Ignatius of Antioch (ca. 116), writing to Rome, associated both Peter and Paul with the church in Rome, and Clement implied their martyrdoms there. Dionysius of Corinth (ca. 170) is the earliest explicit declaration of Peter's martyrdom in Rome, but his testimony is weakened somewhat by the erroneous declaration, if pressed too strictly, that Peter and Paul "were martyred at the same time."

Not long after, the *Acts of Peter* relates an eventful ministry of Peter in Rome and concludes with the story of Peter being crucified head downward at his request (a manner of death referred to also by Origen).

Gaius of Rome, about 200, could point to the "trophies [or memorials] of the apostles," marking the sites of their martyrdoms—of Paul on the Ostian Way (the site of the church of St. Paul's Outside the Walls) and of Peter on the Vatican (which memorial has been found, beneath the high altar, in the excavations under St. Peter's basilica).

Church fathers at the end of the second and beginning of the third century speak of Peter and Paul as the "founders" of the church at Rome. This would not be true in the sense of first preaching the gospel there. The statement, however, could be true of their giving stability and organizational structure to the church, and even more so as referring to the significance of their martyrdoms as giving testimony to the truth of the gospel that lay at the foundation of the church.

The earliest literary and inscriptional sources link the names of Peter and Paul together, and this involvement of both men in Rome seems to be true to the historical situation. The traditions that Paul was beheaded (a swifter and so more merciful death applied to citizens) and Peter was crucified agree with the punishments inflicted on those of their respective social ranks.

Peter in bronze in St. Peter's basilica in the Vatican (by Arnolfo di Cambio workshop, c. 1290–95).

The testimony, therefore, is quite strong that Peter as well as Paul was in Rome late in his ministry; and it is quite probable that Peter was martyred there (less likely that he was crucified upside down), and possible that he held some official position in addition to his apostolic prestige in the church (cf. 1 Peter 5:1, "fellow elder"). This situation would provide the historical core around which grew the later claims made by the Roman church on behalf of Peter as its first bishop and of its relationship to him.

Although legends were sometimes invented "whole cloth," especially in later periods, usually stories that were passed down and claims that were made had some basis in fact. In this case, the basis for later claims about the papacy would have been Peter's presence and martyrdom in Rome and his prestige if not actual position of leadership in the church. Nevertheless, to call Peter "pope" or even sole bishop is anachronistic.

By the end of the apostolic age the Roman church was already a numerous and important community, but the church in Ephesus in the closing years of the first century appears to have been the larger as well as being in the center of the most influential region of Christians.

VI. THE CHURCH IN EPHESUS AND JOHN

The beginning of the church in Ephesus is associated with the work of Paul and his co-laborers. There were already disciples of John the Baptist in the city. One of these, Apollos, was an eloquent speaker, and when brought to faith in Jesus, he became a powerful advocate of the new faith in Ephesus and then in Corinth. Paul's longest recorded stay at one locality—over two years—was in Ephesus in the early fifties. From there he apparently supervised the work of other evangelists who carried the Christian message throughout the province of Asia (western Turkey).

The reports in Acts show Paul in contact (and often in conflict) with a cross-section of the Jewish and Gentile worlds in Ephesus: that is, with government officials, Greek intellectuals, more or less orthodox Jews, wandering Jewish exorcists, pagan magicians, and worshippers of the Ephesian goddess Artemis (whose economic and religious interests were intertwined).

As Paul was the leading figure in the early history of the church of Ephesus, the apostle John, if we may accept church tradition, was the leading figure at the end of the first century. Ephesus early became a center associated with Christian literary activity. Paul wrote 1 Corinthians from Ephesus.

Other New Testament books were written to Ephesus: Ephesians (which may have been a circular letter intended for other churches as well), 1 and 2 Timothy (tradition went further and made Timothy the first bishop of Ephesus), and the first of the seven letters in Revelation (2:1–7).

Early tradition, furthermore, associated the Johannine literature with Ephesus. The strong testimony of early church writers identified the apostle John, son of Zebedee, as the source of this literature.

There was, however, another report of a second John, "the elder," buried at Ephesus from whom some or most of the Johannine literature may have derived. A minority of ancient scholars and a large number of modern scholars attribute the Revelation to yet a different person in the same circle.

These writings address some of the variant teachings that were disturbing the apostolic churches. From 1 Timothy we learn of those teaching a "different doctrine," including myths and genealogies, a

> "But these [signs] are written that you may believe that Jesus is the Messiah, the Son of God, and that by believing you may have life in his name" (John 20:31).

denial of law, asceticism in regard to meat and marriage, a claim to a higher "knowledge," and denial of a future resurrection.

The Johannine letters put a great stress on the original apostolic message and the union of deity and humanity in Jesus Christ in opposition to those who, separating from the Christian community, denied the humanity of Christ and failed to practice brotherly love.

The seven letters at the beginning of Revelation show some of the internal problems of compromise with pagan customs, including its immorality; but the book as a whole draws especially on Jewish apocalyptic themes to strengthen the churches against the challenge of persecution from a pagan society in alliance with the imperial cult. Eschatological fervor endured longer in the interior of Asia Minor than elsewhere in the Greek church.

On the basis of John 19:26–27, later tradition reported that John brought Jesus' mother, Mary, with him to Ephesus and that the two of them died there, so that strong cults of John and Mary developed in the region. On the analogy of the reasoning above about Peter at Rome, it is likely that the apostle John or someone with whom he was

The church of St. John in Ephesus, built under the emperor Justinian in the sixth century.

confused provided a connection between apostolic times and the church at Ephesus at the end of the first century.

The Gospel of John is the only book in the New Testament to preserve anecdotal references to Thomas, and the Gospel of John shares with the *Gospel of Thomas* an interest in the wisdom sayings of Jesus.

VII. THE CHURCH IN SYRIA AND THOMAS

Unless the list of peoples present on Pentecost in Acts 2 is meant to imply regions to which those persons carried the Christian message, the New Testament is largely silent on the eastern spread of the church. There were disciples in Damascus at the time of the conversion of Paul, and he himself went to the province of Arabia for a time after his conversion, although he says nothing about preaching during that time.

From second-century sources it is evident that quite early there was an expansion of Christianity east of Antioch as well as the expansion west of Antioch that Luke describes. The classical church Syriac language developed in eastern Syria (Edessa, Nisibis) from the Aramaic that had been the common language of diplomacy and commerce in Mesopotamia and surrounding regions since the Persian empire.

Syriac-speaking Christianity preserved traditions of an association with the apostle Thomas. Those traditions, incorporated in the fifth-century *Doctrina Addai*, claimed the gospel was first preached in Edessa by Addai at the encouragement of Thomas.

Much of the early literature from the region bears the name of Thomas: the *Gospel of Thomas*, a collection of sayings of Jesus preserved in Coptic and incompletely in Greek (see chapter 3); another *Gospel of Thomas* in Greek about the infancy of Jesus; the *Acts of Thomas*, preserved in both Syriac and Greek versions.

The bilingual nature of the region is shown not only by such dual language editions, but also by uncertainty of the original language of some works, such as the *Odes of Solomon* and Tatian's *Diatessaron*. Western writers reported a mission of Thomas to Persia or to India (also in the *Acts of Thomas*). These traditions, if they are not to be wholly discounted, at the least reflect that the gospel was spread to these regions from Syria and was carried by Christians who revered the name of Thomas.

Syriac Christianity was wider than the Thomas tradition but like it preserved elements from the Semitic heritage of the early church. This included a spirituality shaped by wisdom speculations. Another feature of early Syriac-speaking Christianity, notable in the *Acts of Thomas*, is a decided asceticism, especially in sexual matters. (Further characteristics will be developed in chapters 12 and 16.)

> "The kingdom is within you, and it is outside of you. When you know yourselves, then you will be known, and you will know that you are the sons of the living Father. But if you do not know yourselves, then you are in poverty, and you are poverty" (*Gospel of Thomas* 3).

VIII. CHURCH LIFE IN THE APOSTOLIC AGE

The account above of different regions and different individuals who had a leading role in the early church points to the variety of expressions in the earliest Christianity (and more of this will be seen in subsequent chapters).

When noting that there was not a uniformity in earliest Christianity, one should not go to the other extreme and conclude that almost anything could be covered under the Christian umbrella. Along with the variety of emphases and interpretations, there was a common faith in Jesus and a common core of apostolic teachings that set limits to the diversity. Frequent travel and communication by letters and messengers prevented most communities from developing in isolation from other believers.

Although the Old Testament Scriptures received from Judaism were treated in different ways, there was a common acceptance of them as the Word of God and commitment to interpret them in the light of the new revelation in Jesus Christ.

Moreover, certain common practices served as uniting factors from quite early times. Some of the distinctive practices that were to characterize the church through its history began in the apostolic age: baptism, the Lord's supper, Sunday assemblies, and moral emphases.

Entrance into the Christian community required faith in Jesus as Lord and Savior and baptism in his name. Acceptance of Jesus as the Messiah was the obvious doctrinal dividing line between Christians and Jews. The baptism administered by John the Baptist (and its reception by Jesus) was the immediate antecedent to Christian practice.

John's baptism, like certain Jewish ceremonial washings, was by immersion but was distinguished from them by being a repentance baptism for the forgiveness of sins and by being performed by an administrator rather than being self-administered (hence John's name, "the Baptizer").

Christian baptism shared these features with John's baptism but was further distinguished by including confession of the name of Jesus and the promise of the gift of the Holy Spirit (in Jewish expectation the sign of the coming of the eschatological age). Different theological emphases characterized the interpretation of baptism by different authors—e.g., the imagery of death and resurrection by Paul and of rebirth by John—but the practice itself was essentially the same.

From the beginning the disciples continued the practice of common meals they had known during the ministry of Jesus, only now there was a difference. The breaking of the bread and drinking of the cup, each accompanied by a blessing (or thanksgiving) to God, now was a remembrance of Jesus' last supper with his disciples and his subsequent passion and resurrection. The setting of a common meal

"They devoted
themselves to
the apostles'
teaching and
to fellowship,
to the breaking
of bread and to
prayer"
(Acts 2:42).

was preserved in the names "breaking of bread" (the act at which time a blessing was said and with which Jewish meals began) and "Lord's supper" (as distinguished from ordinary dinners).

The special meaning of the breaking of bread and the cup of blessing, on the occasions of community celebrations, always was distinct in theological significance from the meal itself (even when understood as expressing "communion," or fellowship), and in time was separated in practice from the meal, perhaps as a result of Paul's instructions in 1 Corinthians 11:17–34 and certainly by the time Matthew (26:26–29) and Mark (12:22–25) recorded the institution, although occurring in a meal setting, as something distinct from the meal itself.

The special meetings of Christians included observance of the "Lord's supper," prayer, singing, reading from the Scriptures, and messages of instruction and exhortation. Although Christians might be together more frequently, even "daily," these meetings occurred at a minimum, in commemoration of the resurrection of Jesus, on "the first day of the week" (the Jewish name), that is, the "Lord's day" (the distinctive Christian name), a pattern that John indicates began with the resurrection appearances of Jesus (John 20:19, 26). Jewish Christians continued to observe the Sabbath as well as having Christian assemblies on the following day. Converts directly from paganism found no significance for themselves in the Jewish observance.

Although incorporating some traditional Jewish formulations, Christians related their daily observance of prayer to Jesus and his teachings about prayer. Generosity in giving for the support of the poor, also with antecedents in Jewish practice, characterized Christian communities from the beginning. Christians also continued the moral teachings that had been developed in Judaism. These were applied in the contemporary environment to matters of family, occupation, and social structure.

Matters of morality were not approached, however, in the same way as in Judaism. The relating of all conduct to the commands to love God and love one's neighbor, combined with the motivation of imitating the love of God shown in the life of Jesus, gave a distinctive organizing principle to Christian moral teaching.

FOR FURTHER STUDY

Ellis, E. Earle. *The Making of the New Testament Documents*. Leiden: Brill, 2002.

Witherington, Ben III. *New Testament History: A Narrative Account*. Grand Rapids: Baker, 2001.

Wright, N. T. Christian Origins and the Question of God. Vol. 2: *Jesus and the Victory of God*. Minneapolis: Fortress, 1996.

3

The Subapostolic Age

The second century at one time was described as a tunnel period in the history of Christianity; the imagery is actually more apt for the last one-third of the first century. The absence of a narrative comparable to the book of Acts for this period leaves many gaps in our knowledge. Even those scholars who date a considerable part of the New Testament to the late first century or early second century still must resort to hypotheses and sociological theories to describe the developments in the church in this period.

The apostles Paul and Peter, and James, the brother of the Lord—the "big three" of the apostolic church—were all killed within five years of one another in the mid-sixties. James was killed by the Jerusalem authorities in a period when one Roman governor had died and his successor had not arrived (about 62); and Peter and Paul were executed in Rome under Nero (perhaps in 64 for Peter, before 68 for Paul).

The removal from the scene of three dominant personalities from the apostolic age—combined with the suppression of the Jewish revolt in Palestine against Roman rule (66–70/73) that resulted in the destruction of Jerusalem—brought a significant new situation to the church in the last third of the first century.

I. STRANDS OF JEWISH CHRISTIANITY

The late first and early second century saw an increased alienation of believers in Jesus from the synagogues. One important result of the death of James, the destruction of the temple in 70, and the banishment of Jews from Jerusalem after the Bar Kokhba revolt in 135, was the removal of Jerusalem as a geographical center of the Christian movement. This was accompanied by an increasing marginalization of Jewish Christians in relation to the growing numbers of Gentile believers.

The very terminology "Jewish Christianity" has become problematic, being sometimes used broadly to cover all characteristically Jewish influences on Christianity and sometimes used to refer to Christianity among those ethnically Jews. In the church fathers, this latter usage was narrowed further to refer to those Jewish Christians regarded by the Gentile church as heretical because of their adherence to distinctively Jewish religious observances.

The mutual rejection of each other by most Gentile believers and most Jewish believers effectively removed from the history of the church the potential middle ground of a Jewish Christian viewpoint that could have preserved lines of communication between Jews who did not accept Jesus and Gentiles who did. As a consequence of these developments, little literature from Jewish Christianity survives, so its history must be sketched in broad strokes.

Eusebius, the fourth-century church historian, reports that during the Roman-Jewish War of 66–70, Christians in Jerusalem took flight to Pella, across the Jordan River. The report's historicity has been questioned, and elements of it may not be correct; but there seems good reason to accept a flight by Christians from Jerusalem and a return by some after the war.

Some time before the end of the first century, although the details cannot now be ascertained, many synagogues took actions that effectively eliminated from their membership any Christian presence that may have continued. Jewish Christians found themselves excluded from the synagogue and not accepted by the Gentile churches, which were distinguishing themselves from Jewish practices while at the same time claiming the Jewish scriptural heritage as their own. When Rome forbade Jews from Jerusalem after 135, the Palestinian church itself became largely Gentile.

Three strands of Jewish Christianity are attested in the writings of the church fathers; all are known only fragmentarily and all eventually passed out of existence:

A. Ebionites

The group of Jewish Christians most commented on by Gentile Christian writers, and treated by them as heretical, were called Ebionites. Their hero was James the Just, and they were quite antagonistic toward Paul. They took the position that Gentile converts must submit to the Law of Moses.

Their emphasis on strict monotheism led them to regard Jesus as a man and to reject the virgin birth, while affirming him to be a true prophet, the new Moses, and the Messiah by virtue of his righteous life. The mission of Jesus was to destroy the system of atonement associated with the temple and its cultus, and to bring a new means of forgiveness of sins by immersion in "living" (running) water.

Along with material sacrifices, the Ebionites rejected the monarchy, some aspects of prophecy, and offensive passages in the Old Testament (described as false pericopes, which were regarded as later additions to the text of Scripture).

Other characteristics were a prohibition of meat, emphasis on poverty, and concern with purity (involving ritual washings in addition to the initiatory baptism). They continued the Jewish practices of circumcision, Sabbath (but also observing the Lord's day), and dietary laws. Their Gospel was Matthew, but they also produced other Gospels and Acts of their own.

The church fathers offered various explanations of their name, some speculating (on the analogy of other movements) that they followed a man named Ebion. Origen knew enough Hebrew to recognize that the name came from the word for "poor," and he saw it as appropriate to the "poverty" of their theology that held such a low view of Jesus' nature (only human).

The correct explanation seems to be that the Ebionites continued the religious use of "the poor" in the Old Testament, known also from the Qumran literature and the Gospels, as referring to the humble people who trusted in God.

B. Nazaraeans

There were other Jewish Christians, sometimes called Nazaraeans, who, although living by the Law themselves, accepted Gentile believers without expecting them to submit to the Law. This uneasy middle ground, which failed to draw as much comment from Gentile Christian authors, proved also to be too unstable to survive.

C. Elkesaites

Other Jewish Christians absorbed Gnostic tendencies (chapter 5). This is reflected in the so-called Elkesaites. A prophet named Elkesai is connected with a book of revelations that originated in the early years of the second century. The Cologne Mani Codex relates that Mani, the third-century founder of Manichaeism, grew up in an Elkesaite community, and so establishes a link between its ideas and the later developments in Gnostic thought associated with Mani.

D. Other Jewish Influences

Jewish concepts and concerns continued to be prominent in parts of the church that contributed to its mainstream. This is especially

"[The Ebionites] say that he [Christ] was not begotten of God the Father, but was created as one of the archangels ... that he rules over the angels and all the creatures of the Almighty, and that he came and declared, as their Gospel ... reports: I am come to do away with sacrifices, and if you do not cease from sacrificing, the wrath of God will not cease from you" (Epiphanius, *Panarion* 30.16.4–5).

evident in the work known as the *Didache*, discussed below. Moreover, greater recognition is now being given to the Jewish elements in Gnostic speculations, as will be evident in chapter 5. Non-heretical Jewish Christian ideas are found in Christian additions to the Old Testament Pseudepigrapha, such as *2 Esdras* (*5th* and *6th Ezra*), *Testaments of the 12 Patriarchs*, and *Ascension of Isaiah*.

Apart from fragmentary quotations of Jewish Christian works, the principal surviving source of Jewish Christian material is the Pseudo-Clementine literature. The fourth-century Greek *Homilies* and Latin *Recognitions*, ascribed to Clement of Rome (the *Pseudo-Clementines*), derive from a common source in the third century, which in turn incorporated earlier works, including some "Jewish Christian" (Ebionite?) writings. The *Homilies* are prefaced by purported letters from Peter to James and from Clement to James, in the latter of which James is addressed as "bishop of bishops."

As might be expected from its geographical proximity, Jewish Christianity and its aberrations made their strongest impact in Syria. The early development there of a priestly concept of ministry may be a direct inheritance from Judaism. The asceticism of the Syriac church, which might seem un-Jewish, was perhaps mediated from Jewish sectarian groups, such as those known from Colossians and represented by the Essenes and by Jewish Christian groups.

Much later, Mohammed seems to have had contact with and gained some of his knowledge of Christianity from Jewish Christian groups. This later history of Jewish Christianity in the Middle East is even more poorly known than in its early stages, but, largely cut off from the mainstream of the church, it failed to exert a significant or constructive influence on the history of Christianity.

II. LITERATURE AND PROBLEMS IN GENTILE CHRISTIANITY

In contrast to the little literature preserved from Jewish Christianity, the considerable writings of Gentile Christians from the late first century to the mid-second century enable us to see the organizational and doctrinal developments in the church as it adapted to its new circumstances. This literature, especially the so-called Apostolic Fathers, also reflects perennial Christian concerns and problems, and so prepares for the further unfolding of the church's story in subsequent centuries.

The non-canonical literature of the period may be classified as the Apostolic Fathers, the apocryphal New Testament (extending through the second century and later), and other miscellaneous works. Writings from this period later regarded as heretical will be treated in chapter 5.

A. The Apostolic Fathers

"Apostolic Fathers" is the name given to the earliest orthodox writings not included in the New Testament. The name was given because it was assumed that disciples of the apostles wrote the works, a false assumption in nearly all, if not all, cases. The category is an artificial grouping, encompassing many different literary forms and overlapping other classifications.

The *Didache* and *1 Clement* overlap in time with the later New Testament writings. There is a further overlap in date of the Apostolic Fathers with some of the New Testament Apocrypha and Pseudepigrapha—*Gospel of Thomas, Gospel of Peter*, and perhaps *Odes of Solomon*; moreover, *The Epistle of Barnabas* is perhaps pseudonymous.

The earliest apologists—Quadratus and Aristides—are as early as some of the Apostolic Fathers, and the apology known as the *Epistle to Diognetus* is sometimes included in the Apostolic Fathers (chapter 4). There is also an overlap with the accounts of martyrdom, for one of these, the *Martyrdom of Polycarp* (chapter 4), concerns an apostolic father.

The **Didache** is a manual of church life in three parts: "The Two Ways" of life and death, on the moral teachings given to new converts; instructions on baptism, fasting, prayer, eucharist, treatment of itinerant prophets and teachers, the Sunday assembly, and election of local leaders; and an eschatological conclusion.

The full title of the *Didache* is "Teaching of the Lord through the Twelve Apostles to the Nations." It was a characteristic of the church order literature to claim apostolic origin for the instructions concerning the practical arrangements of church life.

APOSTOLIC FATHERS

Name	Date	Locality	Type of Literature
Didache	c. 100	Syria	Church Order
Barnabas	97/135?	Alexandria?	Letter-treatise
1 Clement	96?	Rome	Letter-treatise
2 Clement	100/150	Corinth?	Sermon
Hermas	100–155	Rome	Apocalypse
Ignatius	d. c. 117	Antioch of Syria	Letters
Polycarp	115/135	Smyrna	Letter(s)
Papias	c. 130	Hierapolis	Explanations

The *Didache* has been variously dated from around 70 or earlier to as late as 180. The question of date is complicated by the compiler's use of earlier materials. Another characteristic of the church order literature is that as practices in the church changed, material was brought up to date, so we cannot rule out later interpolations in the basic document available to us.

Although an argument can be made for an Egyptian origin, rural Syria remains the most likely place of composition. The Jewish setting of early Christianity is quite in evidence throughout the document—in its moral teachings and their framework in the "Two Ways," the language of its prayers, the instructions concerning support of ministers, and the language of eschatology employed.

The *Didache* reflects the continuing concern in Christian history with how properly to conduct church affairs—how to regulate moral life, worship, and polity.

Sharing with the *Didache* a section of moral instruction according to the "Two Ways" is the **Epistle of Barnabas**, with the difference that the "Two Ways" comes at the end instead of the beginning and uses the terminology of "way of light" and "way of darkness" (also, "the way of the Black One"). It is a treatise sent as a letter.

Barnabas is usually dated around 135, which may be about right, although the arguments in behalf of this date (or any other) have problems about them. The author is unknown; both date and content seem to preclude the companion of Paul as the author.

The name Barnabas that appears in the manuscripts but not in the treatise itself can be accounted for in various ways: (1) the author was really named Barnabas, later confused with the apostolic Barnabas; (2) the ascription to Barnabas was a later inaccurate guess; (3) the author issued his work pseudonymously. The likely but not certain place of origin is the vicinity of Alexandria. The author professes not to write as a teacher, but his protests seem to indicate that such was in fact his position.

The principal concern of *Barnabas* was the debate with the Jews over the Old Testament: "Whose is the covenant?" The author answers that it belongs to the later people (Christians) and no longer to the Jews. When the Jews rebelled against God in the incident of the golden calf in Exodus 32, the covenant was broken and it is now given to the people of Jesus Christ.

Barnabas further argues that the institutions and practices of Judaism were never intended to be kept literally and are kept spiritually by Christians: sacrifice (Jesus Christ's atonement), circumcision (hearing the Word of the Lord with the heart and ears), washings (baptism), dietary laws (avoiding sinners), Sabbath (eighth day, i.e., "first day" as a type of the world to come), temple (the heart and people).

The writer seems especially proud of the allegorical interpretation he gives to the circumcision of the 318 servants of Abraham (Genesis 14:14). Since 318 in Greek was represented by the letters *iota* (i = 10), *ēta* (ē = 8), and *tau* (t = 300), and the former two letters were the first two letters of the name Jesus, and the latter letter was in the shape of a cross, he interpreted the circumcision of these men as referring to the sacrifice of Jesus on the cross.

The writer's extreme position of spiritualizing the Old Testament, and denying it to the Jewish people, was not followed by anyone else known to us. Still, *Barnabas* represented one way of addressing the continuing problem posed by the Old Testament, whose authority was accepted by the church, which conversely saw no ongoing need for its religious institutions.

First Clement is the name given to the letter from "the church of God that sojourns in Rome to the church of God that sojourns in Corinth." The letter is attributed to Clement in the manuscripts and also by Dionysius of Corinth about 170 (Eusebius, *Church History* 4.23.11). Hermas mentions a Clement in Rome whose task was to correspond with other churches (*Visions* 2.4.3). However, Clement does not write in his own name. Instead, as a presbyter-bishop, he wrote as a spokesman

Mosaic of Peter and Clement (c. 1125) in the basilica of San Clemente, Rome.

The Subapostolic Age

"The apostles were delivered the gospel for us from the Lord Jesus Christ; Jesus Christ was sent from God.... [The apostles] preached district by district and city by city and appointed their first converts, after testing them by the Spirit, as bishops and deacons of those who were going to believe.... They afterward gave the rule that if [those appointed] died other tested men should succeed to their ministry" (*1 Clement* 42, 44).

of the Roman church. The letter therefore carried communal (rather than apostolic or episcopal) authority.

The date is usually assigned to the reign of Domitian, about 96, but this is not absolutely certain, and some have argued for an earlier date of about 70.

Acording to Irenaeus, Clement was the third successor of Peter as bishop of Rome, following Linus and Anacletus (*Against Heresies* 3.3.3; Eusebius, *Church History* 3.15.34). A rival tradition made him the successor to Peter (Pseudo Clement, *Epistle to James* 2; Tertullian, *Prescription against Heretics* 32). Epiphanius later tried to harmonize the reports by saying Peter consecrated Clement, but he stepped aside until later (*Panarion* 27.6).

As many Protestant and some Roman Catholic historians have observed, the difficulty arises because there was a plurality of presbyter-bishops at this time in the church at Rome, and Irenaeus and others read back into this time the later organization of only one bishop in a church.

The author may have been a freedman of the Roman senatorial Clemens family, either a Gentile convert to Judaism before accepting Christianity or a Jew with some Hellenistic education.

The occasion for the letter was division in the church at Corinth (the Corinthians were taking sides yet again). Some of the presbyters in the church had been unseated. Was this a rebellion of the younger against the older members, or a charismatic uprising against institutional authority? Such interpretations have been advanced, but the letter itself speaks primarily about personal rivalry and envy.

The frequent reference to women in the examples cited and teachings given makes one wonder if women were prominent among those leading the rebellion. The intervention by the Roman church was an effort to allay discord in the church at Corinth.

The letter of *1 Clement* may be divided into two major parts: general moral considerations applicable to the situation at Corinth (1–38) and practical suggestions to solve the problem (39–65). We can perhaps overhear the author's typical methods of preaching and teaching in the way he collects scriptural passages and examples on such topics as jealousy, repentance, obedience, and humility. Although relying primarily on Jewish sources, the author draws on pagan sources as well in order to make his points.

Among the notable contents of the document are:

1. The affirmation of God as creator, with the use of Stoic imagery about the laws of nature, in order to encourage obedience as the human response.

2. The picture of Jesus as "servant of God" and high priest.

3. The affirmation of Paul's doctrine of justification by faith and the quotation of his teaching on love in 1 Corinthians.

4. The description of the organization of the church with bishops and deacons as having been instituted by the apostles with provision for this arrangement to continue ("presbyters" and "bishops" are used interchangeably).

5. The first use of a clergy-laity distinction and of priestly terminology for the ministry of the church (in reference to Old Testament institutions but as analogous to the need for good order in the church).

6. The appeal to the myth of the phoenix bird in support of the resurrection.

7. The implication that Peter and Paul died at Rome under Nero after Paul had preached in the "limits of the west" (Spain?).

8. A long prayer at the end with its positive petitions on behalf of the Roman government.

First Clement reflects the ongoing problem throughout Christian history of division in the church and therefore the need to promote unity and harmony.

Second Clement is a homily of moral exhortation. Although associated with *1 Clement* in the manuscript tradition, it is by a different, otherwise unknown, author. There are few clues to a date, likely early to mid-second century, and the place of composition may have been Rome, Alexandria, or (with slight preference) Corinth. The sermon was delivered by a teacher or reader in the church on the subject of repentance.

A notable theological point is the affirmation of the spiritual church as the pre-existent body of Jesus Christ. The sermon shows the persistent Christian concern with moral conduct, how "to lead a holy and righteous life" (*2 Clement* 5).

The longest work in the Apostolic Fathers is the *Shepherd* (Pastor), a collection of *Visions*, *Parables* (Similitudes), and *Commandments* (Mandates) by **Hermas**. The unity of the work has been questioned, but perhaps the best explanation for the sometimes conflicting data is that the work is from a single author active in Rome over three to four decades in the first half of the second century (and so reflecting different situations in its different parts).

Hermas refers to the idea of the church as eternal and gives information on its contemporary organization. The sometimes tiresome document is valuable for the picture it gives of a Christian community in the third generation. The members were involved in the daily affairs of life, and the world threatened to overwhelm their Christian way of life.

The special interest of the work concerns what to do about sins after baptism. Although the ideal is to preserve baptismal grace untarnished, Hermas gives assurance that there is one "repentance" after conversion for those who have fallen away but warns against presuming that this is always available, for the end of the world is imminent.

The *Shepherd* of Hermas reflects the continuing problem of Christians living in the world while not being "of the world" and how to encourage a faithful life among those whose first love has cooled.

Ignatius, bishop of Antioch in Syria, wrote seven genuine letters that survive, one of which was to the church at Rome pleading with the Christians there not to try to intervene to save him from martyrdom. Ignatius was arrested under the emperor Trajan (98–117), and probably toward the end of his reign was taken under guard to Rome for execution, probably as one of the prisoners to serve as victims in the wild animal games put on to entertain the populace.

On his way across Asia Minor, Ignatius wrote four letters from Smyrna (to the churches at Ephesus, Magnesia, and Tralles in Asia and to the church at Rome) and then three from Troas (to the churches at

Flavian Amphitheater (Colosseum), Rome, in which, according to tradition, many Christians, including perhaps Ignatius, died as martyrs.

Philadelphia and Smyrna, and to Smyrna's bishop, Polycarp). These letters were interpolated and six additional ones were added in the fourth century, and this expanded version was the form in which Ignatius was known until modern scholars recovered the original edition.

The number seven was important in early Christian letter collections (e.g., it was pointed out that Paul wrote to seven churches—nine letters in all to these churches plus four to individuals—and there are seven churches addressed in Revelation—Ephesus, Smyrna, and Philadelphia in common with Ignatius).

Ignatius calls himself Theophorus ("God bearer"). According to tradition he was the third bishop of Antioch, after Peter and an otherwise unknown Evodius. That only one name could be remembered between him and Peter's presence in Antioch suggests that it was late in the first century before a single bishop emerged to lead the church at Antioch.

The exuberant, imaginative style of *Ignatius* contrasts with the sober practicality of *1 Clement*. These two most influential of the Apostolic Fathers may be seen as representing the different tendencies of the Western and Eastern churches—Clement the concern with order and practical unity that characterized the Catholic church, and Ignatius the almost mystical sense of piety and spiritual unity that characterized the Orthodox church.

In understanding Ignatius's letters it is important to remember that he was on his way to martyrdom and hardly traveling in comfort. His own imaginative personality was heightened by the situation to produce flowery figures of speech and mixed metaphors sometimes piled on top of each other. Still, Ignatius had practical concerns with the immediate problems he learned about in churches on his route.

Ignatius was especially concerned about division in the churches, occasioned by the false teachings both of the Docetists, who said that Jesus Christ only "seemed" or "appeared" to be truly human, and of the Judaizers, who promoted Jewish practices. The two kinds of false teaching may come from the same group—a Docetic view of Christ could have solved some problems for Jewish believers in overcoming the paradox of a crucified Messiah.

Ignatius's response to divisiveness was to insist on obedience of Christians to their leaders—the bishop (who took the place of God), the presbyters (who symbolized the apostles), and the deacons (who represented the servant Christ). Ignatius is the first writer to attest this three-fold ministry in each local church.

All activities (eucharist, baptism, agape) were to be under the bishop, either presided over by him in person or by one whom he designated; for Ignatius the requirement was not a question of the validity of the religious acts, but of good order and unity.

"There is one Physician, who is both flesh and spirit, born and yet not born, who is God in man, true life in death, both of Mary and of God, first passible and then impassible, Jesus Christ our Lord" (Ignatius, *Ephesians* 7.2).

In view of Ignatius's strong claims for the one bishop and the later development of church organization, it is worth noting that for Ignatius the bishop was still a congregational and not a diocesan bishop, worked with the presbyters as their leader (a first among equals), and did not have his position by reason of apostolic succession. The absence of an emphasis on the bishop in the letter to Rome has led some to see this silence as an argument against the presence at this time of a monarchical bishop at Rome.

Also to be considered is the subject matter of Ignatius's letter to the Romans, where his interest is martyrdom, making this letter an important early source for the developing theology of martyrdom.

Ignatius is the first to speak of the "catholic church," referring to the universal church composed of all the local congregations and reflecting his concern for the unity of the church.

The letters of Ignatius deal with a continuing problem in Christian history—variant interpretations of the Christian faith by those who withdraw from the life of the local congregation. His response—which was to strengthen the institutional structures of the church—has been the course most often followed in the history of the church, but with mixed results as to its effectiveness in achieving spiritual unity.

Polycarp, bishop of Smyrna, received one of Ignatius's letters and wrote his own letter to the *Philippians* in part in response to their request for copies of the letters of Ignatius. He wrote to them also in order to give instruction in "righteousness," dealing with the qualities of the Christian life. Polycarp further refers to an internal problem at

Agora (marketplace) of Smyrna (modern Izmir), Turkey.

Philippi concerning a presbyter by the name of Valens, who had fallen to the temptation of avarice.

The surviving letter to the Philippians is now commonly thought to be a conflation of two letters, the first (chapters 13–14) written shortly after Ignatius passed through the region on his way to Rome and the second (chapters 1–12) written some twenty or twenty-five years later; but there seems no compelling need for this to be the case.

Polycarp was so saturated with the language of the New Testament that whatever he had to say was expressed in its wording. He wove phrases from the letters of Paul, Peter, and John into new contexts to express his own message. Polycarp remains a representative of the pious Christian leader, filled with the apostolic teaching, who was concerned for righteous living.

Papias of Hierapolis wrote five books of *Explanations of the Oracles of the Lord* (ca. 130), now lost and known only through a few quotations from later writers. Special attention has been given to his testimony that Matthew wrote his Gospel originally in Hebrew and that Mark faithfully set down the preaching of Peter (but not in good order). He likely attested the Gospel of John (and implicitly Luke) as well.

Also notable is Papias's expressed preference for the "living voice" of those who heard the disciples of the apostles over what was written in books. Although this is often taken as a disparagement of Scripture, the frequent use of the word "oracles" for the Scriptures may mean that his very work is a commentary on written texts. In that case, his contrast may be the value of the oral testimony of older disciples over the written books of heretics in interpreting the Christian message.

Papias is also our first non-canonical writer to give a specifically millennial interpretation to the Christian eschatological hope. He advocated, in the manner of some Jewish writings, a materialist understanding of the millennium. Papias thus shows the perennial Christian interest in matters of eschatology.

B. Apocryphal Literature

If one wants to appreciate the genuine article, read the imitations. If one feels a decline in spiritual power from the New Testament to the Apostolic Fathers, there is a plunge into another world in much of the second-century New Testament Apocrypha.

The recent scholarly interest in this literature is an appropriate reaction against its neglect for historical purposes, but is not likely to change the common Christian judgment of its spiritual inferiority. Nevertheless, the Apocrypha remains an important source for assessing the variety of expressions of popular piety in the early church.

> "Faith is the mother of us all, with hope following close after, and the love of God, Christ, and neighbor leading the way" (Polycarp, *Philippians* 3.3).

Some Apocryphal works seem to have been written for entertainment and to satisfy curiosity. Others are more serious works for edification, advocating asceticism and certain doctrinal ideas. These divergent features, however, sometimes are combined in one work.

All of the Apocryphal writings are valuable for reflecting ideas prevalent at the time of composition, itself often difficult to determine. The following discussion is limited to works generally agreed to have the best claim to a second-century date.

The boundaries between orthodoxy and heresy were not clearly perceived in the circles from which some of these works emanated. They are a reminder that departures from apostolic faith as often occurred in popular piety as in theological speculations.

The categories used in the chart below are somewhat artificial, but it is not misleading to group the New Testament Apocryphal writings according to the literary forms of the New Testament itself.

The apocryphal **gospels** reflect types of material found in the canonical Gospels: birth narratives, sayings (but not deeds) of Jesus, and the passion narrative.

Much of the content of the *Gospel of Thomas* sayings had been known, but without a title, in three Greek papyri. The Coptic text contained in the collection of codices found at Nag Hammadi in upper Egypt supplied the missing text and title. Because of its company in the Nag Hammadi codices, the gospel has been described as Gnostic, and it was susceptible to a Gnostic interpretation, but the work may better be described as Encratite (chapter 5) or more broadly as ascetic.

The *Gospel of Thomas* offers, without narrative context, an early collection of sayings of Jesus, often similar to sayings found in the canonical Gospels. Many scholars see the wording as reflecting a quite early stage in the transmission of the sayings of Jesus. New Testament scholars have long conjectured an early collection of the sayings of Jesus called *Q* as explaining the common material in Matthew and Luke. *Thomas* is not *Q*, but it does demonstrate that there

SOME NEW TESTAMENT APOCRYPHA OF THE SECOND CENTURY

Gospels

Gospel of Thomas

Gospel of Peter

Protevangelium of James

Acts

Acts of Peter

Acts of Paul

Acts of John

Epistles

Epistle of the Apostles

Apocalypses

Apocalypse of Peter

was such a thing as collections of sayings of Jesus that circulated independently.

The *Gospel of Peter* is a passion narrative. It was early rejected by church leaders because of its suspected Docetic leanings, that is, presenting a Christ who was not fully human but only "seemed" to be (at his crucifixion he was "as if he felt no pain"). It may not have been specifically written to promote such views, but it could be read as favoring such an understanding of Jesus.

The *Protevangelium of James* concerns the birth of Jesus but especially centers on Mary, promoting her perpetual virginity and presenting Joseph as a widower with children by an earlier marriage. The work was very popular and provided the information for the later elaboration of Marian doctrine.

The apocryphal **acts** in their stories of the travels and adventures of the apostles are most akin to Hellenistic novels. They provide extravagant accounts of the miracles of the apostles. The theme of the chaste love of hero and heroines in the novels is made subservient in the apocryphal acts to a strong ascetic emphasis. The gospel message becomes, "He that believes and renounces sexual union will be saved."

The *Acts of Peter* and *Acts of Paul*, both certainly from the second century, reflect basically orthodox viewpoints. The *Acts of John* is more Gnostic in flavor (chapter 5). Like the *Acts of John*, the *Acts of Andrew*

Gospel of Thomas from Nag Hammadi (Coptic Museum, Cairo).

reflects Gnostic dualism (with even fewer Christian concerns than the *Acts of John)* and is less certainly dated, either to the second or third century. *The Acts of Thomas*, preserved in Syriac and a revised Greek version, is third century.

Epistles are poorly represented in the Apocrypha. The required pseudonymity either was little attempted or proved unsuccessful. The so-called *Epistle of the Apostles* (ca. 150) is an "epistle" only in the broad sense of being sent out supposedly by the apostles. In literary form it is a post-resurrection "revelation" by the Lord to his apostles, a type of writing common in Gnostic documents in order to give authority for teaching not found in the traditions of the ministry of Jesus. The author seems to have adopted this common Gnostic literary device in order to affirm orthodox doctrine against the Gnostics.

Another second-century letter is *Third Corinthians*, included in the *Acts of Paul* but circulated independently and perhaps having been written prior to the *Acts of Paul*. It too is anti-Gnostic in its contents.

An **apocalypse** from the second century is the *Apocalypse of Peter*. Its revelation concerns the punishments of various kinds of sinners in the afterlife. The prominence of the name of Peter in early Christian apocrypha is to be noted: there is also an apologetic work known as the *Preaching of Peter*, and one Jewish-Christian component of the Pseudo-Clementines is the *Preachings of Peter*.

C. Other Writings

Various Jewish writings prompted Christians to enlarge them, interpolate them, or imitate them. The preserved form of the *Ascension of Isaiah* contains—in addition to a Jewish account of the martyrdom of Isaiah—two Christian additions revealing the miraculous birth, life, death, resurrection, ascension, and second coming of Jesus Christ. There is also a description of the condition of the church at the end of the first or beginning of the second century.

The present form of the *Testaments of the Twelve Patriarchs* is a Christian work dating to the second century. The debate continues whether it was a Jewish work that Christian scribes interpolated or was a Christian composition employing earlier Jewish materials. The ethical content is quite close to Christian teaching, but not necessarily of Christian origin. The clearest sign of a Christian hand is found in doctrinal statements about Jesus Christ.

The Jews produced oracles in the style of the pagan *Sibylline Oracles* for propaganda and apologetic purposes. Christians preserved these and wrote many more of their own, so that the existing *Sibylline Oracles* are primarily a Christian composition. Although some of these are fourth century, some are second century, for they are quoted by second-century Christian apologists.

The *Odes of Solomon* may be the earliest surviving Christian hymnbook. The case for a Christian authorship seems stronger than claims for a Jewish or Gnostic origin. Although most scholars date it to the beginning of the second century, some contend for a third-century date. The composition survives complete only in Syriac. The collection consists of forty-two short odes that may have been intended for a worship setting.

Also remembered as a hymn writer was Bardaisan (Latin: Bardesanes) of Edessa (ca. 154–222), one of the first Christian writers in Syriac. His only work to survive is the *Book of the Laws of the Lands*, or *On Fate*, a dialogue transcribed by his disciple Philip. Bardaisan's orthodoxy was found deficient by later Syrian Christian leaders.

D. Limitations and Value of This Literature

Even the writings most acceptable to orthodox Christians—e.g., those from Clement, Ignatius, Polycarp—have been criticized as representing a severe falling away from apostolic Christianity. These authors are indeed inferior to their masters, but they were not as simple-minded as sometimes they are made out to be.

The usual charge is that the Apostolic Fathers retreated from the robust doctrines of grace and faith enunciated by Paul and took refuge in moralism and legalism. Some of this criticism comes from a one-sided understanding of Paul; some from a failure to take into account the specific contexts in which both Paul and the Apostolic Fathers were writing.

A contemporary reader indeed would not confuse the Apostolic Fathers with Paul (or with John or James for that matter), but the contrasts in theology may easily be exaggerated. One would not expect the same theological inspiration and spiritual depth in the second and third generation as in the original leaders, but the later followers did have their own contributions to make.

In their defense, it may further be said that the Apostolic Fathers were sincere, pious persons, striving to preserve the fundamentals of the faith in the face of new circumstances and new challenges. By the testimony of these quite diverse men, the reader can detect what earnest Christians regarded as spurious and what they identified as real.

Certainly some of the enthusiasm of the apostolic age was gone, and the church was beginning to settle down to life in an alien world. In such circumstances more needed to be said about ethical living. This was a situation that called not so much for keen or original thought as scrupulous fidelity in preserving intact Christian doctrine and practice.

"I praise you, O Lord, / Because I love you. / O Most High, do not forsake me, / For you are my hope. / Freely did I receive your grace, / May I live by it" (*Odes of Solomon* 5.1–3).

The Subapostolic Age

Christians of the time did not always respond wisely, but they still proclaimed the same basic message, the same faith, the same Savior, and the same God as their predecessors.

The New Testament Apocryphal writings may have less to commend them, but they too show religious earnestness and give insights into certain strands of early Christianity, in addition to being valuable historical sources (not necessarily for New Testament times but for their own).

Some scholars consider the *Gospel of Thomas* and *Gospel of Peter* to preserve early and valuable material about the teachings of Jesus and the understanding of his death and resurrection.

Among the other works the *Odes of Solomon* reflects a deep spirituality still appreciated by modern readers.

FOR FURTHER STUDY

Foster, Paul, ed. *The Writings of the Apostolic Fathers*. Edinburgh: T & T Clark, 2007.

Jefford, Clayton N. *Reading the Apostolic Fathers: A Students Introduction*. 2nd ed. Grand Rapids: Baker, 2012.

Klauck, Hans-Josef. *The Apocryphal Acts of the Apostles: An Introduction*. Waco, TX: Baylor University Press, 2008.

Idem. *Apocryphal Gospels: An Introduction*. Edinburgh: T & T Clark, 2003.

Lapham, F. *Introduction to the New Testament Apocrypha*. Edinburgh: T & T Clark, 2003.

Skarsaune, Oskar, and Reidar Hvalvik, eds. *Jewish Believers in Jesus: The Early Centuries*. Peabody, MA: Hendrickson, 2007.

The Church and the Empire

I. ATTITUDES TOWARD CHRISTIANS

The relations of the church with the Roman Empire constitute one of the major themes in early Christian history; and, indeed, the relations of Christianity with civil government continued in later centuries to be a key issue. The situation in the first centuries was complex, moving from a period of uneasy contacts to a time of local persecutions and then empire-wide persecution.

A. Attitudes of Early Emperors

In the book of Acts the government did not distinguish Christians from Jews, whose religion was legally recognized. A representative episode occurred in Corinth, when Paul was brought by the Jews before Gallio, the governor of Achaia, who responded, "Since it involves questions about words and names and your own law—settle the matter yourselves. I will not be a judge of such things" (Acts 18:15).

Yet in Acts we do get the background for later unfavorable treatment: the Jews sometimes stirred up trouble, Christian preaching often created wider disturbances (something those in authority always disliked), and Christian teaching threatened pagan society. For instance, the presence of Christians had been the occasion of a disturbance in Rome (ca. 49) during the reign of Claudius, who expelled Jews from the city (Acts 18:2) because of agitation over "Chrestus" (Suetonius, *Claudius* 25.4). Popular turmoil was also a chief cause of persecution later. Everything depended on the attitude of the local officials, who at first were indifferent or at any rate not antagonistic until provoked.

The situation changed under Nero. In response to rumors that he was responsible for the great fire that destroyed much of Rome (AD 64), Nero (or his magistrate) charged and punished Christians for the fire.

Tacitus, the Roman historian who reports the incident (*Annals* 15.44), did not give much credence to the charge of arson, but he did consider Christianity a "deadly superstition" deserving punishment for "hatred of the human race." Nero's officials apparently took action against the group (not individuals) on account of "the name," that is, for being Christians.

Christians were now recognized by the authorities in Rome as distinct from Jews. The persecution under Nero was confined to Rome, but this action set a precedent that could be followed elsewhere.

Domitian (81–96) was remembered in Christian writings as the next persecuting emperor, but there is little external confirmation. He acted, probably for political reasons, against certain high-ranking individuals in Rome who were said to observe "Jewish customs" (Dio Cassius, *Epitome* 67.14). This action was distinct from the troubles that Christians in the province of Asia had during his reign, reflected in the book of Revelation.

Asia had been a center of the imperial cult since the time of Augustus, and the religio-political conflict between the ruling classes and the church came to the forefront there, probably fueled by Domitian's insistence on receiving divine honors. Domitian also had relatives of Jesus in Palestine called in for questioning as part of a search made for descendants of David; again the concern was political (Eusebius, *Church History* 3.20).

The reign of Trajan (98–117) provides important evidence concerning the legal status of Christianity, and for that purpose must be returned to below. Trajan continued the policy that made Christians punishable "for the name," and in this he followed a precedent found in the treatment of Druids, participants in the Bacchanalia, and occasionally worshippers of Isis and Jews.

Sestertius of Emperor Nero, under whose rule occurred the first persecution of Christians in Rome.

When Druidism was suppressed in Gaul, probably for political reasons, on a charge of human sacrifice, no inquiry was made whether an individual actually participated in the shameful activities. The whole group was proscribed. Similarly, when Jews were banished from Rome, no effort was made to determine whether individuals were involved in any illegal or immoral activity; membership in the group was sufficient reason for expulsion.

Hadrian (117–38), in response to popular tumults that forced magistrates to follow mob demands, sought to regularize proceedings to the law courts, in effect reaffirming the policies of Trajan.

The reign of Marcus Aurelius (161–80) was a bad time for Christians, due to disasters and misfortunes at different places in the Roman world. Although Christian Apologists joined the general praise for Marcus Aurelius as a person, his rule saw a worsening of persecution against Christians. There was a wave of persecution in 166–68, a time when the Parthian war, pressure from Germans on the Danube frontier, and an outbreak of the plague came close together. Presumably a general edict called for sacrifice to the gods, which was not specifically anti-Christian in intent, but made Christians conspicuous by their absence.

A new wave of anti-Christian sentiment around 177 produced busy apologetic activity. After a revolt led by Avidius Cassius in 175 was put down, Marcus Aurelius made a tour of the east in 176. New suspicions were aroused against groups not showing the customary forms of allegiance by sacrificing on behalf of the emperor.

B. Attitudes of Pagans toward Christians

Christians aroused considerable popular animosity. People tend to believe the worst about a group that seems aloof, secretive, even foreign. In good times people will tolerate others with strange customs or beliefs, but in bad times they take a more negative attitude. Christians were held responsible for various calamities since they did not worship the traditional gods. Some Jews fanned the flames of hostility, especially on the question of loyalty, by making the authorities aware of the differences between Jews and Christians.

Moreover, early Christians appeared to be obstinate. The Roman governor Pliny the Younger complained of this: It seemed such a simple thing (from a Roman point of view) to burn a pinch of incense on an altar or swear by the emperor, but this was something that committed Christians would not do. Such obstinacy a totalitarian government cannot endure. Under such a regime, the supreme virtue is obedience to the duly constituted authorities.

The ordinary person in the Roman world had no normal obligation to sacrifice—any more than a policeman's order today to "move on" implies a duty of perpetual motion—but the command of a duly constituted magistrate to perform an act of sacrifice required obedience. When Christians, on being commanded to burn incense or acknowledge Caesar as lord, refused to perform these acts of loyalty, the authorities and others took unfavorable notice.

The Christian Apologists repeatedly responded to three other charges: atheism, cannibalism, and incest. These charges seem absolutely incredible to Christians now, so some explanation is required.

Atheism in the ancient world was practical, not theoretical. An atheist was someone who did not observe the traditional religious practices, regardless of what faith he professed. (For example, Epicurus believed in the Greek gods, but since he did not think they interfered in human life—the traditional rites were only for their honor and one

Caecilius, pagan opponent of Christianity: "Why have Christians no altars, no temples, no consecrated images? Why do they never speak openly, never congregate freely, unless for the reason that what they adore and conceal is either worthy of punishment or something to be ashamed of?" (Minucius Felix, *Octavius* 10).

discuss
Gnostics?

should not expect any answer to prayer—his followers often dispensed with the observance of these rituals and so were considered atheists.)

The Christian Apologists insisted that Christians believed in God, Jesus Christ, and the Holy Spirit (Justin Martyr seems to throw in the holy angels as well for good measure), but this did not satisfy the basis of the objection, for Christians still did not perform the customary ceremonies.

The charge of cannibalism may derive from Christian language about the eucharist of eating the body and drinking the blood. Incest may have been suggested by Christians' referring to one another as "brother" and "sister" with men and women sharing the common table at the "love feast."

Other charges of immorality apparently stemmed from a failure of the Romans to distinguish between libertine Gnostics (who claimed to be Christians) and Christians. The early Christians who wrote against heresies made it clear, however, that it was the members of the Gnostic sects who were guilty of sexual immorality.

These and other charges were more readily believed about Christians because they kept themselves removed from the normal activities of society. They remained aloof, however, because almost all aspects—athletics, entertainment, political affairs, and many commercial transactions—were permeated with idolatry.

Another kind of popular contempt of Christians is represented by the graffito found in Rome that shows a person with an ass's head on a cross, while a second raises his hand in tribute, alongside the inscription, "Alexamenos worships his god." The ass's head may have been suggested by the slander known from pagan sources that explained the Jewish prohibition against entering the holiest place in the Jerusalem temple (unlike pagan temples, which were open to the public) as a matter of shame because their cult image (pagan temples always housed an image of the deity) was an ass.

Philosophers like Celsus, who wrote the first major surviving attack on Christians, *The True Word* (the contents of which can be largely restored from the response by Origen, *Against Celsus*), manifested an intellectual scorn and despising of Christians, who were viewed as unprofitable members of society, a miserable bunch of weaklings—women, children, and slaves. Christians, moreover, called on people simply to "believe," and did not engage in rational demonstration.

Celsus raised the philosophical questions that Porphyry and Julian later would elaborate: If Christianity were true, why had it come so late in human history? Were not the miracles of Jesus worked by magic? How can the incarnation be possible, since it involves change in the deity? Is not the immortality of the soul a more desirable goal than resurrection of the body?

Origen responded to these attacks by stating that God prepared the way for Christianity and that fulfilled prophecy demonstrated its truth. The miracles of Jesus were not worked by magic, as is shown by the moral improvement Jesus brought to human life and by the miracles never being used for personal gain. The incarnation brought a change in circumstances but not in nature to the Logos (Word). The resurrection involves a change into a higher form of body. The rapid expansion of Christianity would not have been possible without divine assistance.

Galen shared Celsus's dismay at Christians' substitution of faith for reason, but he did praise their manner of life (chapter 8) as exemplifying what philosophers sought to inculcate on the basis of reason.

The philosophers Epictetus and Marcus Aurelius (the latter also served as the Roman emperor, 161–80) disapproved of the Christians' readiness for martyrdom. Although their own Stoic philosophy permitted suicide in certain situations, they found Christians motivated by blind fanaticism.

The satirist Lucian of Samosata was the mocking rationalist who scoffed at the gullibility of the Christians taken in by the charlatan Peregrinus. Peregrinus was a Cynic philosopher who associated with Christians in Palestine and attained a leadership position among them. When he was imprisoned by the authorities, Christians went to great lengths to provide for his needs, and on his release he acquired a great deal of money from them.

The Christian reader today may recognize behind Lucian's scornful account the putting into practice of the teachings of Jesus Christ about caring for those in prison.

II. THE LEGAL BASIS OF THE PERSECUTIONS

The fact of persecution is not in doubt. Although it was not as constant or as extensive as is often assumed, it was always present as a possibility. Not so clear, in spite of confident assertions, is the reason for the persecutions and their legal basis.

Many explanations have been offered, but they are mostly based on conjecture. Was there a general law forbidding Christianity, going back to Nero? Did governors enforce public order by direct police action without reference to specific legislation? Were Christians persecuted under known criminal laws against treason, illegal assembly, or an alien cult? Was the persecution because of religious reasons—that is, because of opposition to the Roman gods and the perceived threat to the Roman state?

Various factors must be kept in mind in understanding the causes of persecution. Christians, of course, got off on the wrong foot as far as the

Roman authorities were concerned. They worshipped a man who had been crucified by the judicial decision of a Roman governor on a charge of being a messianic (kingly) pretender. That circumstance would always be prejudicial against Christians.

Christians, for religious reasons, could not engage in the accepted expressions of political loyalty, so they appeared as a threat to the Roman state. Moreover, the popular animosity aroused by the aloofness and secretiveness of Christians, and the civil disturbances their presence often caused, were part of the background to persecution.

The correspondence in 112 between Pliny the Younger (*Epistles* 10.96), governor of Bithynia, and the emperor, Trajan, provides a window into the legal situation. From this correspondence it is clear that the standard charge was already "the name": "I asked whether they were Christians." This basis of accusation was not new, and the only time we know when it could have become operative was under Nero. Pliny himself had never been present at investigations of Christians, so he did not know what their crime was.

Pliny found three distinct classes among those against whom accusations had been brought:

Trajan, the emperor under whom the Roman Empire reached its greatest geographical extent and who set imperial policy for the treatment of Christians (Uffizi, Florence).

1. Those who confessed they were Christians and remained steadfast in the confession—these he ordered for execution, or if they were Roman citizens, ordered them to be sent to Rome.

2. Those who denied they had ever been Christians—these he released, since they recited a prayer to the gods and offered incense and wine to a statue of the emperor, "things which those who are really Christians cannot be made to do," and so a reasonable test to determine who was a Christian and who would prove loyal to Rome.

3. Those who apostatized, those who had been Christians but had ceased to be such (a few of these apostatized twenty years ago—that is, under Domitian) and proved it by worshipping the emperor's statue and the gods and cursing Christ—from them Pliny learned what he knew of Christianity, nothing really dangerous, only "a perverse and extravagant superstition."

Pliny asked Trajan three questions: (1) Are any distinctions to be made for age or weakness? (2) Are apostates to be pardoned? (3) Does punishment attach to the name itself or to crimes connected with the name?

The significance here is that if punishment was for the name, those who were no longer Christians could be pardoned, but if it was for crimes attached to the name, the inquiry had to proceed and the guilty punished no matter how long ago it had occurred. Faithful Christians wanted the examination to be on the basis of supposed crimes, for they were guilty of none; apostates wanted it to be on the basis of the name, for they were no longer members. Pliny himself wanted to encourage apostates, for he felt that many could be reclaimed from the Christian superstition.

Trajan gave Pliny the answer he wanted, approving of his procedures. He ignored Pliny's first question, which concerned matters within the discretion of a governor.

Otherwise, Trajan gave three responses:

1. Christians were not to be sought out, but if accused and convicted they were to be punished. This may sound contradictory but was according to normal Roman legal procedure. Rome did not have a public prosecutor, and the legal system was set in motion by an individual making a formal charge before a magistrate.

2. No anonymous accusations were to be received. An accuser had to act in the proper judicial manner by coming forward in his own person.

3. The deniers were to be pardoned; punishment was, therefore, on the basis of the "name." Christian Apologists argued strongly against this procedure, but the course of Roman legal action had been set.

Bust from Cyrene (modern Libya) of Marcus Aurelius, under whose rule there was vigorous apologetic activity by Christians (British Museum, London).

Before Marcus Aurelius, action against Christians was limited, because their numbers seemed few. Since only the governor could pronounce the death sentence, most of the known cases of martyrdom were in the great provincial cities. Governors were allowed a wide latitude by Roman law. The threat of persecution was ever present, but it was not a constant experience.

Before the mid-third century the persecutions were local and occasional. Although they became somewhat more frequent under Marcus Aurelius, the legal situation did not change.

Two responses by Christians to the persecutions resulted in significant literary productions: apologetics and martyrdom.

The apologies get their name from the Greek word *apologia,* meaning "a defense." Martyrdom derives from the Greek word *martys,* "a witness." Christians put in writing the statement of their case and their plea for tolerance. They also told the story of their faithful members who died in testimony to their faith.

III. CHRISTIAN APOLOGISTS OF THE SECOND CENTURY

A. Writings

Possibly the earliest apology to survive in whole comes from Aristides of Athens. Although written in Greek, the better text is the Syriac translation, for the surviving Greek text is a rewriting of the apology by a Byzantine author.

The *Epistle to Diognetus* presents an attractive picture of the Christian life. The anonymous author argues for the divine origin of Christianity as superior to the idolatry of pagans and the ritualistic worship of Jews. The date is uncertain, but the work seems to breathe an atmosphere of an early date. On the other hand, known persons by the name of Diognetus who might be candidates for the recipient of the

APOLOGISTS		
Names	**Place**	**Emperors**
(1) Those known by fragments:		
Quadratus, *Preaching of Peter,* and Aristo of Pella		Hadrian (117–38)
Miltiades, Apollinaris of Hierapolis, and Melito of Sardis		Marcus Aurelius (161–80)
(2) *Epistle to Diognetus*		Date uncertain
(3) Aristides	Athens	Hadrian or Antoninus Pius (138–61)
(4) Justin Martyr	Rome	Antoninus Pius and Marcus Aurelius
(5) Tatian	Syria	Marcus Aurelius
(6) Athenagoras	Athens	Marcus Aurelius
(7) Theophilus	Antioch	Commodus (180–92)
(8) Minucius Felix	Carthage?	Between Marcus Aurelius and Septimius Severus (193–211)

apology belong to the late second century. The present text seems to contain a portion of a homily attached at the end.

Tatian was born a pagan in east Syria and was converted during a journey to Rome, where he became a student of Justin. He composed a harmony of the four Gospels, the *Diatessaron*, which became for two centuries the standard form of the Gospels in Syriac-speaking areas, where he became in his later years a leader of Encratite thought. His approach to apologetics was the negative one of tearing down the pagan alternative. The *Oration against the Greeks* (177–78) is principally a blast against Greek culture, perhaps prepared with Athens in mind. The work has been classified rhetorically either as a "farewell" to Greek culture or as an "exhortation" (*protrepticus*) to accept the "barbarian philosophy" of Christianity.

Athenagoras (176–77) of Athens was the most philosophically accomplished of the second-century Apologists. His *Plea* or *Embassy* (*Supplicatio* or *Legatio*) adapts the model of Middle Platonist philosophical works. In answering pagan charges against Christians, Athenagoras argues the superiority of Christian morality and Christian views of God over pagan descriptions of their gods.

Athenagoras gives an early formulation of the doctrine of the Trinity. His authorship is disputed regarding *On the Resurrection*, a work that argues from nature and reason, and not from Scripture, for the resurrection.

Theophilus, bishop of Antioch, wrote a work, *To Autolycus,* composed of three books, about 180. His view of Christianity has many similarities to Hellenistic Judaism. As an Apologist, he speaks of the Logos but avoids mention of Jesus Christ. He produces a chronological argument for the antiquity of the Jewish Scriptures on which Christianity was based and offers an allegorical reading of the Genesis account of creation.

One Latin Apologist may belong in the late second century — Minucius Felix. There is clearly some relationship in content between Minucius Felix's *Octavius* and Tertullian's *Apology*, dated about 200. Most give priority to Tertullian, but there is enough debate to leave open the possibility that Minucius Felix is earlier. The apology is written as a dialogue between the pagan Caecilius and the Christian Octavius, so there is a statement of the pagan case along with the Christian response, which results in the conversion of Caecilius.

B. Justin Martyr as a Representative Apologist

Arguably the most important and most influential of the second-century Christian Apologists was Justin Martyr, who embodied in his life and death the two Christian responses to persecution that produced

"God does not stand in need of holocausts, although indeed it behooves us to offer a bloodless sacrifice and the service of our reason" (Athenagoras, *Plea* 13).

The Church and the Empire

literary works: apologetics and martyrdom. There survive from Justin two *Apologies* and a *Dialogue with Trypho* and about him an account of his trial, the *Acts of Justin*.

What is known of Justin's life comes mainly from the opening chapters of the *Dialogue*. He was born in Samaria at the Roman colony of Neapolis (modern Nablus), neither a Samaritan nor a Jew. Justin relates his quest for philosophy, studying under a Stoic, an Aristotelian, a Pythagorean, and a Platonist, until he met an old man (at Neapolis or at Ephesus?), who in Socratic method raised questions that only the "Christian philosophy" could answer.

Although Justin's thought fits exactly into the Middle Platonism of the second century, he came to regard Christianity as *the* philosophy, the goal of human searching. In the words of Eusebius, "Justin in philosopher's garb served as an ambassador of the word of God" (*Church History* 4.11).

Justin came to Rome, where, using rented quarters, he taught Christian doctrine in a private school, of which there is some description in the *Acts of Justin*. A Cynic philosopher, Crescens, brought charges against Justin, and he was executed about 167.

Justin fought his apologetic battles on four fronts: against pagan intellectuals, the state, the Jews, and heretics. Eusebius says Justin wrote two apologies. The so-called *2 Apology* precedes the *1 Apology* in the manuscript, but scholars now think it is really an appendix to the latter. The *1 Apology* is an address to the emperor, perhaps occasioned by the martyrdom of Polycarp (c. 156), for it is written against the popular tumults against Christians in Asia. Justin here appeals to a rescript of the emperor Hadrian requiring regular trials and specific charges by individuals against the Christians and argues against the practice of condemning Christians solely for "the name." The *2 Apology*, whether appended to the *1 Apology* or a fragment of another apology, is a petition to the Senate occasioned by another case of martyrdom.

Justin, as the other Apologists, responds to charges of incest, cannibalism, atheism, and being a subversive group. Instead of being immoral, Christianity, he argues, is very moral. Justin further argues from the antiquity of the Jewish Scriptures and the fulfillment of their prophecies in Christianity. He shows considerable self-confidence over against both the state and the synagogue; indeed he aims at the conversion of the empire.

Quite notable is the attention Justin gives to demons, with whom he identifies the pagan gods. Justin finds analogues to Christian beliefs in Greek mythology in order to make Christian teaching understandable and acceptable to pagan readers. Similarities to Christian practices in the mysteries he explains as demonic imitations.

> "Whatever things were rightly said among all men are the property of us Christians" (Justin, *2 Apology* 13).

In order to banish the secrecy about Christian meetings, Justin explains what was involved in baptism and in the Sunday worship. In explaining the relationship of Christ to God, Justin gives expression to the doctrine of the Logos, of which more is said below.

The *Dialogue with Trypho* is the fullest statement from the early church of its arguments with Judaism. It falls in a line of the worsening relations between the church and Judaism extending from Paul's letter to the Romans, the Epistle to the Hebrews, collections of testimonies related to the Old Testament (which Justin may have used), *Barnabas*, the *Dialogue*, Melito's homily *On the Passover*, and *Jason and Papiscus* by Aristo (now lost, but known from other sources to end in the Jew asking for baptism).

The *Dialogue with Trypho* is useful for showing the questions at issue between Jews and Christians. The dialogue was a common literary form, and we should not suppose it was the actual transcript of a discussion. Justin's knowledge of Judaism, however, indicates that he had been in real discussions with Jews, and the contents probably reflect such discussions.

Trypho, the Jew, raised two questions around which the debate centers (chapter 10): First, why do Christians not live different from Gentiles (in regard to Jewish religious customs) as the Scriptures enjoin the covenant people to do? Second, why do Christians put their hope in a crucified man? Stated otherwise, the main issues are three: (1) Christology—is Jesus the Messiah announced by Scripture? (2) The Law—what is the true meaning and purpose of the Old Testament Law? (3) The true Israel—is the church the new people of God?

The central issue of the Messiah is debated mainly in terms of Old Testament prophecy. Related to this issue are such things as the virgin birth, the interpretation of Scripture, and the two comings of the Messiah (the first in humiliation and the second in glory). Justin argues that the Old Testament law was imposed on Israel as a punishment and was temporary in preparation for the coming of the covenant found in Jesus Christ. Christians now are the true people of God. Recurring throughout his writings are other basic differences over practical matters such as the cessation of physical circumcision and the Sabbath.

Justin notes there were two kinds of Jewish believers in Jesus: those who insisted on converted Gentiles keeping the law and those who—although themselves keeping the law—did not insist on Gentile believers doing so. These differences were matched by two views from the side of Gentile Christians: those who insisted that Jewish believers give up the law and those who although rejecting the law for Gentiles allowed Jewish Christians to keep it.

"For the law promulgated on Horeb is now old and belongs to yourselves [Jews] alone; but this [final law and covenant] is for all universally" (Justin Martyr, *Dialogue with Trypho* 11.2).

Christianity had a built-in dialectic in its relations with Judaism. On the one hand, its claims to legitimacy and the authority of ancient Scriptures depended on accepting the Old Testament and the Jewish testimony to these Scriptures. On the other hand, its claims to be the fulfillment of the Old Testament prophecies and the new people of God involved a repudiation of the Jews for their failure to accept Jesus as the Messiah.

In spite of worsening relations, the teachings and traditions of Jews and Christians were mutually influencing each other until the fourth century.

C. The Logos Doctrine

The Apostolic Fathers, like the New Testament, did not give a precise interpretation of the relation of Jesus Christ to God, but they did have formulas involving God, Christ, and the Holy Spirit.

The early Christians, because of their Jewish background and opposition to paganism, stressed the oneness of God, but they knew the Messiah and the experience of the Holy Spirit as the working of God. The Apologists more explicitly state a pre-existent Trinity of God, the *Logos* (Word), and the Holy Spirit, but it is specifically in regard to Christ as the Logos of God that they made their most significant contribution.

The Logos Christology of the second-century Greek Apologists became the basis of later orthodox speculations on the Trinity. A composite description will be offered here of the doctrine pioneered by Justin but most fully expressed by Athenagoras and Theophilus. The Apologists represent the confluence of ideas from both the pagan and the Jewish sides that could be used to support the pre-existence of Jesus Christ.

From the Jewish background came ideas of the Law as pre-existent (rabbinic speculation), pre-existent Wisdom (Jewish wisdom literature), and the pre-existent Messiah and pre-existent Spirit (taken over by Paul). The extent to which any of these in Jewish thought was really hypostatized as distinct entities, in spite of occasional language suggesting a separate existence, is debated.

For the term *Logos* there was a possible background in the Old Testament "word of the Lord" and in the use in the Jewish Targums (paraphrases of Scripture) of the *memra* ("Word") of the Lord as an intermediary between God and his world.

On the Greek side there were the multiple meanings of the word *logos*. Two are important here: *logos* as the reason in the mind, the rational word; and *logos* as the word on the tongue, the spoken word. The Greeks developed the idea that speech is a rational activity: there is a continuity between the thought in the mind and the word on the tongue. In philosophy there was Stoic speculation about the rational principle (sometimes expressed by *logos*) that gave order to the universe.

The Jewish philosopher Philo fused this Stoic idea with the Jewish belief in a personal God by speaking of the *logoi* as the thoughts or reasonings in the mind of God.

Where the prologue to the Gospel of John fits in this development is not clear. Does the "Word" of John 1 reflect primarily the Greek, especially philosophical, usage of *logos*, or does it represent primarily the Hebrew/Aramaic background, or is it already a fusion of these two lines of thought?

In Philo the *logos* has a variety of functions as an expression of God and is seemingly hypostatized, but John makes an affirmation not found in either the Greek or Jewish backgrounds, declaring that the *Logos* became incarnate as a specific historical person.

With Justin and the Apologists these two tributaries are certainly combined in a systematic linking of the Messiah with both Greek preexistent *logos* and Jewish pre-existent Word, Wisdom, or Spirit.

We may schematize their thought as reflecting five stages in the career of the *Logos*:

1. The *Logos* as the reason or wisdom resident in the mind of God—God always has his reason immanent in himself.

2. The *Logos* as the spoken or articulated word—God spoke forth his word, especially in creating the world, giving a separate existence to his word but not emptying himself of his reason.

3. The *Logos* as immanent in the world—God planted his reason in the universe, giving rational order to creation, and in the minds of human beings, thereby inspiring philosophy, art, literature, etc. (both the word or wisdom of God as the agent of creation, and the seminal word in each person, are an image of the divine, so more than human reason is intended).

4. The *Logos* as the revealed word of God in the prophets.

5. The *Logos* as incarnate in Jesus—the divine word became flesh as a personal human being.

The apologetic value of this scheme was great. It connected Jesus, the object of Christian faith, with Greek philosophy and concepts familiar to the Greeks, and it offered a clear illustration of how Jesus Christ could be one with God and yet distinct from him.

As the word in the mind becomes the word on the tongue, so Christ as the eternal reason of God, while remaining one within him, came also to have a separate existence in God's work of creation and

"The Son of God is the Logos [Word] of the Father in form [or thought] and actuality.... He is the first offspring of the Father, not as having come into existence, for from the beginning God, being eternal Mind, had in himself the Logos, since he was always possessed of Logos [Word or Reason]" (Athenagoras, *Plea for the Christians* 10).

revelation. Moreover, he was identical with the rational order of the universe (recognized by philosophy) implanted in it at creation.

Then, going beyond anything in Greek or Jewish thought, this Word of God was not only the means of God's creating activity but also became the means of God's saving activity by taking flesh in the person of Jesus.

Later orthodox thought about Christ in his relation to the one God, although going beyond and thereby correcting the Logos Christology, followed the lines marked out by it.

D. Summary of the Apologists

The Christian Apologists exhibit considerable indebtedness to earlier Jewish apologetics. Among the points on which Jewish thinkers pioneered the way for Christian thinkers were their arguments (1) for the greater antiquity of Moses and the Scriptures than Greek literature and philosophy, (2) for the borrowing by the Greeks of their good ideas from the Hebrews, (3) for the superiority of monotheism to pagan polytheism (drawing also on Greek philosophical thought), and (4) for the interpretation of biblical thought in terms of Greek culture.

As defenders of the faith, the Apologists answered the popular charges against Christians and made a plea for tolerance. Christians, they said, are really good citizens and pray for the empire. On a deeper level, they wrestled with three fundamental questions that, although rephrased, still express the "scandal" of the Christian faith.

1. How can the universality of salvation in one religion that reached back scarcely 150 years be maintained? Their answer connected Christianity with the Jewish Scriptures and the original purposes of God.

2. How can one accept the scandal of the cross, a suffering Messiah who at the same time is God? The answer connected Jesus with the eternal Word of God and blamed the influence of demons for his death.

3. How can the power of demons in paganism and in the persecution of Christians be reconciled with the providence of a good God? The answer could only appeal to faith in the victory of Jesus Christ over the demons and the eventual vindication of God's purposes in the second coming of Christ.

The Apologists were not content with defense. They took the offensive by attacking the pagan cults, which were mythological, irrational, and often connected with immorality.

Moreover, the Apologists sought to prove Christianity. Especially important here was the argument from fulfilled prophecy. A major difference between the modern world and the world in which Christianity arose is that people today consider the latest the best, the most recent the truest. The opposite was the case in the Greco-Roman world: the oldest was the truest.

In a world that valued antiquity, the Apologists argued that Christianity was really not a new religion, but reached back to the original religion of humanity and represented the culmination of God's plans forecast in the prophets of the Old Testament. The argument from prophecy served both to answer the charge of novelty against Christianity and to prove its truth.

The Apologists, furthermore, expounded Christian faith. Doctrinally, they stressed monotheism and the Creator. Jesus Christ and the Holy Spirit were placed in relation to God. They thereby pioneered in the development of Christian theology.

The Apologists mark an important development in the Christian intellectual effort at cultural accommodation and appropriation. They used the philosophy of the day for Christian purposes. As Apologists, they ostensibly addressed outsiders. We do not know to what extent outsiders actually read their works; as has usually been the case since then, their works were probably more read by Christians than by those to whom they were addressed.

Nonetheless, the Apologists represent a new stage in Christian intellectual activity. The New Testament, the Apostolic Fathers, and the New Testament Apocrypha were addressed to those within the Christian movement. The Apologists, regardless of who the actual readers were, wrote with their minds on non-Christians. The New Testament authors, to some extent, had used the rhetoric and moral philosophy of the time to express themselves; the Apologists explicitly used a larger corpus of pagan philosophy and literature to defend and clarify Christian thought.

Educated Christians could either react against their pagan past and reject it, or present Christianity in some sense as in continuity with it and its fulfillment. Converts typically either exaggerate the contrast between the old and the new, or explain the new as what their past logically led them to embrace.

Tatian represents the former approach: he sought to burn bridges from the past. His teacher, Justin, took a different approach: he tried to build bridges.

The future in Christian thought belonged to Justin, but the attitude of Tatian has continued to be one current among the Christian attitudes to the world and society.

IV. MARTYRS OF THE SECOND CENTURY

A. The Literature of Martyrdom

The authentic accounts of martyrdom from the second century come in three literary forms: "letters" by churches that describe the accompanying events and the martyrdoms of those in their number, "passions" that narrate the last days and death of the martyrs, and "acts" that recount their trials before the authorities. The acts have sometimes been thought to be the transcripts of court records of the trials but, although perhaps in some cases based on such records, the surviving accounts clearly reflect Christian editing and adaptation.

By early in the third century leading Christian authors (Tertullian, Origen, Cyprian) also wrote "exhortations" to martyrdom. From the fourth century and after, preachers delivered panegyrics on the occasion of the annual commemoration of the death of a martyr. The concern for edification of the hearers was more important than historical accuracy, and in the later "lives" of the saints legend filled a larger place than fact.

Amphitheater at Lyons, France (built 19 BC), where Christians were martyred in AD 177.

ACCOUNTS OF MARTYRDOM

Documents	Date	Location
Letters of Churches		
Martyrdom of Polycarp	156?	Smyrna
Letter of the Churches of Vienne and Lyons	177	Lyons
Passions		
Martyrdom of Ptolemy and Lucius (in Justin, *2 Apology*)	c. 150–60	Rome
Passion of Perpetua and Felicitas	203	Carthage
Acts		
Acts of Justin and his Companions	167	Rome
Acts of the Pergamene Saints	c. 165–70	Pergamum
Acts of the Martyrs of Scilli	180	Carthage
Acts of Apollonius	c. 184	Rome

One of the most influential documents of martyrdom, and perhaps the earliest to record one in some detail, was the *Martyrdom of Polycarp*. This letter was written by his church at Smyrna to the church at Philomelium in Phrygia. The date of Polycarp's death is disputed between 156, 167–68, and 177, but preference is given to the early date.

The theme of the *Martyrdom of Polycarp* is "martyrdom according to the Gospel." The author writes against the practice of volunteering for martyrdom and refers to an instance when someone did this and then denied the faith under pressure. He commends instead the example of Polycarp, who retired from the city to avoid death, but when captured confessed his faith firmly and endured his trial and execution with dignity and courage.

As described by Justin Martyr, a woman in Rome was converted by the Christian teacher Ptolemy. He was prosecuted on the sole point of being a Christian by the woman's husband when she divorced him for his immoral life. At the trial Lucius spoke in Ptolemy's defense and, when ascertained to be a Christian himself, was condemned to punishment along with Ptolemy.

The *Acts of Justin and his Companions* is one of the oldest surviving *acta* (or *gesta*) of a trial of Christians. The three recensions show the progressive elaboration of the Christian viewpoint that occurred in the transmission of the document. The companions had received instruction in Christianity from Justin (although two expressly stated

Polycarp is especially remembered for his response to the governor's pleas for him to renounce Jesus Christ: "For eighty-six years I have served Christ and he has done me no wrong; how can I blaspheme against my King and Savior?" (*Martyrdom of Polycarp* 9.3).

they received their Christianity from their parents) and they were condemned to be beheaded with him.

The *Acts of Saints Carpus, Papylus, and Agathonice* (the Pergamene saints) is dated by Eusebius to around 165, probably correctly, although the Latin version shows reworking that reflects language more characteristic of the third century. Women were prominent among the early martyrs, achieving an equality in death not often attained in life in the ancient world. Agathonice was a woman, as was one of Justin's fellow martyrs, Charito.

The *Letter of the Churches of Vienne and Lyons* ranks with the *Martyrdom of Polycarp* as the most important documents of the second-century martyr literature. Many of the Christians in the Rhone valley of Gaul (France) came from Asia Minor, and this letter was sent to the churches in the Roman provinces of Asia and Phrygia. Eusebius has preserved this letter, which contains a rich theology of martyrdom, in book 5 of his *Church History*.

The persecution at Lyons is notable (1) for this firsthand account of the rage of the populace that resulted in exceedingly brutal experiences for the Christians and (2) for the large number of martyrs, the

Amphitheater at Carthage (modern Tunisia), probable site of the martyrdom of Perpetua and Felicitas in AD 203.

Photo courtesy of Robin Jensen.

Roman citizens being beheaded and the rest condemned to the wild beast contests in the arena.

The letter gives vivid personal impressions of some of the martyrs, especially of the young heroine of the faith Blandina, who endured particularly unbelievable and excruciating tortures. The martyrs were forgiving of their fellow believers who denied the faith, and they were modest about their own confession, preferring to be called "confessors" and reserving the name "martyrs" for those who had already died.

The *Acts of the Martyrs of Scilli* is notable as the earliest surviving Christian work in Latin. It recounts the examination of twelve Christians from a town in North Africa before the governor in the provincial capital of Carthage. They brought with them a case containing the letters of Paul.

The *Acts of Apollonius* represents another instance of apologetics and martyrdom coming together. It contains two speeches by the philosopher Apollonius, who turned his defense into an apology for Christianity. It seems unlikely that such an apology could have been given in the setting of a trial, but the early part of the account may be accurate.

The *Passion of Perpetua and Felicitas* with its account of martyrdoms in Carthage in 203 is unique in several respects. This Latin narrative incorporates two writings from the martyrs themselves, and one of these is the diary of one of the few women authors known from the ancient church, Perpetua. The contents of the work are the diary of Perpetua, a vision of Saturus from his own hand, as well as an introduction, account of the martyrdoms, and brief epilogue added by the editor (whom some have identified with Tertullian).

Perpetua was a woman of twenty-two, nursing an infant son, of some social standing in Carthage, whose father tried to dissuade her from her Christian confession. She, like the others, was still a catechumen at the time of her arrest, but she was soon baptized. Her diary is notable for her dreams that give insight into popular piety. Felicitas was her slave, who gave birth to a child while in prison.

B. Motifs of Martyrdom

The idea of martyrdom had Jewish precedents but was particularly developed by Christians in the period of persecution. The word "martyr" is the Greek word for "witness."

In Luke's writings the "witness" was one who had seen the resurrected Jesus Christ and could literally bear witness or attest to this event.

John uses the word in the sense of testimony for Christ as the Son of God (comparable to the idea in Matthew 10:32). In Revelation the

The Church and the Empire

word is used in reference to a blood-witness, one who gave his life for his confession, but the word apparently was not yet the technical term it became during the second century. Those who gave their lives in persecution, and they alone, came to be called "martyrs" ("witnesses"); those who gave their confession but for some reason were not killed were called "confessors." The martyrs were not only witnesses in the sense of confessing their faith, but were also in a sense eyewitnesses, for they often received a vision of Christ.

A theology of martyrdom was early elaborated. There is a beginning in Ignatius; it is rather fully developed already in the *Martyrdom of Polycarp*. Since Jesus Christ was the original and true "martyr," a parallelism with Christ was often worked out in the accounts of martyrdom. Moreover, he was thought to be present with the martyrs (as in the *Letter of the Churches of Vienne and Lyons*), sustaining them in their sufferings. The salient points in the theology of martyrdom may be expressed by some basic motifs:

1. Witness

The meaning of the word "martyr" calls attention to the basic motif of witness. The martyrs, by confessing the faith, gave testimony to the authorities and others who heard. The death was a blood witness to Jesus Christ and faith in him. There recurs in the acts of the martyrs the confession, "I am a Christian."

2. Athletes and Heroes

Athletic metaphors are often employed in describing the contest of the martyrs with the forces of evil embodied in their pagan opponents. As victors in the contest they were regarded as the heroes of the church, the outstanding exemplars of the Christian faith. Martyrs thus had a very privileged position in the esteem of the Christian community.

3. Grace

Martyrdom was the supreme form of sanctity, but it was a grace not given to all Christians. Martyrdom was a bit capricious in regard to whom it came, thus there was a sense that one was chosen by God for this experience. God granted the privileges of martyrdom to some but not to all. For this reason, persons were not to force themselves into martyrdom. That would be presumptuous (besides, the church had unfortunate experiences with those who rushed forward to claim the prize). The decision concerning who was to be a martyr rested with God, who gives his grace to whom he chooses.

4. Sharing the sufferings and victory of Jesus Christ.

Martyrdom was a grace because the martyrs' victory was not a human achievement. The martyr was privileged to share the sufferings of Christ and thereby to share in his victory over the devil. Christian existence was a struggle with Satan. As the death of Christ might appear to be a defeat, but was actually a victory over the Evil One, so each martyr's death was a defeat of the devil. Dying without denying the faith was a confirmation of the passion of Christ.

5. Eucharist

As the bread and wine were related to the death of Jesus Christ, so eucharistic language was used for the death of martyrs. Jesus had spoken of his death as "to drink the cup" (Mark 10:38) of suffering and had prayed to "let this cup pass from me" (Mark 14:36). The martyrs too drank the cup of Jesus with trust in God.

6. Holy Spirit

The martyrs endured their sufferings because Jesus Christ was with them, extending his sufferings to be in and with them. This presence of Christ was mediated by the Spirit. The Spirit gave supernatural endurance, and in some cases granted visions to strengthen and console the Lord's witnesses.

7. Eschatology

The martyr was the perfect Christian who brought the eschaton to fulfillment in himself. The martyr was believed to enter directly into the presence of Jesus Christ in heaven and to enjoy special privileges there.

One of these was to share in Christ's role as judge and so to be able to grant forgiveness to weaker brothers and sisters on earth. This became the basis later for the practice of praying for the intercession of the saints.

Martyrdom was viewed as a kind of "radically realized eschatology." The martyrs realized now the blessings intended for all Christians, for in the events surrounding their death they entered into the end-time blessings of the presence of God, the gift of the Spirit, and forgiveness of sins.

8. Baptism

Their death brought forgiveness of sins to the martyrs. Theirs was a "baptism of blood." As Jesus Christ had spoken of his sufferings as a bitter "cup" to be drunk, so he had spoken of them as a "baptism" (Mark 10:38), for he was overwhelmed in suffering. The martyr shared this baptism of suffering, and the same benefits attributed to baptism were ascribed to martyrdom. This was one exception the ancient church made in its normally strong teaching on the necessity of baptism (chapter 8). Often catechumens who had not yet received baptism were caught up in the accusations made against Christians; not all had the opportunity to be baptized, as did Perpetua.

It certainly made no sense for these persons to deny Jesus Christ so as to gain time to be baptized, hence the church assured them that their death for Christ was equivalent to the baptismal confession of faith.

In spite of some defections, the persecutions—instead of crushing the church—strengthened the resolve of devoted believers. Their steadfastness under pressure, even to martyrdom, called attention to Christian faith and attracted inquirers.

Opponents on the outside, however, did not provide the only problems faced by the second-century church.

FOR FURTHER STUDY

Ferguson, Everett, ed. *Church and State in the Early Church.* Studies in Early Christianity 7. New York: Garland, 1993.

Grant, Robert M. *Greek Apologists of the Second Century.* Philadelphia: Westminster, 1988.

Novak, R. P. *Christianity and the Roman Empire: Background Texts.* Harrisburg, PA: Trinity Press International, 2001.

Young, Robin Darling. *In Procession Before the World: Martyrdom as Public Liturgy in Early Christianity.* Milwaukee: Marquette University Press, 2001.

Heresies and Schisms in the Second Century

The last chapter considered the external problems facing the church in the second century: opposition from the state and the synagogue. This chapter turns to the internal problems involved in drawing the boundaries of acceptable doctrine and practice. Modern usage distinguishes heresy (false doctrine) from schism (division over personalities, discipline, and practices, where fundamental doctrinal error is not involved).

As has been observed, "Heretics are brilliantly wrong; schismatics are obstinately wrong." Ancient word usage of *hairesis* ("heresy") and *schisma* ("schism"), however, did not originally make this distinction.

I. MARCION

It may be unconventional to start with Marcion, but his basic position is easier to grasp than that of the Gnostics (this is not to say that there are no problems in interpreting Marcion), and his seems to have been a strictly religious approach without the speculative interests of many of the "Gnostics."

Marcion started from the distinctiveness of the Christian revelation, and he established a new church (something other heretics did not do). His church rivaled the great church and lasted until the fifth century.

Marcion has enough in common with those labeled "Gnostics" to be a good introduction, but enough difference to belong in a class to himself.

In discussing Jewish Christianity we found certain extremes coming from Jewish influences; in Marcion we find extremes from the Gentile side. Marcion took a position decidedly opposing the Jewish roots of Christianity.

Marcion was reared in Sinope, Pontus, where his father was reportedly a bishop. He was a ship-builder and acquired considerable wealth. The false teaching opposed in the New Testament letter to the Colossians and Docetic ideas current in Asia Minor may have been part of his religious background, and anti-Jewish sentiment associated with the Bar Kokhba revolt in Palestine in the 130s likely influenced him, although his basic perspective may have developed earlier.

Marcion went to Rome and gave the church a large sum of money. His teachings, however, were rejected in 144, and his money was returned to him. He proceeded to set up a rival church that in a few years was nearly as widespread as the great church. Marcion's wealth and organizing ability enabled him to take over some of the emerging Gnosticizing groups, but the organization and worship of his communities seems to have been similar to that of the great church.

Marcion is known for his work on the text and canon of the New Testament. He rejected the Old Testament as Scripture for the church and issued a New Testament consisting of edited versions of the Gospel of Luke and ten Pauline epistles (lacking the Pastoral Epistles). He omitted or changed verses, often on a dogmatic basis. His is the oldest known fixed collection of New Testament books.

He wrote the *Antitheses*, presenting contradictions between the Old and New Testaments, in which his theology is set forth. We know the work primarily from the five-book refutation by Tertullian, *Against Marcion*.

Marcion's theology has been described as an exaggerated Pauline gospel of grace. One critic delivered the dictum that in the ancient church "Only Marcion understood Paul, and he misunderstood him." This is no doubt a one-sided Protestant judgment, but it is difficult to see Marcion, or others for that matter, apart from a modern interpreter's own perspective.

The following points reflect the basic views of Marcion as they can be reconstructed from the criticisms leveled against him by his opponents in the ancient church.

> In one of his many witticisms, Tertullian described Marcion as "the Pontic mouse who has gnawed the Gospels to pieces" (*Against Marcion* 1.1).

1. There are two gods—the creator god and the redeemer god. Marcion's dualism seems not to have been a metaphysical matter, but an inference from the human experience of contradictions in life.

2. Law and judgment belong to the creator (the Demiurge), and redemption is the work of the Father (the "Unknown" or "Strange" God).

3. The Old Testament is the revelation of the creator. It predicts the Jewish Messiah (the Jews have read their Scriptures correctly). Jesus is not the fulfiller of the Old Testament (he came

"not to fulfill but to destroy" the Law). The Old Testament God worked evils, contradicted himself, and delighted in wars.

4. Jesus was viewed in a Docetic manner; he only seemed to suffer. Yet, his death was described as a purchase. Jesus' resurrection was of his soul and spirit, and he raised himself. This view again seems not to have originated from a metaphysical standpoint (e.g., the inability of the divine to suffer), but from ordinary experience that recoiled from the flesh as unclean.

5. The physical birth of Jesus was a stumbling block to Marcion, so he began his Gospel in Luke 3 with the statement that in the fifteenth year of the reign of Tiberius Jesus "came down" from heaven "to the Galilaean city of Capernaum."

6. Paul was the only true apostle. The Twelve "Judaized," so the Father had to call Paul to restore the true gospel, but even his epistles were interpolated by the Judaizers.

7. Marcion took his stand on a written revelation. His significance in the development of the canon will be assessed in the next chapter.

8. Asceticism was emphasized. Sex was abhorrent. Water replaced wine in the Lord's supper. Foods associated with sexual reproduction were forbidden—meat and milk products. Fish was the only protein allowed. (How did Marcion think fish reproduced? Or, was the problem with the foods used in pagan sacrifice and not with reproduction as such?)

9. Only the unmarried were baptized, except at the end of life, so there were two levels of adherents in the Marcionite churches, the perfect and the imperfect.

10. The followers of Jesus are not under law. Salvation is by grace alone, and grace needs no law. His views of faith and sin lacked Paul's depth.

The influence of Marcion was considerable, but was overestimated by his twentieth-century interpreters. The catholic church with its creed, canon, and episcopate were not the product of a reaction to Marcion; but reaction to him did strengthen certain tendencies already at work and so speeded up the process of development of these practices.

Marcion's asceticism was very attractive as a fulfillment of Christianity and so was one factor in the ascetic influence in orthodox Christianity. His emphasis on soteriology to the neglect of cosmology was a big problem for the old catholic church fathers (chapter 7).

The severing of Jesus Christ from the Creator God was a great incentive to the orthodox thinkers to begin formulating a doctrine of the Trinity. Justin Martyr held on to the Old Testament by contending that it prophesied two advents of the Messiah—the first in love and the next in judgment.

Tertullian affirmed that God is both justice and love. God had to show discipline before love, and the Sender had to make his authority known (in the Old Testament) before the One Sent would be accepted. In contrast, Marcion's God made a sudden appearance without any preparation.

The church's rejection of Marcion's teaching demonstrated, among other things, its realization that it could not surrender its Old Testament roots and what that entailed about the oneness of God and the goodness of his creation.

Marcion shared with many Gnostics the premise of an unknown God distinct from the creator, a dualism of matter and spirit, a docetic interpretation of Jesus Christ, a negative attitude toward the Old Testament and its God, and a concern with the problem of evil in the world.

He differed from them in rejecting mythology, creating an organization for his followers, avoiding allegorical interpretation, and so engaging in textual criticism to deal with problems he found in the text.

II. GNOSTICISM

The very term "Gnosticism" is problematic. It comes from the Greek word *gnosis*, which referred to immediate experiential knowledge that comes from acquaintance in contrast to propositional or factual knowledge.

There was a group in the second century who called themselves *Gnostikoi* ("Gnostics"), meaning "those capable of attaining knowledge" and then "the knowing ones." But beginning with Irenaeus, Christian heresiologists extended the term to cover opponents in the church in whom they discerned some commonalities yet who had different systems of thought.

So it is well to remember that "Gnosticism" has become something of an umbrella term for what was more a mood and attitude toward the world and its origin (and even these attitudes varied) than a single solution to the problems that some persons felt. That is, Gnosticism was more a movement than a consistent approach.

The religious movement of Gnosticism was characterized by an intuitive knowledge of the origin, essence, and ultimate destiny of the spiritual nature of human beings.

A. Sources for Study

The study of Gnosticism was long hampered by the fact that our main sources of information were the anti-heretical writers of the church. The principal authors who discussed Gnosticism and preserved Gnostic material were Irenaeus, Clement of Alexandria, Tertullian, Hippolytus, and Epiphanius. The Gnostics were also known from the writings against them by the Greek philosopher Plotinus.

Even where these authors preserved quotations from Gnostic writings, these were often out of context and always used for a polemical purpose. It is usually the case in history that losers are known only from descriptions by their opponents, and few persons would like to be remembered only for what their enemies say about them.

Some supplement to what the anti-heretical church fathers said was available from a few original Gnostic works preserved in Coptic, from the Hermetic writings (a pagan form of Gnosticism), and from later Manichaean and Mandaean sources (two movements indebted to earlier Gnosticism).

This situation changed dramatically with the discovery, in 1945 at Nag Hammadi in Egypt, of a collection of twelve codices (plus other sheets) written in the fourth century and containing mostly original Gnostic works in a Coptic translation. The publication of these works in critical editions and reliable translations have made them the primary focus for the study of ancient Gnosticism.

The Nag Hammadi collection can be broadly grouped into five categories of writings (see chart). Of these the most important are the first two, (1) those closer to original "Gnostic" thought—to which the names "Sethian," "Barbelognostic," "Ophite," or others are given and which may represent variations within one school or distinct systems— and (2) those from the Valentinian school.

The accounts of the church fathers give something of the mythical structure of the Gnostic systems, but the new Nag Hammadi documents give more of the living spirit and the methods of interpretation that were employed. The one class of sources helps interpret the other.

B. Question of Origins

Before the discovery of the Nag Hammadi library, three different sources for Gnostic thought were postulated:

1. The view of the church fathers that Gnosticism was a Christian heresy, resulting from Christians explaining their faith to themselves and their neighbors in philosophical terms, has had modern scholarly support.

SOME WORKS FROM THE NAG HAMMADI LIBRARY

(1) Sethian Works
  (a) Some concentrating more on the myth of origins
      Apocryphon of John
      Apocalypse of Adam
      Hypostasis of the Archons
      Gospel of the Egyptians
      Trimorphic Protennoia
  (b) Others relating to the ascent of the soul
      Zostrianos
      Allogenes ("The Foreigner")
      Three Steles of Seth

(2) Valentinian works
      Gospel of Truth
      Treatise on the Resurrection
      Tripartite Tractate
      Gospel of Philip

(3) Works from the Thomas tradition in Syria
      Gospel of Thomas
      Book of Thomas the Contender

(4) Hermetic works
      Asclepius

(5) Other works, including non-Gnostic Christian moral/wisdom writings
      Teachings of Silvanus
      Sentences of Sextus

2. The opposite view, presenting Gnosticism as essentially a non-Christian movement (some tracing it to Persia)—representing the despairing, syncretistic mood of late antiquity that reconstructed a philosophical world view from the old myths and gods, and in the process adopted a veneer of Christianity that in turn provided a model for Christian intellectuals to interpret their faith—was advocated by the history of religions school of interpretation and continues to have many supporters.

3. A less commonly held view that Gnostic speculation began in Jewish circles, perhaps as an effort to find eternity when the kingdom of God did not come (e.g., aeons as "ages" of time in apocalypticism became cosmic components of the divine ple-

roma in Gnosticism), has found renewed support as a result of the Nag Hammadi documents.

There seem to be elements of truth in all three interpretations. Some of the ideas in Gnosticism were older than Christianity, but a complete Gnostic system has not been identified prior to Christianity. Some expressions of Gnosticism, especially those combated by the church fathers, were Christian heresies. Some of the Gnostic systems known from the Nag Hammadi writings show a proximity to Judaism, if not indeed a Jewish origin.

Gnostic works at Nag Hammadi with no explicit Christian features may point to Gnosticism as at first or as also a non-Christian movement, but not necessarily, for if these works could be read by Christians, they could as well have been Christian compositions.

A middle-of-the-road view would be that Gnosticism and Christianity grew up together but from different sources. They had some interactions in the first century and developed into defined forms as separate religions in the second century.

Some contemporary writers make a distinction between "Gnosis" and "Gnosticism," employing the former term for the wider atmosphere congenial to a Gnostic way of thinking and the latter for the developed systems of thought.

As A. D. Nock put it, "Apart from the Christian movement there was a Gnostic way of thinking, but no Gnostic system of thought." He continued, "It was the emergence of Jesus and of the belief that he was a supernatural being who had appeared on earth which precipitated elements previously suspended in solution."

The fully developed Gnostic systems that we know from the church fathers and that are reflected in the Nag Hammadi library, whatever their antecedents, belong to the second century. It was Christian Gnosticism that made an impact, for the Neo-Platonists regarded Gnosticism as a Christian deviation; Gnostics to them were Christians with a kind of claim to be intellectuals characterized by a passionate dualism and extreme anthropocentricity.

To say that Gnosticism is non-Christian in origin is not necessarily to say that it is pre-Christian. Whatever the points of contact between Christianity and Gnosticism, the former statement can be affirmed; the latter is not confirmed.

C. Components of Gnosticism

The debate over origins points to the elements that went into the developed Gnostic systems of the second century. These contained Jewish, pagan, and Christian components.

Many of the Gnostic speculations can be explained as arising from reflections on the early chapters of Genesis. Certain developments in Judaism may be seen as a background to the emergence of Gnosticism: the influence of dualistic thinking, esoteric speculations, personification of Wisdom, intermediary beings found in developed angelology. Hence, many now look to the milieu of heterodox Judaism or specifically to Jews in rebellion against their religious heritage for the origins of Gnosticism.

Greek philosophy provides another large component in Gnosticism. Neopythagorean influences may be seen in the negative evaluation of matter, ascetic practices, and speculations about the cosmos. Some speak of Gnosticism as "Platonism run wild," because of the statements in Plato developed by the Gnostics: a remote supreme being and the soul as immortal and in bondage to the body. Pagan analogies may also be found in the Hermetic literature and the *Chaldaean Oracles*.

Many things in the New Testament, especially Paul and John, proved susceptible of Gnostic interpretation, so that some modern scholars see these New Testament authors as employing Gnostic thinking in formulating their own ideas.

Although we have continued the common practice of speaking of Gnosticism as if it were a single entity, this was hardly the case. Each Gnostic teacher took these component elements and put them together according to a Gnostic way of thinking in order to construct his own system. Thus there is a great variety in the details of the systems of different Gnostic teachers. Gnosticism was an aggregate of a series of individualistic responses to the religious situation made by teachers who did not think of themselves as eccentric.

D. Common Features of the Gnostic Myths

Each Gnostic teacher had his own system of thought for representing reality. What held each Gnostic community together was its myth of origins, the sense of group identity, and the in-group language.

The main features of the various myths were as follows: (1) the original divine element produced other spiritual principles; (2) a "fault" occurred in the divine, spiritual world; (3) as a result matter came into existence; (4) some of the pure spiritual nature was planted in (some) souls; (5) a "redeemer" revealed the way of escape out of the material world for the divine element; (6) the soul passes through the realms of the world rulers in its return to its spiritual home.

The Gnostic attempt to explain the problem of evil posited a fall in the divine world, in deity. This effort to "kick upstairs" the problem of evil was a notable, but ultimately unsatisfying, solution to one of the difficult human philosophical questions.

The way of dealing with this question was one expression of the Gnostic, especially Valentinian, use of the partly poetical, partly philosophical concept of "metaphysical correspondence." Applying the Platonic idea of earthly realities as imitations of the world of Ideas, Gnostics saw the components of the pleroma as equivalent to the totality of the spiritual nature of humanity. There is a heavenly counterpart of the soul. Accordingly, the Gospel narratives were read as reflections of the drama that took place in the heavenly world.

Thus, in spite of its dualism, "The gnosis of Gnosticism involves the divine identity of the *knower* (the Gnostic), the *known* (the divine substance of one's transcendent self), and [the] *means by which one knows* (gnosis as an implicit divine faculty to be awakened and actualized)" (Bianchi).

E. Principal Teachers

The anti-heretical writers of the early church traced "Gnosticism" to Simon Magus, "the father of all heresies." This genealogy of heresy in the church fathers looks artificial, being influenced by various succession lists employed in antiquity, and the account in Acts 8 does not suggest that Simon held any particularly "Gnostic" teaching.

It may be there was a confusion between the Simon of Acts 8 and another Simon, who was a Gnostic; or Acts 8 may not tell the whole story; or Simon was on his way to becoming a Gnostic, and his followers later may have become Gnostic.

At any rate, the attribution of Gnosticism to Simon may point to a Samaritan origin, to which some now look. The teaching later ascribed to Simon does have features of Gnostic schemes in that it includes a fall from divinity and a descent of a heavenly power (Simon himself) to bring salvation.

Seemingly contradictory reports are given of the teaching of Cerinthus, reported to have been opposed by the apostle John in Ephesus. The earliest surviving report (Irenaeus) puts Cerinthus in the Gnostic orbit: A lower Power and not the Supreme God made the world; Jesus was the son of Joseph and Mary who exceeded other persons in righteousness and wisdom; the divine Christ descended on him in the form of a dove at his baptism and flew away before his crucifixion, so the Christ remained an impassible spiritual being.

A slightly later report made Cerinthus a teacher of Jewish millennialism and attributed the book of Revelation to him. A way of reconciling the seeming incongruity of these pictures of Cerinthus is that he anticipated Marcion by saying that the Jewish expectation of a messianic

SOME TEACHERS JUDGED HERETICAL		
Name	Date	Place
Simon Magus	First century	Samaria and Rome
Menander	End of first century	Samaria and Antioch
Cerinthus	End of first century	Asia Minor
Saturninus	Early second century	Antioch
Carpocrates	Early second century	Alexandria
Basilides	Early second century	Alexandria
Valentinus	Second century	Alexandria and Rome
Ptolemy	Second century	Rome?
Theodotus	Second century	Alexandria?
Heracleon	Second century	Italy?

kingdom on earth was a correct reading of the Old Testament prophecies, but Christ revealed the unknown Father and a spiritual salvation.

Irenaeus traced a line leading from Simon to Menander to Saturninus and Basilides. To Saturninus he ascribed a compact summary that corresponds to the principal elements of the basic Gnostic myth: The unknown Father made the various levels of angelic beings; seven of these angels made the world and the first man. The God of the Jews is one of these angels. The Christ, who is incorporeal, came in appearance only in order to overthrow the God of the Jews and to save good human beings. His followers renounced marriage and procreation and were vegetarians.

Carpocrates too affirmed that the world was made by angels, who were far inferior to the unbegotten Father. Jesus was born of Joseph like the rest of men, but because of his purity of soul, power from above came upon him, enabling him to escape the world rulers. Souls which are like Jesus' soul also receive power to escape the world rulers and may even become stronger than Jesus' disciples or indeed Jesus himself.

Carpocrates's followers called themselves "Gnostics," but they had features unlike others known as Gnostics. They taught reincarnation and in contrast to the asceticism in regard to sexuality (characteristic of other Gnostics) were libertines, engaging in sexual immorality. Carpocrates's son, Epiphanes, defended promiscuity on the basis of a "law of nature" that made all things common property.

Basilides had a much more elaborate cosmology than other teachers who sought to combine Christianity with Gnostic speculations. The unengendered Father (or "the non-existent God," i.e., the God beyond existence, in another version) engendered various spiritual qualities and from them produced "powers, principalities, and angels," one set of each for all the 365 heavens. Among the heavenly beings was an Archon who was God of the Jews. The unengendered Father sent his firstborn Mind (or Intellect) to free those who believed in him from the power of the beings who made the world. This emissary corresponds to Jesus, who worked miracles but did not suffer. Simon of Cyrene, who carried Jesus' cross, was ignorantly crucified in his place, while Jesus, taking the appearance of Simon, stood by and laughed at them and then ascended invisibly to the Father who had sent him. Salvation belongs only to the soul, not the body. His followers were ready in times of persecution to deny that they were Christians, since they, like the angels, are not able to suffer.

Of those the church fathers called "Gnostics," by far the most influential teacher was the religious genius Valentinus, who was a Christian reformer of Gnostic theology. Valentinus was educated in Alexandria, and after teaching there, went to Rome, where he was active in the church. Reportedly disappointed in his hope to be elected bishop, and meeting much opposition to his teaching, he dropped out of sight.

Very little that is certainly from Valentinus remains, but it has been suggested that the *Gospel of Truth* found at Nag Hammadi is a sermon of his. Valentinus was more explicitly "Christian" than his Gnostic predecessors, but he also more fully appropriated the language of Plato.

Moreover, Valentinus's mysticism modified Gnostic mysticism by understanding salvation as coming through *gnosis*, knowledge of (or experiential acquaintance with) the savior, the self, and God. His myth of origins starts not with an original monad (the ultimate single entity) but with a pair of first principles, the Inexpressible (Depth) and Silence. Using agricultural language, Valentinus says that they produced other dualities to constitute the first ogdoad ("eight"); from it proceeded twenty-two other powers, making a total of thirty aeons in the *pleroma* (fullness [of the spiritual universe]).

One of these aeons (named Sophia, the Greek word for Wisdom, in other versions of the myth) revolted and engendered Christ and a shadow (matter). Christ returned to the *pleroma*, and the rebellious "mother" emitted the Demiurge (the creator). Jesus was an emanation from the Christ or from other aeons of the pleroma. Earthly entities such as humanity and the church were thus seen as reflections of spiritual realities.

Valentinus's followers were said to have branched into two schools, a Western (e.g., Heracleon and Ptolemy) and an Eastern (e.g., Theodotus and Bar Daisan or Bardesanes). Their own original contributions to biblical interpretation testify to the brilliance of Valentinus as a teacher.

Heracleon wrote perhaps the first commentary on a New Testament book, the Gospel of John, and Ptolemy offered a three-fold scheme for interpreting the Old Testament Law, part coming from God himself, part from Moses, and part from the elders. The church fathers give fuller reports on his successors than on Valentinus himself.

It is often difficult to draw inferences from an intellectual system to the social realities in which it operates, and this is especially the case with Gnosticism. For example, the prominence of feminine elements in the pleroma of the Gnostics does not seem to have necessarily transferred to an equality of women in Gnostic communities.

Nevertheless, there were women teachers prominent in some Gnostic circles: for example, an unnamed woman of the Cainite sect, whose disparagement of water baptism called forth Tertullian's *On Baptism*, and Philoumene, a prophetess and teacher influential on Marcion's disciple Apelles.

Yet there does not appear to be any consistent line of greater openness to women's leadership among "heretical" churches, nor consistent hostility to women as women among the "orthodox."

F. Sample Gnostic Myths of Creation and Salvation

Two extensive elaborations of the basic Gnostic scheme have survived: one from the "Sethian" form of Gnosticism and written by an adherent, found in the *Apocryphon of John* (also known to Irenaeus in a slightly different version); the other from Valentinianism, the system of Ptolemy described in detail by Irenaeus.

According to the *Apocryphon of John,* the First Principle, "the Father of Everything," by means of the Second Principle, "Barbelo," filled up the divine world with emanations. The creator of the world is an evil Craftsman, "Ialdabaoth." The creation of Adam takes place in two stages: first, Adam is made only of soul; at the second stage a material shell encases him.

The *Apocryphon of John* is already a Christian version of the Gnostic scheme, for one of the spiritual beings is a preexistent "Christ," and the content of the work is presented as a post-resurrection revelation of Jesus, yet the true revealer is Barbelo.

Ptolemy's elaboration of Valentinus's version of the Gnostic system is more explicitly "Christian," although "unorthodox," and seeks to give more orderly explanations to the picture of the spiritual world.

There is a doubling of higher and lower Christs and Wisdoms. The higher Christ is an emanation from Intellect and has the Holy Spirit as his consort; the lower Christ, or Jesus, also called Savior, is an emanation from all the aeons and descended on the Jesus who was born of

A VALENTINIAN SYSTEM

According to Irenaeus, Against Heresies 1.1–5

Pleroma (composed of 30 Aeons)

Ogdoad

Tetrad

Bythus (Propator) + Sige = Nous (Monogenes) + Aletheia = Logos + Zoe = Anthropos + Ecclesia

produced   produced

Decad   Duodecad (last of which is *Sophia*, who was seized with passion)

Propator through Monogenes created Horos
(also called Stauros, the supporting and separating power)

   Monogenes produced Christ and Holy Spirit,
   who restored order to the Pleroma

(All these male-female pairs are spiritual fructifications, as the tree is in the seed.)

Thirty is a mystical number.
The Pleroma is encompassed by Horos.
All united to form the perfect being — Jesus (Soter).

Sophia's passion (enthymesis or "inborn idea") was excluded from the *Pleroma* and called *Achamoth* ("Second Wisdom").

Christ took pity and gave her form; Soter then gave her intelligence, so that she was now a hypostasis of ideal matter.

Three kinds of existence formed:

(from passion)	(from her conversion)	(from herself)
Material	Animal	Spiritual
	Demiurge (from Animal substance)	

(Father and King of all things outside the *Pleroma*)
Created Seven Heavens
Created Humans (body from matter, animal soul from *Demiurge*, and spiritual nature from *Achamoth* without knowledge of the *Demiurge*)

When all the spiritual seed come to perfection, *Achamoth* enters the *Pleroma* and is coupled with Soter.

Mary. The higher Wisdom, Sophia, was one of the thirty aeons; her passion for Depth (the perfect Father) gave birth to the lower Wisdom, Achamoth, who in turn gave birth to the Demiurge (creator of the world) and who became ultimately the spouse of Jesus the savior.

Human beings are in three classes—those who are material and will be lost, the psychics or ordinary Christians, and the spirituals or Valentinian Christians. The latter two receive different kinds of salvation.

G. Doctrinal Errors and Significance of Gnosticism

Contrary to the fashion in contemporary study to posit considerable variety in primitive Christianity (discussed further below), the reactions by many second-century Christians to the teachings discussed in this chapter show that some fundamental doctrines were commonly regarded as basic to the Christian faith.

Those who came to prevail as orthodox Christians concluded that the Gnostics, including Valentinians, denied some fundamental doctrines:

1. The identity of the Creator (whom the Gnostics made a lesser and at best morally ambivalent figure) with the one supreme God

2. The goodness of the created order of the universe (most Gnostics treated matter as bad)

3. The full incarnation of Christ (although there were variations in how the divine Christ was related to the human Jesus)

4. Revelation in historical events (rather than in speculative myth and secret traditions)

5. Redemption by the blood of the cross (the cross was treated allegorically even in Valentinianism)

6. A resurrection of the body (and not of the soul only)

It is no wonder that those who pioneered the development of orthodox theology rejected the teachings they associated with the rejection of these doctrines.

In spite of what their opponents discerned as fundamental doctrinal errors, Gnostic thought proved attractive to many. The Gnostic Christians represented an effort to interpret their faith in terms of the philosophical and religious climate of the day and so to wrestle with problems they perceived in the nature of the world and human existence.

Because of these concerns, Valentinianism especially influenced orthodox Christian thinkers in Alexandria in the development of their theology. One learns, sometimes imperceptibly, from one's opponents, and in refuting other ideas, one's own thoughts are advanced by absorbing elements from the viewpoints being rejected.

Gnosticism, furthermore, showed a concern with salvation. Although the means of achieving this was through knowledge, Gnosticism as a religion of redemption testified to the need of human souls for something beyond this world to satisfy their longings.

H. Lessons from the Struggle with Gnosticism

Although culture and philosophy always shape expressions of Christianity to some extent, Gnosticism illustrates the danger of allowing an "outside" system of thought to be determinative of the fabric of Christianity.

The risk is one that has to be taken in attempting to relate the Christian faith to whatever culture one finds oneself in, but the results of such an extreme appropriation warn against moving from communication to acceptance. The threat of Gnosticism may not have been so much to orthodox belief systems as to identity (by reason of assimilation).

A related lesson has to do with the use of words. One may have the right words but the wrong ideas. The Gnostics were able to use the Christian Scriptures and conform to the Christian creed, because they gave these words a different meaning.

Gnosticism, furthermore, may serve a warning against intellectual pride. Individual Gnostic thinkers may indeed have been humble, but the Gnostic approach itself created different classes that placed the ones with the "true insight" in a special camp superior to ordinary Christians. Intellectual elitism is a danger always for those "in the know."

The Gnostic controversy demonstrates the importance of institutions. In a broad sense the Gnostics may be said to have had a "church," but they remained closer to the social organization of a school in which followers continued the teachings and practices of their teacher. Christianity, however, created stronger organizational bonds uniting its members.

For all its failures through history, the "institutional church" has preserved the Christian faith. And so it has been for all teachers and teachings that have endured: Unless an institution embodies and perpetuates an idea, the idea will fail.

The recognition of this reality in the second century, however, should not be given uncritically, for the acknowledgment that orthodox doctrine was preserved among the hierarchical church must be balanced by the acknowledgement that the "heretics" often preserved more biblical views about the freedom and ministry of the church.

III. MONTANISM

Marcionism and Gnosticism became the archetypal heresies over against orthodox Christianity. In a similar way Montanism, as an early movement with sectarian characteristics, after a period of activity within the great church, was forced into schism. No fundamental doctrinal differences were involved, but differences in practice and in disciplinary matters eventually created too much disturbance to be accommodated within the same congregations.

Montanism draws its name from Montanus, who—along with two women, Priscilla and Maximilla—in either the 150s or 170s began a prophetic movement in Phrygia. The adherents of the movement called it the "New Prophecy"; their opponents called it the "Phrygian (or Kataphrygian) heresy."

The movement spread from Asia Minor to Rome and to North Africa. The critics objected that Montanist prophecy involved some kind of possession and speaking in frenzied ecstasy, unlike the biblical prophets, who kept full possession of their understanding.

The Montanists saw prophecy and spiritual gifts as the hallmark of apostolic Christianity. The promised Paraclete (Holy Spirit) of the Gospel of John was regarded as speaking in them, and later opponents quoted Montanus as himself claiming to be the Paraclete.

Montanist epitaph (early fifth century) from Chiusi, Italy: "Here lies Frankios, a spiritual Christian, who lived twenty years. Peace to you."

Photo courtesy of William Tabbernee.

Differences in practice and degrees of emphasis soon emerged between the Montanists and the mainstream of the church. Their most famous convert, Tertullian, was attracted to the greater rigorism of the movement and developed it: observing stricter fasts, prohibiting second marriages even after death of the spouse, and forbidding flight to escape martyrdom.

That the Montanists had a greater eagerness than other Christians to volunteer for martyrdom does not seem necessarily to have been the case. Modern scholars have attributed to the Montanists intense eschatological expectations centering on Pepuza, a village of Phrygia that they called "Jerusalem," but an eschatological interpretation of Pepuza appears to be a later development and a specifically millennial expectation is not attested for early Montanism.

Photo courtesy of William Tabbernee.

Likely site of Pepuza (Phrygia), Turkey, looking toward a later rock-cut monastery.

Besides women's prominence in the beginning of this prophetic movement, they continued to be important in its later development (there may have been a later prophetess named Quintilla) and held church offices not allowed to them by the orthodox.

The dispute over prophecy involved the question of authority in the church: Who has it and how it should be exercised. The Montanists seem not to have opposed the organization of the church, but only to have claimed a place for spiritual gifts as well, but the church's response put the controversy in terms of organization and ministry. The appeal to the authority of the Holy Spirit was countered, it seems, in the church by three developments.

1. The first recorded synods of bishops were held in Asia Minor to consider the proper course of action in relation to the Montanists. Such meetings were comparable to a civil council (*koinon*) that brought leaders of the imperial cult in the cities of a province together to discuss matters of common concern. These early meetings of bishops to discuss the working of the Holy Spirit laid the basis in the actual practice of the church for the theory that the Holy Spirit works through a council.

2. The source of authority in Scripture was emphasized. Montanist prophecy was not true prophecy by biblical standards, it was argued, because it was ecstatic.

3. The bishops claimed to be the true spiritual leaders of the church, possessing the Holy Spirit by reason of their office. As

the bishops claimed apostolic and teaching authority in the church over against Gnostic teachers, so the bishops countered the Montanist appeal to prophets with their own possession of the Spirit. Thus the early triad of apostles, prophets, and teachers began to be centered now in the bishop.

Montanism may be understood as a protest against an increasing worldliness and formality in the church. It won many followers who were dissatisfied with Gnostic "elitism" and with the growing accommodation of the church to the world. Montanism had several appealing features: It represented itself as a return to primitive Christianity, it was a religion of emotional exuberance and less rigid organizational structures, and it offered a direct revelation pertaining to what seemed to be a more committed manner of life.

Montanism's own excesses, however, brought discredit on the movement. Not uncommonly, a reactive movement swings to an opposite extreme and its opponents more strongly confirm the practices being reacted against. Why? Those opponents conclude that since the ones trying to make corrections are clearly in error, then what they were reacting against must be all right.

IV. ENCRATISM

"Encratism" (from Greek, *egkrateia*, "to have in one's power," "self-control") was one of the words used for "asceticism" (Greek, *askēsis*, "athletic discipline") and in a positive sense was present in Christianity from the beginning.

Some ascetic practices, however, were deemed excessive — rejecting wine, flesh meat, and marriage. Where these ascetic practices were accepted by the orthodox, they were criticized in the practice of others as springing from the wrong motives, that is, as deriving not from the foregoing of something good in the service of a higher or spiritual goal (which was approved) but from regarding the created world as bad (which was heretical, as in Gnosticism).

The Encratites — without accepting the Gnostic views on the origin of the world and considering matter as necessarily evil — still regarded certain practices, especially human reproduction, as bad and a hindrance to the higher life. Another factor influencing ascetic behavior was the association of certain animal foods and wine with pagan sacrifice. Thus ascetics abstained from animal food and substituted water for wine in the Lord's supper.

The popularity of the ascetic lifestyle as representing a higher form of spirituality reflects a world-despairing mood found in the second and third centuries in pagan as well as Christian circles. In identifying with this prominent sentiment, Encratism absorbed the spirituality of the surrounding world into its expression of Christianity and attracted many followers. The Encratite tendency is prominent in the apocryphal acts of the apostles and according to some scholars best characterizes the viewpoint of the *Gospel of Thomas*.

The anti-heretical literature associates a heretical Encratism especially with the apologist Tatian. Seemingly after the death of his teacher, Justin, he returned to the East and became a champion of Encratite ideas, condemning marriage and the eating of meats. The anti-heretical writers found particularly objectionable his conclusion that Adam would not be saved.

In spite of some similarities noted by Irenaeus and others, Tatian should not be thought of as a Valentinian; the Syrian East did not treat him as heretical. Nor did he begin Encratism, as Irenaeus claimed, but, associating himself with this general tendency of the Syriac church, he became one of its leading spokesmen.

V. DID HERESY PRECEDE ORTHODOXY?

Modern study of the early history of Christianity has stressed the variety of beliefs and practices present in the early centuries, even in those circles later considered orthodox.

The establishment of "orthodoxy" is seen as the achievement of the bishops and church fathers active around AD 200 who were in communion with the church at Rome. Characteristics of this orthodoxy and the men important in its standards will be examined in the next two chapters. If orthodoxy is defined in institutional terms and fixed statements of belief, then the contention of the late achievement of orthodoxy may be sustained.

Variety was certainly present from the beginning (as the New Testament itself shows, in what it opposes—if not in other ways) and continued after objective standards of orthodoxy were formulated.

On the other hand, those church leaders who opposed the movements discussed above did not see themselves as innovators but as defenders of teachings that had been handed down to them from the apostles and their associates. There were standards of belief and common practices contained in the earliest apostolic teaching.

In this sense, an "orthodoxy" and standards of what constituted "orthodoxy" were present prior to positions that came to be regarded as heretical or schismatic, even if the movements advocating these teachings drew on materials earlier than Christianity. There was an inherited message and inherited norms of conduct that permitted other teachings to be identified as deviant and that could be systematized in the norms discussed in the next chapter.

Problems with doctrinal deviations and schismatic tendencies have plagued the Christian church from the beginning. How is the true faith and practice to be discerned and defended? The early church adopted strategies that with varying degrees of effectiveness continued to be employed in subsequent centuries. To these we now turn.

FOR FURTHER STUDY

Brakke, David. *The Gnostics: Myth, Ritual, and Diversity in Early Christianity*. Cambridge, MA: Harvard University Press, 2010.

Markschies, Christoph. *Gnosis: An Introduction*. Edinburgh: T & T Clark, 2003.

Nock, Arthur Darby. "Gnosticism." *Harvard Theological Review* 57 (1964): 255–79. Reprinted in David Scholer, *Gnosticism in the Early Church*. Studies in Early Christianity 5, ed. Everett Ferguson. New York: Garland, 1993. 1–25. (See other articles in this collection.)

Pearson, Birger A. *Ancient Gnosticism*. Minneapolis: Fortress, 2007.

Tabbernee, William. *Prophets and Gravestones: An Imaginative History of Montanists and Other Early Christians*. Peabody, MA: Hendrickson, 2009.

Williams, Michael A. *Rethinking "Gnosticism": An Argument for Dismantling a Dubious Category*. Princeton, NJ: Princeton University Press, 1996.

The Defense against Rival Interpretations

In the second century developments occurred that have been formative for most Christian churches ever since. These developments took
place in the process of self-definition over against the variant interpretations of the Christian message discussed in the preceding chapter.

The issue between the great church, as Celsus already called it
in the second half of the second century, and its rivals—Marcionites,
Gnostics, Montanists, some Jewish Christians, and Encratites—was the
question, "What is apostolic faith and practice?" Authentic Christianity
had to do with the question of origins. The apostles and first disciples
of Jesus Christ were universally recognized as authoritative sources for
the genuine Christian message.

The second-century church developed a three-fold defense of
"what is apostolic." The logical order of thought was as follows: To
the question, "Where is apostolic teaching to be found?" the church
pointed to the Scriptures. To the question, "How are these Scriptures to
be interpreted?" it pointed to their content in the "rule of faith." To the
further question, "What is the channel through which this teaching has
been preserved and where is it to be found now?" the church pointed
to its succession of duly appointed bishops and presbyters.

According to the historical order in which each achieved definitive
form, the church claimed an apostolic ministry (episcopate), an apostolic faith (rule of faith and creed), and apostolic Scriptures (canon). It
is in their historical order of emergence that these three developments
will be discussed.

All three developments had their roots in the Christian communities apart from the major conflicts of the second century, but all three
were influenced by these conflicts and received sharper definition and
greater emphasis in response to the issues that were raised.

I. MONEPISCOPACY AND APOSTOLIC SUCCESSION

The later books of the New Testament and some of the Apostolic
Fathers provide impressive evidence of a wide geographical spread for

a particular church order. In each church, that order involved a plurality of elders or bishops (the terms were used interchangeably) assisted by deacons:

1. Jerusalem and Judea—Acts 11:30; 15:6; James 5:14
2. Syria—*Didache* 15:1
3. Galatia—Acts 14:23
4. Asia Minor—1 Peter 5:1–4
5. Ephesus—Acts 20:17, 28; 1 Timothy 3:1–13
6. Philippi—Philippians 1:1; Polycarp, *Philippians* 6
7. Corinth—*1 Clement* 42:4; 44:3–6
8. Crete—Titus 1:5–7
9. Rome—*1 Clement* 42; 44; Hermas, *Vision* 3.5.1

If we accept the testimony of later writers, Alexandria could be added to this list.

The emergence of one bishop at the head of the presbytery (monepiscopacy) is attested first at Antioch of Syria and in Asia Minor by the letters of Ignatius. The bishop, as portrayed in the letters of Ignatius, was still a local bishop in a city (not a territorial bishop), and nothing is said of apostolic succession or a priestly function. The bishop appears in close relation to the rest of the clergy—the presbyters and deacons—who with him provided the unified leadership of the church. Ignatius was concerned about false teaching and schismatic assemblies, and he attempted to counter their influence by an insistence on obedience to the clergy and on not doing anything without the consent of the bishop.

The three-fold ministry of the local church became the general pattern by the mid-second century. Justin Martyr's "president" of the Sunday assembly was presumably the "bishop." Marcion's church organization (with a bishop) apparently copied that of the great church. Hegesippus and Irenaeus at the end of the second century drew up lists of bishops in various cities, an indication that persons fitting the description of a single head of the community could be identified for some generations previous. Dionysius, bishop of Corinth around 170, refers to the bishops of the churches to which he wrote and indeed sometimes wrote to bishops of churches (unlike Clement and Polycarp, who wrote to churches, not to fellow bishops).

Some of the factors involved in the emergence of a single head of the presbyteries would have included the following: presidency of the eucharist, administration of church funds, representation of the church in correspondence and hospitality, and the giving of authoritative teaching. Ordination was not yet mentioned in the sources; the limitation of the right of ordination to a bishop is first attested in the *Apostolic Tradition* presumably from the early third century.

The strengthened position of the bishop by the end of the second century is shown in Irenaeus's argument from apostolic succession. Sometimes Clement of Rome is stated to have been the first witness to apostolic succession, but Clement claims apostolic appointment of the office of bishops and deacons and provision for these offices to be filled when the original holders die. This is simply a succession in the office according to a pattern established by the apostles.

"Apostolic succession" becomes something more than this in Irenaeus's controversy with the Gnostics; it becomes a powerful argument for the faith taught in the churches. The claim to an apostolic succession of teachers, on Irenaeus's own testimony, was first made by Gnostic teachers. They certified their teaching on the basis of a claim to have received it from a succession going back to disciples of the apostles.

Drawing on Hegesippus's lists of bishops in various cities, Irenaeus formulated the orthodox counter-claim. In the hands of Irenaeus, apostolic succession was an argument, not an article of faith; but it often happens to successful arguments that they become integral to the position they support and are no longer solely an argument for the position.

The position for which Irenaeus was contending was that the apostolic faith was preserved in the churches by the public succession of bishops and presbyters (Irenaeus included presbyters in the succession) going back to the apostles, not in the sequences of Gnostic teachers.

Irenaeus's argument—each bishop in each church taught the same doctrine—took the following form.

1. The stability or uniformity of the teaching was guaranteed by its publicity. The same teaching was heard from Sunday to Sunday in the church. In secret transmission there is the possibility of faulty communication or deliberate alteration, but in public teaching too many people hear the same thing for significant changes to go undetected.

2. The correctness of the doctrine was confirmed by the agreement among the teachings given from the different teaching chairs. That the same teaching was given in Rome as in Philippi, Smyrna, Ephesus, and so on showed a common origin in the same apostolic message.

3. Moreover, Irenaeus argued that if the apostles had any secrets to impart, they would have delivered them to the men in whom they had enough confidence to entrust the care of the churches as bishops and presbyters.

The Hellenistic world had its successions of teachers in the philosophical schools; the Jews had succession lists of rabbis and of high

"Therefore it
is necessary to
obey the pres-
byters who are
in the church,
those who, as
I have shown,
possess the suc-
cession from the
apostles, those
who together
with the suc-
cession of the
episcopate have
received the cer-
tain gift of truth,
according to the
good pleasure of
the Father; but
to hold in suspi-
cion others who
depart from
the primitive
succession and
assemble them-
selves together
elsewhere"
(Irenaeus,
Against Heresies
4.26.2).

priests at Jerusalem. Against this background of interest in succession lists, Montanists claimed a succession of prophets, and Gnostics a succession of teachers.

In response to the latter, Irenaeus had a collective succession (presbyters of the churches) as well as individual (bishops), and he emphasized a succession of faith and life rather than a transmission of special charismata.

Each holder of the teaching chair received the truth as a gift from his predecessor, but not a gift that guaranteed the truth of what he taught. The true succession required a holy life and sound doctrine (*Against Heresies* 4.26.5); just to be in the succession was not enough, although it did mark off the heretics who withdrew.

In contrast to what apostolic succession became later, for Irenaeus it passed from the one sitting in the teaching chair of a church to the next holder of the chair, and not from ordainer to ordained.

Tertullian, with his characteristic sharpness and exaggeration, carried Irenaeus's argument further. Whereas Irenaeus let the church at Rome stand for his argument, Tertullian appealed to other churches of apostolic foundation in addition to Rome. He mentions only the bishop and not presbyters in his argument. With brilliant satire, contrasting the uniformity of teaching in the churches with the variety in different heretical groups, he asked how all the churches, if not maintaining the one apostolic faith, could have accidentally stumbled into the same "error."

In the language of Hippolytus (early third century) we meet apparently for the first time the idea that bishops are not merely in the succession from the apostles, but are themselves "successors of" the apostles.

This becomes clear in one passage in Cyprian (mid-third century), for whom the bishop was *a* bishop in the whole church rather than just *the* bishop of his own community. The episcopate was one property, ruling the church, a property jointly shared by each bishop (chapter 9). The identity of episcopate and apostolate became the rule in the fourth century.

II. RULE OF FAITH AND APOSTLES' CREED

The correct teaching passed down in the churches by their bishops and presbyters was summarized for Irenaeus by the "rule of faith," or—in his wording—the "canon of truth." For Irenaeus, the canon of truth represented the plot of Scripture, the unfolding of which was the arrangements or dispensations in God's saving plan.

Earlier investigators of the history of the development of creeds often obscured matters by confusing the rule of faith with the creed. The content of the two is related, but they had different functions that account for the variety of wording employed in reference to the rules of faith and the comparative fixity of wording in the Apostles' Creed.

The rule of faith was a summary of the apostolic message and expressed the legitimate content of Scripture, not a separate body of doctrine. In content it was roughly similar to the *kerygma*, as now used in New Testament studies, to stand for a summary of apostolic preaching. The creed, on the other hand, was the faith confessed by those converted to the apostolic preaching, a faith confessed especially as part of the baptismal ceremony. The faith preached (rule of faith or canon of truth) was also the faith believed and confessed (Apostles' Creed).

The statements of the former served in many situations and so the wordings were flexible according to an author's purpose, whereas statements of the latter occurred principally in definite liturgical contexts and so soon were stabilized with a relatively fixed wording.

The statements of the rule of faith focus on the historical acts of God's saving work in Jesus Christ: his virgin birth, ministry, death, resurrection, and coming again in judgment. In an anti-heretical context, these summaries are often given a Trinitarian structure, relating the work of Christ to God the Father as Creator and to the Holy Spirit, who prophesied the coming of Christ and is now at work in the church.

The earliest confession of faith to acquire a creedal elaboration was the baptismal confession of the church at Rome, known as the Apostles' Creed or Apostles' Symbol. A "symbol" meant a sign, a badge of identity, or token of a pact, and so stood for one's faith.

Scholars had earlier reconstructed the Old Roman Symbol, the baptismal confession of faith in use in Rome in the third century, from two fourth-century sources. The confession of faith that Marcellus of Ancyra communicated to the church at Rome (in Greek) and Rufinus's *Commentary of the Apostles' Creed* (in Latin) were so similar that it was deduced that they must have had an earlier (at least third century) common origin in Greek.

Then the discovery of *Apostolic Tradition* ascribed to Hippolytus revealed the same content in the three questions asked of the candidate for baptism, one before each immersion. The major difference was that in the *Apostolic Tradition* the creed is interrogatory: the candidate was asked "Do you believe ...?" and responded to each question, "I believe." The Old Roman Symbol as reconstructed from Marcellus and Rufinus was declaratory: the person recited the creed, and did not simply respond in the affirmative to questions.

It seems that Hippolytus reflected the actual liturgical practice of his time, an interrogatory confession of faith. Those questions were then made declaratory and became the basis of instruction in the faith given to new converts and, in the developed practice of the fourth

"The rule of faith which is believed: there is but one God, and he alone is the creator of the world, who by the sending forth of his Word in the beginning brought the universe into being out of nothing; and this Word, called his Son,... was brought down into the virgin Mary ..., was made flesh in her womb and was born from her as Jesus Christ; thereafter he proclaimed a new law and a new promise of the kingdom of heaven, worked miracles, was nailed to the cross, was resurrected on the third day, was taken up to heaven to sit at the Father's right hand and to send in his place the power of the Holy Spirit to guide believers, and will come again in glory" (Tertullian, *Prescription Against Heretics* 13).

century, a statement that the converts had to memorize and recite as part of the baptismal preparation.

The Roman church appears to have been the pioneer in the production of a crystallized creedal formula. The name "Apostles' Creed" or "Apostles' Symbol" was given because the content was thought to be an accurate summary of the apostolic faith. Under the influence of Rome it attained wide currency in the West, but seems not to have been used in the East. Eastern baptismal creeds show more variety and tended to be more speculative and to give a more cosmic setting to the faith.

Not until the Council of Nicaea in 325 did creeds expand their function as confessions of faith to become tests of fellowship.

By the time of Rufinus, around 400, the Apostles' Creed was believed to be not simply "apostolic" in content but to have been actually drawn up by the apostles to assure that—as they dispersed to preach the gospel—they would deliver a common message. Eventually the creed was distributed into twelve clauses, each contributed by one of the apostles. The present form of the Apostles' Creed still used by many Western churches received its wording in the eighth century, but the differences are minimal from the form known already in the fourth century.

Some of the terminology in the Apostles' Creed probably reflects points at issue with Gnostics and Marcionites. But the beliefs stated were already present in Christian teaching prior to these controversies. In regard to the Rule(s) of Faith and the Apostles' Creed, the church took what was at hand and in use and gave an emphasis, formality, and (in the case of the Creed) a fixity to it. The same occurred in regard to the development of episcopacy and in determining the limits of the canon.

THE OLD ROMAN SYMBOL

I believe in God the Father almighty;

And in Christ Jesus his only Son, our Lord;

who was born of the Holy Spirit and the virgin Mary,

who under Pontius Pilate was crucified and buried,

on the third day rose again from the dead,

ascended into heaven,

sits at the right hand of the Father,

whence he shall come to judge the living and the dead;

And in the Holy Spirit,

the holy church,

the forgiveness of sins,

the resurrection of the flesh.

III. THE BIBLICAL CANON

The church began with a canon of Scripture. That is, it took over and claimed the Jewish Scriptures as its own. From the beginning, however, Christians placed Jesus at the center of their faith, so they followed the Old Testament as related to Jesus and as interpreted in reference to him.

The Gospel of John reflects the early situation by saying "they [the disciples] believed the scripture and the words that Jesus had spoken" (2:22). The Old Testament was followed in the light of the coming of Jesus: "'Everything must be fulfilled that is written about me in the Law of Moses, the Prophets and the Psalms.' Then he opened their minds so they could understand the Scriptures" (Luke 24:44–45). The Scriptures were read through the eyes of faith in Jesus: "the Holy Scriptures, which are able to make you wise for salvation through faith in Christ Jesus" (2 Timothy 3:15). Alongside the Old Testament, then, the first Christians added its interpretation by Jesus, the words spoken by Jesus, and salvation through faith in Jesus.

Marcion had, so far as we know, the first fixed collection of New Testament books, but by his time the letters of Paul were certainly available in collections and very probably the four Gospels also. Marcion did not originate the idea of canon within the church, and the church's immediate reaction was that his was a narrowing down of the apostolic message that lay at the foundation of the church (cf. Eusebius, *Church History* 2.25).

The church would have had its own canon in spite of Marcion, but he may have hastened the process of bringing the authoritative books together, for there was no need to pronounce judgment on what was not in dispute.

A. The Old Testament Canon

By the time of the birth of Christianity the main lines of the Jewish canon were clearly drawn. Of the three parts of the Hebrew Bible — Law, Prophets, and Writings (corresponding in a different order to the thirty-nine books in the present Protestant Old Testament) — the limits of the first two parts were already firmly established. The evidence does not permit the same degree of certainty about the contents of the third part at the time of Jesus. Although a case can be made for its being fairly well determined in his day, there were doubts among the Jews about some books, such as Esther, Ecclesiastes, and Song of Solomon.

Moreover, some books not included in the Hebrew canon were highly regarded by some — *Sirach* and *Wisdom of Solomon* (which were among the books that achieved Deutero-canonical status among Christians) and *1 Enoch* (which had more limited acceptance in Christian circles but was included in the canon of the Ethiopian church). Christians received, along with their Jewish heritage, not only the Jewish Scriptures, but also other writings that were found useful. Thus, in manuscripts of the Greek translation of the Old Testament (Septuagint) preserved by Christians, there were often included varying numbers of other books not found in the Hebrew canon of Scripture.

The Defense against Rival Interpretations

No common agreement was reached on which of these additional books to count as canonical, and indeed it was not until the age of the Reformation, when Protestants insisted on limiting the Old Testament to the thirty-nine books accepted by the Jews, that the Roman Catholic church made an official determination of which books (those called the "Apocrypha" by Protestants, Deutero-canonical by Catholics) would be included in its Old Testament (Council of Trent, 1546). The Orthodox Church accepts, in addition to the books recognized by Roman Catholics, 1 Esdras, the Prayer of Manasseh, Psalm 151, and 3 Maccabees as Deutero-canonical.

Early Christian scholars who researched the matter listed the Old Testament books according to the Jewish canon. The earliest we know who did so was Melito of Sardis (whose list corresponds to the Hebrew canon except for the absence of Esther) in the second half of the second century. Later, Jerome argued for the Jewish canon and the exclusion of the apocryphal books.

On the other hand, there were those who argued for a broader canon than that found in the Hebrew Bible, notably Origen (to a limited extent), who recognized the Jewish canon but defended additions found in the Greek text (notably of Daniel, against criticisms from Julius Africanus), and especially Augustine, whose authority determined the attitude of the Latin church and established the tradition that culminated in the decision at Trent.

Athanasius's intermediate approach was typical of many. He listed as "included in the canon" the books accepted by the Jews (except that he too omits Esther), but commended other books as useful for those who "wish to be instructed in the word of true religion": *Wisdom of Solomon, Sirach, Esther, Judith,* and *Tobit.* In practice he quoted these books, especially the *Wisdom of Solomon,* without distinction from the canonical books.

The acceptance by Christians of the earlier view expressed by Hellenistic Jews (*Epistle of Aristeas,* Philo) that the Septuagint was an inspired translation opened the way for the acknowledgement of the books that might be found in Greek manuscripts of the Old Testament as Scripture.

The situation for many in regard to the Old Testament was this: they acknowledged the priority of the Jewish canon and were in common agreement on nearly all the books in its collection, but allowed some fluidity in defining its exact limits and using some other related books circulated in Greek and in the translations dependent on it.

Much greater unanimity was attained, and at a much earlier date, in regard to the books of the New Testament.

B. The New Testament Canon

The determination of the limits of the canon went through four stages, and failure to distinguish these stages has produced much confusion in efforts to write the history of the New Testament canon. The formation of the canon passed through these different stages at different times at different places and in the thought of different authors, but the lines of development are clear.

1. The Scripture principle

The first stage was marked by the transition from the oral to the written form of the Christian message. This was gradual, and for a long time the sayings of Jesus and the teaching of the apostles were preserved in both oral and written forms side by side. The acceptance of the Scripture principle was the recognition of written authority. And in a sense all the later stages are implicit in the Scripture principle.

There are many early indications of the recognition of the authority, not just the use, of certain Christian writings. The date of 2 Peter is in dispute, but it shows a collection of Paul's writings was included among the "Scriptures" (3:15). Clement of Rome, Ignatius of Antioch, and Polycarp of Smyrna knew and quoted from Paul's letters, presumably in a collection. Indeed Polycarp quotes Ephesians 4:26 as "Scripture" (*Philippians* 12.1).

Both *Barnabas* (4.14) and *2 Clement* (2.4) quote Matthew as "Scripture." It is true that the interest of both writers is in the authority of the Lord, but they find his words in a literary work that is treated as an authoritative source.

Papias and Justin Martyr (1 *Apology* 67.3) referred to the "Memoirs" of the apostles, referring to the Gospels, and Justin records that they were read in the Sunday assembly of the church alongside the Prophets.

The recovery from Egypt of Gospel fragments written on papyrus codices beginning in the early second century are an indication of more than use, for the copies were circulated far from the place of composition and collected to be preserved. The production of apocryphal literature in the second century according to the four types of New Testament writings (Gospels, Acts, Letters, and Apocalypses) shows that these genres had impressed themselves on the Christian consciousness.

The significance of Tatian's *Diatessaron* (c. 170) may be argued in two directions, either that he had so little regard for the text of the four Gospels that he could treat them freely in creating one composite text or that these four Gospels were held in such high regard that he wanted to harmonize them into one Gospel. The latter has been the motivation of other producers through the centuries of Gospel harmonies in one continuous narrative (not synopses in parallel columns) and seems to

"From the Scriptures we have our being" (Tertullian, *Prescription Against Hermeneutics* 38).

be closer to Tatian's attitude and the status the four Gospels held by his time. The acceptance of the *Diatessaron* for a long time in the Syriac church as the standard form of the Gospels would seem to argue that it was a compilation of authoritative books.

The Gnostics of the second century argued from the Christian Scriptures (e.g., Basilides) and among the Gnostics the first commentaries of New Testament books were written (e.g., Heracleon on John).

Overlapping with the second stage, the canonical principle, is the translation of Christian writings from Greek into other languages. Books now acknowledged as belonging to the New Testament were translated into Latin and Syriac as early as the second century and into Coptic (the word is derived from the Greek for "Egypt" and refers to the vernacular language of the native Egyptians) in the third century if not earlier. This practice is a clear indication of the importance and authority of these books and the need to have them available in the language of believers.

Several second-century authors (Polycarp, Ignatius, Irenaeus, Clement of Alexandria) refer to a three-fold standard of authority for Christians: the prophets, the Lord, and the apostles. This may reflect a natural Christian periodization of history, but the grouping into three authorities may reflect a Christian alternative to the three-fold division of the Hebrew Scriptures into Law, Prophets, and Writings.

The prophets for Christians stood for all the Old Testament, since Christians regarded Moses as a prophet and the Psalms and other books in the Writings as prophetic. The Lord and the apostles soon stood for two parts of the New Testament, the Gospels and the apostolic writings, if that was not already implicit in those who first used this formulation. The Lord is central, and the prophets before him and the apostles after him bear witness to him.

2. The canonical principle

The second stage in the formation of the canon is marked by the transition from recognition of written authority to the explicit recognition that the number of authoritative written documents is limited, although the line of where precisely these limits are has not been drawn.

At this stage the canon is theoretically a closed canon but practically still open. There is the positive acknowledgement of certain documents as forming the source of authority, but there is not the negative determination that only these documents form the authority, for there may be other documents unknown at the time or about which a final determination has not been made.

In principle, the idea of canon was established by about 180. When Tertullian wrote his *Prescription against Heretics* at the beginning of the third century, one of his arguments (37; cf. 36) concerned who has the right to the "Christian Scriptures." There must have been some idea of an identifiable entity (however imprecise the boundaries may have been) for there to be an argument over who owns Scripture and has the right interpretation of it (cf. *Against Marcion* 4.1.3; *Against the Jews* 2.7).

Eusebius quotes from an anti-Montanist writer in 192 who presupposes that the revelation of the new covenant was complete and was to be found in authoritative documents (*Church History* 5.16.3; cf. 5.24.7). The writer makes a rhetorical exaggeration in stating his reluctance to write lest he appear to be "adding ... to the word of the new covenant of the gospel," to which one cannot add or take away, a thrust aimed at the (latter day) Montanist prophecies. For him to make this exaggerated pretense of humility, there must have been some set of recognized writings, or he could not have identified the period of revelation with certain written records.

Irenaeus's writings in the last two decades of the second century build from Scripture as a whole, Old and New Testaments. He goes through the words of Jesus, the Gospels, Acts, the letters of Paul, and other apostolic writings (citing nearly every New Testament book) in order to refute the heretics.

Irenaeus is quite explicit about there being only four Gospels, even as there are four corners of the universe and four winds. Before we are too quick to dismiss his words as making a weak case for a weak position, we should remind ourselves of the importance of number symbolism in the ancient world. Moreover, Irenaeus is not arguing for an innovation as far as those Christians whom he represented were concerned.

Over against Marcion's narrowing of the Gospels to one (Luke) and the Gnostic enlargement through the production of new gospels, Irenaeus knew only four as authoritative. His number symbolism is not an argument to establish something new. It is not the case that because there are four winds that he has four Gospels. It is because he has four Gospels that he thinks of other aspects of the nature of things that come in fours. If he had had five Gospels, he would have used another analogy, or if three, another. An appropriate symbolism could have been found whatever number of Gospels he had received.

The term "New Testament" or "New Covenant" was a title of a collection of books for Clement of Alexandria, Tertullian, and Origen, if not already for Irenaeus. For there to have been a collective title, there must have been an identifiable entity to be given a name. These writers may have differed among themselves where the precise limits belonged, but at least they thought they had something to talk about and give a name to.

The date of the *Muratorian Fragment* has entered into the discussion of how early a canonical principle was recognized in the church. The traditional date for the *Muratorian Fragment* from the end of the second century supports the position indicated by the other evidence adduced above, but that position is hardly dependent on a second-century date for the *Muratorian Fragment*. Dating it in the fourth-century scarcely necessitates rewriting the history of the New Testament canon. The *Muratorian Fragment* reflects in broad outline the situation that can be determined from Irenaeus, Clement of Alexandria, Tertullian, and Origen.

By the end of the second century there was a core canon recognized virtually everywhere in the great church: four Gospels, the Acts of the Apostles, thirteen letters of Paul, and varying other apostolic writings. In general, Revelation was accepted in the West but not in the East; Hebrews was accepted in the East as a writing by Paul, but not in the West. Of the general epistles, the widest acceptance was given to 1 Peter and 1 John; the others were less well known.

The canon described in the *Muratorian Fragment* reflects a similar situation, but its exact contents are something of an anomaly in the church, whether second or fourth century, whether East or West. Of our twenty-seven books, the *Fragment* does not mention Hebrews, James, 1 and 2 Peter, and perhaps one letter of John (whether some of these were mentioned, as certainly Matthew and Mark were, in the now missing parts of the document cannot be determined). In addition the document includes, if it is transcribed accurately, the Wisdom of Solomon and the Apocalypse of Peter in its New Testament canon.

3. A closed canon

The third stage is the logical move from the recognition of a canon to the attempt to define its exact limits, from an "open" canon to a "closed" canon. At this stage there was the endeavor to prevent more additions or deletions from an accepted list. Thus from the fourth century there come a number of lists of the canonical Scriptures. This fact has been used to support a fourth-century date for the *Muratorian* canon, but in form it is not a bare list, as the others are, but a discussion of the different books.

Eusebius represents this stage in the history of the canon. Since he was very interested in determining the limits of the canon, he sought to determine the canon of Origen from Origen's writings (Eusebius, *Church History* 6.25; cf. Origen, *Homilies on Joshua* 7.1, not cited by Eusebius). Eusebius's own conclusion about the canon matches what he found in Origen, with the difference that he reduced the results to lists and classified books in various categories (*Church History* 3.25).

"Formerly an older covenant was given to the older people [Jews], and the law instructed the people with fear ... but a new and fresh covenant has been given to the new and fresh people, and the Word has become flesh and fear has been turned into love" (Clement of Alexandria, *Instructor* 1.7.59).

Eusebius noted as books accepted everywhere: four Gospels, Acts of the Apostles, Epistles of Paul (including Hebrews, mentioned by name by Origen but not by Eusebius), 1 John, 1 Peter, and Revelation (which Eusebius himself questioned).

The following were widely acknowledged but were disputed by some: James, Jude, 2 Peter, 2 and 3 John.

Other books that were not genuine but not regarded as heretical included: *Acts of Paul, Shepherd, Apocalypse of Peter, Barnabas,* and *Didache* (Eusebius wanted to put Revelation here also).

Finally, there were heretical books to be avoided altogether: *Gospel of Peter, Gospel of Thomas, Gospel of Matthias, Acts of Andrew,* and *Acts of John.*

The situation had not really changed from Origen's time to Eusebius's.

Any lingering doubts or lack of knowledge of the books in Eusebius's second category were soon removed, for the contents of his first and second categories are combined without any reservations in the canon list of Athanasius of Alexandria (*Festal Letter* 39 for 367), the first ancient list to correspond exactly to our present canon of twenty-seven books.

4. Recognition of the same closed canon

In the fourth and fifth centuries there came to be general agreement in the Greek and Latin churches about the extent of the New Testament canon, although several Greek authors did continue to omit the book of Revelation from their lists and some Latin sources were ambivalent about the Pauline authorship of Hebrews.

Jerome treated the New Testament canon as a "given" not subject to modification, and councils at Hippo in 393 and Carthage in 397 followed Augustine in ratifying a twenty-seven-book New Testament.

The Syriac churches were slower in reaching this stage, for it was not until the sixth century that a Syriac edition of the New Testament included 2 Peter, 2 and 3 John, Jude, and Revelation, and the Church of the East (Nestorian) never accepted these books.

C. Criteria of Canonicity

There was no systematic treatment of canonicity in the ancient church, but the *Muratorian Fragment* is typical in the considerations it urges in incidental remarks.

1. Inspiration

"[A]ll things [in the four Gospels] are declared by the one sovereign Spirit." The attitude of the church at large seems to have been that inspiration was assumed as a minimum requirement, but not all

---

CANON OF ATHANASIUS, *FESTAL LETTER*, 367

[After listing the books of the Old Testament, Athanasius says,] We must not hesitate to name the books of the New Testament. They are as follows:

Four Gospels — according to Matthew, according to Mark, according to Luke, according to John.

Then after these the Acts of the Apostles and the seven so-called catholic epistles of the apostles, as follows: one of James, two of Peter, three of John, and after these, one of Jude.

Next to these are fourteen epistles of the apostle Paul, written in order as follows: First, to the Romans; then two to the Corinthians, and after these to the Galatians and next that to the Ephesians; then to the Philippians and one to the Colossians and two to the Thessalonians and that to the Hebrews. Next are two to Timothy, one to Titus, and last the one to Philemon.

Moreover, John's Apocalypse.

These are the "springs of salvation." ... In these alone is the teaching of true religion proclaimed as good news. Let no one add to these or take anything from them....

There are other books outside these, which are not indeed included in the canon, but have been appointed from the time of the fathers to be read to those who are recent converts to our company and wish to be instructed in the word of true religion. These are the *Wisdom of Solomon*, the *Wisdom of Sirach, Esther, Judith, Tobit*, the so-called *Teaching of the Apostles* [*Didache*] and the *Shepherd*. But while the former are included in the canon and the latter are read, no mention is to be made of the apocryphal works. They are the invention of heretics.

---

works treated as in some sense inspired were necessarily included in the canon of Scripture.

2. Apostolicity

One reason for rejecting Hermas's *Shepherd* was that "it cannot be published for the people in the church, neither among the Prophets, since their number is complete, nor among the Apostles for it is after their time." Apostolic authorship was not literally insisted upon, for the compiler of the *Muratorian* canon acknowledged that Luke had not seen the Lord in the flesh and was only a companion of Paul. The apostolic writings included, therefore, in addition to books written by apostles, the books also that came from apostolic circles and carried apostolic authority.

3. Antiquity

Closely related to the preceding is the exclusion, if the translation above is correct, of works "after their [apostles'] time." John's works, on the other hand, are commended because he was "an eyewitness and hearer ... of the wonderful things of the Lord."

4. Applicability to the whole church (catholicity)

In explanation that Paul in writing to seven churches (two letters each to Thessalonica and Corinth) was actually writing to all churches, the analogy to the Apocalypse of John was made, "For John also, though he wrote in the Apocalypse to seven churches, nevertheless he speaks to them all."

The number seven represented completeness and so stood for the whole, the "one church diffused throughout the whole globe of the earth." Canonical writings had to be useful to the universal church. That is likely a factor in some inspired writings not being preserved (e.g., letters that Paul says he wrote): they did not have wider applicability to other churches.

5. Public reading in the assembly

Closely related to general applicability was the use in worship, "to be read in the church." Non-canonical works were occasionally read in the assemblies for special events or for special reasons, but regular reading was limited to authoritative texts.

6. Right doctrine

"There are many others [epistles] which cannot be received in the Catholic Church, for gall cannot be mixed with honey." Whether a writing agreed with the teaching that had been received was important in the reception of the writing itself.

No one of these criteria by itself was sufficient to assure canonical standing, but all had to be taken together. They appear not so much to have been thought-out standards that were then applied to documents as to have been somewhat "arguments after the fact."

That is, Christians received certain documents and then reflected on why these had come down to them. When other works were brought forward, the comparison with the received works was made according to standards recognized in the accepted writings.

Works that had most of the characteristics, but not all, yet were found to carry the authentic apostolic message, might gain general acceptance but more slowly. Orthodox writings lacking some of the criteria continued to be used but without canonical standing; writings containing unsound teachings were rejected.

D. Theological Reflections

The organized church did not create the canon, but recognized it. This is evident in the way that the decisions of church councils did not enter the process until its later phases. It was only in connection with the final closing of the canon in the West around AD 400 that the church authorities had an effect.

The canon was in a sense "inherited." Writers from the second century on repeatedly referred to the canonical writings as the books "handed down to us." Authoritative books were received as part of the deposit of faith handed down in the church. Succeeding centuries ratified a situation already established.

The approach of the church was not "We determine," but "We recognize" these books as apostolic. The canon represented the books "received" by the church.

The church, therefore, functioned as a witness, not as the judge in the process of canonization. In that sense, the church gave us the Bible. It received and preserved the sacred Scriptures.

So, to an extent, if contemporary Christians take the Scriptures, they must also take the church. But that does not mean they must accept the authority of the church per se, or the authority of the church on all other matters. Certainly the church is part of the apostolic faith and the living of the Christian life, so accepting the faith includes accepting participation in the ongoing life of the church.

On the other hand, when the later church departs from the faith and practice described in the New Testament writings, its witness to the authority of those writings becomes all the more significant, for a witness is more credible when giving testimony against his or her interest.

Instead of being an indication that the church has authority over the Scriptures, the church's role in recognizing the canon of Scripture is a testimony against the authority of the church. Recognizing a canon was an act of placing herself under another authority. If the church wanted to have unlimited authority, it would not have said, "These books are our authority in doctrine and life." The act of canonization was an act of declaring that the church was not her own authority, but that she was submitting to another authority.

Church order, standards of belief, and recognition of the Scriptures have continued to be foundational to the churches. Forms of church polity vary, different creedal statements are accepted, and differences in the content of Scripture (Catholic and Protestant Bibles) remain; but the steps begun in the second century have marked the path on which the churches have walked ever since.

FOR FURTHER STUDY

Ferguson, Everett. *Early Christians Speak*. Abilene, TX: ACU Press. Vol. 1 (3rd ed., 1999): 163–75; vol. 2 (2002): 23–99.

Ferguson, Everett, ed. *The Bible in the Early Church*. Studies in Early Christianity 3. New York: Garland, 1993.

Idem. *Norms of Faith and Life*. Recent Studies in Early Christianity 3. New York: Garland, 1999.

Idem. *Orthodoxy, Heresy, and Schism in Early Christianity*. Studies in Early Christianity 4. New York: Garland, 1993.

McDonald, Lee Martin, and James A. Sanders, ed. *The Canon Debate*. Peabody, MA: Hendrickson, 2002.

Westra, L. H. *The Apostles Creed: Origin, History and Some Early Commentaries*. Turnhout, UK: Brepols, 2002.

The Fathers of the Old Catholic Church and Their Problems

I. BEGINNINGS AND EARLY DEVELOPMENT OF CHRISTIAN THEOLOGY

Theology may be defined as rational reflection on the data of Christian faith. The basic teachings of the Christian faith had been proclaimed in the apostolic age. Those teachings were presented and some effort at interpreting them had been made in the New Testament documents. The Apostolic Fathers sought to preserve this faith and further interpret it.

The beginnings of Christian theology may be found in the Apologists of the second century, who sought to explain Christian teachings to non-Christians by using the philosophy of the day. At the turn from the second to the third century the Church Fathers furthered the process of philosophical reflection on Christian doctrines. Only now, in addition to addressing outsiders (they continued to write apologetic works), they wrote for those inside the church with a twofold purpose: to refute false teachers and to strengthen believers in their faith.

So, in broad terms, there is a progress in Christian literature from addressing insiders by expounding the faith (New Testament and Apostolic Fathers), to addressing outsiders by using philosophy with little appeal to the New Testament (Apologists), to addressing insiders by using philosophy and rational arguments as well as dealing with the Bible as a whole in order to develop a theological understanding of Christian doctrine in opposition to heresy (fathers of the old catholic church).

As early participants in the development of Christian theology, the old catholic fathers often took positions that were found inadequate by the standards of later thought. Hence, only Irenaeus, Cyprian, and Gregory Thaumaturgus are consistently regarded as saints. Possibly three (certainly Novatian, probably Hippolytus, and possibly Tertullian) were in schism from the main body of the church, and one was later explicitly condemned as a heretic (Origen). Yet, they were themselves decisive in the refutation of competing forms of the Christian faith. Irenaeus, Tertullian, and Hippolytus wrote major anti-heretical works, and Clement and Origen developed a philosophical theology that incorporated what was appealing in Gnosticism but subverted its unorthodox premises.

A biographical approach of some of these literary figures will reveal not only their distinctive temperaments, but also some of the characteristics of different regions, as well as much about the life and controversies of the church at the end of the second and beginning of the third century. (The leaders who flourished in the mid-third century will be discussed in chapter 9.)

A. Irenaeus

Irenaeus was a key figure in the orthodox defense against Gnosticism — and as such we have already encountered his name. He was also an important bridge figure between the sub-apostolic age and the development of the old catholic church, for as a youth in Smyrna he had listened to teaching by Polycarp, a reputed follower of the apostle John. He went West and became a presbyter in the church at Lyons in Gaul, which had close contacts with Asia Minor.

In 177 Irenaeus carried a letter to Rome, attempting to mediate in the controversy over Montanism. During his absence, there occurred the persecution described in the *Letter of the Churches of Vienne and Lyons* that took the life of the aged bishop Pothinus. Irenaeus succeeded him as bishop. He continued to live up to his name "irenical" by writing to bishop Victor of Rome to mediate in the Paschal controversy (see III.C below).

FATHERS OF THE OLD CATHOLIC CHURCH			
Name	Date	Location	Language
Irenaeus	c. 115–202	Lyons	Greek
Clement of Alexandria	c. 160–215	Alexandria	Greek
Tertullian	c. 160–220	Carthage	Latin
Hippolytus	c. 170–236	Rome	Greek
Origen	c. 185–251	Alexandria/Caesarea	Greek
Novatian	fl. 250	Rome	Latin
Cyprian	c. 200–258	Carthage	Latin
Gregory Thaumaturgus	c. 210–265	Cappadocia	Greek

Still belonging to the Greek period of the church in the West, Irenaeus's works survive mainly in translation. His principal work, known as *Against Heresies* but described by himself as "Five Books of Unmasking and Overthrow of the Gnosis Falsely So-Called," apart from some passages quoted by later writers, survives in its entirety only in an early literal Latin translation. His *Demonstration [or Proof] of the Apostolic Preaching*, which survives in an Armenian translation, gives an instruction to be delivered to new converts based on the biblical story of God's saving activity set within a Trinitarian context.

In advancing his own theological interpretations in order to defend the mainstream church and to refute heresy, Irenaeus was a "traditional innovator." Irenaeus's theology is based on unity. Against Gnostic and Marcionite dualism, he stresses the one God, who is Creator and Redeemer; the one Lord Jesus Christ, the same pre-existent being who became incarnate; and the one history of salvation that is the plan of the one God centering in the one Christ. He is the first major author known to us to argue from Scripture as a whole, witnessing to the emerging New Testament canon and insisting on the harmony of the Old and New Testaments as successive covenants in God's plan of salvation.

One of Irenaeus's key theological ideas is that of "recapitulation," a word that in rhetoric referred to the summary of a narrative, but with a scriptural meaning supplied by Ephesians 1:10. Irenaeus applies the idea to Jesus Christ as not only a "summing up" but also the "bringing to a head" or climax of God's saving plan. Jesus Christ as the new Adam, both man and God, is the "new head" of humanity who reversed the steps of the old Adam. He shared fully in humanity, except for sin, in order to unite human beings with God by effecting the salvation of the flesh. Christ overcame the Enemy of humanity and swallowed up mortality in immortality.

Irenaeus's argument from apostolic succession for the validity of the church's teachings, and his appeal to the canon of truth as the proper standard for the interpretation of Scripture, were lasting contributions to the catholic understanding of the ministry of the church and tradition.

Significant for the future, and controversial in its meaning, was the place Irenaeus gave to the Roman church. The crucial passage (preserved only in Latin) literally reads as follows, "For with [*or* to] this church [Rome] on account of the more potent principality it is necessary that every church should agree [*or* come together, resort], that is those who from every place are faithful, in which [church] there is always preserved by these who are from every place the tradition which is from the apostles" (*Against Heresies* 3.3.2). Almost every

"The Word of God became man; he who is Son of God was made Son of Man in order that humanity, by being taken into the Word and receiving adoption, might become the child of God" (Irenaeus, *Against Heresies* 3.19.1).

key word is controverted, but it seems that Irenaeus is presenting the Roman church as a mirror of the universal church; representatives from churches all over the empire came to Rome as the capital city, and so there was found in the Roman church witness to the common apostolic tradition.

Irenaeus is important for representing the orthodox reaction to the problems of heresy in the second century. His approach articulated the premises on which the old catholic church developed. He stressed the fundamental Christian doctrines: one God, goodness of creation, redemption through the one Jesus Christ, the resurrection of the body, the historical roots of the Christian faith, and the authority of Scripture rightly interpreted.

He was typical of the old catholic church in anticipating doctrines that were to assume greater importance in the future: the apostolic succession of bishops, the rule of faith [apostolic tradition] as the standard for interpreting the Bible, the appeal to the material elements of the eucharist as embodying spiritual realities, and a place for Mary (the new Eve) in his theology of recapitulation. Irenaeus was thus both a "biblical" theologian and a "catholic" theologian.

B. Tertullian and the Church in North Africa

Tertullian, who flourished in Carthage in the first two decades of the third century, was the most prolific Christian writer in Latin before the fourth century. He began writing in Greek, but as the Western church became increasingly Latin in its language, only his numerous Latin works survived, a fact that assured his continuing influence (in contrast to Hippolytus of Rome, who wrote only in Greek and fell into obscurity).

It is notable that Latin-speaking Christianity emerged as a literary influence first in North Africa, not in Rome. Old Latin versions of the Scriptures were being produced in North Africa and Italy by the end of the second century. In the second century the centers of Roman culture were in the western provinces—Africa, Spain, and Gaul.

Tertullian is commonly regarded as the prototypical rigorist and legalist for his approach to Christian living and manner of argumentation, but for the best appreciation of Tertullian's intellectual formation one must see him as a Latin rhetorician. He was converted to Christianity as an adult in the late second century; he was married, perhaps a presbyter, and active in the church at Carthage.

About 207 Tertullian was attracted to Montanism, and he became an outspoken exponent of its more rigorous approach to disciplinary questions related to Christian behavior. On the basis of Augustine's later report that he brought Tertullianists back into the Catholic Church, it has been thought that Tertullian led a faction that broke away even from the Montanists, but "Tertullianists" may have been a term for the Montanists in North Africa and it is not even certain that Tertullian's support of Montanism ever led him into actual schism from the church.

Tertullian's literary fame rests on his ability to coin sharp, original, technical phrases. His crabbed, abbreviated Latin is often difficult to read, but he was witty, vigorous, and incisive. He set the language of the Western church on such key concepts as original sin, person and nature in the Trinity, sacrament, merit, and others.

Readers are alternately repelled by Tertullian's "Christian" bigotry and fascinated by his startling, striking turns of phrase. He gave many rugged, memorable expressions to Christian language, including:

1. "The more we are cut down by you, the more in number we grow; the blood of Christians is seed" (*Apology* 50), often paraphrased as "the blood of the martyrs is the seed of the church."

2. "It is credible because it is unlikely" (*On the Flesh of Christ* 5.4), often misquoted as, "I believe because it is absurd." Tertullian's statement is not a declaration of Christian irrationalism, but an argument that the sheer improbability of the key Christian claims means they were not invented by men.

3. "What has Athens to do with Jerusalem? What concord is there between the Academy and the church?" (*Prescription against Heretics* 7). This was part of Tertullian's argument that heresy, like philosophy, derived from human groping for truth apart from God's revelation. Tertullian did not actually renounce reason and philosophy, and he indeed spent much time in a philosophical defense of Christianity.

Some of Tertullian's writings may be singled out for comment. His literary masterpiece is usually regarded as his *Apology*, the greatest Latin apologetic for Christianity before Augustine. He has many of the arguments found in Justin Martyr, but his legal knowledge acquired in the practice of rhetoric makes him more cogent. It turns out that Jerusalem has nothing to do with either Rome or Athens. He argues, in opposition to the State's persecution, that the essence of religion is voluntary acceptance.

Another apologetic writing, *On the Testimony of the Soul*, argues that, although "one becomes a Christian and is not born one," yet common human language and attitudes witness to Christian truth. Tertullian's tracts against Roman customs, such as *On Idolatry* and *On the Crown*, include a rejection of military service by Christians, a position he shared with other leading Christian thinkers such as Hippolytus, Origen, and Lactantius.

Tertullian's anti-heretical writings are particularly important for the information they contain about alternative interpretations of Christianity and the development of orthodox theology. His *Prescription Against Heretics* attempts to preempt the heretics' case by arguing from a Roman legal principle in order to claim that the Scriptures belong to the church, and so only catholic Christians have the right to use them. The rule of faith preserved in the tradition of the church is the right key to understanding them.

Tertullian's argument *Against Praxeas* employed the terminology of "three persons" (*tres personae*) and "one substance" (*una substantia*) that, when combined into one formula, became the accepted way in Latin to express the doctrine of the Trinity.

Against Marcion is his longest work. Tertullian defends the oneness of God and the goodness of the law. The polemical purpose should be recognized, but the outcome makes Tertullian an "Old Testament Christian" in whom the Sermon on the Mount becomes a new law. (But, as has been observed, Tertullian himself never turned the other cheek in an argument!)

The tendency to legalism in the Western church, as exemplified in Tertullian, was a wedding of Rome's legal traditions with the Mosaic law read as applying directly to the church's institutions. The result of Christianizing the law was to lead to understanding salvation through meritorious conduct as now possible—through Jesus Christ.

The treatise *On the Soul* is the first Christian writing on psychology. Drawing on Stoic anthropology, Tertullian understands the soul as "material," but of a higher and finer grade of matter than the body.

On Baptism, the earliest extant writing on this subject, opposes a small group of Gnostics who denied the necessity of water baptism.

On Repentance is important for its description of "second repentance," the humiliating disciplines imposed in "confession" of post-baptismal sin in order for a sinner to be restored to the fellowship of the church (which are worth submitting to because "temporal mortification removes eternal punishments").

In his Montanist period, Tertullian rejected the church's practice of allowing forgiveness of post-baptismal sins. Tertullian's practical works from this period take an increasingly rigorist position on moral theory and practice.

Tertullian had a great influence on a leader of the Carthaginian church in the next generation, Cyprian, who moderated Tertullian's views into a form less sectarian and more churchly (see chapter 9).

C. The Church in Alexandria and Clement of Alexandria

Alexandria, founded in the fourth century BC by Alexander the Great, was the second city of the Roman Empire. It was the home of Hellenism, where Greece and the Middle East met.

The city was also home to the largest Jewish community in the Greco-Roman world. Jewish Hellenism planted deep roots in Alexandria. There the Septuagint—the Bible of the old catholic fathers—was produced. There too Philo, the Jewish philosopher, in the early first century had attempted the harmonization of revelation and philosophy. This task of accommodating Scripture to Greek philosophy was inherited by the Alexandrian Christian philosophers, who—in contrast to Tertullian's question—sought to show that Jerusalem was Athens.

The introduction of Christianity to Alexandria is shrouded in darkness. The later Alexandrian church preserved a tradition of its founding by Mark, disciple of Peter, and in its early history links were maintained between Alexandria and Rome. There also were links with Palestine. If the variant reading in the Western text (Codex Bezae) of Acts 18:25 rests on historical information, then Apollos first learned teaching about Jesus already in Alexandria. Some early Christian literature, *Barnabas* and the apocryphal *Gospel of the Egyptians*, may have been written there.

The church at Alexandria early showed some distinctive characteristics:

1. Gnosticism was greatly influential there. Hellenistic Jews may have drifted into a Jewish Gnosticism. Certainly a number of Gnostic teachers were active there, including Basilides, Carpocrates, and Valentinus. Some contemporary scholars have suggested that the early history of the church in Alexandria was suppressed by the orthodox because the earliest form of Christianity there was "Gnostic." Clement and Origen sought to develop an orthodox Gnosticism in place of its heretical form.

2. There were wealthy members of the church in Alexandria. A growing number of converts recruited from the well-to-do leisure class were apparently disturbed at the words of Mark 10:17–22. In response, Clement's sermon *Who Is the Rich Man that Is Saved?* explained that Jesus did not condemn possessions as such, but only the love of money.

3. The polity of the church differed from that developing in the church elsewhere, or at least maintained an older pattern longer than other churches did. The twelve presbyters elected and appointed one of their number as bishop. Teachers main-

tained an independence in Alexandria longer than elsewhere, perhaps because the bishop was not so strong a figure as he became in most churches.

The term "school" is used in three senses, and all three are applicable to the ecclesiastical use of the phrase "school of Alexandria." It may refer to pupils grouped around a teacher, as Justin or Valentinus in Rome and Clement in Alexandria. It could refer to a group of thinkers holding similar opinions (a "school of thought"). The special concerns of the Alexandrian school in this sense were maintaining free intellectual inquiry in the church, exploring the relations of faith and reason, the allegorical interpretation of Scripture, and the Logos Christology.

The "school of Alexandria" also refers to the organized program of catechetical instruction developed in the church there. It is disputed whether the work of Clement and his teacher Pantaenus was already under direct church control or, as is more likely, was a private undertaking like "school" in the first sense.

We know that Origen, while under commission from bishop Demetrius in Alexandria, abandoned his teaching of the classics and devoted himself to the study and teaching of Scripture. This program was under strong episcopal supervision. Later Origen brought in Heraclas to help with the catechetical work so that he could devote himself to advanced instruction, something of a private "university."

Clement was born (c. 160) of non-Christian parentage. He represents the educated and cultured convert to Christianity. A seeker, like Justin, of philosophical truth, he found—after a period of travel around the Mediterranean—a Christian teacher who gave a vigorous interpretation of Christianity in a philosophically acceptable manner.

This "Sicilian bee," as Clement describes him, was presumably Pantaenus, who settled in Alexandria. Clement continued his work and was recognized as a presbyter. He left Alexandria in 202–3 during a persecution under Septimius Severus and spent his later years in Cappadocia, dying about 215. His spirit as a learned and broad-minded man of culture and a conservative moralist has been caught in the phrase "a liberal Puritan."

Clement's three great works form a trilogy. The *Exhortation to the Greeks* (*Protrepticus*) is an apology, drawing intimations of Christianity from Greek philosophy and literature. The *Instructor* (*Paedagogus*) is the first Christian work on ethics (chapter 8). Jesus Christ as the teacher (in his capacity as the divine Logos) instructs in morals and Christian conduct in society. The *Miscellanies* (*Stromata*) is a "patchwork" of reflections on various aspects of Christianity in relation to intellectual concerns of the day. Some of the work is tedious, but it is enlivened by

The Fathers of the Old Catholic Church and Their Problems

profound thoughts. The center of the work is the description of the true Christian Gnostic, who seeks knowledge not for the purpose of salvation, but for its own sake. In the ideal Gnostic the vision of God is attained. Becoming like God is a moral action, possible through grace.

Clement suggested three different theories concerning the validity of philosophy for believers:

1. His most original suggestion was that, as the covenant was given to the Jews, philosophy was given to the Greeks. It was given to the Greeks not by the Logos, however, but by angels—and so was an inferior knowledge.

2. What truth the Greeks had was taken from the Scriptures. This view had been suggested by Jewish thinkers and was taken over by several Christian apologists.

3. What truth existed among the Greeks came from God and could be rightly claimed by Christians for their own use. "Plundering the Egyptians" (based on Exodus 12:33, 36) was an idea later popularized to justify Christians taking over whatever was of value from pagan literature and philosophy.

Furthermore, Clement saw philosophy as having three uses for the Christian: (1) to unmask philosophers' errors, (2) to make the content of the faith more precise, and (3) to help one pass from naïve to scientific knowledge.

Clement's view on the relation of faith and reason has been described as a "double faith" theory. One kind of faith is simple assent to the teaching of Scripture that gives an immediate sort of knowledge; this faith, when demonstrated by reason (rational faith), is gnosis—a knowledge that is not different from faith, but a different sort of faith. Clement affirmed the equality of these two forms of faith against the extremes both of Gnosticism, which gave a higher value to gnosis, and of those believers who rejected philosophy.

The significance of Clement's position may be seen by contrasting it with the views of Tertullian and Origen. Tertullian had a "single faith" theory that gave preeminence to simple faith (the search for philosophical demonstration reduced faith's merit). Origen's "single faith" was the opposite: rational faith is superior to simple faith and is of more merit.

In 1958 in a monastery near Jerusalem a letter was discovered purporting to be by Clement, to someone named Theodore, in which he refers to a *Secret Gospel of Mark* and gives two quotations from this "more spiritual" form of the Gospel intended for those "attaining perfection." Although still disputed, the genuineness of the letter seems to be established. The quotations record contents of the type found in apocryphal and Gnostic gospels, with perhaps more claim to authenticity than most such stories.

Where this material fits in the transmission of the canonical Gospel is uncertain. Was it (1) an early form of the Gospel later edited out, perhaps because of heretical misuse; (2) an interpolated form of the original Gospel; or, as Clement thought, (3) one of two editions issued by Mark himself?

The manuscript of the letter breaks off at the point where Clement offers his interpretation of the episodes in contrast to the use being made of the passages by Carpocratian heretics.

D. Origen in Alexandria and Caesarea

Origen was the most prolific Christian writer before Augustine. He was a pioneer in the scholarly study and interpretation of the biblical text, a creative thinker with a prodigous memory, who remained a ferment in Christian theology for centuries.

Origen was born into a Christian family in Alexandria about 185. We know something of his life and anecdotes from his youth because Eusebius of Caesarea, who belonged to the Origenist school, preserved much about Origen in the sixth book of his *Church History*. Origen's proud father, Leonides, thankful "to be the father of such a boy," was said many times to stand over the sleeping boy, uncover his breast, and kiss it with reverence, "as if a divine spirit were enshrined therein."

The persecution under Septimius Severus (202–3) claimed Leonides as a martyr, and Origen was spared a similar outcome because his mother hid his clothes so the modest youth would not leave the house. He contented himself with writing a letter to his father in prison urging him not to yield to the persecutors out of concern for the family. Origen received a good education, not only the basic literary studies of the Greek world, but also in philosophy, studying in the same atmosphere out of which came Neoplatonism.

Origen supported the family by secular teaching, but at the age of eighteen he was entrusted by bishop Demetrius with teaching inquirers, so he devoted himself to studying the Scriptures, sold his secular books, and lived austerely off the proceeds. Because many women were among his students, Origen, taking Matthew 19:12 literally, "made himself a eunuch for the sake of the kingdom of heaven," an act successfully kept secret for some time. Wealthy patrons began to assist Origen's studies, early on a wealthy lady and later Ambrose, whom Origen converted from Valentinianism.

As Origen's studies progressed so did his fame as a teacher, and he was called on to make many trips for speaking and teaching, including an audience with Julia Mamaea, the mother of emperor Alexander Severus. On one trip to Palestine the bishops invited him to interpret the Scriptures publicly in the church at Caesarea although he had not yet received ordination to the presbyterate.

Bishop Demetrius—whether from jealousy, a desire to strengthen the authority of the bishop, or concern for the orthodoxy of some of Origen's speculations—increasingly made trouble for Origen. The bishops in Palestine, criticized for allowing Origen—as a layman—to preach in church, on a later visit laid hands on him. Demetrius now brought up the matter of Origen's castration, which was considered to disqualify a man from church office, and called him home. The difficulties were so great that Origen in 232 moved to Caesarea, where he continued his teaching.

Among those who came to study with Origen was Gregory (later known as Thaumaturgus), whose *Panegyric to Origen* gives a vivid picture of Origen's teaching. In florid style, this important document for Christian education describes the wide scope of instruction—dialectics, natural science, geometry, astronomy, philosophy, ethics, theology, and Scripture. Origen encouraged his students to read all the philosophers except those who did not believe in God. Employing both lectures and the Socratic method of questioning, he communicated more, in Gregory's tribute, by example than by precept.

In the persecution under Decius in 251, Origen suffered imprisonment and torture, which likely hastened his death some time thereafter. Pamphilus inherited his library at Caesarea and—along with his student Eusebius—wrote an apology in defense of Origen. That library was the foundation of Eusebius's own historical and theological works.

One of Origen's great scholarly achievements was the *Hexapla*, six parallel columns comparing line by line the Hebrew Old Testament, a Greek transliteration, and the Greek translations of Aquila (the most literal), Symmachus, the Septuagint, and Theodotion. The work was intended to lay a sound textual basis for Origen's commentaries on the Old Testament and his argument with the Jews over its interpretation. There was probably never more than the one copy of the work, which did not survive, and copies made of the fifth column did not reproduce Origen's textual signs marking where the Septuagint had additions and subtractions from the Hebrew text.

Much of Origen's study took the form of interpreting the biblical text—scholia or notes on difficult passages, homilies preached on the books of the Bible, and large-scale scientific commentaries on biblical books. Most extensively preserved of the commentaries is the *Commentary on John*, of which nine of the thirty-two books survive. It was never completed; an indication of the detail is shown by the fact that it took ten books to reach the end of the second chapter of John.

In *On First Principles* 4, Origen outlined a tripartite hermeneutical principle, finding three levels of interpretation of Scripture corresponding to the three parts of human nature: (1) the bodily sense is the literal, historical meaning of Scripture; (2) the psychic (soul) sense refers to the moral teaching; (3) the pneumatic (spiritual) to the allegorical or eschatological interpretation that reveals the mysteries of the faith.

Origen's basic distinction, however, was between the literal and the spiritual or non-literal, the latter of which might have multiple applications. In actual practice, his exegetical procedure was to go from the linguistic meaning to the meaning "hidden under the letter." The latter was first of all the Christian doctrinal sense, and then the moral practice dependent on that teaching, as well as its eschatological implications.

For Origen, the Scripture, as inspired by the Spirit, always has a non-literal meaning, but may not have a literal meaning (if the latter spoke anthropomorphically about God, legislated irrational laws, or recorded impossibilities in the historical narrative). In his homilies Origen gave special attention to the moral lessons to be drawn from Scripture. Origen's usage varied, but from his formulations there was later developed a fourfold meaning of Scripture: historical (literal), moral, allegorical (doctrinal), and anagogical (eschatological).

Origen's intellectual framework was a kind of Neoplatonism, which was just emerging at his time. If one thinks in Platonist terms that there is a true spiritual world of which this material world is only an imperfect imitation, then allegory is a congenial method of interpretation, for one looks at "material" texts in order to see a true spiritual reality behind or beyond them.

If instead of such an ontological view, one takes a more historical perspective of before, now, and after, such as the Hebrews did, then typological interpretation (fulfillment in history) is more likely to develop, which it did as we will see (chapter 13) at Antioch.

Origen's *Against Celsus*, the longest and greatest of the Greek apologies for Christianity in the ancient church, raised Christian apologetics to a higher level. Origen responded to Celsus's detailed as well as general criticisms: Christians welcomed bad and ignorant people; Christians immodestly claimed that everything was made for human beings and that Christians had an exclusive claim to truth; and Christianity introduced a new religion that was hostile to traditional society and its religion.

In addition to the usual Christian arguments from fulfilled prophecy and miracles, Origen developed the moral argument for the truth

The Fathers of the Old Catholic Church and Their Problems

of Christianity in order to counter the charge that the miracles of Jesus were worked by magic. Jesus and his followers, unlike the magicians of the time, did not receive any earthly reward or gain for their deeds, but instead brought benefits to others. The growth of Christianity in spite of opposition and persecution was a further proof of its divine power.

Two shorter works show Origen as not only a deep thinker and learned interpreter of Scripture, but also as a concerned churchman and spiritual guide. The *Exhortation to Martyrdom* and *On Prayer* discussed basic expressions of spirituality in the early church, one for the elect few and the other for all Christians.

Origen, furthermore, produced the church's first systematic theology, *On First Principles*, comparable to works at that period on first principles of philosophy.

At the beginning Origen lays down the "rule of faith" delivered to the faithful as the foundation of Christianity: the one God, Christ Jesus both God and man, the Holy Spirit who inspired the prophets and apostles, resurrection of the body with rewards and punishments for souls, free will, existence of evil and good angels, and inspired Scriptures with both obvious and hidden meanings.

The theologian's task is to clarify, define, and make vocal what is implicit in this deposit of faith. This work is controlled by the teachings that have been revealed, but speculation with the purpose of producing a unified body of doctrine is possible in areas not clearly defined in the church's traditional teaching.

Whereas others would have spoken of the Logos as "emitted," Origen introduced the term "generation," from the language of Father and Son, into the Logos speculation. The problem, as others would make explicit, was that human beings think of a father as existing before a son and that would introduce a time element into eternity. For Origen and Platonic thinkers, there was no before and after in eternity, and the language of generation had the advantage of securing the same essence for the Son as the Father. Thus Origen could affirm an eternal generation.

Nonetheless, there was an element of subordination in Origen's thinking, because the Son is derived from the Father. The subordination becomes more explicit in regard to the Holy Spirit, whom he described as the chief of spirits.

Although lacking the exact formulation of later theologians and not using the terms consistently according to the later precision, Origen employed the words that became the orthodox language to discuss the Trinity: Origen used *ousia* and *hypostasis* as interchangeable, but they became the words respectively for the oneness and the individuality in the Godhead.

Origen also speculated about matters for which he became controversial in his own time and for which he was later condemned (in the sixth century—see chapter 16). He gave a more spiritual definition to the nature of the resurrection body than was becoming common in his time. Origen considered the possibility of the pre-existence of souls as explaining the fall of human nature and the separate circumstances of human beings. Moreover, his understanding of God's saving purposes allowed for universal salvation.

E. Hippolytus and Callistus in Rome

Ancient sources transmit contradictory information about Hippolytus (ca. 170–ca. 236). Was he presbyter or bishop, at Rome or Porto, a churchman or a schismatic? Modern scholars have complicated the situation by postulating that the works attributed to Hippolytus come from at least two different authors.

Statue restored as Hippolytus (entrance to the Apostolic Library, Vatican City, Rome).

Moreover, the apparently successful reconstruction in the twentieth century of the influential *Apostolic Tradition* of Hippolytus is now being called into question. The common material from the church orders dependent on this document will be drawn on in the next chapter in describing the life and worship of the church in the second and third centuries.

A still plausible interpretation is that Hippolytus was a presbyter in Rome who went into schism when Callistus was elected bishop, was exiled—along with the later Roman bishop Pontianus—by the emperor Maximinus Thrax to Sardinia, where they both died, and was reconciled (or at least his followers were) to the main church and so treated as a martyr.

The following account will continue to use the name Hippolytus with the understanding that the person represented thereby may not have been so named.

For our purposes now, the questions of Hippolytean authorship may be passed by in order to focus on one work that has been attributed to Hippolytus, *The Refutation of All Heresies*, and one episode described in that

"We, as being successors of the apostles and participants in this grace, high-priesthood, and office of teaching, as well as being reputed guardians of the church, must not be found deficient in vigilance, or disposed to suppress correct doctrine" (Hippolytus?, *Refutation of All Heresies* 1.preface).

work, the conflict of the author with two bishops of Rome, Zephyrinus and Callistus (*Heresies* 9.7). No passage in Christian literature gives such a vivid impression of the social realities of the early church.

Despite the ire of the author, the slave Callistus must have shown shrewdness and ability in the service of his master Carpophorus. Then Callistus lost a considerable amount of money that had been entrusted to him, perhaps through bad luck or speculative investments, although the author implies embezzlement.

When called for an accounting, Callistus ran away, not surprising in view of his master's harsh character. Carpophorus captured him on a boat still in the harbor, but then on the entreaties of others freed Callistus in order to give him an opportunity to recover the assets.

Callistus went to the Jewish synagogue, he said, to approach those who owed him money but, according to the author, actually in order to create a disturbance by claiming to be a Christian and so bring about his death.

At any rate, an uproar resulted, and the city prefect scourged Callistus and sent him to work the government mines in Sardinia. Marcia, a believer who was a concubine of emperor Commodus, obtained release for martyrs in Sardinia. The author states that, although the name of Callistus was not on the list of those to be released, he persuaded the official to add his name (this seems wholly incredible).

After Callistus's return to Rome, bishop Victor provided him with a place of retirement and an allowance of food. When Zephyrinus replaced Victor as bishop, he made Callistus a deacon in charge of the church's cemetery. As a close associate of Zephyrinus, Callistus then succeeded him as bishop. Instead of being the "catholic church," the author says they should be called the school of "Callistians."

The conflict of Hippolytus (if that be the author's name) with Callistus illustrates the difficulties within the church at Rome in the third century in becoming truly inclusive (i.e., "catholic"). Both Hippolytus and Callistus were victims of persecution, but their similarities end there. They came from different social classes—Hippolytus an educated Greek-speaker with contacts in the Greek East; Callistus a former slave who rose to prominence by his wits. They became personal rivals within the Roman church.

Hippolytus and Callistus especially differed in their Christology. Hippolytus represented the Logos theology of the Greek apologists, a position Callistus branded as "ditheist" (a charge that really stung). Callistus then tried to affirm both the unity of God and the separate suffering by the Son, an attempt Hippolytus judged a failure as alternating between the teachings of Sabellius and Theodotus (see below).

The disagreement that broke fellowship concerned church discipline: What sinners could be reconciled to the church and on what terms, and what was to be the church's attitude on social and moral questions?

Hippolytus took the rigorist position that certain sinners, such as murderers and adulterers, could not be reconciled to the church (some sins only God could forgive). Instead, Callistus claimed to be able to forgive such and readmit them to the fellowship of the church. Hippolytus charges Callistus with conniving to condone adultery and murder, yet by reading between the lines in some of the details of the account it is possible to attain a more sympathetic understanding of Callistus's policies.

According to Roman law, for instance, the marriage of a free woman with a slave was not recognized. The greater number of Christian women than men in the free classes led some to choose a Christian slave as a mate. Hippolytus considered such unions "adulterous," but Callistus took an important step in social ethics in recognizing marriages not sanctioned by law.

When some of these women sought abortions rather than have their children considered illegitimate (such abortions were regarded as murder and unforgiveable by Hippolytus), Callistus was willing to extend forgiveness. What remains unclear is the basis on which Callistus claimed to grant forgiveness, that is, extend the reconciliation of the church. Did he do so as "close to Peter" (i.e., as successor to Peter or as close to the bones of Peter?), as a bishop, as a bishop in council with his presbyters, or as a "spiritual man" (technically a martyr)?

Both Hippolytus and Callistus defended valid principles: Hippolytus the ideal of the church as a pure community and Callistus the possibility of forgiveness and reconciliation. Both men made mistakes: Hippolytus a personal vindictiveness and lack of love for sinners, and Callistus acting in a high-handed manner, being too quick to forgive, and condoning abuses accompanying his measures.

Callistus's position represented the course the Roman church was going to take in understanding the church as an inclusive church, a saving society. He compared the church to Noah's ark, containing both clean and unclean animals. Hippolytus, on the other hand, wanted a church of the pure.

These differing understandings of the nature of the church, which came to conflict on the treatment of those guilty of serious post-baptismal sins, had disturbed the Christians in Rome since at least the days of Hermas.

The conflict was resumed a generation after Hippolytus and Callistus when their respective views were taken up again by Novatian and Cornelius (see chapter 9).

II. THE RISE TO PROMINENCE OF THE CHURCH AT ROME

By the end of the second century, the church at Rome was beginning to assert itself as the leading church in the Christian world. This situation was far from finding institutional expression and did not mean that everyone was prepared to follow Rome's lead.

Yet the way in which so many prominent teachers found their way to Rome and sought acceptance of their teachings in Rome, and the involvement of Rome in the controversies that affected Christians at the end of the second century, do show the increasing influence and importance of the Roman church.

A number of factors contributed to the increasing prominence of the church in the capital:

1. Administrative ability of the bishops—they may have been undistinguished theologically, but they acted prudently in holding the diverse elements in the church together.

2. Size of the church—the Roman church grew enormously in the second and third centuries, both through people moving in and through conversions, and it had international contacts.

3. Capital city—people naturally looked to Rome for leadership, a political habit that influenced thinking in the church.

4. Orthodox reputation—in a century of considerable theological variety, Rome maintained a reputation of steadiness and balance in preserving the apostolic traditions.

5. Charity—the Roman church acquired considerable wealth and used it to care for its poor and send money to the relief of Christians elsewhere (money attracts authority).

6. Influence in high places—it is difficult to assess whether evidence from the end of the first century indicates the presence of Christians in senatorial families or only in their households, but by the end of the second century there is no doubt some Christians held positions of influence with the government.

7. Only apostolic church in the West—controversy had given prominence to contacts with the apostles, and Rome was the only church in the western part of the empire with confirmed direct contact with apostles.

8. Martyrdom of Peter and Paul—these apostolic contacts with Rome were not of the ordinary kind, for the two chief apostles had not only been there but had honored the city with their martyrdom and thus the site of their bones.

The church at Rome was Greek-speaking from its beginning, for Rome as the capital had many nationalities represented in its population. It maintained close ties with Alexandria, Corinth, and Carthage.

Victor (c. 189–c. 198), if his name is an indication, may have been the first Latin-speaking bishop. The Latin-speaking element increased through the third century, but it was not until the fourth century that the liturgy (always the most conservative feature of church life) completed the transfer to Latin.

After Peter and Paul, a host of prominent Christian teachers— orthodox and others—found their way to Rome: not only martyrs like Ignatius, but also teachers as diverse as Justin, Marcion, and Valentinus. Therefore, it is no surprise that some of the important controversies affecting the churches at the end of the second century set off sparks in Rome.

III. PROBLEMS FACING THE OLD CATHOLIC FATHERS

In addition to their principal problem of defending orthodox faith and practice against the challenges of heresy and schism (chapters 5 and 6), the old catholic fathers faced other problems.

A. Paschal Controversy

The Paschal controversy is significant for indicating the increasing importance of the church of Rome. The point at issue was the date for commemorating the events of salvation connected with the death and resurrection of Jesus.

Some churches, especially in the province of Asia, were called— by those who disagreed with them—Quartodecimans ("those who observed the fourteenth of the month"). This name came from their practice of observing an annual remembrance of the passion of Jesus on the date of the Passover ("Pascha" in Greek). In the Jewish calendar that date was the fourteenth of Nisan, which might fall on any day of the week. Most of the churches had abandoned the Jewish calendar and remembered the death and resurrection of Jesus on the Sunday after the first full moon of spring.

An observable corollary of this difference in calendar was that Christians in the different traditions broke their penitential fast on different days, some on the day on which the Jewish Passover fell and others on Sunday. Such an annual observance, although not attested in the New Testament, is not unexpected in view of the annual observances that characterized Jewish and pagan religious activities. Jewish converts would have observed Passover with a new meaning, and

The Fathers of the Old Catholic Church and Their Problems

Gentile converts would have been programmed to give special emphasis to the season at which redemption was accomplished.

The earliest documentation for different customs is Irenaeus's reference to bishop Sixtus (115–25) of Rome not making a test of fellowship over the different customs (Eusebius, *Church History* 5.24.14). He further records a visit of Polycarp to Anicetus (155–66) in Rome, in which they disagreed on the Paschal observance yet maintained peace with each other. Anicetus yielded celebration of the eucharist in the church to his distinguished visitor from Smyrna (ibid. 5.24.16). According to Irenaeus, Polycarp claimed the precedent of John and other apostles on behalf of the Quartodeciman practice, and Anicetus appealed to the example of the presbyters before him.

The sign of fellowship among the various house churches in Rome was receiving the eucharistic bread from the bishop's table. Victor provoked a conflict by not sending the communion to congregations that followed the Quartodeciman practice. His motives for seeking to establish uniformity of practice escape us. Asian bishops, led by Polycrates of Ephesus, came to the defense of their custom.

Others like Irenaeus tried to mediate, contending that different customs did not threaten the unity of the faith. Councils of bishops were held in many different places, and the Asian churches were isolated on this issue. The great majority declared that the Lord's resurrection should be celebrated on no day other than Sunday and that the paschal fast should end on that day.

The Quartodeciman practice did not end, but it was increasingly marginalized. Different methods of calculating which Sunday was to be observed persisted until the Council of Nicaea in 325 (and in some places until later).

The Paschal controversy demonstrates several points of importance:

1. The dependence of the church on Jewish customs was evident, but their influence was waning, especially in those regions where the Jewish presence was less felt or where the church wanted to distance itself from that presence.

2. The lack of a uniform apostolic tradition indicates there was no apostolic authority on the custom. The controversy illustrates the problem of following what was old but lacked explicit (written) apostolic authorization. An annual remembrance of the resurrection likely goes back to apostolic times, but the attempt to establish a uniform practice revealed the absence of a verifiable apostolic sanction.

3. The strong feeling for the importance of the resurrection and for Sunday witnessed to the centrality of the event and its

indissoluble connection with a certain day. The weekly Sunday observance had been so established in Christian practice that this superseded any other calendrical considerations.

4. The transfer of leadership from Ephesus to Rome was symbolized by the outcome of the controversy.

B. Patripassianism

The Logos Christology advanced by the second-century Apologists (chapter 4) was not the only interpretation of Jesus Christ put forward in the early centuries. The Gnostics presented Christ as an emanation from the spiritual realm (variously described). Traces of an angel Christology (Christ as "the angel of the Lord") also find expression (e.g., Hermas). According to Tertullian, however, the most threatening idea was Modalism, also known as "Patripassianism."

The old catholic fathers, countering Gnostic speculation, stressed that the Supreme Father is the same as the Creator. Irenaeus used the terminology of the Logos, but differed from the Apologists in allowing only one stage (the generated Word existed from eternity) instead of two stages in the pre-existent Logos. Moreover, instead of using Word and Wisdom as two terms for the pre-existent Christ, he distinguished them, applying Wisdom to the Holy Spirit and speaking of them as "the two hands of God." Thus, in countering the Gnostics, the old catholic fathers refined further the Logos Christology of the apologists.

Other approaches to the relation of Jesus Christ to God placed more emphasis on the oneness of God than on the threeness. Indeed, the problem for the early church was not (as it seems for many contemporary believers) how three can be one, but rather how one can be three. Early Christianity came out of a strong affirmation of the oneness of God in Judaism—although Judaism included speculations about other divine entities.

Also to be found in this Jewish heritage was the Old Testament picture of God suffering with and for his people. This was impossible in Greek speculation, where deity by definition is impassible (incapable of suffering). All the old catholic fathers accepted the idea that God is impassible, hence they rejected "Patripassianism" (that God the Father suffered) and found in a distinction between the Father and his Word (the Son) a solution to the problem of salvation by redemptive suffering without God himself directly suffering.

A number of other theories, however, were advanced to defend monotheism while worshiping the Redeemer Christ alongside the Creator God.

Monarchianism ("one rule") was a common word for monotheism, and two principal forms of a strict and literal monotheism were put forward in the second century. Modern scholars have distinguished these by the terms Dynamic Monarchianism and Modalist Monarchianism (to this latter alone the term Patripassianism applies).

Dynamic Monarchianism was a development of early Adoptionism, wherein Jesus was so worthy that God adopted him as a son, either at the resurrection, at his baptism, or in foreknowledge of his virtues at his birth. Some early expressions could be found in the Gnostic orbit with Cerinthus and apparently were combined with Docetism in the *Gospel of Peter*. "Dynamic" in the name comes from the view that the power (*dynamis*) of God rested upon Jesus.

In the later second century, exponents (the two men named Theodotus and their circle) combined the view with a rationalist concern for the moral, human development of Jesus and an effort to give the precision of mathematics to Christian theology. This intellectual approach, opposed to the philosophical formulation of the Logos, communicated a different motivation from that of the earlier expressions of Adoptionism.

Paul of Samosata (third quarter of the third century) gave the most sophisticated and most plausible presentation in this line of development. He was willing to use the term Logos, but in an impersonal sense as equivalent to God's Wisdom in the Old Testament. Jesus was born of the virgin Mary by the Holy Spirit; the Wisdom that had dwelt in others resided supremely in Jesus.

Since this impersonal Logos was united with Jesus, Paul of Samosata was not strictly speaking as an "Adoptionist." Paul employed Trinitarian formulas, for in the Father there was always his Logos and his Spirit. The term "Son" applied to the person of the human Jesus.

Paul was an important Roman official in Antioch and became bishop of the city. Some of his practices that aroused criticism from his opponents—maintaining a bodyguard, use in the church building of a high throne and small chamber for private meetings, replacing the psalms addressed to Jesus Christ with hymns to himself sung by a chorus of women—may have come from his civil position or from his transferring those practices to his role as bishop.

Synods in Antioch, climaxing in 268, secured his condemnation. Paul of Samosata was able to maintain control of the church building, however, until an appeal by his opponents to the emperor Aurelian secured a judgment. The judgment stated that the property should belong to those in communion with the bishops in Italy and Rome. This was the first occasion on record of an appeal to civil authorities to decide a dispute among Christian factions over ownership of church property.

MONARCHIAN TEACHERS		
Name	**Date**	**Place**
Dynamic Monarchians		
Theodotus the Leatherworker	c. 185	Byzantium/Rome
Theodotus the Banker	c. 199	Rome
Artemon	c. 210	Rome
Paul of Samosata	c. 260–68	Antioch
Modalist Monarchians		
Noetus	c. 200	Smyrna
Praxeas	c. 200	Asia/Rome
Epigonus	c. 200	Rome
Sabellius	c. 215	Rome

According to Tertullian, Modalism offered a greater religious threat than Dynamic Monarchianism, because large numbers of ordinary believers were naïve Modalists. Modalism is the name for the view that Father, Son, and Holy Spirit were successive modes of activity and revelation of the one God. This teaching was what ancient authors referred to as Monarchianism, or in a derogatory sense, "Patripassianism" ("Father suffering").

The term "Patripassianism" was used because one implication of the Modalistic identification of the Father and the Son was that the Father suffered on the cross. This idea is perhaps possible (if not so starkly stated) in biblical thought, but it was clearly unattractive in the prevailing philosophical sentiment of the day. (One can always depend on one's opponents to bring out the implications of one's teachings in the most uncomplimentary way possible.)

Tertullian turned his sarcastic wit on one of the early representatives of Modalism, Praxeas, who also opposed Montanism, with the comment, "Praxeas did a twofold service for the devil at Rome: ... he put to flight the Paraclete, and he crucified the Father" (*Against Praxeas* 1).

The most important representative of Modalism was Sabellius, who became so influential that he gave his name (Sabellianism) to the doctrine in the East. The crucial difference between Sabellius and the Logos Christology was that for Sabellius the one God revealed himself successively as Father, Son, and Holy Spirit, whereas for the Logos theologians these distinctions in the Godhead were simultaneous distinctions.

Philosophically minded Christians in the tradition of the Logos Christology developed an internal Trinity to combat Gnosticism, pagan philosophy, and the various forms of Monarchianism. This development revolved around the Logos and Hellenistic thought.

Tertullian represented the Western emphasis on the unity of God by identifying "God" with the Father and by identifying the Son and Holy Spirit with the same substance as God, but like the Greek fathers he found the source of deity in the Father. His differentiations between the persons in the one divine substance were associated with God's saving plan (hence, the designation "economic Trinity" is sometimes employed).

Origen represented the Eastern tendency to emphasize the distinctions between the three by emphasizing their functional differences. That is, from the one Father were derived the Son and Spirit, who had a relative subordination to the Father but were one in nature with him.

All the possible alternatives in explaining the relationship of Jesus Christ to God were present by the end of the second century. Little was expressly said about the Holy Spirit, for the doctrine of Christ bore the brunt of controversy. Early thinkers may have been "Trinitarian" in thought, but they were "binitarian" in passion.

C. Persecution

Relations of Christians with the government and pagan society continued to provide the setting for the work of the old catholic fathers. The problem was how to be law-abiding in the face of a deified empire requiring worship of the state.

The church did not turn revolutionary in spite of provocation. Instead, one old catholic father died as a martyr (Cyprian), one died in exile (Hippolytus), and another suffered such tortures in persecution as to die shortly thereafter (Origen).

In addition, three wrote exhortations to martyrdom (Tertullian, Origen, and Cyprian). Two wrote treatises on the evil aspects of pagan society, especially the public games (Tertullian and Novatian). Three wrote apologies (Tertullian, Clement of Alexandria, and Origen) that in literary style, comprehensiveness, and cogency of argument constituted the greatest apologies for Christianity to come out of the pre-Nicene period. Furthermore, internal tensions produced by persecution brought Hippolytus and Novatian into schism and provoked the major ecclesiastical problems confronting Cyprian.

Although sometimes taking the stance that Christians were really the best citizens and would provide the basis for the best society, the general attitude in this period was one of sharp separation from the state, represented in the view that Christians could not fill magistracies or serve in the military (Tertullian, Hippolytus, Origen).

Nevertheless, the early third century brought a period of peace that began to weaken these sectarian sentiments, as the church grew in numbers and began to attract favorable attention in the highest government circles (see chapter 9).

D. Penance and Polity

Persecution brought into tension two conflicting ideals of the church. "Rigorists" saw the church as the saved people separated from sin; "laxists" saw the church as the instrument of salvation (a hospital for sick souls). The former position is represented by Tertullian, Hippolytus, and Novatian; the latter by Callistus, with Cyprian attempting a mediating position but rejecting the consistent "rigorist" view.

These competing interpretations of the nature of the church were reflected in the dispute over the discipline that should be meted out to the *lapsi*, those who had "fallen" away from the church in times of persecution. The rigorists wanted to keep them in a state of discipline for the rest of their lives, saying that God could in the end save them if they were truly penitent but the church could not presume to offer its forgiveness by restoring them to full communion. Laxists wanted immediate forgiveness in order to strengthen the faith of weak members by restoring them to the life of the church.

A related question that emerged was the authority of the confessors and martyrs. On the basis of Jesus' promise that those who confessed faith in him in times of persecution would possess the Holy Spirit, confessors claimed authority to forgive the lapsed. This further expression of the tension between the authority of the individual and the authority of the institution (also to be seen in the conflicts of teachers, of prophets, and—in the fourth century—of monks with the organized church) ended with the bishops gaining sole authority to represent the church in granting forgiveness (Cyprian).

By the end of the second century the procedure for public confession and repentance was generally established. When a person who had fallen away returned to the church, a public confession of sin was made; repentance was expressed by wearing mourning clothes, weeping, and fasting; request for the prayers of the church was made while kneeling or prostrating oneself before the church; prayer was offered; and restoration to fellowship was shown by the laying on of the hands of the clergy and admission to communion. It was often stated that only one such formal "second repentance" was available.

Four stages of development in thinking about the nature of the church may be discerned:

1. All members are saints—reflected in the New Testament. Montanism involved an effort to reclaim this view.

2. The clergy must be saints. The Novatianists and then more explicitly the Donatists represented this position.

3. The church embraced "saints" (martyrs and confessors) and "sinners." This view was taking shape in the mainstream of the third-century church, and in the fourth century found expression in the distinction of monks from ordinary church members.

4. The sanctity of the church belongs not to individuals, but to the sacraments of the church. Augustine articulated this later stage in the development.

In the second century the bishop had presided at worship and the presbyters had largely been responsible for church discipline. By the mid-third century (Cyprian), however, the bishops secured control of discipline and with the growth of city churches presbyters were delegated liturgical functions in the separate assemblies.

Sacerdotal language became increasingly common during the third century for the bishop and his functions. With the transfer of the bishop's role in worship to presbyters in "parish" churches, the priestly interpretation began to be extended to them as well.

FOR FURTHER STUDY

Crouzel, H. *Origen*. San Francisco: Harper & Row, 1989.

Osborn, Eric F. *The Beginning of Christian Philosophy*. Cambridge: Cambridge University Press, 1981.

Idem. *Irenaeus of Lyons*. Cambridge: Cambridge University Press, 2001.

Idem. *The Philosophy of Clement of Alexandria*. Cambridge: Cambridge University Press, 1957.

Idem. *Tertullian: First Theologian of the West*. Cambridge: Cambridge University Press, 1997.

Trigg, J. W. *Origen*. London: Routledge, 1998.

Church Life in the Second and Third Centuries

I. CHRISTIAN INITIATION

Tertullian's treatise *On Baptism* and the *Apostolic Tradition* attributed to Hippolytus provide sufficiently similar accounts of Christian initiation to show the general pattern of how one became a part of the Christian community in the early third century. By that time the simple procedures recorded in the New Testament and early second-century sources had been elaborated considerably, but the basic pattern remained the same. Much of the elaboration represented the addition of actions designed to embody the doctrinal ideas associated with conversion.

A lengthy period of instruction and a rigorous moral examination preceded admission to the final stage of preparation for baptism. The *Apostolic Tradition* required that candidates receive instruction for three years, but conceded that conduct—not length of time—was the decisive factor. The following description resembles the *Apostolic Tradition*, but parts may represent fourth-century additions.

Regarding conduct, slaves were taught to please their master, married persons to be content with their spouse, and unmarried persons to avoid fornication. Prostitutes, sodomites, and magicians were not even considered for membership. Brothel keepers, actors in the pagan theater, charioteers, gladiators, officials who put on the public games, pagan priests, military officers, and magistrates had to cease from these professions or were rejected for baptism.

Sculptors and painters must not make idols or else they too were rejected.

Educators, who had to teach the pagan literature of the time, would do better to cease but if they had no other craft were permitted to continue. Soldiers should not kill or swear the military oath, and a catechumen or believer who wanted to join the army was rejected. A man who had a concubine must marry her legally or was rejected, and a concubine must be faithful to the man with whom she had relations.

The intensive preparation for baptism began on the Thursday before Easter Sunday (the preferred time for baptism). The time was spent in fasting, prayer, confession of sin, attendance at Scripture reading and instruction, and receiving exorcism of demons. Early on Sunday morning the administrator prayed to God to bring the sanctifying power of the Holy Spirit on the water. The candidates removed their clothing—the children, then men, and finally women were baptized separately. The candidates made a verbal renunciation of "the Devil, his pomp, and his angels"—a declaration of repentance—and were anointed with the oil of exorcism.

While the one being baptized stood in the water, the bishop or presbyter conducting the baptism laid a hand on the head of the person and asked in turn, "Do you believe in God the Father almighty?" "Do you believe in Christ Jesus the Son of God ...?" and "Do you believe in the Holy Spirit, the holy church, and the resurrection of the flesh?" To each question the one being baptized responded, "I believe," and after each confession the administrator guided his head under the water (or, alternatively, if the hand on the head was not functional, the water may have been scooped over the head, as often is the practice in later Orthodox baptisms). Quite notable in the sources is the association of a confession of faith with baptism. The triple immersion is first attested by Tertullian, but appears to have been the general custom and remains the practice in the Eastern Orthodox churches.

After the third immersion, the administrator anointed each person with the oil of thanksgiving. The newly baptized persons dried off, put on clothes, and entered the assembly. The bishop laid his hand on the head of each and prayed (Tertullian associated the coming of the Holy Spirit with this post-baptismal imposition of hands) and then (according to the *Apostolic Tradition*) gave another anointing. The persons then joined the congregation in prayer and the kiss of peace.

There followed the baptismal eucharist, which according to the *Apostolic Tradition* included also a cup of water, symbolizing the washing that had occurred, and a cup of milk and honey, symbolizing the food of infants and entrance into the Promised Land.

Exceptions to the practice of immersion were made in two circumstances. The *Didache* 7 prefers baptism in running ("living") water; in its absence, cold water is preferred to warm. If there is neither, the *Didache* approves pouring water three times on the head "in the name of the Father, and of the Son, and of the Holy Spirit."

Other than in cases of the lack of sufficient water for immersion, an alternative action was allowed for persons on their sickbed and facing death. Cyprian defended "the divine abridgements" of pouring or sprinkling in place of washing. When "necessity compels and God bestows his grace," he claimed the divine benefits were not weakened, as long as the modified baptism was done in church and the faith of the giver and receiver was sound.

Not all agreed, however, that sickbed baptism made one a legitimate Christian. When Novatian recovered and his bishop appointed him a presbyter, the other clergy and many laymen objected that someone who had received pouring while in bed due to sickness could not become a member of the clergy.

The *Apostolic Tradition* is one of the early references to the baptism of little children. Tertullian is the earliest certain reference to the practice, and he advised against it, but a half century later in his church in Carthage, Cyprian gave strong advocacy to infant baptism, even of the newborn.

The *Apostolic Tradition*'s description of the ceremony of baptism shows that it was designed for those who had attained sufficient years to take an active part. The confession of faith was so integral to baptism that provision was made for the parents and or someone else in the family to speak for those unable to do so for themselves. Even the later liturgies show their origin in a time when baptism presupposed believers. The whole catechetical practice of the fourth and fifth centuries likewise presupposed persons of responsible age.

Christ emerging from the baptismal waters as a dove flies toward him (painting in the cubiculum [bedroom] of Lucina in the Catacomb of San Callisto, Rome).

Justin Martyr reflected the normal situation in early times when he said, "As many as are persuaded and believe that the things taught and said by us are true and promise to be able to live accordingly ... are led by us to where there is water" (*1 Apology* 61). Still, infant baptism became routine in the fifth and sixth centuries.

Tertullian alluded to cases of "necessity" as the occasion for bringing small children for baptism. It seems that the threat of imminent death was the probable situation in which infant and child baptism arose. Influential was John 3:5, the most cited baptismal text in the early church, understood as requiring baptism in order to enter heaven.

Burial inscriptions that give information on the time of baptism, and on the age at death of the deceased, show a close correlation in time between the baptism and the death, whatever the age of the person. These inscriptions would argue that infant baptism was not routine, but whenever death threatened (and the infant mortality rate was high in the ancient world, as it still is in some parts of the world today), the family wanted their child to depart this life having received the grace of baptism.

Christian art early developed a standard iconography for baptism, depicting the hand of the administrator on the head of the one being baptized. Literary sources such as the *Apostolic Tradition* show that this was the moment of the confession of faith. The posture could also have been functional in an immersion and contrasts with later medieval

The standard iconography of baptism, with the hand of the administrator on the head of the candidate while the dove of the Holy Spirit approaches, and two other scenes elaborating the meaning of baptism as conversion (fisherman) and forgiveness or deliverance (healing of the paralytic) (from the Catacomb of San Callisto).

paintings, after another method of baptism had become normal in the West, which show John the Baptist pouring water on the head of Jesus.

That in many of the early scenes the candidate stands in a small amount of water has been thought to argue against immersion as the usual practice, but the hand of the administrator on the head of the candidate as well as the latter's nudity weaken this interpretation. It may be for artistic reasons that the presence of water is merely alluded to.

In the early representations Jesus (or the candidate) is often shown smaller than the administrator. This may be an allusion to the idea of new birth, but the recipient was not shown as an infant and the relative sizes may again have resulted from artistic considerations.

II. CHRISTIAN ASSEMBLIES

From the earliest days, the church had established the custom of meeting for communion and worship on the first day of the week, Sunday, to which Christians gave the name "Lord's day," in honor of Jesus' resurrection. This name was consistently distinguished from the Sabbath day. Many Jewish Christians continued to observe the Sabbath (the seventh day) as a day of rest, in addition to meeting for the Lord's supper on the first day of the week.

The Roman governor Pliny noted the custom of Christians meeting to worship Jesus Christ on a fixed day before sunrise, a practice necessary because Sunday was not a holiday before the time of Constantine. They met again in the evening for a meal, perhaps the agape (love feast) described by Tertullian as consisting of prayer, holy conversation, and chanting praise, along with the common meal of fellowship at which the needy were also fed. Christian meetings primarily took place in the homes of more well-to-do members. By the third century Christians had begun to rent or purchase property for their own use, remodeling houses and by the end of the century constructing their own meeting halls.

Justin Martyr provides our earliest explicit account of activities in the Sunday assembly: readings from the memoirs of the apostles or writings of the prophets, a sermon based on the readings, prayer, the eucharist of bread and wine mixed with water, and a voluntary contribution for those in need. These items are attested in other sources, as is also the singing of psalms and hymns. Perhaps by the end of the third century there was a separation of two parts of the service. The first part centered on instruction in the Word, to which all were welcome. The second part centered on the Lord's supper, to which only baptized believers not under discipline were admitted.

The common name in the early church for the Lord's supper or communion was "eucharist" ("thanksgiving"), calling attention to its principal aspect. It held a central place in each Sunday assembly. Other aspects associated with the eucharist were fellowship, remembrance, eschatological hope, and offering.

Both the recitation of Jesus' words at the Last Supper and the invocation of the Holy Spirit might be included in the prayer that effected the consecration of the elements to a new meaning. Realist language about the presence of Jesus Christ was common, often with an anti-heretical thrust, emphasizing that the material elements were the means of spiritual blessings.

Ignatius complained of Docetists who abstained from the eucharist because they did not confess it to be the flesh of Jesus, "who suffered for our sins." Irenaeus insisted that the eucharist supported the orthodox against the Gnostics, because the invocation of God added a heavenly to the earthly reality and so brought the hope of the resurrection to participants.

The most popular text concerning the eucharist was Malachi 1:11, indicating that Christians offered the pure sacrifice desired by God. In contrast to the bloody sacrifices of paganism and the Jewish temple, sacrificial

The blessing of bread on a table (painting in the Catacomb of SS. Pietro e Marcellino, Rome).

language moved from the prayers of thanksgiving as a spiritual service (Justin Martyr), to the elements as first fruits of the earth (Irenaeus), and then to the sacrifice of Jesus Christ on the cross that was commemorated by the bread and wine (Cyprian).

In the first two centuries Christian apologists like Justin Martyr noted the difference from pagan religions in the absence of temples, altars, images, and material sacrifices. In the third century, as part of an increasing distinction between the clergy and the laity, the language of priesthood began to be more regularly applied to Christian ministers (perhaps more comparatively by Origen but in a straightforward way by Cyprian).

The Christian assimilation to the environment in cultic terminology increased throughout the third century and became standard in the fourth century. By then, ministers were priests, church buildings were temples, communion tables were altars, and sacred art was common.

III. CHRISTIAN LIFE

In addition to the meeting on the Lord's day, the *Didache* provided for Christians to fast on Wednesday and Friday in contrast to the fasts by

Jews (Pharisees) on Monday and Thursday. It further enjoined praying the Lord's Prayer three times a day. Different sources reflect other practices for daily private prayer: at meals, three times a day, and at night (Clement of Alexandria) or five times a day and at night (Tertullian).

The *Apostolic Tradition* instructed believers to begin the day by meeting together where teachers gave instruction in the Word and prayer was offered, or if there was no instruction on that day, to read the holy book and pray at home. One version of the document specifies six other hours of the day and night for prayer.

"The Two Ways" in the *Didache* and *Barnabas* reflect the Jewish moral teaching adopted by early Christianity. The Ten Commandments were elaborated so that the prohibition of killing included abortion and abandoning young children, and the prohibition of adultery included fornication and homosexual practices. There is an emphasis on the attitudes of the heart as well as the outward actions.

Accordingly, the *Didache* expanded its version of the "Way of Life" by adding the teachings of Jesus on non-retaliation and love of others (including enemies) found in the "Sermon on the Mount." Jesus' interpretation of the law continued to provide the summary of Christian moral teaching in the Apologists, and seems to have been basic to the earliest instruction of new converts about the manner of life expected of Christians.

Christian Apologists made the Christian moral life central to their argument for the truth of Christianity. The *Epistle to Diognetus* and the *Apology* of Aristides give beautiful pictures of Christians living "in the world, but not of the world." The practices mentioned include honesty in business, sexual purity, family solidarity, doing good to enemies, caring for the poor, obedience to the laws, and daily prayer.

Even allowing for a certain idealizing, there must have been some basis in reality for the appealing descriptions. The Christians' manner of life and even more the Christians' manner of dying (willing to accept martyrdom) proved a powerful factor in converting pagans to the faith.

Where Christian moral teaching coincided with the moral philosophy of the times, Christians claimed that their religion gave the spiritual power for even ordinary, uneducated people to live the life that philosophers felt only the few could attain. Failure by Christians to live according to the standards of the gospel could result in church discipline (see chapter 7 on "Penance").

Indeed, the Christian manner of life attracted the favorable attention of some pagans. Galen, physician and philosopher, observed that Christians by following their beliefs in "rewards and punishments in a future life" attained a manner of life "not inferior to that of genuine philosophers." He noted especially their "contempt of death" (martyrdom), "restraint in cohabitation," "self-control in matters of food and drink," and "keen pursuit of justice."

Sexual practices came under careful scrutiny by Christian moralists. Moderate moralists like Clement of Alexandria not only opposed fornication, adultery, and homosexuality, but also defended the goodness of marriage against the ascetic tendencies of the time. Like many other Christian writers, he limited the purpose of intercourse in marriage to the producing of children, a view also shared by Stoic moralists of the early empire.

Tertullian, in his Montanist period, regarded celibacy as better than marriage and advised against a second marriage, even in the case of the death of a spouse. In his treatise *On Monogamy* he connected marriage (only once) and monotheism (only one God). Despite his sometimes negative characterizations of women, he nonetheless gave a very positive picture of Christian marriage: the two becoming one in flesh and spirit, sharing one hope, one desire, a common discipline of life and service—together praying, singing, fasting, going to church, and doing good works.

Clement of Alexandria produced a manual on manners for Christians called the *Paedagogus*, or *Instructor* (chapter 7). He went through the course of a day's activities, giving instruction on how Christians should behave in different circumstances. As far apart as he and Tertullian were in temperament and approach, there is remarkable agreement on the details of conduct.

Charity for the poor and the underprivileged was a characteristic of early Christianity. The strong sense of brotherhood brought a cor-

Meal scene in the Catacomb of San Callisto.

responding sense of obligation to alleviate the physical needs of other believers. Benevolence toward others was seen as an imitation of God's philanthropy for human beings. Already in the early second century Ignatius had to caution against excesses in the use of church funds to purchase the freedom of slaves.

Justin and Tertullian report that the contributions collected in the assemblies were used to provide for the sick, elderly, widows, orphans, prisoners, travelers, and burial of the poor. Clement of Alexandria counseled that it was better to do good to the unworthy than, by guarding against the unworthy, to fail to do good to the worthy.

Christians were serving in the military by the end of the second century, at the latest, but many leaders in Christian thought—such as Tertullian, Hippolytus, Clement of Alexandria, Origen, and Lactantius—viewed Christian involvement in war negatively and either denied that Christians should be in the army or advised those who were soldiers not to participate in the religious observances of the Roman army and not to kill (much of the army's time was spent in keeping order and building roads).

IV. CHRISTIAN WOMEN

The lives of women may not be covered extensively in the surviving literature of the early church, but women certainly were prominent in its story. The names of only a few are known, but the numbers of women believers were greater than those of male believers.

Women are mentioned principally in their traditional roles of wives and mothers, where they were expected to be loving and faithful to their husbands, to manage their households in an orderly manner, and to educate their children in the fear of God.

On the other hand, a celibate lifestyle was adopted by many— both virgins who never married and widows who did not remarry. The ascetic life was initially lived individually and privately in one's own household, but by the third century there were small communities of virgins living together.

Some of the most heroic martyrs of the early church were women, such as Blandina at Lyons and Perpetua at Carthage. Women were also involved in the missionary outreach of the gospel, accompanying apostles and evangelists on their travels and working in the women's quarters of households to which men did not have access. The apocryphal *Acts of Paul* gave prominent notice to Thecla, who became an object of cult as a saint in Asia Minor. Despite the feeling of some that women were untrustworthy teachers, they were often engaged in private teaching.

Veiled woman in a posture of prayer (orant) between a teacher and Mother with Child (Catacomb of Priscilla).

Widows and virgins were recognized as having special serving roles in congregations from early times. Certainly by the third century, if not earlier, there were women appointed with the title deaconesses. Only in Montanism and some Gnostic sects did women engage in public preaching and presiding at liturgical functions. Tertullian, for one, objected to women performing baptism, but other sources indicate their assisting at the baptism of women.

New Testament strictures against women doing public teaching in church, and against women filling the position of elders, seem to have been uniformly observed in the mainstream of the church.

V. CHRISTIAN HOPE

Two patterns of eschatological hope emerged early in Christianity. From a certain strand of apocalyptic Judaism there developed a chiliastic eschatology. According to this view, all the deceased wait in the Hadean world for the coming of the earthly, temporary messianic kingdom, with the righteous and the unrighteous separated in different compartments.

Christian chiliasm placed the resurrection of the righteous (the first resurrection) at the time of Jesus Christ's return and the inauguration of his earthly rule from Jerusalem. Based on Revelation 20:3, this view fixed the length of this rule as 1,000 years, hence the designation millennium (Latin) or chiliasm (Greek). At the end of this period the remainder of human beings will be raised for judgment with the subsequent eternal separation in either heaven or hell.

Chiliasm was an integral part of the polemic against Marcion and the Gnostics in Justin Martyr, Irenaeus, and Tertullian. Irenaeus integrated the millennial kingdom into his whole theology by interpreting the millennium as a time in which resurrected bodies are accustomed to spiritual existence and prepared for the heavenly vision of God. Tertullian posited that the martyrs were an exception and did not have to wait in Hades for the resurrection as others did, but went directly to the presence of Jesus Christ. Other champions of chiliasm in early Christianity were Papias, Victorinus, and Lactantius.

An alternative, non-chiliastic, pattern of eschatology understood the future kingdom of God and Christ as heavenly, not earthly. According to this view, also derived from Jewish sources, the righteous dead are already in the kingdom of heaven (i.e., paradise) and there is no trace of an interim earthly kingdom.

In place of the ideas of the abode of the dead in Hades and an earthly millennium, this view embraced the belief in an intermediate stay by the righteous in the heavenly realm in the presence of Christ. Often there was expressed the conviction that Christ at his resurrection delivered the righteous dead of the Old Testament from Hades and took them with him to the intermediate heavenly realm.

This non-chiliastic form of the Christian hope interpreted Revelation 20:3–4 as referring (1) to the binding of Satan by the ministry, death, and resurrection of Jesus; (2) the coming to life of those beheaded for the sake of Jesus as the resurrection of their souls at death in order to enter paradise with Christ; and (3) the thousand years as symbolic of this present interim rule of the faithful with Christ in the heavenly Jerusalem. At the second coming there will occur the resurrection of bodies and final judgment.

This non-chiliastic current of eschatological thought was widely pervasive in early Christianity and is represented in such writers as Hermas, Polycarp, the authors of the *Epistle to Diognetus, Ascension of Isaiah, Apocalypse of Peter, Martyrdom of Polycarp,* and *Letter of the Churches of Vienne and Lyons,* Clement of Alexandria, Origen, and Cyprian.

There is no evidence of Christian use of separate burial grounds in the early period. About 200 the church in Rome acquired what became the nucleus of the catacomb of Callistus, but the

Burial niches *(loculi)* in the Catacomb of San Callisto.

shared use of the same tombs by pagans and Christians continued to be common into the fourth century. Christians followed the usual burial practices of society (these will be examined in the next chapter in connection with the development of the cult of the saints). They sometimes gave expression to their faith and hope by inscriptions, symbolic images, and paintings at their burial places.

Present in all forms of the orthodox eschatological hope was belief in the bodily resurrection, in contrast to Gnostic views of the resurrection of the soul only. Both Gnostic and orthodox non-chiliasts believed the righteous go immediately after death into the presence of God in heaven, but the non-orthodox did not link this belief with a further expectation of a resurrection of the body. Origen emphasized the "spiritual body," but most (perhaps in direct opposition to Gnosticism) emphasized a resurrection of the "flesh."

Apart from Origen, who entertained the possibility of universal salvation after a period of purification and education of souls in the afterlife, those who spoke to the subject understood an ultimate division of humanity in heaven or hell. The expectation of eternal reward sustained Christian endurance in the face of persecution and other hardships.

FOR FURTHER STUDY

Bradshaw, Paul F. *Early Christian Worship: A Basic Introduction to Ideas and Practice*. Collegeville, MN: Liturgical Press, 2001.

Ferguson, Everett. *Early Christians Speak*. 2 vols. Abilene, TX: ACU Press, 1999, 2002.

Development of the Church during the Third Century

I. PERSECUTIONS

A. Principal Phases

From the time of the Roman emperors Domitian (d. 96) to Decius (d. 251), Christianity was understood as distinct from Judaism and, since it was not an ethnic religion, it had no right to protection. Christianity was occasionally repressed in sporadic persecutions, but there was no general effort to root it out. Christianity often had its hardest times under the strongest emperors—Marcus Aurelius and Septimius Severus.

The period from Marcus Aurelius (d. 180) to Decius saw a decline in the empire's vitality. Religions from the eastern part of the empire continued to spread into the West. Following an outburst of persecution under Septimius Severus, who in 202 had forbidden conversion to Judaism and Christianity, there followed the first long peace of the church from 211 to 250, interrupted by a brief persecution under Maximinus in 235. Christianity grew tremendously during this period, but the attitudes of the populace were still negative.

Christianity experienced a particularly favorable situation under Alexander Severus (222–35), who was interested in various philosophers and religious teachers (including Jesus), and Philip the Arabian (244–49), under whom the situation was so favorable that Eusebius thought that he was a Christian. There is inscriptional evidence of the penetration of a confident Christianity into Phrygia by the mid-third century. During the third century Christianity grew extensively not only in Asia Minor, but also in Egypt and North Africa.

Under Decius (249–51) and Valerian (253–60), the empire declared war on the church with an effort at systematic oppression. When these persecutions were relaxed, other problems in the empire gave Christianity a second long period of peace, from 260 to 303, when Diocletian once more attempted to suppress the church.

B. The Decian and Valerian Persecutions

The reign of Decius marked the turning point from local, sporadic persecution to an empire-wide assault on Christianity.

The situation in the empire provides the setting for Decius's policies. There was a continuing barbarian threat on the frontiers, made more perilous by economic difficulties within the empire. Revival of Roman fortunes occurred in the Roman army of Illyricum, perhaps the least Christianized part of the empire. The celebration of the one-thousandth anniversary of the traditional founding of Rome (753 BC) sparked a revival of ancient customs.

The first action of Decius was the arrest of the higher clergy. The second was a universal order to sacrifice to the gods of the empire (burn incense, pour a libation, and taste sacrificial meat). Those who sacrificed received a certificate testifying that they had complied.

After a generation of peace, the church as a whole was unprepared for the challenge. Many had grown comfortable in the acceptance of Christianity, and vast numbers lapsed from the faith by obeying the command to sacrifice. The effects on the church might have been even greater if the persecution had lasted longer. Decius was killed in 251, and the outbreak of an epidemic in 251/2 turned people's attention to other concerns.

Emperor Decius, who began the first empire-wide persecution of Christians (Uffizi, Florence).

Valerian resumed the persecution in 257 by sending bishops into exile and forbidding Christian assemblies. In 258 the clergy were recalled and many were executed. Christians of high rank were degraded and their property seized, and Christians in the imperial service were sent in chains to work the imperial estates. The church's corporate property and funds were also seized.

Scholars have suggested various motives for the intense attack on the church: avarice by the rulers, the economic collapse blamed on the disfavor of the gods, popular hostility leading to an effort to suppress a foreign body in the state and require loyalty to the emperor, and the psychological desire to rally the subjects behind the emperor. Probably more significant was a conservative religious policy aimed at strengthening traditional Roman paganism.

Valerian's son, Gallienus (253–68), reversed the policy of persecution and returned property to the churches.

C. The Cult of the Martyrs

More church members compromised their faith than became martyrs. Nonetheless, the number of martyrs was considerable and gave impetus to the martyr cult (activities associated with worship).

The extravagant regard for the martyrs and the special privileges assigned to them were the basis for their cultic veneration. The high honor for martyrs is already evident in the *Martyrdom of Polycarp*, but the care for Polycarp's remains need not be read as going beyond normal human regard for a loved one. Marks of respect and veneration were not in themselves cultic manifestations.

In the background of the development of the Christian cult of martyrs are ideas associated with the cult of heroes in Greek religion and with funerary practices of the Greco-Roman world. The heroes were those who were strong in this life and who remained strong to help after death. Their influence was confined to their relics and where they were buried. Respect for the dead included meals taken in memory of the deceased at the tomb by the family periodically after a person's death, and then annually on that person's birthday.

Christian practice made some changes in these customs. The funerary meals were eucharistic in the church (*Acts of John* and Tertullian). Cyprian is the first to call the eucharist a sacrifice offered in memory of the martyrs, commemorating their victory as well as praying for their repose. The day of the death was treated by Christians as the "birthday" (the birthday to immortality), and so the anniversary of the death—instead of the birth—was commemorated. Ordinarily burial (the *depositio*) was on the same day as the death.

The list of the anniversaries to celebrate in each church became the basis of the first martyrologies. The family of the deceased was the Christian community, and this assured the perpetuity of the anniversaries, but the commemorations were strictly local at first.

The latter half of the third century shows the cultic veneration of martyrs had penetrated everywhere. Inscriptions began to appear in Rome, "Peter and Paul, pray for us all." Terminology, however, lagged behind practice, for the word *sancti* in Christian Latin in the fourth century still designated all the faithful dead, not just "saints."

"Paul and Peter pray for Victor" — inscription at the Catacomb of San Sebastiano (c. AD 260).

The principal expression of cult, or worship, was prayer addressed to the martyr, so that prayer to the deceased became more prominent than prayer for the repose of souls. The martyr was already in the presence of God and had won "freedom of speech" (*parrhesia*) so as to be able to serve as an intercessor. The invocation of the saints was based on this idea of intercession.

Given the exceptional place of martyrs in the church, and ideas current about the rapport of the dead with the living, the practice of invocation to the dead would not have been strange to the people of Greco-Roman culture.

The practice of prayer to the martyr was preferably in the presence of the tomb, for there the power was most evident. In Origen explicitly, but also in the fourth-century theologians, the veneration of martyrs stood in relation to Jesus Christ and not in competition with him, for the martyrs were his servants.

II. CYPRIAN AND SCHISM

At the crisis occasioned by the Decian and Valerian persecutions, the North African church received capable leadership from Cyprian as bishop of Carthage.

Sources for the study of Cyprian's life include the following: (1) his *Life* written by his deacon Pontius, the first Christian biography; (2) the *Acts of Cyprian*, one of the authentic accounts of martyrdom from the early centuries; (3) Cyprian's own treatises and a considerable body of his correspondence, a major source of information about the times as well as of the internal working of the church; and (4) secondary notices by Jerome and others.

Caecilius Cyprianus Thascius was born in the first decade of the third century, probably in Carthage, to a rich and cultured pagan family. He received a good education, but his disgust at the corruption of public life led him to seek something higher. A presbyter in Carthage, Caecilius, converted him about 246. His education, position, and abilities led him almost immediately to be made a presbyter. He was elected bishop in 248 "by the voice of the people" against the opposition of some of the elderly presbyters who remembered Paul saying something about a bishop not being a new convert (1 Timothy 3:6).

The Decian persecution of 250 caused his flight from the city. The persecution took the life of Fabian, bishop of Rome, and Cyprian had to defend his flight. He kept in touch with the church by letters.

During Cyprian's absence, some confessors gave letters of pardon to the *lapsi*, those who had fallen away during the persecution, and demanded their immediate reconciliation to the church. They relied on the church's view that those who confessed their faith under persecution received a special measure of the Holy Spirit and so were entitled to forgive and to exercise the privilege of presbyters (who had charge of the discipline of the church).

Cyprian objected, saying that such action should await a return of peace when the bishops could meet and the whole church could agree on a unified policy toward the apostates who wanted forgiveness and a return to the church.

A deacon, Felicissimus, led a schism, joined by five presbyters who had opposed Cyprian's election, in support of the actions of the confessors.

Cyprian returned to Carthage in 251 on the death of Decius, and a synod of bishops confirmed his position and ex-communicated his antagonists. At this same time there occurred a schism in Rome, this time by the rigorists, led by Novatian, who opposed any reconciliation of apostates to full communion in the church.

The remaining years of Cyprian's life were filled with activity during a stormy time for the church. He continued to work for unity in the church at Carthage and elsewhere and to restore order and stability to a threatened and discouraged church. A devastating plague, during which Christians were active in care for the sick, did much to mitigate the opposition of pagans.

Cyprian also became involved in a controversy over rebaptism with Stephen, bishop of Rome, which was not immediately resolved because of Stephen's death in 256 and Cyprian's banishment in 257. Cyprian was brought back to Carthage and beheaded in 258.

Cyprian was a man of action, interested in administration and the direction of souls rather than in theological speculation. He was thoroughly converted, but he naturally brought concepts from his pagan past to his interpretation of Christianity. For instance, he freely used the language of pagan religion to describe Christianity. Although he did not create the terminology, he was among the first extensively to speak of the bishop as a priest, the eucharist as a sacrifice, and the Lord's table as an altar.

Cyprian was thrust into a position of leadership at a time filled with immediate practical problems before he could assimilate fully some aspects of Christianity. His principal asset was his practical wisdom, which he brought to bear in the interests of preserving the church as a unified community with the clergy and laity acting in concert. The strength of the church in North Africa and elsewhere that emerged from the ordeal of the Decian persecution is a tribute to his moderation and statesmanship.

The treatises of Cyprian dealt mostly with practical matters. Of greatest theological interest is *On the Unity of the Church*, an important contribution to the doctrine of the church. Of greatest historical interest is *On the Lapsed*, which reveals much about the persecution and church life. His *Letters* constitute the largest body of correspondence from the ante-Nicene church, sixty-five letters by Cyprian and sixteen addressed to him or to the clergy of Carthage.

Cyprian was involved in three controversies. The major one, around which the others revolved, concerned the reconciliation of the lapsed.

Cyprian confronted the extremes of both rigorism, which said apostates could not be restored to full fellowship, but must be kept in the condition of penitents for the rest of their lives, and laxism, which said that penitent apostates could be restored to full communion immediately. The former course of action would teach the seriousness of sin and strengthen the faithful to confess during any renewal of persecution. The latter course would restore the numbers of the church and strengthen the fallen in the face of further temptation.

Cyprian advocated a middle course that would make distinctions according to the gravity of the transgression. Those who actually sacrificed were to be placed under discipline and could be reconciled to the church at the moment of death. This would teach the gravity of their sin, but would enable them to die in the peace of the church and thus give their conscience an assurance of salvation.

Those who had obtained certificates of sacrifice without actually sacrificing (something that could be done by bribing an official or by sending a slave or pagan friend to perform the sacrifice) were to be placed under discipline and could be reconciled after an appropriate time.

> "How can they say that they believe in Christ who do not do what Christ commanded them to do?" (Cyprian, *On the Unity of the Church* 2).

Finally, those who had entertained the thought of denial, but had not actually done so, since their sin was private, were to make a private confession to the bishop.

In Cyprian's day, the public penitential discipline included the same elements as fifty years earlier, but was more structured. After a person confessed to the bishop and sought reconciliation to the church, it comprised three stages:

1. The performance of works of penance — praying, fasting, lamenting and weeping, wearing sackcloth, observing vigils, and giving alms — while being excluded from the eucharist.

2. Confession (*exomologesis*), which may not have required a detailed statement of the sin, in the presence of the church, for the people had to agree to the reconciliation.

3. The reconciliation by a laying on of the hands of the bishop and clergy and by prayer.

Cyprian's policy established discipline as a prerogative of the bishop and clergy (acting in concert with the congregation) and brought the martyrs under the authority of the bishops (a step that may have inspired the idea that a true bishop has the worth of a martyr).

The second controversy in which Cyprian participated, this one at second-hand, was the Novatian schism at Rome. Whereas the schism at Carthage was prompted by the "laxists," who wanted immediate reconciliation of the lapsed, the schism at Rome involved the "rigorists" led by Novatian, who viewed the church as the church of the pure and so would not restore to full communion those guilty of apostasy.

Novatian had been a leading presbyter in the church at Rome and authored the first major surviving theological treatise in Latin from the Roman church, *On the Trinity*. He had himself ordained bishop by three neighboring bishops after the Roman church elected Cornelius, a representative of the moderate position favoring restoration of the "fallen" who were penitent. Cyprian supported Cornelius as the rightful bishop of Rome. It may be that his treatise *On the Unity of the Church* was prompted by this schism at Rome, but it may have been intended for the Carthaginian church as a consequence of the schism of Felicissimus.

Cyprian became involved in a third controversy with Stephen, second bishop of Rome after Cornelius, over the validity of baptism administered by those outside the catholic church.

Stephen, relying on the tradition of the Roman church, said that a person in a schismatic or heretical group who had received water baptism in the name of the Father, Son, and Holy Spirit did not have to be baptized again on seeking fellowship with his church. Instead, only the laying on of the hand of the bishop was necessary to receive the person into communion (perhaps a bestowing of the Holy Spirit in fulfillment of the person's baptism, or more likely an act of reconciliation of one regarded as a penitent being restored to the fellowship of the church). Stephen regarded himself as a successor of Peter and so as maintaining an apostolic tradition in taking his position against rebaptism.

In contrast, Cyprian argued in his letters that baptism administered outside the church is invalid, for "a person cannot have God as his Father who does not have the church as his mother" (*Epistle* 74.7). One who "does not possess the Holy Spirit cannot impart the Holy Spirit," that is, one outside the church does not have the Spirit and so in performing baptism cannot give the Spirit (*Epistle* 70.2–3). Against Stephen's argument from tradition, Cyprian replied that because something is old does not make it right: "Custom is the antiquity of error" (*Epistle* 74.9).

An anonymous North African opponent in the treatise *On Rebaptism* turned the flank of Cyprian's position. Granting that heretical baptism of itself did not confer the gift of the Spirit, the author argued that it created the possibility of spiritual receptiveness that made repetition superfluous. The imposition of hands supplied all defects. Thus one might receive baptism in water as a heretic and baptism in the Spirit (which ordinarily ought to be associated with the former) at entrance into the church through the laying on of hands. He added that sound faith or good character was not necessary in the administrator and that the invocation of the name of Jesus possessed peculiar powers.

The subject of heretical and schismatic baptism was discussed by other church leaders. Cyprian's view made the validity of baptism dependent on the administrator of baptism, and that always introduced an element of uncertainty into one's salvation. The affirmation of the objective validity of a baptism properly performed had a greater appeal. The position of Stephen, therefore, came to prevail, although Cyprian's view lived on in North Africa, being powerfully revived by the Donatists in the next century.

These three controversies impinged on Cyprian's attitude toward the church at Rome. In his treatise *On the Unity of the Church*, Cyprian presents the church as originating in unity from the Lord's promise to Peter (Matthew 16:18–19), and he affirms that the episcopate is one and must preserve this unity.

Cyprian saw the bishops as having a parallel position in the church to that of the apostles. As the apostolate was jointly shared by all the apostles, who had their source of unity in Peter, so the episcopate is a universal property, jointly shared by all the bishops.

Some manuscripts of *On the Unity of the Church* carry this idea of Peter as the center and symbol of the unity of the church further. Although Cyprian identified Peter as representing the local bishop, these statements could be read, in view of Rome's claims, as referring to the bishop of Rome as successor to Peter; and there is a short recension of the treatise omitting these statements. It may be that both forms of the text go back to Cyprian himself.

A possible explanation is that Cyprian first wrote the long recension in the context of his stress on unity and the need for a visible symbol of that unity, but that when his controversy with Stephen showed him that the bishop of Rome could be in error and so was not to be agreed with on everything, he issued a revised text leaving out the strong statements that could be an embarrassment to him in that controversy.

Another possibility is that the short recension was addressed to the North African situation and the longer recension was the form sent to Rome in response to the Novatian schism. Even in the long recension Cyprian had in mind primarily the chronological priority of Peter over the other apostles as a symbol of unity, and not a primacy to which others were subject.

III. THE BEGINNINGS OF CHRISTIAN ART AND ARCHITECTURE

Most accounts of Christian history have been based almost exclusively on literary sources, and the study of Christian art has been pursued separately as part of art history, and that minimally as virtually a footnote to late antique art. There is now a growing recognition of the value of treating the literary and artistic sources as complementary, since both emerged from the same community.

The first identifiable Christian art appears about the year 200. Its absence for nearly two centuries after the beginning of the church is usually attributed (1) to a continuation of the Jewish aversion to images based on the Decalogue (Exodus 20:4–5a), (2) to Christianity being a spiritual religion antithetical to material manifestations, or (3) to Christian opposition to a pagan culture closely associated with visual imagery. More recently this absence has been attributed to (4) the economic and social circumstances of most Christians, not to any inherent opposition to pictures or other expressions of art.

One theory of the origins of Christian art is that it began in small objects of everyday use which everyone had to have, such as seal rings and household lamps. Clement of Alexandria spoke of images appropriate for Christians to employ on their seal rings: dove, fish, ship, lyre,

Mosaic (fifth century) of the third-century Roman deacon Lawrence, who was reported to have been roasted on a gridiron, with the copies of the Scriptures for which he was responsible (Galla Placidia, Ravenna).

anchor, fisherman. Not to be used were images of idols, implements of war like sword or bow, and drinking cups (since Christians were temperate).

Another theory derives Christian art from the larger pagan environment. Certainly in style and technique, Christian art borrowed from both classical and non-classical influences on late antique art. As a specific context for the beginnings of Christian art, since pagans decorated their tombs, Christians did too. And, in fact, our earliest identifiable examples of Christian art come from the catacombs, the underground burial chambers, around Rome.

The catacombs were not hiding places in times of persecution (the authorities knew of their existence), nor were they normally places of assembly, although funerary meals in memory of the deceased were held there. The rooms (*cubicula*) and their entrances were sometimes decorated with small paintings, and the stone slabs covering the burial niches (*loculi*) in the galleries were sometimes chiseled with inscriptions or simple pictures.

The paintings were often decorative scenes of plants and birds, but many depicted events from the Old or New Testaments. Most popular from the Old Testament was the story of Jonah; from the New Testament, the raising of Lazarus. Symbolic representations were even more common, and the symbolic nature of early Christian art is often noted.

Particularly frequent in Christian art as a whole, as well as in the catacombs, were the pictures of the Good Shepherd (besides its biblical precedents, it was an image associated with philanthropy) and a figure in the posture of prayer with arms extended and hands uplifted (*orans*—a symbol of piety). Occasionally Christian ceremonies are depicted, such as baptism and meal scenes, of which the feeding miracles of the Gospels, the Last Supper, the eucharist, the agape, and funerary meals are now indistinguishable. Because of the difficulty of working underground with limited light from small lamps or torches, the pictures for the most part employ a limited range of colors and a minimum of detail, more alluding to the scene than describing it.

From the latter half of the third century there began to appear among Christians evidence of a more expensive form of burial, sarcophagi (stone coffins for depositing the bodies of the deceased) with sculptured scenes. The same repertoire of biblical and symbolic subjects continued to be employed, the selection and form of which was often governed by the existence of an image available from Greco-Roman art. Free standing, three-dimensional sculpture is rather rare in Christian art for many centuries, but from the third century there do survive small images of Jesus Christ as the Good Shepherd and as a teacher, as well as images from the Jonah cycle.

The funerary character of so much of the surviving early Christian art may give a one-sided view, because in this setting the main concern is the afterlife, deliverance from death, and Jesus Christ as a powerful savior. On the other hand, these themes may reflect the appeal of Christianity to the people at large. The biblical history of God saving his people, and of Jesus as a teacher and miracle worker more powerful than any human enemies, were at the heart of the Christian faith and its success in spite of persecution in the Greco-Roman world.

Some Christian art derived from internal everyday religious considerations, either as an expression of the doctrinal content of Christianity or as a result of Christian worship and piety. A generation after

The fish—a common early Christian symbol—from a grave slab in the Catacombs (Vatican Museum, Rome).

the earliest catacomb paintings, biblical scenes appeared on the walls of the room used as a baptistery in the house church at Dura Europus in Syria (240s). These included a Good Shepherd and Adam and Eve (added later) immediately behind the font, and on side walls, the woman at the well of Samaria, Jesus healing the paralytic, Jesus and Peter walking on the water, and a procession of women to the tomb of Jesus. Notable is the absence of paintings from the assembly room.

The earliest Christian meeting places were commonly in the houses of more well-to-do members ("house churches"). As numbers grew and resources increased, local congregations purchased houses as church property (*domus ecclesiae*, "house of the church"), often remodeling the interior according to the needs of the community (as at Dura Europus).

Sometimes warehouses or other buildings were acquired by local churches for their meeting places (as in Rome), and by the end of the third and beginning of the fourth century new structures in the shape of halls (Aquileia and Ostia) appeared (*aula ecclesiae*, "hall of the church").

Only under Constantine did the characteristic form of Christian architecture, the basilica, appear, and it developed from earlier secular buildings.

The story of Jonah (three scenes read right to left), the most commonly occurring Old Testament scene in early Christian art (Catacomb of San Callisto, Rome).

Jonah sarcophagus
from the late third
century (Vatican
Museum, Rome).

IV. A NEW CHALLENGE: MANICHAEISM

Receiving a heavenly call in 240 to become the "apostle of light," Mani (216–76) founded a new religious movement in Mesopotamia and Persia along the lines of the Gnostic sects of the preceding century.

Aiming at a universal religion, Mani drew on elements from the Jewish Christian Elkesaites, among whom he had been brought up, from other Christian heretical groups (such as the Marcionites), from Zoroastrianism and Buddhism, and from orthodox Christianity itself.

Mani's teaching is based on an extreme dualism of light and darkness, good and evil, spirit and matter. Particles of light are trapped in the material world, and redemption is the liberation of these particles of light so that they can return to the pure heavenly realm. The "elect" or perfect members of the sect were vegetarians, abstained from sex, and avoided most forms of work. They were supported by the "hearers," who lived in the world until they approached death.

Aggressive evangelism spread Mani's new religion into the Roman Empire in the West (where the pagan emperor Diocletian attempted to proscribe it in 295) and in the East to central Asia and as far as India and China. The Manichees produced beautiful manuscripts containing their teachings and liturgies.

Warnings against Manichaeism from within the church appeared early, but surviving written refutations begin mainly with the fourth century.

V. THE CHURCH IN THE LAST HALF OF THE THIRD CENTURY

The Christians' care for their sick during the epidemic of the 250s, which was mentioned above, gave them a higher survival rate than pagans, who often fled their communities or abandoned the sick for fear of contagion. This survival factor gradually left Christians with a higher percentage of the population even without making converts. More converts soon followed, however, in part because Christians had cared for non-Christians as well as their own.

The church experienced tremendous growth during the third century, a growth that precipitated a climactic conflict with the Roman state. The latter half of the third century was a period of rest, growth, and moral relaxation for the church. The external history was more important than writings and the internal development of the church, so there is relatively little information until the resumption of warfare against the church under Diocletian.

Nevertheless, there are glimpses into the development of the church provided by additional documents and writers that should be noted.

A. Church Order: *Didascalia*

The *Didascalia Apostolorum* ("Teaching of the Apostles") comes from approximately the mid-third century in Syria and, although originally written in Greek, survives complete only in Syriac.

The Christian community reflected in this document was in close contact with its Jewish roots. The author insists that Christians keep only the Ten Commandments of the Old Testament. The other requirements were a "Second Legislation," from which Jesus Christ set his followers free.

The document shows the bishop as the necessary head of the local church—its teacher and preacher, moral watchman, judge in cases of discipline, pastor who seeks the lost sheep, and spiritual physician healing sick souls who repent. The bishop also was steward of the church's possessions from which he, the clergy, and the poor were supported. In addition, he was the administrator of baptism, anointing, and eucharist and the church's priest (offering spiritual sacrifices).

The bishop was assisted by presbyters as counselors, but especially by deacons, about whom more is said than about presbyters. There was also an order of widows, whose responsibility was primarily to pray, but not to teach or baptize, and an order of deaconesses, who ministered in the women's quarters of houses and gave the anointing and teaching to women at their baptism.

In addition to warnings about accepting Jewish customs, being involved with idolatry, and avoiding of heresies and schisms, the *Didascalia apostolorum* also gives instructions about marital fidelity, bringing up children, care for orphans, treatment of those imprisoned for the faith, the resurrection of the dead, and the events of Jesus' passion week.

"O bishops, imitate God, that you may be quiet and meek, and merciful and compassionate, and peacemakers, and without anger, and teachers and correctors and receivers and exhorters; and that you be not wrathful, nor tyrannical; and that you be not insolent, nor haughty, nor boastful" (*Didascalia* 7).

B. Theology: The Two Dionysii

The Logos theology had triumphed to the extent that even Paul of Samosata (condemned 268) spoke of God's preexistent Logos (chapter 7). The situation in regard to speculation on the Godhead in the latter half of the third century is illustrated by the brief literary controversy between Dionysius, bishop of Alexandria (c. 247–c. 265), and a second Dionysius, bishop of Rome (c. 260–c. 268).

Dionysius of Alexandria cut a large figure in the controversies of the third century. He (1) sided with Cornelius of Rome in opposing Novatian's denial of forgiveness to those who lapsed in the Decian persecution, (2) shared Stephen of Rome's position against Cyprian's insistence on rebaptism of heretics and schismatics, and (3) opposed the millennialism of the Egyptian bishop Nepos by arguing that differences in style indicated that the apostle John to whom the Fourth Gospel was attributed could not have been the prophet John who wrote the book of Revelation.

In (4) refuting the Sabellians, Dionysius of Alexandria emphasized the differences between Father, Son, and Holy Spirit to such an extent that he came close to tritheism. For these statements he was rebuked by Dionysius of Rome. His clarification vindicated his orthodoxy. This discussion concerning the likeness of nature between the Son and the Father, and the question of whether and how the Son came into existence, anticipated key issues in the Arian controversy of the fourth century.

The exchange between the bishops of the two most powerful churches in the Christian world illustrates the way Western theologians typically emphasized the oneness of the Godhead, whereas eastern theologians often stressed the threeness.

C. Missions: Gregory Thaumaturgus

Gregory Thaumaturgus ("Wonderworker") (c. 210–c. 265) was born a pagan in Neocaesarea in Pontus. Intending to study law at Berytus (Beirut), he spent time at Caesarea, where attending several of Origen's lectures proved to be the turning point of his life.

After five years with Origen, Gregory became a missionary to Pontus and Cappadocia and the bishop of Neocaesarea. Accounts of his life report numerous miracles, which gave him his nickname and attest his prominence in evangelizing his homeland.

Gregory's work heralds the importance of this region for Christian theology in the fourth century and provides the connecting link between Origen and the great Cappadocian church fathers. One of them, Gregory of Nyssa, whose grandmother was taught by Gregory Thaumaturgus, wrote the most important account of his life.

D. Literature: Methodius, Lactantius

Methodius (d. 311) and Lactantius (c. 250–c. 325) illustrate some of the concerns of Greek and Latin authors respectively at the turn to the fourth century.

Methodius was bishop of Olympus in Lycia and died a martyr. Many of his works are lost, but some survive in an Old Church Slavonic translation. From one of these, *On the Resurrection,* we know his argument that the glorious body of the resurrection will be identical with the mortal body—in opposition to Origen's view of a spiritual resurrection body.

Methodius's treatise *On Free Will* continues the insistence of early church thinkers on human freedom as the basis of morality and of rewards and punishments at the judgment—in opposition to Gnostic views on the origin of evil.

One work by Methodius survives in its original Greek, the *Banquet,* a long dialogue that takes up many theological topics but centers on the ascetic life and praises virginity.

Lactantius was the master stylist of Christian Latin, borrowing heavily from Cicero, Virgil, and other classical Latin authors. A native of North Africa, he was invited to Diocletian's new capital at Nicomedia in 303 to set up a school of rhetoric there. He soon lost that position after being converted to Christianity, but a few years later he was chosen by Constantine to teach his eldest son, Crispus, at Trier in Gaul.

Lactantius's principal work is the *Divine Institutes,* in which he not only refutes paganism, but also undertakes an apologetic Christian philosophy of religion. That philosophy involves a history of religion, a moral system built on a Christian understanding of the classical virtue of justice, and a worldview centered on providence.

Like his model, Cicero, Lactantius used oratorical form and style for philosophical thought. Although his exposition of Christian doctrine was found deficient by later thinkers, he is important for the Christian appropriation of Latin literature and culture in order to appeal to the cultivated class of the Roman world.

Lactantius wrote *On the Deaths of the Persecutors* to show the just vengeance of God against those who persecuted the church. He constitutes one of the principal sources of information for the persecution under Diocletian.

VI. WHY DID CHRISTIANITY SUCCEED?

By the end of the third century Christians made up a sizeable minority of the population of the Roman Empire. Historians have pointed to

---

"There is no occasion for violence and injury, for religion cannot be imposed by force; the matter must be carried on by words rather than by blows, that the will may be affected.... For nothing is so much a matter of free will as religion" (Lactantius, *Divine Institutes* 5.20).

various factors to account for this success. Even if one appeals to divine providence, what were the human or natural circumstances through which providence worked?

External conditions at the beginning of Christianity were favorable: (1) the spread of Judaism provided a base of operations for Christian preaching throughout the Roman world, (2) the Hellenizing of the eastern Mediterranean provided a common language and ideas, and (3) the political unity under Rome provided peace, stability, and possibilities for travel. These external conditions were available to all, however, so why did Christianity outdistance its potential rivals?

Internal conditions suggested by various historians as part of the appeal of Christianity include the following: (1) the firm belief in the truth of the Christian religion (although Christian insistence that it was the one and only way was a scandal to many, then as now), (2) the universal outlook of the Christian faith that was open to all, (3) the effective practice of brotherly love and charity that produced a society meeting all needs of its members, (4) the disciplined self-government of individual Christian communities that were united with one another, (5) the practice of fellowship that gave a strong sense of community, and (6) the combination of the strengths of religious practice and philosophical thought.

Christian ideas were for the most part acceptable to pagans: high moral standards, monotheism, and a claim to prophetic revelation. On the other hand, the idea of the incarnation of deity was strange (especially in the distinctively Christian version of incarnation) but not unintelligible. The resurrection of the body, though, was the most repellent aspect of Christian teaching. Yet Christian miracles seemed more powerful than what magicians could accomplish.

The psychological factor of the weariness of paganism contrasted with Christianity's hope, which was worth living for since it was worth dying for.

Sociological factors involving the positive attitudes toward women, family, and children, as well as the care for the sick in times of illness and epidemic, also favored Christian numerical growth.

Ultimately, however, such attempts to account for the success of Christianity turn out to be more descriptive than explanatory. In the end, many of the items selected above are merely modern judgments about what is assumed to have been appealing.

The success of Christianity on the political level in the fourth century turned on the conversion of one man—Constantine the Great. After him, political support was an important factor in the further growth of the church.

FOR FURTHER STUDY

Burns, J. Patout. *Cyprian the Bishop*. London: Routledge, 2002.

Jensen, Robin Margaret. *Understanding Early Christian Art*. London: Routledge, 2000.

Spier, J., et al. *Picturing the Bible: The Earliest Christian Art*. New Haven: Yale University Press, 2007.

Diocletian and Constantine

On the Threshhold of the Fourth Century

I. THE PERSECUTION UNDER DIOCLETIAN

A. Reorganization of the Empire

A brief survey of Roman governmental administration is necessary in order to understand the course of the empire-wide persecution against Christians. The latter was very much bound up with the political history of the early fourth century.

The monarchy during the principate since Augustus had its theoretical basis in the Senate of Rome giving its sanction to imperial power. The real basis was the army, when it gave its recognition of the emperor by acclamation. A religious confirmation came from the practice of apotheosis, the acceptance of the deceased emperor into the number of the gods. The court protocol of Persia was taken over, emphasizing the distance between the ruler and his subjects. The increased emphasis in the course of time on the divinized deceased emperor passed into divinization during the ruler's lifetime. Attestation of the ascension of the deceased emperor became routine.

Head of Diocletian (Archaeological Museum, Istanbul).

During this time, the principle of legitimacy was provided by passing authority from father to son. Orderly succession, however, became the exception rather than the rule in the third century. None of the traditional bases of the monarchy served to solidify the throne. The rivalries of greedy armies led by ambitious generals produced frequent civil wars. Economic instability and crumbling defenses on the frontiers accompanied and intensified the internal conflicts.

Diocletian (284–305) combined the earlier bases of imperial rule with a reorganization plan. His purpose was to provide an orderly succession to the throne and to offer the top military commanders an assured turn at supreme rule without having to resort to rebellion to attain it. The empire was divided into four regions (prefectures) to be governed by two Augusti assisted by two Caesars. The theory was that after ten years the situation would be reviewed and the Augusti would resign, the two Caesars would become Augusti, and two new Caesars would be appointed.

Under this reorganization plan, Diocletian and Maximian became Augusti and took the names of Jupiter and Hercules. Galerius and Constantius Chlorus were named Caesars with primarily civil administration. Each emperor ruled a prefecture. Each prefecture had its own capital (after 284 Rome was no longer an imperial residence).

The empire was further divided into twelve dioceses and approximately one hundred provinces. The latter number varied as provinces were created, divided, or combined. (It should be noted that this terminology differed from what came to prevail in the ecclesiastical world, where provinces designated larger territories than dioceses.)

The reforms of Diocletian recognized that the strength of the Roman Empire—numerically, financially, and culturally—was in the East. The distribution of power may be shown in chart form.

DIVISION OF THE EMPIRE UNDER DIOCLETIAN			
Prefecture	Dioceses	Capital	Ruler
Oriens (East)	Oriens (including Egypt), Pontus, Asia	Nicomedia	Diocletian
Illyricum	Thrace, Moesia (Macedonia, Dacia), Pannonia	Sirmium	Galerius
Italy	Africa, S. Italy, N. Italy	Milan	Maximian
Gauls	Spain, S. Gaul, N. Gaul, Britain	Trier	Constantius Chlorus

B. The Course of the Persecution

As a prelude to the empire-wide persecution of Christians, Hierocles, governor of Bithynia and later prefect of Egypt, claimed that the empire could survive only if it was united in religion. Drawing on Porphyry's (c. 232–c. 305) intellectual attack *Against the Christians*, Hierocles called Christians an "empire in the empire" and insisted on sacrifice to the gods by Christians in the army.

The "Great Persecution" began in 303 at the instigation of Galerius, but with support from Diocletian. Four successive edicts were issued:

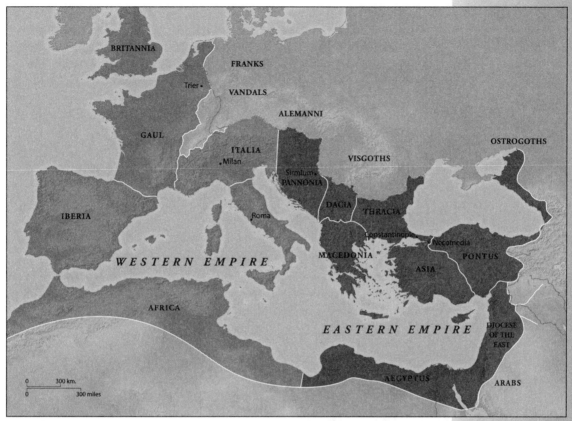

The division of the western and eastern empires under Emperor Diocletian.

1. Christian buildings were to be leveled, Scriptures were burned, and anyone appearing in a court of law had to sacrifice (thus debarring Christians from the judicial system), as did anyone when challenged to do so (thus removing those who would not sacrifice from high office).

2. Governors were ordered to arrest and imprison bishops.

3. Bishops could be released if they sacrificed.

4. Sacrifice to the gods was made obligatory on everyone.

The persecution was more systematic than under Decius, but initially was not so brutal. A new phase was entered when Diocletian, who took his reforms in the government seriously, pressured a reluctant Maximian to join him in retiring. Galerius and Constantius Chlorus became the new Augusti, and the new Caesars were Severus in Italy and Maximinus Daia in Oriens. Persecution was renewed in the East, and Daia turned to capital punishment. In the west, however, civil war ensued. Maximian supported his son Maxentius in seizing control in Italy, but then attempted unsuccessfully to depose him.

Constantius Chlorus had been mild in persecution, not going beyond a token show of enforcing the first edict of Diocletian, but he died in 306. His troops, in rejection of the new constitutional arrangements of Diocletian, proclaimed his son Constantine as emperor. An ailing Galerius issued an edict of toleration for Christians in 311, asking them to pray for his recovery, but the request (if complied with) did not prevent his death. Licinius, allying himself with Constantine, gained control of the East.

The future lay with Constantine, and our narrative will follow his story.

II. CONSTANTINE THE GREAT

The conversion and reign of Constantine mark a major turning point in the history of Europe and the Near East. On many topics in Christian history, the distinction pre-Constantinian and post-Constantinian is more than a convenient chronological division that historians employ. The terms represent both real and symbolic differences. Some of these major shifts will appear in the course of our narrative.

A. Interpretation

As with other great figures of history—whose careers have changed human history or have been bound up with significant changes—Constantine has been subject to various interpretations. Conflicting interpretations were present from the beginning of his rise to power, and these correspond to his family background.

Constantine's father, Constantius Chlorus, was a Neoplatonist who was tolerant of Christianity. Constantine's mother was Helena, who came from humble circumstances. She was a Christian and later was known as Saint Helena. Pagan sources say that Constantine, on the death of his father (306), had a vision at a temple of Apollo that was interpreted to mean he

Statue of Constantine outside the church of St. John Lateran, Rome.

would be emperor. Christian sources describe a vision in 312 before the battle of Milvian Bridge that marked his espousal of the Christian religion.

In the Orthodox church, Constantine has sometimes been called a "saint," but not consistently. Yet like the saints, his name continues to be one of the more popular given names in Greece. The opposite evaluation treats him as a politician, at the most a prudential Christian, whose primary concern was to hold the empire together and who let his subjects think of him as either a pagan or a Christian according to their preference.

A mediating position sees Constantine as a syncretist in religious matters, who started out as a Neoplatonist and who never clearly distinguished between the worship of the Sun and the Son.

It is possible that we should consider another option, namely that Constantine was both sincere in his conversion and used Christianity for his own purposes. Sometimes one's faith and convictions prove to be the politically expedient course of action at a given juncture in human events. Constantine's own understanding of Christianity probably increased with time.

Since it is difficult to know our own motives, much less those of others, especially in the past, judgment on why Constantine supported Christianity must be reserved. Certainly he wanted unity and harmony, and consequently pursued policies in regard to all his subjects—especially in church conflicts—that favored inclusiveness and flexibility.

For most believers the favor that Constantine extended to Christianity was the appropriate goal toward which the early growth of Christianity was moving. This goal was the creation of Christendom—a civil society composed mostly of Christians and in which Christianity was the dominant force. Constantine himself did not alone achieve this, and his successors went further in imposing Christianity on the populace and interfering in the affairs of the church.

Other believers have not taken such a favorable view of the "Constantinian church" and have spoken of the union of church and state and developments associated with this as "the fall of the church." They have done so because of the decline of commitment among church members, the lowered standards of the Christian life, and the introduction of coercion as an aspect of religious profession.

Circumstances certainly were dramatically changed, but if the new situation is thought of as more a decline than progress, "fall" may still not be the most accurate word. One might rather speak of a "slide," for the growth of the church in the third century had already brought many accommodations with Roman society, and the entanglements with the state steadily increased after Constantine's time.

B. Conversion and Favor for Christians

After the death of his father, Constantine quickly consolidated his hold on the western part of the empire and marched against Maxentius in Italy. In 312, as his troops were camped north of the Tiber River near Rome, Constantine had a "religious experience" in which he was admonished to adopt the Chi Rho monogram (the first two letters of the word Christ in Greek) as the emblem for his troops. Lactantius says the instructions came in a dream. Claiming to repeat a report from Constantine himself, Eusebius says there was both a sign in the sky, brighter than the mid-day sun, and an appearance of Jesus Christ the following night in a dream.

Once more, various interpretations are possible: Was the whole incident fabricated? Was it a figment of his imagination? And, if he dreamed something or saw something, what was it? A likely explanation is that he did indeed have some kind of experience—a dream, a vision, or both—but that the interpretation was provided by Christian advisers (notably Ossius, or Hosius, bishop of Cordoba, Spain) who accompanied him. They may have helped Constantine to see in his experience the monogram of Christ as the Christian interpretation of what he saw.

At any rate, Constantine was clearly conscious of some divine mission and of the promise of divine help, and that sense of mission continued to characterize his policies and propaganda. He instructed his soldiers to put the Chi Rho monogram of Christ on their shields, and thereafter this Christogram became an almost ubiquitous Christian symbol, often combined with the letters alpha and omega (the first and last letters of the Greek alphabet), for Christ as the beginning and the end.

Constantine's smaller army won the battle of Milvian Bridge (Sax Rubra) and he secured control of Rome—and with it the end of opposition in the West. Eusebius interpreted the event in grand biblical terms, comparing the defeat of Maxentius's army to the destruction of the Egyptians under Pharaoh in the Red Sea.

Whatever the nature of Constantine's "conversion" and whatever his motives, after 312 he slowly but steadily began to favor Christians and to shift the ideological underpinnings of the empire. Constantine entered into an agreement with Licinius at Milan in 313 extending free exercise of religion to "Christians and all others." This agreement, the so-called "Edict of Milan," is known from official letters sent by Licinius to provinces under his control, giving Christians in the East the liberties those in the West already enjoyed under Constantine.

By 320 it was apparent that Constantine and Licinius did not agree. Licinius was more inclined to pagan monotheism, and he began persecution again in the East. Constantine defeated him in 324 and was now the sole ruler of the whole Roman world. Thereafter Constantine dropped the image of himself as a representation of the sun-god and presented himself as representing Jesus Christ, the Sun of Righteousness.

Constantine was uncomfortable with the pagan associations of Rome and the traditions surrounding the Senate, and certain factors drew him to the East as the proper center of the empire: its greater wealth, commerce, culture, and educational opportunities. Consequently, in 330 he founded a new capital, Constantinople (modern Istanbul) on the site of the old Greek city of Byzantium. His rule laid the basis for the orthodox Christian empire known as the Byzantine empire, which would last more than 1,100 years (until 1453).

Constantine himself delayed his baptism until near his death, when in 337 he was baptized by Eusebius, bishop of Nicomedia. He thus set a prominent precedent for others in the fourth century who delayed their baptism until their old age or their death bed so as to obtain the maximum benefit of the forgiveness of sins.

Constantine showed favor for Christians in various ways, but many of his actions were designed not to offend pagans or were subject to ambiguous interpretation. The prayer he composed to be recited by the army, for instance, was religiously neutral between pagan and Christian monotheism. The legislation making Sunday a legal holiday gave leisure to Christians for their church assemblies, but was worded as an honor to the sun. (Christians had been meeting on Sunday, their Lord's day, from the beginning, but the Constantinian legislation made this day a day of rest as well.)

Bread and a Chi/Rho on a slab that covered a grave in the Catacomb of San Sebastiano. After Constantine, the Chi/Rho (the first letters of the name *Christ* in Greek combined in a monogram) became an almost ubiquitous Christian symbol.

In addition, Constantine employed the Chi Rho as a standard for his troops and placed the emblem on some of his coins, but it could have been seen as one more talisman, and indeed Constantine (as well as an increasing number of Christians) seems to have had a rather superstitious regard for the cross. Other legislation favoring Christians put them on the same footing with other religions. Privileges of exemption from civil duties and monetary support from the government long held by pagan priests were given to Christian priests (see below on Donatism).

Other policies gave more recognition to the church. Bishops were given the privilege of adjudicating disputes when the parties referred their cases to them. Their decisions were given the same status as decisions of civil judges, an important step toward setting up separate ecclesiastical courts, and an act that compromised the jurisdiction of the imperial judiciary.

Perhaps the greatest outward show of favor for the church was Constantine's extensive building program. Church buildings were built to celebrate important sites of sacred history (in Palestine, for example, the Church of the Nativity in Bethlehem, the Church of the Holy Sepulcher in Jerusalem, and the Eleona on the Mount of Olives), to commemorate the martyrs (in Rome, St. Peter's and St. Paul's Outside the Walls to mark the places of their martyrdoms), and to enhance the prestige of the church and of Constantine himself (in Rome the Lateran basilica, now St. John's, and in the new capital churches dedicated to Christ as the Holy Wisdom and to the Twelve Apostles, where Constantine was later buried as a thirteenth apostle—or as a new Christ himself?—among twelve empty sarcophagi representing the apostles).

The emperors had long celebrated their rule with monumental building projects, and Constantine continued this practice, but with the difference it was now church buildings that advertised the majesty and munificence of the emperor. The architectural style adopted was patterned on the imperial basilicas used for audience and reception halls, court rooms, and other affairs of state (chapter 12).

C. The New Situation in Church-State Relations

Constantine realized the problems caused by division in the state, so "concord" (or harmony) became the key word of his propaganda and the policies of his reign. He clearly wanted the aid of the Christian God in achieving his goals. There was a long-standing Roman conviction that the welfare of the state depended on right relations with the deity and due performance of religious duties. Constantine's transfer (or addition) of allegiance to the Christian God did not change these convictions.

A model of the Constantinian Basilica of the Nativity, Bethlehem (Museum of Roman Civilization, Rome).

Since there was one supreme God, Constantine felt there should be one earthly rule corresponding to the one divine rule. His mission was to overcome the demons of barbarians without and the divisions within associated with polytheism. Renouncing fate, he affirmed that the empire was under the control of providence. God is connected with order in the universe, and he considered himself God's instrument to accomplish this.

Retaining the dignity of *pontifex maximus* ("high priest" in the religion of Rome), Constantine felt a responsibility for the religious welfare of his subjects. He spoke of himself as "bishop of those (or things) without," either bishop of those outside the church or bishop of the external affairs of the church. His son Constantius went further and called himself "bishop of the bishops."

As a result of the new situation with an emperor supporting and favoring instead of persecuting the church, three major problems thrust themselves on the attention of the church: the competence of the state in church affairs, the nature of the church itself, and the definition of doctrine (what is the orthodox church?).

Church-state relations underwent a paradigm shift, now requiring the definition of the competence of a Christian empire. The church found itself largely unprepared for the change from a persecuted

Resurrection sarco-
phagus with the
labarum, a military
standard with the
Chi/Rho monogram
(Vatican Museum,
Rome).

"The God of
all, the Supreme
Governor of the
whole universe,
by his own
will appointed
Constantine
to be prince
and sovereign"
(Eusebius, *Life
of Constantine*
1.24).

church to a favored church. It was not ready for its responsibilities in a
state that, if not Christian, at least supported Christianity.

Tertullian would have thought a Christian emperor a contradiction
in terms, and the way Constantine and many of his successors ruled
(Constantine had his wife, Fausta, and son Crispus murdered for political reasons), there may have been some truth in this. Eusebius, on the
other hand, exulted as if the kingdom had come.

Eusebius saw the "recognition" of Christianity as an act of God's
providence determining a period of peace and prosperity before the end
of the world. Other theologians, especially those writing in Latin, took
a more sober line, and stressed the responsibilities now placed upon the
authorities charged with Rome's welfare.

The nature of the church itself also required clarification in the
new situation. The Donatist schism raised anew the question of the
holiness of the church: Is the church the church of the pure, or is it a
mixed body, a "hospital for sick souls"? Can a church of the majority
and of a ruling class be a holy church?

Monasticism constituted a new reaction to the changed circumstances. In part responding to the new linking of the church with social
status and acceptance, the monks sought to work out the true Christian
life with the same intensity that had characterized the times of persecution. Denied literal martyrdom, they attempted a martyrdom of self-
denial. (The story of monasticism will be reserved for the next chapter.)

Other changes also resulted from the new condition. Up to Constantine's time the bishop knew his people, but the sense of local fellowship began to be lost in the rapid increase in membership. The
church began to adapt its organization so as to give structure to a real
catholicity.

The definition of doctrinal orthodoxy was brought to the forefront by the Trinitarian controversy, sparked by the teachings of Arius.

Doctrinal controversy threatened the unity of the church and with it Constantine's goal of harmony in the empire. The problems of Arianism and Donatism both arose during Constantine's reign. They raised fundamental questions about the definition of the church and of the deity it worshiped.

D. Eusebius of Caesarea: The Emperor's Historian

Eusebius (c. 260–c. 339) became an heir of Origen's theology and erudition through the influence of his teacher Pamphilius and access to the latter's library, built up from Origen's.

Ordained bishop of Caesarea in Palestine about the year that a temporary peace came to the church (313), Eusebius became actively involved in the intellectual and political issues of his day. He was vitally interested in apologetics, writing two major works (*Preparation for the Gospel*, a refutation of paganism, and *Demonstration of the Gospel*, a proof of the gospel from fulfilled prophecy).

Eusebius also was keenly interested in biblical interpretation, writing commentaries on Psalms and Isaiah, as well as preparing a set of tables to identify parallel passages in the Gospels and a list of place names in the Bible with a geographical and historical description.

Involved in the theological issues of the time, Eusebius worked unsuccessfully for unity in the Arian controversy (of which more is said below). Eusebius is especially remembered for his historical work, writing a *Church History* that collected information from the beginning of the church to his time. In successive editions, Eusebius detailed events of the persecutions under Diocletian and his associates and successors.

Eusebius is also important for the political theology he developed in his *Life of Constantine* and *Praise of Constantine*. Although not as close personally to Constantine as it might appear, he promoted Constantine as God's appointed messenger to bring peace to the church and healing to the nations.

III. THE DONATIST SCHISM

Schisms occurred in Alexandria (prompted by the rigorist position of Melitius) and in Rome in the aftermath of the "Great Persecution" initiated under Diocletian, but the Donatist schism in North Africa became the most important.

The Donatists continued the sectarian understanding of the church from pre-Constantinian times, but in many places in North Africa they formed the majority church. The underlying problem was the old issue of laxism versus rigorism in the treatment of those who were thought

"Although it is clear that we are new and that this new name of Christians has really but recently been known among all nations, nevertheless our life and our conduct, with our doctrines of religion, have not been lately invented by us, but from the first creation of humanity have been established by the natural understanding of divinely favored persons of old" (Eusebius, *Church History* 1.4.4).

Diocletian and Constantine

"Donatus of
Carthage was
responsible,
for through his
poisonous wiles
the question of
unity was first
brought into
question....
While all those
who believed
in Christ were,
before the day
of his insolence,
called Chris-
tians, he ven-
tured to divide
the people of
God, so that
those who fol-
lowed him were
no longer called
Christians,
but Donatists"
(Optatus, *On
the Schism of the
Donatists* 3.3).

to have compromised in some way with the governing authorities during the persecution. Only now the issue was complicated by the entrance of the emperor into the decisions, and as the controversy unfolded, social and cultural differences intensified the conflict.

The occasion of the schism in North Africa was the election of Caecilian to succeed Mensurius as bishop of Carthage. A Catholic opponent of the Donatists, Optatus, later charged that the schism came about "by the anger of a disgraced woman, was fed by ambition, and received strength from avarice." Allowance must be made for the polemical nature of the statement, but it is well to notice the charges, for they show so well the human side of church history.

Lucilla, a wealthy and pious woman, had practiced the custom of kissing the bone of a martyr before taking communion. Mensurius, in an effort to keep the cult of the martyrs under church control and out of private ownership, had forbidden unauthorized honor to those killed in persecution and undue veneration to confessors, and his chief deacon Caecilian had rebuked her for her practice. This took some courage, for she was wealthy, but her practice was extreme, as well as representing a challenge to church authority.

The unhappy Lucilla became a focal point of the opposition to the election of Caecilian on the death of Mensurius in 311. Two men who desired to be chosen bishop, failing to obtain their desire, turned against Caecilian.

Another problem was that Mensurius, in order to protect the possessions of the church during the persecution, had entrusted them to some of the older members of the church, who were no longer able (or refused) to return the goods when Caecilian demanded an accounting. A further complication came from the custom for bishops from Numidia to participate in the election and consecration of the bishop of Carthage, yet Caecilian was raised to office before their arrival.

The Numidian bishops, at the instigation of the disaffected elements in the Carthaginian church, proceeded to the appointment of Majorinus, who belonged to the household of Lucilla, as a rival bishop.

The doctrinal point used to justify the schism was the participation of Felix, bishop of Aptunga, in the consecration of Caecilian. Felix was accused of surrendering copies of the Scriptures to the authorities during the persecution, making him a *traditor* ("one who handed over" the church's books).

The critics of Caecilian argued that such a one had in effect denied the faith and so could perform no ecclesiastical functions; therefore the consecration of Caecilian was invalid. The question was raised: What does the moral character of a clergyman have to do with the validity of his actions on behalf of the church?

Later investigations cleared Felix of the charges, but the Donatists questioned the impartiality of the investigations and, indeed, by then the schism was so set that the determination of the facts was beyond objectivity.

On Majorinus's death in 313, Donatus succeeded him as head of the rival church in Carthage, which he led until 355, a sufficiently long enough time that those in communion with him came to wear his name, the "Donatists."

Already in 313 the imperial government became involved in the dispute when Constantine made two grants to the Christian clergy that extended to them privileges that belonged to pagan priests: a distribution of money and an exemption from the civic responsibility of collecting taxes. The Donatists claimed the money and the exemptions on the grounds that they were the true church in North Africa. They appealed their case to Constantine, who referred the matter to the bishop of Rome, Miltiades. The latter assembled a small synod, but the results were inconclusive. In contrast to his swift certainty in dealing with military and political matters, Constantine was hesitant in how to deal with church conflicts.

In response to the Donatists' demand for another trial, a larger synod met at Arles in Gaul in 314. Bishops came from all the territories under Constantine's control at the time, including three bishops from Britain. Arles had the distinction of being the first church council called by an emperor, and of representing the largest geographical area of any council up to its time. It far exceeded all earlier councils, which primarily represented a province but sometimes also adjoining areas.

Among the twenty-two canons adopted at the council were decisions about determining the date of Easter (since British bishops were not present at Nicaea in 325, the newer method of determining the date arrived at there was not observed in Britain), forbidding Christians to reject military service in peacetime (that is, positively, allowing their participation in police functions), approving Christians to hold local and state offices if they are submissive to their bishop, regulating matters of marriage and remarriage, forbidding rebaptism of those baptized in the name of the Trinity, and (although calling for *traditores* among the clergy to be removed) upholding ordinations performed by lapsed clergy.

The Council of Arles set a precedent for how the state would deal with ecclesiastical problems, but it also set an unintended example for later councils in failing to bring to an end the problem for which it was called.

In 316 Constantine decided definitively in favor of Caecilian and in 320 directed persecution against the Donatists, but gave this up the following year. The Donatists were missionary-minded and grew. They erected rival buildings, some bigger and better than those of the catholic churches. They appealed to the North African theological tradition of Tertullian and Cyprian and represented themselves as continuing their view of the martyr church.

Disappointed in their earlier appeal to the imperial authorities, the Donatists came to reject the alliance of the church with the government forged by Constantine and his successors. Donatus put it succinctly, "What has the emperor to do with the church?" (quoted by Optatus, *Against the Donatists* 3.3). The Donatist church understood itself in terms of the holy assembly of Israel in the midst of her impure enemies and, in keeping with this self-image, interpreted all Scripture as holy law.

The Donatists' greatest success came among the rural Punic and Berber populations, who resented the class and economic privileges of the ruling Latins. The economic and social deprivations experienced by many fed the violent reactions against wealthy landowners by the *Circumcelliones*, whose connection with the Donatists is unclear, although their violence was deplored by Donatus. These aspects of the Donatist-Catholic conflict lead some scholars to interpret Donatism primarily as a social movement.

Even as personal factors were present in the beginning of the schism, so social factors were certainly involved in the spread of Donatism. It would not be safe to say, however, that the religious differences were merely the excuse justifying the real points of conflict. How theological concerns are intertwined with personal and social concerns is often difficult to disentangle, and this is particularly the case with Donatism. Issues seldom come as individual questions, more often as a complex of factors, but that does not mean that individual factors (in this case the religious aspects) cannot be discussed separately on their own merits.

The golden age of Donatism came under the successor of Donatus, Parmenian (bishop 362–c. 392). During this time the Catholic literary response appeared in the work *Against the Donatists* by Optatus of Milevis.

A rival to Parmenian for intellectual leadership among the Donatists was Tyconius, who took a broader view of the church and came out against the practice of rebaptism of those converted from the Catholic church. In opposing Donatist sectarianism he articulated views on the sacraments and the distinction between the visible and the invisible church that were later elaborated by Augustine. Tyconius produced a book of rules of hermeneutics that Augustine employed, but the millennialism expressed in his commentary on Revelation was eventually rejected by Augustine.

The later history of Donatism is so involved with Augustine's refutation as to be better told in connection with him (chapter 14). Even if

Donatism's real motives were social, the movement raised legitimate theological issues that challenged Augustine's creative mind.

IV. ARIUS AND THE COUNCIL OF NICAEA

A. Background of the Arian Controversy

The political background to the Arian controversy has been sketched above in connection with Constantine's rise to power and his goals for unity in the empire. The Donatist schism had raised religio-political questions in regard to the nature of the church in the western part of the empire. The teachings of Arius raised similar questions in the eastern part of the empire with regard to the nature of Jesus Christ.

Beginning with Constantine, the church entered imperial history in such a way that one cannot deal with the secular history of the fourth century without discussing the church and cannot deal with the religious history without considering the state. Constantine clearly set a precedent of state involvement in church affairs.

Previously a bishop in council with his presbyters decided questions for the church under his jurisdiction. When it came to disputes between bishops and issues with broader than local implications, the "congregationalism" of the early church left no machinery for their resolution.

Councils of bishops became the characteristic Christian way of dealing with these problems. In the second century, meetings of bishops in a province or region dealt with Montanism and then the Paschal observance.

There still was no means, however, of handling something involving larger areas. The case of Paul of Samosata and the possession of church property in Antioch (third century) had set a precedent for referring some matters to the Roman government. Then came the Donatist appeal to Constantine.

In the early stages of the Donatist controversy, both sides felt it proper for the state to arbitrate, although Constantine initially preferred to throw the question back to the churches. With a "Christian" emperor interested in the affairs of the church, it was natural for church leaders to look to him. Constantine was cautious, but his sons were more open in their attempts to define dogma.

The ecclesiastical background to the theological controversies of the fourth century is provided by the rivalries of the bishops of the great sees. The churches of Alexandria and Antioch had developed competing theological traditions. Constantinople, emerging late as a Christian center, was dependent on one or the other for its bishop and

Letter of Arius to his Bishop Alexander: "God, being the cause of all things, is without beginning and altogether sole, but the Son, being begotten apart from time by the Father, and being created and found before ages, was not before his generation; but, being begotten apart from time before all things, alone was made to subsist by the Father. For he is not eternal or co-eternal or co-unoriginate with the Father, nor has he his being together with the Father" (quoted by Athanasius, *On ~~the Synod~~ 16*)

for its theological orientation. Rome, for some time not involved in Eastern doctrinal controversies, offered its mediation, but initially was more often allied with Alexandria. To its previously honorific authority Rome increasingly asserted a jurisdictional and teaching authority.

By the beginning of the fourth century the bishop of Alexandria, called *papas* ("father," "pope"), had preeminence in all of Egypt and some adjoining territories. Presbyters presided over local churches in Alexandria. Arius was a leading member of the Alexandrian clergy as presbyter of a church in the harbor area. His bishop was Alexander.

The theological background to the early Arian controversy is provided by the two different ways in which the successors of Origen worked out his theology in relation to the Monarchian controversies of the third century. The catholic viewpoint had followed the lines of the Logos doctrine instead of either of the two Monarchian positions (chapter 7). In Greek philosophy God is impassible, and that premise controlled theological speculation among intellectuals. After the Gnostic and Marcionite controversies, no distinction was possible between Creator and Redeemer.

Origen, making the relation between the incarnate Logos (i.e., the Son of God) and the supreme God the same as that of the pre-existent Logos to the One God, had employed the metaphor of "begetting." This assured that the Logos was of the same nature as the Father, but Origen's thought still posited a subordination of the Son to the Father.

Origen's theology could be developed either in the direction of emphasizing the unity of nature (this Alexander did) or of emphasizing the subordination to the extent of saying different natures (this Arius, with a penchant for pushing things to their logical conclusions, did). Since the exact relation of the Logos to the supreme God was still not clearly agreed upon, further formulation was needed.

B. Events Leading to Nicaea

Arius was a Libyan by birth but received his religious education from Lucian of Antioch (a martyr in 312). He was already a popular preacher in Alexandria when he challenged his bishop Alexander's teaching that the Father and the Son possess equal eternity.

Arius affirmed, "There was (once) when Christ was not." Understanding "begetting" as equivalent to "creating," Arius taught that Jesus Christ was not derived from the substance of the Father, but, as the first and highest of God's creations, became the instrument of all the rest of creation.

Bishop Alexander secured a condemnation of Arius's teaching at a synod in Alexandria (317 or 318) that sent a letter to other bishops concerning the exclusion of Arius from fellowship. Arius put his views in writing and appealed to his friends, notably Eusebius, bishop of Nicomedia, for support. Both sides circulated conflicting correspondence.

The dispute came to the ears of Constantine, who sent his chief ecclesiastical advisor, Hosius of Cordova, to look into the situation. The issue came to the fore at a synod in Antioch in early 325. The synod condemned the Christology of Eusebius, bishop of Caesarea, and two others; Eustathius, a strong opponent of Arius, became bishop of Antioch.

A synod was to meet at Ancyra to hear Eusebius's recantation, but Constantine saw the opportunity of combining this planned gathering with a celebration of his recent victory over Licinius and the approaching twentieth anniversary of his acclamation as emperor, so he invited the bishops to come in May 325 to the royal palace at Nicaea. He offered the assistance of the imperial post in providing transportation to the meeting. Probably between 250 and 300 bishops responded.

C. The Council of Nicaea, 325

The presence of bishops who showed the injuries sustained during the recent persecutions, now gathered under the favor and in the presence of the Roman emperor, was a moving experience. Constantine called for unity.

The supporters of Arius offered confessions of faith drawn from scriptural language, but since these did not address the difference of interpretation between Alexander and Arians like Eusebius of Nicomedia regarding the origin of Christ, they were inadequate.

The viewpoints on the doctrinal issue represented at the council may be listed as follows: (1) the convinced adherents of Arius's teaching led by Eusebius of Nicomedia; (2) the moderate subordinationists in the tradition of Origen who, although they would not have stated matters as sharply as Arius, did not see his teachings as dangerous, of whom Eusebius of Caesarea may be taken as representative; (3) conservatives hostile to new formulas and concerned with unity, many without theological education; (4) those who found Arius's teaching dangerous and wanted to outlaw it, such as Alexander and Hosius; and (5) the Monarchians, whose views were perceived by many as carrying an implicit Modalism, such as Eustathius of Antioch and Marcellus of Ancyra.

An overwhelming majority of the bishops did not agree with Arius, but it was harder for them to agree on a positive statement of doctrine. (It is always easier to get agreement on what people are *against* than on what they are *for*.)

Eusebius of Caesarea wrote a letter to his home church indicating that he had a more prominent place in the proceedings than is probably the case. He submitted the baptismal creed of his church in order to secure his rehabilitation. According to his report of the events, however, it became the basis of the creed approved by the council.

The major concern in Eusebius's report, and no doubt in the minds of many others, was the addition to the creed of the Greek word *homoousios* (in Latin, *consubstantialis*), "of the same substance." Eusebius explains the word, "which it has not been our custom to use," as affirming that the Son of God "bears no resemblance to creatures," was like the Father "in every way," and did not derive from any other substance than that of the Father himself. He no doubt had the encouragement of Constantine and others to understand the word in this broad way, "peace being the aim which we set before us."

The council adopted the word *homoousios* in order to eliminate Arian teaching, as well as to affirm that Jesus Christ was fully God, sharing in some way the same divine nature as the Father. *Homoousios* at this time had a looser and more ambiguous sense than it came to acquire as a result of the ensuing theological discussions. A word not found in Scripture was considered necessary because the Arians interpreted every scriptural phrase in accordance with their teaching, but in a way that the majority felt was inconsistent with the intended meaning of Scripture.

THE CREED ADOPTED AT NICAEA IN 325

We believe in one God the Father All-sovereign, maker of all things visible and invisible;

and in one Lord Jesus Christ, the Son of God, begotten of the Father, only-begotten, that is, of the substance of the Father, God of God, Light of Light, true God of true God, begotten not made, of one substance [*homoousion*] with the Father, through whom all things were made, things in heaven and things on the earth; who for us men and for our salvation came down and was made flesh, and became man, suffered, and rose on the third day, ascended into the heavens, is coming to judge the living and the dead;

and in the Holy Spirit.

And those who say "There was when he was not,"

and, "Before he was begotten he was not,"

and that, "He came into being from what-is-not,"

or those who allege that the Son of God is "of another substance or essence," or "created," or "changeable," or "alterable,"

these the Catholic and Apostolic Church anathematizes.

The council's affirmation of the identity of substance between the Father and the Son, if "substance" was understood in a materialistic way, carried dangers either of a tritheistic interpretation, as referring to three entities consisting of a common matter, or a Sabellian (Modalist) interpretation, as referring to identically the same being.

Hence, Eusebius was at pains to remove a materialistic meaning from this word that was plainly troubling to him and, as the subsequent events unfolded, to many others. *Homoousios* was a word the Arians could not accept, and it was approved for this negative reason. Only as the post-council debates proceeded did the word come to acquire a more precise meaning as a safeguard of monotheism, the oneness of substance. It often happens that in the development of thought provoked by debate, a person comes to see strengths and virtues in a position originally adopted for other reasons.

Eusebius says that the emperor insisted on the addition of the word *homoousios*. This is likely the case, but it is unlikely that the initiative lay with him, since many of the bishops themselves did not understand the issues. It may have originated with Hosius, who would have seen it as equivalent to the Latin term with which he was familiar, *consubstantialis*; with Eustathius, for whom the implication of Monarchianism was perhaps congenial; or with Alexander, for whom its unacceptability to the Arians was sufficient justification.

If, on the other hand, we accept Eusebius at face value that Constantine was the source of *homoousios* at Nicaea, it may be that the emperor derived the term from pagan religious philosophy that spoke in this way about the two divine substances, Mind (*Nous*) and Word (*Logos*).

After making their positive affirmations in the creed, the council anathematized the main errors alleged against the Arians: (1) that "There was when he was not" or "He came to be from nothing" and (2) that the Son of God is "created," or "alterable," or "mutable." In the latter anathema the words *hypostasis* and *ousia* (both of which can be translated "substance") are used interchangeably; later consideration would distinguish these words. Eusebius had a harder time explaining the statement of anathemas. He took this part of the council's decision as forbidding the use of these terms not explicitly found in Scripture. Alexander surely understood much more to have been intended.

Other matters came before the assembled bishops. They approved the method for determining the date of Easter that would henceforth be observed in Christendom. They set policies for treating followers of Novatian, Melitius, and Paul of Samosata who returned to the church. The twenty-two canons give us a picture of the institutional life of the church. These canons, along with those approved at other councils, entered into the corpus of canon law for the Greek church.

Athanasius would later observe the difference in wording employed in regard to the creed and in regard to the canons. On the former, the bishops said, "We believe," for the faith cannot be changed but only confessed; on the latter they said, "We decide," because matters of discipline, liturgy, and organization allowed for ecclesiastical judgment.

D. The Importance of Nicaea

The Council of Nicaea is one of the significant turning points in church history. Three aspects may be highlighted.

1. Nicaea was the first ecumenical ("universal") council, although it was not so called for another dozen years. Such general assemblies of church leaders became *the* way to deal with dogmatic problems that affected the church universal.

   Nicaea was an assembly conscious of its uniqueness, because it was very different in extent from previous councils. It was unprecedented for Rome to send legates to an Eastern council, and although the number of Western bishops was small (the names of only five, including Hosius, plus the two presbyters representing the Roman bishop, are known), their presence gave a consciousness of a truly universal representation.

   The bishops had a sense of authority. The unanimity was impressive and felt to be a manifestation of the Spirit's presence. Although many had to do contortions with their conscience, as did Eusebius of Caesarea, in the end only two Libyan bishops withheld their signatures, and they may have acted for nontheological reasons, either out of desire for independence from Alexandria or out of friendship for Arius. It was wonderful to get 250 bishops together, and even more wonderful to get them to agree.

2. Nicaea served as a symbol of imperial involvement in church affairs. It was different from previous councils because of the personal presence of a formidable new factor, the emperor Constantine. The aura of authority that came from Nicaea resulted from those who bore the marks of persecution now being assembled by the emperor with great publicity and signs of favor.

   The age of persecution was over and the age of Christendom—Christianity as a religion favored by government—had begun. In many ways, Nicaea was a "victory" celebration for the church. The banishment of Arius, however, was a reminder that there was a price to pay for imperial involvement, and many in later ages would question the spiritual effects of the political victory. Nonetheless, the alliance of church and state was set on a course that would prevail for most Christians for twelve to fourteen centuries, and that in many places still prevails.

3. Nicaea marked a crucial development in doctrinal history. By adopting a creed backed up by anathemas, it made creeds into something more than confessions of faith. Instead of being summaries of catechetical instruction to be confessed at baptism, as they had been, creeds in the fourth century became formulations of councils. At Nicaea it was not catechumens who needed a creed, but bishops.

The use of nonbiblical language in the Nicene Creed was not so great in significance as many then and since have thought. The problem was safeguarding a biblical thought. Any time sermons are preached or theological treatises are written, words and expressions not in the Bible are used in order to communicate and clarify the biblical message. Although confessions of faith are customarily more privileged forms of discourse, they need not be more restrictive in their terminology. The question is whether the language is true to the meaning and intent of Scripture.

What was new at Nicaea was putting a nonbiblical term in a creed enforced by anathemas. (The preceding Council of Antioch is the first known instance of appending anathemas to a statement of faith.) Instead of being only a confession of faith, the creed of Nicaea became a test of fellowship. The precedent of Nicaea was capable of considerable extension: the First Creed of Sirmium (351) contains twenty-seven anathemas.

It is true that any positive affirmation implies a rejection of its opposite, but Nicaea took an important step in its language of exclusion, a step whose consequences were made more severe by the new potential of state enforcement.

FOR FURTHER STUDY

Anatolios, Khalid. *Retrieving Nicaea: The Development and Meaning of Trinitarian Doctrine*. Grand Rapids: Baker, 2012.

Drake, H. A. *Constantine and the Bishops: The Politics of Intolerance*. Baltimore: Johns Hopkins University Press, 2000.

Frend, W. H. C. *The Donatist Church: A Movement of Protest in Roman North Africa*. 3rd ed. Oxford: Clarendon, 1985.

Kelly, J. N. D. *Early Christian Creeds*. 3rd ed. London: Longmans, 1972. 205–62.

Odahl, C. W. *Constantine and the Christian Empire*. London: Routledge, 2008.

11

The Church in the Fourth Century

Doctrine, Organization, and Literature

I. THE ARIAN CONTROVERSY AFTER NICAEA

A. From 325 to 361

The first phase of the Arian controversy was the brief period from its outbreak until the Council of Nicaea in 325. The second phase lasted from Nicaea until the death of Constantius II and the accession of Julian the Apostate in 361.

What is traditionally called the "Arian controversy" is somewhat of a misnomer. After igniting the conflict, Arius virtually disappeared from the scene, almost never referred to by those who continued his line of thought. Moreover, the ensuing theological discussions were more a search for an agreed definition of faith than a constant controversy.

Political events provided the background for the ecclesiastical developments. On Constantine's death in 337, in spite of all his rhetoric about restoring unity to the empire, the rule was divided among his three sons. He may not have been consistent in his policy of unity, but he was constant in naming his children: Constantine II received Spain, the Gauls, and Britain; Constans received Africa, Italy, and Illyricum; and Constantius II received the East. (Constantine also had a daughter, Constantina.) After 340 Constans took over all the west. Constantius overcame Constans in 350 and the usurper Magnentius in 353 so as to rule over the whole empire. He was an Arianizer.

The Nicene Creed was designed to comprehend all who wanted to be comprehended, but it was troublesome on both sides. Eustathius was distressed that Eusebius of Caesarea could sign it, and Eusebius returned the compliment. Many sought to supplement the Nicene Creed with other creeds and interpretations that would narrow the comprehension. The Nicenes tried to picture the Eusebian moderates as Arian, and the latter tried to depict the supporters of Nicaea as Sabellian.

Eusebius, bishop of Nicomedia, assumed the leadership of those whose sympathies were with Arius. Athanasius became bishop of Alexandria in 328. The two sides were now the Eusebians and the Athanasians, but the options were never this limited, and even these parties saw fractionalization under the attacks of opponents and the pressures of imperial politics.

Constantine himself, in his desire for unity, became increasingly conciliatory: He reinstated the two bishops who had not signed the Nicene Creed, and when he died in 337 he left his sons under the spiritual care of Eusebius of Nicomedia. The latter proved a skilled ecclesiastical statesman and survivor in the tangled doctrinal and political maze of the fourth century.

Many of the champions of Nicaea (and others as well) experienced depositions by synods of bishops, whose decisions were now often enforced by the civil authorities' power to send into exile. Constantine turned against Athanasius for the latter's administrative acts, if not his theology, which in itself may have concerned Constantine little.

Although as long as Constantine lived the authority of the Nicene Creed was unchallenged, Arianism has the appearance of spreading rapidly. Why did this happen so soon after it had been officially condemned? This appearance was not simply due to the political skills of Eusebius of Nicomedia. Coalitions, after achieving their immediate purposes, often begin to fall apart.

Nicaea was more a triumph of an anti-Arian majority than of a pro-Alexandrian sentiment. The great majority of Christians had no clear views on the Trinity and did not understand what was at stake in the issues. The Arian sympathizers were able to exploit a long-standing "subordinationism" in the thinking about Jesus Christ.

Moreover, the new word *homoousios* had a suspect history: (1) it was not used in Scripture; (2) it had been used by the Gnostics; (3) it had been used by Paul of Samosata in some way not now clear; and (4) it sounded Sabellian (and some Nicenes were close to this position).

So the apparent resurgence of Arianism after Nicaea was more an anti-Nicene reaction exploited by Arian sympathizers than a pro-Arian development.

Attacks on individuals brought down some of the most disliked champions of the Nicene Creed. About 330 a council in Antioch removed Eustathius, bishop of Antioch. The charges were moral: disregard for the royal family (and he did have a sharp tongue). About the same time in Constantinople Marcellus of Ancyra was deposed, charged with Sabellianism, and he was close to it. He did not take steps to reconcile Arians, so disrespect for the emperor was also a lever to get rid of him.

The crowning achievement of the opponents of Nicaea was the banishment of Athanasius in 335 by a council at Tyre. Most of the Eastern clergy at this council favored the restoration of Arius. Athanasius was condemned on moral grounds: acts of violence unworthy of a bishop. A synod at Jerusalem lifted the excommunication of Arius and asked the emperor to reinstate him as a presbyter. The news apparently so excited Arius's weak heart that he died in 336 before it could be done. The symbol of the new ascendancy of pro-Arius thinkers was the translation of Eusebius from Nicomedia to become bishop of Constantinople in 339.

Through this time the bishop of Rome stood by Nicaea and Athanasius. Julius (bishop 337–52) convened a local synod in 341 that declared all the banishments illegal. Since the western emperor was not Arian, the bishop of Rome was more independent, and Julius offered his support to Athanasius. The West as a whole was largely unaffected by the conflict during its early stages. The alliance between Rome and Alexandria became an important factor in the eventual triumph of the Nicene cause.

As the Arian controversy unfolded during the fourth century, the following broad positions may be distinguished:

1. The *Homoousians* supported the wording adopted at Nicaea (the Son is of "the same substance" with the Father). Their theological spokesmen were Athanasius in the East and Hilary of Poitiers in the West. The bishops of Rome stood by this position, although with some wavering, and it became the "catholic" position.

2. The *Homoiousians* (who said the Son is of "similar or like substance" to the Father) were concerned about possible Sabellian implications of *homoousios* and wanted to preserve the distinctness of Father, Son, and Holy Spirit, while rejecting the extreme Arians. An early leader was Basil of Ancyra, who advocated the phrase "like the Father in *ousia*." This was a

---

POSITIONS ON THE RELATION OF THE SON TO THE FATHER

Homoousians — the Son is of the same substance with the Father

Homoiousians — the Son is of similar substance to the Father

Homoeans — the Son is like the Father

Anomoeans — the Son is unlike the Father

position that commanded wide support in the eastern part of the empire.

3. The *Homoeans* (from *homoios*, "like" or "similar") preferred to avoid the word *ousia* altogether. This is the least clearly defined of the positions. Some were willing to say that Jesus Christ is like God "in all things," as Eusebius encouraged his church members at Caesarea to understand *homoousios* and as Basil of Ancyra agreed to accept. Others used *homoios* as a vague cover term, for they wanted to preserve the distinction between the Father and the Son. Acacius, successor to Eusebius as bishop of Caesarea, an Arian at heart who wanted to be orthodox in language, represented the *Homoean* position. This view gained the most support for a time, both among those who agreed with Arius and those who did not like *homoousios*, and it had the support of Constantius II.

4. The *Anomoeans* (the Son is "unlike" the Father) were a later development of the extreme Arian view, sometimes known as "Neoarians." For them, it is possible to define the essential nature of God as "ungenerated," and since the Son is "generated," he is unlike the Father in essence. The advocates of this view rejected the label *anomoios* given by their opponents, because they agreed the Son was like the Father in energy, power, and activity, but said he was unlike in substance, so they preferred as their watchword *heterousios*. Aetius and Eunomius were leaders of this position.

A long series of councils met in the fourth century to deal with the doctrinal problems. These showed the extent to which the Nicene Creed was a novelty, but initially were not explicitly Arian. Increasingly imperial pressure from Constantius II forced agreement to Homoean creeds, which he thought had the best chance of uniting the church. (In spite of the harsh things said by Homoousians, Constantius was mild for the times in his treatment of those who did not agree with his policies.)

A series of councils (in the years 347, 351, 357, 358, 359, and disputedly in 378) met at Sirmium, in the province of Pannonia II (present-day Hungary) on the route of travel between East and West. The Nicenes labeled the second creed to come out of these councils (357) as the "Blasphemy of Sirmium," because the influence of Ursacius and Valens secured the rejection of *homoousios* and *homoiousios*, even forcing the signature of the aged Hosius.

The climax of imperial pressure came at the councils at Ariminum (Rimini) in Italy and Seleucia in Isauria, 359, which were intended to be joint parts of an ecumenical council. Although the westerners were Nicene in sentiment, they were worn down by imperial pressure to accept a Homoean creed, a victory for Valens and Ursacius. A similar scene at Seleucia resulted in the Homoiousians accepting the Homoean formula championed by Acacius and Eudoxius. Jerome later expressed the judgment, "The whole world groaned and marveled to find itself Arian."

There was clearly now a need for a fresh statement of views. As sometimes happens in the course of events, the success of the anti-Nicene forces was their failure. It was their failure because they were more united in what they were *against* than in what they were *for*.

A local synod at Ancyra in 358 under the leadership of Basil of Ancyra and George of Laodicea, and another at Alexandria in 362 under Athanasius, laid the groundwork for new formulas. The former synod tried to take a position between *homoousios* and *homoios*, sometimes called "Semiarian" but better "Neonicene." The latter synod acknowledged that those who spoke of *homoiousios* had the same intentions as those who used *homoousios*.

The other creeds drawn up in the 340s and 350s, then, were an implicit criticism of Nicaea. Criticism made Nicaea's adherents fight for it and see its value.

Among the arguments for the Nicene Creed were the following:

1. The emperor ratified the decisions. Victorinus in 359 was the first to declare that Constantine confirmed the creed of Nicaea.

COUNCILS IN THE MID-FOURTH CENTURY

Place	Date	Creed	Position
Antioch	341	Dedication	Moderate, Anti-Sabellian
Sardica	343		Western bishops reaffirmed Nicaea; Eastern bishops condemned Athanasius
Antioch	344	Macrostich	*Homoios*; condemned Marcellus
Sirmium	351	First Sirmium	Opposed Photinus
Arles	353		Western bishops forced to abandon Athanasius
Sirmium	357	Blasphemy of Sirmium	*Homoousios* and *Homoiousios* condemned
Sirmium	359	Dated Creed	Son like the Father "in all respects"
Ariminum – Seleucia	359		*Homoios*

2. The bishop of Rome ratified the decisions. Documents were forged to that effect, and Damasus of Rome said Nicaea was authoritative because the bishop of Rome had confirmed it.

3. The bishops at Nicaea were good men, many of whom were confessors in the persecution.

4. The most influential consideration, surprising to modern students, was number symbolism.

We know the names of 220 signatories to the Nicene Creed. Eusebius says over 250 bishops attended. Athanasius at one time said about 300. But Hilary in the year 359, and then Athanasius himself, gave the number as 318 who approved the creed. The significance of this number was its correspondence to the number 318 for the servants of Abraham (Genesis 14:14), which had already been interpreted as a cipher for Jesus Christ and the cross (see on *Barnabas* in chapter 3). Hence, "the 318" bishops at Nicaea had confessed the full deity of Jesus Christ, who was crucified for human salvation.

It was not obvious in the 330s to 360s that the Nicene Creed was the one universal creed of Christendom. That it became so was largely the achievement of Athanasius.

B. Athanasius

Athanasius, one of the giants of church history, was born in a Christian home in Alexandria about 300. He studied under Peter the Martyr and was influenced by those who emphasized Origen's view of the common nature of Father and Son. As a deacon under bishop Alexander, he served as his secretary at the Council of Nicaea in 325. He succeeded Alexander as bishop of Alexandria in 328.

The vicissitudes of imperial and ecclesiastical politics are mirrored in Athanasius's five exiles from Alexandria:

1. 335–37, deposed by the Council of Tyre, he was sent by Constantine to Trier.

2. 339–46, banished by Constantius as still canonically deposed, he went to Rome.

3. 356–61, outlawed again by Constantius, he went into hiding among the monks in the deserts of Egypt, from which he was able to direct the affairs of his church.

4. 363, exiled by Julian, he was concealed again in Egypt.

5. 365–66, forced to leave the city by Valens, he found refuge once again in the Egyptian desert.

Each time changing political fortunes brought Athanasius back to the enthusiastic welcome of his parishioners. Nearly sixteen of his forty-five years in the episcopate were spent in exile. He died in 373.

The bulk of Athanasius's writings are polemical works dealing with the Arian controversy, the largest of which are the *Orations against the Arians* (two of the four are certainly genuine and probably the third) and *Apology against the Arians*. A good introduction to the issues is his *Defense of the Nicene Definition*, which defends the language of the Nicene Creed against criticisms, arguing that the affirmations are scriptural although not using the words of Scripture (the Arians too, Athanasius points out, used unscriptural words in presenting their views) and were in accord with earlier teaching in the church. The polemical works of Athanasius as well as those of other writers show how much the "Arian" controversy was a debate over the meaning of Scripture texts.

Two other works by Athanasius are notable. *On the Incarnation* sets forth Athanasius's basic theological position. He emphasizes the incarnation as the means of salvation. The reverse side of the incarnation is the view of salvation as deification. By Jesus Christ's presence in a body he is united with all, bringing truth and knowledge of the Father in place of ignorance and bringing immortal life in place of death.

For Athanasius, in his understanding of salvation as divinization, it was important that Jesus Christ is fully divine. Otherwise, the salvation he brought would be incomplete. This was the crucial soteriological concern that Athanasius brought to the Arian controversy.

The Arians' view of salvation was different. For them, Jesus Christ as a created being, and so subject to change, serves as an example of obedience and moral change for the better.

We can better appreciate the significance of the Arian controversy if we remember that it was not only a dispute about the metaphysical definition of the Godhead, but also was a struggle about the very nature of Christianity and human salvation.

For Athanasius, the incarnation included the death and resurrection of Jesus. Nevertheless, it may be said by way of generalization that Eastern theology gave more attention to the incarnation and Western theology to the crucifixion as the means of atonement. Neither gave the same centrality the New Testament does to the resurrection, although the resurrection was by no means neglected.

Two different eschatologies were at work: in the East a more realized eschatology in which Jesus Christ brought salvation now, and in the West a more futuristic eschatology in which the task now is to imitate the humble Jesus.

Regarding imitating the humble Jesus, Athanasius's *Life of Anthony* was very influential in advertising monastic ideals. Its translation into

> "He was made man that we might be made gods, and he manifested himself in a body that we might receive the idea of the unseen Father" (Athanasius, *On the Incarnation* 54.3).

Latin promoted monasticism in the West. Initially the Donatists and Arians identified with the rigorist elements in the church. Athanasius's treatment of Anthony, however, helped to keep the impulse to rigorism within the orthodox church. He presented the hermit Anthony as coming to Alexandria, rebuking Constantius, and speaking out on behalf of Nicene orthodoxy. After this, monks were brought into the doctrinal conflicts of the church.

The importance of Athanasius is bound up with the Nicene position, of which he became a symbol. The opponents of Nicaea brought many charges against him, and "sweet reasonableness" was not characteristic of him as a controversialist.

Athanasius's steadfastness and his writings blocked the Arians' progress and prepared for the eventual victory of the Nicene cause. In this respect his career is an illustration of the principle that issues are settled when someone convinces the majority. Of course, the majority are not necessarily right, and they may base their decisions on other reasons than the logical (or in Christian issues, the theological) merits of the respective positions.

Others besides Athanasius were important in the Nicene victory, and Athanasius's career certainly shows the difficulties under which he labored, but it is difficult to imagine the Nicene cause triumphing as completely as it did without him.

Statue of the emperor Julian, remembered by Christians as "the Apostate" (Baths of Cluny, Paris).

C. From 361 to 381

The accession of Julian the Apostate (361–63) to the imperial rule marked the turning point to the third phase of the Arian controversy. Although raised as a Christian, Julian reacted against the insincerity he saw around him. Keeping his sentiments private until he came to power, he became an earnest supporter of an enlightened pagan monotheism. His goal was a universal pagan monotheistic cultus.

In Julian's efforts to revivify paganism, Gregory of Nazianzus charged that he imitated Christians by urging the pagan priests to preach morals and to organize benevolence programs. Julian did not attempt direct persecution (although there were a few martyrs in the military), but he did seek to remove Christians from positions of privilege.

Julian allowed banished bishops to return to their sees, interpreted by some as a cynical move to destroy Christianity from within by fostering theological conflict. (If that was the purpose, little did he realize that theological debate is an expression of deeply held convictions and that Christians thrive on such conflict.)

At any rate, the result was that Julian's brief reign brought together the disparate elements favorable to Nicaea and opposed to the Homoean interpretation imposed by Constantius. Julian was killed in battle in Persia. Christian legend quoted his last words as, "O Galilean, Thou hast conquered."

Valentinian I (364–75) was a Catholic, but he believed the government should not interfere in matters of dogma. Associated with him as ruler in the East was Valens (364–78), who revived the Arian persecution of bishops. Gratian succeeded to rule in the West (375–83) and Theodosius I (379–95) in the East. The latter became for the orthodox a "second Constantine," whose decree of 380 declared the faith of bishop Damasus of Rome, and bishop Peter of Alexandria, the faith of the empire. Theodosius I also summoned the Council of Constantinople in 381.

During the third phase of the Arian conflict, four theological issues confronted church leaders:

1. The theological authority of the Council of Nicaea

The Athanasians called themselves "Nicenes" and developed the arguments noted above regarding the authority of the Nicene Creed. Some who agreed with the anti-Arian thrust of Nicaea, however, would not accept the Council or its wording as sacrosanct and irreversible.

2. The semantic problem

The terms *ousia* and *hypostasis* had been used interchangeably at Nicaea. The willingness of supporters of Nicaea to make semantic concessions was important to the resolution of the doctrinal uncertainties. A compromise emerged to use *ousia* for the common nature of the Father and Son and to use *hypostasis* for the individual identity of each.

3. The core problem of unity and distinction in the Godhead

The *homoiousian* party insisted that "like (or similar) substance" safeguarded the separateness of the three persons against Sabellianism, but went far enough in showing identity of substance. To say "same substance" meant for this group that there was no distinction and therefore encouraged Sabellianism.

4. The place of the Holy Spirit

Some Homoiousians would not grant to the third person of the Trinity what they did to the second person. They considered the Holy Spirit the chief of the angels. The earliest sources call them "Pneumatomachians" ("Those who fight against the Holy Spirit"). Athanasius also called them

"Tropicists" because they wanted to take literal passages about the "wind" metaphorically of the "Spirit." They were also called "Macedonians" after Macedonius, bishop of Constantinople, but his connection with this position is not proved. A leading figure was Eustathius of Sebaste.

Four men emerged as leaders in the settlement: Athanasius and Hilary of Poitiers from the Homoousians and the two Basils (of Ancyra and Caesarea in Cappadocia) from the Homoiousians. Hilary and Athanasius knew both Greek and Latin and so could clear up the confusion in the Trinitarian terminology employed in the two languages. Latin used *substantia* for the common "substance" or nature of the Godhead. The etymological equivalent in Greek was *hypostasis*, a word coming to be commonly used by the Homoiousians for the individual persons in the Godhead. Therefore, the impression was given to the Greeks that the Latins in saying "one substance" meant "one individual" and to the Latins that the Greeks were saying "three substances." A clarification of the different senses in which the two words were being used facilitated mutual understanding.

In regard to the difference among the Greeks themselves over the use of *ousia* and *hypostasis*, Basil of Ancyra agreed to use the Nicene term *homoousios* in the Homoiousian sense to protect the distinctions of the persons. Athanasius, for his part, said the common faith, not the wording, was important. At a synod in Alexandria in 362 he made his contribution to doctrinal unity by distinguishing *hypostasis* and *ousia*. The synod also affirmed, over against the Pneumatomachians, that the Holy Spirit is inseparable from the *ousia* of the Father and the Son.

The three great Cappadocian church fathers, Basil of Caesarea, Gregory of Nazianzus, and Gregory of Nyssa, sometimes called "Neonicenes," by building on the foundation laid by the Homoiousians, became the great theologians of the new synthesis. For them, the Father is the fount and cause of the other two co-equal Persons. They helped establish the terminology of *hypostasis* for the threeness and *ousia* for the oneness of the Trinity. Their theological expositions were the basis for the position endorsed by the second ecumenical council, Constantinople 381.

D. The Council of Constantinople, 381

Once a person allows for a plurality within the understanding of monotheism, something that Christian thinkers in the second and third centuries had come to do, there was no necessity that a Trinity would be the result. The biblical data, not logical or theoretical considerations, determined that three entities were described as God, not two or four.

The Council of Constantinople, called by the emperor Theodosius in 381, was not immediately considered ecumenical. In fact, we are poorly informed on its proceedings, and evidence for its creed is confused. The council affirmed that its creed was the same as Nicaea's, but the creed that has been handed down as approved by this council is fuller than the creed adopted at Nicaea and omits its anathemas. This is the creed recited in many churches as the "Nicene Creed"; more accurately, it is the "Nicaeno-Constantinopolitan Creed."

A problem occurs because the text of the creed is quoted in a work of Epiphanius dated before the council. Either the council approved an already existing creed, or (more likely) a scribe substituted the form of the creed with which he was more familiar for the text in Epiphanius.

The council's creed reaffirmed that the Son was consubstantial (*homoousios*) with the Father and confirmed the divinity of the Holy Spirit.

The council anathematized the Eunomians (Neoarians), Pneumatomachians, Sabellians, the followers of Marcellus and Photinus, and the Apollinarians (see chapter 13).

Among other decisions was a canon that gave to the bishop of Constantinople the prerogative of honor after that of the bishop of Rome, "because Constantinople is New Rome," a decision that foreshadowed later controversy between Rome and Constantinople over the basis of their prerogatives (chapter 13).

Theodosius's edicts after the council made the pro-Nicene version of the Christian faith the official religion of the empire.

The church of Hagia Eirene (St. Irene), on the site of the Second Ecumenical Council, AD 381, in Constantinople (Istanbul), Turkey.

> ## NICAENO–CONSTANTINOPOLITAN CREED
>
> We believe in one God the Father All-sovereign, Maker of heaven and earth, and of all things visible and invisible;
>
> and in one Lord Jesus Christ, the only-begotten Son of God, begotten of the Father before all the ages, Light of Light, true God of true God, begotten not made, of one substance with the Father, through whom all things were made; who for us men and for our salvation came down from the heavens, and was made flesh of the Holy Spirit and the virgin Mary, and became man, and was crucified for us under Pontius Pilate and suffered and was buried, and rose again on the third day according to the Scriptures, and ascended into the heavens, and sits on the right hand of the Father, and comes again with glory to judge living and dead, of whose kingdom there shall be no end;
>
> and in the Holy Spirit, the Lord and the Life-giver, that proceeds from the Father, who with Father and Son is worshipped together and glorified together, who spoke through the prophets;
>
> in one holy catholic and apostolic church;
>
> we acknowledge one baptism unto remission of sins;
>
> we look for a resurrection of the dead, and the life of the age to come.

Why did the Nicenes (albeit in the modified form of the Neo-nicenes) win the doctrinal debates? Why did Christians pick out certain councils as authoritative and not others? It was a matter of reception—by whom and how.

Gregory of Nazianzus, for instance, considered the small synod assembled at Alexandria in 362 as Athanasius's finest achievement. Nicaea is a paradigm of the problem of the authority of councils. Its supporters succeeded because the majority decided this was the right way to express the *consensus fidelium* ("agreement of the faithful").

In practical terms, other creeds did not win because they did not have Athanasius and Rome for them. That does not mean, however, that Athanasius and Rome got all they wanted. They supported Paulinus's claims as bishop of Antioch, for instance, but the majority of Eastern churches backed Meletius as bishop of Antioch.

II. ORGANIZATION OF THE CHURCH

The fourth century saw an increasing institutionalizing and intellectualizing of the church. The processes had begun before, but the organizational developments and the literature produced made the fourth century a significant period for the church and its culture.

The fourth-century Trinitarian debates were marked by a large number of church councils, many of which were called for specific purposes and did not fit the regular pattern of councils that came to prevail. Synods of bishops had been meeting since the latter part of the second century to deal with common problems (like Montanism) or to settle disputes (like the observance of Easter).

Before the fourth century the bishop of a city and his presbyters would have been together often, but with the growth of the church the bishop was expected to call together his clergy several times a year—a diocesan or parochial council.

During the third century councils on a regional level became a common feature of organized church life.

The Council of Nicaea required bishops of a province to come together twice a year under the presidency of the bishop of the metropolitan or mother church—a provincial synod. Rome for Italy, Carthage for North Africa, Alexandria for Egypt, and Antioch for Syria already in the third century were seen as having a jurisdiction larger than a province, and Nicaea recognized such expanded jurisdictions. These arrangements anticipated the later patriarchal synods, first notably in the case of Alexandria's leadership in Egypt and neighboring territories.

Nicaea was the first of the councils that came to be recognized as ecumenical, representing the universal church. The Council of Chalcedon in 451 defined which councils up to its time were to be so acknowledged. A special kind of council developed at Constantinople, the *synodos endemousa*, the permanent holy synod of Constantinople. After Constantinople became the capital of the empire, several bishops from other places would be in the capital at any given time. The emperor would convene a council of the local clergy and whatever visiting bishops were available in order to advance his concerns.

When councils dealt with matters of faith, their statements were known as "symbols" or "dogmas." Decisions in regard to organizational, disciplinary, or procedural matters were known as "canons."

The fourth century saw greater refinement in the differentiation of clergy beyond the three-fold ministry of the second century. Already in the mid-third century the church at Rome boasted of having forty-six presbyters, seven deacons, seven sub-deacons, forty-two acolytes, fifty-two exorcists, readers, and doorkeepers, and about 1,500 widows on the roll. Few other churches were so large, but most cities required the development of a parish system. The bishop became more of an administrator, and the local pastoral care and liturgical leadership passed to presbyters.

Rural areas near a city were served by a presbyter, a deacon, or a "rural bishop" (*chorepiscopus*)—a functionary known mainly in the

East in the fourth century, who was dependent on the city bishop and limited in his right to ordain.

The ranking of bishops was determined by two factors: the mission methods of the early church, by which the gospel spread from cities on major trade routes to surrounding regions, and the meeting of synods for dealing with common problems. The metropolitan was usually the bishop in the capital of the political province, where the emperor had his official representative, but in some cases the bishop of another city had seniority as the first church in the province. The metropolitan could also be called archbishop, which became the normal term in the West from the tenth century. Nicaea recognized four bishops with an authority greater than that of a metropolitan—the bishops of Rome, Alexandria, Antioch, and Caesarea. From these special jurisdictions emerged the patriarchs, not fully in place until the fifth century, and not usually called patriarchs until the sixth.

The influence of Ambrose, Jerome, and Augustine made celibacy virtually obligatory in the West on all clerics in major orders. Increasingly in the fourth and fifth centuries bishops were chosen from among the monks, in both East and West, and under Justinian celibacy was imposed on bishops in the East. The privileges granted by the state from the fourth century on tended to make the clergy even more a class apart, a feature enhanced by drawing bishops from the higher social classes.

From the fourth and fifth centuries the clergy began to wear special clothes, at first in the liturgy only. The change in clerical garments was especially the result of failure to keep up with changing fashions in secular life, as the clergy continued to wear long Greco-Roman tunics and cloaks and laymen adopted Germanic trousers. Toward the fifth century clergy took over the tonsure of monks. Celibacy and distinctive attire were a part of an increasing "monasticizing" of the clergy (see chapter 12 on monasticism), at least in the ideal.

III. THE FATHERS OF THE NICENE AND POST-NICENE CHURCH

The century and a quarter from Nicaea (325) to Chalcedon (451) is the "Golden Age of Patristic Literature." In quantity and quality of literature this was the flowering period of the ancient church. There is nothing comparable again until the twelfth and thirteenth centuries. Hence the fourth and early fifth centuries form one of the better known periods in church history. This "great patristic century" provides a fixed point in the discussion of almost any topic, for we enter a period of full light.

On many matters the formulations reached during this time dominated the Christian approach for the succeeding centuries. The thinkers and writers of this period—especially Augustine in the Latin West and the three Cappadocians (Basil, Gregory of Nazianzus, and Gregory of Nyssa) in the Greek East—laid the intellectual foundations for the Christianization of classical culture.

The Roman Catholic Church recognizes eight great doctors of the church from the patristic period: four Latin writers—Ambrose, Jerome, Augustine, and Gregory the Great; and four Greek writers—Athanasius, Gregory of Nazianzus, Basil the Great, and John Chrysostom. All but Gregory the Great fall in the period under consideration. Some of these receive fuller treatment elsewhere (Athanasius, Augustine, Gregory the Great). The remainder, plus a few other important writers, receive some biographical treatment here.

GREEK PATRISTIC WRITERS, 4TH – 5TH CENTURIES

Name	Dates	Country	Importance
Eusebius of Caesarea	260 – 339	Palestine	Church historian; apologist; moderate Origenist
Athanasius	c. 300 – 373	Egypt	Champion of Nicaea
Cyril of Jerusalem	d. 387	Palestine	Bishop; catechetical lectures
Basil of Caesarea	330 – 79	Cappadocia	Ecclesiastical statesman
Gregory of Nazianzus	329 – 90	Cappadocia	Orator and theologian
Gregory of Nyssa	331 – 95	Cappadocia	Philosophical theologian
John Chrysostom	347 – 407	Syria	Preacher
Cyril of Alexandria	375 – 444	Egypt	Theologian and ecclesiastical statesman

LATIN PATRISTIC WRITERS, 4TH – 5TH CENTURIES

Name	Dates	Country	Importance
Hilary of Poitiers	315 – 67	Gaul	"Athanasius of the West"
Ambrose	339 – 97	Italy	Ecclesiastical statesman
Ambrosiaster	4th cent.	Italy	Commentator on the Bible
Rufinus	345 – 410	Italy	Translator
Jerome	347 – 420	Italy	Translator of the Bible and champion of monasticism
Augustine	354 – 430	North Africa	Most influential Latin theologian
John Cassian	365 – 433	Gaul	Mediator of Eastern theology and monasticism to the West
Vincent of Lerins	5th cent.	Gaul	Doctrine of tradition

A. Basil the Great of Caesarea

The three great Cappadocians—Basil and the two Gregories—represent the height of Christian culture in the fourth century, a uniting of Greek literary and rhetorical education with a deep Christian faith and loyalty to the church.

Cappadocia was once regarded as backward, and in the fourth century part of it was still within a century of its evangelization. Yet this region in the fourth century moved to the forefront of the Christian intellectual enterprise and to a position of leadership in the affairs of the church. Although gifted in many areas, Basil was foremost as an administrator and ecclesiastical statesman among the Cappadocians.

Born around 330, Basil came from one of the outstanding Christian families of the region. His father, a rhetorician at Neocaesara in Pontus, was the son of Macrina the elder, a convert of Gregory Thaumaturgus. His mother, Emmelia, was the daughter of a martyr in the Diocletian persecution. These parents had ten children, of whom three

Mosaic (twelfth century) of Basil the Great and John Chrysostom in the Palatine Chapel, Palermo, Italy.

sons became bishops (Basil, Gregory of Nyssa, and Peter of Sebaste) and their eldest daughter (Macrina) became a model of the ascetic life. Besides his father's instruction, Basil studied at Caesarea in Cappadocia, where he became a friend of Gregory of Nazianzus, as well as at Constantinople and Athens.

Back home, Basil's career as a rhetorician was short, for a spiritual awakening and a journey to Egypt and Palestine to meet ascetics led to his baptism. He divided his fortune among the poor and went into solitude at Annesi near Neocaesarea. He was soon surrounded by companions and a monastery began, for which he drew up his monastic rules. In 364 he was ordained a priest at Cappadocian Caesarea and in 370 became its bishop.

As bishop, Basil became a pioneer in establishing Christian benevolent institutions—homes for the poor, hospices for travelers, and hospitals. The latter was anticipated by Eustathius, bishop of Sebaste (356–80). These three Christian benevolent institutions became common in the fifth and sixth centuries.

Basil stood his ground in the Arian controversy, successfully resisting efforts at his banishment, and began the literary refutation of the Neoarian Eunomius. He worked for unity among the opponents of Arianism and for better understanding between the Eastern and Western churches. His doctrinal treatises, letters, and sermons laid the basis for the theological accomplishments of the two Gregories.

B. Gregory of Nazianzus

Gregory of Nazianzus was the greatest orator of his day, but he is distinguished in the Orthodox tradition by the designation "The Theologian." Like Basil, who was about the same age, Gregory came from a wealthy aristocratic family. He shared with Basil a desire to unite ascetic piety with literary culture, but unlike Basil, his preference for quiet contemplation left no taste for the active ecclesiastical life. Gregory's accommodating disposition gave a lack of resoluteness, however, allowing him to be drawn into various positions of responsibility and leadership for which he had little liking.

Other lovers of reading and contemplation can identify with Gregory's sentiment, "Quiet and freedom from affairs is more precious than the splendor of a busy life" (*Epistle* 131). Recurrent bad health also limited his involvement in responsibilities to which he was called. His life is characterized by a succession of flights from and returns to the world.

Gregory was born at Arianzum, near Nazianzus, where his father was later bishop. His mother, Nonna, was the daughter of Christian parents and was responsible for the conversion of her husband and the early religious training of her son, as we learn from Gregory's tribute to her many abilities.

Gregory studied at Cappadocian Caesarea, Caesarea in Palestine, Alexandria, and Athens. After his studies, he returned to Cappadocia and was baptized. He joined Basil in his retirement in 358–59, where together they worked on the *Philocalia*, excerpts from Origen's writings (preserving the Greek of many passages otherwise known only from Latin translation), and on Basil's monastic rules.

Very much against his will, Gregory's father ordained him a presbyter in 361. In 371 Basil ordained him bishop of the small town of Sasima, as part of his program of appointing supporters throughout the province in order to strengthen his eccesiastical influence, but Gregory never obtained possession of the see. In 374 he took over the see of Nazianzus but a year later he retired to the region of Isauria. A call

With regard to philosophy, Gregory of Nazianzus said, "Avoid the thorns; pluck the roses" (*Letter to Seleucus* 1.61), and on its relation to faith, "For faith according to us gives fullness to reason" (*Orations* 29.21).

came in 379 to become preacher for the small orthodox congregation in Constantinople.

At the Council of Constantinople in 381 Gregory was appointed bishop of the capital, but he resigned during the council because of opposition claiming it was uncanonical for a bishop to transfer to another see. He took charge of the church at Nazianzus until 384, when he again went into retirement until his death.

Gregory is best known for his *Orations*, especially the five theological orations, in which he clearly and persuasively set forth the Cappadocians' understanding of the Trinity. Within the one God three individuations can be distinguished according to their modes of existence. These distinctions are derived from biblical language: the Father is ungenerate, the Son is generated, and the Holy Spirit proceeds from the Father through the Son.

Gregory was less successful as a poet, using classical forms with a Christian content, but his autobiographical poems are quite revealing. His letters, too, reproduce classical style.

Mosaic (eleventh century) of Gregory of Nyssa in the monastery of Hagios Loukas, Greece.

C. Gregory of Nyssa

Born in Pontus in the early 330s, Gregory was named for Gregory Thaumaturgus, whose life he was later to write. His grandmother Macrina, mother Emmelia, and sister Macrina were formative home influences, and his education came primarily from his older brother Basil. He was appointed a reader in the church, became a teacher of rhetoric, and was probably married. Basil's example as a bishop and his mother's death may have turned Gregory to a more committed church life.

Learned in philosophy, rhetoric, and medicine, Gregory of Nyssa is remembered as the philosophical theologian of the Cappadocians, effecting a synthesis of Greek philosophy and Christian theology. His Christian Platonism transformed philosophy according to Christian presuppositions.

Basil appointed Gregory bishop of the small town of Nyssa in 372. Gregory reluctantly accepted the position, and appropriately so, for he showed a lack of firmness in dealing with people and an unfitness for church politics. His carelessness with financial affairs gave Arians occasion to charge misappropriation of church funds, and he was deposed by a synod in 376 and banished by the emperor Valens.

Recalled along with other banished bishops by Gratian in 378, Gregory returned to a triumphant welcome by his church. His main period of literary activity came after Basil's death in 379. Gregory attended the Council of Constantinople in 381, and the emperor Theodosius named him among those bishops with whose doctrine on the Trinity all should agree.

In addition to his contributions to Trinitarian thought, Gregory of Nyssa is important for making the distinction between the Creator and the created the basis of his metaphysics, for his distinction between what humanity is by nature and what it may become by participation in the divine life, for his clear affirmation of the infinity of God (his most distinctive contribution to Christian thought), and for his development of the ransom theory of the atonement.

According to Gregory's explanation of the atonement, the devil, after seeing the miracles of Jesus Christ, chose him as the ransom price for humanity. The veil of humanity prevented the devil from recognizing Christ's deity, so the devil was not able to keep him in his power. The deceiver was thus deceived and God's justice was strictly served.

Gregory of Nyssa influenced greatly the moral and spiritual theology of the Eastern church. He defined perfection in the spiritual life as always making progress in virtue. Perpetual progress in perfection is the human corollary of the divine infinity. Perfection cannot be attained by human free will and effort alone. Instead, divine grace comes in to help and complete human moral efforts.

The relationship between patristic Christianity and Greek culture, usually phrased as the question of the Hellenization of Christianity, is typified in the interpretations of Gregory of Nyssa. Gregory knew directly the Platonic tradition through acquaintance with the writings of Plato and Plotinus and perhaps even more through influence from Porphyry, and he knew Stoicism from Posidonius and those elements of Stoicism that had been absorbed in Neoplatonism. This circumstance led to the view that Gregory was a Hellenizer of Christianity.

The growing consensus of contemporary scholarship, however, is that Gregory's theology makes him one of the most successful Christianizers of Hellenism. Few Christian thinkers knew Greek philosophy as well as he did. Even fewer transcended it as completely as he did. Like other Cappadocian thinkers, Gregory thought Greek philosophy could contribute positively to the exposition of Christian doctrine.

"For the perfection of human nature consists perhaps in its very growth in goodness" (Gregory of Nyssa, *Life of Moses* 1.10).

D. John Chrysostom

John was born about 347 at Antioch. His mother, Anthusa, lost her husband when she was twenty and John was an infant. She renounced another marriage and devoted herself to her son. She provided him with the best education possible, both in Scripture and in the classics. For the latter, John studied under the most famous pagan rhetorician of the time, Libanius, who paid Anthusa the compliment, "God, what women these Christians have!"

Baptized at the age of eighteen, John became a reader in the church. He was drawn to the ascetic life and spent two years in a mountain cave, an experience that ruined his health. Back in Antioch, he was ordained a deacon in 381 and a presbyter in 386. In the latter capacity he served as the preacher in the principal church in the city until 397.

Over time, John established his fame as the greatest of Christian pulpit orators and expositors. His designation Chrysostom ("Golden Mouth") has been current since the sixth century. His typical method was to preach through a biblical book, a passage at a time, first giving an exposition of the main points in the text, and then going back through it with application to his hearers. He had a gift for seeing the meaning of the text and how to make an immediate and practical application of it.

Constantinople often looked to Antioch to find its theological and ecclesiastical leaders, and in 397 John was chosen bishop of Constantinople and consecrated to that office in 398. It proved to be a great personal misfortune. His efforts to raise the moral tone of the capital met with strong opposition. After he had six bishops deposed, his enemies joined forces: the empress Eudoxia and local clergy, who resented his preaching against luxury, and Theophilus, bishop of Alexandria, who was jealous of an Antiochian at the capital.

When Theophilus was summoned to answer charges by some monks and Chrysostom presided over the court, Theophilus resolved to destroy him. Thirty-six bishops met at the "Synod of the Oak" outside Chalcedon. Chrysostom refused three times to answer its summons to appear, and the synod declared him deposed in 403. The emperor accepted the decision and exiled John. The people of Constantinople rioted, and the emperor, frightened by the people's response, recalled John the next day.

Chrysostom's preaching angered Eudoxia again. The Gospel text on the beheading of John the Baptist occasioned Chrysostom's undiplomatic remark, "Once more Herodias demands the head of John on a platter."

Chrysostom's enemies sought his banishment for unlawfully resuming the duties of a see from which he had been canonically deposed. Their argument: a synod of bishops could depose a bishop from office; the emperor could exile or recall from exile, but could not

"Everything done by God is full of both righteousness and loving-kindness. If he had demanded righteousness only, then everything would have been destroyed; but if he had employed only loving-kindness, then the majority of people would have become indifferent. Varying his approach to the salvation of human beings, he employed both of these for their correction" (John Chrysostom, *Commentary on Psalms* 111.6 on Psalms 111:7).

put a person back into office. Chrysostom, however, did not recognize the bishops' jurisdiction.

The emperor then ordered Chrysostom to cease performing ecclesiastical functions, but he refused to do so. While he was gathering catechumens for baptism, soldiers showed up and drove him from the church. The soldiers' violence ended up staining the baptismal waters with blood.

Chrysostom remained in exile from 404 until his death in 407. In 438 his remains were brought back to Constantinople and interred in the Church of the Apostles.

E. Ephraem the Syrian

The classic writer of the Syriac-speaking church is Ephraem (c. 306–73), from Nisibis and later Edessa, where he established a school and formed a women's choir. His prose works include commentaries on biblical books, notably on Tatian's *Diatessaron*, sermons, and refutations of heretics, but he is especially honored for his metrical homilies and hymns, for which he is called the "Harp of the Holy Spirit."

Ephraem represents a basically pre-Nicene (but anti-Arian) Semitic Christianity, so much so that all branches of later Syriac Christianity looked back to him as a spiritual teacher. Drawing his imagery from both nature and the Bible, Ephraem's rich and suggestive language

> "Who, Lord, can gaze on your hiddenness
> which has come to revelation? Yes, your obscurity
> has come to manifestation and notification; your concealed Being
> has come out into the open, without limitation.
> Your awesome self has come into the hands
> of those who seized you.
> All this happened to you, Lord,
> because you became a human being.
> Praises to him who sent you.
> Yet who will not fear
> because, even though your Epiphany is revealed
> and so too your human birth,
> your birth from the Father remains unattainable;
> it has baffled all those who investigate it."
>
> (Ephraem the Syrian, *Hymn on Faith* 51.2–3,
> Sebastian Brock translation)

The Church in the Fourth Century

finds all reality as providing symbols of spiritual truth. He integrated theological commitment with spirituality, orthodox faith with worshipful humility. His hymnody influenced Byzantine hymnody through Romanus Melodus (sixth century).

In an age when Greek theologians split churches over terminology to describe the Godhead, Ephraem defended the essential mystery of God. Rather than use philosophy, he found poetry (as deeper if less precise) to be a more suitable vehicle for expressing theological discourse.

F. Ambrose

Ambrose is a doctor of the church in special reference to his teaching on the proper relationship of church and state.

A Greek in education, Ambrose also contributed to the Western exposition of the Trinity and to moral theology.

Born in Trier, Ambrose was the son of the praetorian prefect of Gaul. He studied law and was appointed governor of Aemilia-Liguria at Milan. In 374 he was elected bishop of Milan, although an unbaptized catechumen, through an unprecedented set of circumstances.

At the time there was a sharp dispute between the Arian and Catholic factions over the election of a new bishop. The story goes that when Ambrose stepped into the pulpit to restore order, a young child, seeing him in the position usually occupied by the bishop, called out, "Ambrose, bishop!" The congregation, remembering that "A little child shall lead them," took the voice as the will of God. Ambrose took some persuading, but finally he too acknowledged the call of God, received baptism from the Catholic clergy, and a week later ordination as bishop.

Ambrose was involved in four conflicts with the Roman government.

> "The emperor indeed is within the church, not above the church" (*Sermon against Auxentius* 36).

1. In 384 the senate requested restoration of the altar dedicated to the goddess Victory that the emperor Gratian had removed two years before. Ambrose influenced the emperor Valentinian II to reject the restoration of this symbol of paganism to the traditional seat of Roman government.

2. In 385–86 Ambrose successfully maintained orthodox possession of a basilica in Milan that the Arians, at the instigation of Valentinian II's mother Justina, requested for their use. Ambrose organized a "sit-in" by the orthodox, whose spirits he maintained by hymn singing, until the emperor's troops withdrew.

3. In 388 a Jewish synagogue was destroyed by rioting Christians and the emperor Theodosius demanded that Christians rebuild it. Ambrose successfully opposed this order on the grounds that Christian money could not be used to build a Jewish synagogue.

4. In 390 Theodosius ordered the massacre of 6,000 to 7,000 citizens of Thessalonica for sedition after a riot resulted in the murder of several imperial officials. When Theodosius appeared at church in Milan, Ambrose refused him communion until he did penance for the executions. Theodosius, unlike his predecessors, was already baptized and thus subject to the discipline of the church.

Mosaic (fifth century) of Ambrose in the church of San Ambrogio, Milan.

Ambrose achieved the success he did because he had the Christian populace behind him and the emperors themselves were devoted Christians (moreover, Gratian and Valentinian II were young). It was through the emperors' personal faith that Ambrose influenced state policy. He had a spiritual view of the church and did not aim at a state church, but that was virtually the result.

Decisions Ambrose reached with a religious motive appear intolerant now, especially the rebuilding of the synagogue. Less intolerant is the episode of the altar of the goddess Victory, for the issue was not religious toleration, per se, but a symbol of paganism at the center of government.

Ambrose formulated a theory of two powers—civil and ecclesiastical—but in his actions he represented an authority of the church over the state, and that became the significance of his precedent in the Middle Ages. Yet Ambrose had a different conception of the church from those in the Middle Ages who looked to his example, for he was not seeking political power for the church.

There are other notable things in Ambrose's career. His treatise *On the Duties of the Clergy* was an influential work on the pastoral role of priests. The title (*De officiis*) was borrowed from a work on ethics by Cicero, but Ambrose makes clear the Christian differences. The *sacerdos* (still usually the bishop) was also a *prophētēs* (prophet) who must rebuke while guiding the people in moral conduct. His *De Fide* was an important contribution to the Latin doctrine of the Trinity. Indeed, Ambrose's position as bishop of Milan made him more important than the bishop of Rome in the church's victory over paganism and Arianism in the West.

Ambrose was an able preacher whose expositions of Scripture had a part in the conversion of Augustine, something that in itself would have earned him a place in church history. He promoted the cult of the relics and was one of the first to transfer relics to a place beneath the altar of a church. He also promoted the ascetic ideal for virgins and clergy. His liturgical activity included the writing of hymns and the introduction of Greek antiphonal singing to the West.

His *On the Mysteries* and *On the Sacraments* (his authorship of the latter, although questioned, is to be accepted) are important in liturgical history for the rites of Christian initiation. He is an early witness to the metabolic theory of the eucharist in which the bread and wine are changed by consecration into the body and blood of Christ.

The manuscript tradition attributes to Ambrose a commentary on the epistles of Paul by an anonymous writer of the fourth century to whom modern scholars have given the name Ambrosiaster. This person was also the author of a work on *Questions on the Old and New Testaments* transmitted under the name of Augustine. From his works we can gather that he probably served in the imperial court and had contacts with Judaism. He used the Old Latin version of the Bible instead of Jerome's new translation.

Ambrosiaster opposed Damasus, bishop of Rome, who sought to bring the practices of the church into conformity with its new role as a state religion and adopted a corresponding lifestyle. Instead, Ambrosiaster insisted that the bishop should live in humility, not in the glory of the emperor. He also pointed out that in the New Testament there was no difference between a bishop and a presbyter.

G. Rufinus

A native of Aquileia, Rufinus studied in Rome and traveled in the east visiting monks. He joined with Melania in setting up a double monastery for men and women at Jerusalem. Returning to Aquileia, he became a presbyter there in 399.

Rufinus's principal contribution was as a translator of Greek works into Latin: Origen's *On First Principles*, the Pseudo-Clementine *Recognitions*, Eusebius's *Church History*, and other works. An important original work is his *Commentary on the Apostles' Creed*.

Rufinus was involved in a bitter controversy with Jerome over the orthodoxy of Origen, whom Rufinus defended. He had the effrontery to point out Jerome's earlier dependence on Origen, a fact that irritated Jerome's thin skin.

A painting (c. 1400) of Jerome, Gregory the Great, Ambrose, and Augustine by Stephano di Giovanni (Sienna, Italy).

H. Jerome

The two men above both incurred Jerome's wrath, but that hardly makes them distinctive, for Jerome was peevish and ill-tempered. His life story is that of fallings out with associates and controversies over religious issues of the time.

Jerome was born in Dalmatia to Christian parents, who gave him a good education. He was baptized in Rome toward the end of his student days. About 370 he was part of an ascetic group in Aquileia, but it broke up and he went East.

During an illness at Antioch Jerome had a dream in which he was rebuked as "a Ciceronian, not a Christian." He resolved to give up his classical studies and devote himself to Christian writing, but the renunciation of pagan learning was not as absolute as he professed, for his work continued to show the influence of classical authors.

Withdrawing to the desert as a hermit (*Epistle* 22.7), Jerome learned Hebrew. His fellow hermits disliked his company, however, so Jerome went back to Antioch, where the bishop of the Nicene community, Paulinus, ordained him a presbyter.

Back in Rome in 382, Jerome was set to work by Damasus on a new Latin translation of the Psalms and the New Testament. The literal and unliterary character of the Old Latin versions of the Bible offended many educated persons, and Damasus wanted the best for the church. Jerome promoted asceticism, declaring that "all who are afraid to sleep alone should have wives" (*Epistle* 50.5).

"I praise marriage because it brings virgins into the world" (Jerome, *Epistle* 22.20).

Among Jerome's supporters was a circle around the wealthy Paula and her three daughters. Jerome's attacks on luxury and on a less than ascetic lifestyle provoked opposition from the clergy, and his disappointment over the election of Siricius as bishop led him to leave Rome in 385. With Paula he toured Palestine, and they settled at Bethlehem, establishing dual monasteries for men and women. Thus began his most fruitful period of studying and writing.

Although living in Palestine, Jerome remained essentially a westerner. He wanted to appear orthodox, but he did not care for the details of Eastern theological controversy. He hoped to be a Christian Cicero, a comprehensive teacher of Christian culture, and in addition be a monk and a saint. Although committed to the philosophical and outward ideal of asceticism, however, Jerome was not really a monk at heart. The inconsistency of his ideals, it has been suggested, reached to the roots of his being, driving him to relentless work and perhaps explaining some of the contradictions of his character.

Jerome was drawn into a series of controversies involving asceticism and the ecclesiastical issues of the day, writing against: (1) Helvidius, who denied the perpetual virginity of Mary; (2) Jovinian, who denied that monasticism was a superior form of the Christian life; (3) Vigilantius, who denied the cult of the martyrs; (4) Rufinus, who supported Origen's orthodoxy; and (5) Pelagius, who supported the possibility of human sinlessness. In each case the positions Jerome championed, albeit with exaggeration and bitter invective, ended up prevailing in the Catholic church.

It is as a literary man that Jerome is remembered. His outstanding contribution to the future of Western Christendom was the Latin translation of the Bible. Although not immediately winning general acceptance, it became the common version and hence is known now as the Vulgate.

Unlike the Old Latin versions, which translated the Old Testament from the Greek Septuagint, Jerome translated from the Hebrew, giving his translation a value as an independent witness to the Hebrew text of his day. His knowledge of the Hebrew Scriptures led him to reject the Apocrypha from the canon. Under pressure from his friends, he did translate (although hurriedly) some of the Apocryphal books, all of which books came to be included in the Vulgate.

Jerome made other translations of Greek Christian authors, and wrote a number of commentaries on biblical books. These drew heavily on earlier Greek commentators, including Origen. As time went on, the "mystical" interpretation was increasingly crowded out by historical and philological exposition. He did employ typology in interpreting the

Old Testament. He affirmed that Scripture contained no contradictions and was infallible, but he did not develop a hermeneutic of his own.

Although Jerome was committed to the original languages in which the Bible was written, he recognized the pastoral responsibility of the interpreter: "We have the obligation to expound the Scripture as it is read in church, and yet we must not, on the other hand, abandon the truth of the Hebrew" (*Commentary on Micah* 1.16).

The extensive correspondence of Jerome is a window into his personality and into the life and controversies of the time. To single out a few of his letters, *Epistle* 15 to Damasus illustrates the semantic problem between Greek and Latin in the Trinitarian discussions; *Epistle* 146, written against the presumptions of the Roman deacons, testifies to the original identity of presbyters and bishops in the New Testament; *Epistles* 107 and 128 give instruction on education; and *Epistles* 22 and 130 promote virginity.

Jerome's *Lives of Illustrious Men* is the first history of Christian literature. His lives of the monks Paul, Hilarion, and Malchus are his most polished works from a stylistic point of view, but their historical core is minimal.

Jerome always wrote with emphasis. His works were haphazard (he often wrote too fast), but he was extremely erudite (although much of his learning was secondhand). He read extensively and had a tremendous memory; without his works much information would be lost to us now.

Despite his personality—described as bitter, vindictive, vain, and inconsistent—Jerome's scholarship left future centuries in his debt.

IV. THE IMPORTANCE OF THE BIBLE

The dominance of these figures, and others to be noted in subsequent chapters, within the Greek, Latin, and Syriac churches should not blind the student to the centrality of the Bible in all aspects of the early church and in the theology and spirituality of these men.

For nearly all these leaders the major part of their surviving writings are commentaries on biblical books or homilies preached on them. Their doctrinal controversies were argued in terms of biblical interpretation. The Bible was important in all expressions of spirituality—inspiring martyrdom, guiding prayer and meditation, supplying a source of wisdom for ascetics, and providing themes for art.

The Scriptures especially were the focal point of the liturgical assemblies, where large segments were read. The earliest lectionary that we know was developed in Jerusalem at the end of the fourth and beginning of the fifth century, but in the following centuries lectionary texts were produced in profusion and are now one of the sources for the textual criticism of the Bible.

Moreover, all the Church Fathers of the fourth century promoted the ascetic lifestyle as the highest and most authentic form of the Christian life, even if they themselves were presbyters and bishops instead of monks. To that development we now turn.

FOR FURTHER STUDY

Allen, Pauline. *The Heavenly Trumpet: John Chrysostom and the Art of Pauline Interpretation*. Tübingen: Mohr, 2000.

Ayres, Lewis. *Nicaea and Its Legacy*. Oxford: Oxford University Press, 2004.

Barnes, Michel. *The Power of God in Gregory of Nyssa's Trinitarian Theology*. Washington: Catholic University of America Press, 2001.

Brock, Sebastian. *The Luminous Eye: The Spiritual World Vision of St. Ephrem*. Rev. ed. Kalamazoo, MI: Cistercian Press, 1992.

Gwynn, D. M. *Athanasius of Alexandria: Bishop, Theologian, Ascetic, Father*. Oxford: Oxford University Press. 2011.

Hanson, R. P. C. *The Search for the Christian Doctrine of God: The Arian Controversy 318–381*. Edinburgh: T & T Clark, 1988.

Kelly, J. N. D. *Jerome: His Life, Writings, and Controversies*. San Francisco: Harper & Row, 1975.

McGuckin, John Anthony. *St. Gregory of Nazianzus: An Intellectual Biography*. Crestwood, NY: St. Vladimir's Seminary Press, 2001.

Meredith, Anthony. *The Cappadocians*. London: Chapman, 1995.

Mitchell, Margaret M. *The Heavenly Trumpet: John Chrysostom and the Art of Pauline Interpretation*. Louisville: Westminster John Knox, 2002.

Moorhead, J. *Ambrose: Church and Society in the Late Roman World*. London: Longman, 1999.

Raddle-Gallwitz, A. *Basil of Caesarea: A Guide to His Life and Doctrine*. Eugene, OR: Cascade, 2012.

Young, Frances. *From Nicaea to Chalcedon: A Guide to the Literature and Its Background*. Philadelphia: Fortress, 1983.

Monasticism, Expansion, Life, and Worship

The Church in the Fourth Century

The greater abundance of literature from the fourth and early fifth century make this period a convenient time to review some major developments in the early history of Christianity. This was a significant period in regard to monasticism, missionary expansion, the relation of Christianity to Roman society, and the elaboration of the liturgy.

I. MONASTICISM

A. Origins

In its monastic expression, Christianity has close approximations to some other world religions, most notably Buddhism.

Tributaries of Christian monasticism include the following:

1. Jewish

Judaism, although generally non-ascetic in its approach to life, in the first century included some ascetic strands. We know of celibate Essenes and, perhaps related to them, the Therapeutae in Egypt, who maintained a separation of male and female members. Moreover, some of the Old Testament prophets and later figures like John the Baptist offered potential models of solitary, seemingly homeless religious life.

2. Pagan

Pythagoreans were vegetarians and exercised a disciplined life that may have been the model for the Therapeutae. The Gnostics typically viewed matter as evil. Some Cynics "denied the world" in an uncompromising protest against the norms of society.

3. Eastern

The Manichaeans may have provided precedents of celibate communities. The Hellenistic world was also intrigued by reports of the gymnosophists (naked wise men), holy men in India.

4. New Testament

Jesus' sayings, such as "sell your possessions and give to the poor" (Matthew 19:21), had a great influence in monastic circles. Jesus and the Twelve became images of ideal monks. The Apocryphal Acts brought the ascetic motif into prominence.

5. Secular

Social factors, such as escape from the burdens of society, led pagans to withdraw to the deserted regions bordering the settled Nile valley.

6. Christian

Asceticism in varying degrees of self-denial (in matters of marriage and diet) had been practiced by some Christians from the early days of the church. Largely this was individual, with the person maintaining his or her home with the family or in personal quarters. So, the early asceticism was not withdrawn from everyday life.

In contrast to unorthodox ascetic practices (in Marcionism, perhaps Encratism, and some forms of Gnosticism), early asceticism did not regard matter as evil. Instead, it adopted self-denial as the renunciation of the good in pursuit of a higher life and to be more fully dedicated to religious ministry.

Many females adopted the ascetic life, something obscured by the fact that most of the literature was written by males for males. Although women seem to have preceded men in living an ascetic life at home or together in small groups for mutual support, men in greater number made the break to withdraw into the desert areas.

By the end of the third century the ascetic impulse began to express itself in a greater degree of withdrawal from society, at first near cities and villages, but soon by flight to greater solitude in the uninhabited or sparsely inhabited regions near the Nile valley.

In Egypt, Manichaean and Melitian communities arose at least as early as did organized communities among the orthodox. The connection of the Nag Hammadi codices with a Pachomian monastery suggests that asceticism was sometimes more important than ideology in bringing the early ascetics together.

Although the Egyptian contributions to Christian monasticism are better known, asceticism in Syria had earlier and deeper roots (Encratism, Marcionism, and within orthodox circles ascetics living with the mainstream community), with the result that the Syrian church had a strong ascetic impulse from an early date.

Terms employed for ascetics included "monk" (a solitary man, one who lived alone), "anchorite" (one who withdraws), and "hermit" (from the word for a deserted region). In common usage, monk has become the general word, and both anchorite and hermit are used for those who adopted a solitary life. The term used to describe community is "cenobite," from the Greek for "common" or "community life." Ascetics living together in small groups—whether in cities, towns, or villages—were called *apotaktikoi*.

The ascetic flight from the world, taking the form of a spatial separation from society, exploded in popularity in the fourth century and left an indelible impact on Christianity in subsequent centuries. The social factor mentioned above affected Christians as well as pagans. Specifically Christian motivations have sometimes been cited as involved in the new popularity of asceticism. There was also an element of protest, both against the institutional church and against the increasing secularization of the church. In addition, an effort was made by some to work out the true Christian life in terms of the self-denial that had been required in times of persecution.

Less worthy motives were also at work among some who sought escape from responsibilities, and their disorderly behavior brought some discredit on the whole movement, whose champions sought to correct these expressions of escapism.

In the fourth century, champions of monasticism treated it not as a special form of the Christian life, as it came to be later, but as the actualization of what was in principle a life demanded of all Christians.

At the beginnings of the movement, however, monasticism often competed with the church and was, in a sense, a rejection of it, until ecclesiastical statesmen (Athanasius, Basil of Caesarea, Augustine) captured and domesticated the monastic impulse as a part of the total life of the church.

Three forms of monasticism developed in Egypt: (1) the hermit life, where individual monks lived an isolated and austere life of spiritual struggle in prayer and meditation, typified by Anthony; (2) the cenobitic or communal model, where a group of monks lived, prayed, and worked together under a superior, a model developed by Pachomius; and (3) an intermediate form, where a loosely organized group of small settlements (of 2 to 6 persons) in close proximity looked to a common spiritual leader, a type pioneered by Ammun.

Similar to the last was the *laura* that developed in Palestine. Cells or caves for individuals were located in close enough proximity that a person could live as a hermit, but come together with others for worship and other occasions. Among the several who developed lauras, Saba(s) (439–532) is most famous.

In Syria a distinctive development of the hermit life was living on a small platform atop an abandoned column. The first of these "pillar saints" was Symeon Stylites (c. 390–459), who progressively raised the height of his pillar to increase his separation from the earth and people. Other Stylites followed his example.

B. Motifs of Monasticism

The literature of monasticism included lives of the monks (e.g., Athanasius, *Life of Anthony*, and the anonymous *Life of Pachomius,* preserved in various forms), collections of sayings by the desert fathers (*Apopththegmata Patrum*), histories that are largely biographical and anecdotal (Palladius, *Lausiac History*, and Theodoret, *History of the Monks of Syria*), and rules for monasteries (Basil of Caesarea and later Benedict of Nursia).

From this literature certain motifs emerge as prominent interpretations of the monastic life.

1. Military

The monks were the fourth-century Christian soldiers. Military imagery had been prominent in the popular philosophers and was employed by Paul in the New Testament and by pre-Nicene Christian writers. As nominal Christianity became more common and the best minds were occupied with theology, many who wanted to go back to the ideal of moral Christianity interpreted their spiritual struggles as warfare against evil. Some took their military mission too literally and employed violence against pagan temples and philosophers and even against other Christians in the fifth-century Christological conflicts.

2. Martyr

The monks saw the martyrs as important prototypes and sought to imitate their sacrifice for the Lord. A new kind of persecution was afflicting the secularized church, requiring "athletes of piety" to champion the faith. The monks came to be regarded as the successors of the martyrs, the spiritual equivalent of the confessors in times of persecution.

3. Demonic

The warfare of the monks and their resistance to enemies of Christianity were directed against "demons." In Justin Martyr the demons were external enemies, causing persecution and heresy. In Origen, the demons were still external but worked inside persons, causing temptations. In Athanasius' *Life of Anthony*, where the demonic element is prominent, the demons are internalized, psychologized as the temptations themselves.

4. Angelic

As opposed to the demonic forces, namely the fallen angels who tempted them, the monks lived the angelic life. Renouncing sexual relations in order to live "like the angels" (Luke 20:36), they anticipated the life in paradise. Sustained by grace, they hoped to restore paradise by keeping women (and sexuality) out of their life. Of course, women too undertook this style of life.

5. Gnostic

Clement of Alexandria and Origen had appropriated many Gnostic motifs for Christian spirituality. Claiming this legacy, many intellectual monks saw their intense contemplation of the truth as removing the need for the ordinary communion and discipline of the church. The goal of the monks was the "imitation of God," to become "like God." They sought to know God not just intellectually, but in an experiential way.

6. Philosophic

Philosophy had become a "way of life," and the "philosophic life" was equated with asceticism. Christian authors developed this terminology, so that to live as a philosopher was to live ascetically. One branch of Greek philosophy in particular, the Cynics, provided a precedent for the lifestyle of Christian monks. Even as many had previously sought guidance for life from philosophers, so now many individual Christians went out into the desert to seek spiritual guidance from these new heroes of the faith.

7. Baptismal

Becoming a monk was described in baptismal terms. Adopting the monastic life was a new birth. The abbot (*abba*) was the spiritual father of the monks. (The monasticizing of the clergy that soon began encouraged the clergy also to be called "Father"—*Papas* was already in use for the bishops of Alexandria and Carthage by the third century.)

8. Eschatological

The theme of paradise recovered is prominent. The cells and caves of the monks were called a paradise. There was present in the Bible an ambiguous attitude toward the desert. On the one hand, the wilderness was a place of testing for Israel and for Jesus. On the other hand, the wilderness was God's honeymoon time with Israel and it could be interpreted positively in the post-conversion experience of Paul.

So, this place of discipline, where the serpents and scorpions represented the devil tempting the saints, was also the place of contemplating nature as idyllic. It was a place, supposedly, where there was no disharmony between creatures and where even the wild animals recognized the true saint.

C. Early Leaders

Many of the important leaders in the early history of monasticism are discussed elsewhere:

1. Athanasius's *Life of Anthony* set the style for lives of monks and popularized the hermit type of monasticism, while claiming its energies for the cause of doctrinal orthodoxy.

2. Basil of Caesarea encouraged a communal monasticism based on love and integrated monasticism into the Great Church.

3. Jerome, an early Western exponent of the monastic life, established a monastery at Bethlehem and encouraged women in the ascetic life.

4. Augustine was influential in providing a model for combining monastic life with pastoral duties.

Anthony was not the first hermit, for Athanasius says that he took counsel from an old man who had lived as a hermit from his youth in a nearby village. Yet Anthony became, by his withdrawal into the desert east of the Nile and by his holiness, the exemplar for future hermits. Whether or not Athanasius's *Life of Anthony* is accurate, its importance is in its influence. The imitation of God was Anthony's basic motif.

IMPORTANT NAMES IN THE EARLY HISTORY OF MONASTICISM

Name	Date	Place	Contribution
Anthony	251 – 356	Egypt	Model of hermit life
Pachomius	292 – 346	Egypt	Promoted cenobite monasticism
Martin of Tours	316 – 397	Gaul	Missionary bishop and founder of an episcopal monastic community
Basil of Caesarea	330 – 379	Cappadocia	Monastic rules that govern Greek and Slavic monasteries to the present
Evagrius of Pontus	345 – 399	Egypt	Origenist theology of monasticism
John Cassian	365 – 433	Gaul	Introduced Egyptian monasticism to the West
Symeon Stylites	390 – 459	Syria	Pillar saint
Saba(s)	439 – 532	Palestine	Lauras

Anthony's counterpart among the cenobites was Pachomius, whose monasteries first developed in connection with villages as an extension of the earlier forms of asceticism, only later expanding to fringe and desert areas. Pachomius's rule was mildly rigorous, but made provision for those who wanted to work harder at the ascetic life.

Other important names in the history of Egyptian monasticism include Ammun, who founded semieremitic communities of cells of hermits living in close proximity to one another, and Shenoute, whose writings in Sahidic, the dialect of Coptic used in upper Egypt, represent the indigenization of monasticism among the native Copts in Egypt.

Evagrius of Pontus spent his later life in Egypt. Under the spell of Origen's theology, he carried some of Origen's ideas to lengths judged unacceptable by most in the church, but he became the philosophical theorist of the monastic life. His spiritual writings stated a high theology for monasticism that was quite influential in spite of his rejected ideas.

Whereas Evagrius was the philosophical theorist of monasticism, Basil of Caesarea in Cappadocia was its practical theorist who gave institutional organization to Greek monasticism. Quite common were double monasteries of men and women in one community under one head, but with separate living quarters for men and women. Basil's older sister Macrina was the real originator of what is known as Basilian monasticism.

As Jerome was a Western champion of monasticism who went East, so John Cassian was an easterner who went West (see chapter 14). Cassian's *Conferences* and *Institutes* brought the wisdom and ideals of the Egyptian monks to southern Gaul. He thought of the cenobite life as training for the higher spiritual life of the hermit. Benedict of Nursia (sixth century) disagreed on this evaluation of the hermit. Otherwise, Cassian's writings were influential enough that if Benedict is the father of Western monasticism, then Cassian is the grandfather.

Martin of Tours was one of the early Western adherents of monasticism. After his conversion, he evangelized northern Gaul and became an important influence on British monks. After he became bishop of Tours, he continued a monastic type life, living on the edge of town, and thus set an example of monastic clerical life. Martin exemplified the important role monks came to play in missions, for many became traveling missionaries.

An Eastern example of the influence of the monks in evangelization was Symeon Stylites, who became so famous that crowds came out to seek his advice, and many conversions of pagans resulted.

II. MISSIONARY EXPANSION IN THE FOURTH AND FIFTH CENTURIES

The fourth and fifth centuries provided one of the significant periods in the history of Christian missions. Especially important for Western history was the mission work of Ulfilas among the Goths, a story that will be reserved for chapter 15.

Although often undertaken with the blessing of bishops, mission work in the fourth century was not officially organized and directed by ecclesiastical authority. The missionary movement was more spontaneous and resulted from the initiative of individual Christians in very special circumstances.

Since the western expansion of the faith into Ireland and Scotland will be touched on later (chapter 18), the following presentation will trace its eastern geographical expansion beyond the Greek and Latin language areas as well as outside the boundaries of the Roman Empire.

A. Syria

Syriac-speaking Christianity emerged within the borders of the Roman Empire relatively early. Syriac translations of parts of the New Testament were present in the second century, but these Old Syriac versions were revised and eventually replaced by the Peshitta, associated with the name of Rabbula, bishop of Edessa (411–35), who endorsed it. Syriac-speaking Christianity spread outside the borders of Roman rule and continued vital for centuries.

A late legend claimed that Addai, sent by the apostle Thomas, converted King Abgar of Osrhoene, whose capital was Edessa. The story pushed back into apostolic times the claim of the conversion of Abgar VIII (177–212), supposedly the first Christian king. Edessa was the first center of Syriac-speaking Christianity, already in the latter half of the second century, but soon followed by Nisibis.

During the fourth century a Syriac literary culture flourished. The first major writer was Afrahat (Aphraates in Latin, early fourth century), known as the "Persian Sage," who wrote essays on Christian doctrine and practice, many of which treat points at issue with Jews. The greatest representative of Christian Syriac is Ephraem (chapter 11).

Syriac Christianity exhibited the following characteristics:

1. Emphasis on schools—educational establishments, perhaps continuing the Jewish emphasis on religious education, trained especially clergy but others as well.

2. A missionary thrust—Syriac-speaking Christians carried the faith as far as India (how early is disputed), and eventually China, and many regions on the way (chapter 17).

3. Asceticism—celibacy was highly prized. Among the "Sons and Daughters of the Covenant" or "Covenanters," single persons were devoted to various forms of service to the church. Yet a married clergy (including bishops) was permitted.

4. Doctrinal separation—due to theological, political, and geographical reasons, most Syrians and those influenced by them followed a different Christology than most Greek and Latin churches (chapters 13 and 16).

B. Persia

Syriac-speaking Christians early spread the faith into Mesopotamia and Persia. By the time the Sassanid dynasty overthrew the Parthians about the year 225, there were a number of Christian congregations in Persia. The Sassanians made Zoroastrianism the state religion, but Christians, persecuted by Persia's long-standing opponent, the Roman Empire, enjoyed peace.

When Constantine espoused Christianity and ill-advisedly wrote to the Persian emperor on behalf of the Christians, the loyalty of Christians became suspect. Not only did they not recognize the official religion, but they belonged to the religion now favored by the Roman enemy.

Persecution of the Persian Christians began in 339 and lasted forty years, producing more martyrs and fewer apostacies than the Roman persecutions of the preceding three centuries. The fifth-century Christian historian Sozomen claimed that the names of 16,000 martyrs were known.

Another period of persecution began in 420, but in 424 a synod of bishops declared their independence from the jurisdiction of Roman and Greek bishops and reached a working agreement with the government.

Already in 410 a synod at Seleucia-Ctesiphon had recognized its bishop as leader of the whole Persian church (the title "catholicos" was in use by the end of the fifth century).

C. Armenia

Armenia was the first country as a nation to accept Christianity. In a pattern to be followed at many places later, it was the work of a single great man—in this case Gregory the Illuminator—who converted the king (Tiridates III, d. 314). Christianity then spread from the king and aristocracy down.

The church was organized around a single see, now known as Echmiadzin, occupied by Gregory and then by his descendants. The title "catholicos" for this head of the Armenian church has been used in an official sense from the fifth century. The bishop Nerses (339–73) deepened the religious life of the country.

During the fifth century, with the encouragement of the Catholicos Sahak, Mashtots (Mesrob) and his disciples (notably Eznik, who wrote *Against the Sects*) developed a written alphabet for the Armenian language and established an important school of Christian literature.

The impetus for this was translation of the Bible, undertaken from Syriac about 415 and from the Greek about 435. Mission work has often gone hand in hand with translation of the Scriptures, and for peoples without a written language this has required the creation of an alphabet.

D. Georgia

The Caucasus region, including Georgia, was evangelized from Armenia, and Mashtots was credited also with the creation of the Georgian alphabet, making possible a national Christian literature. There were Christians in Georgia already in the third century, and the royal court accepted Christianity in the fourth century.

The conversion of the land was due to the miracles and virtues of Nino (c. 330), a Christian slave girl from Cappadocia who healed the queen Nana of a serious illness. Her conversion was followed by that of king Mirian. Adherence to the Greek tradition was more a cultural than a doctrinal move. Close connections were also maintained with Jerusalem.

EARLY MISSIONARY EXPANSION		
Place or Peoples	**Missionary**	**Dates**
Edessa, East Syria	Addai (?)	2nd century
Persia		By 3rd century
Armenia	Gregory the Illuminator	Late 3rd – early 4th century
Ethiopia	Frumentius	4th century
Goths	Ulfilas	c. 311 – c. 383
Georgia	Nino	c. 330
Scotland	Ninian	c. 360 – c. 432
Ireland	Patrick	d. c. 460

The Bible was translated into Georgian in the fifth and sixth centuries, either from the Syriac or the Armenian, but with strong influence from both. The "Syrian Fathers" in the sixth century founded monastic communities on the Syriac model.

From the sixth century the Georgian church has been an independent national church whose Catholicos resides in Tbilisi. The patron saint is George, but not because his name has any connection with the name of the country.

E. Ethiopia

Two young men from Tyre, Frumentius and Edesius, were the sole survivors of a voyage that met disaster on the Red Sea coast of Ethiopia (or Abyssinia). Made slaves, they were carried to Axum, the capital. They rose to high positions and had charge of the education of the royal children.

When allowed to return home, Edesius returned to Tyre but Frumentius went to Alexandria and requested that a bishop be sent to Ethiopia. Athanasius ordained him, and he returned to Axum, which is still the ecclesiastical capital of the Ethiopian church, although no longer the political capital of the country. The king Ezana was baptized before AD 350.

The "Nine Saints," monks of possibly Syrian origin who arrived in the late fifth century, spread Christianity among the populace and promoted monasticism, which has maintained a dominant influence in Ethiopic Christianity.

At some point traditions associated with Jewish history became influential, including the claim to possession of the ark of the covenant from the temple in Jerusalem.

The national language, Ge'ez, had developed a form of writing derived from a south Arabic alphabet. It is the only Semitic language that normally takes note of vowels and is written left to right. The translation of the Bible was completed between the fifth and seventh centuries, and a national Christian literature emerged, a feature of the Christianizing of each of these lands.

The Ethiopic church has a broader definition of the canon of Scripture than other churches, counting eighty-one books in its canon, which includes Jewish pseudepigraphal writings and Christian works of church order.

Ge'ez continues as the language of the liturgy, but today it has been replaced by Amharic as the spoken language.

III. CHRISTIAN LIFE AND SOCIETY

The steady growth of the church within the Roman Empire reached its climax in the fourth and early fifth centuries. The fourth century saw Christianity become the official religion of the Roman world. The process of Christianizing Europe was slow and before completion received the setback of the barbarian invasions of the fifth and subsequent centuries.

The empire's peasants of the countryside and its cultivated aristocracy, these opposite ends of the social scale being traditionally the most conservative elements of a society, offered the greatest resistance to Christianity. But steadily over time (often extending into the fifth and sixth centuries) even they were penetrated with the new religion.

Statues of the gods were torn down, defaced, or abandoned. Temples were burned, converted into churches, or left as spoils for new building projects. Pagan deities and sacred sites saw their functions and rituals taken over by Christian saints and ceremonies. More than once, the "Christianization" of pagan practices went so smoothly that the church replaced the pagan sanctuary with no interruption in the continuity of the life of a given district. Pagan festivals began to die out or be replaced by Christian counterparts.

The interior of the sixth-century basilica of Sant' Apollinare in Classe, Ravenna.

Gradually a Christianizing of space and time occurred. For many, however, the old pagan mentality continued to persist. One scholar (A. D. Nock) described the result as "the old firm [the old religion] doing the same business at the same location, only under a new name and new management."

A. Imperial Support of Christianity

Constantine began a policy of imperial favor for Christianity (see further in chapter 10), some of his measures having social ramifications. In 318 he permitted churches to receive legacies. Out of deference it seems for Christian ascetics, Constantine repealed the legislation of Augustus (seldom enforced) requiring marriage. The care of orphans was left to the church. Christian emblems began to appear on coins and in other official places. Overtly anti-pagan legislation was rare, but private haruspicy (taking of omens) was forbidden in 319. Constantius II took a more vigorous official stand against paganism, prohibiting all pagan sacrifice in 341 and ordering the closing of temples in 356, but his measures were not uniformly enforced.

Julian sought to reverse the tide, revoking the privileges of the "Galilaeans" and restoring those of paganism. In his efforts to remove Christians from positions of privilege he forbade them to teach pagan literature, which was the basis of the educational curriculum and so of the path to advancement. Apollinaris of Laodicea went beyond those who fought for the Christian right to teach pagan literature with a Christian interpretation. In association with his father, who had the same name, Apollinaris rewrote some of the biblical books in classical meter and classical style in order to provide an alternative curriculum.

Jovinian, Valentinian, and Valens relegated paganism to its position under Constantine, but did not further molest it.

Gratian (375–83) in the West renounced the title Pontifex Maximus, discontinued state subsidies of pagan temples, confiscated the revenue of pagan priests and landed property of temples, and removed the altar of Victory from the Senate house in Rome.

Similarly severe was Theodosius I (379–95), under whom came the climax of imperial legislation making Christianity the official religion of the Roman Empire. In addition to his edict of 380 establishing the faith of the bishops of Rome and Alexandria as the standard of official orthodoxy, and his edict of 381 depriving heretics of their places of worship and forbidding their holding assemblies in cities, he sought the suppression of paganism. His decrees of 391–92 forbade even private pagan worship. Later emperors renewed the laws against paganism, showing that it was by no means dead.

The Jews also fell under Christian emperors' repressive measures. Constantine in c. 335 ordered the manumission of Christian slaves belonging to Jews and forbade Jewish attacks on Christian converts from Judaism. Constantius II required Christian converts to Judaism to forfeit their property to the state. Measures aimed at restricting Jewish social and political influence came mainly in the fifth century under Theodosius II (408–50)—prohibiting mixed marriages, barring Jews from political office, forbidding the building of synagogues, and prohibiting proselytizing.

No doubt the imperial support of Christianity was a significant factor in the growth of the church in the fourth century. The church developed further the catechumenate, which had begun by the end of the second century (chapter 8), to handle the influx of new members (see further below).

Despite the many advantages of accepting the Christian faith, Christian emperors at least did not execute pagans, although Constantius II threatened to do so in some cases.

B. Christian Influence on the Roman World

Christian influence on life in the Roman world was not as great as might have been expected. Nevertheless, one can see that influence in a number of positive ways in the legislation of the Christian emperors.

Married men were forbidden to keep a concubine. Adultery and rape were severely treated, and obstacles were put in the way of divorce. Infanticide was forbidden in 374, presumably including the exposure of children. Measures were taken to improve the condition of slaves, and the church encouraged emancipation. There were efforts to introduce a little humanity into prison conditions.

Christian preachers continued, as they had before, to protest against the immoralities and expenses associated with public entertainments—the mimes and pantomimes at the theater, the chariot races at the circus, and the gladiator and wild beast contests at the amphitheater. In regard to the last, state action banned gladiator fights in 325, but this ban was not fully applied until the 430s. The public entertainments were closely bound with the calendar of pagan and state festivals, but slowly the Christian calendar (see below) began to regulate the rhythm of social and business life.

Churches took the initiative in establishing charitable institutions—shelters for travelers, the sick, and the poor. In one crucial area of cultural life Christianity had a negligible impact in the fourth and fifth centuries—the educational system. Christians trained in the classical studies. Indeed, all of the church's literary figures—most notably

Basil, Gregory of Nazianzus, Jerome, Augustine—used their rhetorical and literary skills in the service of the Christian faith. But it was only slowly that a significantly modified educational curriculum emerged.

Christians depended on the religious instruction in the Bible and in the faith that took place in the home and in church to counter the pagan influence in the schools. Basil, John Chrysostom, and Jerome offered specific recommendations on religious teaching and how to select proper works from classical literature according to their moral quality.

C. Negative Factors in the Late Empire

There were negative factors built into the society of the ancient Roman world that mitigated Christian influence. More and more Christians had come to serve in the army during the third century, and Christian involvement in the affairs of state in the fourth century now meant even larger numbers were participating in war. This seemed an inevitable part of taking responsibility for the empire with its many external enemies.

Moreover, there is an inertia in any civilization that impedes major change. It was no easy task to Christianize the pagan society of the Roman world. The Christian emperors inherited a totalitarian regime that was accustomed to coercion and cruelty. The increasing barbarism of the late empire was reflected in the frequent use of torture, and treason was broadly interpreted. In the church itself, religious intolerance toward paganism and Judaism was extended to variant forms of Christian doctrine.

On the social and economic level, the church was not in a position to make fundamental changes in the trend toward feudal structures, nor to make basic reforms in the power of the great landlords.

As the numbers of Christians increased, discipline was relaxed, many were nominal Christians, and the level of Christian life was shallow. That seems to be the story of human nature. It was in that atmosphere that the monastic life appealed to many "athletes of virtue."

We should not overlook, however, the many ordinary Christians who sought to give Christian expression to their fundamental human religiosity.

D. Pious Practices

The fourth century saw distinctive Christian developments of certain aspects in Greco-Roman religious life. The basic elements in the cult of the saints were already in place during the third century (chapter 9). The cult of the saints had a Christian development, but pagan

Edict of Gratian, Valentinian II, and Theodosius I, 380: "It is our will that all the peoples who are ruled by the administration of our clemency shall practice that religion which the divine Peter the Apostle transmitted to the Romans.... this is the religion that is followed by the Pontiff Damasus [of Rome] and by Peter, bishop of Alexandria, a man of apostolic sanctity; that is, ... we shall believe the single Deity of the Father, the Son and the Holy Spirit, under the concept of equal majesty and of the Holy Trinity. We command that those persons who follow this rule shall embrace the name of Catholic Christians" (*Codex Theodosianus* 16.1.2).

"[The church] as it gained strength, grew by persecution and was crowned with martyrdom, but then, after reaching the Christian emperors, increased in influence and wealth but decreased in Christian virtues" (Jerome, *Life of Malchus* 1).

ideas influenced it, and more so as time went along. The ways in which beliefs and veneration for the saints were expressed largely stemmed from traditional practices.

When peace came to the church, the Christian enthusiasm for the martyrs could not be restrained. By the end of the fourth and beginning of the fifth centuries the cult of the saints was fully developed.

The annual commemoration of the martyr's death took on more the character of a popular feast than of a solemn religious occasion. Great numbers of the faithful participated. There was a procession. An oration extolled the example of the martyr.

The burial places had previously been places of prayer, and now *martyria* (shrines or church buildings) were set up over the tombs of martyrs. *Martyria*, unlike the rectangular basilicas, were typically constructed on a central plan in order to focus on the tomb or sacred place.

In the fourth century, calendars of martyrs were compiled. New names were added to martyrologies, and the churches borrowed one another's saints' days. The relics of the martyrs became popular and were thought to have power over demons and to effect healings.

Christian leaders like Ambrose declared that the saints were neighbors to the living. The saints knew the weakness of the flesh and could intercede for the weakness of others, and since they shared human infirmities, their perfection could be imitated. (Perhaps the doctrinal controversies concerning the deity of Jesus Christ affected popular piety by leaving a need for intercessors who seemed more human.)

In the panegyrics and lives of saints, edification was more important than historical accuracy. So began the huge production, which continued in subsequent centuries, of hagiographies with their accounts of extraordinary miracles and exaltation of specific moral virtues.

Believers preferred to be buried in the vicinity of a martyr's tomb. The faithful gave the name of a holy person to their children.

A characteristic phenomenon was the finding of relics hitherto forgotten or unknown, usually as the result of a dream or a vision. Three types of relics came to be recognized: the body or body parts of a holy person, objects closely related to the person (such as clothing), and objects such as sand, oil, or water that touched these remains and was stored in ampullae (small flasks).

According to the hagiographers, miracles were worked not by the relics themselves, but by God working through the saint. Toward the end of the fourth century the sentiment against disturbing a grave began to be overcome, and relics of martyrs were moved to be placed under the altar of churches. Thus the cult of the martyrs brought a change in burial practice, so that dead bodies were no longer considered impure (a major change from the Jewish roots of Christianity).

Octagonal martyrium
of Philip the Apostle
(fifth century) at
Hierapolis (modern
Pamukkale), Turkey.

Instead of being buried outside the cities (as in Greco-Roman practice),
dead bodies began to be brought into the churches. This uniting of the
relics of the saints with the eucharistic altar was important in bringing
the cult of the saints under the supervision of bishops and priests.

Also, during the fourth century cultic veneration began to be
extended from martyrs to include monks and bishops, whose ascetic
sacrifice and service to the church were considered equivalent to that
of the martyrs. Origen, denied the martyrdom he desired, had already
spiritualized ascetic piety as an interior martyrdom. This ideal became
the spiritual basis of Christian monasticism.

Before the fourth century, Christians spoke of holy persons, the
holy church, and the holy Scriptures, but in the fourth century they
began to speak of holy places. Although Christians had made journeys
to Palestine for religious reasons from the early days of the church,
pilgrimages as acts of religious devotion to sites associated with the life
of Jesus and the apostles began to be extensively documented in the
fourth century.

Two important early records are the itinerary from Bordeaux to
Jerusalem dated 333 by an anonymous pilgrim, and the more extensive
travel diary of the noble woman Egeria from Gaul or Spain to Sinai,
Egypt, Palestine, and Asia Minor at the end of the fourth century.

Going on pilgrimage combined various elements: devotion to the
historical roots of the Christian faith, the ascetic and in some cases penitential discipline of the journey, curiosity and sight-seeing, and sometimes emotional restlessness. Gregory of Nyssa in one letter warned

against the moral dangers of travel and professed there was nothing more holy about Palestine than other places, but in another letter he spoke of the thrill of seeing the holy sites there.

During the fourth century journeys were undertaken to visit holy people as well as holy places. Many went to observe the life of the desert monks and to consult them for spiritual advice. The more superstitious took back blessed oil, water, or soil from the site associated with the holy person.

As the practice of pilgrimage grew, great pilgrim churches began to be built in the fifth and sixth centuries at sites associated with popular saints—e.g., Abu Mena in Egypt, Qal'at Sim'an (Symeon Stylites) in Syria, and St. John at Ephesus.

IV. WORSHIP

The maintaining of the Jewish Scriptures as part of the Bible of the church meant that many concepts from the Old Testament ended up influencing Christian practice even without direct contact with Jews. Thus, the distinction between clergy and laity was reinforced by the Old Testament distinction of priests from the people. A priestly understanding of ministry, a sacrificial understanding of worship, and the view of the church building as a holy temple, were among the earlier religious ideas that developed under the influence of the Old Testament.

A. The Liturgy of Baptism and Eucharist

The *Catechetical Lectures* delivered in 348 by Cyril of Jerusalem, who represented "orthodox" Trinitarian thought in the East, and the *Apostolic Constitutions* (especially book 7), compiled probably in Syria or Asia Minor in the late fourth century by someone of "Arian" sympathies, provide descriptions of baptismal practice not greatly different from what appeared in the West a century earlier (chapter 8). Cyril's lectures do seem to reflect a greater formality, above all a more developed explanation of the various practices and an elaboration of symbolism.

Ordinary catechumens, the "hearers" (*audientes*), were allowed to remain at the Sunday service for the Scripture readings and sermon, but were dismissed before the eucharist. No one was allowed to witness the "mysteries" of baptism and the eucharist, or hear them described, until the time of initiation.

Those desiring to receive baptism turned in their names shortly after the beginning of the new year. During the forty days of Lent there was instruction in the Christian faith, based primarily on the creed, but giving some attention to the biblical story of the history of salvation. There was also teaching on Christian morals but, in comparison to doctrinal instruction, considerably less than in the second century.

Baptism was administered on Easter Sunday. The special preparation for baptism involved not only instruction, but also time spent in penitence and confession of sin. Several exorcisms were performed to remove the person from the sphere of evil forces. Those undergoing the immediate preparation for baptism were called in Greek *photizomenoi* ("those being enlightened") and in Latin *competentes* ("candidates").

The ceremony of baptism itself began with a renunciation of Satan. The candidate, facing west and stretching forth the hand, said, "I renounce you, Satan, and all your works, and all your pomp, and all your worship." Then, turning to the east, the candidate made profession of faith, "I associate myself with Christ," and recited the creed.

The candidate put off the undergarment as a symbol of putting off the old person and received an anointing with oil. The priest invoked the Holy Spirit on the water to consecrate it with a new power of holiness. Standing in the water, the candidate made the "saving confession," probably in question-and-answer form, and was immersed three times.

There followed an anointing with consecrated ointment, which Cyril regarded as representing the anointing of Jesus by the Spirit at his baptism. The church in Syria, in contrast, made the pre-baptismal anointing the symbol of reception of the Holy Spirit and so a central act of the ceremony.

During the week following the baptism there was instruction on the meaning of baptism, eucharist, and chrism (anointing).

Photo courtesy of Robin Jensen.

A baptistery (fourth or fifth century) at Sbeitla, Tunisia.

By the late fourth century the Sunday service took the shape it was to maintain for centuries. There were individual differences in different regions, and these came to be recorded in the written liturgies of the subsequent centuries (chapter 16). The women sat apart from the men. There is a clear separation of the liturgy of the Word, which all could attend, from the liturgy of the table for the faithful.

The first part of the service might include up to four Scripture readings: from the Law, the Prophets, the Epistles or Acts, and the Gospels. Between the Old Testament and New Testament readings, a cantor sang psalms, to which the people sang responses. The presbyters and bishop delivered homilies. Then came the dismissal of the catechumens, those possessed by evil spirits, and those under discipline.

From Cyril of Jerusalem's *Catechetical Lecture* 23, *Mystagogical Catecheses* (which some, probably incorrectly, have ascribed to Cyril's successor, John) 5, "On the Sacred Liturgy and Communion," we may learn a sample liturgy of the faithful as celebrated in Jerusalem. The presbyters began with a ceremonial washing of their hands (the *Lavabo*) as a symbol of freedom from sin. At the invitation of the deacon there was exchanged the kiss of peace, signifying brotherly love and reconciliation.

The presiding priest called out "Lift up your hearts" (*Sursum corda*), to which the people replied, "We lift them up to the Lord." Then the priest said, "Let us give thanks to the Lord," and began the prayer of thanksgiving. This led into the singing of the *Sanctus* ("Holy, Holy, Holy" from Isaiah 6:2–3). The *epiclesis* called on God to send his Holy Spirit upon the bread and wine.

In the Great Intercession, "over that sacrifice of propitiation" a prayer was offered to God, first on behalf of the living and then in commemoration of the dead. (There was much controversy on the subject of prayers for the dead in Cyril's time and he tries to answer some of the objections. There is nothing in any other early liturgy corresponding to Cyril's expectation that "at their prayers and intercessions God would receive our petition.")

Next, there was recited the Lord's Prayer. Then the priest invited to communion with the words, "Holy things for the holy," to which the people replied, "One is Holy, One is Lord, Jesus Christ." The chanter sang Psalm 34, verses 8 and 11. The bread and the cup were received reverently with a voiced "Amen." A thanksgiving and benediction closed the service.

B. Sacraments

The word *sacrament* in English derives from the Latin *sacramentum*, an "oath." Tertullian used the word in a Christian sense in reference to the oath of loyalty to the heavenly commander at the time of one's

OUTLINE SUMMARY OF SOME COMMON FEATURES OF SUNDAY LITURGIES IN THE FOURTH AND FIFTH CENTURIES

(Placement of these features varies in different liturgies, not all features are present in every liturgy, and some items are not included here.)

I. Service of the Word (the Mass of Catechumens, also known as the Synaxis)

  1. Preliminary Prayers and Songs

  2. Readings from both Old and New Testament

  3. Psalms sung between the Scripture lessons

  4. Sermon

  5. Prayers and Benedictions for different groups

  6. Dismissal of catechumens and penitents

II. Service of the Supper (the Mass of the Faithful, also known as the Eucharist)

  1. Prayers of the faithful. Series of biddings by the deacon with the people responding, *Kyrie eleison* ("Lord, have mercy"). Completed by prayer by the bishop

  2. Kiss of peace

  3. Offerings brought by the people

  4. Anaphora or Canon of the Mass:

    a. *Sursum Corda* ("Lift up your hearts")

    b. Preface — "Let us give thanks"

    c. *Sanctus* (or *Trisagion* — "Holy, Holy, Holy")

    d. Thanksgiving prayer:

      (1) *Epiclesis* — Invocation of the Holy Spirit

      (2) Words of Institution

      (3) *Anamnesis* ("Memorial" of passion and resurrection)

      (4) Oblation — Offering or sacrifice

      (5) Intercession for the living and the dead

    e. Lord's Prayer

  5. Communion

  6. Benediction

baptism. By a broadening of meaning the word was extended to other rites.

The Greeks used the word *musterion*, "mystery," a secret sacred ceremony. Jews and the apostle Paul had used the word for God's secret counsels that he then revealed to human beings, but since Clement of Alexandria some Christians had appropriated the terminology of the Greek mystery religions for comparison to Christian rites. During the fourth century some Christian ceremonies began to be treated in the same way as the Greek "mysteries," that is, as secret ceremonies revealed only to the initiated.

By the fourth century three acts had sacramental significance according to the later theological definition of a sacrament, that is, the use of material elements or outward actions as channels of inner spiritual blessing: baptism (water), eucharist (bread and wine), and chrism (oil of anointing). There was significant development also in regard to other acts that later were considered sacraments.

Baptism from the earliest times of the church had been the initiation into the people of God, who were defined now by faith and not by race (in contrast with Judaism). Water in the ancient Near East had been ambiguous—a necessity of life, but also representing chaos and death. Christians appropriated these ideas in interpreting baptism as the means of imparting life and understanding the passing through the waters of immersion as a deliverance from the forces of evil.

The blessing of the font served to emphasize the water as imbued with the power of the Holy Spirit. The Church Fathers of the fourth century made frequent use of imagery identified with baptism from an earlier time—regeneration, new birth, death and resurrection, washing, illumination, and seal. They associated baptism with grace, confession of faith, forgiveness of sins, freedom from slavery to the devil, and the beginning of a new moral life—all of which concepts belonged to earlier baptismal theology, only now more elaborated.

What became known as confirmation in the later Western church was not clearly separated from baptism, for the imposition of hands and the anointing that symbolized the imparting of the Holy Spirit, whether administered before (as in Syria) or after the baptism (as elsewhere), were a part of the baptismal ceremony itself.

As infant baptism grew, the anointing was often separated in time from baptism, at least in the West, where it was administered by the bishop, unlike in the East where the officiating priest could also anoint as well as baptize.

The use of oil in the baptismal ceremony is first confirmed among the Valentinians in the second century, but whatever its origins it quickly became common. It enforced the imagery of dying with Jesus

Christ (for oil was used in embalming), the idea of cleansing (for it was used by athletes to clean the body and by everyone following a bath), and of preparation of the bride for the heavenly bridegroom. Moreover, for the Christian to be anointed, as was Jesus Christ, enforced the idea of the royal priesthood.

The baptismal oil ("chrism") was described by several of the church leaders as sacramental, representing the Holy Spirit. Cyril of Jerusalem, it seems, regarded baptism as conveying both remission of sins and the gift of the Holy Spirit, but as signifying only the former with chrism signifying the latter. It prepared the person for an active participation in Christian duties through the power of the Holy Spirit.

The eucharist was the center of the Sunday assembly from the beginning of the church, and by the fourth century was being observed in some churches on Saturday as well. The commemorative and eschatological features of the early eucharist were by the fourth century being supplanted by other understandings. In the Eastern churches the eucharist was viewed as an epiphany of the divine with an emphasis on the epiclesis of the Holy Spirit. In the West it was viewed as a sacrifice with an emphasis on the words of institution. But the two ideas intermingled, and both components were often found together in the liturgies.

The belief in the presence of Jesus Christ with his people gathered for the breaking of bread, and the association of the elements with his body and blood, went back to the beginning of the church. Third-century authors sometimes spoke realistically of the identification of

"Sarcophagus of the Trees" (c. 375), showing an orant (praying) figure in the center flanked on each side by three miracles of Christ, each separated by a tree (Archaeological Museum, Arles, France).

the elements with the body and blood. At other times they spoke of the elements as "symbols" (Greek) and "figures" (Latin).

Some fourth-century bishops began to speak of a change in the elements effecting the presence of the body and the blood. Thus the *Mystagogical Catecheses* of Cyril of Jerusalem said that the Holy Spirit "made the bread the body of Christ and the wine the blood of Christ," a marked advance over earlier statements.

Gregory of Nyssa coined a word to express his thought: "By the power of the benediction through which he transelements the natural quality of these visible things to that immortal thing."

Ambrose identified the consecration that made the bread into the body and the cup of wine and water into the blood with the repetition by the priest of Jesus' words of institution.

The view that the elements were changed, not just in their function but in a realistic sense, gained greater currency in subsequent centuries. This realistic understanding of the presence of Jesus Christ in the elements preceded by several centuries the doctrine of "transubstantiation," which is a theory of how the change occurs, not the fact of a change itself (chapter 21).

Sacrificial ideas associated with prayer and thanksgiving were explicitly related to the eucharist by the second century if not earlier (*Didache*). Cyprian in the third century had used the language of sacrifice freely for the eucharist, declaring that the priest (bishop), while imitating what Christ did at the Last Supper, "offers a true and full sacrifice." He went further in identifying this sacrifice with the Lord's passion, for not only is mention made of his passion but also, Cyprian explains in an aside, "the Lord's passion is the sacrifice which we offer."

Sacrificial ideas were fully developed in Ambrose, Cyril of Jerusalem, and the *Apostolic Constitutions*. Ambrose stays closer to earlier thought in saying that "the holy bread and cup of eternal life" are a "spotless offering, reasonable offering, unbloody offering." The *Mystagogical Catecheses* mark the future development by combining the real presence with the sacrifice: "We offer up the Christ who was sacrificed for our sins, propitiating ... the merciful God."

The penitential discipline of the church was well developed by the end of the second century (chapter 7), and Tertullian had called the public humiliation and confession of sins a "second plank" of salvation after shipwreck.

The *Canonical Epistle* attributed to Gregory Thaumaturgus of the third century listed the classes of penitents: (1) mourners, who had to stay outside the door of the church, where they implored the faithful—as they entered—to pray for them; (2) hearers of the word, who could stand inside the door to hear the Scriptures and the preaching;

(3) kneelers, who were within the assembly room, but were still dismissed before the eucharist; (4) bystanders, who were associated with the faithful but did not commune; (5) restored ones, who now shared in communion. We do not hear of the first two classes in the West, unless those from whom fellowship had been withdrawn are the same as the mourners.

In the fourth century the canonical legislation elaborated this structure with prescribed periods in each category for each sin, but the bishop ultimately decided on the amount of penance. The forms of penitential exercises and reconciliation remained the same as in the third century.

The term "confession" (*exomologesis*) continued to be the regular designation for public discipline, but a confession before the faithful (in addition to a private confession to a priest) was not always obligatory. The rule of only one post-baptismal penance continued to be affirmed.

We hear of punishments for moral offenses mainly in the canonical legislation, and most references to excommunication occur in the efforts to enforce doctrinal uniformity. Basil of Caesarea already indicates that he had to deal with a state of relaxed discipline. A systematic theology of penance as a sacrament did not come until the twelfth century.

The ancient practice of election of the bishop by the people maintained itself in post-Nicene times, but more influence was wielded by the clergy, neighboring bishops, or even (in the case of some sees) imperial authority.

Consecration of a bishop ordinarily required three bishops. The manner continued to be prayer and the laying on of hands. The laying on of hands was understood as conferring the Holy Spirit.

This sacramental character of ordination was slow in evolving, but in the fourth century Gregory of Nyssa gave expression to the idea of a sacramental change in the status of the one ordained. He paralleled the changes in regard to the elements in baptism, eucharist, and chrism to the change in the person ordained. He attributed to the prayer of benediction the Spirit's transformation of a person who had been one of the common mass of people and who remained in outward appearance the same. By an inner grace and power the individual was transformed into "a guide, a president, a teacher of righteousness, an instructor of mysteries."

It remained for Augustine, however, to lay the basis for the sacramental understanding of ordination by formulating its indelible character.

The place of the laity in the liturgy came to be reduced to a minimum. The diaconate became a rung on the ladder of advancement, not

A model of a basilica in the museum of the Catacomb and Basilica of San Sebastiano, Rome.

a particular lifetime office. (The term archdeacon was in use at Rome by the end of the fourth century.)

Canon 18 adopted at Nicaea decreed that presbyters pass the elements of the eucharist to the deacons, reversing the earlier practice of deacons serving the presbyters, who were the only ones to have seats in the house churches. The canon made clear that the presbyters were definitely priests (with functions delegated by the bishop), and that the deacons were servants of the presbyters as well as of the bishop. The bishops became more administrative officials, at least in the larger cities, and were the only ones with votes in the councils.

C. The Church Calendar

The commemoration of saints days (see above) added to the number of festival days, but the main contours of the church calendar depended on the feasts of salvation.

The Jewish religious calendar provided Christianity with its observance of Pascha and Pentecost. With the outcome of the Quartodeciman conflict of the second century Christianity had departed from the Jewish calculations for Passover and moved the observance to Sunday. Each year the bishop of Alexandria sent a Paschal Letter announcing the date for Easter of that year. The Council of Nicaea determined that the Paschal Sunday would be the first Sunday after the first full moon following the spring equinox.

The major new fourth-century addition to the Christian calendar was the celebration of the birthday of Jesus. The followers of the Gnostic teacher Basilides in Egypt celebrated the manifestation (epiphany) of Jesus in his baptism on January 6, a day important in the cult of Dionysus and associated in Egypt with the beginning of a new year. When orthodox Christians in Egypt and the East observed the day, they associated Jesus' appearance with his birth. There were various other speculations about the day of Jesus' birth, centering mainly on the spring, but for the first three centuries the church realized the day of Jesus' birth was unknown and attached no theological importance to it. There are accounts in the East of both the birth and the baptism of Jesus remembered on January 5–6.

Christmas was a Western feast, first celebrated in Rome in the second quarter of the fourth century. The date of December 25 was influenced by the sun cult, which was promoted by third-century emperors and continued to be recognized by Constantine. December 25 as the birthday of Jesus began to be introduced into the eastern part of the empire at the end of the fourth century. This date forced a separation from Epiphany. In the West January 6 became associated with the visit of the Magi to the infant Jesus, but in the East the day continued an association with the baptism of Jesus, and in Armenia maintained itself as the birthday of Jesus. Theological considerations were important in the spread of the festival, because of the emphasis on the incarnation.

As Jerusalem became more important as a pilgimage site in the fourth century, a celebration of Palm Sunday a week before Easter developed there by about 400.

D. Basilicas and Art

The churches built under Constantine set the pattern for church buildings over the next few centuries. The Christian basilicas were rectangular halls, normally with a narthex (an entrance room), an apse (the semi-circular focal point on the opposite end from the narthex), a clerestory supported by columns above the central nave, and two (sometimes four) side aisles. The rectangular shape focused attention on the altar and the seating for the presbyters and the bishop's chair at one end. Although not true of all Constantinian basilicas, most church buildings were oriented to the east.

Indeed, within this general description there was much diversity in local styles. With support from the emperor and other wealthy patrons, fine marble was incorporated in the construction, and furnishings and communion vessels were made of precious metals.

Evidence of the decoration of Christian meeting places becomes more extensive in the fourth century. At the beginning of the fourth century, Bishop Theodore of Aquileia covered the floor of his new

Inscription of Bishop Theodore in the mosaic floor of the basilica he built in Aquileia in northeast Italy at the beginning of the fourth century.

church building with mosaics that incorporated biblical motifs and nautical and floral designs. The apse of basilicas was the most important place to make an artistic statement. It was adorned with pictures in mosaic or fresco of Jesus Christ as lawgiver or teacher.

The figural decoration of the catacombs became much more extensive, and more elaborate sarcophagi began to be produced, with the repertory of biblical scenes expanded. In general terms there was a move in content from a primarily symbolic to a more "historical" art.

There was also in the Theodosian age the beginning of some of the features that would characterize later Byzantine art—frontality, symmetry, and abstract idealizing. The various portrayals of Jesus Christ showed him taking over the features of pagan deities.

FOR FURTHER STUDY

Ferguson, Everett, ed. *Missions and Regional Chracteristics of the Early Church*. Studies in Early Christianity 12. New York: Garland, 1993.

Frank, Georgia. *The Memory of the Eyes: Pilgrims to Living Saints in Christian Late Antiquity*. Berkeley: University of California Press, 2000.

Goehring, J. E. *Ascetics, Society, and the Desert: Studies in Early Egyptian Monasticism*. Harrisburg, PA: Trinity Press International, 1999.

Harmless, J. W. *Desert Christians: An Introduction to the Literature of Early Monasticism*. Oxford: Oxford University Press, 2004.

Johnson, L. J. *Worship in the Early Church: An Anthology of Historical Sources*. 4 vols. Collegeville, MN: Liturgical Press, 2009.

Christological Controversies to Chalcedon (451)

I. AN OVERVIEW OF THE FIRST FOUR ECUMENICAL COUNCILS

The Trinitarian conflict of the fourth century was associated with two councils that came to be regarded as ecumenical, and so was the Christological controversy of the fifth century.

As an oversimplication, the relationship of these four councils can be expressed according to the following scheme:

1. Nicaea (325) emphasized the *oneness* of God (Jesus Christ is *homoousios* with the Father).

2. Constantinople (381) emphasized the *threeness* of God (Father, Son, and Holy Spirit).

3. Ephesus (431) emphasized the *oneness* of Jesus Christ (Mary is *theotokos*).

4. Chalcedon (451) emphasized the *twoness* of Jesus Christ (two *physes* or "natures").

According to the unfolding logic of the theological debate, it may be said that the solution of the Trinitarian problem heightened the Christological problem. If Jesus Christ is fully and completely God, what is the relation of the deity to the humanity of Jesus?

THE FIRST FOUR ECUMENICAL COUNCILS

Nicaea — The oneness of God

Constantinople — The threeness of God

Ephesus — The oneness of Christ

Chalcedon — The twoness of Christ

II. RIVALRIES BETWEEN ALEXANDRIA AND ANTIOCH

The Christological controversies were primarily fought in the eastern half of Christendom. The westerners did not get as heavily involved as the easterners did, although Rome did have a crucial role in the official decisions.

Political rivalries, especially between Alexandria and Antioch, became even more prominent than before. If one is distressed by the political machinations in the Arian controversy, there is more to lament in the Christological controversies. The elevation of the see of Constantinople to second rank behind Rome at the Council of Constantinople in 381 was a humiliation of Alexandria and may be a factor in that see's policies against Chrysostom, Nestorius, Flavian, and others.

In addition to ecclesiastical jealousy, one must note the different cultural and theological traditions influencing the churches of Antioch and Alexandria.

The church in Antioch was in closer touch with Palestinian Jewish sources. It had more of a tradition of critical, rational inquiry. The Antiochene school developed a typological interpretation of the Old Testament that gave full historical reality to the events it recorded and to the setting of its prophecies, while seeing those acts and words as foreshadowing Christian revelation. Church leaders at Antioch gave more emphasis to the humanity of Jesus Christ.

The intellectuals in the church at Alexandria, on the other hand, were more under the influence of the philosophical Judaism represented by Philo and transmitted to later Christian thinkers by Clement of Alexandria and Origen. They had more of a tradition of contemplative piety. In the interpretation of Scripture the school of Alexandria developed the allegorical method that had been employed by Greek philosophers in interpreting Greek mythology and by Philo in interpreting the Bible. This method saw the true meaning of Scripture to be the spiritual realities hidden in its literal, historical words. The leaders of thought in Alexandria put more emphasis on the divinity of Jesus Christ.

The differences between the Antiochians and Alexandrians had already surfaced in their different approaches to the refutation of Arianism, differences that set the stage for their Christological conflict.

The Arians made much of those New Testament passages that suggested a subordination of the Son of God to God the Father. Verses they quoted included John 14:28, "the Father is greater than I," and Matthew 24:36, "No one knows ... not even the angels in heaven, nor the Son, but only the Father."

In their response to the Arians, the theologians at Alexandria argued that such passages were properly applied to the Son of God, but in his incarnate state.

The theologians at Antioch thought that this approach was in effect surrendering to the Arian claims of subordination. Taking another course, they referred such passages not to the divine Logos, but to the man Jesus—the human person. Both approaches provided a defense of the Nicene theology, a refutation of Arian arguments, and a framework for interpreting the Gospels.

The Alexandrian approach had no difficulty recognizing Jesus as God, but tended to diminish the importance of the human portrait of Jesus.

The Antiochian approach seldom had trouble taking this portrait seriously, but always found it difficult to say how this Jesus could be one with God.

This difference is why Arianism and the Nicene creed kept coming up in the Christological controversy. Each side thought the other was selling out to Arianism (church leaders always seem to prefer to fight new battles in terms of old controversies with whose arguments they have become comfortable). Nestorius of Antioch and Cyril of Alexandria in the fifth century were unable to distinguish the defense of the Nicene creed from the doctrine it sought to defend.

Although by the end of the fourth century Nicene dogma had become catholic orthodoxy, its defense rested on different theological approaches. By the fifth century these different defenses had shaped two different theological traditions, which as a result undercut the appeal to tradition.

There was a time—to about the end of the second century—when bishops could appeal to a common tradition. In the Christological controversies, however, we see the crumbling of the classical argument from tradition.

ALEXANDRIAN AND ANTIOCHIAN THEOLOGIANS

Alexandria	Antioch
Cyril, bishop (412 – 44)	Diodore, bishop of Tarsus (368 – c. 390)
Dioscorus, bishop (444 – 51)	Theodore, bishop of Mopsuestia (392 – 428)
Eutyches, archimandrite in Constantinople (fl. 450)	Nestorius, bishop of Constantinople (428 – 51)
Severus, bishop of Antioch (512 – 18)	Theodoret, bishop of Cyrus (423 – c. 460)

The three phases of the Christological controversies of the fourth and fifth centuries concerned three positions that were judged heretical: Apollinarianism, Nestorianism, and Eutychianism.

III. PRELIMINARY PHASE, 362–81: APOLLINARIANISM

The problem in understanding the nature of Jesus Christ has been characterized as the conflict between two Christologies. Alexandria followed a Word-flesh Christology, based on John 1:14, "The Word became flesh." Over against it, Antioch followed a Word-man Christology, speaking of the Word joined to a human being.

An extreme representative of the former approach was Apollinaris of Laodicea (c. 315–92), one of the defenders of the Nicene creed. He explained that the divine Logos took the place of (replaced) the human soul or spirit in Jesus Christ. In other words, Jesus had a human body in which dwelled a divine spirit. The synod of Alexandria in 362 under Athanasius condemned those who rejected the belief that the Savior had a soul or mind, but the object of that condemnation may have been Arians (who also held to a Word-flesh dichotomy) rather than Apollinaris. The Council of Constantinople in 381 condemned Apollinarians by name.

Gregory of Nazianzus supplied the decisive argument against Apollinarianism with his aphorism, "What was not assumed was not healed" (*Epistle* 101). That means, for the entirety of human nature (body, soul, and spirit) to be saved, Jesus Christ must have taken on a complete human person.

A column capital with Christian cross in the ruins of the Serapeum in Alexandria, destroyed under Bishop Theophilus in 391.

IV. THE SECOND PHASE, 381–433: NESTORIANISM

Cyril of Alexandria said that Nestorianism had its roots in Diodore. Diodore was a teacher in Antioch and later bishop of Tarsus (378–c. 390). His students included John Chrysostom, later bishop of Constantinople (chapter 11), and Theodore of Mopsuestia. He was an opponent of Arianism and of Apollinarianism.

In his Christology, Diodore distinguished the Son of God from the Son of David. "Never let the Word be thought of as Mary's son," he declared. The indwelling of the Logos in the human nature is like a person in a temple or a person in his garments. There are two sons of God—one by nature and one by grace.

Verbally, Diodore maintained the unity of the Savior, but he insisted on the completeness of Jesus Christ's human nature, which the Apollinarians denied. The latter accused him of the error that the Word dwelled in Jesus as it did in the prophets.

Theodore of Mopsuestia was born in Antioch (c. 350) and also studied under Libanius with John Chrysostom. He then entered a monastery, where he studied under Diodore. He was ordained a presbyter in Antioch by bishop Flavian in 383 and then became bishop of Mopsuestia in Syria in 392.

This bishop was known in the West as an exegete and biblical critic who practiced a literal interpretation of the Scriptures based on historical context. In the Syriac-speaking "Church of the East," which continued the tradition of the Antiochian church and of Nestorius, he rather than Nestorius is remembered as the authoritative theologian.

Theodore wanted a real humanity of the Lord. In describing the union of the divine and human he favored the language of indwelling. The Logos lived in the man Jesus. While there is a complete distinctness between the human and the divine in Jesus, yet there is also such a unity of will and operation that the result is one person. Since the union is not in essence, nor by activity, however, this union was understood by his critics as no more than a moral union.

Theodore thought in terms of the human Jesus who became God. Apollinaris thought in terms of the divine Christ who became man.

Another important theologian and biblical scholar in the Antiochian tradition was Theodoret (393–c. 460). Born in Antioch, he had Chrysostom and Theodore as his teachers, and Nestorius and John of Antioch as fellow students. He became bishop of Cyrus in Syria in 423, where he began a purge of heresy, an extensive building program, and the writing of historical, polemical, and exegetical works.

The name of Nestorius became attached to the Antiochian theological tradition by its opponents because of the condemnation of Nestorius at the Council of Ephesus in 431. Nestorius was a presbyter and head of a monastery in Antioch when the emperor Theodosius II chose him to be the bishop of Constantinople, a position to which he was consecrated in 428. He soon started a harsh campaign against heretics, but became himself accused of heresy, charges prompted in part by jealousy and in part by his own aggressive personality.

The sticking point in the controversy about Nestorius was the word *Theotokos* ("God bearer") as applied to Mary. The term became the flash point of conflict between the two separate theological traditions that had taken root in Alexandria and Antioch. To supporters of the Alexandrian

"[Christ] united the whole man assumed with Himself, causing Him to share with Him in all the honor which He, the Son by nature indwelling him, enjoys" (Theodore of Mopsuestia, *On the Incarnation* 7).

"I hold the natures [divine and human in Christ] apart, but unite the worship" (Nestorius, *Sermon* 1).

theology, the term seemed entirely appropriate. The divine Christ in the process of taking flesh was truly in the womb of Mary; to say anything less was to deny the full divinity of Christ and the completeness of his union with the flesh. Nestorius and those of his theological tradition were concerned that the title made Mary a goddess. She was the mother of the man who was assumed by God, and nothing should be said that might imply she was the "Mother of God."

In November of 428, Anastasius (chaplain to Nestorius) in a sermon denied that Mary is *Theotokos*, and Nestorius supported him against the protest that ensued because of the increasing honor to Mary in popular piety. In 429 the presbyter Proclus (later bishop of Constantinople) asserted that Mary is *Theotokos*, and Nestorius, who was present, began an extemporized answer. The controversy was under way.

Nestorius was banished by the emperor after the Council of Ephesus in 431. While in exile, Nestorius wrote a book preserved in Syriac under the title *Bazaar* (more accurately *Proceedings*) *of Heracleides*, setting forth his life and defending his position. He warned against Apollinarianism and "paganism" (i.e., the idea that God changes). He claimed that the Word was associated with the human person at the first moment of life, but he offered *Christotokos* in place of *Theotokos* as a more appropriate title for Mary, for she was the mother of the resultant new person.

Modern efforts to rehabilitate Nestorius find him more of a schismatic in temperament than a heretic, for he denied the teaching for which he was accused, namely that the human Jesus and the divine Christ were two different persons, although he lacked a vocabulary and the theological sophistication to relate the divine and human in a convincing way.

The principal opponent of Nestorius was Cyril of Alexandria (bishop 412–44). Like other bishops of Alexandria before him (Athanasius, Theophilus), Cyril was a passionate theologian and determined politician. In his Paschal letter of 429, Cyril defended the term *Theotokos*. The key text for Cyril's Christology was John 1:14, "The Word became flesh."

Cyril applied a grammatical model to the understanding of the incarnation. The Word is the subject; the flesh is the attribute that the Word took on. Becoming flesh involved no change in the divine nature. The self-emptying of the incarnation was a change in the circumstances in which the divine exists, but not a change in divinity itself.

Hence, the unity of Jesus Christ's person is maintained, so much so that Cyril could speak of "one nature" because there is only one acting subject. The Logos unites flesh to himself. The one person is not constituted by the union, but the one person of the Logos extends himself so that humanity is included with himself.

This appropriation of the flesh is what Cyril meant by "composition." His essential analogy was predication, not physical analogies. His comparison of the incarnation to the union of soul and flesh was not an illustration of how the union occurred, but of the change of circumstances in which the one subject lives.

A central theological difference between the Antiochians and the Alexandrians had to do with their approach to the question whether the divine was subject to suffering.

Nestorius maintained the divine impassibility and so insisted on the difference between the divine and human in Jesus Christ. Because the divine impassibility was an axiom of Greek philosophy, the Alexandrians hesitated to assert that the divine suffered in Christ, but Cyril's emphasis on the union of the divine and human in Christ approached an acknowledgment of this in his paradox that Christ "suffered impassibly."

When bishop Celestine of Rome heard of the dispute, he selected John Cassian (c. 365–c. 433) to respond to Nestorius, which he did in *On the Incarnation* (430). Celestine determined to side with Cyril and to try to reclaim Nestorius.

The alliance of Rome and Alexandria still held: a synod in Rome condemned Nestorius in 430, and Celestine asked Cyril to conduct proceedings against him. Cyril had Nestorius condemned in a synod at Alexandria and sent notice of the action to Nestorius with a covering letter and a statement of *Twelve Anathemas* that stated the Alexandrian position in an uncompromising form.

V. THE COUNCIL OF EPHESUS (431) AND ITS AFTERMATH

Theodosius II and Valentinian III called a general council for Ephesus. As the bishops began to gather in 431, the tactical maneuvering resulted in the most confused set of proceedings of any of the ecumenical councils. Cyril and the Egyptian bishops had the support of Memnon, bishop of Ephesus, and the bishops in Asia.

The council opened on June 22, 431, with 153 bishops present. Forty more bishops later gave their adherence to the decisions. Cyril presided. Nestorius was served citations, but he repudiated them. He was then declared deposed and excommunicated, and the city of Ephesus rejoiced.

On June 26, John, bishop of Antioch, and the Syrian bishops, who had been delayed, arrived. John held a rival council in his lodgings, consisting of forty-three bishops and a count representing the emperor.

"If anyone does not confess Emmanuel to be very God, and does not acknowledge the Holy Virgin consequently to be *Theotokos*, for she brought forth after the flesh the Word of God become flesh, let him be anathema" (Cyril of Alexandria, *Third Letter to Nestorius* 12.1).

They declared Cyril and Memnon deposed. Further sessions of the rival councils extended the number of excommunications.

Reports of the activities reached Theodosius II, and representatives of both sides pled their respective cases against their opponents. Theodosius's first instincts, probably correct, were to confirm the depositions of Cyril, Memnon, and Nestorius. Finally, lavish gifts from Cyril and the intercession of his friends carried the day. Theodosius dissolved the council and sent Nestorius into exile, and a new bishop of Constantinople was consecrated. Cyril returned triumphantly to Alexandria.

From the standpoint of church history, the post-council activities were more important than the council itself. John of Antioch sent a representative to Alexandria with a compromise creed. This asserted the duality of natures, in contrast to Cyril's formulation, but accepted the *Theotokos*, in contrast to Nestorius. This compromise creed anticipated decisions to be reached later at Chalcedon. The church at Antioch sacrificed Nestorius for the sake of peace. Cyril assented to the creed and a reunion of the churches occurred in 433.

Judgments on Cyril's action varied: Did he make a statesman-like compromise for the sake of peace, having achieved his main point on the *Theotokos*, or did he cynically accept a creed that contradicted his basic insights, having achieved his purpose of getting rid of Nestorius?

The restored apse of the Church of the Virgin Mary in Ephesus, perhaps built after the Council of 431.

Either way, the real loser was Nestorius. Theodosius had his books burned, and many who agreed with Nestorius's theology tacitly dropped their support.

Those who represented his theological emphases continued to carry on their work in eastern Syria, becoming the Church of the East. For a time, it was a flourishing separated church that spread in Persia and in lands to the east. Today it is greatly reduced in numbers (see further chapter 17).

VI. THE THIRD PHASE, 433–51: EUTYCHIANISM

Both sides of the conflict had their extremists. Nestorius was judged an extreme representative of those who stressed the "twoness" of Jesus Christ, although he later denied that he taught the position he was accused of holding, that Christ represented "two persons." The Cyrillian emphasis on the "oneness" of Christ was continued by Eutyches and Dioscorus, both of whom lacked Cyril's balance and exhibited some of Nestorius's pugnacious personality.

Eutyches was condemned for an extreme advocacy of the one nature of Jesus Christ (so-called Monophysitism). As an aged presbyter and monastic leader in Constantinople, he had opposed Nestorius. He adhered to the phrase that came to characterize his party: "Two natures before the union; but after it one." This formula gave lip-service to the humanity of Christ, but only as an abstraction, for from the moment of the conception of Christ the divinity was the acting subject in the person of Christ. Christ was essentially divine.

At a synod in Constantinople in 448, at which its bishop, Flavian, presided, Eutyches was deposed and excommunicated for teaching the one-nature of Christ (Monophysitism).

Cyril was succeeded as bishop of Alexandria by his arch-deacon Dioscorus (444–51). He has been described as a brutal, proud, fierce ecclesiastic. Eager to vindicate Eutyches, and seeking to duplicate the success of his predecessor, he planned another general council for Ephesus.

Meanwhile, the Roman bishop, Leo I (440–61), had confirmed the actions of the synod of 448 and had written *Tome*, a letter-treatise to Flavian giving an analysis of Christology from a Roman perspective.

Dioscorus presided over a gathering of 135 bishops at Ephesus in 449. Theodoret was excluded from the gathering. The orthodoxy of Eutyches was affirmed, the *Twelve Anathemas* of Cyril were approved as correct doctrine, and representatives of a two-nature Christology (Dyophysitism) were condemned. Theodoret, Flavian, Ibas, and others were deposed.

The club-wielding Egyptian monks who accompanied Dioscorus showed their anger at Flavian by so beating him up that he died later of the wounds inflicted. The atmosphere of intimidation was so strong that the papal delegates feared to read the *Tome* of Leo to the assembly.

Dioscorus had overreached himself and the Roman-Alexandrian alliance—so important in the theological controversies of the fourth and fifth centuries—now snapped.

Leo protested the actions at Ephesus in 439 and called the meeting not an ecumenical council but a "Synod of Robbers." The Alexandrian theology lost its imperial patronage when Theodosius II died in 450. He was succeeded by his sister Pulcheria, who chose the general Marcian as her consort. Pulcheria favored Leo and the Dyophysites.

VII. THE COUNCIL OF CHALCEDON, 451

Pulcheria and Marcian called a general council for Nicaea in 451, but turbulent conduct forced them to move the meeting place to Chalcedon, nearer Constantinople. Between 500 and 600 bishops assembled, the largest of the ancient councils. They were all easterners except for the Roman delegates and two North African bishops.

The first three sessions were concerned with the trial of Dioscorus and related matters. When the minutes of the Robber Synod were read, Theodoret was shown into the assembly at the mention of his name. The minutes of the synod at Constantinople in 448 were read, and Flavian was declared orthodox.

"... in two natures, without confusion, without change, without division or separation ... one person and one hypostasis" (Chalcedonian Definition of Faith).

It was now clear where majority sentiment lay. As a result, Juvenal of Jerusalem and the bishops of Palestine and Illyricum abandoned Dioscorus and went over to the Dyophysite side. Leo's *Tome* was read and greeted with the acclamation, "Peter speaks through Leo," although to some it sounded Nestorian. Dioscorus's deposition was pronounced and signed by the bishops.

The fourth to sixth sessions dealt with the question of drawing up a new Definition of Faith, which many were reluctant to do. It was agreed that the faith was to be based on the Creed of Nicaea as confirmed by Constantinople, expounded by Cyril at Ephesus, and set forth in Leo's *Tome*.

Several efforts to find an acceptable wording failed, but a committee finally produced the Chalcedonian Definition of Faith. The crucial affirmation was that Jesus Christ consisted of two natures (divine and human), but was only one person.

The official promulgation occurred in the sixth session before the emperor, with Pulcheria given the honor of presiding. The bishops gave the following acclamation: "Many years to our emperor and empress, the pious, the Christian.... To the priest, the emperor. You have straightened out the churches, victor of your enemies, teacher of the faith. Many years to the pious empress, the lover of Christ ... to her that is orthodox. You have put down the heretics, you have kept the faith."

The remaining nine sessions settled questions involving various bishops and adopted canons regulating affairs and relationships among the churches.

There were four aspects of the Council of Chalcedon, 451, of importance for the history of the church.

A. Dogmatic

The Definition of Faith in regard to the mystery of the incarnation is the chief element for which the Council of Chalcedon is remembered. The Logos was made man, so he had two natures: two *physes* or *ousiai* in Greek, two *naturae* or *substantiae* in Latin.

Cyril of Alexandria had a different nomenclature. Instead of using *physis* for each substratum of Jesus Christ's being, he used *physis* or *hypostasis* for the unity of personality. Hence, he became the great saint of those called by their opponents Monophysites. For the duality of Christ, he used such expressions as "quality of existence," "natural quality," or "property."

Both sides claimed Cyril for themselves. The so-called Monophysites maintained his literal language of "one nature." The Chalcedonians claimed they were preserving his intentions by establishing a more precise terminology.

At Chalcedon the word *persona* or *hypostasis* was adopted for the unity of Jesus Christ's being, and the word *physis* or *natura* for the duality. Christ was affirmed to be not only *homoousios* with the Father, but also *homoousios* with humanity, sin excepted.

The Chalcedonian formula rejected the tertium quid of Apollinarianism, the two persons alleged against Nestorius, and the one nature affirmed by Eutyches. The formula does not really explain how the two natures became one person; rather it adopts a terminology for the "oneness" and the "twoness" and marks out the boundaries of acceptable speculation. It preserved the mystery rather than explaining it.

B. Conciliar

The Council of Chalcedon was important for defining the authority of councils. It identified the three preceding ecumenical councils: Nicaea, Constantinople, and Ephesus.

Up to this time, no one could have spoken of two or three ecumenical councils, for only Nicaea had general recognition as such. Indeed, there was considerable resistance to the idea of drawing up another creedal statement, for that implied the inadequacy of the one definition of Nicaea.

The council also defined which councils' canons would be authoritative for the churches, so this was an important step toward codifying a common canon law for the church.

C. Monastic

The canons of Chalcedon defined the place of monks in the church. It was decreed that monks may not invade other parishes (no more of the Egyptian monks intimidating bishops at general councils). It also decreed that monks must be subject to the bishop in whose diocese their monastery was located. No new monasteries were to be set up without the bishop's permission.

Chalcedon was a further step in bringing what was almost a rival church under the control of the episcopally organized great church.

D. Constitutional

The Council of Chalcedon confirmed the place of the church of Constantinople as next to Rome. The twenty-eighth canon grounded the authority of the Roman bishop in his place of residence, and not on his connection to the apostles. Thus was laid the basis for a long-standing dispute between Rome and the East on the constitutional basis of the church.

The East followed a principle of accommodation, so the ranking of churches could be accommodated to political realities. Since Constantinople was now the capital of the empire, the new Rome, its bishop should be given a rank reflecting that reality. A primacy of honor was accorded to the bishop of Rome because of the historic associations of Rome as the old capital of the empire.

The bishop of Rome, on the other hand, steadfastly insisted on a principle of apostolicity: Rome had its position because of its connections with Paul and Peter. Leo accepted only the dogmatic part of the Council of Chalcedon as an ecumenical council, because his legates had the prudence to withdraw before the session at which the twenty-eighth canon was approved. He protested that the canon unfairly elevated Constantinople ahead of the apostolic sees of Antioch, Alexandria, and others.

The ranking of Rome, Constantinople, Alexandria, Antioch, and Jerusalem as the principal sees of Christendom established a proto-patriarchal system of church government. (The language of Patriarchs for these sees would be employed in the next century under Justinian.)

The Council of Chalcedon formally closed the Christological controversy for the West, but in the East it inaugurated a new period of debate. Although the wording adopted at Chalcedon has been accepted by the Western churches and many of the Eastern churches as the definitive statement on Christology, the council by no means settled the controversy.

Instead, the controversy continued to rage in various places throughout the East with ever sharper intensity (see chapters 16 and 17).

FOR FURTHER STUDY

Grillmeier, Alois. *Christ in Christian Tradition.* Vol. 1, 2nd ed. Louisville: Westminster John Knox, 1975.

Kelly, J. N. D. *Early Christian Doctrines.* 5th ed. New York: Harper & Row, 1978. 280–343.

McGuckin, John Anthony. *St. Cyril of Alexandria and the Christological Controversy.* Crestwood, NY: St. Vladimir's Seminary Press, 2004.

Studer, Basil. *Trinity and Incarnation: The Faith of the Early Church.* Collegeville, MN: Liturgical Press, 1993.

14

Augustine, Pelagius, and Semipelagianism

I. AUGUSTINE

Augustine is a towering figure in church history. He serves as the climax of patristic thought in Latin and was the dominant influence on the Latin Middle Ages—so much so as to be called the "Architect of the Middle Ages." Augustine has continued to be a major influence in theology for both Catholics (especially in his views on the church and the sacraments) and Protestants (especially in regard to grace and salvation).

A. Life (354–430)

We know the outward facts of Augustine's life and the inner development of his thought better than any other person in the ancient world. There survives a biography by his disciple Possidius, bishop of Calama, that brings out Augustine's daily activities.

There is also Augustine's own *Retractions,* which shows his intellectual development, for he enumerates nearly 95 works, gives the purpose and circumstances under which each was written, and adds corrections and explanations.

Of greatest importance and influence is Augustine's *Confessions,* the first spiritual autobiography in Christianity. "Confession" can mean three things, and probably means all three here: (1) a confession of sin, (2) a profession of faith, and (3) a praise of God (this work is written as a long sustained prayer to God).

Confessions became a religious classic because of its penetrating analysis of sin and human nature, but it is also great source material for the psychology of religion. Books 1–9 are autobiographical, praising God for his graces earlier in Augustine's life despite his own sins; book 10 is epistemological (on knowledge, time, memory, and the church); and books 11–13 are an allegorical exegesis of Genesis 1, praising God with regard to Augustine's present state (having found God, he loves to rediscover him in all his creatures and in the Scriptures). Augustine wrote this classic about 400, twelve years after his mother Monica's death.

Additional source materials include Augustine's numerous writings, especially his letters, which reveal one of the great intellects of all time working creatively and flexibly with topics of perennial concern.

Augustine's life may be divided into five periods.

1. Childhood, 354–70

Augustine was born in Tagaste, a minor commercial city in North Africa. His mother was a Christian and later a saint, pious but superstitious and ambitious for her son. His father, Patricius, was a member of the local ruling class, a pagan but baptized just before his death. Augustine received an elementary Christian education, but was not baptized as a youth.

2. Classical period, 370–75

During his student days Augustine was converted to philosophy in general, but not to any particular philosophy. Cicero's now lost *Hortensius* was his first intellectual turning point. Enamored with classical Latin, Augustine was repelled by the grammar and style of the old Latin versions of the Bible. Early in this period he acquired a concubine, to whom he was faithful and by whom a son was born, Adeodatus ("gift from God"). After studying at Madaura and Carthage, Augustine taught at Tagaste and then in Carthage.

3. Manichaean period, 375–82

Like many Christians, Augustine was attracted by the radical dualism and rational piety of Manichaeism, which presented itself as Christianity for intellectuals. A particularly alluring philosophy, it gave an easy solution to the problem of good and evil. He became an auditor in the religion, in contrast to the perfect observants, the elect.

Augustine, however, began to have some doubts about Manichaeism and looked forward to the coming of Faustus, who was expected to answer his questions, but failed to do so. Magic and astrology then caught Augustine's attention. The beauty of the heavens, considered a manifestation of the divine, led him away from Manichaean dualism. He moved from North Africa with his mother to Rome. Although disappointed with Manichaeanism, he had not totally broken with it. A young man with ambitions, he found the students in Rome better behaved than those in North Africa, but worse about paying their fees.

4. Neoplatonic and catechumen period, 382–89

This transition period in Augustine's life is the least clearly marked on each end. Apparently he went through a brief period of skepticism, not to be surprised at, for when a complete system (like Manichaeism) begins to crumble, often one loses all faith. He was rescued from his doubts by Neoplatonism: the dualism of Manichaeism was dissolved in the spiritualism of Neoplatonism. He learned from Plotinus that all beings are good and that there are incorporeal realities.

In 384 Augustine was appointed professor of rhetoric at Milan, in part through the influence of Manichaean friends in Rome. As much out of professional curiosity as anything, he went to hear the city's most famous public speaker, bishop Ambrose, preach. From him, Augustine heard a much more intellectually respectable interpretation of the Scriptures than he had learned growing up in North Africa.

The presbyter Simplicianus took on Augustine as his personal project. Augustine read the commentary on Paul written by Marius Victorinus, who had been converted in 355 from Neoplatonism to Christianity. Augustine underwent an intellectual conversion, but not yet a moral conversion. It took him some time to get his relationship with his concubine straightened out. When his mother finally convinced him to put her away so that a respectable marriage could be arranged, he had another companion within two weeks (his bride-to-be was still underage). After this failure of sexual self-control, Augustine heard about the austere lives of uneducated monks, who could control themselves in a way that the intellectual Augustine could not. Conversion for him, as for so many in this period, meant a decision for the highest type of Christianity, asceticism. The problem became now not so much one of belief as of action.

Augustine's "conversion experience" occurred in 386. While agonizing in the garden of his house over his moral failures, he heard a child in a nearby house repeat in a sing-song voice the refrain, *Tolle, lege* ("Pick up and read").

There was a book of the letters of Paul on a bench, and Augustine picked it up and read, "Let us behave decently, as in the daytime, not in carousing and drunkenness, not in sexual immorality and debauchery, not in dissension and jealousy. Rather, clothe yourselves with the Lord Jesus Christ, and do not think about how to gratify the desires of the flesh" (Romans 13:13–14).

It was as if the Lord had spoken directly to Augustine. He retired to a country estate to contemplate Christianity seriously. Augustine then enrolled for baptism, which he received from Ambrose on Easter Sunday, 387. He had found his way back to the faith of his childhood and turned his back on his oratorical career.

Augustine and his mother started back to North Africa, but Monica died at Ostia while they awaited passage. The *Confessions* describes in detail a kind of mystical conversion. The language is still colored with

Neoplatonic elements, so the relationship of Neoplatonism and Christianity at this time in Augustine's life is controverted. Nevertheless, Augustine had found peace and assurance that his final destination was God's heavenly Israel.

5. Clerical period, 389–430

Augustine returned to Tagaste and gathered some friends around him in a monastic community. He was ordained presbyter in 391 for the catholic church at Hippo (a city largely Donatist), where he did the preaching because the bishop was Greek and could not handle Latin and Punic fluently. He became a co-bishop in 395 and within a year the sole bishop of the community.

Augustine continued a monastic community life with his clergy, which was later to be imitated by others. The Augustinian Rule is based on his ideas and kind of life. He led an extraordinarily busy episcopal career. Many hours each day were spent judging and counseling those with disputes and problems. Besides, he had an enormous literary output.

B. Writings

Reference has already been made to Augustine's *Retractions* and *Confessions*, and the controversies discussed below in which he was engaged occasioned some of his polemical writings. One authority cites 113 books and treatises by Augustine, close to 250 letters (some of which are equal in length to treatises), and more than 500 sermons.

Perhaps the best introduction to Augustine's thought, in spite of some careless phrases, is his *Enchiridion*, or *On Faith, Hope, and Love*. Faith is an exposition of the Apostles' Creed (sections 9–113), hope is summed up in the Lord's Prayer (sections 114–16), and love is the summary of the commandments (sections 117–21).

Augustine's *On Christian Teaching* (*De doctrina christiana*) is not so much a treatment of Christian doctrine as it is a treatment of Scripture—what it teaches (Book 1), how it is to be interpreted (2–3), and how it is to be presented (4).

On Catechizing the Uninstructed (*De catechizandis rudibus*) gives advice on instruction to inquirers concerning the Christian faith. It provides a long and a short form of a sample instruction, which takes the form of a survey of biblical history within which the teacher can develop any points of special need by the student.

His *On the Good of Marriage*, although upholding the superiority of virginity to marriage, affirmed the benefits of marriage as bringing children into the world, promoting fidelity, and being an indissoluble sacrament symbolizing the union of Christ and the church. It was the

"Whoever, then, appears in his own opinion to have understood the Sacred Scriptures, or even some part of them, yet does not build up with knowledge the twofold love of God and neighbor, 'has not yet known as he ought to know.' Yet, if anyone has derived from them an idea that may be useful in building up this love, but has not expressed by it what the author whom he is reading truly intended in that passage, he is not erring dangerously nor lying at all" (Augustine, *On Christian Teaching* 1.36.40).

textbook on the theology of marriage for the Middle Ages, as Jerome's *Against Jovinian* was the textbook for celibacy.

Augustine is best known, after the *Confessions*, for his *City of God*, the climax of Latin Christian apologetics and the blueprint for the Middle Ages. Written between 413 and 426, the *City of God* was a response to the sack of Rome in 410 by Alaric, leader of the Goths (chapter 15). Although Rome was no longer the capital of the empire, the city was important to all as the symbol of the empire. Pagans were saying that what happened to Rome was a punishment by the gods of the Republic for forsaking their worship. The work grew from an occasional piece to become a comprehensive apologetic responding to paganism and to offer a providential philosophy of history based on the two cities, the city of the world and the heavenly city.

In the *City of God* the question of providence in relation to the Roman Empire proved too narrow a frame of reference for Augustine, who undertook to study the providential action of God with regard to the whole of human history. Books 1–10 are the negative, apologetic part, an attack on paganism, dealing with such questions as: Was Christianity responsible for the fall of Rome? What spiritual power presided over the rise of Rome? Has any pagan system a serious claim against Christianity, the true spiritual religion?

Books 11–22 in the *City of God* are the positive, philosophy of history part, explaining the origin, progress, and end of the two cities.

The basilica at Hippo (in modern Algeria), probably Augustine's episcopal see.

Photo courtesy of Patout Burns.

"City" is broadened to mean "society." There are two cities: of the just (of God, the celestial city) and of the wicked (of the devil, the terrestrial city). Through their love, human beings adhere to either the one or the other, to God or to self. The two cities are confused always and everywhere in this world and are in constant strife. God by providence prepares for the victory of the celestial city to be consummated in the fullness of time. God's judgment consists in giving people what they love most, life with him or separation from him.

Augustine had earlier schematized human history as "before the law," "under law," "under grace," and "in peace"—a scheme that he also applied to the stages of spiritual development in the individual believer—or alternatively as seven periods corresponding to the creation week: five periods of Old Testament history, the period of the new covenant, and the seventh as the millennial rest of the saints after the second coming.

In the *City of God*, however, Augustine elaborated a view of history that involved a non-millennial eschatology. He understood the 1,000 years of Revelation 20:3, 7 as a symbolic figure for either the age of the church or the completeness of human history. This interpretation largely supplanted a literal millennial eschatology throughout the Middle Ages and beyond in much of Western Christendom.

As the *Confessions* was theology experienced in a soul (God's action in the individual), the *City of God* was theology lived in the historical framework of humanity (God's action in the world). Augustine treated current questions from such a noble standpoint that the work remains a classic statement of Christian philosophy, offering profound and original views on common problems of the human mind. He covers concerns that still present moral dilemmas—rape, abortion, suicide.

In stating the principles guiding Christians' relations with human kingdoms, Augustine's analysis often becomes practically threefold: kingdom of God, kingdom of Satan, and kingdoms of men. This led, in the medieval reading of the work, to a confusion of the two cities with church and state.

On the Trinity (*De Trinitate*, written 399–419) is Augustine's major doctrinal work, in which he gave definitive Western formulation to the doctrine of the Trinity. Books 1–7 seek to establish the doctrine according to the Scriptures and to answer objections.

Books 8–15 of *On the Trinity* explore analogies in human nature. Since human beings are made in the image of God, the trinitarian nature of God is imprinted on human beings; for instance, the mind consists of three aspects: memory, intellect, and will. Developing the biblical revelation that "God is love," Augustine hypostasizes love as the eternal relation (the Holy Spirit) between the Father (the Lover) and the Son (the Beloved).

"O Lord the one God, God the Trinity, whatever I have said in these books that is of you, may they who are yours acknowledge; if anything [is] of my own, may it be pardoned both by you and by those who are yours. Amen" (Augustine, *On the Trinity* 15.28.51).

Augustine moved beyond Eastern formulations in a significant way by giving special content to the Third Person, and by laying the basis for seeing the procession of the Holy Spirit as coming from the Father *and* the Son, not simply from the Father *through* the Son (as in Eastern formulas).

C. Controversy with Donatists

The Donatists (see chapter 10) presented the chief ecclesiological problem of Augustine's episcopacy, occupying his attention especially from 400 to 412. Since the time of Constantine, Donatism had been the majority church in North Africa, which was nearly all nominally Christian.

By making the holiness of the clergy the hallmark of Christianity, the Donatists stood mid-way between the early view that all Christians are saints and the later view pioneered by Augustine that the holiness of the church is in its sacraments (chapter 7). They asked, "How can a bishop give [in the sacraments] what he does not possess [holiness]?"

The Donatists' moral rigor, ethnic identification with the native populations of North Africa, and their appeal to the fathers of the North African church (Tertullian and Cyprian), all gave Augustine a hard job.

Augustine's position at first was to be moderate and amicable. He engaged in discussions in hope of converting the Donatists, and he interceded on their behalf when the imperial government sought them out.

In the end, finding this method unsuccessful, Augustine moved on to the position that the government should compel them to come in, appealing to Jesus' parable of the wedding feast (Luke 14:23). This failure to distinguish the church from the Christianized state had very unfortunate consequences later, for this passage in Augustine was used to justify the Inquisition. Augustine himself thought the policy was justified, however, because many Donatists came into the church, and their children grew up to be faithful Catholics.

In answering the Donatist argument against the Catholic clergy and their sacraments, Augustine developed the sacramental view of ordination and the objective character of the sacraments, which prevailed in Western Christendom until the Reformation.

Augustine argued that a royal seal (*signum regale*), an indelible character (*character indelibilis*), was imprinted on one at baptism and ordination. As long as the person intended to be baptized or ordained and the correct action was done and the proper words were spoken, a change in the person was effected. This understanding was later described by the phrase *ex opere operato*, "It is worked by the work." In other words, from the action performed the work is accomplished.

Augustine thus made ordination a permanent possession of the cleric. Sacraments administered by him continued to have validity regardless of his moral character or faithfulness to the church, because ultimately it was God who was doing the work, not the human administrator. This view made ordination no longer an organ of the community, but an individual possession that could be exercised apart from the congregation.

With regard to baptism, this interpretation meant that baptism was valid, whoever performed it, because it imparted an objective character. Whereas strict Donatists rebaptized Catholics who came to their churches, Catholics did not rebaptize Donatists. Instead, by the laying on of hands they reconciled them to the church.

These practices might seem to devalue Catholic baptism, and indeed Augustine acknowledged that many Catholics sought to cover all bases by receiving Donatist as well as Catholic baptism, since everybody agreed that baptism as administered by the Donatists was valid. Augustine saved *Roman* catholicity by saying that the sacraments administered outside the church, although having a formal validity, became actually effective for salvation only in communion with the church.

The Donatists, by maintaining their schism, appeared to be sinning against brotherly love, and although persons baptized by the Donatists did not have to be rebaptized, they could not be saved as long as they maintained their separation from the Catholic church.

A conference in Carthage in 411 assembled 284 bishops from each side. The Donatists were not impressed with Augustine's arguments, and the effort at unity failed. The imperial tribune, however, declared

Photo courtesy of Robin Jensen.

The basilica of Dermech, just outside the walls of Carthage (in modern Tunisia), usually dated to the fifth century and thought by some to have been a Donatist church.

against the Donatists, and an edict in 412 suppressed Donatism, but did not impose the death penalty. The movement declined but did not disappear until the coming of the Muslims in the seventh century.

D. Controversy with Pelagians

Both Donatism and Pelagianism placed an emphasis on human perfectionism instead of divine grace, the one of the church and the other of human nature. The ultimate results of the controversies were not as Augustine intended, but his writings supported the accommodation of the Catholic church to the existing society that marked the transition from late antiquity to the early medieval world.

In the case of the Donatists, Augustine prepared for the end of a separatist view of the church in favor of a "catholic" view of the church. In the case of the Pelagianists, he prepared for the rejection of the old ideals of the autonomy of human ethics and reason in favor of a pessimistic view of unaided human morality.

As Donatism was important for Augustine's elaboration of the sacrament of ordination and the nature of the church, Pelagianism was important for his elaboration of the sacrament of baptism and the doctrine of original sin. With regard to the latter, Augustine argued that baptism imparts an indelible character: there is no more possibility of being held guilty of Adam's sin.

By its very character, asceticism took good works seriously and as advocated by Pelagius (see below) raised questions of free will, original sin, grace, and predestination. Pelagianism has been regarded as the great "heresy" in the West comparable in significance to Arianism in the East. Pelagianism was akin to the Arian controversy in that both had a soteriological interest—Arianism from the divine side and Pelagianism from the human viewpoint.

Almost amounting to one of the "laws of church history" is the repossession of heresy in the name of orthodoxy. Account was taken of Arius's insistence on the difference between the Father and the Son in the final Trinitarian formulation, and although no comparable creedal document resulted from Pelagianism, the dominant viewpoint that emerged maintained his emphasis on the necessity of good works, while affirming Augustine's doctrine of the priority of divine grace.

Augustine began to oppose Pelagius and his associates about 412, and he wrote on the subject up to his death in 430. He went through three stages in his thinking in regard to human free will.

1. Related to overcoming Manichaeism, Augustine could affirm, "I will choose this day whom I will serve" (cf. Joshua 24:15).

Manichees held a fatalistic view: They were the predetermined elect to see the truth. Augustine opposed them with the older Christian position that affirmed free will in respect to faith. The individual makes his or her own decision as to salvation. From Neoplatonism, Augustine borrowed the image of the attractiveness of the highest good moving the human will as a way of overcoming fatalism.

2. Next, Augustine could say, "It is the same God who works all things in all" (cf. 1 Corinthians 12:6), but nowhere is it said that it is God who believes all in all. "That we believe well is our affair; that we do well is his affair." Faith is a human response, but sanctification belongs to the Holy Spirit.

3. Around 396 Augustine moved to a predestination position: Faith too is given by God. God "is at work in you, enabling you to will and to work" (cf. Philippians 2:13). This found expression in a statement in the *Confessions* to which Pelagius took such exception, "Give what you command, and command what you will" (reported by Augustine, *Predestination of the Saints* 2.53). Thus Augustine internalized and individualized the Hebrew doctrine of the chosen people. Before one comes to God, there must be a predisposition to do so, and God gives this.

Not until the later stages of the Pelagian controversy did Augustine meet first-class opponents; they pushed him to such extreme positions that the church at large at the time did not follow him.

More than fourth-century commentators on Paul, Augustine explored the conflict between law and grace, and plumbed the depth of sin as not just wrong acts but as something in human nature. The anti-Pelagian views of Augustine may be listed under the following heads.

1. Adam, made in the image of God, possessed lordship over creation, reason, and ability to live with Eve without lust. Even in paradise he had a fleshly body, not just the resurrection body, as the Eastern fathers said. Moreover, he had a superadded grace that enabled him to choose the good.

2. This grace that gave the possibility of living without sin was removed when Adam did not exercise the gift and chose sin instead. The whole human race was involved in the fall, and as a result of this original sin became a corrupt mass (*massa perditionis*).

3. The transmission of original sin to all human beings is associated with sexual generation. Augustine saw the sexual drive as

a principal expression of concupiscence, which may be defined as the "lust for power," the "drive for control," or more simply the "weakness of the will" that resulted from the fall.

4. Many things contributed to Augustine's generally negative views on sex: Jesus and Paul were unmarried, sex was important in pagan cultus, Augustine had been unable to control his own sexual drives, and certain sexual desires and responses are involuntary. These factors made sex the most conspicuous form of concupiscence. Nonetheless, the evil was not sexuality itself (as in Manichaeism), but the loss of control.

5. After the fall, human free will is not implemented, for the fallen nature inclines the will toward sin and away from God. The human will is moved by what delights it, and this delight escapes self-control. Hence, there is a need for the supernatural activity of grace, not only to aid the will (as the Greek fathers would have said), but also to give (restore) free will.

6. Grace not only turns one toward salvation, but also gives perseverance in it, hence all the means of salvation are absolutely gratuitous.

7. Predestination of the elect to faith, to holiness, and to eternal glory is not just God's foreknowledge, but is based on God's gracious choice. Although in *On Free Will* Augustine had argued that God's foreknowledge did not determine future contingents, the doctrine of predestination involved the conclusion that it did. The non-elect are abandoned to the way of perdition, their natural state without God's gracious intervention.

8. As a personal act of God, this predestination is different from ancient fatalism (which was impersonal), but it was also different from the earlier emphasis in the church on human free will. Human history may be summarized in three periods: "Able not to sin" [Adam in paradise], "not able not to sin" [the human condition after the fall], and "not able to sin" [the heavenly state].

9. God's will to save all refers to the elect, so the number of the saved is limited.

Augustine insisted on infant baptism because each person is a part of a mass of perdition. Baptism removes the guilt of original sin, but not the weakness that it imparts, hence the need for sustaining grace to impart perseverance in faith to the elect.

Pelagius felt no necessity for infant baptism, but was willing to conform to the custom of the church. Augustine used the practice of infant baptism to argue for original sin. Baptism was "for the forgiveness of sins"; since the infant had not committed any sin, though, the forgiveness must be for the sin associated with the fallen human nature. Thus Augustine found his doctrine implicit in the practice of the church, even if he could find few predecessors who taught his view of original sin and lack of free will in regard to salvation.

The relationship of infant baptism and original sin illustrates a frequent occurrence in religious history, namely that a practice precedes the doctrinal justification for it.

Grace for Augustine was more than a soteriological concept. It was also important for epistemology. Human beings are unable to see and know God, not only because of their sinfulness, but also because of their created condition and the limitations of time. Hence, revelation is necessary for knowledge of God, and grace's effect on the reason is primarily revelatory. The model of all revelation is the incarnation, in which Jesus Christ in humility accommodated his divine nature to the human condition. The illumination that makes knowledge possible is an infusion of divine grace. This occurs in salvation, but also in preaching and in the sacraments, whose efficacy derives from Christ acting in them.

For all of his undoubted genius and positive achievements, Augustine has had a problematic influence on Western Christianity in several areas.

1. Augustine's identification of sexuality with the fall and the transmission of original sin has given an unhealthy, negative view of sexuality.

2. His objectification of grace, closely tied to the sacraments, provided the background for the Reformation protest that the biblical understanding of grace was different.

3. His emphasis in later life on individual election gave an anxiety about predestination to Western religious thought.

II. PELAGIUS AND CELESTIUS

Pelagius was born c. 350 in Britain. His father was a physician who had accompanied the bureaucrats there and had married a Celt. Both were Christians and had high ambitions for their son, who was a commanding figure.

By 390 Pelagius was in Rome, where he had come to study law and where he was baptized. He gained influence as a moral reformer and spiritual director. Although an ascetic in reaction against the looseness of Christian life in Rome, he did not advocate a withdrawal from society.

Pelagius had a good background in the classics and the earlier Church Fathers, but he was especially well grounded in the Scriptures. There he found such ideas as free will, moral conduct, doing the will of the Father, good works, following the example of Jesus Christ, and a system of rewards and punishment.

Pelagius distinguished capacity, will, and action. Grace applies only to the first, as the creation of God. Will and action are altogether in human power. So, he located grace in things external to ourselves, in the law and teaching of Jesus Christ, in forgiveness, and in the example of Christ.

Pelagius was not a theologian, much less a mystic; rather, he was a moralist. His view is summed up in the statement, "We confess that man always has free will." God, the Father of all justice, makes no exception of persons, and he does not demand the impossible. Human perfection is possible; therefore, it is obligatory.

Two circumstances make it necessary to treat Pelagius and his follower Celestius together. There is considerable dispute over the authenticity of some of Pelagius's writings (the most important of his acknowledged works being the *Expositions of the Thirteen Pauline Letters*); hence, it is difficult to distinguish his views from those of his associates. Moreover, the controversy that developed from the spread of his ideas in North Africa by Celestius permits the identification of what opponents found objectionable in the teaching.

Pelagius left Rome in 410 with other refugees from the Visigoths, and his ideas provoked sharp reaction in North Africa by the bold and extreme way Celestius presented them. In c. 411 the church in Carthage rejected Celestius for ordination and condemned him for his teachings.

Two points were particularly singled out: his teaching that the sin of Adam and Eve injured themselves alone; and his teaching that a newborn child is in the same state as Adam before the fall (so an infant without baptism has eternal life, but Celestius and Pelagius accepted the church's practice of infant baptism for the forgiveness of sins, but not for transmitted sin).

Other teachings of Celestius that were controverted are these: Adam was made mortal and would have died even if he had not sinned; the law as well as the gospel leads to the kingdom of heaven; before the coming of Jesus Christ there were people who lived without sin; and the whole race does not die because of the sin of Adam and Eve or rise because of the resurrection of Christ.

The implication of these teachings was that a person can live without sin and observe all the commands of God.

Celestius moved to Sicily, and Pelagius departed for Palestine. Augustine began a formal refutation specifically directed at Pelagius. At a conference in Jerusalem, Pelagius successfully defended himself, but Jerome, with encouragement from Augustine, began writing his *Dialogue against the Pelagians*. The Eastern theologians, however, were disposed to give more attention to free will and human deeds, and a council at Diospolis (Lydda) in 415 declared Pelagius and Celestius orthodox.

The North Africans were of a different mind, and a council at Carthage in 416 called on the bishop of Rome to condemn Pelagius. Innocent I in 417 confirmed their condemnation. In response, Pelagius wrote his *Libellus fidei* ("Book of Faith") to Innocent I. The brand-new bishop of Rome, Zosimus, a Greek more favorable to Pelagius, reinstated him in 417.

The angered North African bishops at a council in Carthage in 418 approved nine canons dealing with Pelagianism. Three canons were on original sin, pronouncing anathema on those who say death is not the result of Adam's sin, on those who say a newborn child is not condemned to eternal punishment for what was acquired from Adam, and on those who assert a distinction between the kingdom of heaven and eternal life (the Pelagians made a distinction in order to avoid the argument from John 3:5 on the necessity of baptism for newborn children to receive eternal life).

Three more canons were on grace, anathematizing those who say grace only brings remission of past sins, those who say grace aids us not in understanding (Augustine said grace enables us both to know and to will the right, but Pelagius allowed only an exterior grace), and those who say grace only enables us to do more easily what we do.

The last three canons, on sin, pronounced anathema on those who say 1 John 1:8 confesses sin only from humility; on those who say the petition in the Lord's Prayer, "Forgive us our trespasses," applies only to the congregation, not necessarily the individual; and on those who say this phrase out of humility, not truly.

At this point the state intervened, and the emperor Honorius in 418 banished Pelagius and his followers. Zosimus followed suit, excommunicating Pelagius and Celestius. Pelagius soon passed from the scene. Eighteen Italian bishops, however, refused to sign Zosimus's condemnation of Pelagius, and Julian of Eclanum assumed leadership of the Pelagian position. Julian and his associates took their stand in favor of creation, of marriage, of God's law, of free will, and of the merits of the holy persons of old.

"That we are able to see with our eyes is no power of ours; but it is in our power that we make a good or a bad use of our eyes.... [T]he fact that we have the power of accomplishing every good thing by action, speech and thought comes from him who has endowed us with this possibility, and also assists it.... [W]henever we say that a man can live without sin, we also give praise to God by our acknowledgement of the power which we have received from him, who has bestowed such power upon us" (Pelagius, *On Free Will*, quoted by Augustine in *On the Grace of Christ* 5).

The Council of Ephesus in 431 in its letter to Pope Celestine confirmed the depositions of "Celestius, Pelagius, Julian" and other Pelagians, so while Alexandria was getting what it wanted in regard to Nestorius, Rome was getting what it wanted in regard to Pelagius.

III. SEMIPELAGIANISM

The name "Semipelagianism" is something of a misnomer, for the people included under the label had nothing to do with Pelagius. Even as what was called from the strict Nicene standpoint "Semiarianism" was more nearly the general orthodoxy of Eastern thought on the Trinity, so what was called from the strict Augustinian standpoint "Semipelagianism" was a Western formulation of the general Christian orthodoxy on human nature.

The first phase of the Pelagian controversy was Augustine's controversy with Pelagius and then with Julian of Eclanum. A second phase had already begun before Augustine's death when in 427 his writings on grace and predestination reached Gaul. Monks in southern Gaul sought a middle course between what they saw as the extremes of Pelagianism (limiting grace to the gifts of creation and to the externals of Jesus Christ's example and death) and the extremes of Augustine (limiting human freedom and the extent of God's will concerning salvation).

The leading intellectual figure in monasticism in southern Gaul was John Cassian, abbot of St. Victor in Masillia (modern Marseilles). Born in Scythia (c. 365), Cassian joined a monastery in Bethlehem and then left to study monasticism in Egypt. After a time in Constantinople, Cassian established himself in the West. He founded twin monasteries (one for men and one for women) in Marseilles and promoted the ideals of Egyptian asceticism in this new environment (chapter 12). He became an important monastic theorist and organizer for other ascetic communities in the region, including the earlier foundation on the island of Lerins.

Furthermore, Cassian gave an early formulation of the four meanings of Scripture (see chapter 7 on Origen) that guided biblical interpretation throughout the Middle Ages. He applied the four meanings to Jerusalem: historically, Jerusalem is the city of the Jews; allegorically, it is the church of Christ; anagogically, it is the heavenly city of God; and tropologically, it is the human soul. Each passage of Scripture could be approached in this fourfold way so as to draw out relevant teachings.

A medieval formulation stated: "The letter teaches the things done; allegory [teaches] what you are to believe; the moral meaning what you are to do; and anagogy what your goal is" (Nicholas of Lyra, ca. 1340).

Modern Biblical exegesis has swept away all except the historical sense. In the process, it has cut off access to a rich patristic and medieval theology and spirituality derived from meditation on the biblical text.

Cassian presented his own views on the relation of grace and free will in *Conferences* 13. He rejected Pelagianism, but he also rejected Augustine's predestination, particularism of grace, and complete bondage of the will. He affirmed the paradox that everything is the work of God's grace, yet everything can be ascribed to free will. The divine image and human freedom were weakened but not destroyed by the fall; human beings are sick, but not dead. A person cannot help himself, but can desire help and can accept or refuse it when offered. Either the human will or God's grace may take the initiative in an individual's salvation.

The stories in the Gospels of two tax collectors illustrate the possibilities. In the case of Zaccheus, the will determined itself to conversion before the Lord spoke his words of grace. In the case of Matthew, the Lord's call and grace anticipated the will.

Theologically, Cassian affirmed that every beginning of human salvation is founded on God's grace. But he argued that this external grace is supplemented by inner grace, which acts on mind and will to effect sanctification. He also argued that God wills the salvation of all, and that predestination is based on foreknowledge of those who accept or reject his grace.

"If you wish to attain to a true knowledge of Scripture, then, you must first hasten to acquire a steadfast humility of heart ..., for it is impossible for the impure mind to receive the gift of spiritual knowledge" (John Cassian, *Conferences* 14.10.1).

"Special care must be taken that we hold to that which has been believed everywhere, always, and by all" (*quod ubique, quod semper, quod ab omnibus* — Vincent of Lerins, *Commonitorium* 3).

In addition to Cassian and others who articulated an alternative to Augustine's theory of grace, there were also those conservatives who simply reacted against the novelty of Augustine's teaching.

One such conservative, Vincent of Lerins, pointed out what were to him the illogical and blasphemous deductions from Augustine's doctrine, namely that God was responsible for sin and damnation.

Vincent presumably had the novelty of Augustine's teachings at least partly in mind when in his *Commonitorium* (434) he constructed the classic statement of the ancient church's doctrine of tradition. As is often the case, this polished formulation came after the position had lost its validity. The appeal to tradition, by reason of the passage of time, was no longer viable. In his survey of previous doctrinal controversies of the church, Vincent's history is a striking example of history written by the victors.

Vincent declares that we fortify ourselves in the true faith, first, by the authority of the canon of Scripture. Second, Scripture is to be interpreted by the tradition of the church, especially as expressed in the decisions of ecumenical councils. If a question has not been addressed by the councils, Scripture is to be interpreted by the agreement of the Church Fathers on the matter.

In matters of faith, then, Vincent said the "catholic church" follows the principles of "ecumenicity, antiquity, and consensus."

Vincent argues in a circle by circumscribing such a general consensus to the "orthodox" fathers. Even if one assumes that such a consensus can be found, this rule is limited as a guide since it throws no light on the path in front, only on that which has already been traversed.

Indeed, those churches that claim to follow the authority of tradition as laid down by Vincent do not come off too well by his standards. While they explain that what fulfills the conditions is to be accepted, it does not follow that a doctrine lacking one of these characteristics should be excluded. Of course, such was the very thing Vincent wanted to exclude!

Nevertheless, Vincent's exposition does allow for progress in dogma: there can be development, if it does not involve change in essentials.

The first stages of the Pelagian controversy were over, but the issue was not settled. Pelagianism was rejected, but many were not satisfied with the later formulations of Augustine.

Nor did the Semipelagians carry the day, for the Augustinians had their responses to Augustine's critics (next chapter).

More immediately, other problems demanded attention: The barbarians were at the gates.

FOR FURTHER STUDY

See Reference Works at back of book.

Brown, Peter. *Augustine of Hippo: A Biography.* Berkeley: University of California Press, 1967.

Chadwick, Henry. *Augustine of Hippo: A Life.* Oxford: Oxford University Press, 2009.

Harmless, William, ed. *Augustine in His Own Words.* Washington: Catholic University of America Press, 2010.

Stump, Eleonore, and Norman Kretzmann, eds. *The Cambridge Companion to Augustine.* Cambridge: Cambridge University Press, 2001.

Weaver, Rebecca H. *Divine Grace and Human Agency: A Study of the Semi-Pelagian Controversy.* Macon, GA: Mercer University Press, 1996.

Transitions to the Middle Ages

Germanic Migrations, Doctrinal Developments, and the Papacy

When Augustine died in 430, the Vandals were at the gates of Hippo. While the Council of Chalcedon was in progress in 451, Leo the Great was negotiating with the Huns to save Italy from their ravages. Western history was dominated in the fifth and sixth centuries by the movement of (principally) Germanic peoples into the territory of the old Roman Empire. The accompanying displacements and interchanges of population had a profound effect on Christianity in the western regions.

Medieval civilization was built up from the culture of the later Roman Empire (especially Roman literature, law, and governmental institutions), the customs of Germanic peoples, and the church with its faith and practices (specifically the theology of Augustine and the preeminence of the papacy).

The Byzantine civilization (chapter 16), in contrast, was built up from the culture of ancient Greece, the institutions of the Roman state, the customs of the Hellenized peoples of the Near East, and Christianity.

I. WHEN DID THE MIDDLE AGES BEGIN?

Periodization is helpful for getting a handle on major changes in history, but the continuities in history make the assignment of exact dates for these changes somewhat arbitrary.

The very terminology of "Middle Ages" is a prejudice of the Renaissance due to its program of recovering the classical past before "barbarism" prevailed in the intervening centuries. Without accepting the prejudice involved in the term, students still realize that there were new developments.

The beginning of the Middle Ages is often taken as equivalent to the fall of Rome, but other factors were involved. There was a break in the history of western Europe with the Germanic invasions, but the question of the beginning of the Middle Ages is too complex for these invasions to provide the simple answer it did for older historiography. There was a gradual but steady decline in the institutions of the Roman world from the third to the eighth centuries that makes an exact dating difficult.

Various dates for the beginning of the Middle Ages have been proposed:

1. 330, when Constantine moved the capital to Byzantium, but Rome had already ceased to be an administrative capital. This event was significant for church and cultural history.

2. 395, the death of Theodosius I, the last of the great emperors. There was no effective single ruler after him, and the administration of the empire was never again reunited under one head.

3. 410, when Alaric sacked Rome, an event that sent considerable shock waves across the Roman world.

4. 451, the date of the Council of Chalcedon, sometimes taken in the history of doctrines as the end of the Patristic Age.

5. 476, when the last emperor in the West, Romulus Augustulus, was deposed by the Germanic chieftain Odoacer. This event was long taken as the symbolic event marking the end of the Roman Empire. Since the Roman Empire still continued in Constantinople, however, contemporaries apparently did not mark it as all that significant.

6. 604, the death of Pope Gregory I, an alternative to 451 in patristic studies, so as to include this "doctor of the church" in the patristic period.

7. Seventh and eighth centuries—when Arabs swept around the Mediterranean, limiting contacts based on trade and travel across the Mediterranean between East and West, and weakening the cultural continuity of the region.

8. 754, when Pope Stephen II anointed Pippin as king of the Franks, an event marking the turn of Rome's attention to the West instead of to the Mediterranean and the East.

Various factors have provided the basis of theories concerning the decline of ancient civilization:

1. Political—the decline of the role of cities, the weakening of government by civil wars and military emperors in the third

century, the bureaucracy at the expense of the senate that continued in the reorganization of Diocletian and Constantine.

2. Economic—the failure of industry, the decline of trade, the turn to a "house economy," the impoverishment of the soil (which has been disproved).

3. Biological—some form of racial degeneration (for which there is no proof).

4. Christianity—turning human attention to another world and draining off the best minds from affairs of state (but most of the faults attributed to Christianity existed apart from Christianity).

5. Social—higher classes, who were the custodians of classical culture, were overwhelmed by the illiterate masses.

6. Military—constant wars on the frontiers so that "Roman civilization did not die a natural death; it was murdered."

In regard to these and other factors that have been mentioned, the question may be asked: what is symptom and what is cause? Most of these items, instead of answering "why," are more descriptive than causal.

The principal factors that produced a new situation, from a church history standpoint, for the western Middle Ages have already been examined in previous chapters:

1. Constantine—the state-church that emerged in the fourth century, an alliance of the government with Christianity, and the consequent large scale conversion of half-instructed people.

2. Augustine—the theological reconstruction of Augustine that gave a new pattern of thinking for Western Christians.

3. Monks and popes—the development of monasticism and the papacy as the dominant religious and social institutions.

To these factors another may be added:

4. Missions—the conversion of Germanic peoples to a form of Christianity.

II. THE MIGRATION OF NATIONS IN THE WEST

The Germanic incursions of the fifth century were but the first of four great waves of migration and invasion to sweep into the territory of the old Roman Empire: (1) the Germans especially in the fifth century, (2) the Mongol Avars and the Slavs into the Balkans beginning in the sixth century, (3) the Muslim Arabs beginning in the seventh century, and (4) the Northmen or Vikings from Scandinavia in the eighth to the tenth centuries.

The resulting ethnic, cultural, and religious changes produced significant developments affecting the history of the church. Our concern now is with the first of these, the Germanic invasions.

The fifth century was the culmination of a long process of somewhat controlled immigration in which the Germans found land, settled within the frontiers of the empire, and served in the empire's military. In some respects these barbarians preserved, rather than destroyed, the empire by filling gaps in the population and manning the armies.

Depending on their proximity to Roman institutions, the different Germanic tribes entered the empire with varying degrees of Romanization. Pressures from the movement of peoples out of central Asia, broken treaties between the Romans and the Germans, and search for better living conditions turned the tide of migration into an armed flood.

Certain key dates in the first half of the fifth century mark the transition:

1. 410—Alaric, leader of the West Goths, sacked the city of Rome, a traumatic event for the western Roman world. His successor Ataulf married the sister of the emperor Honorius.

2. 430—Augustine, who had written the *City of God* to explain the fall of Rome in 410, died the year before the Council of Ephesus in the East and the fall of his city of Hippo in North Africa to the Vandals.

3. 451—Attila and the Huns from central Asia, who were sweeping through western Europe, were defeated by an alliance of Romans and Germans led by Aëtius and were persuaded by Pope Leo to turn back from Rome. The same year the Council of Chalcedon was meeting in the East.

4. 455—Aëtius and the emperor Valentinian III were assassinated, and the Vandals under Gaiseric sacked Rome.

III. CHRISTIAN MISSIONS AMONG THE GOTHS

It was of great significance that when the barbarian Germans swept through the western Roman world in the fifth century, they came (for the most part) not as pagans but as Arian Christians. The first of the Germanic peoples to be reached with the Christian gospel were the Goths. One of their bishops, Theophilus, was at Nicaea.

The principal missionary among the Goths was Ulfilas (c. 311–c. 383), consecrated bishop in 341 by Eusebius of Nicomedia. He was of mixed ancestry and spoke Greek, Latin, and Gothic. He signed the Homoean creed of the Council of Ariminum (Rimini, 359) while at Constantinople in 360. As far as Ulfilas knew, he was carrying the proper form of Christianity to the Goths.

The task of conversion was facilitated by two historical realities: (1) the Germanic peoples' old religion was in decline at the time of contact with Christianity and (2) the Germanic peoples all spoke a common tongue.

Ulfilas was active in communicating the gospel and translating the Scriptures until his death. He left the books of Samuel and Kings out of his translation (the Goths knew enough about warfare already!). His activity is a reminder that translation has often accompanied mission work, even to the extent, as in this case, of creating a written alphabet for the language.

To the Goths, accustomed to three chief gods (Tu, Thor, and Woton), who had no control over the lesser gods (called demons by the missionaries), Ulfilas insisted on monotheism. He used the figure of Jesus as a prince, the hero (*held*), under the Father as King. In this simple form he taught the people and avoided Logos speculation. From the Goths Arian Christianity spread to other Germanic peoples (with the exception of the Franks).

Arian Christianity among the Goths had the following characteristics:

1. They spoke of the Father and the Son as of "one blood," instead of the Greek philosophical language of one substance, and so avoided theological debate.

2. The liturgy and the Scriptures were in the vernacular.

3. No distinctive church community was created, but social ties remained those of the family and the clan.

4. The bishops and priests from the beginning were rather like military chaplains, for there were no fixed geographical dioceses, and there were no metropolitan bishops (there were no cities!). Synods were assembled by the ruler, since there was no hierarchy between the bishops and the ruler.

5. The prevailing organizational pattern was the "proprietary church" (*eigenkirche*), or "church of the ruler" or of any lay patron, since a prominent member of the "folk" who built a chapel and secured the services of a priest considered the church as in a sense belonging to himself. This authority of

the proprietary lord over priests weakened episcopal jurisdiction. Later the most prominent free bishop of the church in the West was the Roman bishop, so he had to fight for the freedom of the church from the control of secular authorities. The proprietary church arrangement survived after the Arian theology was gone.

6. As in the empire, the ritual side of Christianity counted more than the moral.

7. The saints came to be viewed more as helpers than as models.

IV. MOVEMENTS OF SPECIFIC PEOPLES

We will make a half circle around the western Mediterranean, following the course of events affecting the different Germanic tribes.

A. The Vandals and North Africa

When Rome removed its armies from the Rhine in 406 in order to protect Italy, the Germanic tribes poured into Gaul, Spain, and North Africa. Gaiseric (king 428–77) led the Vandals across western Europe into North Africa (429). Carthage was taken in 439 and made the capital of an Arian Vandal kingdom. Gaiseric was an intolerant Arian. In 455 he felt so powerful that he sent his ships across the Mediterranean to sack Rome.

The Donatists in North Africa initially rejoiced in the coming of the Vandals. A Donatist-Catholic synod met in 484 to try to heal their theological differences. There was an abatement of persecution of Catholics under king Gunthamund (484–96), but his brother Thrasamund (496–523) resumed persecution. This religious persecution of Catholics did more to give the Vandals their bad name than any acts of "vandalism," for the Vandals were no more "barbaric" than the other Germans.

Justinian's general, Belisarius, reoccupied North Africa for the Byzantine empire in 534.

B. The Visigoths (West Goths) and Spain

The first contact of the Romans with the Goths came under Decius. During the time of Constantine the Goths became allies (*foederatae*), and they often entered the army in high offices. The West Goths were hard-pressed by the Huns, and in 376 they sought refuge on the Roman side of the Danube. The emperor Valens granted this, and there began a mass conversion to Arianism.

Three Visigothic votive crowns from the seventh century (Cluny Museum, Paris).

Due to mistreatment, the Goths revolted in 378 and killed Valens in the battle of Adrianople, an event that marked the real beginning of the Germanic invasions and shocked the East in a way comparable to the effect of the sack of Rome in 410 on the West. The emperor Theodosius moved the Goths west.

The Gothic king Alaric died in the same year (410) as the sack of Rome, but by 419 his successor, Ataulf, had mastered southern Gaul and all of Spain. Under their king Theodoric (420–51) the Visigothic army fought with Rome against the Huns in 451. The pro-Roman Theodoric II (451–56) was succeeded by Euric (456–84), a cruel ruler. During the reign of Alaric II (484–507) the Visigoths were forced out of Gaul, and Toledo [Spain] became the center of the Visigothic kingdom.

By 565 Justinian had regained much of the West, including part of Spain. King Reccared (586–601) accepted Catholic Christianity in 587. This conversion was signaled by the third synod of Toledo in 589, where the Nicene creed was accepted.

In an effort to establish orthodoxy, the synod may have overdone it by adding the *filioque* clause ("and from the Son") to the creed. Whereas the current form of the "Nicene Creed" (approved in 381) said that the Spirit "proceeds from the Father," the Latin of the creed adopted in 589 said the Spirit "proceeds from the Father and the Son," an expansion based on Augustine's theology of the Trinity and designed to emphasize the full deity of the Son.

This addition was later to alienate the Eastern Christians, who argued that the Nicene creed was inviolable and not subject to change and that the addition introduced two sources of deity into the Godhead. In any case, the Arians and Catholics in Spain united to drive out the Byzantines.

Instrumental in the conversion of Reccared to Catholic Christianity was Leander (not himself a Goth but from the old Italian aristocracy), bishop of Seville and friend of Gregory the Great. Leander was succeeded by his brother Isidore, metropolitan of Seville (599–636), who is remembered as the most important religious figure of Visigothic Spain. His *Etymologiae*, or *Origines*, was an encyclopedia of the knowledge of the time. As a transmitter of learning he became one of the educators of the Middle Ages. In 633 the Fourth Council of Toledo systematized the liturgy of the Mozarabic Rite.

In 711 the Muslims brought an end to the Visigothic kingdom.

C. The Suevians

The Suevians occupied the northwestern Iberian peninsula. They became Catholic early under Rechiarius (448–57) but then passed back to Arianism. Their final conversion came about 550–55 under King Charriaric, thanks largely to the influence of Martin, bishop of Braga (after 561–80). Their kingdom was annexed by the Visigoths in 585.

D. The Burgundians

The Burgundians had their center on the middle and upper Rhone river. They were divided between Arians and Catholics, and they were speedily and thoroughly Romanized. The Burgundian kingdom was absorbed in 534 by the Franks.

E. The Franks

The Franks were the least mobile of the Germanic peoples, settling in what is now northern France and expanding their political rule from there. They joined other German tribes and the Romans in defeating the Huns in 451. They also had been the most immune to Christianity, before coming directly from paganism to Catholic Christianity under their king Clovis (c. 466–511).

Clovis's conversion to Catholic Christianity was significant for future European history. Since the Vandals, Visigoths, Ostrogoths, and most of the Burgundians were Arian, it was possible that Arianism would take over the West as the empire broke down. Moreover, alone of the Germanic kingdoms, the Frankish kingdom (under the Merovingian dynasty) survived, perhaps in part because Clovis early embraced the same faith as the majority of his subjects.

Avitus, bishop of Vienne (c. 490–518), planned the marriage of the Burgundian princess Clotilda, a Catholic Christian, to Clovis (c. 492). They had a son, who was baptized but died while still in his baptismal robes. Clovis said his gods would not allow such a thing to happen. Later they had another son who lived. In war against the Alemanni, another Germanic tribe, Clovis asked for the aid of the Christian God. When the Alemanni were defeated and their king killed, Clovis submitted to baptism, bishop Remigius of Rheims performing the baptism on Christmas day (496 is the traditional date).

The principal source for Clovis's conversion is the *History of the Franks*, written by Gregory, bishop of Tours (538–94). In this work and others Gregory gave to the Franks a sense of identity and shaped their self-understanding for the future.

As a propagandist for the orthodox, Gregory viewed Clovis as a new Constantine and developed the symbolic importance of his bap-

The invasion of the western empire by Germanic peoples during the fifth century.

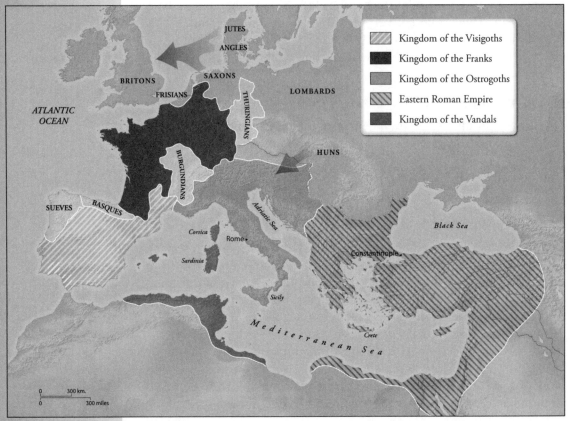

> ## THE VASE OF CLOVIS
>
> Clovis plundered a number of churches, and at one a large vase was taken. The bishop pleaded with Clovis to return it, and he was going to do so, claiming the vase as part of his share of the booty. One of his men, however, insisted that it should be assigned by lot as was the rest of the booty and shattered the vase with his axe. Later, at a muster of the soldiers, the man who broke the vase did not pass inspection. Clovis seized the man's battle-axe and threw it to the ground. As the man bent to pick it up, Clovis took the axe and buried it in the man's head, exclaiming, "Thus you did the vase at Soissons" (Gregory of Tours, *History of the Franks* 2.27).

tism, placed at the age of thirty (the age of Jesus' baptism) and accompanied by the baptism of 3,000 of his soldiers (cf. Pentecost in Acts 2). Consequently, many details associated with the conversion remain undetermined and even the date uncertain (496 or 498).

The anointing of Clovis after his baptism became a custom among the Franks at the appointment of kings. The resulting aura of sacred Christian kingship gave a justification for the Frankish control of the church. Clovis's character, however, remained little changed by his acceptance of Christianity.

After defeating the Visigoths in 507, Clovis seized their treasury and gave it to the shrine of St. Martin of Tours. At Tours in 508 Clovis received a cloak from the eastern emperor, completing an alliance in faith with Rome and in politics with Constantinople. Following the conquest of Aquitania from the Visigoths in 507, the Frankish kingdom added Burgundy in 534 and Provence from the Ostrogoths in 536.

In 511 the bishops of the Frankish territory met in Orleans for the first synod of the Merovingian kingdom. Bishops had assembled on the level of civil provinces, regions, or the empire as a whole before, but it was new for them to meet on the level of a kingdom, with the king in some respects taking the place of the emperor.

F. The Ostrogoths and Italy

In 476 the Germanic general Odoacer (Odovacar) deposed the young Romulus Augustulus, the last ruler of the West before Charlemagne to wear the name of emperor, and Odoacer became the effective ruler of Italy. He was slain in 493 by Theodoric, ruler of the East Goths (Ostrogoths) since 471 and in the imperial service since 488.

Mosaic of Theodoric, later reascribed to Justinian, in the church of Sant' Apollinare Nuovo, Ravenna.

"Reason belongs to the human race alone, just as the true intelligence is God's alone.... We should then think it most just that human reason should yield itself to the mind of God, just as we have determined that the senses and the imagination ought to yield to reason" (Boethius, *The Consolation of Philosophy* 5.5).

Next to Clovis, Theodoric was the most important ruler of the new barbarian kingdoms. Theodoric made Ravenna his capital. He was an Arian and a barbarian, but he supported Byzantine culture. Personally tolerant, he found his Catholic subjects not so tolerant. His rule (493–526) brought the last flowering of late Roman culture in the West.

The Ostrogothic kingdom continued until 553, when Justinian retook much of Italy for the Byzantine empire. The cultural revival from 493 to 553 may be called the "Indian summer of Christian antiquity." During this period flourished a number of significant persons who laid the basis for early medieval society.

Boethius (c. 480–524/26), a philosopher and statesman, was a member of a leading Roman family and became a minister in the government of Theodoric. Although loyal, Boethius came under suspicion and Theodoric had him imprisoned and later executed for treason. While in prison, Boethius wrote his most famous work, *Consolation of Philosophy*.

Boethius represents a transition from the Fathers to the Scholastics, for his approach anticipated the work of the later Schoolmen. He communicated to the Middle Ages, through his translations, what was known of Aristotle—his ethics and logic, including Porphyry's commentary on the latter (chapter 21). The Schoolmen esteemed Boethius the greatest authority in philosophy after Aristotle.

Dionysius Exiguus ("the Less," an expression of his humility) was a Scythian who came to Rome toward the end of the fifth century and died about 527. He collected and translated the canons of the Eastern church into Latin. He also collected the canons of the Western church and papal decretals. As his work grew, it soon attained great authority.

Dionysius has a wider cultural significance because he introduced a system of dating based on the Christian era, beginning with the incarnation (AD for *anno domini*, "in the year of the Lord") instead of the secular method according to the consuls of Rome and the empire of

Diocletian. Unfortunately he miscalculated the date of Jesus' birth, so that according to contemporary reckoning Jesus was born at least 4 BC ("before Christ").

The relative security of the period made possible an interest in dates and archives. The *Liber Pontificalis* ("Book of Popes"), composed under Pope Boniface II (530–32), contains the "Liberian Catalogue" (from the fourth century; Liberius is the last pope mentioned), and then a continuation about the later popes up to Felix IV (526–30). The work was then kept up by contemporary accounts until the ninth century.

Cassiodorus (c. 485–c. 580) was another important Catholic in the administration of Theodoric, holding various offices from the age of twenty. He became the soul of Theodoric's government, contributing to the greatness of the reign and being honored by his successors. He preserved the laws of the Ostrogoths in his *Variae*, and the collection of his letters while in public office became the model for chancelleries in the Middle Ages.

When Cassiodorus retired from public life in 540, being granted a "second life," he said, he established the monastery of Vivarium on his estate on the southern coast of Italy. His monks translated some works and copied manuscripts of others by dictation, an activity important in the transmission of Jerome's Vulgate.

Cassiodorus's *Institutes of Divine and Secular Readings* presented a union of sacred and secular knowledge, providing an introduction to theology and Scripture and a summary of the liberal arts. Although his monastery did not survive, its ideal of learned celibacy was picked up in part by the Benedictines later.

Another important figure of the period, Benedict of Nursia, born about the same time in 480 as Boethius and Cassiodorus, will be considered in relation to Gregory the Great (chapter 16).

G. The Lombards and Italy

The Lombards in 568 broke through the northern bounds of Justinian's empire and entered Italy. Gregory the Great in 593 turned them back and secured peace with a division of Italy between Lombard and imperial holdings.

Not united, the Lombards ruled from three centers: The kingdom at Pavia in the north threatened Ravenna; the duchies of Spoleto and Benevento in central Italy were a danger to Rome and Naples respectively.

The Lombards were Arian. Their acceptance of Catholic Christianity did not come until the seventh century.

"Every word of the Lord written by the scribe is a wound inflicted on Satan. And so, though seated in one spot, with the dissemination of his work he travels through different provinces. The product of his toil is read in holy places; people hear the means by which they may turn themselves away from base desire and serve the Lord with heart undefiled. Though absent, he labors at his task" (Cassiodorus, *Institutes of Divine and Secular Readings* 1.30).

Two gold crosses from the Lombards (seventh–eighth century) found near Pavia (Museo Civico Medievale, Bologna).

V. EFFECTS OF THE BARBARIAN INVASIONS

A. The Christian Literary Response to the Invasions

Others besides Augustine undertook literary responses to the Germanic invasions. Although the plunder of Rome in 410 seemed to some to mark the end of the ages, Orosius, at the suggestion of Augustine, wrote *Seven Books against the Pagans* (417–18) in order to show that the pre-Christian world suffered no less than the present and to interpret the invasions as a chastisement from God. The work became a manual of universal history in the Middle Ages.

Orosius gave an important place to the Roman Empire in the divine scheme, so that his theological history placed on the Western mind the idea of the divine role of the Roman people. Jerome had already interpreted the fourth kingdom of Daniel as Rome and concluded that it was to continue as long as the church did, a significant idea in the future. Orosius promoted the view that both the Hebrew and Roman peoples had a part to play in the salvation of the world.

Salvian's *On the Divine Government* in 440 added the historical significance of the Germanic people. He exaggerated the good qualities of the Germans in contrast to the corruptions of the Romans, so that the invasions served as chastisements for Rome's sins.

Augustine held that political success and failure are ultimately indifferent: his focus was on the world to come. Orosius, on the other hand, retained the belief of Eusebius of Caesarea that Christianity was the guarantor of the empire's prosperity. Salvian claimed that the empire was punished for its sins. These appeared to be the three possible attitudes open to Christian apologists in the aftermath of the invasions.

Later Christian historians in the West began to write the history of the Germanic peoples, expanding Salvian's incorporation of them into God's providential rule. Thus Cassiodorus (c. 485–c. 580) wrote a *History of the Goths* (now lost), Gregory of Tours a *History of the Franks* (written 576–91), Isidore of Seville (c. 560–636) a *History of the Goths, Vandals, and Suevi*, and the Venerable Bede the *Ecclesiastical History of the English Nation* (completed 731).

B. Effects on Society

The Germanic Christian kings for the most part regarded themselves as Roman, acknowledged the emperor in the East, and respected Roman traditions and customs.

Nevertheless, the old Roman and the new Germanic peoples were divided by language (Latin or Gothic), customs of food and dress (Latins wore togas and Germans trousers), and legal systems (often different laws were applied to the different peoples within the same kingdom). It took centuries for the two peoples to blend and become the nations of modern Europe.

Greco-Roman civilization had been based on cities, but the Germanic invasions brought a decline in cities. A purely rural economy developed in the West, accelerating the development of feudalism. Bureaucracy, civil service, and mercenaries were possible in the East because of a money economy.

Whereas in the East cities remained the backbone of the social organization, in the West country estates held this position. The kings had to subsist essentially on their own landed possessions, so there was a decentralization of government services.

C. Effects on the Churches

With the decline in central government in the West, the church took over many public services, for example education, that retained their traditional basis in the East.

In the West, churches and monasteries were bound to the agricultural economy and profited by the prominence of local powers.

The church had advantages over the monarchies. The idea of a universal authority associated with the church created a potential superiority over the more limited authority of regional kings. No secular authority in the West was able to control the church as an organ of state to the same extent as the eastern emperors.

On the frontiers of the empire, Christianity was less well established. This fact, plus the destruction caused by the invasions, resulted in an almost total obliteration of the church's presence or, if not, at least a temporary withdrawal.

In regions farther back from the frontiers, the settling of new populations and other effects of the invasions disrupted the church's life for varying periods of time, but did not completely interrupt it.

As the empire crumpled, the church almost alone of the old institutions survived, and to it Christians looked for support and continuity. The bishops often mediated with the invaders and the new kings.

Nearer the Mediterranean core of the western empire, in southern Gaul and Italy, the upheaval was less extensive, and Roman civilization was able to lead a tenuous life for several generations. Churchmen there could continue to indulge in the luxury of theological controversy.

VI. THE LATER STAGES OF THE AUGUSTINIAN-PELAGIAN CONTROVERSY

As we saw in chapter 14, the first phase of the Pelagian controversy was Augustine versus Pelagius, and the second phase was the Semi-Pelagian reaction against Augustinianism in southern Gaul. A third phase opened with the defense of Augustine by his supporters in Gaul.

From the literary viewpoint the principal champion of Augustine's ideas was Prosper of Aquitaine (c. 390–after 455). He replied to Cassian in *Contra Collatorem* (432) and sought the aid of Pope Celestine against the "Semipelagians." At first Prosper appears more faithful to strict Augustinianism and tried to hang the already condemned heresy of Pelagius on Cassian.

For Prosper the key issue was the utterly gratuitous character of grace, and he saw the cause of disagreement as differing estimates of the effect of the fall on the human capacity for good. Prosper's response to the objections others lodged against Augustine's teaching defended predestination and perseverance, but introduced foreknowledge of wrongdoing as the reason for God's withholding the grace of perseverance from some.

Prosper's *On the Calling of the Gentiles* wrestled with God's will to save all, a troublesome concept for Augustinians. He explained that God's general grace invited all, and he interpreted 1 Timothy 2:4 as God's will that prayer be made for the salvation of all. Although he was conciliatory about the place of the human will in salvation, Prosper's case was ultimately unsatisfactory because his emphasis on the necessity of special grace for salvation was inconsistent with the universal saving will of God.

A fourth phase in the controversy saw renewed opposition to strict Augustinianism as expressed by Lucidus, whose views on predestination were condemned in a synod at Arles in 473. Faustus, abbot of Lerins in 433 and then bishop of Rhegium (Riez) in 458, wrote *On Grace* to oppose predestination. He sought to locate a middle position between Pelagius and Augustine, affirming both the freedom of the will and the necessity of grace. Avitus, bishop of Vienne (c. 490–c. 518) and Fulgentius, bishop of Ruspe in North Africa (c. 507–c. 533) affirmed a thoroughgoing Augustinianism against Faustus.

The final phase of the conflict over human nature and salvation saw the triumph of what may be called "Semiaugustinianism," as expressed by Caesarius, bishop of Arles (502–42). Caesarius was one of the most important bishops of his time. He was known for his benevolence and pastoral care, his homilies were used as models of preaching, and he drew up the first rule specifically written to regulate the communal life of nuns.

Although Caesarius had been trained at the monastery at Lerins, he adopted a moderate Augustinianism that incorporated Augustine's emphasis on the priority of grace, accepted the monastic emphasis on good works and their reward at the judgment, and passed over the more controversial aspects of Augustine's teaching on predestination and perseverance.

Caesarius's views were approved by a small synod of bishops gathered at Orange in 529 and given wider currency by Pope Boniface II's endorsement in 531. The main points were the following: Humanity is under original sin and has lost all power to turn to God. Prevenient grace (grace preceding any good will or work) is affirmed against the Semipelagians. Baptism is the decisive conferral of grace, forgiving original sin and renewing the capacity to choose the good. All who receive grace in baptism can be saved if they work faithfully. Thus the basis was laid for the medieval compromise that insisted on the theological priority of grace and the pastoral emphasis on achieving merit by good works.

Even though Caesarius and the Council of Orange were largely Augustinian, their views allowed for predestination to grace, but not for predestination to glory (the absolute gift of perseverance).

Although there continued to be adherents of a strict Augustinianism, the general view in the Latin West was that of Pope Gregory the Great (chapter 16), who accepted prevenient grace without its irresistible or particularistic aspects.

"I beg and exhort with great humility that whoever receives this little book in his hands should both read it frequently himself and instill it into others.... [M]any people, and perhaps pious ones, want to keep their numerous books shining and beautifully bound; they keep them locked up in chests so that they may not read them themselves or give them to others to read. They do not know that it is of no advantage to have books and not read them.... [A book] which is continually read ... is not beautiful on the outside, [but] makes a soul beautiful within" (Caesarius of Arles, *Sermon* 2).

VII. THE DEVELOPMENT OF THE PAPACY: FOURTH AND FIFTH CENTURIES

A. Fourth and Fifth Centuries before Leo the Great

Some of the same factors that had lifted the church in Rome to prominence by 200 were still operative, but some underwent significant changes.

Theologically, Rome claimed the apostolic authority of Peter and Paul, but in the fourth and fifth centuries Paul dropped out of the formulations, as the historical memories faded and the textual argument based on the three "Petrine passages" (Matthew 16:16–19; Luke 22:31–32; John 21:15–19) assumed centrality.

The personal factor of the steadfastness of the bishop of Rome during the Arian controversy (except for the dubious case of Liberius) maintained Rome's reputation for orthodoxy. The bishop of Rome never attended an ecumenical council and so kept clear of the machinations and pressures accompanying these gatherings.

Organizationally, Rome kept to the usage of a local provincial synod held twice a year. This stable, conservative body of bishops—always in league with Rome—gave a consistent organ through which the pope acted, in contrast to the synod at Constantinople, which depended on visiting bishops and so was subject to fluctuation of policy.

Geographically, the Roman bishop, by reason of his location, had a voice that could be heard everywhere. Ecclesiastically, Rome was the only patriarchate in the West.

Politically, Rome in this period was not as important as it had been earlier. Milan was the capital for the region, and later Ravenna was to become the capital. Nevertheless, Rome still had importance, at least symbolically, and with the absence of the royal court its bishop was the most important figure in the city. The associations of imperial Rome began to surround the church's government.

The word *pope* is from the child's word for "father" in Greek (*pappas* or *papas*). It was used in Latin for the bishop of Carthage by the beginning of the third century. "Pope" was the common word for the bishop of Alexandria by the mid-third century and is still the title of the Coptic patriarch of Alexandria. The first known use of the word at Rome for its bishop is in an inscription of 303 for Marcellinus, but the word became common at Rome in the fourth century. It was used almost exclusively in the West for the Roman bishop from the sixth century.

Julius (bishop 337–52) stood by Athanasius in the Nicene cause but, more significant for the development of the papacy during his tenure was the third canon of Sardica, 343. That canon provided that a deposed bishop in the West could have an extra hearing before the bishop of Rome, an important step in the recognition of his appellate authority.

Liberius (352–66) used the term *papa* of himself. At Sirmium he signed a creed that sacrificed the Nicene terminology, doing so in order to stay in office against a rival Arian bishop.

By far the most important bishop of Rome for advancing the claims of his see in the fourth century was Damasus (366–84), who came to the office after a contested election in which there was bloodshed between his supporters and those of his rival Ursinus. Damasus made frequent reference to Rome as "the apostolic see" and spoke of the "primacy of the Roman see" on the basis of Matthew 16:18.

Damasus honored his predecessors' burial sites in the catacombs with ornate inscriptions, undertook reform of the liturgy (in Latin rather than Greek), and commissioned Jerome to make a revision of the Latin Bible. Since he insisted on conducting himself in a manner consistent with the importance he ascribed to being bishop of Rome, the pagan historian Ammianus Marcellinus observed that he too might become a Christian if he could be bishop of Rome.

Siricius (384–99) considered his letters as having the place of authoritative edicts and styled them "apostolic." Innocent I (402–17) pushed back Sardica's canon 3 to Nicaea. In the Pelagian controversy he claimed the highest teaching authority for the apostolic see. He extended his authority into Illyricum and began the use of the term "vicar" for the bishop of Thessalonica. Boniface I (418–22) used the term "papal vicar" and forbade any appeals beyond Rome.

B. Leo the Great and Gelasius

Leo I (440–61), who shares the designation "Great" with two other popes—Gregory I and Nicholas—may be justly called "the first pope" in something like the sense that title carries for people today. He combined the themes of authority over councils, authority over emperors, and successor of Peter in constructing his theory of the papacy.

Leo's *Sermon* 3, on the first anniversary of his election as bishop of Rome, elaborated the Petrine theory in terms of the Roman law of inheritance, according to which an heir assumed fully the position of the testator. Peter had the keys of the kingdom and authority over other apostles, Peter became the first bishop of Rome, and his authority was transmitted to later bishops of Rome. Therefore, the perpetual authority of Peter is found in the Roman bishop, "the vicar of Peter" and "primate of all bishops." Leo took the passages of John 21 and Matthew 16 and disposed of the primitive theory of episcopacy, making the authority of bishops dependent on him.

"You were asked to share our responsibility, not in the fullness of our power" (*plenitudinem potestatis*).... [Bishops are not equal, and] the care of the universal church converges toward Peter's one seat" (*Epistle* 14.2, 11).

Canceling out the position of Cyprian that all bishops share Peter's authority by faith, which did not pass exclusively to Rome, Leo held that in John 21 Jesus Christ extended to all bishops their authority through Peter and his successors.

The bishop of Rome now stood between Jesus Christ and other bishops: "It is true that all bishops taken singly preside each with his proper solicitude over his own flock, and know that they will have to give account for the sheep committed to them. To us [bishop of Rome], however, is committed the common care of all; and no single bishop's administration is other than a part of our task" (*Sermon* 5.2).

In that same *Sermon* 3, Leo states, "He is speaking whose representative we are," using the royal plural. When Leo's *Tome* was read at Chalcedon, the bishops echoed his claim with the acclamation that Peter was speaking through Leo. Chalcedon gave an assent to Rome's teaching authority previously unknown and later seldom acknowledged in the East, but Rome's competence in discipline and jurisdiction was endangered.

The primacy of Rome was well established in the West, but the story was different in the East, as shown by canon twenty-eight's ranking of Constantinople next to Rome. Rome never accepted that canon (chapter 13).

In implementation of his theory of the papacy, Leo tried to secure a practical primacy. One challenge came from the metropolitan of Arles, who moved toward development of a patriarchate of his own. In 445 Valentinian III supported Rome, a decree that was later an embarrassment to Rome, for it represented the state deciding the constitution of the church.

In his political theory, Leo drew a comparison between the two natures of Jesus Christ and the two parts of the empire, the priesthood (*sacerdotium*) and the kingship (*regnum*). He compared Peter and Paul as founders of the Roman church to Romulus and Remus as the founders of the city of Rome, and presented the *pax Christianum* (the Christian peace) as the counterpart of the *pax Romanum*.

Leo's policy toward the barbarians was both to civilize and sanctify them. They called him the *consul dei* (the consul of God). Leo negotiated with the Huns under Attila to get them to turn back from Rome. He claimed the title of the pagan chief priest of Rome, "pontifex maximus," for himself, and he was the first Roman bishop to be buried in St. Peter's.

In sum, the powers and prerogatives of the future papacy are outlined in Leo's methods, policy, and ideals: acting as head of the city government, checking the advance of the barbarians, enforcing his authority on distant bishops, preaching on doctrine, and intervening successfully at Chalcedon. Augustine provided the intellectual substance for the medieval Western church, and Leo outlined its institutional form.

Gelasius (492–96) developed the religio-political theory of Leo. Gelasius realized that the acclaim of emperor Marcian at Chalcedon as teacher of the church and priest-king was fraught with danger. The Old Testament functionaries of prophet, priest, and king, Gelasius proclaimed, were filled by Jesus Christ, fully God and fully man. Only one who was divine could fill all three. Among human beings, these functions must be kept separate.

Gelasius's viewpoint of the superiority of priests over kings was to be echoed throughout the Middle Ages. Gelasius repeated the claim that it was the office of the Roman church to judge other churches, but to be judged by no human tribunal. The West now regarded the kingdom of Jesus Christ as embodied in the church, whereas the East persisted in the Eusebian ideal of a Christianized empire, embodied in the rule of Justinian (chapter 16).

The sixth-century popes will be considered in the next chapter.

FOR FURTHER STUDY

Deanesly, Margaret. *A History of Early Medieval Europe from 476 to 911.* 2nd ed. rev. London: Methuen, 1969.

Russell, J. C. *The Germanization of Early Medieval Christianity.* Oxford: Oxford University Press, 1994.

Wessel, Susan. *Leo the Great and the Spiritual Rebuilding of a Universal Rome.* Leiden: Brill, 2008.

Wolfram, H. *The Roman Empire and Its Germanic Peoples.* Berkeley: University of California Press, 1997.

"There are two chief factors by which this world is ruled, the sacred authority of priests and the power of kings. Of these, that of the priests is the more weighty" (Gelasius, *To the Emperor Anastasius* 2).

Eastern and Western Churches in the Fifth and Sixth Centuries

The late fifth and sixth centuries saw important developments in the theology, liturgy, and spirituality of the Eastern church. The sixth century was also the age of the man who became the model Byzantine emperor, Justinian.

Two other men flourished during the sixth century and made important contributions to the most important institutions of the medieval church in the West: Benedict of Nursia to monasticism and Gregory the Great to the papacy.

By the end of the sixth century the distinctive characteristics of the Eastern and Western churches had shaped two different ecclesiastical traditions, and in the East various subsets emerged.

I. THEOLOGICAL DEVELOPMENTS IN THE EAST BEFORE JUSTINIAN

The councils of Ephesus and Chalcedon (chapter 13) produced a three-way split in Eastern churches that continues to the present: (1) the Chalcedonians or Byzantine Orthodox, (2) those usually called Monophysites or Oriental Orthodox (claiming the heritage of Cyril of Alexandria), and (3) the Church of the East (unfairly called "Nestorian").

There was much dissatisfaction in the East with the Western-inspired formula at Chalcedon (451), which sounded Nestorian to the followers of Cyril (chapter 13). The objections to Chalcedon were both doctrinal and jurisdictional.

The Cyrilline opponents of Chalcedon, which said that Jesus Christ was "one person in two natures," wanted to say that he was "out of two natures" before the union, but after the union was one nature. This latter formula left the humanity of Christ rather abstract and impersonal, but it emphasized the unity of his being and the predominance of the divine in the resultant person.

Because the presence of humanity was not denied, the name "Monophysites" commonly given to them is not wholly accurate and not acceptable to the modern heirs of the position. The Greek *monos* in the word Monophysite implies "only one" nature. A better term would be Henophysite (or Miaphysite), for the Greek *hen* (feminine *mia*) says "one" without the implication of "only."

Just as the Antiochians did not regard themselves as "Nestorian" and rejected the position of "two persons" with which Nestorius was charged, so the later followers of Cyril of Alexandria did not regard themselves as Eutychian and rejected the view that the human nature was wholly lost in the divine, the view to which the term "Monophysitism" would apply.

There were also national feelings against the Council of Chalcedon. Egypt was virtually in revolt after the council, for it was loyal to its deposed patriarch, Dioscorus. Both Alexandria and Antioch were displeased with the prestige given to Constantinople in its canon 28. Those bishops who supported Chalcedon were called "Melchites," royalists, supporters of the imperial church.

Rival bishops competed for possession of the sees of Alexandria and Antioch, but popular sentiment favored the Monophysite/Henophysite claimants. One of these, Peter the Fuller, off and on the bishop of Antioch, added to the Trisagion ("Holy, holy, holy") the phrase, "who was crucified for us." This addition became a focal point of controversy, but not only as something new in an important part of the liturgy. The phrase could be orthodox on the understanding that what was said of the human nature of Jesus Christ could be said as well of the divine, and what was said of the divine could also be said of the human (*communicatio idiomatum*, "communication of the properties"), since he was one person; but by emphasizing the deity of the one who was crucified it was especially congenial to Monophysites. Liturgical changes like this, joined with doctrinal differences, were often occasions of controversy.

A tombstone from Egypt (fifth-to-seventh century) with a Greek inscription for the Reader, Pheinos, an only son who died at age twenty-six (British Museum #679, London).

Imperial policy for two centuries had to come to terms with Henophysite sentiment in the eastern provinces. With the slipping away of imperial control in the West, the emperors could safely disregard the views of Pope Leo I, but they wanted to keep the loyalty of their eastern possessions. They attempted to make modifications within the

"We confess that the Only-begotten Son of God, himself God, who truly took upon himself humanity, our Lord Jesus Christ, who in respect of his Godhead is consubstantial with the Father, and consubstantial with us in respect of his humanity; we confess that he, having come down and been made incarnate of the Holy Spirit and the virgin Mary, the God-bearer, is one, not two; for we assert that both his miracles and also the sufferings which he, of his own will, endured in the flesh, belong to one single person; we in no wise admit them that make a division or confusion, or bring in a phantom" (*Henoticon*).

framework of Chalcedon, which they were not willing to repudiate, since it had established the canon law of the church and recognized the special position of Constantinople in the church.

The contest for the imperial office between Zeno (474–75, 476–91) and Basilicus (475–76) produced the first imperial efforts to settle theology apart from a council. Basilicus in 476 issued the *Encyclion*, prepared by the Henophysites Timothy the Cat of Alexandria and Peter the Fuller of Antioch. It accepted the first three ecumenical councils, but condemned the *Tome* of Pope Leo and "all things done at Chalcedon" that were contrary to Nicaea. Zeno regained power and in 482 modified the repudiation of Chalcedon with the *Henoticon*, an edict of reunion. It condemned both Nestorius and Eutyches, exalted the *Twelve Anathemas* sent by Cyril to Nestorius, and made no mention of Leo's *Tome*. This compromise intended to please moderates on both sides failed, as compromises so often do, to satisfy either the Henopysites or Chalcedonians.

The patriarch of Constantinople at the time was Acacius (471–89), who supported the effort to achieve unity. However, Pope Felix III in 484 excommunicated him on the grounds of his interfering in other Eastern churches, something he felt was an exercise of his rights under canon 28 of Chalcedon. For Rome the rights of bishops were more at stake than was orthodoxy. The "Acacian Schism" between Rome and Constantinople was brought to an end by Emperor Justin in 519.

Moderates did accept the *Henoticon*, and it is now a doctrinal standard of the Jacobite Church (named for Jacob Baradaeus discussed below). In 512 Severus became bishop of Antioch, and he gave a definitely anti-Chalcedonian interpretation to the *Henoticon*. The Mono/Henophysitism which has lasted to modern times in Syria is Severan in theology.

Severus continued, as Cyril, to use "nature" (*physis*) and "person" (*hypostasis*) as synonymous. For him there is a logical, not a real, distinction between the two natures in Jesus Christ. Against the more extreme Monophysites (the Aphthartodocetae), who said the body of Christ even before the crucifixion was not corruptible, he ascribed incorruptibility to the body of Christ only after the glorification.

Following Severus's death in 538, there was a dual succession to the patriarchate of Antioch, one Melchite or "Orthodox" and the other anti-Chalcedonian or "Henophysite."

The church in Armenia adopted the Henophysite position in 491. The Synod of Dvin in 506 included bishops from Armenia, Georgia, and the Caucasus who rejected the creed of Chalcedon. The church of Georgia thereafter elected its own catholicos/patriarch. Around 600 it returned to Byzantine orthodoxy, however, and was excommunicated by the Armenian church.

Henophysite Christology spread from Syria to Persia in the sixth century. Henophysite writers in Syriac included Jacob of Sarug (d. 521) and Philoxenus of Mabbug (d. 523). In Egypt the Henophysites had no strong leader. Their common slogan was "one is the enfleshed nature of the God-Word." The Coptic church supplied the Ethiopian church with its catholicos or patriarch (the *abuna*—not until 1959 did the Ethiopians gain a native in this office), and the church in Ethiopia followed Egypt into Henophysitism.

Whereas the largest Christian party in Syria was Henophysite, in Persia it was Dyophysite, but in Persia, unlike in Syria, Christians were a minority in the population.

The Church of the East in Persia maintained the Antiochene Dyophysite (two-nature) Christology. Although officially accepting the creed of Nicaea (325) since a synod in 410, the church adopted an explicitly "Nestorian" creedal statement at a synod in 486 and then in 497 rejected the *Henoticon*. Another synod in 585 approved the writings of Theodore of Mopsuestia as the church's theological standard while anathematizing the "heresy of Eutyches."

The Church of the East never taught, however, the heretical Dyophysitism of two Sons or two persons. As usual in the Antiochene tradition, the emphasis was on an impassible deity. Theological leaders included Narsai (d. c. 503), head of the school of Nisibis, and Babai the Great (d. c. 628), abbot of St. Izla near Nisibis.

The irony of the situation is that modern students conclude that the Chalcedonians, the Henophysites, and the Church of the East were essentially trying to say the same thing about Jesus Christ—somehow he was at the same time two (divine and human) yet one individual. Their different starting points gave different formulations that opponents found unacceptable.

In the period around 500 flourished one of the influential persons in Greek Orthodox spirituality, Pseudo-Dionysius the Areopagite. The real name of the person is unknown. He ascribed his combination of Christianity and Neoplatonism to a convert of Paul in Athens (Acts 17:34), and his contemporaries accepted his writings as genuine.

Pseudo-Dionysius, later claimed by both Chalcedonians and non-Chalcedonians, was imprecise in his Christology, speaking of Jesus Christ as a composite being with a single theandric (divine-human) energy. Learned in Neoplatonism, he was also a mystic. Mysticism in its narrow, technical sense, refers to an experience of union with deity, but in current study is often broadened, as a species of spirituality, to refer to an experience of the presence of God. Pseudo-Dionysius fits the narrower definition, and he became the fountainhead of a strain of mysticism widely influential in Greek Christianity and, after

"[The One] is a Unity which is the unifying Source of all unity and a Super-Essential Essence, a Mind beyond the reach of mind and a Word beyond utterance, eluding Discourse, Intuition, Name, and every kind of being. It is the Universal Cause of existence while Itself existing not, for It is beyond all Being and such that It alone could give a revelation of Itself" (Pseudo-Dionysius the Areopagite, *On the Divine Names* 1.1).

being translated into Latin in the ninth century, influential in the West also.

Through confusion with the first bishop of Paris and martyr, Dionysius (Denys), Pseudo-Dionysius became the patron saint of France. His writings had some claim to the authority of Paul as containing the sort of teaching he supposedly communicated to philosophical Athenians.

Pseudo-Dionysius's writings—*On Celestial Hierarchy, On Ecclesiastical Hierarchy, On Divine Names*, and *Mystical Theology*—stressed the tendency already found in Greek Christian authors like Origen, Athanasius, and Gregory of Nyssa to define the goal of human salvation as divinization. This deification is attained by purification, illumination, and perfection (union with God), which became the standard three stages of mysticism.

He further identified three stages in describing God: give him a name (affirmative theology), deny this name (negative theology), and reconcile the contradiction by looking beyond terms of human experience (superlative theology). The way of negation (*via negativa*) leads to contemplation (mystical theology), a simpler and purer idea of God.

His arrangement of angels into nine tiers became the basis of the medieval doctrine of angels. As part of his positive appropriation of Neoplatonism (in this case, the philosopher Iamblichus, c. 245–c. 325), he describes the sacraments as a kind of "Christian theurgy" (actions that produce divine power).

II. THE AGE OF JUSTINIAN (527–65) IN THE EAST

A. Military-Civil Achievements

Justinian's court members still thought of themselves as ruling the Roman Empire; to call it the Byzantine empire is modern terminology, which (however) we will use. Latin remained the official language of government, even though the heart of the empire was the Greek Near East.

Justinian sought to regain the lost lands of the empire. In this goal he was aided by the able general Belisarius. In 534 the Byzantines put an end to the Vandal kingdom in North Africa. The Gothic War, 553–55, reestablished rule in Italy. In 554 a foothold was gained in Spain. These conquests drained the economic resources of the empire. The Lombards invaded Italy in 556 and weakened the Byzantine position. They gained control of the peninsula except for a strip of land (the garter on the leg of Italy) from Ravenna to Rome.

Under Justinian there was undertaken a compilation of civil law, the *Corpus Iuris Civilis* (the editor in chief was Tribonian), which was to be the basis of legal codes in Europe for centuries. It contains four parts: (1) the *Institutes*, a manual explaining the principles of law for students; (2) the *Digests*, juridical decisions (pandects) classified and harmonized; (3) the *Code* proper, over 4,000 laws from Hadrian to Justinian, based on the earlier compilation of Theodosius II; and (4) the *Novellae*, new laws of Justinian and later two of his successors.

From the eleventh century Justinian's compilation of law slowly established itself in the western European countries except for England, where the old common law prevailed.

Often seen as a restorer of imperial power, Justinian saw himself as in many ways an innovator making improvements in law and government. Later historians assess his policies of military expansion as so exhausting financial resources as to be more or less disastrous for the empire. An outbreak of the Bubonic Plague in the last decades of Justinian's rule further weakened his empire.

B. Religio-Political Policy

Justinian took an active interest in church affairs. He was a good canon lawyer and theologian, so he entered church conflicts not as an outsider invading a foreign domain, but as an insider trying to fulfill better the duties incumbent upon him. He regarded the patriarch of Constantinople as his chief minister for ecclesiastical affairs.

In the legislation of Justinian the word "patriarchate" and the idea expressed by it of the church ruled by five patriarchs (pentarchy) was made official. Thus was completed the constitutional work of Chalcedon, recognizing five chief churches in Christendom—Rome, Constantinople, Alexandria, Antioch, and Jerusalem. Justinian's wife Theodora was of Henophysite sympathies, unlike Justinian himself, who nonetheless sought a compromise that would keep the Henophysites in the Orthodox church and loyal to the empire.

A series of controversies filled Justinian's reign and he was personally involved in many of them. The Theopaschite controversy involved the expansion in the liturgy to include the formula "One of the Trinity suffered for us in the flesh." The statement could be orthodox, but it was suspect to the Chalcedonians, for it sounded Monophysite and it was new. Justinian secured acceptance of the Theopaschite formula in Rome and Constantinople in 534.

Both Dyophysites and Henophysites were afraid that Chalcedon could not be interpreted without Nestorian implications. The Neochalcedonians—Justinian himself, John of Scythopolis, Leontius of Byzantium, and later Leontius of Jerusalem—gave a way of interpreting Chalcedon consistent with the Christology of Cyril of Alexandria.

"If the priesthood is everywhere free from blame, and the empire full of confidence in God is administered equitably and judiciously, general good will result, and whatever is beneficial will be bestowed upon the human race. Therefore we have the greatest solicitude for the observance of the divine rules and the preservation of the honor of the priesthood" (Justinian, *Novellae* 6.preface).

Since Chalcedon had spoken of two natures in one *hypostasis* (person or individual), the philosophical question was how there could be a hypostatic union of the natures. Using Aristotelian distinctions, the Neochalcedonians said that in Jesus Christ one nature found its attributes in the other nature. The human nature subsists in the Logos. Between the state of existing in one's own self and being non-existent or lacking self-existence, there is a middle state of subsisting, that is, having existence or individuality, in another *hypostasis*.

"Christ and Apa Menas," a painting on wood (sixth century) from Bawit, a monastery in Egypt named in honor of Father Menas, a Coptic martyr (Louvre, Paris).

Jesus Christ's humanity is not without *hypostasis*, since it exists, nor is it a *hypostasis*, since it does not exist "by itself." But a nature without a *hypostasis* would be an abstraction, so Christ's humanity exists in the Word, to whom it belongs and who gives it power to exist by taking it into himself. This way of describing the union provided a reasoned way of continuing adherence both to Chalcedon and to Cyril.

The Origenist controversy began among the monks, some of whom were the bitterest foes of Origen's spiritualizing theology. There had been an anti-Origen reaction at the end of the fourth century, especially against the use to which Evagrius of Pontus put the theology of Origen.

During Justinian's reign there was a fresh growth of Evagrian Origenism. It was opposed by Saba (d. 532), monastic superior in Palestine whose followers continued to persecute Origenist monks. In 543 or 544 Justinian condemned nine points from Origen's *On First Principles* and Origen himself. There began the destruction of Origen's works that has resulted in the loss of many of his writings in their Greek originals. In 553, in advance of the official opening of the Fifth Ecumenical Council, Justinian secured fifteen anathemas against Evagrius from the bishops already assembled.

The special concern of the Fifth Ecumenical Council (553), the second at Constantinople, was the "Three Chapters." There was considerable opposition to three Antiochian theologians: Theodore of Mopsuestia, Ibas of Edessa, and Theodoret of Cyrus, who because of their greater stress on the humanity of Jesus Christ were suspect of Nestorianism. In order to appease the Alexandrian church, Justinian agreed to condemn them.

In 544 Justinian issued an edict, the "Three Chapters," against their writings. He was careful not to impair formally the Definition of Faith at Chalcedon, but the condemnation of the writings of these Antiochenes was designed to remove any possibility of giving it a Nestorian interpretation. The Cyrillic interpretation of Chalcedon (Neochalcedonianism) was now the only official one.

The Eastern churches, even the Orthodox, have continued to give more emphasis to the divinity than to the humanity of Jesus Christ.

A concurrent controversy to the Fifth Ecumenical Council was connected with Pope Vigilius. Vigilius was an ambitious deacon appointed papal representative at Constantinople. He was advanced by Theodora, who thought he would be favorable to her. After Rome was retaken by the Byzantines in 536, Pope Silverius was deposed in 537 and Vigilius was consecrated as his successor.

The new pope, however, did not favor the Henophysites and refused to join in the condemnation of the three Antiochian theologians. He was brought to Constantinople and, after considerable waverings, agreed in 548 to their condemnation, but with express reservations in favor of Chalcedon.

This condemnation provoked strong opposition in the West, and a council at Carthage even excommunicated him. Vigilius retracted his condemnation of the Antiochenes. He was brought to the East again, but he declined to preside at the Second Council of Constantinople (553). He finally consented to its decrees. Before reaching Rome, he died (555). Northern Italy withdrew support from the papacy, and Grado and Aquileia raised themselves to the level of patriarchs, so that part of Gregory the Great's policy was to regain control in the region.

ECUMENICAL COUNCILS

325	Nicaea I
381	Constantinople I
431	Ephesus
451	Chalcedon
553	Constantinople II
680 – 81	Constantinople III
787	Nicaea II

ADDITIONAL COUNCILS RECOGNIZED BY THE WESTERN CHURCH

869 – 70	Constantinople IV
1123	Lateran I
1139	Lateran II
1179	Lateran III
1215	Lateran IV
1245	Lyons I
1274	Lyons II
1311 – 12	Vienne
1414 – 18	Constance
1438 – 45	Florence
1512 – 17	Lateran V
1545 – 63	Trent
1869 – 70	Vatican I
1962 – 65	Vatican II

Ultimately Justinian's policy of winning back those he called "Monophysites" failed. They continued strong in the eastern provinces, now with an increasing national consciousness. Justinian's concessions were not enough, for the "Henophysites" demanded express condemnation of Chalcedon. Justinian turned to repressive measures, which dealt them severe blows.

In the decade after 540 a real separated church emerged. This was due in Syria largely to the unflagging work of Jacob Baradaeus (Jacob the Ragged), who was consecrated metropolitan of Edessa in 542, but spent most of his life traveling on foot throughout the Near East, appointing clergy of "Henophysite" sympathies, strengthening his fellow believers, and defending their doctrine.

From Jacob derives the name "Jacobite" for the "Henophysites" in Syria, whose own name for themselves is the Syrian Orthodox Church. Monasticism was important in the Syrian church, and the monastery of Mar Barsauma (founded in the fifth century) became an important Jacobite center until its destruction in the fourteenth cenutry. In Egypt the Coptic church was also "Henophysite."

C. Christian Culture of the Period of Justinian

The opposition to Origen may be taken as indicative of a certain narrowing of intellectual interests in contrast to the large-mindedness of Origen.

Justinian closed the Academy in Athens in 529, a date symbolically significant for the transition from the ancient to the medieval world, for it was the same year as the Council of Vaison in Gaul that instructed all priests to give a Christian education to children admitted to the rank of readers (symbolic of the transfer of education to the church in the West), the Council of Orange that established Semiaugustinianism as the faith of the West, and the founding of the monastery of Monte Cassino in Italy by Benedict.

Justinian took measures against pagans and heretics. The canonical decisions of the church were enshrined in civil law. For example, rebaptism was prohibited (according to the church's rejection of the necessity of rebaptizing converted heretics).

In theological controversies the argument from authority assumed an ever more important place. Whereas the fourth-century theologians argued from Scripture, after 381 arguments increasingly appealed to the earlier Fathers as well as to Scripture.

At the Council of Ephesus in 431 the reading aloud of written documents with the bishops giving their judgment replaced conciliar proceedings composed primarily of oral debate. Accordingly, the

Byzantine theologians increasingly argued using quotations from the Fathers. This is shown in the production of catenas (quotations from earlier commentators in exegesis of Scripture) and florilegia (quotations on theological topics).

There was another side, however, to the sixth century. Much literature was produced, and there was enough subtle theological thought to demonstrate that creativity had not ceased with Cyril—witness for starters Leontius of Byzantium and Leontius of Jerusalem.

Orthodoxy's greatest liturgical poet, Romanos Melodos, also flourished during the first half of the sixth century. He mastered the form of hymn known as the Kontakion, which flourished from the fifth to the seventh centuries. The Kontakion was a sermon in verse, chanted by the preacher or a cantor, that consisted of an introduction and varying numbers of stanzas connected to the introduction by a refrain and to one another by an acrostic and by a shared metrical structure.

In response to Justinian's command that tribes on the periphery of the empire be converted to Christianity, much of Nubia (in modern times southern Egypt and northern Sudan and more nearly corresponding to the "Ethiopia" of the Bible than modern Ethiopia) accepted Christianity (eventually in its Henophysite form), accelerating a movement that had begun as early as the fourth century. The Nubian Christian kingdom flourished in the ninth and tenth centuries, but the rising tide of Islam from the twelfth century led to the extinction of Nubian Christianity by the fourteenth or fifteenth century.

The reign of Justinian saw the flowering of the first great period of Byzantine art, and some of its masterpieces are still to be seen, especially in Ravenna, Italy. Ravenna in the fifth and sixth centuries was the meeting place of East and West and already in the fifth century was the site of some of the greatest of Christian mosaic decorations of religious buildings—the so-called Mausoleum of Galla Placidia, the Baptistery of the Orthodox, and the churches of Sant' Apollinare Nuovo and Sant' Apollinare in Classe. As a contemporary wrote concerning some of the mosaics in Ravenna, "Light is captured here, yet reigns in freedom."

To the sixth century belongs one of the greatest glories of Christian mosaic art, the interior of the church of San Vitale.

The high point of artistic achievement under Justinian was the domed basilica of Hagia Sophia in Constantinople, designed by Anthemius of Tralles and Isidore of Miletus, one of the great architectural accomplishments of all time. On viewing the completed building, Justinian is reported to have exclaimed, "Solomon, I have surpassed you!"

In Eastern orthodoxy, the basic manifestation of the church is the eucharistic assembly. The orthodox liturgy came to exhibit increased

Mosaic, showing Mary with the child Jesus being presented with a model of the church and of the city of Constantinople, in the Hagia Sophia in Istanbul.

pomp, display, and splendor. It emphasized the sense of holy awe before the divine mysteries. Especially characteristic was the dramatic community spirit of the celebration. Here the deacon played an irreplaceable role as the intermediary between the celebrants and the people; he directed the congregation's prayer, called on the people to answer, and indicated the important moments of the ceremony.

Popular devotion developed along lines already traced: veneration of martyrs and now saints, trust in their intercessions and miraculous powers, attachment to their relics, and fondness for pilgrimages.

The veneration of Mary also assumed a preeminent place. The title *Theotokos* ("God bearer" or "Mother of God"), which had been approved in the fifth century, was at first a Christological and not a Mariological statement, but it furthered the exaltation of Mary.

In hymns and homilies to the Virgin, Mariology (as poetry rather than speculative theology) appeared in the East several centuries in advance of the West, which did not catch up until the twelfth century, but then eventually took the lead in Marian devotion.

Mary was invoked in prayer among Greek speakers in the third or fourth century, but the first Latin hymn involving an address to Mary is from the fifth century. In the East, churches were named for Mary, Marian feasts were introduced in the liturgical calendar, and pictures of Mary were produced.

Rome added the name of Mary with the title "Mother of God" (*mater Dei*) to the Mass in the sixth century, and in the seventh century added the Eastern feasts of the Annunciation, Visitation, Birth, and Purification.

The church came to permeate society to an extent hitherto unknown. In fact, in the East there did not exist to the same extent the gulf that emerged in the West between clergy and laity. There was not, however, a confusion of the two realms, spiritual and temporal, but rather a close association of them. The Byzantine ideal was the interpenetration of religion and society.

Indeed, for both the East and the West during the Medieval and Byzantine periods, church and state may be viewed as two sides of one coin—that is, of one society. Nevertheless, there was a stronger sense of separation of the two spheres in the West, hence more open conflict between the pope and the emperor occurred in the West.

The eastern emperor certainly exercised much influence in the affairs of the church. But Orthodox thinkers have rejected the term "Caesaropapism" (the emperor functioning as the equivalent of a pope) to describe the involvement of the emperor in the affairs of the church. They insist that the distinction of the emperor from the clergy was always maintained.

III. BENEDICT OF NURSIA, THE "PATRIARCH OF WESTERN MONASTICISM"

Benedict (c. 480–540), after his education in Rome, retired to Subiaco to live as a hermit in a cave. When confronted with a temptation, he would throw himself on the bramble bushes, sure to get his mind on something else.

Deciding he could be of service to other monks, Benedict set up twelve monasteries of twelve monks each. Some resented his efforts to impose a stricter rule on them, and Benedict once avoided a poisoned cup.

In 529 Benedict moved to Monte Cassino, where he established his famous monastery. Benedict seemed to contemporary believers to have powers not given to ordinary people and extraordinary miracles were attributed to him. He does not appear to have been ordained, nor to have contemplated an order for clerics; at first monastic life and ecclesiastical duties were felt to be incompatible. His sister, Scholastica, formed a convent for women nearby that became the basis for Benedictine houses for women.

Benedict brought the traditional Roman virtues of gravity, stability, authority, and moderation to the monastic life. His rule for his monks is notable for its qualities:

1. Exactness and comprehensiveness

2. In contrast to Basil's rules, which were primarily moral, Benedict's rule provides not just maxims, but detailed instructions about what to do when.

3. Moderation

4. It was severe enough to overcome human inclinations, but was not concerned to torment the body as Pachomius and Cassian did and so did not discourage its followers.

5. Order

6. It introduced stability into monastic life in contrast to wandering monks or the small groups that had no discipline. The life of Benedictine monks was to be a balanced regimen of divine praise (*opus Dei*, the "work of God"), spiritual reading (*lectio divina*, "divine reading"), and physical work (*labor manuum*, "work with hands").

The monastery was to be organized under an abbot, who held the powers of a Roman householder as the *pater familias* of the monastery. The monks elected the abbot, who then appointed the other officers. The abbot's chief assistant was the prior. "Deans" were heads of ten monks. One monk was over the cellar and one over other supplies. The abbot assembled the whole community to deliberate matters of common concern, the chapter.

The rule in chapter 4 presents the "instruments of spiritual progress," moral instructions of what to do and what not to do. Chapters 5–7 discuss the virtues of obedience, silence, and humility—with much attention to the latter. The twelve steps of humility became the basis of Benedictine spirituality.

In the rule, ten hours out of a day were to be spent in worship and meditation. On the basis of Psalms 119, verses 62 and 164, eight times of prayer were appointed: the night office or vigils (2:00 A.M. in winter), lauds (at daybreak), prime, terce, sext, and none (the four little offices, which were field hours), vespers (a half-hour before sunset), and compline (before retiring). Beginning with the night office each Sunday, the whole psalter was sung every week.

An example of the practical wisdom in the rule is the instruction for the monks to sleep in their habits so as to be ready to rise as soon as the bell rings for the night office, but not with their knives at their side, "lest they hurt themselves in their sleep."

"The first degree of humility is to have the fear of God ever before our eyes; never to forget what is his due and always to remember his commands" (Benedict, Rule 7).

The Benedictine Rule came to supplant all other rules so that Western monasticism in the eighth to twelfth centuries was Benedictine. Benedictine monasteries became a symbol of stability in a world of flux. They were important in the transmission of culture and in the conversion of peoples north of the Alps. An irony of the early Middle Ages is that at the end of ancient civilization, it was those who withdrew from society who built the new order.

The great future of Benedict's rule came not only from its own qualities, but also from the support Gregory the Great gave by telling the story of Benedict in his *Dialogues*.

Statue of Benedict of Nursia (sculpted in 1736) in the courtyard outside the church of the abbey of Monte Cassino, Italy.

IV. GREGORY THE GREAT, THE FIRST MONKISH POPE

Pope Gregory I (590–604) has been called "the Great" since the eleventh century. Recognized by the Roman church as one of its four great Latin doctors, Gregory's greatness was as a pastor, a builder of the church, a popularizer of a modified Augustinianism, a moral theologian, and a spiritual master.

Born into an aristocratic Roman family and well educated for his time, Gregory became prefect of Rome in 573, learning every detail of the municipal administration. Shortly afterwards, he retired from public life to become a monk, establishing seven monasteries on the pattern of Monte Cassino, although there is no evidence that he adopted the Benedictine Rule, which was drawn up for a house, not an order. Because of this background, Gregory brought the ethos of a monastic community to Roman church administration with his papacy.

Pope Pelagius II sent Gregory as his representative to Constantinople, where he lived from 579 to 586 and was impressed with the Eastern liturgy, but failed to learn Greek. After his return to Rome, the city suffered from flood and a plague. The latter claimed the life of Pelagius II, and the people acclaimed Gregory his successor.

In Gregory's correspondence he was deferential in addressing the emperor, but his tone was more superior toward barbarian rulers. In contrast to Gelasius's quite separate spheres for church and state, and Augustine's view of the state as essentially secular (he did not really expect anything spiritual from the state in spite of his approval of the use of force against the Donatists), Gregory had a rather Byzantine view on church-state relations, seeing a mutuality in which the church gives direction to the state and the state helps the church and reforms it if necessary.

In dealing with the East, Gregory had a special problem with the claim of John IV the Faster (for his frequent fasts), patriarch of Constantinople (582–95), to be "ecumenical patriarch." "Ecumenical" in Eastern usage had come to be widely used with reference to patriarchs in order to express their power in their patriarchates. John now made a simple application of the word to the supreme position of Constantinople in the East. It was not a claim to authority over Rome, but Gregory saw the title as a matter of pride and thought it could only mean "sole" patriarch. He rejected the title for himself as well, and in this context stated his own concept of his office as "servant of the servants of God," which itself later became a papal title.

Gregory was more important in the West than the exarch of Byzantium, whose authority was largely confined to his capital in Ravenna. As the effective image of authority, Gregory made peace with the Lombards. Gregory had to reassert papal dignity against the bishops of Ravenna, Milan, Grado, and Aquileia, who claimed patriarchal dignity.

Gregory laid the basis for the temporal power of the papacy. In the vacuum of power he took over certain functions of civil government, not from ambition but from necessity. Here he profited from his civil experience. He appointed governors of Italian cities, and he administered the landed properties that over the years had been bequeathed to the Roman church. These estates (*latefundia*) were scattered throughout Italy, Corsica, Sardinia, Sicily, and North Africa. Known as "the patrimony of Peter," they furnished food and finances for Rome. Many of Gregory's letters deal with administration of these estates and show him to have been knowledgeable of the details of administrative, economic, and social life.

While in Constantinople, Gregory began writing his *Moralia*, an exposition of Job, which he finished while pope. As the title indicates, Gregory was especially interested in the moral sense of Scripture, more than the literal or the mystical sense, and this holds for his homilies as well.

Gregory modified John Cassian's and Evagrius's lists of eight principal sins, and his list was then transmitted, with some variation, to medieval moral teaching as the "seven deadly sins": pride (or vain-glory), covetousness (or avarice), lust, envy, gluttony, anger, and sloth (or acedia—weariness of heart, apathy).

Gregory's expositions of Scripture contained an analysis of spiritual experience that was to be influential on monastic devotional life. This analysis involved a compunction for sinful tendencies, detachment from sin, self, and the world, and an ardent and patient desire for God—all leading to peace.

The *Pastoral Rule*, written on his accession to the papal throne, remains Gregory's most influential work, through its incorporation in the breviary for daily reading by Roman priests. The *Pastoral Rule* had a comparable influence on Western clergy as Benedict's rule had on Western monks.

The *Pastoral Rule* may be characterized as an essay on humility as the key to the unity of the church. The pastor should be greater than the people, as a shepherd goes before his flock. He should be pure and a leader. A preacher must reach all types of people; he must be loved in order to be heeded. Moreover, he must be careful of extremes.

Gregory recommends substituting lesser evils for greater vices as a good technique for the person who cannot rise to the heights of spiritual life at once. Gregory possessed in an eminent degree the art of spiritual oversight, endowed with common sense and a genius for practical affairs.

In theological matters Gregory transmitted to the Middle Ages the Semiaugustinianism represented by the Council of Orange (529). He supported the reverence for saints and relics and the idea of purgatory, teaching that the sacrifice of the mass helps souls there. Gregory was pessimistic about conditions of his time and expected the imminent end of the world. The paradox has been observed that just when the church in its imagination dealt more and more with the other world—angels, demons, purgatory—in practice it was becoming more and more involved with the things of this world—land, serfs, politics.

Gregory's *Dialogues* show the uncritical credulity and superstitions of the time. These accounts of monks promoted monasticism. Gregory, moreover, granted privileges to monks that served to loosen episcopal control and so opened the way for the eventual bringing of monks under direct papal control. He did not hesitate to raise monks to the priesthood and saw the possibility of using monks as missionaries. One of his most important influences was the mission to England (a story told in chapter 18).

Gregory took an interest in the liturgy of the church, but the so-called *Gregorian Sacramentary* is later (see below).

Likewise, the Gregorian Chant (plainsong or plainchant, which was monophonic) has minimal if any association with him (despite the

"The government of souls is the art of arts" (Gregory the Great, *Pastoral Rule* 1.1).

later tradition that he reformed the chants used at Rome). It may derive from an ancient Roman melody, earlier than Gregory, used in singing the Psalms, but it achieved its classical form after him during the ninth century in the Frankish kingdom.

Nor did Gregory have a role in developing the *schola cantorum* ("school of singers") in Rome, which probably originated at the end of the eighth or beginning of the ninth century.

V. THE DEVELOPMENT OF LITURGY

The great liturgies arose in the fourth to sixth centuries, and most were codified in the sixth to seventh centuries (although this is sometimes attested only by later documents). They represent much more elaboration than was found in the second- and third-century liturgies.

Several factors favored the creation and utilization of written liturgies.

1. There are natural tendencies to uniformity in the language of worship. Things well said, or impressive ways of doing things, tend to be repeated.

2. Unlearned bishops and presbyters needed guidance in the conduct of worship.

3. A stable written liturgy made the services more orderly.

4. The desire to hold to what was ancient and believed to be apostolic became even more deeply engrained, and this tendency worked against any desire for change.

5. The concern for orthodoxy and fear of heretical doctrines further sanctified what was old and blocked major innovations. What liturgical changes were made sparked controversy.

6. The Jewish synagogue liturgy received classical formulation at a comparable period. Whether there were any mutual influences, or only parallel developments in the two religions at a comparable stage of their development, is not now clear.

The main families of liturgies show certain broad similarities in structure, themes, and occasionally even in wording, but had distinctive features. These main families may now be listed.

The principal Eastern families of liturgies and their main representatives are the following:

1. Alexandrian or Egyptian

   Early attestations are in the prayers of Serapion and the Der Balizeh papyrus. The first complete text is the *Liturgy of Mark*. The Coptic Liturgy of St. Cyril is in use today.

2. Jerusalem

   Its practice is represented by the *Liturgy of James*. Along with the next two families (as well as the liturgy of the Armenian church), it may be grouped together under the heading West Syrian.

3. Clementine

   This is the pseudonymous name for the liturgy found in book 8 of the *Apostolic Constitutions* from the end of the fourth century. It may derive from Antioch, which provided the basis for the next liturgy.

4. Constantinopolitan

   Two liturgies are associated with the eastern capital and are known by the names of two of the great Eastern fathers. The *Liturgy of Basil* is the older and in its eucharistic prayers may go back to Basil and his church at Caesarea of Cappadocia. The *Liturgy of Chrysostom* was in use before 431, but was linked with Chrysostom only from the tenth century. The latter is the liturgy in common use in the Greek church, with the former used on certain special days.

5. East Syrian

   This family includes the "Nestorian," Syro-Malabar, and Addai and Mari liturgies.

The principal families of Western liturgies are the following:

1. Roman

   Important manuscript witnesses are later and include the following *Sacramentaries*: *Leonine* or Verona (early seventh century, preserving earlier prayers), *Gelasian* (mid-eighth century), and *Gregorian* (end of eighth or beginning of ninth century, represented by the *Hadrianum* sent by Pope Hadrian to Charlemagne)—both of the latter preserving sixth-seventh-century material. The later *Ordines romani* give detailed descriptions (*Ordo XI* is the earliest).

2. Gallican

   This is best typified in the *Missale Gothicum* (c. 700). The *Bobbio Missal* (end of seventh century or eighth century) is a mixed Gallican and Roman liturgy. The next three may be considered subspecies of the Gallican.

WESTERN LITURGIES

Roman Rite	Gallican Rite
Liturgy of the Word	*Liturgy of the Word*
Introit by two choirs	Entrance
Kyries ["Lord, have mercy"]	Celebrant's salutation and response
Celebrant's salutation	Kyries
	Benedictus or Gloria in excelsis
Collect (Gathering of the petitions of the congregation into one prayer)	Collect
Old Testament Reading	Old Testament Reading
Antiphonal chant	
Reading from Epistle	Reading from Acts or Epistle
Gradual (Psalm sung responsorially by cantor or choir)	Benedictus es
Alleluia	
Reading of Gospel with lights/incense	Reading of Gospel, procession/incense
	Chant — Tersanctus or Kyries
	Sermon
	Deacon's Litany
Dismissal of those not communicating	Dismissal of catechumens
Liturgy of the Supper	*Liturgy of the Supper*
Offertory (Psalm sung)	Offertory (Psalm sung)
	Reading of diptychs (dead remembered in prayer)
	Collect
	Kiss of Peace
Salutation and Sursum corda ["Lift up your hearts"]	Salutation and Sursum corda
Prayer of Consecration	Prayer of Consecration
Preface	Preface
Sanctus ["Holy, holy, holy"]	Sanctus
Canon (including intercessions, words of institution, anamnesis)	Words of institution and Collect
Kiss of Peace	
Fraction (breaking of the bread)	Fraction (Collect, Antiphon, Commixture of bread and wine)
Lord's Prayer	Lord's Prayer
	Celebrant blesses people
Communion	Communion
Thanksgiving prayer	Thanksgiving prayer
Dismissal by Deacon	Dismissal by Deacon

3. Ambrosian

   This was the liturgy of Milan, which survives in use there; whatever part Ambrose had in formulating it, later accretions make his elements impossible to identify.

4. Mozarabic

   Developed in the sixth century, this was in use in Iberia until the eleventh century and survives at Toledo.

5. Celtic

   The *Stowe Missal* (eighth century and later) preserves a Hiberno (Irish)-Gallican liturgy.

The term "Mass" (from the Latin *missa* or *dismissio*) was in use in the fourth century for a liturgical rite and by the mid-fifth century was applied to the eucharistic service. The formula of dismissal, *Ite missa est* ("Go, this is the dismissal"), apparently gave the name of "Mass" to the whole service, perhaps from the dismissal's association with a blessing.

The two principal Western liturgies as practiced in the sixth and seventh centuries, the blending of which became the medieval mass, may be compared (see chart on preceding page).

VI. THE DIFFERENCES BETWEEN THE EASTERN AND WESTERN CHURCHES

The development of the church in the first six centuries has been outlined in the following manner: an "early catholic" church (the second century and some would push this back into the later documents of the New Testament); an "old catholic church" (late second and third century); a "state catholic church" (fourth century); a "Roman catholic church" (fifth century in the West), and a "Byzantine orthodox church" (sixth century in the East).

A SCHEMATIC OUTLINE OF EARLY CHURCH HISTORY	
Second century	Early Catholic Church
Third century	Old Catholic Church
Fourth century	State Catholic Church
Fifth century (West)	Roman Catholic Church
Sixth century (East)	Byzantine Catholic (Orthodox) Church

The Germanic invasions brought political instability to the West, but stable government continued in the eastern half of the empire.

Events of the year 451 may serve to symbolize the differences: An alliance of Visigoths, Franks, and Romans in Gaul turned back Attila the Hun, who then entered Italy, where Leo the Great negotiated his withdrawal; a vast assembly of bishops met in Chalcedon to discuss the nature of Jesus Christ.

After the division of the empire in 395 between the sons of Theodosius I, the unity of East and West was never re-established. The land bridge of the Balkans between East and West suffered the heaviest from barbarian invasions after 380, and Roman influence withdrew to the Dalmatian coast. The invasions of the Avars and Slavs in the sixth century finally blocked direct communication across this region.

This, plus the subsequent Arab conquest of the eastern provinces and control of the sea routes, added to the Germanic conquest of the West, caused the separate development of Eastern and Western Christianity, and accentuated the differences that already existed between the Greek and Latin mentalities of these two major branches of Christianity.

It is characteristic that we call the Eastern church "orthodox" and the Western "catholic." In the East the controversies were over God and Christ; in the West over the nature of the church and of human beings. The East was more concerned with the great philosophical issues raised by the faith; the West was more legal and practical in its concerns.

Accordingly, the fourth century in the East was dominated theologically by the Arian controversy over the Godhead; in the West, in North Africa, the major ecclesiastical problem was Donatism, concerned with the nature of the church and the sacraments.

In the fifth century, similarly, the East was conflicted over the theological issue of the nature of Jesus Christ, whereas the West was torn by a controversy over the anthropological issue raised by the conflict between Pelagius and Augustine.

All the major controversies may be seen as concerned with salvation: Arianism with how God saves and Donatism with how the church fits into salvation; the Christological debates with the divine role and Pelagianism with the human role in salvation.

Other developments mentioned in this chapter reflect other differences. In regard to the eucharistic liturgy the East emphasized the divine presence, the West the act of sacrifice. Hence, the East put more emphasis on the epiclesis, the invocation of the presence of the Holy Spirit; the West on the words of institution, reliving the sacrifice of Jesus Christ.

In regard to church organization, the patriarch of Constantinople operated in the shadow of the emperor; the bishop of Rome faced no such competing political power.

Differences between the Western church and the Byzantine church (and between western society and Byzantine society) may be summed up by saying that the Eastern church did not have a Middle Ages. Much more continuity was maintained by the Orthodox churches (but this is not to say that they had no significant developments, as the further unfolding of their history will show) than by their Western counterpart.

The major factor here was the Germanic invasions and the subsequent conversion of the Germanic peoples. The Eastern churches had somewhat comparable experiences in the conversion of the Slavs and the Muslim invasions, but the results were different. The conversion of Slavs did not change the Byzantine church in a way comparable to the effects of the Germanic peoples on the Latin church.

Furthermore, the Muslim invasions were much more devastating to the churches that came under Muslim control than the Germanic invasions were in the West, because the Muslim conquerors were not converted to Christianity.

FOR FURTHER STUDY

Frend, W. H. C. *The Rise of the Monophysite Movement.* 2nd ed. Cambridge: Cambridge University Press, 1979.

Grillmeier, Aloys. *Christ in Christian Tradition.* Vol. 2, Part 1: *From the Council of Chalcedon (451) to Gregory the Great (590–604).* Vol. 2, Part 2: *The Church of Constantinople in the Sixth Century.* Louisville: Westminster John Knox, 1987, 1995.

Jungmann, Josef A. *The Early Liturgy: To the Time of Gregory the Great.* Notre Dame: University of Notre Dame Press, 1959.

Kardong, Terrence G. *Together unto Life Everlasting: An Introduction to the Rule of Benedict.* Richardton, ND: Assumption Abbey, 1984.

Maas, M., ed. *The Cambridge Companion to the Age of Justinian.* Cambridge: Cambridge University Press, 2005.

Markus, Robert A. *Gregory the Great and His World.* Cambridge: Cambridge University Press, 1997.

The Eastern Churches from the Seventh to Eleventh Centuries

This chapter covers several decisive and defining developments in Eastern Christianity.

Doctrinally, there was the final definition of Christological dogma, the continuing rejection of dualist heresy, and—after a great struggle—the rejection of iconoclasm.

In terms of the numbers of Christians, there were the great losses due to the expansion of Islam, offset to some extent by mission work by the Orthodox among the Bulgars and the Slavs, especially the Russians, and by the separated Eastern churches to the Far East.

The aftermath of the Iconoclastic controversy saw a great flowering of Middle Byzantine architecture and art. Significant developments occurred also in monasticism, the life of piety, and literary productions.

Relations with the Western church were punctuated not only by Christological controversy, iconoclasm, and competition for the allegiance of converts in central Europe, but also by the Photian schism. That schism identified some of the points of estrangement between the Western and Eastern forms of Christianity that were to climax in the great schism of 1054 (chapter 19).

No doubt the principal development, of far-reaching consequences not only for Eastern Christians, but also ultimately for them all, was the emergence of Islam.

Events in the Western church to be surveyed in the next chapter stand in marked contrast to the situation we find in the East.

I. THE AGE OF HERACLIUS AND THE MONOTHELETE CONTROVERSY

As the years 400–600 had been in western Europe, the years 600–800 were the time of barbarian invasion and settlement for the East. The Indo-European Slavs and the Mongol Avars and Bulgars overran the Balkans. Moreover, the Persians invaded Egypt, Syria, and Asia Minor.

To face this crisis, a great emperor, Heraclius (610–41), emerged. He brought military victories over the Persians in 628–29, but soon a more serious threat was to come from the Arabs (section III below).

On the theological front, Emperor Heraclius undertook again the task of reconciling the separated Christians of the East to the Byzantine version of orthodoxy. As other emperors, he was concerned to preserve the authority of Chalcedon because it represented the participation of Rome, had given prominence to Constantinople, and had drawn up the canon law of the church.

Heraclius's goal was to preserve the doctrine of the two natures, but to find the oneness of Jesus Christ in some other aspect than person. By the seventh century the lines had hardened to the extent that theology was not the real problem in the separation of the Henophysites, but it would be cynical to say that theology was not important.

Sergius, patriarch of Constantinople (610–38), advocated the formula "one energy" (operation or activity)—employing language to be found in Cyril, Pseudo-Dionysius, and Severus—to represent the unity of the two natures in Jesus Christ. Sophronius, a Palestinian monk who in 634 became patriarch of Jerusalem, opposed the formula, saying that monenergism ("one energy") was a covert revival of Monophysitism. He explained that there was *one* working agent who perfomed *two* operations according to the appropriate nature.

Both Sergius and Sophronius wrote to Pope Honorius (625–38), who advised against the use of "one energy," but in his own exposition said Jesus had "one will." Honorius presumably was speaking concretely of the act of willing, not theoretically of how many "wills" there were in Jesus, but his suggestion was taken up by Sergius in the theoretical sense.

Heraclius promulgated the *Ekthesis*, written by Sergius, in 638, forbidding discussion of "one energy," but affirming "one will" (Monotheletism), the last of a series of compromises (the *Henoticon*, Neochalcedonianism, the *Three Chapters*) aimed at reconciling the Chalcedonians and the Henophysites. It failed to conciliate the Henophysites, though, and only succeeded in dividing the Chalcedonians. Pope John IV (640–42) condemned Honorius, and the Monothelete controversy caused a schism between Rome and Constantinople between 646 and 681.

Emperor Constans II (642–68) in 648 issued the *Typos*, forbidding discussion of the "wills" in Jesus. The ambitious Pope Martin I (649–55) in a synod at Rome in 649 proclaimed the doctrine of two wills in Jesus and condemned Honorius and Sergius.

"The spiritual attraction of sacred song expresses the intense pleasure to be found in divine things, which stirs souls to the undiluted and happy desire of God and awakens them to an intensified hatred of sin" (Maximus the Confessor, *Mystagogy* 11).

Maximus the Confessor (c. 580–662), one of the great theologians and spiritual masters of the Greek church, was the leading advocate of the two wills in Jesus. Maximus had fled to Rome when he was banished by the eastern emperor, who also sent Pope Martin into exile in the Crimea.

Maximus's position was that there is *one* who wills and he cannot perform two contrary volitions. It is impossible that Jesus Christ's human will, which is a truly human will, but deified like the whole of his humanity, should not agree with the divine will. The human will does agree, freely and of spontaneous volition, with the divine will.

This theology was the basis of Maximus's spirituality: Jesus Christ heals our freedom so that the imitation of Christ brings a voluntary submission to the will of God.

In his *Mystagogy*, Maximus drew a comparison between a church building, the universe, the human soul, and the liturgy. The church building with its sanctuary set aside for priests, and nave for all the faithful, is an image of the universe, divided into an invisible spiritual world and a visible corporeal world. It is also an image of the soul, which consists of two forces, intellect and vitality. Each act of the liturgy, with its two parts (of the Word and of the sacrament), marked by the first entrance of the priest into the building and the second or great entrance of the holy sacrament, is symbolic of some aspect of Christian faith.

The Monothelete theologians were the patriarchs Cyrus of Alexandria, Pyrrhus of Constantinople, and Macarius of Antioch. They declared that will is a matter of person, not nature (*physis*). Since Chalcedon had said Jesus Christ is "one person," the will of that person is the will of the Logos. The result was a theological psychology. The human nature of Christ became a passive instrument that the divine activity and will employs, devoid of any initiative of its own. The Monothelete view placed the principle of the Savior's human activity in the divine Word.

Cyrus of Alexandria instituted a persecution in Egypt against the Coptic church (Henophysite in its theology) on behalf of the Melchite (imperial) cause that supported the "one will" position. That persecution was most unfortunate, for it alienated much of the Egyptian population from the emperor on the eve of the Arab conquest.

The emperor Constantine IV (668–85) tried to ease the strained relations between Rome and Constantinople. Islam (below) had overwhelmed the eastern provinces, so it seemed more important to appease Rome than the Henophysites. He convened the sixth ecumenical council, Constantinople III (680–81), also called the First Trullan Council from its meeting in the Trullos (domed room) Hall. Pope

Agatho (678–81) was the new Leo behind the decisions of the council, and Maximus provided the theological basis. The Monotheletes were willing to say, instead of one will or energy, one hypostatic will and one theandric (divine-human) energy. That would have been good theology under Justinian, but it was not accepted by those committed to the language of "two wills." So, the theology of Constantinople III was another Roman victory.

The council condemned Sergius, Cyrus, Pyrrhus, Macarius, and Honorius. It preserved the oneness in Jesus Christ by saying that the human will submitted to the will of the Logos.

The four Christological councils may be interpreted as representing a pendulum swing between the emphases of the schools of Alexandria (the oneness of Christ) and Antioch (the twoness of Christ): an Alexandrian emphasis at Ephesus (431), Antiochian at Chalcedon (451), Alexandrian again at Constantinople II (553), and Antiochian again at Constantinople III (681).

Roman Catholics have defended Honorius's orthodoxy (and so papal infallibility) by various explanations: (1) he used "one will" in a moral, not physical, sense; (2) his was a private view not expressed *ex cathedra*; (3) the council was wrong in attributing to him the same view as the others condemned, and because of his careless use of language he was condemned along with others; (4) his name was substituted for another's in falsified acts of the council.

On any explanation, even if infallibility is technically saved, Honorius proved not to be a safe theological guide in the controversies of his time.

The Syrian Christians of Lebanon maintained the Monothelete viewpoint and pulled away. They became known as the Maronites, named for a hermit, Maro, of the fourth-fifth century, but actually founded by St. John Maron (seventh-eighth century).

During the exile of the patriarch of Antioch to Constantinople in the first decade of the eighth century, the Lebanese Christians began the practice of electing their own patriarch. They later accepted the two-will position and since the twelfth century have been a uniate church with Rome, that is, a church preserving its own customs and liturgy, but in communion with Rome.

Many Byzantine monks and churchmen fled to the West from Islam and the Monothelete emperors and brought with them Byzantine art, monastic discipline, and liturgy. Among these was Theodore of Tarsus (chapter 18). Among the devotional practices that spread to the West was the veneration of the cross.

In contrast to Rome's theological victory at Constantinople III, its sequel was a defeat for Rome, even more of a defeat than the canons on church organization of Chalcedon had been. Since neither the fifth nor sixth ecumenical councils had framed disciplinary canons, Justinian II (685–95; 704–11) called the Second Trullan Council (692), also known as the Quinisext (fifth-sixth) Council in respect to canonical legislation.

This entirely Eastern gathering, not recognized by Rome, approved 102 canons. Among the decisions that differed from Western practice were the renewing of the twenty-eighth canon of Chalcedon that gave Constantinople equal privileges to old Rome, allowing deacons and presbyters to be married if the marriage was contracted before ordination (the requirement of celibacy for bishops meant that bishops were drawn from the monks, resulting in the monks ruling the church), renewing the prohibition on eating blood, prohibiting the representation of Jesus Christ as a Lamb (demeaning to the Logos, who had become man, not an animal, and illustrating the Eastern church's higher sacramentalism with respect to religious art), prohibiting fasting on Saturday in Lent except on the Great Sabbath, and rejecting from the liturgy the Theopaschite addition to the Trisagion (chapter 16).

In establishing the disciplinary code for the Byzantine church, this council confirmed the practices that were to form a barrier to unity with the Western church.

II. PAULICIANS

Byzantine sources say the founder of the Paulicians was a certain Constantine from Armenia in the seventh century who adopted the name of Silvanus. Those sources attribute a dualistic, Manichaean doctrine and a Docetic Christology to the Paulicians, who actually took their name from either the apostle Paul or, more likely, Paul of Samosata (third century).

Armenian sources are not so explicit on historical details but indicate the movement was active in Armenia a century before it was known to Byzantine writers. Some features of the group may have been found among Armenian Christians earlier. The Paulicians joined with the Muslims against the empire, but they were favored by the Iconoclastic emperors.

The *Key of Truth*, of medieval origin (perhaps seventh to ninth century), but known from an Armenian manuscript dated 1782, appears to be an authentic Paulician source and gives a different perspective on the group's beliefs. The doctrines presented include the unity of God; the humanity and adoption of Jesus; the importance of baptism for Jesus and the believer (no infant baptism); the rejection of the sacraments and hierarchy of other churches; the rejection of asceticism, cult of saints, and image worship (including even the symbolic use of the cross); and the claim that Mary did not remain a virgin. They affirmed that they were true Christians, alone possessed of the apostolic faith. Except for the doctrines of God and Christ, these positions are confirmed by the Byzantine sources.

It seems that by the ninth century there was a split in the Paulicians. One group in Byzantium adopted a dualist-docetic position. This Western group was the one known to the Byzantine polemicists and influenced the Bogomils in the Balkans, who followed the Manichaean dualist viewpoint. The charge of Manichaeism against the Paulicians as a whole may have had special reference to Iconoclasm, because dualism was perceived to give a theoretical basis for the rejection of images.

The *Key of Truth* preserved the position of another group in Armenia that stayed nearer the earlier doctrines. Its close similarity to Paul of Samosata, taken with the Syrian influence in the Christianity of Armenia, does not require a direct descent from Paul of Samosata, but may suggest that the name was given from the acceptance of a similar Adoptionist Christology.

III. THE IMPACT OF ISLAM

During the age of emperor Heraclius arose another force of world historical significance—Islam. By the time of Heraclius's death (641), both Persia and Byzantium were severely weakened by the Muslim invasions from Arabia. In the end the church lost three patriarchates (Jerusalem, Antioch, and Alexandria), and many Christians in the East lived under Islam. Its influence is still felt in Eastern churches today and to a lesser degree its influence lingers in the West in the Iberian peninsula and hence in South America.

To anticipate the next chapter, we note that the success of Islam in the southern and eastern Mediterranean not only weakened the eastern empire and broke the unity of the Mediterranean world, but also brought about a political and cultural shift in the West. Ultimately, the success of Islam created the circumstances in which the Frankish kingdom came to dominance and the papacy began to look northward and westward to the Franks for political support and to develop as an independent state itself.

A. Muhammad and His Christian Background

Many Arabs had been converted to one form of Christianity or another. In south Arabia, for instance, the Himyarites were Christians, against whom there was a native uprising at Najran in 523 that produced at least 200 martyrs.

The Henophysite (Syria) and "Nestorian" (Persia) forms of Christianity were alienated from the Byzantine Orthodox and often swung the balance in favor of the Islamic conquest in Palestine, Syria, and Mesopotamia.

Many of the Arab peoples had remained pagan, and Muhammad set about to convert them.

Muhammad (570–632) married a wealthy widow who died in 595, leaving only daughters. He worked on camel caravans and thus came into contact with Jews and Christians. In 622 he moved from Mecca to Medina. This move, the Hegira, marks year 1 in the Muslim calendar.

The Koran shows some knowledge of Christian customs and beliefs. Some are disapproved, such as religious pictures and monasticism (the Koran knows mainly monasteries and not churches). Some are misunderstood, such as the Trinity consisting of the Father, the Virgin Mary, and the Son.

The "creed" of Islam stated: "Oh, you who have believed in Allah and his messenger (Muhammad) and the book (Koran) which he sent down through his messenger and his book (Bible) which he sent down before; whoever disbelieves in Allah and his angels and his books and his messengers and the last day has strayed far into error."

"Believed" meant "submission," which is the meaning of "Islam," and "Muslim" is "one who submits."

According to Muhammad, strict monotheism allowed for no "Son" or "Spirit." The angel Gabriel supposedly gave the Koran to Muhammad, who is "the apostle" or "prophet" of Allah. The Koran in time was supplemented by tradition (Hadith), custom (Sunna), and consensus (Ijma). The Old and New Testaments had their place, and so Jews and Christians as "people of the book" were more highly regarded than pagans. Jesus was considered an earlier prophet, but the understanding of him was quite Docetic.

Islam's radical monotheism, strict morality, simplified list of duties (daily prayer, fasting during the month of Ramadan, and pilgrimage to Mecca), and fanatical zeal appealed to many.

B. Muslim Expansion

After the battle of Yarmuk, 636, the Muslims marched into Jerusalem. The city's patriarch showed Mount Moriah (as the scene of Abraham's intended sacrifice of Isaac) to the conquerors, who were considered by many as liberators from Byzantine rule. Antioch fell in 638. Alexandria was somewhat harder to take, falling in 641, after the Arabs had taken Babylon in the East. Armenia was conquered in 654, and the region of Georgia voluntarily submitted to Arab rule.

Carthage, the last vestige of Byzantine resistance in Africa, fell in

697 and by 709 all of North Africa was in Muslim hands. Unlike the situation in the countries of the Middle East, Christianity completely disappeared in North Africa. Several factors may have been at work: similarities of culture between the Muslims and the Punic and Berber populations of North Africa, the social and economic differences between the Romano-Byzantine peoples and the native population, the major split between the Donatists and the Catholics, and especially the Vandal view of Christ as a deified chieftain that offered no strong alternative to the Muslim view of Muhammad.

From North Africa the Muslims spread into Spain, controlling most of the peninsula by 711 and taking Toledo in 712. Expansion north of the Pyrenees was checked by Charles Martel's defeat of the invaders between Tours and Poitiers in 733 (traditionally dated 732). The century of greatest Muslim expansion is neatly bracketed by the death of Muhammad in 632 and the defeat at Tours in 733.

As was suggested above, Islam was often received as a liberating force against the Byzantine emperor. The rapid expansion of Islam in the lands where Christianity had first taken root (Palestine, Syria, Egypt) demonstrates how superficial the Christianization had become. The people had been harassed by doctrinal controversies and sectarianism. Many persons' Christianity was bound up with former pagan beliefs and practices, prayers to the saints, reverence for Mary, and use of amulets and other features of magic.

When the Muslims came saying Muhammad was the last of the prophets, many people accepted the new religion. The purified ethical monotheism, and opposition to superstitious practices and pictorial representations, seemed to represent a higher religious ideal.

Islam initially made no effort to convert non-Arab Christians, and there is no evidence of destruction of church buildings until the ninth century. The conquerors did destroy images in the churches. As the bureaucracy of the Arab rulers developed, taxes and indemnities were imposed on Christians. In addition to the financial burdens, Christians could not hold certain offices in the government.

The education and experience of many Christians, however, made them indispensable to the new rulers. This was especially so in Egypt, but also in Baghdad, where "Nestorian" scholars who had mastered Greek, Syriac, and Arabic translated Greek philosophical and scientific works into Arabic.

Nonetheless, the popular support for Christianity began to disappear. Only one-half of the churches in some areas of the East were in use. By the early eighth century there was great pressure on the churches in the Near East. Some pockets of Christianity left in the East, however, have endured until today.

The spread of Islam from the seventh century to today.

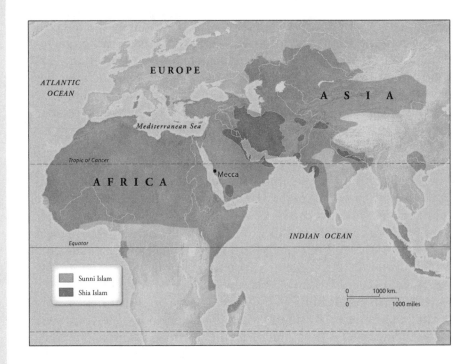

C. The Christian Response to Islam

When Christian apologists began to respond to Islam, they offered three not mutually exclusive explanations for the phenomenal expansion of this new religion.

1. Islam was a Christian heresy. There were enough points in common with its belief structure—monotheism, prophetic revelation, judgment, and afterlife—to make this plausible.

2. Islam was God's judgment on the shortcomings of the church. There are always enough deficiencies in the Christian life of believers to make this a possible explanation for misfortunes.

3. Islam was a demonic imitation of the true religion. The early Christian apologists had used this argument to account for similarities between Christianity and pagan mystery religions.

We can trace three stages in the Christian response to Islam. The first response was to see Islam as a chastisement for Christians' sins (#2 above) and to say that if enough Christians would repent the plague would go away.

The second response (beginning in the late seventh century) was to advance an apocalyptic interpretation of Islam. Its coming preceded the end of the world, and soon the Muslims would experience worse afflictions than they inflicted.

Only about a hundred years after the rise of Islam did Christian writers begin to engage in serious polemics against Islam (the third response to Islam).

The first writer to articulate the Christian case in Arabic was Theodore Abu Qurrah (c. 745 – c. 825), whose work was more designed to keep Christians from being influenced by Islam than to try to convert Muslims.

IV. THE ICONOCLASTIC CONTROVERSY

The Iconoclastic ("image breaking," that is, picture destroying) controversy was sparked, in part, by response to Islam's opposition to images.

The debate concerned the pictoriability of Jesus Christ (among other persons), especially the divine in Christ, so the Christological arguments that were employed made the whole question an epilogue to the Christological controversies.

The first phase of iconoclasm lasted from 726 to 787; the effort was revived from 815 to 843. The controversy touched the nerve of popular piety, for the most significant form of Eastern devotion had become the cult of holy images or icons (the Greek word means "pictures," not "statues") depicting Jesus Christ, Mary, saints, and angels.

Christian art had arisen by the beginning of the third century (chapter 9). This was nearly simultaneous with the first evidence of Jewish pictorial art, so the theory that Christianity inherited a tradition of religious iconography from the Hellenized synagogues lacks evidence.

The earliest distinctive Christian art represented scenes from the Bible. It was decorative, but some have claimed that it helped to teach. The funerary art may further have served to enhance the sacred character of the monuments.

Marks of devotion to pictures seemingly evolved from the marks of respect paid to official portraits of reigning emperors during the late empire. These portraits were considered a substitute for the emperor's presence, so the same signs of respect due the emperor were shown to his pictures: draperies to set them off, prostration before them, burning of incense and lighting of candles beside them, carrying them in solemn processions.

The first Christian images known to have been surrounded with these marks of cult were portraits of persons venerated as holy while they were still alive. A cult of images is first attested during the fifth century and became suddenly popular during the last half of the sixth and the seventh century. The reserve that church leaders such as Epiphanius and Augustine had shown toward the first images at the end of the fourth century had now disappeared.

The pictures provided a more concrete and direct representation of the presence of spiritual powers. Prayer, faith, and hope were addressed beyond the symbol to the person or mystery represented, but the image itself became an object of veneration possessing its own power of intercession or even miraculous properties.

The ascribing of miracles to objects related to holy pilgrimage sites and the increased devotion to Mary (chapters 12 and 16) provided precedent for ascribing miraculous powers of healing and intercession to images.

Leo III the Isaurian (or Syrian) (717–41) was a soldier emperor who gave himself to holding the boundaries against the military and ideological threat of Islam. One of his first achievements was to drive the Arabs back from Constantinople in 717–18, not long before Charles Martel checked their advance in the West. He is reported to have said, "I am both priest and king," a view with a long precedent in the East.

In 721–22 emperor Leo III decreed the forced conversion of Jews, a decree repeated by later emperors, all unsuccessful. In 726 he issued a law code that made both parties to adultery equally culpable, made betrothal binding, and imposed mutilation as a symbolic punishment for certain crimes.

The bases of Leo's opposition to pictures in the churches are very much disputed, and the initiative may actually have come from bishops in Asia Minor. Possible influences include (1) those who attributed the success of Islam to the idolatry of Christians, (2) those who hoped that a purified Christianity would convert Muslims and Jews, (3) Paulician associations in his background, or (4) Leo's desire to control the church by weakening the powerful monasteries, where the monks made icons and sold them for a great price to pilgrims.

After declaring his opposition to images in 726, Leo III issued an edict against them in 730 and deposed the patriarch Germanus for resisting his policy. Major support for the pictures came from the monks. Pope Gregory III opposed the emperor in two synods held in Rome in 731, and Leo III responded by relieving papal jurisdiction from Illyricum, south Italy, and Sicily.

Emperor Constantine V (741–75) was an opponent of the cult of saints as well as of religious pictures. He called and took an active part in a council that convened in 754 at Hiereia, an imperial palace across the Bosporus from Constantinople. The iconoclasts regarded it as the seventh ecumenical council, but Constantinople was the only patriarchate represented.

Both iconoclasts and iconodulists (those who venerated icons) agreed that the divine in Jesus Christ could not be represented in pictures, but Jesus Christ had two natures.

The iconoclasts argued that to represent the human nature was to lapse into the Nestorian heresy by dividing Christ, but to represent both natures was to go against their distinction (Monophysitism) and was to make an image of deity. To worship the pictures was to worship the human nature (Arianism).

The iconodulists replied that not to represent Jesus Christ was Monophysitism. (These arguments illustrate the practice of debating new issues in terms of already condemned errors.)

Against pictures of Mary and the saints, the iconoclasts reasoned that one cannot depict their virtues, so pictures were a vanity. Other arguments by the iconoclasts were that the only true image of Jesus Christ is the eucharist or a holy person, that the most perfect image was the emperor himself, saintly by office, and that the early Church Fathers such as Eusebius of Caesarea had said that it was not possible to have an image of Christ.

The supporters of the pictures used arguments that were most effectively articulated by John of Damascus (d. c. 750), an Arab Christian who wrote in Greek. John came from a Christian family to whom the task of collecting taxes for the Muslim rulers had become hereditary. He succeeded his father in this job, but he became a monk at the monastery of St. Saba(s) in Palestine, where he became a priest and devoted himself to the spiritual life and literary work. Outside the Byzantine empire, he was safe from retaliation by the iconoclastic rulers.

John of Damascus was the most systematic and comprehensive theologian in the Greek church since Origen. His most important work is the *Fountain of Knowledge*, part three of which (*On the Orthodox Faith*) gives an excellent summary of the teaching of the Greek Fathers on the principal Christian doctrines. He also produced homilies, hymns, and a commentary on Paul.

John of Damascus's *Three Apologies against Those Who Attack the Divine Images* took a fourfold approach to the issue.

1. It is impossible and impious to picture God, who is pure spirit, but Jesus Christ, the virgin, saints, and angels who have appeared to human beings may be depicted. The Bible forbids idols alone.

2. It is permissible to make images. The Old Testament prohibition of images was not absolute, for some images are commanded there (the cherubim over the mercy seat and other adornments of the temple). Moreover, we are not under the Old Testament

"Since God, who is good and more than good, did not find satisfaction in self-contemplation, but in his exceeding goodness wished certain things to come into existence that would enjoy his benefits and share in his goodness, he brought all things out of nothing into being and created them, both what is invisible and what is visible" (John of Damascus, *On the Orthodox Faith* 2.2).

now; by the incarnation God has prompted us to make the image visible. (John set the incarnation at the center of his defense of images, elevating the debate from a question only of practices of piety to a matter of doctrinal orthodoxy.)

Since human beings are created as body and soul, the physical senses are important in human knowledge of the divine. There are images everywhere — human beings are images of God. The tradition of the church allows images, and this suffices without the Bible.

3. It is lawful to venerate the images. Matter is not evil. There are different kinds of worship: true worship belongs to God, but honor may be given to others.

4. Finally, there are advantages to images and their veneration. They teach and recall the divine gifts, nourish piety, and become channels of grace.

"The venerable and holy images, as well in painting and mosaic as of other fit materials ... should be given due salutation and honorable reverence (*proskunesis*), not indeed that true worship of faith (*latreia*) that pertains alone to the divine nature" (*Decree of the Second Council of Nicaea*).

Despite John's arguments, the emperors drove the iconodulists from their positions of power and began a vigorous persecution. Many works of art in church buildings from before the eighth century were destroyed. Constantine V took strenuous measures against monks, the chief spokesmen for the pictures, secularizing their property and forcing them to marry nuns. Many of them fled to the West. Some of the best formulations of the independence of the church, arguing that the emperor was not the teacher of the church, were made in letters of the popes.

In the end, the iconoclasts sealed their own defeat by refusing to give to pictures of Jesus Christ a reverence they gave to pictures of the emperor.

The reaction against iconoclasm finally set in after Constantine V. First, Emperor Leo IV (775–80) was milder in his policies, and then his widow Irene brought a complete reversal. Irene was cruel (blinding her own son, Constantine VI, in 797), but she was sincere in her veneration of the pictures.

Irene was deposed in 802, but before that she held the seventh ecumenical council, Nicaea II (787), presided over by the patriarch Tarasius, which supported the iconodulist position and was confirmed by papal legates sent by Pope Hadrian I. This council declared the council of 754 heretical.

The key decree of the Second Council of Nicaea made a distinction between "honorable reverence," which could be given to pictures, and "true devotion," which belongs to God alone.

Moreover, there was a distinction made between the image and what was worshiped. The theological defense of images, however, still left them more pregnant with the divine essence than was true for some of the idols of paganism.

The Second Council of Nicaea argued that this is true because an image partakes of the nature of that which it represents: "For the honor that is paid to the image passes on to that which the image represents, and he who reveres the image reveres in it the subject represented" *(Decree of the Second Council of Nicaea)*. In other words, the pictures become "God with us" in visible form.

The popular imagination of people, however, does not always observe the theological distinction between true worship and lawful veneration. That has been true down through the ages.

The council's rejection of the church's aniconic past included the exclusion of the option of being Messianic Jews with its requirement (canon 8) that Jewish converts give up Jewish customs.

A later phase of the iconoclastic controversy opened in 814 when Leo V the Armenian again implemented an iconoclastic policy. Opposition to him came from Nicephorus, patriarch from 806 to 828, and Theodore (759–826), head *(hegoumenos)* of the monastery of Studium in

The church of Hagia Sophia, Nicaea (modern Iznik), Turkey, site of the Second Council of Nicaea.

Constantinople, an outstanding representative of Greek monasticism, who legislated a way of life for monks and made Studios an influential urban monastery in the capital.

The second phase of the controversy brought greater erudition and philsophical depth to the debate. A council in 842 reaffirmed the decisions of Nicaea II, and this victory for the images is celebrated by the Orthodox churches on the first Sunday in Lent as the "Triumph of Orthodoxy."

The pictures had come a long way from their earlier use in decoration, instruction, and aids to piety to become objects of veneration. And, it should be noted, the iconoclastic controversy in the East concerned only pictures; statues were regarded as idolatrous.

In the West no such limitation was involved, although it was some time before there was extensive production of free-standing images. The veneration of images occupied a somewhat lesser place in the Western church, for there the image was an intermediary and a modality of worship to the object depicted and so received a relative veneration, whereas in the East the image received a direct veneration as infused with the nature of the object represented.

As a result of the iconoclastic controversy, art became in the East an ecclesiastical competence and subject to dogmatic definition. The decisions of Nicaea II surrounded icons with an aura given previously to relics of the saints. Relics, however, were not neglected, for Nicaea II required that relics of saints be placed in the altar at the consecration of a church (canon 7).

In later history art had a freer development in the West than it did in the East, where it was surrounded with theological restrictions.

The victory for the icons was also a victory for the monks in the Greek church. Monasticism became the standard for what is the Christian life. The monks regarded themselves not only as those who had renounced the world, but also as those who set the norm for the church, its doctrine, and the spiritual life.

Nevertheless, the union of church and state continued to give the emperor—as theocratic representative—tremendous influence in the church. State-church arrangements in practice characteristically give the state preeminence over the church and promote traditionalism in society.

The Orthodox Church considers as ecumenical only seven councils and so the official statements of its doctrine as closed. As the arguments in the iconoclastic controversy show, tradition as enshrined in the ecumenical councils and the consensus of the early Fathers is authority for Orthodoxy, for these provide the criteria not to be deviated from in interpreting the Bible.

V. THE PHOTIAN SCHISM

Photius was a learned scholar, skilled politician, and captivating person, who served twice as patriarch of Constantinople (858–67 and 878–86). The patriarch Ignatius either resigned or was deposed in 858, and Photius, a layman and first secretary to the emperor Michael III the Drunkard, was elected to succeed him.

The details of the situation illustrate the practical realities faced by the Byzantine church. Ignatius had refused communion to Caesar Barda, uncle of the emperor, for his immoral life and was removed from office. Photius was ordained by a bishop who had been suspended by Ignatius, whose followers declared Photius deprived of office and excommunicated. The supporters of Photius responded in kind. Pope Nicholas the Great sent legates to investigate. Exceeding their powers and passing a judgment the pope had reserved for himself, the legates confirmed the deposition of Ignatius, who refused to recognize their competence. The pope deposed his legates and declared Photius deprived of office.

An encyclical of Photius in 867 complained of the intrusion of Roman missionaries into Bulgaria and of certain practices of the Western church: fasting on Saturday in Lent, clerical celibacy, and refusal to recognize the validity of confirmation by Greek priests (in the West confirmation was restricted to the bishop).

Photius also objected to the Western teaching on the procession of the Holy Spirit from the Son as well as from the Father, thereby exposing a difference in the Latin and Greek understandings of the Trinity, for the Latins saw the principle of unity in the one divine nature common to the three persons and the Greeks saw the unity in the one God the Father.

A synod in 867 declared the pope deposed and excommunicated. Basil I seized sole power in Constantinople later in 867 and reinstated Ignatius as patriarch. A synod in Constantinople in 869–70 (counted by the Latins as the eighth ecumenical council) excommunicated Photius and over the protest of the papal legates received the Bulgarians under the jurisdiction of Constantinople.

When Ignatius died in 877 or 878, Photius again became patriarch. Pope John VIII was willing to accept him if he would repent of his previous conduct. At a synod in 879–80 Photius again won the papal legates to his side, and when he read the papal instructions, he carefully omitted the demand for repentance. He was, however, recognized even by the pope. In 886 the new Emperor Leo VI, for political reasons and out of dislike for his former teacher, deposed Photius and placed him in a monastery.

The schism between Rome and Constantinople connected with Photius was temporary and only one of several through the early centuries, but it did bring out the issues that made certain a final break in communion.

Photius stated the arguments against the Western teaching on the procession of the Holy Spirit that would be repeated in later theological discussions, and he highlighted some of the differences in customs between the Latin and Greek churches. He objected to Roman interference in what he considered Constantinople's affairs and sphere of influence, but he was not the relentless foe of the primacy of Rome that he has often been pictured to be.

The Greek theory of pentarchy (rule by the five patriarchs) did not imply equality of the patriarchs and was not placed in opposition to a primacy by Rome until the twelfth and thirteenth centuries. The so-called Photian schism was more of an internal struggle in the Byzantine church, into which Rome was drawn, than a controversy between Rome and Constantinople.

Photius drew up a law code that gave a comprehensive guide to relations between the emperor and the patriarch. The emperor was to be responsible for the welfare of the empire, the defense of orthodox doctrine, and the interpreter of the laws. The patriarch was to be the sole judge in regard to the canons and conciliar decrees of the church. As a theorist of imperial power, Photius set forth the position that was to govern the relation of political power and religious affairs in the Byzantine and Slavic worlds.

VI. THE FLOWERING OF THE MIDDLE BYZANTINE CHURCH

Byzantine culture had its second golden age (after the age of Justinian in the sixth century) in the late ninth through the eleventh centuries, associated with the Macedonian dynasty (867–1056), a time when the West was culturally still struggling in comparative darkness (chapter 19).

This period was highlighted by the reign of Emperor Basil II (976–1025), who revived the military power of the Byzantine empire. Evidence of this Byzantine achievement is found in the spiritual life nourished by monasticism, literary productivity, and the flowering of art.

The Sunday eucharistic liturgy remained the focal point of church life and spirituality. In addition, three movable feasts highlighted the church year: Palm Sunday, Easter, and Ascension (Pentecost). Nine fixed feasts structured the rest of the church calendar: Annunciation to Mary, Nativity of Christ, Epiphany of Christ (his baptism), Hypapante (the "meeting" of Simeon and Anna with Mary and the infant Jesus at the latter's presentation in the Temple), Transfiguration of Christ, Birth of the Virgin, Presentation of the Virgin, the Dormition of the Virgin, and Exaltation of the Cross. The commemorations of the martyrs filled the remainder of the church year.

During the eighth century the type of hymn known as the Kontakion was replaced by the Kanon. The Kanon consisted of eight- or nine-verse paraphrases of the nine biblical odes that previously had a place in the liturgy. A model stanza introduced the hymn and set the melody and rhythm.

Marian piety flourished. In the fourth century Mary became a symbol of the virginal life, in the sixth century the protectress of cities, but in the ninth century she became much more human, as in the prominence in literature and art of the theme of the "Lament of the Mother of God" at the foot of the cross. Theodore of Studios developed this theme, and the sermon on the "Lament of the Virgin" by George of Nicomedia (bishop from 860) on Good Friday was influential. He was the first to develop salvation from a Mariological point of view.

The essential elements in the cult of the saints developed in the fourth and fifth centuries and so were parallel in the Eastern and Western churches. Relics as well as icons were tangible reminders of saints' examples and powers to aid. Relics were believed to protect from enemies, bring good harvests, bring healing, and work other miracles. The consecration of a new church required placing relics of saints in the building. Parts of a saint were placed in containers that could be displayed for veneration on the saint's feast day, and fragmentary parts were worn in phylacteries by the clergy and laity. Hagiographers reported that on the death of a holy man crowds tried to

A Byzantine reliquary (eleventh century) for a fragment of the "True Cross" (Louvre, Paris).

obtain remains by cutting off part of his garment and pulling out hairs from his beard.

There were three principal types of monasticism practiced in the Byzantine world:

1. Large cenobite monasteries located close to cities. These were involved in the life of the city, serving as centers of worship and pilgrimage, providing hospitality for travelers and care for the sick and aged, and producing items of everyday use as well as objects of religious art.

2. Hermits or solitaries, who withdrew far from towns for a life of prayer and asceticism.

3. A small community of "hermits" living away from towns under the spiritual direction of an old man. Since the sixth and seventh centuries a typical process had emerged of a young monk (a) entering a *coenobion*, (b) then the head of the monastery allowing him to lead a life according to his own pattern of spirituality under the direction of an old man at a colony of hermits, and (c) then, as he became experienced in the spiritual life, his living in complete solitude.

A special case of a large cenobite community developing apart from a town occurred on Mt. Athos, the rocky peninsula jutting out into the Aegean from the northeast coast of Greece. Hermits had lived there in the ninth century, but cenobite monasticism began about 961 when St. Athanasius built the Great Laura and gave a rule for the monks. Since that time other monasteries have been established at the site, and Mt. Athos became the chief center of Orthodox monasticism.

Two strands of influence were present in Byzantine civilization—the ascetic/monastic element from Christianity and the humanistic element from classical Greece. Both influences found expression in the literature and art of the Middle Byzantine period.

A cursive, or minuscule, script began to replace the uncial script (capital letters) in the ninth century, first in religious writings, and many of the surviving Greek manuscripts of the Bible come from the ninth and tenth centuries.

Much of the literature produced, being compilations, was of a secondary nature. In the ninth century Photius compiled notes on his wide reading, his *Library*, valuable for preserving the contents of many lost works.

In the tenth century Suidas compiled a lexicon of Attic Greek (the *Souda*), containing grammar and biography as well as definitions, still consulted by lexicographers.

Simeon Metaphrastes (fl. c. 960) made the chief collection of Byzantine hagiography, the *Menologion*, which recounted the lives of saints arranged by the liturgical calendar.

In the eleventh century Michael Psellus was a historian and enthusiast for the revival of classical learning, especially Platonic philosophy.

The most creative theologian of the period and greatest of the Byzantine mystics was Simeon the New Theologian (949–1022). Lacking much acquaintance with traditional theological literature, Simeon gave priority to directly revealed inner experience. The characteristic form of his mysticism was the experience of light. On several occasions he had visions of brilliant divine light, which he recorded in his writings. Simeon's principal teachings involved the primacy of a spiritual father in guiding the disciple to a direct experience of God and the importance, in the midst of one's tears and grief, of feeling the divine grace.

Byzantine culture of the Macedonian period has been described as only a thin layer at the top of society, but the tenth and eleventh centuries have left us more manuscripts and mosaics than any other period. This was the flourishing period of Middle Byzantine art. Illuminated manuscripts (from Patmos, Athos, and other monastic centers), ivory

Mosaic of the nativity of Christ in one of the four pendentives (dome supports) of the monastery of Daphni, outside Athens (eleventh century).

carvings, and other arts had a splendid development, but especially impressive is the architecture with its mosaic decoration. This Byzantine art is defined by hieratic dignity and monumental solemnity.

Many eleventh-century church buildings are still to be seen in Athens, and others are scattered about the Greek world. These are mostly small buildings in the shape of a Greek cross (like a plus sign with arms of equal length), a dome over the crossing, a narthex on the west end, and an apse or apses on the east end. The pattern was set by the palace church of Basil I in 881, no longer extant.

Byzantine church buildings were an image of the cosmos, giving the impression of hanging from above and developing downward. The dome represented heaven, and the movement is downward toward the earth (in contrast to the basilicas of the ancient church, where the movement is forward, like time, and in contrast to the later Gothic churches of the West, where the movement is upward). Beautiful mosaics or frescoes covered the interior walls in three zones. In the dome was Christ the Pantokrator (Almighty), in the pendentives and other higher places are narrative scenes of the festival cycle of the church (representing the holy land), and on the lower walls (representing the earth) are individual representations of saints. Second in importance to the dome was the apse, which often depicted Mary.

Impressive examples of Middle Byzantine mosaics in Greece itself are found at Nea Moni on the island of Chios and on the mainland

Mosaic of Pentecost (twelfth century) in one of the domes of San Marco, Venice.

at Daphni near Athens and Hosios Loukas west of Delphi. Two tendencies in Byzantine art are exemplified at the latter two sites. The mosaics and frescoes at Hosios Loukas have a hieratic style—rigid and austere scenes, frontal poses, and a limited range of colors. The mosaics at Daphni show the influence of classical art with lifelike portrayal of figures and flowing garments.

Middle Byzantine religious art in mosaic has some of its best surviving representations at Venice and in Sicily, where the West was in contact with Byzantium and Byzantine mosaicists were employed. St. Mark's in Venice, where Byzantine artistic influences are evident in the architecture and in the mosaics, which date from the eleventh to the fourteenth century, provides one of the best places to gain an impression of a Byzantine church. The Norman rulers of Sicily in the twelfth century borrowed heavily from Byzantine mosaic art, as well as incorporating Arab influences, in decorating the Palatine chapel at Palermo and the cathedrals of Monreale and Cefalù.

The flourishing of Middle Byzantine civilization had a counterpart in Armenia, where the first third of the tenth century was an intellectual and architectural golden age under the Bagratid dynasty. So we are led to look at the fortunes of Eastern churches outside of Byzantium.

VII. MISSIONARY EXPANSION

Of great significance for the future of the Eastern Church were the missions to central Europe that converted the Slavs and Bulgars to Orthodox Christianity.

In 864 Emperor Michael III, in response to a request from the king of the Slavs in Moravia, Rastislav, sent two brothers—Constantine (better known by the monastic name he took at the end of his life, Cyril), and Methodius—as missionaries to Moravia. Cyril, born in Thessalonica, grew up speaking Greek and the Slavic language, learned the Semitic languages, and was a student of Photius. Both brothers had served high officials. Out of their mission came the adaptation of the Greek alphabet for the Slavic language (later named, for Cyril, the Cyrillic alphabet), perfected in Bulgaria, whence it spread among the southern Slavs. After Cyril's early death, Methodius carried on.

The work of Cyril and Methodius is an example of what came to be the policy of the Eastern church, that is to organize churches on racial and national lines, leading to a federation of autonomous churches with different customs but one doctrine and spirit. The Roman practice in missions was different, insisting on the same liturgical language (Latin, which persisted in all Roman Catholic churches until Vatican II's Constitution on Sacred Liturgy, 1963) and customs.

Cyril and Methodius secured papal support for their mission. Rome won jurisdiction in the area and permitted for a time a Slavonic liturgy, which was welcomed in Bulgaria and eventually found its home in Russia. This Old Church Slavonic of the liturgy, however, became increasingly remote from the spoken language of the people.

There were Christians among the Bulgars since the seventh century, but Christianity was established in Bulgaria under King Boris (852–84). He decided for Constantinople over Rome since its patriarch would recognize a self-governing church, and in 870 a council in Constantinople put Bulgaria under its jurisdiction. His grandson, Czar Symeon, created a culture that was Slavonic in language, but Byzantine in spirit.

The first Bulgarian speaking bishop was Clement of Ochrid (893), a disciple of Methodius, who established a monastery in Ochrid (modern Macedonia) that became an important religious center. The Bulgarian patriarchate was established in 925. The Bulgarian church thus became the first national Orthodox Church outside the empire. The Rila monastery, founded in the tenth century, became the cultural center of Bulgaria.

The beginnings of the conversion of Russia eventually led to bringing the largest numbers into the Orthodox fold. The Vikings or Northmen (chapter 19) who migrated east in the eighth to tenth centuries became known as Rus. They penetrated modern Russia by following the Dnieper and Volga rivers south, opening trade routes with Bagh-

Statues of Cyril and Methodius in front of the National Library in Sophia, Bulgaria.

dad and Constantinople. Some settled among the Slavic population, adopted the Slavic language, became the rulers, and gave their name to the native people, with whom they merged.

Although there was earlier missionary activity, the first convert from the nobility of the Rus was Queen Olga at their capital of Kiev (Ukraine). The real founder of Russian Christianity, however, was her grandson, Vladimir, himself a ruthless libertine, yet he formally embraced Orthodox Christianity.

The story is related in the *Russian Primary Chronicle* that Vladimir investigated Islam, Judaism (accepted by the neighboring Khazars in the eighth century), Roman Catholicism, and Greek Orthodoxy. Each of the first three had features that displeased him. His delegation to Constantinople brought back a glowing report of the splendors of Hagia Sophia and of the liturgy, in which God seemed to dwell on earth.

Vladimir was baptized on January 6, Epiphany, 988, followed by a mass baptism of the people of Kiev a few months later (either Easter or Pentecost)—events celebrated in 1988 as the thousandth anniversary of the beginnings of Russian Christianity. He instituted policies that won a majority of his people to Orthodox Christianity by his death in 1015.

Although adopting the Greek form of Christianity, Russia did not appropriate the Greek intellectual heritage, but it did borrow heavily from the Byzantine artistic tradition. The ties with Constantinople were also maintained on the administrative level: The Russian church was for long administered mostly by Greeks, and the metropolitan bishop of Kiev was appointed by Constantinople. The metropolitan moved from Kiev in 1299 and in the fourteenth century settled in Moscow, which became a patriarchate in 1589.

One of Vladimir's sons, Yaroslav the Wise (1019–54), advanced the independence of the Russian church from Byzantium—codifying Russian law, providing for the translation of canon law, building the cathedral of St. Sophia in Kiev, collecting religious books, and opening schools.

The early center of Russian Orthodox spirituality was the Kievan Caves Monastery, founded by Antonii, who returned to his homeland after time spent at Mount Athos (see above). The chronicler distinguished his work in this way: "Many monasteries have indeed been founded by emperors, nobles, and magnates [with silver and gold], but they are not such as those founded by tears, fasting, prayer, and vigil."

The Hungarians (chapter 19) and the western Slavs (Bohemians, Poles, Croats, and Slovenes), in contrast, came under Frankish and Roman influence.

The Jacobite church in Syria was not well located for missionary work, but the first half of the ninth century was a golden age in its production of Syriac literature.

Meanwhile the Church of the East was living up to its name by carrying the Christian message even to the Far East. From their home base in Persia these Christians were prepared to follow the trade routes that lay open to the East. The members were energetic, monks were ready for self-sacrifice as missionaries, the hierarchy was intelligent, and effective methods involving educational and medical services were employed. As new episcopal sees were established, the Church of the East also set up schools, libraries, and hospitals.

It is estimated that in the Middle Ages more Christians gave allegiance to the catholicos of Seleucia-Ctesiphon than to either the patriarch in Constantinople or the pope in Rome. In 775 the catholicos moved his seat to Baghdad, the new capital of the Muslim 'Abbasid dynasty (750–1258).

Much of the intellectual achievement under the 'Abbasid caliphate of the eighth and ninth centuries was due to Dyophysite (Nestorian) Christian scholars, who had translated works of Greek science and philosophy into Syriac and then into Arabic. One of these is among the great names in the history of translation—Hunain ibn Isḥāq (809–73). Notable among those who held the position of catholicos were Yeshuyab II (628–43) and Timothy I (780–823).

Varying reports place the introduction of Christianity into India as early as the first and second centuries, other evidence increases the probability of Christianity there in the fourth century, and a strong presence is certain in the sixth. Large numbers of Christians existed on the southwest (Malabar) coast of India and smaller numbers in the northwest. From the earliest times their associations were with Syriac-speaking Christianity by way of Persia, and Syriac was the ecclesiastical language. During the seventh to ninth centuries the Church of the East provided episcopal leadership for the Christians in India and sent missionary monks there. (The arrival of a west Syrian bishop in 1665 meant that Syrian Orthodox [Jacobite] influence replaced the east Syrian.)

From as early as the fourth century there were Christians around the Caspian Sea and in Bactria. By the end of the fifth century East Syrian missionaries were working among the Huns. Bishoprics came to exist at the major cities along the "Silk Road" to China.

A long inscription in Chinese set up in 781 at Xi'an, the capital of the T'ang dynasty, tells of the arrival there in 635 (at the time the Irish missionary Aidan went from Scotland to England—chapter 18) of an East Syrian missionary monk, A-lo-pen, who was favorably received by the emperor. The inscription gives an effective presentation in Chinese of the doctrines of the "Luminous" religion (Christianity).

Opposition brought physical destruction to Christian property in the early eighth century, but imperial favor was restored in 742.

Another persecution in the mid-ninth century brought suppression of Christianity in China, and in 980 a Syrian Christian priest and five others who had been sent to aid the mission in China returned to Baghdad reporting that Christianity was extinct there, perhaps not totally true.

Somewhat later in the tenth to eleventh centuries Christianity was spreading by a more northerly route into Mongolia. The king of a nomad tribe, the Keraits, accepted Christianity, and there were Christians among the Mongol tribes, perhaps the grain of truth behind the western legend of a Christian king and priest called Prester John. Later, in the thirteenth century, Christians missed their opportunity to launch a major mission effort under Kublai Khan (chapter 24).

The Korean Chronicles speak of East Syrian Christians in the country during the Silla dynasty (661–932), perhaps as a result of Korean contact with Xi'an during the time of Christian favor there. Japanese sources report that in 737 an envoy to Xi'an returned with a Persian representative of "the Church of the Luminous Religion," and there is evidence of a Christian building in Kyoto dating apparently to the seventh century.

VIII. THE COPTIC CHURCH

The Coptic church in Egypt experienced a time of revival under the Fatimid caliphs (969–1171), its members achieving artistic excellence and filling high government positions under their Muslim masters. The period was marred by persecution at the end of the tenth and beginning of the eleventh century.

The eleventh century saw the first composition in Arabic of a grammar for the Coptic language. Coptic scholars saw a need to resist the overwhelming influence of Arabic and renewed the production of grammars and dictionaries in the thirteenth century, but this late burst of literary activity was unsuccessful in preserving Coptic as a living language outside the liturgy, where it is still used.

The patriarch Christodoulos (1047–77) transferred the seat of the patriarchate from Alexandria to Cairo. In the next century was compiled the *History of the Patriarchs of the Egyptian Church*, a major source of Coptic church history in spite of containing much legendary material for the early centuries.

FOR FURTHER STUDY

Besançon, A. *The Forbidden Image: An Intellectual History of Iconoclasm.* Chicago: University of Chicago Press, 2000.

Bowersock, G. W. *Mosaic as History: The Near East from Late Antiquity to Islam*. Cambridge, MA: Belknap, 2006.

Dvornik, Francis. *The Photian Schism: History and Legend*. Cambridge: Cambridge University Press, 1970.

Evans, Helen C., and William D. Wixom, eds. *Glory of Byzantium: Arts and Culture of the Middle Byzantine Era, A.D. 843–1261*. New York: Metropolitan Museum, 1997.

Garsoïuan, Nina G. *The Paulician Heresy: A Study of the Origin and Development of Paulicianism in Armenia and the Eastern Provinces of the Byzantine Empire*. The Hague: Mouton, 1967.

Giakalis, A. *Images of the Divine: The Theology of Icons at the Seventh Ecumenical Council*. Leiden: Brill, 1994.

Griffith, Sidney H. *The Church in the Shadow of the Mosque: Christians and Muslims in the World of Islam*. Princeton: Princeton University Press, 2008.

Louth, Andrew. *St. John Damascene: Tradition and Originality in Byzantine Theology*. Oxford: Oxford University Press, 2002.

Tollefsen, T. *Christocentric Cosmology of St. Maximus the Confessor*. Oxford: Oxford University Press, 2008.

The Western Church from the Seventh to Ninth Centuries

I. CELTIC AND ANGLO-SAXON CHRISTIANITY

A. Early History of Christianity in Britain and Ireland

According to Tertullian (*Against the Jews* 7), there were Christians among the Britons by the end of the second century.

Three British bishops were at the Council of Arles in 314, where they learned the way to date Easter. When the method was revised at Nicaea in 325, however, the new dating did not reach Britain, and the difference became a point of conflict when the new method was introduced later by Roman missionaries.

Archaeological finds associate Christianity in Britain in the fourth century mainly with Roman land-owners, but any poorer Christians would not have left material remains.

Ninian (360–432) was the "apostle of Scotland." Ninian was British, but trained in Rome. He also visited at St. Martin's in Tours, France, where he was influenced by the idea that a monk should be a missionary. From his base at Whithorn in Galloway, he worked mainly among the southern Picts between Hadrian's Wall and the Antonine Wall.

Patrick (389–461) was the "apostle of Ireland." Born into a Christian family in northwest England, he was seized as a youth by pirates and sold in Ireland. After an escape to Gaul, where he learned monasticism, he returned to Ireland as a missionary. Although not the first missionary to the Irish (being preceded by Palladius, who was sent by Pope Celestine in 431 to work among "the Irish believing in Christ"), Patrick laid the basis for the vitality of later Irish Christianity.

Although Christianity had existed earlier in Wales, the region's patron saint is David (d. c. 601), known for his extreme asceticism and promotion of monasticism.

The withdrawal of Roman troops from Britain in 402 and the invasions of Angles, Saxons, and Jutes brought a recrudescence of paganism, now in its Germanic form, to Britain. The British Christians, not eager to see their Anglo-Saxon conquerors again in Paradise, showed no concern to take the gospel to them, but the Celtic Christians took great interest in going on missions to the continent.

When Roman missionaries came to England at the end of the sixth century, there were already three expressions of Christianity in the British Isles: (1) the old Romano-British Christians, pushed back to Wales and Cornwall; (2) Irish Christians, representing a purified and intensified form of Christianity introduced by Patrick; and (3) Iro-Scottish Christians, who came from Ireland to Scotland. The term "Celtic Christianity" is sometimes applied to all three, and sometimes only to the Irish form that also spread to Scotland and northern England.

Celtic Christianity, especially as practiced in Ireland, had the following characteristics:

Ardagh Chalice (eighth century) from Ireland (National Museum of Ireland, Dublin. Used by permission.)

1. It cultivated the monastic life. The mid-sixth century saw the foundation of a group of important monasteries: Derry (546), Clonard (549), Durrow (c. 553), Bangor (c. 555), Clonmacnoise (554–58), and Clonfert (558–64).

2. It was associated with clan life. The bishop was a less important figure than elsewhere, being almost superfluous except for performing ordinations. Abbots were the important religious leaders. As an illustration, Armagh, which later was the episcopal center of Ireland, began as a monastery.

3. It was characterized by missionary zeal. Each Christian should communicate the gospel to others, so they exhibited considerable mobility. Pilgrimage (or wandering) was a penitential duty.

4. It identified the Christian life with penance. A penitential discipline was in force that was to become more widely observed later. Public confession was known, but a system of private confession with a schedule of satisfactions was worked out.

5. It had its own date for Easter, distinctive tonsure for monks, and liturgy (in Latin, but preaching was in Gaelic).

Two notable and representative Irish monk-missionaries were Columba (Columcille) (521–97) and Columbanus (543–615). Columba was educated at the monastery at Clonard in Ireland under Finnian. In 563 the island of Iona off the southwest coast of Scotland became the center of his missionary activity and the spiritual center from which Celtic Christianity spread in Scotland and northern England. From Iona, Aidan was to go to Lindisfarne and missionize Northumbria (635) at the invitation of its king Oswald.

Columbanus was educated at Bangor in northern Ireland and was one of the most learned Latin Christians of his day. Before the Roman missionaries arrived in England, he was missionizing the Germans on the continent. He established monasteries at Luxeuil in eastern France (590) and Bobbio in northern Italy (613) and evangelized the Alemanni around Lake Constance. An independent man, he corresponded with Pope Gregory the Great.

Columbanus brought to the continent Irish penitential books that spread the practice of repeatable private penance. Irish and Welsh monasteries in the fifth and sixth centuries developed a method of discipline that was formulated in the penitentials and later became widespread on the continent. An individual private penitential discipline largely replaced the one-time collective and public discipline of the early church.

According to the newer system confession was made under a seal of secrecy to a priest, who imposed acts of satisfaction that were ordinarily done in private. The penitential books with their scales of penance encouraged a system of equivalent punishments for sins and of commutations of punishment in return for works of satisfaction. Among the disciplines prescribed were reciting the Psalms, fasting, vigils, flagellation, pilgrimages, and monetary satisfactions.

An associate, Gallus, about 612 established a hermit's cell at a site that became in the eighth century a Benedictine abbey, St. Gall, whose library and school from as early as the ninth century was a center of culture north of the Alps.

The careers of these Irish monks and of Augustine of Canterbury illustrate the fact that before 1100 the missionaries were most often monks (or kings), not the ordinary clergy. Columba's death in 597 correlates closely with Augustine's arrival in England.

B. The Mission of Augustine to England

The story was later told that Gregory the Great saw some English youths being sold as slaves and was told that they were Angles (English). So impressed with their appearance, Gregory remarked, "Say not *Angli*, but *Angeli*" (not Angles, but angels).

Whatever the origin of his interest in England, a century after the conversion of Clovis to Catholic Christianity, Pope Gregory in 596 dispatched Augustine and forty other monks to England.

"Take down their idols and consecrate their temples" (Gregory the Great, *Epistle* 11.76).

Convinced of God's favor by a vision, Edwin called his councilors together to persuade them to accept Christianity. The chief pagan priest declared the old gods had done him no good, and he smashed the altars he had himself dedicated. An unnamed thane told the story of a sparrow flying through the mead house in winter. Man's life, he said, is like that, appearing on earth for a little while but coming from darkness and vanishing again. "If this new teaching can reveal any more certain knowledge, it seems only right that we should follow it" (Bede, *Ecclesiastical History of the English People* 2.13).

Augustine's party landed in the region of Ethelbert, king of Kent, in southeastern England. Ethelbert's spouse was Bertha, the daughter of the Frankish king, great-granddaughter of Clotilda (wife of Clovis), and a Christian. A Frankish interpreter accompanied Augustine. Ethelbert permitted them to stay in his realm if they did not use coercion in making converts. He himself was baptized in 597. The center of Augustine's work was Canterbury, so he is distinguished from his more famous namesake by the designation Augustine of Canterbury.

The correspondence of Augustine with Gregory gives details of the problems of adapting Roman Christianity to pagans. Gregory's replies provide classic exposition of the Catholic strategy in missions: What was clearly inconsistent with Christianity was to be destroyed, but what could be taken over or adapted to Christian purposes was to be used in such a way as to provide as much continuity in the religious life as possible. Gregory's mission policy meant to Christianize holy places and times.

Although Gregory anticipated London and York becoming metropolitan sees, Canterbury retained precedence in the south.

Augustine moved about 602 or 603 to meet with the British bishops. A holy man had told the bishops that if the Romans came in humility they were to be welcomed as men of God, but if they came in pride they were to be rejected. In keeping with his status as archbishop and representative of Rome, Augustine remained seated when the British bishops approached. They accepted this as a sign that they should refuse his demands.

Augustine's position was that the British Christians should accept the Roman dating of Easter, administer baptism according to the Roman Rite, and join with him in evangelizing the English. The failure of this meeting led to a century of conflict between Celtic and Anglo-Roman Christianity. The failure of the British Christians to evangelize their English invaders proved especially disastrous to their future.

C. Developments in Northumbria

The king of Northumbria (northeastern England), Edwin, was married to Ethelburga, daughter of Ethelbert and Bertha, and through her the influence of Christian queens continued. She brought with her to her new home a representative of Roman Christianity, Paulinus, who evangelized the area.

Edwin and his people were baptized by Paulinus. This early missionary work, however, was later either wiped out by the heathen king Penda of Mercia (the large central area of England) or absorbed by the work of the Celtic missionaries.

Whitby Abbey
(thirteenth-century
buildings) on the site
of the monastery
where the Council of
Whitby met in 664.

King Oswy of Northumbria grew up a Celtic Christian. He was being pressed hard by Penda, but won a crucial battle over him in 655. Oswy's wife, the daughter of Ethelburga, was a Roman Christian, and he called a council in 664 to consider the differences between Celtic and Roman Christianity. It met at Whitby in the double monastery for men and women founded and led by the remarkable abbess Hilda, who patronized Caedmon, the first known poet in the English language. The spokesman for the Roman side was the monk Wilfrid of York; for the Celtic side, Colman, successor of Aidan at Lindisfarne. (The most intense form of Christianity on each side was monkish.)

The British and Celtic Christians calculated Easter as the Sunday between the fourteenth and twentieth day of the moon, the Roman Christians on the Sunday between the fifteenth and twenty-first. The Roman tonsure left the hair in the form of a crown around the head; the Celtic shaved the hair at the front of the head. Behind the debate over the date of Easter and the proper tonsure for monks, there were more significant cultural differences, so the considerable learning was compromised by sharp acrimony.

The outcome was finally settled by Wilfrid's remark that Peter possessed the keys of the kingdom of heaven, to which Colman agreed. Oswy would take no chances on offending Peter and decided in favor of the customs of Peter's successor instead of those of Columba. Thereafter Roman Christianity prevailed in England for centuries.

A second Roman mission to England arrived in 668–69 in the person of Theodore of Tarsus, a Greek-speaking follower of Rome who fled west during the Monothelete controversy and was appointed arch-bishop of Canterbury. Theodore gave ecclesiastical organization to the church in England, starting a parochial system and separating the diocesan organization from civil governments. He thus made an English nation in anticipation, but the completion of the church hierarchy with two provinces of Canterbury and York was not accomplished until 755.

Theodore's associate Benedict Biscop, an Anglo-Saxon monk from Lerins, introduced the Benedictine Rule and founded monasteries at Jarrow and Wearmouth. Intellectual life flourished in the "Northumbrian renaissance" of the seventh and eighth centuries. Greek and Latin were studied, and manuscripts were gathered and copied (including the best copy of the complete Vulgate — Codex Amiatinus, produced at Wearmouth/Jarrow during the lifetime of Bede, now in Florence).

Art found stunning expression in illuminated manuscripts, most spectacular of which are the Lindisfarne Gospels (696–98) and the Book of Kells (c. 800, perhaps prepared at Iona) — with flamboyant colors; intricate patterns; profusion of entwined animal, plant, and human figures; and humorous details characteristic of Celtic art.

St. Martin's Church, Canterbury, a church of the Roman Christians, later the chapel of Queen Bertha at the time of the coming of the missionary Augustine to the realm of King Ethelbert in Kent, England.

> Over the tomb of Bede in Durham Cathedral, England: "Christ is the Morning Star who when the night of this world is past brings to his saints the promise of the light of life and opens everlasting day" (Bede, *Commentary on Revelation* 2:28).
>
> Prayer of Bede: "I implore you, good Jesus, that as in your mercy you have given me to drink in with delight the words of your knowledge, so of your loving kindness you will also grant me one day to come to you, the fountain of all wisdom, and to stand for ever before your face. Amen."

"My chief delight has always been in study, teaching, and writing" (Bede, *Ecclesiastical History of the English People* 5.24).

By the year 700 European learning was being kept alive largely in the monasteries of Ireland and England, and from there were to come the scholars that lit the fires of the Carolingian renaissance on the continent a century later.

The pride and glory of English scholarship and piety was the Venerable Bede (673–735), an almost exact contemporary of John of Damascus (chapter 17). He was brought to Wearmouth at seven years of age for an education and service to the church; later he was identified with the monastery at Jarrow.

Bede gained such knowledge of Latin that he no longer spoke his native Anglo-Saxon. His commentaries on the Bible show knowledge of Greek available at few places in western Europe at the time. This grandchild of pagans produced impressive exegetical, spiritual, and historical achievements.

Bede is especially remembered for his *Ecclesiastical History of the English People*, which exhibits three themes: fostering a self-understanding of the varying peoples in England as one English people; supporting the Roman church and its practices; and providing models of behavior for kings, monks, and bishops that would in turn promote a Christian society.

A Benedictine, Bede was the first to include in a historical work the BC–AD system of dating worked out by Dionysius Exiguus in the early sixth century (chapter 15). He gives an attractive picture of the Celtic Christians, even though he was a Saxon and came out clearly for the right of the Roman form of Christianity.

Bede did for England what Cassiodorus did for Italy, Gregory of Tours for France, and Isidore for Spain: giving the Germanic peoples a sense of identity and of place in God's purposes, transmitting classical learning to the Middle Ages by putting it to the service of the church, and providing a basis for a new Christian civilization.

II. ANGLO-SAXON MISSIONS ON THE CONTINENT

The earlier wave of Celtic missionaries was followed a century later by Anglo-Saxon missionaries loyal to Rome. Between 690 and 770 large numbers of Anglo-Saxon missionaries went to the continent.

Having been recently converted to Christianity, these missionaries now worked especially, but not exclusively, among their fellow Saxons and related Germanic peoples. They came not so much to put down Celtic Christianity as to preach to those who had not heard and to bring organization to the surviving Christian presence.

Christian territorial losses to Islam in the south and east were partially compensated for by gains in the west and north, beginning with Great Britain and then moving to the continent, whence Christianity spread to northern and central Europe. Two representatives are Willibrord (Clement) and Winfrid (Boniface).

A. Their Strategy

The Anglo-Saxon missionaries adopted several useful strategies to achieve their goals on the continent.

1. They placed their work under the pope. They thus established the northern bounds of papal control.

2. They worked under the protection of local rulers and with the support of the *major domo* (House Mayor or Mayor of the Palace—something like "prime minister") of the Frankish kings. This had practical advantages, but it often created barriers before the people whom they sought to convert, for they appeared as agents of an enemy political power.

3. They offered a direct challenge to the superstitions of the people, whom they sought to impress with the frailty of the pagan gods.

4. They gave simple, practical catechetical instruction.

5. They practiced mass conversion, gathering their converts for baptism at Easter or Pentecost.

6. They organized dioceses with parishes. The Celtic missionaries had paid little attention to diocesan arrangements and had moved freely without political patronage. The Anglo-Saxons, on the other hand, thought of themselves as restoring the ecclesiastical order of the old Roman Empire.

7. They instituted auxiliary bishops or revived chorepiscopi (rural bishops).

8. They established a sprinkling of monasteries that served as anchors for their work.

B. Willibrord (658–739)

Willibrord (Clement) had studied under Wilfrid, bishop of York in northern England, as well as in Ireland. He went to Frisia (modern Benelux countries) with eleven Saxon comrades in 690. Although others had preceded him in this area, when he came this was a pagan land beyond the old Roman boundaries, but it had been exposed to the higher culture and religion of the empire. Some Christian communities continued after the Roman legions departed, so in those cases there was some Christian knowledge, but this was not true among the native Frisians, where syncretism abounded.

Willibrord's main base was at Echternach (Luxemburg), but the outpost at Utrecht (Netherlands) eventually became the archepiscopal headquarters. The Frisian mission was given a severe setback by an uprising against the Franks, but the region was converted by 784 through the efforts of Charlemagne, under whom Alcuin wrote the life of Willibrord.

C. Winfrid (673–754)

We know the career of Winfrid (Boniface) from his biography by Willibald and his own correspondence. Born in Wessex (a West Saxon), Winfrid at seven was placed in the monastery at Exeter as an oblate. Dissatisfied with the meager library there, he removed to the monastery at Nutsall near Winchester where he remained until he was forty. Then he went on a mission to the Frisians where he worked briefly under Willibrord.

After a visit to Rome, where his name was changed to Boniface, he was sent by Pope Gregory II to work in Thuringia and Hesse. A second visit to Rome was followed by further mission work among the Saxons. A famous incident was his demonstration of the impotence of paganism by cutting down an oak tree sacred to the god Thor at Geismar and using the wood to build an oratory dedicated to St. Peter at Fritzlar.

Boniface's correspondence with his royal patron in France and with the popes shows his mission strategy. His was a practical approach avoiding elaborate philosophical argument. He had the advantage as a missionary of coming as a representative of the superior Roman culture. With a renunciation of paganism and a confession of faith, the converts received baptism.

Boniface's missionary work included reorganizing and restoring church life in the former border areas that had been devastated by the

A reliquary containing part of the skull of St. Boniface, and on the right, the knife (so it is claimed) that killed him (Fulda Cathedral, Germany).

barbarian invasions. His principal monastic establishment was at Fulda (744), organized on the Benedictine model. For most of his career as bishop (appointed in 722 by Gregory II) and archbishop (appointed in 732 by Gregory III) he had no fixed see, but from 747 he made Mainz his headquarters, and Mainz later became the largest bishopric in Europe.

His correspondence included rebukes for his royal patrons and even the popes Gregory II and III, whose full support he enjoyed. To the latter he said that unless conditions improved in Rome he could not send any more pilgrims there: in conjugal relations the pagans of the North were more exemplary than the nominal Christians of the South.

Boniface's reform efforts included active involvement in the councils of the Frankish realm. These were a combination of civil diets and ecclesiastical synods that issued capitularies with the force of both church canon law and civil law.

The second of these German councils (the first was in 742), held at Estienne in what is now Belgium in 743 or 744, took an important step in the development of feudalism. The king was allowed use of lands to which the church retained the title and received in return a nominal rent. This practice provided a precedent for the concept of a fief—the grant of a use of property, but with military service given in return instead of rent.

The Council at Soissons in 744 is the first council that dated itself from the birth of Christ. Boniface was made the head with the other bishops under him; there was to be an annual synod of the bishops.

Since cities were few, the dioceses were large and divided into many parishes; the priests were to remain in their parish and be visited by the bishop once a year. The choosing of the bishops belonged to the Merovingian House Mayor.

Some of the capitularies, drawn from various councils between 742 and 747, illustrate life of the times and the difficulties faced by the church:

1. Money that had been appropriated from the churches by rulers was to be restored, but this principal concern of the councils proved to be overly ambitious.

2. The clergy were not to carry weapons or fight—they often went to war with relics, shouting "Hallelujah" and praying antiphonally.

3. Celibacy was required of the clergy, not uniformly attained.

4. Monks were obliged to live by the Benedictine Rule.

5. Bishops were not to keep falcons.

6. Priests were to use only oil consecrated by the bishop, an effort to maintain a symbol of unity under the bishop.

7. There was to be a suppression of syncretism, which was a problem in this shadowland of Christendom (e.g., the ceremonial fires of the Germans that were the origin of the bonfire).

Boniface returned to Frisia in 753. He was martyred in 754 while preparing converts for baptism. He and his co-laborers made no resistance to their pagan attackers.

In his work, Boniface tied the knots that held together the ecclesiastical structure in the Frankish realm and its adjoining lands to the north, but he was never successful in mission work among the Saxons.

III. THE AGE OF CHARLEMAGNE IN THE WEST

A. Charlemagne's Predecessors: Pippin and the Papacy

Charles Martel, House Mayor of the Merovingian king, was remembered for two things: halting the Muslim advance (733) into France and secularizing church property in order to finance his enterprises. The Carolingian dynasty takes its name from him. Charles Martel died in 741 and was succeeded in his position by his sons Carloman and Pippin. The next decade and a half was to be a decisive turning point in western political and religious history.

In 747 Carloman for religious reasons retired to a monastery, leaving his brother Pippin (Pepin) III the Short the sole ruler in fact as the House Mayor to Childeric III, the last of the "do-nothing" Merovingian kings. In the same year a Frankish council sent requests on canon law to Pope Zachary, marking the first overture of Frankland to Rome and the restoration of relations with the papal see after a period of decay.

Pippin sought the royal dignity, so he sent a delegation in 751 to Rome with an inquiry concerning the situation in France, where the one who had the title of king had no real royal authority. Pope Zachary replied "that it would be better that he who actually had the power should be called king rather than him who held the title without the royal power." Childeric was sent to a monastery and Pippin was elected king. It is possible that Boniface as representative of the pope was among the bishops who anointed him; if so, that would have been the culmination of his work of reorganization.

Pippin desired a more direct papal confirmation of his authority, and in 754 Pope Stephen II went north to bestow a personal papal anointing on Pippin and his two sons at the abbey of St. Denys, near Paris. Anointing gave the Frankish king a Christian holiness as an epiphany of Jesus Christ in place of the inherited pagan holiness. It is possible that earlier Visigothic and Merovingian kings were anointed, but express mention of anointings in 751 and 754 was probably due to the usurper Pippin's desire to legitimate his kingship.

Thereafter kings at their anointing and on ceremonial occasions wore vestments that were essentially ecclesiastical. They were anointed with the holy oil used in the consecration of bishops; their sword, scepter, ring, and crown were blessed. No wonder the kings thought of themselves as having a sacred character and as set above bishops and priests.

Stephen II proclaimed Pippin and his sons "patricians of Rome" with responsibility to protect Rome from the Lombards, and in return Pippin declared the Byzantine corridor of land between Rome and Ravenna as belonging to the papacy.

It was argued back and forth in the Middle Ages whether this was a restitution of lands already the pope's or was a bestowal by the king. At issue was the question, "Who was the 'man' of the other?" Actually the land was neither Pippin's to give nor the pope's, but the eastern emperor's, but the excuse was that he had failed to give adequate defense. The "Donation of Pippin," later repeated by Charlemagne, changed the private papal lands, the "Patrimony of Peter," into papal civil jurisdiction, "the Republic of St. Peter."

The papal state represented the coming together of several elements: the estates left to the church, the administrative achievements of individual popes in Rome, the theory that Rome belonged to the pope since the "donation of Constantine" (see below), and the view that the pope as representative of the emperor had prerogatives in the Byzantine corridor in Italy. What had been taking shape for some time was now given a larger legal recognition.

In 751 Ravenna fell to king Aistulf of the Lombards, the last of the Germanic invaders of Italy. They replaced the Byzantine power in Italy save for the extreme south and the Rome-Ravenna corridor. The Byzantine emperors were pursuing an iconoclastic policy (the iconoclastic Council of Hiereia met in 754) and so were considered heretical in Rome. Besides, they were harassed by the Muslims and so could not offer protection to Italy. Pippin sent expeditions against the Lombards to relieve their pressure from the north and the south on Rome. In 752 Zachary, the last Greek pope, died.

So, by 754, the year of Boniface's death, the West was looking to Rome, and Rome had turned away from Byzantium to look to the Franks. Stephen II was the last effectual representative of Roman imperial power in the West, and when he arrived in Gaul in 754 to anoint Pippin, he represented the spirit of what was to be medieval Western Christendom.

Some would say this event symbolized the end of the transition period from the fifth to the eighth centuries between the end of the Roman Empire in the West and the beginning of the new medieval civilization.

Certainly the year 754 was significant for religious as well as political history: the papacy turned from Byzantium to the Franks, now governed by a new dynasty, the papal states as a legal entity came into existence, and the papal anointing gave a sacred character to kingship.

Pippin III died in 768 and was succeeded by his sons Carloman and Charles, to be known as "Charles the Great." On Carloman's death in 771, Charlemagne became sole ruler. He sought a Frankish-Roman Empire inspired by Augustine's *City of God*.

Concurrently with the Iconoclastic controversy, the pope in 754 turned from the East to the West for political and military support. In 800 Charlemagne was viewed in the West as the true successor to the Roman emperor. The Franks, culminating in Charlemagne, snatched western Europe from decline and brought a brief cultural revival, the Carolingian Renaissance.

B. Military-Missionary Expansion under Charlemagne (768–814)

Charlemagne captured Pavia in 774 and became king of the Lombards as well as king of the Franks. He renewed concessions to the pope, now Hadrian, who began to mint coins in his own name and to date documents according to the year of his pontificate, sure signs of political independence from the Byzantine emperor. Charlemagne annexed Bavaria in 787 and began its ecclesiastical reorganization. He pushed his borders south of the Pyrenees and secured the allegiance of the surviving Visigoths in northern Spain (788). Frisia was conquered by 790.

Charlemagne's principal foe was the Saxons. He conducted eighteen military expeditions into Saxon land over thirty-three years. Many missionaries had labored among them with little success, for the Saxons remained loyal to Germanic religion. They continued to raid Frankish territory.

Charlemagne saw missions as part of his military policy, but his demand for all to be baptized caused massive resistance led by the chieftain Widukind. The brutal policy of Charlemagne left a scar on the whole people. After the Frankish victory at Verdun, Widukind surrendered and was baptized in 785.

A capitulary of a council from 781 or 785 concerning Saxony made the baptism of infants under one-year of age obligatory, enforced by the death penalty for hiding a child (the death penalty was common for many offenses). Such legislation made failure to baptize one's child a sign a paganism. As a contemporary observed, "Charlemagne preached with the iron tongue."

Peace was finally achieved after 10,000 Saxons were transplanted to Frankish soil and Frankish settlers colonized Saxony.

An insight into the Christianity that emerged among the Saxons is provided by the *Heliand* ("The Healing One"). It was composed in the first half of the ninth century by a Saxon in the old Saxon language at the request of Charlemagne's son, Louis the Pious. Known as "The Saxon Gospel," since it is a retelling of the four Gospels in epic poetry, the *Heliand* presents a synthesis of Christianity and the Saxon warrior society.

Employing terminology and concepts familiar to his hearers, the poet-monk speaks of Jesus' disciples as his "warrior companions," highlights the virtue of loyalty to the chieftain (thus contributing to the later picture of Christian knighthood), juxtaposes fate with the biblical God, and borrows from magic (for example, stressing the performative power of words and shifting the emphasis in the sacra-

A model of Charlemagne's palace complex at Aachen, including his octagonal chapel (Landesmuseum, Bonn).

ments from the working of God to the effectiveness of the elements themselves).

Missionaries set about Christianizing the Avars, a Mongolian/Turkic people who settled in the Danube basin.

Except for isolated incidents, Jews lived peacefully and prosperously, and Charlemagne and his successors protected them.

C. Ecclesiastical Organization and Practices under Charlemagne

Charlemagne took it into his hands not only to missionize without, but also to organize the church within. Charlemagne, holding a sacral kingship by reason of his divine anointing, was viewed as a new David or a new Josiah, who, like those Old Testament kings, supervised the religious as well as the secular life of his territories.

A chief concern of the Carolingian church was for order, and this meant a stable hierarchy loyal to the crown. Charlemagne's chief advisor, Alcuin, addressed him as "David" at court. There was a mixing of sacerdotal and kingly power.

This was seen, for example, in the pan-Frankish synods that contained lay and ecclesiastical representatives. Decrees affecting the church were issued not as decisions of bishops but as capitularies from the ruler. *Missi dominici* (a lesser noble and a cleric) were sent out to keep check on frontier regions. Bishops and abbots, especially under Charlemagne's successors, became vassals of the king and their offices were benefices bestowed by the ruler.

Charlemagne had Augustine's *City of God* read to him each night, but he seems to have understood it in terms of using the state to submit the world to the church. The two powers, royal and sacerdotal, were now confused. Not even the bishop of Rome opposed the emerging arrangements; only Alcuin could have, and he was so florid in his style that Charlemagne never got the point.

The term "archbishop" had been in use for patriarchs and bishops who were special representatives of the pope, but it now began to be used for the metropolitan bishops (bishops of important sees such as provincial capitals), who received the pallium (a white woolen shoulder piece) from the pope as a sign of being his deputy.

Eight new dioceses were formed during Charlemagne's reign. There were supposed to be annual synods of bishops under their archbishop, but Charlemagne preferred pan-Frankish synods in which there was no distinction between bishop and archbishop. At the end of his reign there were in his territories twelve French archbishops, five Italian, and four German.

Unlike the situation in the early years of the church, ecclesiastical dioceses and provinces were determined by agreement between the secular power and the pope, and the bishops were named by the king, as had been the custom for Frankish kings since Clovis. They were expected to preach, were to make regular visitation to the parishes, and were to avoid sumptuous living.

There was now firmly in place a network of local parishes, which became more important as the old city-based organization of the church was no longer possible in the primarily agrarian economic and social system that had emerged.

Each parish had its own cemetery and baptistery. No church was to be consecrated without the presence of holy relics (reviving a provision of a council at Carthage in 401 that relics be placed in altars). Although clergy had worn special clothes—at least while celebrating the liturgy—since the fourth or fifth century, distinctive clothing for them was now required at other times in order to discourage their presence at brothels and taverns under the anonymity of lay dress.

A distinctive feature of the Carolingian period was the development of canonical clergy at cathedrals. A cathedral (from the Greek *kathedra*, "chair," by way of Latin) was the church of the bishop, where he had his "seat." Previously, there were two types of clergy: the "secular" clergy, who lived in the world (*saeculus*) and performed pastoral duties in the parishes, and the "regular" clergy, ordained persons who lived as monks by a monastic rule (*regula*). The "canonical" clergy combined both features, serving parish responsibilities in the world but living according to a rule.

The chief of the cathedral clergy was the bishop himself, but from the ninth century sometimes a dean was chosen to assist the bishop in the administrative affairs of the diocese, and archdeacons were appointed by regions to oversee the financial administration of the dean and archpriests. In collegiate churches (larger parish churches where there were several priests), a provost (a kind of secular abbot) or an arch-priest led the clergy. Chrodegang, bishop of Metz (d. 766), had already under Pippin sought to regulate the life of canons by adapting the Benedictine Rule for local clergy.

The great Saxon monastery at Corvey (modeled on the French monastery at Corbie) was established, comparable to Fulda in importance. Benedict of Aniane (d. 821) aimed at greater uniformity of customs among monasteries by reforming them according to the Rule of Benedict of Nursia. It was made the standard for monastic houses in the West by Charlemagne's son, Louis the Pious, thereby giving the idea of a "family" of monasteries that later influenced the Cluniacs and Cistercians.

Benedict of Aniane emphasized manual labor over study and asceticism over culture. Several unmarried and widowed women of the Frankish nobility founded convents and became their abbesses. In the next century Dunstan (909–88), as abbot of Glastonbury and then archbishop of Canterbury, brought English monasticism into line with Benedict's rule. Monasteries averaged 70 to 150 members. Corbie was exceptional in reaching 300 members.

A copy of the canon law was received from Rome, the Dionysio-Hadriana, based on the collection of Dionysius Exiguus and supplemented by Pope Hadrian.

Under Pippin and Chrodegang the Roman liturgy and chant began to be introduced into France. In 785 Pope Hadrian sent to Charlemagne's court in Aachen a copy of the *Gregorian Sacramentary*. It was reworked by Alcuin, using some Gallican elements. This liturgical rite, which had passed from Rome to Gaul, in its modified form came back to Rome. The resulting Gallic-Roman Rite purported to be Roman but actually contained a large admixture of Gallic elements. It largely replaced the other Western liturgical rites. The goal of greater uniformity in monastic regulations, canon law, and liturgy was associated with materials received in France from Rome.

Good order included regulation of the religious life of the people: baptizing their children at birth, abstaining from work on Sunday, confessing sins and communing three times a year, and tithing. Baptism was "christening" (making one a Christian), which included giving one a "Christian" name under the sponsorship of godparents, who now became a part of one's kinship for reckoning the degrees within which marriage was forbidden.

During the eighth century in the administration of baptism, triple immersion of the newborn was normal, but affusion (the pouring of water over the head of the candidate) began a long process of replacing immersion in the West not only in cases of sick-bed baptism (in which it was normal) but as the ordinary practice. Baptism was supposedly administered soon after birth, but unless there was an emergency it was delayed until Easter or Pentecost.

Education in the Christian life often left much to be desired: Jonas of Orleans in the first book written *On the Lay Estate* (820) lamented that so many of the laity thought that—because they had been christened—no matter how they lived they could not be lost and would face only purgatorial fire. In contrast, he offered the opinion that the unbaptized who lived well would be better off than the baptized who lived in wickedness.

The economic basis of the church was regularized and strengthened by the state levying and collecting tithes. Besides tithes, churches received offerings and bequests and earned rent from its properties. The tithes were divided into four parts: one for the bishop, another for the clergy, the third for the poor, and the fourth for rebuilding churches (this distribution of offerings was an older practice, included in Gregory the Great's instructions to Augustine).

The intellectual and literary activity of the Carolingian age resulted in the first manuscripts in musical notation (called neumes), dating from the ninth and tenth centuries, elaboration of liturgical music, and the first anticipations of polyphonic melody. Treatises on music continued earlier practice of treating the subject theoretically and not dealing with its actual performance. Congregational participation in the liturgy was already much reduced; in larger churches choirs carried the chant.

The Byzantine court gave an organ to Pippin in 757 and another to Charlemagne in 812. This is sometimes taken as the introduction of organ music into the Western liturgy, but the organ was used in Byzantium only in court functions, not in the liturgy, and it would seem the same was true in Aachen. Organs were used on ceremonial occasions also at the great monasteries, variously dated between the Carolingian age and sometime around 1000, and then at the introduction and conclusion of the service (not initially as an accompaniment to the liturgy).

The first use of church bells seems to have been in North Africa and Gaul in the sixth century. They were employed by Celtic missionaries in the seventh century and became more common in the Carolingian period. Bells announced the hours for prayer, calling the faithful to pray and chasing the demons away.

Pagan practices still survived among the people, especially elements of magic, sorcery, and astrology. Clergymen made an effort to Christianize customs by substituting the "Our Father" and the Apostles' Creed for incantations, and consecrating trees and fountains to saints.

Pious practices that had begun earlier and became characteristic of the Middle Ages, such as the cult of relics and pilgrimages, are attested in Carolingian times, as are their attendant abuses. The desire for relics was the occasion for their theft. Pilgrimages (St. Martin of Tours was the most popular site in France) brought moral temptations, so that some tried to discourage women from making the journeys. One disillusioned observer wrote: "To go to Rome, great fatigue, little profit. You will find the King you went there seeking only if you brought him with you."

Bishops were great builders of civic as well as ecclesiastical structures. Modifications of the early Christian basilica, which would prepare the way for Romanesque architecture in the eleventh and twelfth centuries, began to occur. On a different, centralized, plan was the cathedral at Aachen—sixteen sides with an octagonal dome. Its design

> "Although correct conduct may be better than knowledge, nevertheless knowledge precedes conduct.... We have recognized [in letters we have received] both correct thoughts and uncouth expressions; because what pious devotion dictated faithfully to the mind, the tongue, uneducated on account of the neglect of study, was not able to express in the letter without error. Whence it happened that we began to fear lest perchance, as the skill in writing was less, so also the wisdom for understanding the Holy Scriptures might be much less than it rightly ought to be" (Charlemagne, *Epistle Concerning Letters*).

was inspired by the octagonal church of San Vitale at Ravenna. The cathedral was built 794–98 and consecrated by Leo III in 805.

D. The Establishment of Schools and the Intellectual Renaissance

The late eighth and ninth centuries in the West are called the Carolingian renaissance. The return to some measure of political stability and security, with added encouragement from Charlemagne and his court, permitted some revival of intellectual life that had suffered greatly on the continent in the wake of the barbarian invasions. Charlemagne directed every monastery and diocese to conduct a school, but this was difficult to enforce.

Moreover, Charlemagne surrounded himself with capable men, drawing scholars from other countries—Spain, Italy, and especially Britain—to promote the spread of learning in his territories. This interest in education had as a special goal that pastors and people be able to understand the Scriptures. The premise was that right knowledge was a prerequisite to right acting.

Latin Bibles were the most frequently copied books of the period. With Charlemagne's encouragement, scholars at various centers labored to provide a reliable text of the Vulgate. A new form of writing, the Carolingian minuscule script, emerged. Glosses to manuscripts of the Psalter provided prototypes for the twelfth-century *Glossa Ordinaria* to the Bible as a whole. Paul the Deacon prepared a collection of sermons from the Church Fathers, arranged by scriptural texts and according to the liturgical year, to serve as models for use all over the realm.

Many "lives of saints" were also produced. Indeed, the primary literary genre of the Middle Ages, in the West and the East, was hagiography. These works drew on classical traditions of biography and funeral orations, but included legendary material about miracles with the purpose of exalting the virtues of the saint and promoting Christian living in the readers.

Alcuin made the court of Charlemagne at Aachen a center of learning, and he later became head of a monastic school at Tours. He had previously been master of the school in York that was begun by its archbishop Egbert, a pupil of Bede. Prior to schools under court patronage, there had been three kinds of schools in Christendom: monastic, episcopal or cathedral (designed for the recruitment of clergymen for the diocese), and in some cases parish. Only in Italy had lay grammar teachers continued to teach for fees. Alcuin wrote the first known catechism, *Questions and Answers for Children*.

In antiquity the teacher had no social standing, but in Christianity in this period the teacher was a holy man, a cleric and learned. For the Germanic peoples the teacher was a revered figure, and there was an awe for books, especially since they were in the venerable language of Latin, which stood for cultural antiquity and was the language of redemption.

Instruction followed the seven liberal arts of classical antiquity: the Trivium of grammar (including philology, literature, and literary criticism), rhetoric (letter writing, preaching, and the art of convincing), and dialectic (logic, and later the whole of philosophy), and the Quadrivium (not pushed to any extent) of astronomy (so as to calculate the date of Easter), music (ecclesiastical), arithmetic (for church accounts), and geometry. The prominence of dialectics in the curriculum contained the germ of later Scholasticism.

The basic requirements of priests were to know the creeds, the Lord's Prayer, the Mass, the sacramentary (prayers) and lectionary (Scripture readings), church music, and the homilies of the Fathers. The principal categories of literature produced in the preceding three centuries available for study were commentaries on the Bible, theological treatises, saints' lives, historical works, treatments of the liberal arts, calendars, encyclopedias and compendia, and collections of laws.

E. Theological Developments and Controversies

The theological controversies of the age of Charlemagne and his successors were related to the nature of Jesus Christ and the church and were argued in terms of the correct interpretation of tradition.

Some church leaders on the Iberian peninsula in the late eighth century, notably Elipandus, archbishop of Toledo, and Felix, bishop of Urgel, taught a Christology that their opponents Beatus and Alcuin labeled as "Adoptianism," not to be confused with the early Christology of "Adoptionism." The name came from a characterization of the teaching stating that the Son of God by nature adopted the son in his humanity.

Charlemagne's theologian Alcuin wrote the major refutation, *Against Felix*, in which he insisted that it was doctrinally more exact to speak of the divine Christ assuming human nature (*homo assumptus*) rather than adopting a son (*filius adoptivus*). He charged (incorrectly) that Felix's teaching was a revival of Nestorianism. The Iberians' Christology was actually based on Philippians 2:6–7, the self-emptying of the Son of God. Their view was condemned as heretical—both at the Council of Frankfurt in 794 called by Charlemagne, and by Pope Leo III in 798.

The addition of the *filioque* clause (affirming that the Holy Spirit proceeded from the Father *and the Son*) to the Nicene Creed, adopted at Toledo in 589, was added to the Gallic liturgy under Charlemagne. Pope Leo III ordered it omitted from the Roman liturgy rather than alienate the Greeks further, and it was not added in Rome until the eleventh century.

The Second Council of Nicaea, 787, in opposing the Iconoclastic movement, made a distinction between lawful veneration to images and adoration that belonged to God alone. When the decisions of the council were translated into Latin, this distinction was confused. Since no Frankish bishop was at the council, Charlemagne said the council was not ecumenical. He commissioned a theologian, probably Theodulf of Orleans, to produce the *Libri Carolini* ("Books of Charlemagne") that stated a fairly common Western view on religious art as suitable for instruction and decoration, but not for worship.

Rejecting both the councils of Hiereia (754) and Nicaea II (787), the author says, "We neither destroy in common with the former nor adore in common with the latter." The Council of Frankfurt in 794 repudiated the decree of the Council of Nicaea II, in spite of the latter having papal endorsement and so ultimately prevailing as official policy. The religious art of the Carolingian period reflected the empire's renewed cultural contacts, drawing on Italian and Byzantine art as well as on Celtic and Germanic art.

"We permit the use of images in the churches of the saints, not that they should be adored, but in order to recall past events and for the adornment of the walls" (*Libri Carolini*).

F. Charlemagne's Coronation as Emperor

On Christmas day, 800, Pope Leo III in Rome crowned Charlemagne as emperor. The event was clearly planned, but by whom? A plausible reconstruction is that both Charlemagne and Leo III had something to gain from the event. Charlemagne strongly desired the imperial title, but he had to deal with a pope who was under suspicion of adultery, did not want himself to be judged by any, and wanted his enemies banished for treason.

Charlemagne's thought that he would receive the crown in return for accepting the pope's oath of his innocence without a trial, which he did. In earlier times a new emperor was acclaimed and then the crown was bestowed. What Charlemagne did not foresee was Leo converting the crowning into the constitutive act so that the acclamation became a "spontaneous" approval by the people in the church. That change in the meaning of the event, so that the imperial title was the gift of the pope, would explain why the biography of Charlemagne by his servant Einhard says Charlemagne was displeased by what happened.

Charlemagne and the pope held two different conceptions of empire that would contend for supremacy in subsequent centuries: Did the emperor have a supervisory role over the church, or did the pope make (and so could unmake) emperors?

In the background to the crowning of Chalemagne was Irene's seizure of power in Byzantium in 797. Since a woman alone was not considered properly to hold the imperial title, the West could interpret the situation as being that the imperial throne was vacant. The Byzantines, however, reacted negatively to the crowning of Charlemagne (although a Byzantine chronicler reported that Irene contemplated marriage with Charlemagne). Finally, a compromise was negotiated whereby the emperor Michael I in 812 recognized Charlemagne as his brother with rule in Italy except for Venice and the surrounding region. As for Charlemagne, he evidently saw himself as a new Constantine.

The coronation of Charlemagne is often described as the beginning of the "Holy Roman Empire." Such terminology is anachronistic. With the hindsight of what later came into being, we can see that something new was occurring, although the actual terminology was some centuries in emerging.

The intention by the participants was to elect a new emperor in the existing empire. Charlemagne was already king of the Franks and king of the Lombards. In addition, in the eyes of those who elected him, he was now emperor in the existing Roman Empire. He acquired a new dignity, but he did not become the emperor over any new land.

IV. LATER CAROLINGIAN CULTURE AND ITS PROBLEMS

The ninth century saw the beginning of a disintegration of the unified empire and culture Charlemagne had sought to achieve. In that setting occurred controversies affecting church organization and theological questions in which a few men of notable learning showed the results of the preceding educational revival.

A. Political Background

If Charlemagne had not had his son Louis the Pious (814–40) raised to the purple before his death, the title of emperor would have died with Charlemagne. The influence of the clergy over his actions gave Louis his nickname. According to his father's wishes, he crowned himself, but he permitted his coronation to be repeated by the pope, Stephen IV, who also gave him the first imperial anointing, at Rheims in 816. Thereafter the two rituals of anointing and crowning were often combined.

The *Constitutio romana* (824) spelled out the relations of emperor and pope. The emperor had supreme jurisdiction, while the pope as a local ruler was to exercise ordinary judiciary and administrative power in his territories. The pope was to be chosen by the Roman people without constraint. The emperor was to confirm his election, and before his consecration he was to take an oath of loyalty to the emperor. The pope had the right to crown and anoint the emperor.

Mosaic (reconstructed in the eighteenth century) in Pope Leo III's dining hall of the Lateran Palace in Rome, depicting in the center vault Christ sending forth the Apostles to preach, on the left Christ giving the keys to Peter and the labarum (imperial cross) to Constantine, and on the right Peter giving a Roman standard (now the banner of Christianity) to Charlemagne and the pallium (papal stole) to Leo III.

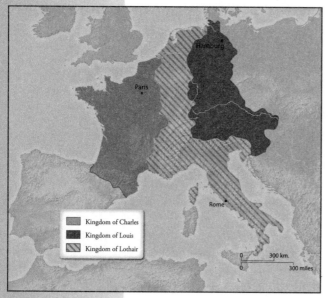

The division of Charlemagne's empire under his grandsons in 843.

Louis's sons — Lothair, Louis the German, and Pippin — had been sub-kings under their father. In 840 Lothair claimed the whole realm, but the situation was complicated by the ambitions of Charles the Bald, son of Louis by a second spouse. The result at Verdun in 843 was the division of the realm three ways, a settlement that foreshadowed later political divisions in Europe: Charles the Bald ruled the west (France), Lothair the middle region (including Italy), and Louis the German the east (Germany). The title of emperor remained a personal rank.

The fortunes of the Carolingian dynasty are symbolized by the names of its leaders, beginning with Charles Martel (the Hammer), Charles the Great (Charlemagne), followed by Charles the Bald, Charles the Fat (son of Louis the German), and Charles the Simple (grandson of Charles the Bald). (The translation of the name given to the last does him an injustice, for *simplex* was used in the sense of "without guile.")

Nevertheless, churchmen maintained the clerical idea of a "Christian empire," and Carolingian churchmen advanced important ideas on political theory. The Anglo-Saxon Catwulf stated the view that as there are two natures in Jesus Christ, so there are two natures in society, the body politic and the body ecclesiastical. This has remained until modern times a good Anglo-Saxon view, but it declined as the Carolingian realm disintegrated.

Smargeus in *Royal Way* speaks of unction giving the king a sacramental power so that he becomes an adoptive son of the king of heaven. Jonas, bishop of Orleans, in writing on the *Royal Institution* affirms that royal power is from God, not lineage; even an unjust ruler is to be obeyed as God's chastisement on his people. Hincmar, archbishop of Rheims, *On the Authority of Kings*, insists that bishops are superior in that they consecrate kings, but are not consecrated by them.

When Pope John VIII crowned Charles the Bald in 875, developing the thought that the consecrated king is an imitation of the true king, Christ, he declared that what Christ possesses by nature the king possesses by grace, words that would echo in future coronations. Such treatments of political theory advanced the idea of divine kingship in the West.

The gateway of the monastery at Lorsch, Germany, an example of Carolingian architecture.

B. The Pseudo-Isidorian Decretals

Ecclesiastical problems in ninth-century Gaul centered around the authority of bishops over against archbishops. Hincmar, archbishop of Rheims (845–82), was trying to promote unity and found the bishops to be a decentralizing force. The popes had favored the revival of archbishops, but now became afraid of the archbishops having too much power and found it to their advantage to strengthen bishops against both kings and archbishops.

The date of the *Pseudo-Isidorian Decretals* is uncertain, perhaps as early as the eighth century (c. 774–78) or as recent as about 850. The alleged compiler was Isidore Mercator (a pseudonym), perhaps intended to be associated with Isidore of Seville. One purpose of the *Pseudo-Isidorian Decretals* was to show the popes as defenders of bishops against their metropolitans. The material probably originated near Rheims and, if the later date is accepted, had Hincmar himself as its target. There were other forgeries of a similar kind at this time, but this collection became the most influential forgery in the history of the Roman Catholic church. It became the basis of the claims for the papal monarchy in the later Middle Ages.

After the preface there are four parts to the collection:

1. Papal communications (all forgeries)—fifty "Apostolic Canons," and sixty decretals from Clement of Rome (the Pseudo-Clementine literature is used as apostolic) to Miltiades.

2. "Donation of Constantine"—the legend that Pope Sylvester healed and converted Constantine, who then moved his capital to Constantinople and gave rule over the West to the pope, from whom he received the imperial crown, had been widely accepted in Rome in the late fifth century and had circulated in an eighth-century forgery in connection with Stephen's anointing of Pippin. It is easy to ridicule this devoutly believed story, but the legend points to the actual result of the emperor's move of the capital to Constantinople.

3. Canons of councils from Nicaea to the seventh century, mostly authentic.

4. Letters of popes (forty of which are apocryphal) from Sylvester (d. 335) to Gregory II (d. 731).

The overall effect of the collection was to give a legal basis for papal authority over the jurisdictional structure of the church. The "Donation of Constantine" had the further significance of giving a basis for the claim that the pope is supreme over all rulers, even the Roman emperor.

C. Pope Nicholas I the Great (858–67)

Nicholas I, who was involved in the dispute with the Eastern church (chapter 17) over the election of Photius as patriarch and over jurisdiction of missionary work among the Slavs, was the first pope to make use (perhaps innocently?) of the *Pseudo-Isidorian Decretals*. He did so in forcing Hincmar to recognize the right of the papacy to intervene in his dispute with a bishop, whose cause Nicholas upheld. Nicholas also suppressed the claims of John of Ravenna to a patriarchal title and jurisdiction.

Moreover, Nicholas established a precedent for papal interference in politics, on this occasion on moral grounds, in forcing king Lothair II to take back his first wife.

D. Controversy over the Lord's Supper

The first eucharistic controversy occurred in the mid-ninth century. Paschasius Radbertus (d. ca. 860) wrote the first doctrinal monograph on the Lord's supper, *On the Body and Blood of the Lord* (831, revised 844). Radbertus was a monk and later abbot at Corbie. He made a realistic identification of the eucharistic body with the human body of Jesus Christ that was born of Mary, was crucified on the cross, and is miraculously multiplied on the altars of Christendom at the consecration of the bread and wine. The elements become nothing less than the flesh and blood of Christ under the figure of bread and wine regardless of the faith of participants—a faith which is necessary, however, for spiritual blessings to be received.

The view of Radbertus drew opposition from various perspectives—from Gottschalk, Rabanus Maurus, and John Scotus Eriugena. Charles the Bald commissioned Ratramnus (d. c. 868), another monk at Corbie, to reply. Ratramnus opposed the realistic interpretation of the bread and wine, saying that the body and blood of Jesus Christ are present in a figure, not literally. The spiritual presence of the body of Christ is a mystery, available only to faith. As the elements nourish the human body, the spiritual reality nourishes the soul. The Holy Spirit works in the bread and wine to bring spiritual blessing even as he does in the baptismal waters.

In the background of this discussion were two different traditions of interpreting the words of Jesus at the Last Supper and in John 6. Ambrose had set forth a metabolic view of the Lord's supper in which by consecration the sign becomes the reality. Augustine made a subtler distinction, maintaining the symbolism of the sign and the realism of the supernatural invisible gift. By the time of Bede the two views were brought together synthetically, using the terms of both.

Accordingly, both Radbertus and Ratramnus assumed that both Ambrose and Augustine agreed, for it was assumed that there was no contradiction in the tradition, but each of the former men interpreted each of the latter men according to the perspective of the other. Over time, the position espoused by Radbertus gained ground, especially in popular piety.

E. Gottschalk and Predestination

A son of a Saxon count, Gottschalk (c. 804–c. 869) was brought as an oblate (a child "offered" to a monastery) to Fulda to be educated. Louis the Pious had ordered that an oblate at maturity could choose whether to stay in monastic life, but Gottschalk had entered under Charlemagne, when oblates did not have this privilege. A Synod at Mainz (829) apparently allowed him to leave Fulda, but did not release him from his monastic vows and required that the property given by the father remain with the monastery.

During several years as a wandering monk and preacher, Gottschalk defended an extreme form of double predestination. Believing he had really understood Augustine, Gottschalk said God elected some to eternal life and assigned the reprobate to eternal fire. This was because of God's decree, not because of God's foreknowledge.

Synods at Quiercy in 849 and in 853 (the latter under Hincmar) condemned Gottschalk's doctrine and affirmed that God elects only to life, that free will lost in Adam is restored in Jesus Christ through baptism, that God intended the salvation of all, and that Christ died for the sins of all, not just the elect.

A council at Valence in 855, on the other hand, upheld double predestination. Gottschalk himself, however, died still condemned. The varying responses to his teaching showed that strict Augustinianism was still alive, although most held back from many of its implications.

F. Rabanus Maurus and John Scotus Eriugena

Rabanus Maurus (c. 780–856) was a participant in the discussion of the eucharist and an opponent of Gottschalk. He moved in the highest circles of influence in the Carolingian world: student of Alcuin, abbot of Fulda, archbishop of Mainz, and teacher of some of the outstanding Carolingian scholars (so much so that he was known as the "teacher of Germany").

Rabanus Maurus was especially influential through his commentaries on the books of the Bible, drawn from patristic works and presenting allegorical interpretations applied to Jesus Christ and the church.

When the Irish discipline of private penance spread and many different penitentials were compiled, some champions of a public and more rigorous discipline, although acknowledging that it had fallen into disuse, objected. Rabanus Maurus took a middle way and advocated public confession for public sin and private confession for secret sin. He was representative of the traditional scholars and churchmen of the age, quite in contrast to John Scotus Eriugena.

John "the Scot" (c. 810–c. 877), an Irishman (his name means "Erin born") who went to the continent and enjoyed the patronage of Charles the Bald, was the one outstanding original thinker of the ninth century in the West. As a master of Greek (knowledge of Greek remained longer in Celtic areas than in Gaul), he translated the works of Dionysius the Areopagite into Latin.

John Scotus Eriugena developed his own philosophical system that was later suspected of pantheism because of its attempted reconciliation of Neoplatonic emanation with Christian creation. His work *De Divisione Naturae* divided nature into four categories: nature that is not created but creates (God), nature that is created and creates (the Platonic ideas), nature that is created and does not create (the natural order that is perceived through the senses), and nature that is not created and does not create (God, to whom all things return).

"[The sacramental and the historical Christ differ] not indeed in nature but in form; that body of the Lord which is daily ... consecrated from the substance of the bread and wine for the life of the world, and which is ... offered by the priest, is one thing, and the body of Christ which was born of the virgin Mary and into which the former is changed, is in form another thing" (Rabanus Maurus, *Letter to Egolonem*).

V. SUMMARY

The preceding and the following chapters as well as this one include sections on missionary expansion. Different models were present. The Irish monk-missionaries worked on their own and offered an individual holy person as the center of loyalty. The Benedictines let a monastery serve as a Christian center. The Carolingians used ecclesiastical structures to promote political unity. The Byzantines allowed "national" churches with their own language to provide cohesion among new converts.

The popes planned an independent episcopal organization united by allegiance to Rome. The three popes Gregory sought to avoid the extremes of imposing counsels of perfection on new converts or settling for superficial conversion. However, their adapting Christianity to the pagan pattern of religious thinking and behavior resulted in a folk catholicism within a church with a more learned leadership.

Greek missionaries had the advantage that political pressure and cultural superiority from Byzantium led barbarian rulers in Moravia, Bulgaria, and Russia to request Christian teachers to instruct them. Missionaries in the West, although often enjoying political support, usually took the initiative in entering new areas. The Byzantine leadership put more stress on doctrine, whereas the popes stressed morals and loyalty to Rome. All the missionaries emphasized the weaknesses of the pagan gods and the advantages of accepting Christianity.

During the seventh through ninth centuries the building materials for medieval Europe were assembled. The Carolingian age laid the groundwork for a medieval European civilization whose bond of unity was to be religious rather than political. The damage done by the Germanic invasions of the fifth and sixth centuries was partially reconstructed. The renewal on the continent was encouraged especially by missionaries and teachers from Britain and Ireland, well illustrating how mission fields often maintain a higher religious vitality than more established areas do.

A revival of learning associated with the establishment of schools brought with it the copying of manuscripts and renewed theological activity. The Carolingian age set the contours for the religio-political map of Europe for some time to come.

A blending of the character of political and religious offices occurred. The institution of sacral kingship and a revival of a Roman emperor in the West crowned by the pope gave a holy character to civil rule. On the other hand, civil jurisdiction by the papacy was advanced with the creation of the papal states.

The revival associated with the Carolingian age, however, was soon threatened by a new wave of invaders, this time from Scandinavia.

FOR FURTHER STUDY

Moore, M. E. *Sacred Kingdom: The Bishops and the Rise of Frankish Kingship*. Washington: Catholic University of America Press, 2011.

Riché, Pierre. *The Carolingians: A Family Who Forged Europe*. Philadelphia: University of Pennsylvania Press, 1993.

Talbot, C. H. *The Anglo-Saxon Missionaries in Germany*. New York: Sheed & Ward, 1954.

Wallace-Hadrill, J. M. *The Frankish Church*. Oxford: Clarendon, 1983.

Ward, Benedicta. *The Venerable Bede*. London: Chapman, 1990.

Decline and Renewal of Vitality in the West

The Ninth to the Eleventh Centuries

I. THE "DARK AGES"

Medieval historians, for good reasons, prefer to avoid the term "Dark Ages." To the extent that it is appropriate, it applies to the time in the West between the later ninth century and the early eleventh century.

In contrast to the flourishing of Middle Byzantine civilization, this was a time when civilization in western Europe reached a low ebb, but even then there were forces of renewal at work. There was more continuity than the language of "Dark Ages" allows, and the tenth century prepared for the great progress of the eleventh and twelfth centuries.

Threats to European Christianity came from both the East, represented by the Magyars, who moved into what is now Hungary at the end of the ninth century, and from the North, to which we will give more attention. Those very invaders from the north, when incorporated into the feudal society of western Europe, combined with the Benedictine monks to provide the impetus to an age of renewed vitality in the West.

With roots in the troubled times of the tenth century, efforts at institutional revival—monastic, imperial, and papal—came to a culmination in the eleventh century.

A. Invaders from Scandinavia

The Northmen or Norsemen (hence, Normans), including the Vikings and Danes, were Germanic peoples from Scandinavia, who represented the last wave of migration into the heart of Europe. The word "Viking" meant pirate raiders, which few of these people were,

Viking raiders
depicted on a tomb-
stone from the eighth
or ninth century
(Museum of
Lindisfarne Abbey,
England).

but the name was given a wider significance to refer to invaders from the North, barbaric pagans who threatened to snuff out the light of civilization kindled during the Carolingian renaissance. Between 800 and 1100 the Vikings went from the Iron Age to a fully medieval society.

The Vikings had invaded Ireland in the eighth century and by the end of that century had ravaged the Northumbrian monasteries in England. The first recorded Viking attack is described in the *Anglo-Saxon Chronicle* for the year 793, and a stone was set up at Lindisfarne a century later as a memorial. King Alfred (871–99) of Wessex checked their advance into England. An unusually learned and able ruler for his time and place, Alfred translated Gregory the Great's *Pastoral Rule* and Boethius's *Consolation of Philosophy* from Latin into Anglo-Saxon.

The Normans by the tenth century were raiding around the Mediterranean Sea and into Russia. Under an arrangement with Charles the Simple, Rollo settled his followers after 911 in the region of France since known as Normandy, where they were Christianized. Where Christians had not taken the gospel, the people came to the Christians. The vitality of the Normans gave them a great religious significance in the renewal of Western Christianity.

B. The Decline of the Papacy

Meanwhile, civil wars and petitions had reduced the territory over which the Roman emperor ruled to a small Italian principality. This enabled the papacy to establish a hold over the title of emperor in the late ninth century and to suppress the title in 924.

One incident will illustrate how the barbarity of the times affected even the heart of the Western church. Pope Formosus (891–96) was involved in political treachery: he crowned Lambert, duke of Spoleto, emperor and then repudiated him and crowned Arnulf. After Formosus's death, a successor, Stephen, had his body exhumed, placed in the papal chair, and judged. All Formosus's acts were condemned, the three fingers with which he conferred the papal blessing were cut off, his vestments were stripped from his body, and his corpse was dragged through the streets and thrown into the Tiber River.

During much of the tenth and eleventh centuries the Roman aristocracy dominated the papacy. The ruling influences in Rome and on the papacy for the first sixty years of the tenth century were Theophylact and his daughters Marozia and Theodora. Marozia's son Alberic controlled affairs in Rome from 932 to 954.

One bright spot was the papacy of Gerbert, who took the name Sylvester II (999–1003), recalling the first Sylvester to whom Constantine supposedly made the donation of rule in the West and thus the harmony of emperor and pope. Known as the "wonder of the world" for his learning (he had studied in Spain, where he became acquainted with Arabic scholarship), Gerbert declared, "I always tried to combine the art of speaking with the art of living well," a combination typical of the education of the time. He had taught at Rheims, to whose cathedral school he bequeathed his precious library, and had been abbot of Bobbio and then archbishop of Rheims and later of Ravenna before becoming pope. He pioneered the use of Arabic numerals (although still without the zero) instead of Roman numerals.

The papacy fell back again under the Tusculum popes, 1012–46. Count Alberic of Tusculum was descended on the female side from the Theophylact family. He raised to the papacy his brother Theophylact as Benedict VIII (1012–24) and then another brother as John XIX (1024–32). He finally seated his son, Theophylact, as Benedict IX (1032–44), under whom the papacy sank to a new moral low.

At this point the reformed empire stepped in to rescue the papacy, and the reforming popes in turn dissociated themselves from the empire (below and chapter 20). The shameful abuses of the papal office in the tenth and eleventh centuries did not shake the institution, because since Augustine's controversy with the Donatists it was customary to make a distinction between the office and its holder.

C. Missionary Counterattack

At a time when Western Christianity at its center seemed hopelessly mired in political intrigue and moral corruption, on the frontiers new gains were made for the Christian faith. The coming of the Norsemen brought to Christians an awareness of the pagans to the North. As British scholars had sparked the Carolingian renaissance, so two centuries later the contact of Scandinavian chieftains with Britain provided some of the fuel for the evangelization of Scandinavia.

Willibrord had visited Denmark briefly in the early 700s, but the principal mission work in Scandinavia began with Anskar (or Ansgar) from the Frankish kingdom in the ninth century. Pagan reactions largely wiped out his efforts.

More lasting work began with the conversion about 965 of King Harald Bluetooth, who built the first church on the site of the twelfth-century cathedral at Roskilde, where Danish kings and queens are buried. Under the kings Svein (Svend, 985–1014) and Canute (Knut) the Great (1014–35) the Christian faith spread in Denmark.

King Olaf of Sweden was baptized in 1008 by Sigfrid, a monk from England, but heathenism was not overthrown until about 1100.

The Norwegian king Olaf Tryggvason had been baptized in England about 995 after a hermit on the Scilly Isles foretold his future to him. The Christianization of Norway, however, owed more to Olaf Haraldsson (king 1016–30), whose harsh measures against paganism

The redbrick cathedral at Roskilde, Denmark, founded in the eleventh century, with the present church built and modified later on.

provoked opposition, but who became the patron saint of Norway after he was killed in battle. From 1150 to 1300 there flourished in Norway the construction of the distinctive wooden stave churches (named for the upright posts that formed their framework).

The spread of Christianity in Scandinavia was aided by the expansion of the Germanic empire in the tenth and eleventh centuries.

To the East, encroachments by the German empire also advanced Christianity in Bohemia and Poland. Despite the ninth-century mission work of Cyril and Methodius in Moravia, paganism continued there and in neighboring Bohemia.

"Good King Wenceslas" of Christmas carol fame was actually the duke of Bohemia (910–29), who enthusiastically and successfully promoted Christianity in his half-pagan realm. Political conflict caused his assassination in 929, but the largely legendary "Lives" of Wencelas (Vaclav in Czech) correctly emphasized his piety, humility, and charity, so that he became the patron-saint of his homeland. His successors consolidated the hold of Christianity in the region, and the episcopal see of Prague, established in 976, was subordinated to the archbishop of Mainz.

Christianity entered Poland with the baptism of Prince Mieczyslaw (or Mieszko) I in 966. He donated his realm to the papacy in 992 in order to block German and Bohemian claims, and under Boleslas (Boleslav) Polish independence was recognized by the German emperor Otto III (1000) and a metropolitan see was established at Gniezno.

The Magyars (their own name for the Hungarians) accepted Christianity under King Stephen I (997–1038). On becoming king, he made his vow to Mary; earlier the Christian rulers had made their vows to Christ. Stephen styled himself *kral*, a variant of Karl (or Charles), showing the continued aura emanating from the rule of Charlemagne. One half of the expense of his crown was a present of Pope Sylvester II and the other half a gift of the Byzantine government. This fact is a reminder of the close competition between East and West that preceded Hungary's allegiance to the Western church.

II. MONASTIC REVIVAL: CLUNY

A. Protection and Autonomy

Because of the Viking invasions, lack of protection, and secularizing influences, monastic life declined with other aspects of Western society. Lay abbots were often appointed due to the feeling that the monasteries needed someone to defend them, but these lay abbots did not always put spiritual interests first. The center from which the monastic renewal in the eleventh century was to come was Cluny, founded in 909/910.

William the Pious of Acquitaine placed Berno (abbot 910–27) in charge of a new monastic foundation at Cluny. He worked out a charter that was destined to have a great influence. The monastery had autonomy under the protection of Peter and Paul (not even the bishop of Rome could give the land to another) with the purpose of freeing it from the control of the local bishop and nobles.

Although not the first monastery to have papal protection, Cluny utilized its position to exercise great influence. It operated under the *Rule* of Benedict. After Berno the monks were to elect their own abbot. The long tenure of the early abbots showed the stability of the new foundation. Four of the first six (all but Berno and Aymard) were venerated as saints.

B. Characteristics of Cluny

1. Independence

The right of election of the abbot by the monks, and exemption from episcopal oversight and from taxes, had precedents but became common with the example of Cluny.

A canon adopted at Chalcedon had prohibited monks from moving around without permission of their bishop, and an important concern of Benedict had been *stabilitas* ("staying in one place")—both aiming to bring the monks more under control.

Left to right:

Statue of Wenceslas, Duke of Bohemia, in front of the National Museum in Prague.

Statue of Stephen, first Christian king of Hungary, in Budapest.

Now, however, there was a need for greater freedom, and this could be secured only by placing the monastery under the "outside" supervision of Rome (under the circumstances of the tenth century an authority far removed).

EARLY ABBOTS OF CLUNY	
Berno	910 – 27
Odo	927 – 42
Aymard	942 – 54
Majolus (Mayeul)	954 – 94
Odilo	994 – 1048
Hugh the Great	1049 – 1109

2. Kinds of monks

A distinction developed between lay monks, who were subject to the rules of the monastery but had not received orders, and monks who were priests. Originally monasticism had been a lay movement; then priests were appointed to minister to them. Now the two distinct classes of monks introduced the concept of a "regular clergy," that is, clergy who lived by a monastic rule (*regula*). In addition, there were serfs to work the land.

3. Emphasis on liturgy and learning

With others present to do the hard work, the monks became overseers of estates that came into their possession. They filled their time with more elaborate worship. Because of the liturgical interest, Cluny is associated with the introduction of a new feast in the church calendar, All Souls Day on November 2, to follow All Saints Day.

C. The Influence of Cluny

During the eleventh century a number of monasteries received exemption from the jurisdiction of bishops, for which they made a payment to Rome, and associated themselves with Cluny. A close alliance developed between the papacy and the Cluniac movement. Cluny began to bring under its leadership other Benedictine monasteries, which had been isolated, to form a congregation of monasteries. These monasteries were ruled by priors under the Abbot-General of Cluny, so that Cluny became the head of a movement within Benedictine monasticism.

A feeling of being a "church apart" developed among the Cluniacs, a consciousness of being a third force (in addition to the papacy and the empire) in Christendom. Such a vast congregation had a concern with all of society.

The impact of Cluny was felt in four areas.

1. Religious and monastic reform

The practice of free election of abbots and priors spread to other monasteries. Many Cluniac monks became bishops, and Cluniac abbots attended diocesan and provincial synods. In the eleventh century, popes Clement II, Gregory VII, and Urban II were Cluniac monks. Many pagan practices and beliefs continued to be held by the people (especially peasants), so there was much teaching to be done by bishops and monks.

2. Civil peace

The "Peace of God" and the "Truce of God," although not a product of Cluny, were promoted by Cluny and became the first popular religious movement of the Middle Ages. The terms refer to enactments of many councils between 975 and 1040 designed to promote peace. Councils of bishops, also attended by abbots, met. Monks brought their relics of saints to serve as heavenly witnesses to agreements reached at the councils and sworn to by the nobles. Large enthusiastic crowds, drawn by the presence of the valuable relics, gathered.

"[We] prescribe according to God's commandment and our own that no Christian shall kill any other Christian, for without a doubt, whoever kills a Christian sheds Christ's blood" (Council of Narbonne, 1054).

The first of these gatherings met in an open field near LePuy in 975. The earliest council from which canons of the Peace movement survive met at the monastery of Charroux in Aquitaine in 989. Its enactments, typical of those to follow, pronounced an anathema, unless reparations or satisfactions were made, on those who attacked the church or took anything from it, those who seized animals from the poor, and those who robbed or seized an unarmed cleric. Similar protections were extended later to other defenseless persons—widows and unaccompanied women, pilgrims, and merchants—and to other aspects of food production. With its promise of protection for the weak the Peace of God was a popular movement of the poor with social implications, and so opposed by the privileged.

The "Truce of God" began to be enacted in the 1030s and reached definitive expression in councils at Arles, 1037–41. It protected all classes at certain seasons—at first only on Sunday, then from Wednesday evening to Monday, then on liturgical feasts, so that, if observed, only eighty days a year were left for private warfare. As a commentary on the times, provision was made for the use of arms to enforce the Peace and Truce, but bishops and nobles took up the proposals as a means of reducing bloodshed and limiting feuds.

The advocates of the Peace and Truce of God saw a religious sanction for peace on earth as an image of divine peace. Some of these proposals continued to be enacted into the twelfth century. Although setting ideals, they met with little practical success. Warlike energies were later to be channeled into the Crusades, fighting the enemies of Christian faith rather than shedding the blood of Catholics. The Peace and Truce of God did promote the idea of a Christendom that transcended political divisions.

3. Celibate clergy

The Peace of God was related to a broader reform movement, for the councils that promoted it also enacted reform canons in regard to clerical celibacy and the independence of the church from secular lords.

The connection of the Peace of God and clerical reform was a concern for the purity of the church from abuses that were polluting the clergy: marriage and unchastity, simony, and the use of arms. The monks wanted to impose chastity on the "secular clergy," that is the clergy who lived in the world. They called the practice of married clergy "Nicolaitanism" (from Revelation 2:6, 15, traditionally interpreted as referring to sexual immorality) and the wives of clergy "concubines." The priests who had wives, however, did not consider them concubines.

There was a tendency to have the son of priestly marriages inherit the parish church with the result of trapping the church in feudalism, to say nothing of what spiritual qualifications the son might or might not have for his duties.

The reforms of Cluny with its development of priestly monasticism sought to impose the ideal of celibacy on all clergy and to make noncelibacy a matter of "heresy" for the clergy. This was not a new development, for earlier canonical legislation in the West had opposed the marriage of priests, but this had not been uniformly observed in recent years. Monastic reform now brought new pressure to have a celibate priesthood, which provoked opposition. This could take a cynical turn, as in one writer's comment on clerical celibacy: God had taken sons away from bishops, but the devil gave them nephews.

4. Purchase of clerical office

The term "simony," from Simon Magus's offer to buy from the apostles the power of conferring the Holy Spirit (Acts 8:18–19), referred to buying spiritual gifts. There was agreement that simony was wrong, but there was uncertainty about what constituted simony, and reformers applied the word to practices against which they protested.

In particular, the Cluniac monks applied the word to the common practice of paying money in order to receive a benefice. Defenders of making gifts to the proprietor of a church or monastery saw these as tokens of obedience to the secular lord and distinguished the property belonging to the church from the ecclesiastical office itself, a distinction denied by those who wanted to separate the church from lay control. Many with good intentions paid money according to the general custom on receiving clerical offices, which often carried with them temporal administration and its accompanying remuneration.

On the other hand, clergymen who received payments for administering the sacraments did not see this as the sale of the gifts of the Spirit.

The word *simony* was later applied to the supplier of a church office as well as the purchaser and extended to any appointment to church office by a lay ruler.

The Cluniac reform, defending the independence of the church, opposed these practices.

D. Related Developments

Other reform movements arose. In Lorraine (led by Gerard), Burgundy, and Acquitaine there was opposition to married clergy. In Italy reform found expression in a revival of anchorite (hermit) piety. Peter Damian (more below) was its foremost representative.

Monasteries in the tenth and eleventh centuries became the centers of the cult of relics. Reliquaries (chests or caskets, often expensively and elaborately ornamented, to house and display the relics of saints) were created, and larger church buildings were required at monasteries, especially abbeys, to accommodate the crowds of pilgrims. Oaths were sworn on the reliquaries; and they were carried in processions to ward off plagues, obtain good harvests, or drive away an approaching enemy.

The reform of monastic life, the renewal of the cult of the saints, and the extensive building and rebuilding of churches gave a strong sense of renewal to the early eleventh century.

III. IMPERIAL REVIVAL

Political leadership in western Europe had been with the Franks, but after the Viking incursions it passed to the Germans. (With the election of Hugh Capet as king in 987 the Carolingian dynasty was replaced in France by the Capetians, who ruled until 1328.)

Five duchies (ruled by dukes) in Germany became the basic framework of the empire—Saxony, Franconia, Lorraine, Swabia, and Bavaria—from whom the king of Germany was chosen. In addition to these, the king of Burgundy and the king of the Lombards were part of the structure of the empire.

A. The Saxon Kings—the Ottonian Age

The Saxon line of German kings (919–1024) began with Henry the Fowler (he was falconing when he was elected), who avoided a liturgical coronation. His son, Otto I the Great (936–73), began the imperial revival that brought the broader Ottonian cultural renewal of the tenth and eleventh centuries.

Otto I the Great was anointed and crowned king at Aachen, being installed on the very throne of Charlemagne. The archbishop on handing him the sword, said: "Receive this sword to repulse the adversaries of Christ, the barbarians and evil Christians, as a symbol of the divine authority that is conferred on you and of your power over the empire of the Franks for the abiding peace of Christendom." These words summarized the Christian kingship of the Carolingians and the Ottonians.

Not content to be a "first among equals," Otto strengthened the national monarchy. He attached much importance to receiving papal coronation as emperor in Italy, which he obtained in 962. When he was crowned by the pope, he revived the imperial title, based on the ninth-century theory that an emperor (in contrast to a king) ruled over a number of peoples. He was King of Germany, King of Lombardy, and now *Imperator augustus* (there was no "Roman" in the title). The imperial dignity only brought rule of the diminutive duchy of Rome, and Otto did not revive Charlemagne's empire in West Frankish lands.

Otto had led an expedition to Italy in 951, but a rebellion in Germany prevented his establishing his authority there. Alberic ruled Rome and placed many popes on the throne, including his immoral sixteen-year-old son, consecrated in 955 as John XII, who set the precedent for a pope to change his name. Otto returned to Italy in 961, and John XII crowned him emperor in 962, a significant date for the relations of the papacy and the empire. Their agreement regulated the election of the bishop of Rome: he was to be elected by the people and clergy of the diocese; the election was to be announced to the king of Germany for approval before consecration.

Otto swore to honor papal authority, and after his coronation he confirmed and extended the Carolingian grant of the papal states. John XII, however, concluded Otto was too powerful and turned against him. Otto then had him deposed at a synod, and a new pope, Leo VIII, was elected. The Roman people sided with John XII and rioted, but Otto put to flight the Roman populace.

In Germany, Otto I the Great used bishops and abbots in securing authority over the powerful duchies. He formed prince-bishoprics with church prelates as an integral part of the structure of government, advancing the gradual evolution of ecclesiastical properties into ecclesiastical principalities. The archdioceses of Germany were Trier, Cologne, Mainz, Salzburg, Hamburg-Bremen (since Louis the Pious), and Magdeburg (elevated under Otto I in 962).

An ivory depiction of the crucifixion, ascension, and second coming of Christ, from Cologne in the tenth or eleventh century (Cluny Museum, Paris).

Otto strengthened the position of archbishops and imperial abbots, using them in the administration of the empire, in order to counterbalance the authority of dukes and counts. The control of the elections of abbots and bishops passed almost entirely to the king. He conferred the shepherd's staff at their consecration. Henry III later extended to the ceremony the bestowal of the bishop's ring (indicative that the only lawful spouse was the prelate's diocese). Among the regal rights given to bishops were the collection of tolls, coining money, exercising judicial power, and fortifying their cities.

Not all the clerics were loyal to the king—some joined a revolt in 953—but, in general, the bishops were pillars of royal support. Clerics were appointed from the nobility. Louis the Pious had appointed serfs because they were more pious, but this was not done again until Henry II, who appointed them because they were more compliant.

Monasteries continued to provide education in Scripture and the seven liberal arts. The monastery of St. Gall (Switzerland) was a center of learning under the Ottos. In the tenth and eleventh centuries cathedral schools added an emphasis on *mores*, manners and conduct, so that education was summarized in the combination "letters and manners" (or literature and conduct, learning and virtue).

Brun, who ended his career as archbishop of Cologne (953–65) and was brother of Otto I, served a similar educational role in Ottonian circles as Alcuin did for Charlemagne, except that his activity focused more on preparation of clerics for civil service than for their religious duties. Cathedral schools prepared churchmen for service in an imperial church with frequent dealings in the secular world. A common sequence under Otto was from cathedral school to the court chapel to a bishopric.

In three regions Otto I the Great carried on missionary activities with territorial interests: among the Magyars (modern Hungary), whom he defeated at Lechfeld in 955, the Norsemen (subjugating the Dane-mark, now Denmark), and the Slavs (east of Saxony). The pope permitted the king to do the ecclesiastical organization in these areas.

Diplomatic contacts with the eastern empire, including the marriage of Otto II to the Byzantine princess Theophano, opened the way to Byzantine influence on Ottonian art, seen especially in wall paintings of churches and illuminations of biblical and liturgical manuscripts.

Otto II (973–83) took the title "Roman Emperor." He did so in conscious opposition to the Byzantine emperor (whose title was

"Roman Emperor") Basil II. The title stuck with his successors. In the background was the continuing influence of the interpretation of the fourth kingdom in Daniel 7 as Rome, an interpretation going back to Hippolytus and Jerome. There was the feeling that the name must continue for the kingdom to endure until the end.

The reign of Otto III (983–1002) was significant for church-state relations. He appointed the first German pope, his cousin Bruno, as Gregory V, and the first French pope, his tutor Gerbert, as Sylvester II.

B. The Salian Dynasty and the Papacy

With Conrad II (1024–39) the Salian dynasty (1024–1125) succeeded the Saxons as German rulers. Under him, about 1034, the title "Roman Empire" came into use for all the lands under the sway of the German emperor.

The emperor Henry III (1039–56), who no longer styled himself "king of the Germans" but "king of the Romans," provides the connection between the monastic revival and the imperial revival, for he was married to the daughter of the duke of Acquitaine, whose family had founded Cluny, and he was himself a genuinely religious ruler and a great patron of the Cluniac order.

Henry III also provides the connection between the imperial revival and the papal revival, for he removed three rival popes and placed his own nominees in office. This situation came about because in Rome the first half of the eleventh century repeated the first half of the tenth century, as the papacy sank again to a miserable condition.

Benedict IX (1032–44) was only eighteen years old when raised to the papacy and was one of the worst popes. He was driven from Rome, but was able to return and held the church of St. John Lateran. Sylvester III was bishop of Sabina when elected to replace Benedict in 1036; he held St. Peter's Vatican. Gregory VI (1045–46) came from a family of converts from Judaism and wanted to rescue the papacy. He bought the office for 1,000 pounds of silver from Benedict, who then sought to regain his position. Gregory occupied Santa Maria Maggiore.

Emperor Henry III convened three synods in 1046: at Pavia, at Sutri (where Gregory VI abdicated and Sylvester III was divested of office), and at Rome (where Benedict IX was deposed). Henry III secured from the Roman people the right to designate the bishop of Rome.

As a reform-minded ruler, Henry III opposed Nicolaitanism and favored celibacy. He did so not only to safeguard the purity of the church, but also to control ecclesiastical benefices that otherwise would be inherited by the sons of married clergy. The popes favored celibacy not only for long-standing religious reasons, but also in order to avoid a hereditary priesthood that would sink the church further into feudalism (chapter 20).

Both the emperor and the popes opposed simony, but the rulers felt bound to appoint good men to office, while righteous popes had to oppose appointments by the rulers in the interest of the independence of the church.

IV. PAPAL REVIVAL

Until the mid-eleventh century the actual influence of the pope, although theoretically head of Western Christendom, was largely provincial. The papal revival at this time began a process of changing the theory into more of a reality.

The emperor Henry III named Suidger, the bishop of Bamberg, as Pope Clement II (1046–47), followed by Damasus II (1047–49). The year 1046 begins a new era in church history. The popes had started taking new names, and a large number of "the seconds" occur: Victor II (1055–57), Nicholas II (1058–61), Alexander II (1061–73), and Urban II (1088–99), who initiated a series of eight consecutive popes who were "the second." There was a consciousness that something new was occurring.

In 1049 there came a great pope, Leo IX (1049–54). He was a product of the reform efforts in Lorraine that came from the secular clergy and he had been bishop of Toul. He did not consent to becoming pope without proper election by the clergy and people of Rome.

Leo IX brought with him into the administration of the church the following associates:

1. Frederick of Lorraine—archbishop of Liege and brother of Godfrey, duke of Tuscany and the second spouse of Beatrice (beginning the alliance of Tuscany with the papacy), who became Leo's Chancellor, then abbot of Monte Cassino, and finally Pope Stephen IX.

2. Humbert—from Lorraine, a monk at Cluny who thought Cluny had compromised the ideals of its founders and who was made a cardinal.

3. Hugh White—monk and then cardinal, who later turned against the reform.

4. Hildebrand—appointed archdeacon of papal finance, who later became Pope Gregory VII.

5. Peter Damian, who became a cardinal under Stephen IX. Peter Damian was important as an author and eloquent spokesman

of asceticism. He promoted the celibacy of the clergy and its separation from secular involvement, but was more moderate in his approach than Hildebrand.

The college of cardinals grew out of the old advisory presbyteral council of the bishop of Rome. By 736 seven bishops of suburban sees (Ostia, Porto, Alvano, Sabina, Tusculum, Frascati, and Praenesti) were a part of the pope's regular advisory council. The archpriests of the titular churches and other churches of special note were the cardinal priests, and eighteen deacons were included in the cardinalate.

Under Leo the cardinals became more institutionalized as a "senate of the Roman church" with less importance for the liturgy and spiritual life of individual Roman churches and more for serving as assistants of the popes. Leo's strategy was to put into as many of these positions as possible fellow reformers from Lorraine. Although the feeling survived that a bishop was married to his original church and should not be translated, Leo internationalized the cardinalate.

On the model of the German emperor at imperial diets, Leo IX journeyed up and down to convene synods and local councils, to adjudicate disputes, and promote reform. He elaborated the Petrine authority of the papacy and advocated celibacy for the clergy and canonical election of prelates.

Leo's first policy in Italy was directed not against the Saracens or Byzantines, but against the Norman freebooters who had been a threat in south Italy since 1016. Leo claimed this area as part of the patrimony of Peter on the basis of the *Donation* of Constantine. He devised the first papal banner and took it into battle, but his troops were defeated in 1053 and he was held captive for nine months. His military action alarmed the Byzantine emperor, who was concerned for the Byzantine holdings in south Italy.

The further story of the revived papacy can be told in terms of the break in communion with the Greek church (below) and the Investiture controversy (chapter 20).

V. THE SCHISM BETWEEN WEST AND EAST (1054)

A. Differences between West and East

Leo IX's counterpart in the Greek church was Michael Cerularius, Patriarch of Constantinople (1043–58). An unusually assertive patriarch, he was in many ways like Leo IX—interested in the independence of the church, holding a high ideal of his office, and promoting education.

Decline and Renewal of Vitality in the West

Michael was ambitious for the extension of Byzantine dignity. Remembering the popes of the preceding century, he looked on the Roman see as uncouth and barbarian. When Leo IX was captured by the Normans, Michael ordered the Byzantines in Italy to abstain from helping the Romans, and he closed the churches in the East that used the Latin liturgy.

Michael operated within the Eastern theory of one empire with one emperor, and of the church as one body in which the five senses were represented by the five patriarchs.

The reality, however, was that after the Photian schism in the ninth century the bond between East and West never grew strong again. There were differences of language, national character, ecclesiastical organization, liturgy, and theology. These differences were more of emphasis than of contradictions.

The Eastern church drew its self-understanding more from the local assembly united in eucharistic fellowship, from the sacraments, and from the ecumenical creeds. In contrast, the Western church was coming to define itself more in terms of canon law and hierarchical submission to a monarchic head.

To these differences had been added serious political complications: loss of Byzantine control in central and northern Italy, the alliance of the popes and the Franks, the formation of the papal states at the expense of Constantinople, the revival of the western empire under Otto I, the loss of Byzantine territory in south Italy to the Normans in the early eleventh century that ended the last geographical link between East and West, and Ottonian and then papal military policy in south Italy.

The question of authority over lower Italy and different views over the primacy of Rome aroused Michael, who skillfully directed popular sentiment in such a way that the long threatened schism between Rome and Constantinople appeared to be almost entirely his work.

Michael attacked the Latins as heretical for a variety of reasons. The Latin church used unleavened bread in the eucharist (the Greeks, arguing that the Gospels use the word for ordinary bread in the accounts of the Last Supper, used leavened bread), making them no better than Jews. They forced celibacy on all the clergy. They pictured Jesus Christ as a Lamb (because of the incarnation he should be pictured as a man). They sang Hallelujah at Easter only, omitting it from Lent. They did not forbid the eating of strangled meat (the Germans liked their blood sausages!).

The question of the addition of the *filioque* clause to the Nicene Creed, criticized by Photius, played only a minor role in the dispute before the twelfth century.

These differences had been lived with for some time. More important than all the differences, political and religious, between East and West was the loss of the will to unity. Where that will to unity is present, major differences can be overcome; where it is lacking, minor differences can be an occasion for division.

Leo IX replied to Michael's attacks with letter-dissertations: *In terra pax* and *More Romano*. These treatises argued that a variety of usages could prevail and therefore he would not close the Greek churches in Rome. Among Greek customs that he found objectionable were clerical marriage, rebaptism of Latins by Greeks, waiting until the eighth day before baptizing children, Cerularius's use of the title "ecumenical patriarch," and his claims to authority over the patriarchs of Alexandria and Antioch.

Leo IX insisted that Rome was the mother church and those separated from her were synagogues of Satan. Constantinople, he said, was a daughter of Rome. Furthermore, he pointed out the heresies that some patriarchs of Constantinople had embraced, in contrast to the successors of Peter who could never fall from the faith. Leo included an appeal to the *Pseudo-Isidorian Decretals* to support his claims for the Roman bishop.

B. The Excommunications

Emperor Constantine X (1042–54) made efforts at reconciliation. Leo IX sent two more letters: one to the emperor appealing for help against the Normans and one to Michael, referring to his errors, including the false title of "ecumenical patriarch." The administrators of the Roman church (the Curia), aiming at repudiation of the title "ecumenical patriarch" and acceptance of the Roman primacy, sent a three-man embassy to the emperor: Humbert, Frederick of Lorraine, and Peter of Amalfi.

Humbert was a champion of papal authority, claiming the apostolic see of Rome as the source and norm of all church law and advocating the freedom of the church from lay control. Humbert wrote a *Dialogue between a Roman and a Constantinopolitan*, in which he defended the celibacy of the clergy not as a matter of discipline but of faith (any priestly marriage was "concubinage") and said that sacraments administered by married clerics were invalid.

Humbert's later work *Against the Simoniacs* in three books made a similar claim: Any cleric appointed to office by a layman, no matter how honestly, could not administer valid sacraments, a doctrine that revived the viewpoint of Donatism, which made the validity of sacraments depend on the status of the administrator.

Nicetas, a monk at the Studium monastery, wrote against the Latin use of unleavened bread, and Humbert, angered at the reply, attacked the monk. The emperor went to Studium and insisted that Nicetas retract his book and burn it.

This was the atmosphere in which the papal delegation went to Hagia Sophia in 1054 and laid on its high altar a bull of excommunication against Michael Cerularius and his associates, while declaring the emperor and people of Constantinople orthodox.

Michael asked for a conference with the three legates. They feared this and asked for the presence of the emperor, a request that was refused on the grounds that only ecclesiastical matters were at stake. The legates, carrying gifts from the emperor to the pope, left Constantinople, but Michael issued a counter excommunication of the papal legates and their supporters. Leo IX, however, had died a few months before, not knowing that the excommunication had been consummated.

There had been breaks in communion between Rome and Constantinople before—notably, according to the terminology of the Western church, the Acacian schism (482–519), the Monothelete schism (646–81), and the Photian schism (869–80). After two centuries it was time for another break in communion, and there was no reason to think that this one would not be repaired as the earlier ones had been.

Moreover, since the excommunications did not apply to the respective churches as a whole, and not even to their heads, the pope and the emperor, little changed in the relations of the two churches for some time. However, the recriminations were more vehement and the sense of estrangement greater. The schism remains unhealed, although in 1965 Pope Paul VI and Patriarch Athenagoras cancelled the excommunications of 1054.

Already since the sixth century it has been necessary to tell the story of the Latin and Greek churches separately. With the separation of the two churches our story will follow developments in the West and include the East primarily as the respective histories intersect.

FOR FURTHER STUDY

Chadwick, Henry. *East and West: The Making of a Rift in the Church: From Apostolic Times to the Council of Florence.* Oxford: Oxford University Press, 2003.

Evans, Joan. *Monastic Life at Cluny, 910–1157.* Hamden, CT: Archon, 1968.

Runciman, Steven. *The Eastern Schism: A Study of the Papacy and the Eastern Churches during the XIth and XIIth Centuries.* Oxford: Clarendon, 1955.

The Papal Reform Movement and the First Crusade

Two themes dominated Western church history in the late eleventh and early twelfth centuries: the efforts inspired by the papacy to reform the church and free it from secular control, and the rallying of secular rulers by the papacy to undertake an armed reconquest of the Holy Land from the Muslims.

The result of the former was conflict between the pope and the emperor over lay investiture (secular princes giving to churchmen the symbols of their office). The papal reform movement revived the papal theory of the empire as the secular arm of the church. When the church—defending the principle of independence—opposed appointments of good men to church offices by pious laymen, the feelings were bound to be bitter, for it was originally appointments by pious lay rulers that showed the church her mission.

The other side of church-state relations was that the church needed the support of secular rulers, especially as it turned the warlike energies of the western nobles to the religious cause of the Crusades.

I. THE PAPACY AND GREGORY VII

After the death of Leo IX in 1054 it seemed possible for a time that the gains of reform would be lost, but the reformers kept their goals in mind.

Notable for the future was the papacy of Nicholas II (1058–61), the first pope, it appears, to have been crowned like a king or emperor. The *Pseudo-Isidorian Decretals* had been firmly woven into canon law by the eleventh century, and Nicholas II stood on them. In his foreign relations, the principle of holy warfare carried on by Leo IX was acknowledged as part of papal policy, relations with Tuscany were furthered, and peace was made with the Normans, who now controlled the former Byzantine lands of southern Italy and Sicily.

The Lateran decree of 1059 confirmed Leo's assertion of papal independence from royal power and issued regulations for the election of the pope, with some modifications the "world's oldest constitution" still in force. The election of the pope was to be by the cardinal bishops, confirmed by the cardinal presbyters and deacons (later all the cardinals had an equal voice in the election of the pope—see chapter 22 on the Lateran Council of 1179), and ratified by the people of Rome. Notification was to be sent to the emperor. The pope might be chosen outside the city of Rome, might come from anywhere in the church, and took office immediately on election. This decree established the exclusive right of cardinals to elect the pope and reduced the role of the "clergy and people" (that is, the nobility of Rome and the emperor).

The political situation in Italy and Europe had introduced new factors and added new dimensions to old factors in papal power since the times of the "Greats"—Leo, Gregory, and Nicholas. These factors included: (1) territorial jurisdiction over the papal states prevented the rise of a single Italian power and afforded the pope a measure of political independence; (2) this led to a policy of balancing the powers of secular rulers in Italy; (3) the consolidation of feudalism confirmed the hierarchical understanding of the church; and (4) the papacy afforded a useful source of arbitration as an "appeal court" for Europe.

The papal revival reached its climax under Hildebrand, Gregory VII (1073–85). He had been associated with Gregory VI's efforts to rescue the papacy (chapter 19), thus his choice of name. As archdeacon and a diplomat under Alexander II (1061–73), he was already the real power in the papal court. During the funeral for Alexander II, the people seized Hildebrand and carried him to be installed as pope, an action later ratified by the cardinals. This action was uncanonical according to the constitution Hildebrand had helped inaugurate under Nicholas II, and it would be used against him in his later struggle with King Henry IV.

Gregory VII was a man with a strong conviction of his divine calling, hence a man who acted out of moral and religious motivation, and a man with strong commitments to justice and to the see of Peter. He took a dim view of the state of the church in his time. Nevertheless, with unshaken confidence in his convictions, he made aggressive and rigid claims for papal authority and church rights. Gregory thus was a key figure in the development of the papal monarchy. In pursuing his program of church reform he had three sources of political support: the Normans in south Italy, commercial interests in north Italy, and the counts of Tuscany in central Italy.

Gregory kept a file of legal authorities relating to the office of pope. About 1075 a summary or perhaps a "table of contents" of this collection

CLAIMS OF THE *DICTATUS PAPAE*

(Selected statements arranged by topics)

Preeminence of the Roman See

1. The Roman Church was founded by God alone.
2. The bishop of Rome alone is to be called universal.

Special Privileges of the Popes

8. The pope alone may use imperial insignia (e.g., tiara, red carpet, which had been borrowed from Persia by Emperor Diocletian).
9. All princes should kiss his feet, and his alone.

Inerrancy of the Church of Rome

22. The Roman Church has never erred, nor will it ever, according to Scripture.
23. The pope, if canonically ordained, is by merits of Peter rendered holy.
26. No one is to be reckoned a Catholic who does not agree with the Roman church.

Jurisdiction of the Popes

4. His legates take precedence over all bishops in council, and his legates can give sentences of deposition.
7. The pope by himself has power of making laws if necessary.
16. No synod is to be called ecumenical except with his permission.
17. No legal statement, nor any book of canons, is to be accepted apart from his authority.

Authority over Bishops

3. The pope alone has power to depose or reconcile bishops.
13. The pope may translate a bishop to other dioceses in case of necessity.

Authority in Adjudication

18. The pope alone can revise one of his sentences.
19. The pope can be judged by no one.
20. No one dare condemn an appellant to the apostolic see.

Papal Rights in Respect to Secular Authorities

12. The pope may depose emperors.
27. The pope may absolve subjects of wicked rulers from their allegiance.

was copied into the register of his letters. Gregory was a canonist, and these twenty-seven statements, known as the *Dictatus Papae*, served as an index to the principles of papal primacy. The claims expressed in it were the basis of his policy toward the Eastern church, the emperor, and ecclesiastics who were recalcitrant.

Gregory I had exercised a spiritual primacy, and Gregory VII now claimed a supreme temporal power as well. Later popes had more effective power, but there was no need to extend Gregory VII's claims.

II. THE INVESTITURE CONTROVERSY

The conflict between Pope Gregory VII and King Henry IV of Germany was so important for the future course of the church, the papacy, and church-state relations, is so revealing about the circumstances of the time, and so captured the imagination of people then and now that it deserves being recounted in some detail.

In spite of its name, the conflict involved more than investiture. Two long-standing but contrasting conceptions of the relationship of the religious and political spheres clashed: the church as free but under the supervision of the superior state (the royal viewpoint) versus the church as independent and deferred to by the state (the papal viewpoint).

Or, put another way, the two leaders of Christendom contended for two different views of kingship: for Gregory it was a political office subject to the pope; for Henry it was a theocratic office filled by one who was king by the grace of God and as liturgically anointed served as mediator between the people and the clergy.

Their conflict came to a head in the city of Milan over the selection of the city's bishop. The situation was complicated by the opposition of the Patarenes ("beggars") to the bishop and clergy for their corruption and loose morals; Gregory VII took up their cause against the royal nominee. Milan became a test case for which viewpoint would prevail.

The real issue in what has come to be called the "Investiture Controversy," therefore, was the relation of spiritual and temporal authority. The German king/emperor claimed authority as the representative of the laity, and the pope required obedience from even the emperor.

The controversy was narrowed down to the practice of "lay investiture" (the bestowing of the symbols of spiritual office in the church by lay rulers) and the compromise resolving the controversy was in these terms.

In their textbooks of theology and canon law, students learned of the wickedness of "simony" (defined as receiving spiritual office from lay rulers), the necessity for celibacy of the clergy, and the supremacy of the Roman see. The eleventh and twelfth centuries saw the translation of these old theories into something like practice with the creation of the papal monarchy.

In the propaganda war between the papacy and the empire, the papal position had clarity and consistency: The spiritual is superior to the temporal, and the pope represents spiritual authority. The imperial position had tradition and political expediency behind it: Why is the church upset now? Why not continue to do what has always been done?

A. The Context of the Conflict

Bishop Adalbero of Laon in 1015 identified three classes of society: clergy, whose task was to pray; the military, whose task was to fight; and peasants, whose task was to produce food. This was a simplistic classification even then, but during the eleventh century the relationships of the elements in society became more complex. The definitions of clergy and laity, for instance, underwent refinement. The clergy became more distinct from the laity, and during the lowest ebb of the papacy a third force had arisen, the congregation of Cluny with its monastic priests. In Rome the "plebs" were not the people as a whole but the aristocrats. Outside Rome the laity meant counts and kings; a special kind of layman was the German king, elected by the dukes and anointed by the pope.

The church was very much involved in the social, economic, and political structures given the modern name feudalism (from *feudum*, possession of a gift, which carried obligations). Feudalism became more clearly delineated in tenth-and-eleventh-century France and spread from there.

Modern interpretations differ, but three elements in feudalism may be identified: the social element of lordship and vassalage (which were the medieval words for the relationship), the economic element of property (a fief), and the political element of decentralized government and law (which provided the setting and the need for these arrangements).

A key element in the relationship, vassalage, is attested already in the eighth century: a lord protected his "man," who as a vassal aided his protector. From late Carolingian times the duty of service became linked no longer simply with a person but with a gift of land, and the latter became understood as no longer a temporary enjoyment of the fruits of an estate but as an outright gift.

Feudalism thus refers to the personal relationship between two persons of knightly or noble status (and so from the upper class socially) in which one granted to the other income-producing property (usually land), the fief, in return for various forms of assistance. Vassalage affected all the upper levels of society: the knight held his fief from a baron, a baron his fief from a count, and a count his fief from the king.

A ceremony of homage sealed the relationship, the vassal upon receiving a fief or benefice and promise of protection pledged service to the lord. By the end of the eleventh century the developed ceremony included a promise by the vassal kneeling without weapons, placing his hands together between the hands of the lord, who raised him up and kissed him. (The extended hands placed together is apparently the origin of the gesture that came to symbolize prayer.)

The lord had to defend his "man," give him gifts, receive him at table, and bring up his sons and marry off his daughters if need be. The vassal provided the lord with financial aid, lodgings, military service, and counsel. When a fief passed into possession by the church, the church made a financial compensation for the loss of services.

Many persons had willed land to the church or a monastery, so that bishops and abbots inherited feudal obligations and became themselves great feudal lords with serfs working the land. Ambitious and greedy men wanted these major offices in the church, for these positions, which gave control of great church holdings, were more than spiritual offices.

Moreover, nobles had control over the selection of bishops and abbots because, unless they accepted a person as a vassal, they could withhold possession of the lands associated with these offices. Often a noble's private chapel (*eigenkirche*, "proprietary church") served as the village church, but the noble wanted to keep on selecting the priest.

The reform movement of the eleventh and twelfth centuries sought to remove these places of worship from laymen and give them to bishops. The landowners preferred, if they must give them up, to give them to monasteries in return for prayers by the monks for their souls. Church officials, moreover, had assumed many civil functions in the collapse of the western empire and so had duties to civil rulers.

Church and state, therefore, were intertwined in a great variety of societal functions. Every secular ruler was dependent on the resources and personnel of the church. All administrative and secretarial departments were staffed by churchmen, and so the way was prepared for the eventual change in the meaning of the word "cleric" from clergyman to one who performed "clerical" duties. The income from church lands was important to ecclesiastical and civil rulers. The kings and other rulers thought they should be able to choose their own officials, but the church did not think it should accept prelates chosen for political reasons.

"Lay investiture" was the narrow issue about which the struggle over conflicting interests and opposing viewpoints was fought. The term technically meant the conferring of the insignia of ecclesiastical office, such as the bishops' ring and staff, by secular rulers. (The ring symbolized the marriage of the bishop to his church and the staff his role as shepherd.) It has been observed that the twofold duties of churchmen, often inconsistent with each other, made a conflict inevitable but at the same time insoluble, since neither the church nor the state could afford to lose their services.

Four actions were involved in the handing over of the rights and privileges of a church office, but these actions were not so clearly distinguished in the eleventh century as they came to be. Ivo of Chartres (1040–1116), a pupil of Lanfranc at Bec, bishop of Chartres from 1090, and a canonist, whose *Decretum* and *Panormia* influenced the development of canon law, took a mediating position in the Investiture Controversy.

Ivo prepared for the resolution of the conflict by distinguishing the different actions involved in the appointment of a bishop: (1) election by the canons of a cathedral and acclamation by the people; (2) consecration by an archbishop, who bestowed the staff and ring as symbols of office; (3) oath of allegiance to the temporal lord, who granted possession of the property of the diocese; and (4) bestowal of jurisdiction, which an auxiliary bishop did not have and from which one could be removed by the pope.

In the eleventh century election was almost "designation" by the king or local noble. A free election would often have meant a free fight. (In the thirteenth and fourteenth centuries the papacy began to replace lay choice of bishops with papal provision.)

Consecration was the liturgical action in which the Holy Spirit was imparted.

The property, whether belonging to the diocese, monastery, or parish, was the benefice that provided the income for the office.

Jurisdiction was the right to perform the duties (including civil) that went with the office.

B. The Dispute between Gregory VII and Henry IV

Beginning in 1074, a series of reform synods under Pope Gregory VII proclaimed again the requirement of priestly celibacy, forbade lay investiture (those who received it were placed under the penalty of excommunication in 1078), and in 1075 renewed the excommunication (first decreed in 1073) as simoniacs of five of king Henry IV's councilors, with whom he had continued to associate.

Papal legates called provincial synods to promote the reform agenda. Much of the German episcopate, however, opposed these measures. There was tension between the German bishops and Gregory because of his treatment of them; Gregory's claims to authority were seldom challenged, but frequently ignored or avoided. Henry, in the flush of victory over Saxon rebels, proceeded to appoint the archbishop of Milan. Gregory denounced him in a letter of 1075.

Henry IV was in a rage, and the Diet of the empire that met at Worms in January, 1076, declared that Gregory VII had wrongfully become pope. The German bishops sent a letter of defiance to Gregory:

> You have done your best to take away from bishops all of the power which was conferred upon them from God through the Holy Spirit.... We cannot complain enough of the outrages you have done to bishops whom you call the sons of harlots. Therefore, since your accession was initiated by such perjuries and since the Church of God sinks to ruin by reason of the terrific storm occasioned through your innovations and since your life is besmirched by ill report, we renounce the obedience we never promised you and will not observe it for the future, but as you say we are not bishops, so we say you are not pope.

This strong language was exceeded by Henry IV in his letter to the pope:

> Henry, king not by usurpation, but by the holy ordinance of God to Hildebrand, not now pope but a false monk.... Come down, then, from the usurped apostolic seat. Let another ascend who will preach the sound doctrine of the blessed apostle without the cloak of violence. I Henry, king by the grace of God, and all my bishops say, "Come down, come down and be forever damned."

Gregory VII responded at the Lenten synod, February 22, 1076, by excommunicating Henry:

> For the honor and defense of thy Church ... by thy power and authority, I deprive Henry the king,... who has risen against thy church with unparalleled pride, of the governance of all Germany and Italy and I absolve all Christians from the bond of the oath which they have or shall make. I prohibit any one from serving him as king.

Although Henry answered by having his bishops excommunicate Gregory, he was nonetheless left in a precarious position. His enemies in Germany now had the upper hand and gave him one year to remove the papal ban. The pope set out for Germany to preside at a Diet at Augsburg to settle German affairs. Henry, determined to forestall a coalition of the pope and the princes, started across the Alps.

Gregory, not knowing Henry's intentions, took refuge in the castle of the countess Matilda of Tuscany at Canossa, a precaution that led to the charge of "hiding behind a woman's skirt." Henry, however, appeared in penitential garb, walking barefeet in the snow for three days outside the wall of the castle. Gregory had promised to take no action without consulting the princes, but as a priest (and throughout the controversy he had acted from what for him were spiritual motives) he could not refuse absolution to someone genuinely penitent. The clever Henry took advantage of this, and Gregory lifted the excommunication.

The contrast of Henry IV's humiliation at Canossa in 1077 with his father Henry III's removal of three rival popes in 1046 shows how much papal fortunes had changed in thirty years.

Henry won a diplomatic victory at the price of personal humiliation. He regained his power in Germany, and the recalcitrant princes went their own way without regard to the pope. Since Henry continued his old policies, Gregory issued a new excommunication against Henry in 1080. This time it had little effect, because the king's opponents, having been left in the lurch by the pope before, paid little attention to it. Two-thirds of the German episcopate supported Henry, declared Gregory deposed, and supported the antipope, Clement III. Henry invaded Italy in 1081 and in 1084 set up the antipope, who gave him the imperial crown.

Gregory fled to Salerno, where he died in 1085 with the words, "I have loved righteousness and hated iniquity, therefore I die in exile"

From left to right:

A tapestry of King Henry IV, created in the eighteenth century (Museum of Canossa Castle, Italy).

A view of Canossa, Italy.

(contrast Psalm 45:7). Gregory had lost the immediate political struggle, but he had won a moral victory. The picture of the king begging forgiveness before the pope was a symbol and precedent worth the loss of the alliance with the German princes.

In spite of the circumstances of Gregory's death, the monarchical form of government of the Roman church was now solidly in place.

C. The Final Settlement

Gregory VII's pontificate had left the prestige of the church greatly enhanced, and that new prestige could not be destroyed by brute force. On the other hand, the practical influence of the monarch was only slightly diminished. Henry IV died in 1106 still under excommunication and with much turmoil in Germany.

Pope Paschal II reached an agreement with Henry V in 1111 whereby Henry would renounce his rights to investiture, confirm the papal states, and guarantee the churches their offerings and non-royal possessions, and the bishops would renounce their royal properties and their place as princes of the empire. This far-reaching and radical solution would have been revolutionary in its economic and political consequences; such a return to apostolic poverty would leave the church poor and subservient, so the bishops rejected this compromise and it failed.

In 1122 the Concordat of Worms between Emperor Henry V and Pope Callistus II resolved the conflict between the empire and the papacy over investiture. The monarch gave up the custom of investing prelates with ring and staff (the symbols of ecclesiastical office), but kept his influence in the choice of prelates and the right to bestow the regalia (the symbols of temporal authority including the non-ecclesiastical property and material possessions).

The First Lateran Council of 1123—the Ninth Ecumenical Council according to Roman reckoning, and the first in the West and first to be called by a pope—ratified the Concordat of Worms and the gains of the reform movement. (It was "ecumenical" not because the bishops came from all countries, but according to the new definition that it was summoned, presided over, and confirmed by the pope—a view already anticipated in the *Dictatus Papae*.)

Proprietary churches were another aspect of the entanglement of the spiritual and the temporal. In spite of earlier denunciations by popes and councils, they continued into the twelfth century, when the transformation of owners into patrons was accomplished.

Lay investiture in the narrow sense was abolished, but the conflict between empire and papacy continued on through the Middle Ages. So did Hildebrand's ideal.

III. THE SACRAMENT OF PENANCE

Penance is the name given to the procedures for obtaining forgiveness of post-baptismal sins and so the means for the removal of an excommunication. Although the theology of penance was not formulated until the twelfth century, the practices were rooted in the pre-Nicene church. The penitential discipline of the early church, however, had been altered in various ways, from being public and non-repeatable to becoming private and repeatable, and from being a punishment to becoming a positive part of the religious life.

Since the time of Gregory I the basic framework followed during the Middle Ages had been in place. The essential parts were contrition, confession, and works of satisfaction. Although the guilt (*culpa*) of sin was forgiven on the basis of penitence and confession, the medieval practice, influenced by Germanic legal theory, required in addition punishment (*poena*), "satisfactions." These "punishments" for sin might be worked off either on earth or in purgatory, which received greater stress in the twelfth century.

Instead of the severe fasts and public displays of penance that earlier served as a satisfaction for sins, "redemptions" or commutations that substituted praying the Psalms or giving alms were in use from Carolingian times. These practices set the background for the development of indulgences to be noted below.

Private confession once a year at Lent, common since Carolingian times, was made obligatory by the Fourth Lateran Council of 1215. Public confession, however, did not disappear, and the penitential exercises continued to be rather public.

From the beginning of the eleventh century it was customary to grant absolution after confession and before imposing the satisfaction. From the twelfth century a declarative formula instead of a prayer was in use, and by 1350 "I absolve you" was the common formula. Large volumes of casuistry replaced the penitential books mentioned in chapter 18.

> The sacrament of penance was one religious component of the investiture controversy and of the Crusades.

IV. THE FIRST CRUSADE

The First Crusade is connected with the assertions of papal authority and developments in the sacrament of penance. Many of the families involved in the First Crusade had ties with the papal reform movement of the eleventh century. Gregory the VII explained that military service could be an act of penance when directed against his opponents in the Investiture Controversy. This early emphasis on penitential warfare soon became bearing arms in God's service. The First Crusade was the culmination of an ideological shift from warfare as a reason to do penance to warfare *as* penance. The idea of violence as an expression of piety was a new development and requires some explanation of how it came about.

A. The Devolution of the Idea of Holy War for Christians

Six strands of thought contributed to the idea of the Crusades.

1. The acceptance of a Christian's participation in warfare

Many early Christians saw themselves as soldiers of one emperor, Jesus Christ, with a duty to inflict no harm on others. Others, seeing no clear distinction between the army and the police power of the state, served in the military but as much as possible avoided the pagan religious aspects of army life.

Under Constantine all the functions of the state came to be thought of as within the sphere of a Christian's activities. The Council of Arles (314), in a canon subject to differing interpretations, refused communion to Christians in the army who threw down their weapons in time of peace.

The main routes of the first and second Crusades.

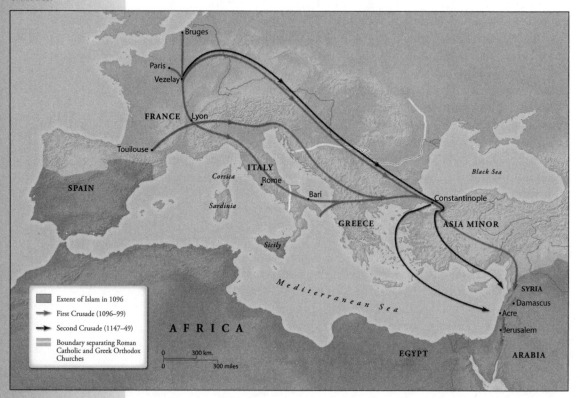

Eusebius suggested the righteousness of war against demonic forces—divisiveness within the empire and barbarian invasions from without. Yet it was a long time before Christian thinkers accepted the idea, itself older than Christianity, of a "just war." Augustine was an exponent of the view, but he still felt even a just war involved an element of sin for which one must do penance.

Although the Muslims came to be regarded as a legitimate object of just war, Charles Martel still thought of his work as self-defense. Charlemagne felt he could undertake missionary warfare, but the idea that war was sin continued on beyond the Carolingian period. (Later, the Americas were taken by the European powers under the theory of missionary warfare.)

It was still a grave sin in the eleventh century to kill a man in a battle waged for secular ends. Even the Normans under William the Conqueror at the battle of Hastings in 1066, a battle blessed with papal approval and fought against a perjurer on holy relics (Earl Harold), were subject to penances for the deaths they inflicted. (By the mid-thirteenth century the theory of "just war" gave the wars of almost all responsible secular rulers the benefit of any doubt, unless they were against the interests of the papacy or those to whom the pope extended his protection.)

2. The devolution of the right of just warfare from the imperial ruler to kings to knights

Charlemagne and his successors had claimed the right of warfare for the emperor alone. Then it was accepted that the anointed kings could undertake a just war as well as the emperor. Feudalism, however, increasingly placed the burden of keeping order on local nobles.

From the tenth century the warrior, his arms, and his banners were liturgically blessed. Under the code of chivalry the knight possessed a hallowed sword so that he was free to use it according to his understanding of justice. The knight with his arms became a symbol of Christian peace. The warlike instincts of the barbarians were limited by the Cluniac reform and in narrow spheres were given church approbation.

The Peace of God movement (last chapter), paradoxically, contributed to the development of the idea that shedding of blood in battle was more than justified and could even be salvific in the service of God when directed against pagans and heretics.

The benediction of the sword was originally used only in royal coronations, but it now devolved so individual knights could freely use their hallowed sword for the protection of churches and of the oppressed.

> ## THE CHRISTIAN KNIGHT
>
> The code of the Christian knight included the following responsibilities: (a) to give his life for his lord—a continuation of the Germanic view of loyalty; (b) not to use his sword for personal gain; (c) not to try to save his own life in defending his lord; (d) to die for his homeland (which could be interpreted as the heavenly Jerusalem); (e) to give his life in fighting heretics, schismatics, and those excommunicated; (f) to defend the poor, widows, and orphans; and (g) to be true to his oath of allegiance.

The blessing of the sword represented a decline in the older view that killing was wrong and demanded penance. The ceremony of dubbing a knight was given a religious character. Chivalry became the Christian form of the military life.

3. The influence of Islam

The acceptance of the idea of holy war by the medieval church may perhaps have been due in part to the influence of this concept from Islam. The privilege of the crusaders to receive forgiveness from punishment for sins (see below on indulgences) had a parallel in the promise to go to paradise given to Muslim warriors in a holy war.

In the reverse direction, religio-political opposition to Islam, even before the call for the crusade, had led Normans in southern Italy to set about retaking Sicily from Islam. It also led French knights to take part in the beginning of the reconquest of Spain. This reconquest was started by Christian rulers in northern Spain in the eleventh century (a task that required two centuries to accomplish and was not completed until the fall of Granada in 1492).

4. The papalization of warfare

The raising of armies on behalf of the papal states by the popes, as with Leo IX, led to the universalizing of the conception of warfare once again. Churchmen came to accept warfare in certain circumstances as something that could be engaged in on God's authority, and theologians interpreted Augustine's views of a just war to mean that soldiers fighting in a war authorized by the pope incurred no blame. The idea of a holy war, however, had vigorous critics (such as Peter Damian).

Alexander II sent papal banners to Count Roger for his attack on Sicily and to Duke William of Normandy for his invasion of England. Gregory VII asserted the superiority of the church over the state and instinctively appealed to military imagery in spiritual things. He used military forces, and, never in doubt about what was right, decided what was a just war.

The right of the church to defend the interests of Christendom with the material sword was extended further by Pope Urban II, for it was now acknowledged that the church as such could engage in warfare. He directed attention away from conflicts within Christendom to a crusade against the infidels. The Crusade was not only a just war; it was a holy war. One fought now not just *as* a Christian but *because* he was a Christian. Christians must retake the holy city from the infidels. In this theory only the pope could engage in a universal holy war; in a sense, he could do what the ancient emperors claimed to do.

5. The practice of pilgrimage

Some went on pilgrimage to a holy site as a penance imposed by a confessor, some as an act of devotion (often to fulfill a vow), and some went to Jerusalem in their old age in order to die there. Pilgrims to Jerusalem had at first been forbidden to carry arms. Then they carried them for self-defense. Finally, the "pilgrims" took the offensive against the Muslims. The Crusades combined the language of pilgrimage and of a military expedition. Pilgrimage to Jerusalem was one of the motifs inspiring the zeal of the crusaders.

6. The motive of reuniting the church

The schism between East and West was still fresh in the minds of Western churchmen, who saw military aid given to the Byzantine empire as a basis for renewing good relations and the restoration of communion.

B. The Preaching of the Crusade—Pope Urban II (1088–99)

Generally the Muslims were tolerant of their Christian subjects, but sometimes there were exceptions that aroused Christian resentment. The caliph Al-Hakim, who ruled from Egypt, claimed to be divine (the Druze are his followers) and started a campaign against those who refused to accept his claims.

When Al-Hakim leveled the shrine of the Holy Sepulcher in Jerusalem in 1009 as part of a larger campaign to convert Christians and Jews, it was a vivid reminder that the holiest sites of Christianity were controlled by unbelievers, and the passions of Christians even in the West were inflamed against Muslims, even though Al-Hakim's successor had the church rebuilt.

The Islamic empire in the East had a similar experience to the earlier Roman Empire in the West: As the Germanic invaders were converted to Catholic Christianity, so the Turkish invaders of the Muslim territories were converted to Islam. The Seljuk Turks in 1070–71 took Palestine, including Jerusalem.

The eastern empire's decline from its peak under the Macedonian dynasty was highlighted by two military losses in 1071: the fall of Bari, the last major Byzantine holding in southern Italy, to the Normans, and the defeat at Manzikert by the Seljuk Turks, who proceeded to occupy much of Asia Minor. Although the practice continued, it was now more difficult for Christians to make pilgrimages to Jerusalem, so the Byzantine emperor Alexius I Comnenus (1081–1118) made a request for aid from the West.

Pope Urban II, a product of the monastery at Cluny and a supporter of Gregory VII, followed the latter's example in working for union of East and West. Urban thought the crusade would impress the Eastern church with the religious vitality and charity of the West. The outcome, however, proved to be quite the reverse.

At a council at Clermont in 1095, Urban brought together the strands leading to a Holy War by combining the motifs of pilgrimage

The church of St. Anne in Jerusalem, built by the Crusaders.

to Jerusalem and of pious violence. He declared that it was no longer possible to go to Jerusalem without weapons; an armed processional was necessary.

War cries received formal authorization—*Deus le volt* ("God wills it"). The crusaders were urged to sew a cloth cross on the back of their outer garment; on their return, to place it on the front. The ancient Romans had said that it is "sweet and fitting to die for one's country"; later the Christian martyrs died for the heavenly homeland; the pope now said that one must be ready to die for the earthly Jerusalem.

Urban II at Clermont offered to crusaders the same remission of the church's penalties for sin that were customarily granted to pilgrims to Jerusalem, but in the subsequent promotion of the crusade preachers extended the promise to a remission of all penalties for sin that God would inflict both in this life and in the next. Thus the Crusades marked an important step in the development of indulgences.

An indulgence was the remission of the temporal punishments (whether inflicted on earth or in purgatory) for sin. The guilt of sin (eternal punishment) was forgiven by absolution in response to the contrition and confession by the sinner, but satisfaction (temporal punishment) still had to be made for sins.

To obtain an indulgence some good work was prescribed. From earlier in the eleventh century, bishops in France and Spain had granted indulgences to those who contributed to church buildings. The rigors of the campaign to retake the Holy Land were seen as satisfying the requirements for temporal punishment for sins. No other satisfaction for sins was necessary. Urban had earlier extended the same promise of remission of penance to those fighting the Muslims in Spain.

Holy war became a new way of gaining forgiveness of sins, an alternative to entering the monastic life. Later the same promise of remission of penalties for sin was extended to those who equipped a crusader. The promise of remission of the punishments due for sin gave a religious character to the whole crusading enterprise.

Urban, himself French and a Cluniac, singled out the French as the special bearers of the crusading idea. French was the language of the crusaders, and "French" (or "Franks") became the term for Europeans among the Muslims, just as "Turks" emerged among Europeans as the generic name for the religio-political enemies of Christendom. A phrase that echoed through the literature of the Crusades was to "avenge the honor of God" that had been offended by the Muslims.

Those who responded to Urban's call and the calls for later crusades did so out of a variety of personal motivations. Various interpretations of the Crusades are reflected in the motivations assigned to the crusaders.

For some there was the expectation of improving their fortunes by plunder, for some there was the love of adventure, for some the ambition for territorial enrichment or social advancement. Expectations of material gain from the enterprise, however, were rarely achieved.

Some acted out of religious hatred for the "infidel Turks," while some out of genuine devotion to Jesus Christ felt a positive commitment to return the site of his crucifixion to the hands of believers.

These aspirations were not mutually exclusive, and for many there must have been a mingling of motives, from a religious perspective some worthy and others unworthy. Whatever the individual motivations, undertaking the armed pilgrimage to Jerusalem required a commitment to a dangerous, demanding, and expensive enterprise. Support by families and religious communities made possible the personal sacrifice of the crusaders.

C. The Crusaders and the Fighting

The pope preached the crusade, but he had very little control over it. The recruitment, organization, and oversight fell to the knights, many of whom came from middle-ranking nobles.

A first contingent led by Peter the Hermit of Amiens and other violent preachers anticipated the main army of crusaders. Made up largely of discontented peasants, this rabble pillaged its way across Europe, on the way inciting in central Europe a severe persecution of Jews, who had received intense persecution in France earlier in the century. Their effort ended in disaster when many were killed by the Turks near Nicaea and Peter fled.

The main body of crusaders started out in 1096. The leaders included Godfrey of Bouillon, duke of Lorraine, whose ideal remained untarnished to the end; Baldwin of Boulogne, his brother; bishop Adhemar of LePuy, the principal religious advisor; Raymond of Toulouse; and Bohemond, a Norman from Taranto in south Italy.

At Constantinople the crusaders learned they were to give an oath of allegiance, which they reluctantly gave, to Emperor Alexius, who preferred mercenaries—not armies under their own commanders. The Turks were defeated at Nicaea; Dorylaeum fell in 1097; Antioch fell in 1098. Disunity among the Muslims contributed to the success of the First Crusade. Jerusalem, the goal of the crusade, fell in 1099, accompanied by much bloodshed. After the hardships and losses experienced on the way, the victory convinced the crusaders that the hand of God had helped them capture Jerusalem.

Much criticism has been given to the crusaders for their brutality. An Arab chronicler declared: "All those who were well-informed about the Franks saw them as beasts superior in courage and fighting ardor but in nothing else, just as animals are superior in strength and aggression." The crusaders, however, were no more brutal than Muslims, nor more brutal than was expected in warfare at the time (and there were examples of chivalrous conduct on both sides).

Successive contingents of crusaders set out by various routes to the East until 1131, including an expedition organized by Italian commercial cities in 1101.

D. The Theological Aspect of Reunion

Amid this fighting there was an effort at theological reconciliation with the Greek church. A council met in 1098 at Bari in southeast Italy, for which the pope enlisted the support of Anselm of Canterbury.

The council discussed some of the points of difference between the Greek and Latin churches: the *filioque* addition to the Nicene Creed and differences in the liturgy of the eucharist. In regard to the latter, the Eastern church summoned the Holy Spirit in the epiclesis (invocation), whereas in the West the recitation of Jesus' words at the Last Supper effected the change in the elements into the body and blood of Jesus.

The outcome of the second eucharistic controversy (chapter 21) made the understanding of the Real Presence more of a problem than the difference between leavened and unleavened bread. The authority of the pope was not discussed.

This council could have been the capstone to the First Crusade, but in the meantime, according to the view of the eastern empire, the crusaders had gotten out of hand.

E. Results of the Crusade

One major result of the First Crusade was the further alienation of the Greeks from the West. The independent actions by the crusaders were not the kind of help Alexius wanted.

Even greater alienation of the Muslims resulted from the subsequent two-hundred-year history of the Crusades, which permanently poisoned Muslim-Christian relations and ended the spirit of tolerance for Christians living under Muslim rule.

Perhaps the only peoples to welcome the crusaders were some of the Christian minorities who had suffered from both Byzantine and Muslim rule, such as the Armenians and the Maronites in Lebanon. The latter affiliated with Rome in 1182 as a uniate church, maintaining their own liturgical rites and customs, but these ties had to be reestablished in the fifteenth century.

For others, such as the Copts in Egypt, the Crusades were a calamity, since they were suspected of Western sympathies by Muslim rulers and treated as schismatics by the Latins. Indeed, they were prohibited by the Latins from making pilgrimage to Jerusalem.

Relations with the Eastern churches were not improved by the erection of two Latin patriarchates, Antioch and Jerusalem. Later, under Innocent III in the wake of the Fourth Crusade, a Latin patriarch was appointed for Constantinople also.

The Crusades weakened the Byzantine empire and so hastened its fall. The Arab governments were also weakened and left susceptible to the Turkish and Mongol invasions.

Jews did not fare any better than Muslims from the Crusades, and indeed the First and Second Crusades were disastrous for the Jews in western Europe who—because of the Crusades' emphasis on the cross of Jesus Christ and the related charge of deicide—experienced anti-Semitic pogroms by the general populace in spite of opposition to such treatment from popes and church leaders like Bernard of Clairvaux.

An immediate result of the First Crusade was the establishment of Latin states in the East: (1) Edessa became a county under Count Baldwin; (2) the principality of Antioch was ruled by Bohemond; (3) the Italian cities founded a state at Tripoli; (4) Jerusalem was declared to be ruled by Jesus as king with Godfrey as Protector of the Holy Sepulcher. Godfrey's scruples about not taking the title "king" over the city where his Lord was crucified were not shared by his brother Baldwin, who succeeded him on his death and assumed the title "king" (1100–1118).

A significant new development in monastic history was the rise of the knightly monastic orders. The first of these was the Knights Templar, founded in 1118 under Hugh of Payens. King Baldwin gave the Templars their name, and from them the idea of fighting for the Temple passed to other orders.

Bernard of Clairvaux (chapter 22), although not the author of the rule for the Templars, as legend claimed, did write *In Praise of the New Militia of Christ*. King Philip IV of France confiscated the property of the Templars in 1307, and Pope Clement V dissolved the order in 1312.

The practices of the Templars were soon imitated by the Hospitallers, who had an earlier origin as a charitable order. They had been organized in 1050 by merchants from Amalfi resident in Jerusalem to protect pilgrims. They provided hospitality and later care of the sick, exemplifying the change in the connotations of the word "hospitality" to those of the word "hospital." Under Gerard (d. 1120) the Hospitallers gained papal sanction. His successor, Raymond of Provence, reorganized the Hospitallers as a military order on the pattern of the Knights Templar. The Hospitallers or Knights of St. John the Baptist were known after 1310 as the Knights of Rhodes and after 1530 as the Knights of Malta.

Another military order, the Teutonic Knights (the Order of St. Mary of Teuton), arose later (papal approval in 1199) in the Third Crusade.

The knightly monastic orders had certain features in common. With them warfare as a temporary act of devotion became warfare as a devotional way of life. They represented a fusion of two meanings of the "militia of Christ," monks and crusaders. The old monastic idea of fighting the demons coalesced with a literal military goal.

Members took the common vows of other monks—poverty, chastity, and obedience—and in addition a pledge to defend other persons by arms. Poverty was not stressed, for the collective means of the order were to be used to benefit others, and the Templars later became an object of envy for their wealth.

As the military mission became dominant, smaller eleeomosynary (benevolent) orders arose. All the knightly orders were devoted to the idea of pilgrimage to Jerusalem. Knights, serving brothers, and priests comprised the membership of the orders. A Grand Master was in control, and there were annual chapter meetings of all the local priors. The Hospitallers and the Templars became international.

CRUSADES

Name	Dates	Participants	Features
First	1096 – 99	Baldwin, Bohemond, Godfrey, Raymond	Captured Jerusalem
Second	1147 – 49	Louis VII, Conrad III	Failure
Third	1187 – 92	Frederick I Barbarossa, Philip II Augustus, Richard I the Lionheart	Captured Acre and coast lands
Fourth	1202 – 4	Venice	Capture of Constantinople
Children's	1212	Children	Disaster
Fifth	1217 – 21	King John of Jerusalem, Papal legate	Capture and loss of Damietta
Sixth	1228 – 29	Frederick II	Failed in Egypt; Jerusalem recovered through negotiation
Seventh	1248 – 54	Louis IX	Failed in Egypt
Eighth	1270 – 71	Louis IX, Prince Edward	Defeated at Tunis; postponed loss of Palestinian coast

In studying the military aspects of relations between Christianity and Islam one should remember that there were peaceful interchanges in the Middle Ages between Muslims and Christians. Some Christians advocated peaceful missions to the Muslims. Non-violent encounters may be seen especially in mutual borrowings in art. Christians prized Muslim metalwork and textiles. Church vestments were often made by Muslim weavers. A sample shown at Canterbury is a cloth that was reused, so a priest was wearing a garment containing in Arabic, "Great is Allah, and Mohammed is his prophet."

On the positive side, the Crusades promoted a greater sense of unity in western Europe. Its various peoples, sharing a common Latin culture, giving allegiance to the pope in Rome, and joined in a common religio-military enterprise, became more aware of their unity.

The Crusades resulted in increased prestige for the papacy. The involvement of the laity in the Crusades stirred religious sensibilities that may be related in some ways to the new religious movements of the twelfth and thirteenth centuries (see chapters 22–24).

Another result of the Crusades was the stimulation of an intellectual revival in western Europe. In a measure this was already present (chapter 21), or there would not have been enough energy to start a crusade. But the crusaders brought back with them new experiences and knowledge from another part of the world that greatly stimulated intellectual life.

Moreover, there was direct contact with Muslim thought in Spain and Sicily that contributed to the twelfth-century renaissance in Europe. A revitalization in theology and other areas can be located especially in Normandy, as at the monasteries of Bec and Comte. That intellectual activity is associated with the development of Scholasticism.

FOR FURTHER STUDY

Blumenthal, Uta-Renate. *The Investiture Controversy: Church and Monarchy from the Ninth to the Twelfth Century*. Philadelphia: University of Pennsylvania Press, 1988.

Cowdrey, Herbert E. J. *Pope Gregory VII*. Oxford: Clarendon, 1998.

Idem. *Popes, Monks, and Crusaders*. London: Hambledon, 1984.

Morris, C. *The Papal Monarchy: The Western Church from 1050 to 1280*. Oxford: Oxford University Press, 1989.

Riley-Smith, Jonathan. *The Oxford Illustrated History of the Crusades*. Oxford: Oxford University Press, 1995.

Idem. *What Were the Crusades?* 3rd ed. Lanham, MD: Rowman and Littlefield, 2002.

Robinson, I. S. *The Papacy 1073–1198: Continuity and Innovation.* Cambridge: Cambridge University Press, 1990.

Tellenbach, Gerd. *Church, State, and Christian Society at the Time of the Investiture Contest.* Oxford: Basil Blackwell, 1940.

Tierney, Brian. *The Crisis of Church and State, 1050–1300.* Englewood Cliff, NJ: Prentice-Hall, 1964.

Ullmann, Walter. *The Growth of Papal Government in the Middle Ages: A Study of the Ideological Relation of Clerical to Lay Power.* 3rd ed. London: Methuen, 1970.

Intellectual Revival: The Rise of Scholasticism

A number of external factors influenced the intellectual revival of the eleventh and twelfth centuries. These factors included the peace movement associated with Cluny, monastic reform efforts, growth of the papal monarchy that drew clerics and lawyers to Rome, and the Investiture Controversy that sparked the study of law and production of a pamphlet literature.

Factors also included the expansion of trade and commerce with the resulting development of urban life, political stabilization that brought a greater degree of internal peace and easier communication, increased prosperity that could pay for the copying of manuscripts and creation of works of art, and translations of philosophical and scientific works from Arabic and Greek resulting from contacts with Muslims and Greeks.

While these factors set the context, intellectual movements can seldom be traced to external factors alone.

Monasteries had operated exterior schools in the liberal arts for those not entering the monastery, as well as interior schools for the training of their monks (chapter 18). The latter emphasized spiritual formation through the reading of the Bible and the church fathers and participation in liturgical life. The monasteries kept a glimmer of learning alive even in the most difficult of times.

Over time, cathedral schools for clerics developed a different approach to learning over against the monastic schools. The cathedral schools put relatively more emphasis on logic and philosophy.

The old learning relied on the personal moral authority of the teacher and was primarily oral in character. The new learning that began to grow up in the later eleventh century relied on disputation and reasoning and became increasingly based on written texts. Previously ethics was the ruling element in liberal arts teaching. By 1180, however, philosophy was no longer the practical discipline of virtuous

"A monastery without a library is like a fortress without arms" (Medieval proverb).

living. Instead, philosophy had become a theoretical discipline concerned with dialectics and metaphysics. Whereas monastic theology was content to admire the divine, scholastic theology began to speculate.

These changes in education were heralded by Berengar and especially Abelard, both of whom challenged their teachers, went beyond tradition, and initiated a new approach that substituted reasoned debate for personal authority.

As a result of these changes, the center of education shifted in the twelfth century from monastic schools to cathedral schools (chapter 18) and out of the latter came the universities.

The teacher in the cathedral schools was commonly known as the *scholasticus*, and the new learning that grew up has, therefore, been called Scholasticism. There was something new in the intellectual life of the eleventh and subsequent centuries, but the term "Scholasticism" has been used in so many ways that for the word not to be useless some careful definition of its different elements must be given.

We will begin with some general characteristics of the intellectual activity of the eleventh to fourteenth centuries, and then turn to the early phases of the intellectual revival.

I. ASPECTS OF SCHOLASTICISM

Because so much attention in the study of Scholasticism is directed to its use of dialectics and philosophy, it is well to be reminded of the importance scholastic theologians gave to the study of the Bible.

The exposition of the books of the Bible was a staple of education in the schools. Annotations to the Latin Bible had been compiled by many since the Carolingian period, but these became standardized in the twelfth century as a textbook for basic courses in theology.

Central in this development was Anselm of Laon (d. 1117), who collected extracts from the church fathers arranged as marginal and interlinear glosses on the text of the Bible. The activity was continued in his school at the cathedral of Laon and resulted in the *Glossa Ordinaria* ("Ordinary Gloss"), which began circulating about 1130. Later revised by Peter Lombard (chapter 22), it became the standard medieval commentary on the Bible that was widely used as a work of reference.

Scholasticism was a text-based culture. Scripture was the primary text, because it put human beings into direct contact with the divine. Commentaries on Scripture, the writings of the church fathers, and the texts of Aristotle and commentaries on him were also authoritative. The making and studying of commentaries on texts were important for Scholasticism. These texts were so inexhaustibly rich that they defied human efforts to grasp them fully. Scholastic thinkers started with the premise of doctrinal unity. Apparent contradictions in the authoritative texts led to the exploration of the relation of authority and reason.

Scholasticism may be defined in relation to attitude (confidence in reason), in relation to method (dialectical reasoning), in relation to content (the philosophical question of universals), and in relation to form (collecting authorities and arguments pro and con on a question).

As to attitude, the Scholastics were characterized by great confidence in the powers of reason. They were convinced that there is no contradiction between faith and reason—Anselm more than most. He sought to demonstrate the propositions of faith—the existence of God, the Trinity, original sin, and the atonement—by the use of reason alone.

Later thinkers were more chastened in their expectations of what reason could accomplish, but they were dedicated to the use of reason in exploring matters of faith. Among nearly all of them the confidence in the powers of human reason was balanced by humility in the presence of the divine.

Among some Scholastics a subtle shift occurred whereby the authority of reason assumed the position formerly held by the authority of the fathers on whom they commented.

As to method, the Scholastics employed dialectical reasoning, which historically meant oral discussion by question and answer. The scholastic method was a technique of interpreting texts and teaching that involved distinctions, definitions, and disputations. The method involved presenting a problem (*quaestio*), stating arguments for and against (*disputatio*), and proposing a solution (*sententia*). Authorities were cited on opposite sides of questions, and some sort of reconciliation was sought.

Thus scholastic theologians were involved in producing commentaries, raising theological questions, and harmonizing authoritative texts. The underlying conviction was that only by combining inadequate partial truths can a glimpse be gained of the whole of reality.

The Scholastics were certainly not the first Christian thinkers to use reason, but they sought to demonstrate and to expound the truths of religion by logic. The study of dialectics or logic was the area where the intellectual revival first appeared. Scholasticism was characterized by the application of critical reasoning to matters of faith.

By reason the early Scholastics especially meant the relation between universals (class concepts, going back to the "Ideas" of Plato) and particulars (individual representatives of a class). Thus Scholasticism was concerned in its content with a special philosophical problem.

Every student even in the "Dark Ages" studied the *Isagoge* ("Introduction" to the logic of Aristotle) written by Porphyry and translated into Latin by Boethius. The crucial passage that raised the question of universals was the following:

> Next concerning *genera* [classes of objects with common characteristics] and *species* [manifestations of a larger class] the question indeed whether they have a *substantial existence* [Realism], or whether they consist in bare intellectual *concepts* [Conceptualism and later Nominalism] only or whether, if they have a substantial existence, they are corporal or incorporeal, and whether they are *separable* [extreme Realism] from the sensible properties of the things (or particles of sense), or are *only in those properties* [Moderate Realism] and subsisting about them, I shall forbear to determine. For a question of this kind is a very deep one and one that requires a longer investigation.

Indeed, the question occupied Scholastics for four centuries. "Realism" (from the Latin *res*, "thing" or a reality) referred to the real existence of universal concepts ("Ideas" or "Forms") and so is used differently from the term "realism" as used in later philosophy. "Nominalism" (from the Latin *nomen*, "name") referred to the position that a class concept was only the name given to the common characteristics of members of the class and had no real existence of itself.

The principal positions that emerged were three:

1. *Extreme realism.* This position is represented by Anselm and corresponds to Plato's view, which said that universals have real existence apart from and prior to individuals. This position, dominant in early Scholasticism, was expressed by the Latin formula *universalia ante rem* ("universals are before the individual thing").

2. *Moderate realism.* This position is represented by Thomas Aquinas and—following Aristotle—said that universals are real, but always exist in actual individuations, existing as form to matter. This position, which became dominant in the thirteenth century, was expressed by the formula *universalia in re* ("universals are in the individual thing").

3. *Nominalism.* This position is represented by William Ockham, who said that universals are only inferences drawn from observing individuals. This position, dominant in the fourteenth century, was represented by the formula *universalia post rem* ("universals are after the individual thing").

DIFFERENT POSITIONS ON UNIVERSALS		
Extreme Realism		
Anselm	*universalia ante rem*	A real existence apart from individuals
Moderate Realism		
Aquinas	*universalia in re*	A real existence only in individuals
Nominalism		
Ockham	*universalia post rem*	Only names for common characteristics

The form in which later Scholastics presented their arguments grew out of their methods (above), being much indebted to the disputations of the schools (chapter 23) and then especially to Abelard's arrangement of citations of authorities on different sides of a question (see further below).

From these methods of teaching derived literary genres. In teaching, the *lectio* (reading, lecture) was the reading of an authoritative text followed by commentary on its meaning. The commentary expounded the literal meaning (*littera*), paraphrased it (*sensus*), and then gave the teacher's view of the doctrinal issues (*sententia*). In the *disputatio* the master posed questions, the students gave responses in favor or opposed, and the master gave a final determination. Even as the *lectio* came to be recorded in commentaries, so the *disputatio* gave rise to the *quaestio*, the literary equivalent of oral disputations.

In the *quaestio* two opposite views were juxtaposed. These views were discussed according to several distinctions so as to arrive at perspectives from which an element of truth was found in each or an ultimate synthesis was possible.

Questions came to be discussed as problems in their own right, independent of the texts that gave rise to them. Exegetical *quaestiones* arising out of the biblical text, especially from the letters of Paul, began to be debated separately, and from these disputations arose "theology" as a separate academic discipline.

Abelard was impatient with the traditionalism of Anselm of Laon, but the form of the disputation was congenial to his creative and critical mind.

II. THE SECOND EUCHARISTIC CONTROVERSY

The first theological controversy in which the new dialectical reasoning of the schools had been employed was the eleventh-century eucharistic controversy.

The cause of the controversy was the teaching of Berengar, born at Tours about 1000 and educated under Fulbert at Chartres. He became Scholasticus at the cathedral of Tours, where he taught students to seek the literal, inner meaning of Scripture, not the allegorical meaning. (By the eleventh century, cathedral schools had begun to take educational leadership from the Benedictine monastic schools.)

Since the ninth-century eucharistic controversy, the view of the physical real presence of the body and blood of Christ in the eucharistic elements had grown in popularity as a center of devotional piety.

The occasion of the outbreak of the second controversy was a letter Berengar sent in 1049 to Lanfranc, prior at Bec and later archbishop of Canterbury, unsuccessfully seeking his support in opposition to this materialist interpretation.

The issue for Berengar was theological, but it became a tool of the ecclesiastical policy of the papacy and the political intrigue of his patrons. Lack of a driving personality prevented Beregar from making an impressive appeal, and his lack of political knowledge and interest made him an easy opponent for astute politicians and a skilled dialectician like Lanfranc.

After raising the issue of the materialist interpretation of the elements, Berengar came to use grammar and logic in arguing against that viewpoint. Jesus' statement "This is my body" cannot mean the substance of the body becomes the substance of the bread, as his opponents claimed, because grammatically the predicate nominative ("body") must take its meaning from the subject of the sentence ("this," that is the bread), not the reverse. Unless the substance of the bread continued, the proposition ("This bread is my body") was meaningless because there was no referent for "body."

Moreover, "qualities" or "accidents" (the sensible properties) of objects cannot exist apart from their substance (correct according to Aristotle), so the qualities of bread could not exist apart from the substance of bread. In addition, there is the obvious point that a change into a physical presence is contrary to the senses. His positive position may be described as dynamic symbolism: The consecrated elements do not become the body and blood, but produce the effects of Christ on the recipient.

Berengar was condemned at Rome in 1050. He received more favorable treatment at a hearing at Tours, where Hildebrand was present as the papal legate. In 1059 at Rome, Berengar was forced to read a grossly material confession and to consign certain of his works to the fire. The literary warfare continued, but a council at Rome in 1079 marked the final defeat of Berengar before Hildebrand, now Pope Gregory VII.

The advocates of a real physical presence who used dialectical reasoning in support of their position succeeded before the end of the eleventh century in establishing the theory of transubstantiation as the mode of sacramental change.

Although the next century credited Lanfranc with the chief part in the overthrow of Berengar's teaching, he was still primarily a monastic theologian with reservations about dialectics. Cardinal Humbert was more important on the official level, and in the literary controversy Durand and Guitmund were more significant.

Among the opponents of Berengar there were traditionalists like Peter Damian who took a realistic interpretation of the change in the elements and rejected the dialectic approach. However, without meeting Berengar on his own grounds of dialectics and grammar it was not possible to overthrow his arguments and establish metabolic realism, that is, a real change in the elements.

Lanfranc used the terms "qualities" and "essence," not the Aristotelian terminology of "accidents" and "substance" that came to prevail. He spoke of the elements as "converted in their essence [*essentiam*] into the body of the Lord," already the concept, but not yet the terminology, of transubstantiation (change of substance). Guitmund popularized the phrase *substantialiter mutari* ("to be changed in substance").

The oath required of Berengar in 1079 included the first official use of the phrase "changed substantially" (*substantialiter converti*). The word *transsubstantiatio* for the change of the elements began to appear about 1140. The idea was that the substance of the bread and wine became the substance of the body and blood, but the "accidents," the accidental qualities (appearance, taste, smell, touch), remained those of the bread and the wine. This Aristotelian distinction gave precision in the thirteenth century to eucharistic doctrine. The result of the controversy supplied what was lacking in earlier advocates of a physical real presence, namely a philosophical explanation of how a change in the bread and wine was effected.

Anselm and others in the twelfth century related the doctrine of transubstantiation to the rest of catholic theology, especially of the incarnation. The Fourth Lateran Council of 1215 used the word "transubstantiation" in its statement of the change of the bread and wine by divine power into the body and blood of Christ, but theologians of the time saw this usage by the council as only a rejection of a non-materialist interpretation, not as a definitive statement on the mode of the real presence.

Liturgical practices reflected the theological development. From the twelfth century, communion in one kind by the laity (the bread) was accepted: The whole Christ was communicated in one element, and there was less danger of spilling or contaminating the wine if it was taken only by the priest. About 1200 the practice of elevating the host (*hostia*, "sacrificial victim," used for the eucharistic bread) and the chalice became common, so the people would know the exact moment of consecration (spoken in Latin, not understood by most of the people).

III. THEOLOGICAL IMPLICATIONS OF THE CONTROVERSY OVER UNIVERSALS

When the philosophical question of universals was applied to matters of faith, the issue became crucial for the doctrines of the Trinity, original sin, the incarnation, and the church.

One can see the potential for difficulty by considering the views of Roscellinus (1050–1120), the founder of Nominalism. He held that universal categories are names and do not have real existence. He used *substantia* ("substance") in its old philosophical sense of individuation or hypostasis. Thus, accepting Boethius's definition of man as "rational substance," he saw only individual human beings as really existing and "man" as only a name for their common features.

Applying this same thinking to the Trinity, Roscellinus said each Person (Father, Son, and Holy Spirit) was a rational individual. He denied that the Trinity could be *una res* ("one thing" or "one reality"), but must be three individuals, in effect "three gods." "Deity" is not a universal, and each of the Three Persons is omnipotent and not subordinate to the others.

With such implications one can see why Anselm wanted this incipient Nominalism quickly rejected. Roscellinus was important because he helped Anselm formulate his own philosophical position of Realism, although the term was not used yet, shown in his treatise *De fide Trinitatis et de Incarnatione Verbi* ("On Faith in the Trinity and on the Incarnation of the Word") written in answer to Roscellinus. The ancient church had a philosophical corpus not available in the Middle Ages, so the problem of the One and Three had to be worked out anew. By way of Augustine, the western Middle Ages was the heir of Platonic Realism and this was reappropriated in saying that the universal is "Being," hence all Three are One, who "is."

The realist interpretation of universals provided a helpful way to explain various doctrines. The transmission of original sin can be accounted for if there is a real human nature—corrupted by the first sin—that exists apart from individual human beings. In the incarnation the Son of God took on this universal human nature. The church as the body of Christ has a reality beyond the individuals who are its members.

IV. ANSELM OF CANTERBURY (1033–1109)

The outstanding intellectual figure of the late eleventh century and turn of the twelfth century was Anselm. His *Life* was written by his devoted disciple Eadmer, of doctrinal importance as an early advocate of the immaculate conception of Mary.

Anselm has been called the "Father of Scholasticism," but it is difficult to assign a singular paternity to such a multiform development as Scholasticism. The use of dialectical reasoning and the renewed exploration of the problem of the one and the many preceded Anselm, and the distinctive form of later Scholastic treatises derived from Abelard's approach.

Anselm certainly typified the Scholastic confidence in the powers of reason, and he employed dialectics and formal logic to demonstrate the truths of the faith. But his use of reason must be set in the context of the intellectual circumstances of his time. His approach was a response to the situation that in the schools ancient texts were being treated less as authorities to be repeated and more as beginning points for further inquiries.

The entrance to Canterbury cathedral, honoring four archbishops of Canterbury: Augustine, Lanfranc, Anselm, and Thomas Cranmer.

The second eucharistic controversy had exposed the difficulty of debating over the meaning of authoritative texts. The way around this impasse was through a careful consideration of words and their meaning: Logic could provide a demonstration of truths beyond simply citing authoritative texts on different sides of an issue.

Anselm was born at Aosta in Italy and was a religiously sensitive youth. He went in 1060 to Bec in Normandy, famous for the teaching of another Italian (from Pavia), Lanfranc. Anselm became prior at Bec in 1063, during which time he wrote the *Monologion* and *Proslogion*, and became abbot in 1078. He continued to follow in the steps of Lanfranc, succeeding him as archbishop of Canterbury in 1093.

In a quietly courageous pontificate, Anselm defended the church against the royal control of William Rufus (d. 1100), son of William the Conqueror. Conflict between the king and the archbishop came to a head at the Council of Rockingham (1095) over the recognition of Urban II as pope over against the imperial antipope favored by Rufus. Most of the clerics were with the king, but Anselm won over the barons to his side. The real issue was the spiritual rights of the church. Anselm took Urban's pallium from the altar, not the pallium in the hand of the king. The king came to recognize Urban, but he fabricated charges against Anselm that forced him to leave the country.

Anselm went to Rome in 1097 and then to Capua, where he wrote *Cur Deus Homo* and worked out his formulation of transubstantiation (*Letter* 54). Chosen as a theologian for the Council of Bari in 1098, he wrote against the Greeks: *On the Procession of the Holy Spirit*; *On the Eucharist*; and *On Unleavened Bread*.

At Bari Anselm met Ivo of Chartres (chapter 20), who worked out the basis for the settlement of the Investiture Controversy adopted in 1122 but first implemented by Anselm in England. The new king of England, Henry I, recalled Anselm in 1100, but Anselm's refusal to do homage to the king led to another exile in 1103. When he returned in 1106, he worked out a compromise recognizing the rights of the church and the crown respectively in appointments to church office.

Some care must be taken in understanding the place of reason in Anselm's approach. He took as programmatic the phrase "faith seeking understanding [or, knowledge]" (*fides quaerens intellectum*), which was the first title he gave to his treatise *Proslogion*. Anselm's slogan was, "I believe in order that I may know" (*credo ut intelligam*), a formula derived from Augustine and based on the Greek and Latin translation of Isaiah 7:9 ("Unless you believe, you will not understand").

Anselm did not claim that reason by itself could discover the truths of Christian revelation, but once these truths were made known by revelation and accepted by faith, reason could demonstrate them. This

A plaque set up in 1908 on Anselm's house in Aosta records this tribute in French: "Here was born in 1033 St. Anselm, Archbishop of Canterbury, Primate of England, Doctor of the Church, Metaphysician, and Profound Theologian. The greatest genius of his age, in his doctrine and in his works he admirably united the splendors of the faith and the worship of reason. He combatted error with the eloquence of philosophy and the ardor of the apostles. He fought against the great of the earth with an indomitable energy for right, justice, and liberty."

"A Christian should advance through faith to understanding, not come to faith through understanding, or withdraw from faith if he cannot understand" (Anselm, *Epistle* 136).

approach shows that in the Middle Ages *fides* ("faith") had become an intellectual, almost a philosophical, term (as was one of its uses in classical antiquity). When later Luther used *fides*, he meant "trust," and Protestants consequently have had only a modicum of content in the word. Medieval Catholicism, in contrast, placed considerable intellectual content in "faith," for as a noun it included the whole deposit of tradition. Although even Protestants have found Anselm an attractive thinker, by faith he meant primarily "believe," not "trust."

Anselm was a man of gentleness and goodness who has remained one of the best respected thinkers in church history. He himself was so full of the traditional authorities for Christian thought and so humble that he was unaware of the originality of his own thought. Modern readers are still captured by the charm of his writing and the care of his argumentation.

Two aspects of Anselm's thought deserve attention as particularly influential: his arguments for the existence of God and his satisfaction theory of the atonement. Both represent his approach of "faith seeking understanding."

Anselm's *Monologion* seeks to prove God's existence from the characteristics of nature. The presence of good in ascending degrees of goodness leads to the one supreme Good. Being points to a first cause, the supreme Being (a form of the cosmological argument). The hierarchy of perfections climaxes in the perfections of God, the Trinity.

In the *Proslogion* (also titled "Faith Seeking Understanding," as noted above), Anselm sought to combine these arguments into one embracing argument—the ontological argument. Even "The fool who says in his heart, 'There is no God,'" must admit that there can be in the mind "something than which nothing greater can be conceived." This "something," however, cannot be only in the mind, for if it did not exist in reality, then anything which exists in reality would be greater.

It was a matter of logic and the nature of Being: "If, therefore, that than which nothing greater can be conceived is only in the mind, that than which a greater cannot be conceived is that than which a greater can be conceived [i.e., something that actually exists], and this certainly cannot be." Or to rephrase, "What cannot be thought not to exist" is greater than "what can be thought not to exist," so, "That than which nothing greater can be thought" is "that which cannot be thought not to exist."

Another monk, Gaunilo, replied to Anselm in "A Plea for the Fool," reasoning that although one can imagine in the mind the most beautiful island, this does not prove such an island to exist.

Anselm answered that the objection applied to islands and anything that has beginning, end, or composition of parts—such "can be

> "I pray, O God, to know you, to love you, that I may rejoice in you.
> And if I cannot attain to full joy in this life, may I at least advance
> from day to day, until that joy shall come to the full.... I will
> receive, that my joy may be full. Meanwhile, let my mind medi-
> tate upon it; let my tongue speak of it. Let my heart love it; let my
> mouth talk of it. Let my soul hunger for it; let my flesh thirst for
> it; let my whole being desire it, until I enter into your joy, O Lord,
> who are the Three and the One God, blessed for ever and ever.
> Amen." (Anselm, *Proslogion* 26)

thought of as not being"—but the objection does not apply to God.
One must distinguish perfection in its own kind from Absolute Perfec-
tion. The argument applies to Being itself, not to particular objects:
Perfect Being exists necessarily.

Ever since Gaunilo, the ontological argument has been controversial in philosophy. Does the argument's formal logical validity correspond to reality, or is the argument only a playing with words, a
mental construct? Thinkers as diverse as Descartes, Spinoza, and Hegel
have followed Anselm; others as varied as Aquinas and Kant have not
accepted the argument.

Anselm also made a major contribution to explaining the atonement, the central doctrine of Christianity, but also its least authorita-
tively transcribed doctrine (never the subject of conciliar definition).
Cur Deus Homo ("Why the God-Man") offered a logical proof for the
satisfaction theory of the atonement. An epoch-making treatise, it is
the most coherent statement of what has been the dominant Western
explanation of the basis of Christian faith.

God's honor bulks large in Anselm's *Cur Deus Homo*. Sin is so serious because sin is against God, who demands unswerving allegiance.
At the same time, God is also concerned for human welfare. Along with
the feudal idea of owing God his due, there is God's purpose of human
fellowship with himself.

God's purpose was temporarily thwarted by human sin. As the
sinner, only a human being ought to make satisfaction for sin, but so
great is the offense (since it was against the supreme God) that only
God can make the satisfaction. Hence, the need for the God-Man, one
both God and man.

Jesus Christ as a human being needed to do no more than remain
righteous, but he did something more—he died. Death was the punishment for sin, so as a sinless person Christ had no need to die. Christ

made his death an offering (sacrifice) to God, presented of free will and not of debt. He offered himself as a man; but what he did as a man was multiplied infinitely in its worth, for he was also Deity. He offered an infinite satisfaction for sin.

Using contractual language, Anselm then says Christ could will the reward for his deed over to human beings as a means of redeeming them.

Anselm drew his imagery from feudalism, but his theory was not simply a reflection of Germanic legal theory. As a student of Augustine, Anselm employed motifs older than feudalism. More of the conceptual basis of his theory was due to a shift that had occurred in sacramental doctrine.

In the ancient church the principal point in a person's religious life and the means by which forgiveness was obtained was baptism. Baptism gave the imagery of victory in the water over the forces of evil that contributed so powerfully to the classical theory of the atonement as a victory won over the Evil One.

That imagery derived from baptism as an individual's decision to renounce a former way of life was no longer meaningful, however, in an age when baptism was a routine act administered to infants. Access to the altar where communion with the death and resurrection of Christ was obtained came now by penance, which was the sacrament where persons were conscious of having their sins declared forgiven.

The eleventh and twelfth centuries saw the doctrinal formulation of the sacraments of eucharist (transubstantiation) and of penance (satisfactions and "redemptions"—see chapter 20). Hence, sacrifice and satisfaction became key categories and provided the imagery for Anselm's theory of the atonement.

With the view that the eucharist is consubstantial with Jesus Christ, it offered more of a participation with Christ than was associated with baptism, and this participation was not with the victorious Christ of early Christian baptism but with the sinless humanity that went to the cross. The center of interest now was Christ on the cross.

The earliest representations of the crucifixion (from the fifth century and after) pictured the victorious Christ reigning from the cross. Art from the late eleventh century began to recover an emphasis on the humanity of Christ, entailing a new interest in his sufferings and wounds that came to fuller expression in the thirteenth century.

The New Testament employs a number of images to convey the reality of atonement—justification, reconciliation, sacrifice, redemption, victory—but strictly speaking offers no "theory" of how the atonement is effected.

Three of the major theories of the atonement popular in the West were present in the early twelfth century.

1. The ransom theory (variously formulated), according to which Jesus Christ paid the ransom to release mankind from the slavery to the devil that resulted from sin, was the most popular theory in the church fathers and so has been called the "Classic" theory of the atonement. It continued to be maintained by Bernard of Clairvaux, who lived intellectually in patristic theology (chapter 22).

2. The moral-exemplary theory of the atonement has had fewer champions throughout history, but it was advanced in the twelfth century by Abelard (below).

3. The sacrificial or satisfaction theory had an initial statement by Tertullian, but found its classic formulation in Anselm. It was the view that eventually won the largest following.

As a rational demonstration of the atonement, Anselm's exposition seems to allow God merely to acquiesce in turning the benefits of Jesus Christ's death over to the world, but Anselm affirms this is an act of the divine mercy. As with any rational theory of the atonement, God is operative in only a minimal way so that the whole transaction is almost impersonal.

The very personal aspects of the ransom theory of the atonement declined not only because baptism and its earlier imagery had lost its significance, but also because of philosophical Realism. It made a real personal devil almost impossible, for in Realism evil is the absence of the good. Even as the divine mercy has a more formal appearance, so too does the devil.

On the positive side, Realism made possible an abstract "humanity" that Jesus Christ could assume. This too, however, had its down side, for the identification of Christ with his brothers and sisters is not so evident with a "God-Man."

The expression of human involvement and human feelings in redemption formerly given to Jesus was now given to Mary. Mary at the cross and at the tomb became two favorite pictures of the later Middle Ages.

V. PETER ABELARD (1079–1142)

Abelard came from a knightly background that perhaps contributed to his sense of superiority. He studied under Roscellinus (a Nominalist), William of Champaux (an exaggerated Realist who introduced dialectic argument into his instruction in metaphysics and theology), and Anselm of Laon. After giving a brilliant refutation of William's

Realism, Abelard began lecturing to enthusiastic classes at Paris with no qualification except his genius. He became head of the school of Notre Dame in 1113 and decided to turn from philosophy (dialectics) to theology.

Abelard's career was cut short, however, in 1118 by the tragic issue of his love affair with one of his students, Heloise, niece of Fulbert, a canon of Notre Dame. When Heloise became pregnant and their affair was discovered, they secretly married, although Heloise attempted to dissuade Abelard from this step, willing to be his mistress rather than his wife so as not to impede his clerical career.

Having been mutilated at the instigation of Fulbert, Abelard decided to dissolve their union by placing Heloise in a convent and becoming a monk at the monastery of St. Denis (Denys). Their correspondence reveals both a self-analysis, prompted by Christian consciences aware of a fall into passion, and an individuality, usually associated with the Renaissance. Heloise shows herself the intellectual equal of Abelard and his superior in disinterested love and personal integrity. Theirs was a union of minds and emotions, and they continued in a relationship of nonromantic friendship.

Heloise, after later receiving the monastery of the Paraclete as a donation from Abelard, became its abbess and made it (with its six daughter houses) one of the foremost women's religious houses in France. She was known for her intelligence, interest in education for all nuns, and competent administration.

Attacks on Abelard's doctrine of the Trinity as Modalist led to his being condemned unheard at a council at Soissons in 1121. His criticism of the legend that the patron saint of St. Denis was Dionysius the Areopagite, Paul's convert at Athens, forced him to flee from there. He established a small oratory called the Paraclete near Troyes, and in 1127 he became abbot of St. Gildas. He resumed teaching in Paris in 1136.

The tomb of Abelard and Heloise at Pére Lachaise Cemetery, Paris.

Bernard of Clairvaux secured Abelard's condemnation at Sens in 1140, a condemnation confirmed by the pope in 1141. The errors charged against him, in addition to his Trinitarian doctrine, were an exaggerated optimism about creation, Nestorian leanings in regard to Jesus Christ, a latent Pelagianism on grace, transforming the atonement into a lesson in charity, and neglecting the objective element in morality by an excessive insistence on the subjective element (the motive).

The conflict between Bernard and Abelard was more than a theological controversy. Theirs was a clash of two kinds of education: Bernard represented the older education based on Scripture, monastic exegesis, and loyalty to tradition and oriented toward prayer and contemplation. Abelard represented the new scholastic philosophy that put the curiosity and investigative power of logic at the service of faith. The career of Abelard marks the birth of the kind of person who is at home in the modern university, the professional academic.

At the end Abelard was received at Cluny by Peter the Venerable and was reconciled to the church and to Bernard. With a nice touch of French romantic sentiment, when Heloise died, she was buried beside Abelard at the Paraclete; their remains were taken to Paris after the French Revolution and now rest in the Père Lachaise cemetery.

Abelard, in contrast to Anselm, used the principle that he had to doubt (in the sense to question or to examine) in order to know. "For through doubting we come to inquiry, and through inquiry we perceive the truth according to Truth himself." Abelard anticipated Thomas Aquinas in his approach to theological language. Abelard recognized that there is a lack of agreement between human language and the divine nature. They have enough in common to make meaningful communication possible, but there are enough differences that all talk of God, who is unique, is ambiguous and subject to misunderstanding. The task of the theologian is to find answers as close to the truth as possible.

The most significant of Abelard's many works was *Sic et Non* ("Yes and No") in which he arranged statements from the Bible and the church fathers on opposite sides of 158 questions. The object was not to discredit the authorities of the church, but to stimulate study. Here he was both a forerunner and the opposite of John Gratian (chapter 22) in treating differences in the councils and fathers of the church. This method exercised a decisive influence on the form of Scholasticism: the citing of authorities pro and con became the pattern of study.

Not only citing the fathers disparately, Abelard (without attempting a reconciliation of viewpoints), suggested five ways to treat differences in their texts, an elaboration of comments by Augustine:

1. One text was not authentic.

2. A given statement was only a summary of an opponent's position to be refuted by the Father.

3. A given opinion had only local significance, later superseded by the opinion of popes or councils.

4. Shifts of meaning due to translation or an author's peculiar use of language required that semantic distinctions be made.

5. If there remain real contradictions, then one must appeal to a determination of authorities according to the scale of the Bible first, Augustine second, and others third.

Abelard's treatment introduced the disputation into university study, made for more care in the use of patristic authorities, and led to a greater use of dialectics.

Abelard stated his moral influence theory of the atonement in his *Commentary on Romans*. In contrast to Anselm's doctrine of an objective theory of atonement, Abelard had a subjective theory. God sent his Son as a revelation of his love and as a teacher and example. In Jesus Christ the love of God was made manifest. This love awakens a loving response in human beings, and this love is the basis of forgiveness.

Abelard's view of ethics, set forth in *Know Yourself* (*Scito te ipsum*), emphasized that right action is determined by motive alone, the intention of doing the will of God. Abelard did not deny, however, that the

---

SOME SCHOLASTIC THEOLOGIANS

Name	Dates	Origin	Place	Feature
Anselm	1033 – 1109	Aosta	Canterbury	Faith seeking understanding
Peter Abelard	1079 – 1142	Nantes	Paris	Doubt in order to know
Hugh of St. Victor	d. 1142	Saxony(?)	Paris	"On the Sacraments of the Christian Faith"
Peter Lombard	1100 – 1160	Novara	Paris	"Master of the Sentences"
Thomas Aquinas	1225 – 74	Aquino	Paris	Grace perfects nature
Bonaventure	1217 – 74	Italy	Paris	Mystical illumination
Albert the Great	d. 1280	Near Ulm	Cologne	Reconciliation of Aristotle with Christian theology
Duns Scotus	1265 – 1308	Duns, Berwickshire	Oxford; Paris	"Doctor Subtilis"

intention must be informed by a knowledge of right and wrong that was dependent on revealed truth.

On the question of universals, Abelard began nearer Nominalism and opposed Realism, but he moved to an intermediate position, Conceptualism. According to this view, universals are conceptions, useful but neither real nor mere names. Concepts in the mind agree with external reality; names or words correspond to the understanding that exists in the mind of God. His formulation proved too vague, but prepared for Aquinas's Moderate Realism.

The great influence of Abelard was not as a writer but as a teacher. Of his students, one became pope, twenty-five became cardinals, and fifty became bishops. Abelard was not the medieval representative of liberal rationalism he is sometimes made out to be, for he saw himself as a faithful servant of the church. He did mark out new lines of approach and identify new issues, once people caught up with him and the problems he recognized.

The career of Abelard is a striking illustration of how today's "heretic" may mark out the lines on which tomorrow's orthodoxy will be defended. Today's orthodox often lack the foresight to recognize such thinkers and confuse them with the enemies because such thinkers are in close combat with them and are not shelling them from entrenched positions far from the line of battle. The church needs its Abelards to point out its inconsistencies and pioneer new approaches.

On the other hand, Abelard was an unstable person—self-willed and arrogant, as too many brilliant persons are—not the kind an institution depends on.

VI. THE LATER HISTORY OF SCHOLASTICISM

Scholasticism continued to be a vital educational curriculum in the fourteenth and subsequent centuries and has had a modern revival in Neoscholasticism. The philosophy of Thomas Aquinas (chapter 23) became the official Catholic philosophy and until the mid-twentieth century was equated with Catholic orthodoxy.

Neoscholasticism made a clearcut distinction between the philosophy and theology of the thinkers studied, although this was not the way the latter saw their work. Diversity among scholastic theologians is now better recognized, and the form and content of their writings is seen as integrally related.

Moreover, Neoscholastics omitted the mystics from their concern, although nearly all the scholastic thinkers (chapter 22) had an element of mysticism in them. The role of Cistercian monks in the creation and dissemination of the *Glossa Ordinaria* shows that contemplative

"We say that an intention is good, that is, right in itself, but that an action is good, not because it acquires any kind of goodness in itself, but because it comes from a good intention. It follows from this that the same thing may be done by the same person at different times, and yet that the action may sometimes be called good, sometimes bad, because of a difference of intention" (Abelard, *Know Yourself* 11).

(monastic) learning and scholastic (in the nascent universities) learning were intertwined.

FOR FURTHER STUDY

Evans, Gillian R. *Anselm.* London: Chapman, 1989.

Gaspar, G. E. M. *Anselm of Canterbury and His Theological Inheritance.* Aldershot, UK: Ashgate, 2004.

Gilson, Etienne. *History of Christian Philosophy in the Middle Ages.* New York: Random House, 1955.

Luscombe, David E. *The School of Peter Abelard: The Influence of Abelard's Thought in the Early Scholastic Period.* Cambridge: Cambridge University Press, 1969.

MacDonald, A. J. *Berengar and the Reform of Sacramental Doctrine.* London: Longmans, Green & Co., 1930.

Macy, Gary. *The Theologies of the Eucharist in the Early Scholastic Period: A Study of the Salvific Function of the Sacrament According to the Theologians c. 1080–1220.* Oxford: Clarendon, 1984.

Marenbon, J. *The Philosophy of Peter Abelard.* Cambridge: Cambridge University Press, 1997.

Pieper, Josef. *Scholasticism: Personalities and Problems of Medieval Philosophy.* South Bend, IN: St. Augustine's Press, 2001.

Monastic, Literary, Political, and Cultural Activities in the Twelfth Century

The intellectual revival of the eleventh century and the energy that produced the First Crusade carried over into a period of economic growth and tremendous building activity in the twelfth century.

Some medieval historians speak of a "Twelfth-Century Renaissance" because of the architectural and other artistic developments, intellectual energy, educational advances (centered on dialectics), literary work (lyric poetry and courtly romances in the vernacular, as well as philosophical works and compendia of the liberal arts in Latin), and anticipation of themes in the Italian Renaissance two centuries later.

A significant difference from the fourteenth-and-fifteenth-century Renaissance, however, was that the twelfth century still felt a sense of continuity with antiquity, both pagan and Christian, that the later movement, which self-consciously turned away from its immediate medieval past toward the remoter antiquity, did not have.

Like the later Renaissance, the intellectuals of the twelfth century desired to return to the more reliable tradition of antiquity, but also like other such movements, they produced something new.

As at other times of crisis or opportunity in the history of Catholicism, new monastic orders arose and provided inspiration and guidance for the new period of vitality.

I. NEW MONASTIC TYPES

A. Renewed Monastic Vitality

From the late eleventh through the twelfth century many efforts were made to reform monastic life and many new religious orders were founded. The variety of options in living a religious life that emerged led the broader-minded spirits to voice the slogan "diverse but not adverse."

Beginning with the mid-eleventh and continuing through the mid-twelfth century, both old and new monastic types saw a huge increase in the number (1) of conversions to the religious life and (2) of monasteries established. Patrons made the monastic expansion possible; their founding and support of religious houses brought social prestige and spiritual benefits, since the benefactions were credited to their souls' welfare and the recipients prayed for the patrons. Many almshouses and hospitals were also founded by laymen in the twelfth century and were run by canons and canonesses.

During the twelfth century the distinctions between monks and clergy lessened with a considerable increase in the percentage of monks who received priestly ordination and with the increase in the number of parish and diocesan clergy who lived under a monastic-type rule ("regular" or "canonical" clergy).

Several new groups representing reform efforts in the eleventh and twelfth centuries followed conventional monastic patterns. These were in part reactions to Cluny, where Peter the Venerable (abbot 1122–57) was the leading figure in the first half of the twelfth century.

Reformers of monastic life (in both older and newer foundations) typically advocated austerity and regularity of life, greater seclusion from the world, silence, and manual labor. The themes of the renewal movements of the eleventh and twelfth centuries that continued through the subsequent centuries (chapter 24) included the imitation of Jesus Christ, the apostolic life, and the ideal of the primitive church. The rhetoric of religious leaders compared the monastery to paradise, to the garden of Eden, and to the heavenly Jerusalem.

The military orders discussed in connection with the First Crusade (chapter 20) were a distinctly new development in monasticism. Hermits and canonical clergy were among the older types that found new expressions in this period.

The Camaldolese were hermits who lived in caves and beat themselves. They began in Italy in 1012, founded by Romuald (d. 1022), with the intention of restoring the primitive ascetic life. Peter Damian became their principal spokesman.

The Carthusians, too, took as their ideal the ancient hermits of Egypt. Beginning in 1084, their founder, Bruno of Rheims (d. 1101), decided to go to the French Alps at Grande Chartreuse (from which their name derives) to establish a colony of German-speaking hermits. Each hermit had independence, but little companies of twelve lived within the hearing of a bell that called them to communal devotions. Going much beyond Benedictine practice, Carthusian asceticism allowed no meat, almost no wine, and cooked meals only twice a week. A strictly contemplative order, the Carthusians took a vow of silence.

The Augustinian (Austin) Canons had their origin in communities of clergy in northern Italy and southern France in the mid-eleventh century who—inspired by the Gregorian reform—lived a common life of poverty, celibacy, and obedience. By the beginning of the twelfth century they had adopted the rule attributed to Augustine of Hippo (compiled from the writings of Augustine to monks and nuns and achieving wide use in the twelfth century). Since they lived by a monastic rule, they were known as regular (from *regula*, "rule") canons. They were the official staff of a cathedral or of a church with several priests.

The Premonstratensians began at Prémontré in France in 1120, founded by Norbert (ca. 1080–1134), a German from Xanten. They were canons, secular clergy who were virtually monks. They followed, as did other canons regular, the Rule of St. Augustine but with more austerities, such as abstinence from meat. Many women as well as men were initially drawn to the order.

B. Cistercians

The most important of the new religious movements was the Cistercians, a reform movement within Benedictine monasticism that ended up creating a new order. They took their name from their first house at Citeaux. Its founding in 1098 was led by Robert, the earlier founder of Molesme, but his return within eighteen months to his previous foundation left his companions with ambiguous feelings about him.

An Englishman, Stephen Harding (d. 1134), who was a chief mover in the founding of Citeaux, became its third abbot and drew up the nucleus of the rule for the community, the *Carta caritatis* ("Charter of Love") in 1119 (in its present form probably to be dated to the mid-century).

Recognizing that there was too much power in the hands of the abbot of Cluny, the Cistercians aimed at decentralization. The organization provided for the four daughter houses of Citeaux at Morimond, La Ferte, Pontinity, and Clairvaux to govern the houses established by each. With this federal arrangement the abbot of Citeaux was a limited monarch. There was to be a uniformity of custom and discipline according to the Rule of Benedict.

The Cistercians were critical of Cluny's wealth, its large and ornately adorned church, elaboration of the liturgy, and easy life with serfs to do the work. Among the topics on which Cistericans and supporters of Cluny debated was their clothing. The Benedictine monks wore black, which they took as an expression of humility. The Cistericians saw black as ostentatious and wore undyed white garments as an expression of simplicity and as resembling the garments of angels, clothing the Cluniacs considered a mark of pride.

Cluny represented tradition, whereas the Cistercians claimed to go back to the original Rule of Benedict. The new movement gained a large following, but against the new orders the old customs had defenders, like Orderic Vitalis (d. 1142) in his *Ecclesiastical History*, otherwise notable for its account of the achievements of the Normans.

For the Cistercians there was to be a return to Benedictine simplicity. The wealth of language in the liturgy was pruned so as to leave time for contemplation. The buildings were to be plain, lacking artistic adornment. The monks were to engage in manual work. Instead of serfs, the Cistercians included in their monasteries unlearned lay brothers (*conversi*) who were fully members of the community except for rights reserved for the priests, but they were willing to employ hired help as well. The lay brothers were not new, but became characteristic of Cistercian monasteries. In their emphasis on self-support the Cistercians pioneered experiments in raising plants and sheep so that they came to have a substantial impact on the economy of northern Europe.

Plan of a Cistercian abbey.

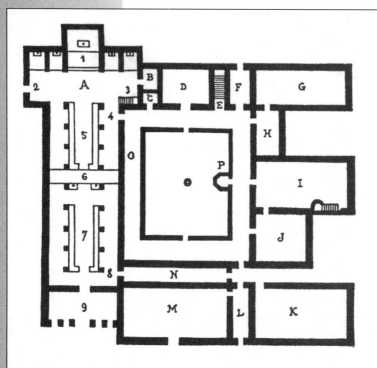

A. Church
   1. Presbytery
   2. Door to the cemetery
   3. Stairway to the dorter
   4. Door of the monks
   5. Choir of the monks
   6. Rood-screen
   7. Choir of the lay brothers
   8. Door of the lay brothers
   9. Vestibule
B. Sacristy
C. *Armarium* (library)
D. Chapter-house
E. Stairway to the dorter of monks
F. Parlor
G. Community room *(scriptorium)*
H. Warming-house
I. Refectory
J. Kitchen
K. Refectory of the lay brothers
L. Passage
M. Storage room
N. Corridor of the lay brothers
O. Cloister gallery
P. Washing fountain

(Adapted by permission from *Cistercians in Texas: The 1998 Jubilee* [Carrollton, TX: Mix Printing Co., 1998].)

Many Cistercian monasteries were built in the twelfth century, by preference in secluded areas. Their impressive ruins now dot the landscape of France, Britain, Ireland, and elsewhere. From the monastery built for Bernard's abbey at Clairvaux by Villiers there came a common plan for Cisterican abbeys. Built around a courtyard, or cloister, the church with a shallow square presbytery rather than an apse occupied the north side, the chapter house and other rooms the east side, the refectory the south side, and guest rooms the west side. A colonnaded walkway surrounded the cloister courtyard. Sleeping quarters for the monks were located on the second floor above the chapter house and refectory. The Cistercians designed efficient water mills, and their development of conduits and drains made them pioneers in plumbing as well as in agriculture.

There were Cistercian nuns relatively early in the history of the order. The Cistercians gave great devotion to Mary. Although at the beginning the Cistercians cultivated the individual religious life, after a generation they were having an impact on the affairs of the world.

As the historian Roland Bainton observed, "When Christianity takes itself seriously, it must either forsake or master the world and at different points may try to do both at once." In these characteristics and others, Bernard of Clairvaux is typical.

II. BERNARD OF CLAIRVAUX (1090–1153)

Bernard was the dominant figure of the first half of the twelfth century, sometimes called "the Age of Bernard." In Catholic circles he is known as the "mellifluous doctor" for drawing out the sweetness of the Christian life.

Born of noble Burgundian parents, Bernard was recognized as an aristocrat among men. He became associated with Citeaux in 1113, and his success in winning recruits (including four brothers) for the monastery saved the new movement. The growth permitted him to establish a daughter house at Clairvaux, where he was the abbot. The great expansion of the Cistercians in the twelfth century was primarily due to his influence. His combination of sincerity and eloquence proved quite persuasive.

Bernard became involved in the wider affairs of church and society. From 1130 to 1153 he was the arbiter of Europe, rebuking kings, clerics, and monks. In the disputed papal election between Anacletus II (1130–38) and Innocent II (1130–43), Bernard favored Innocent, who took shelter in France. Bernard sought the help of the kings of France, England, and Germany and finally carried his point.

A crozier from the abbey of Clairvaux (late twelfth or early thirteenth century) (Cluny Museum, Paris).

One of Bernard's disciples became Pope Eugene III (1145–53), and he wrote his *De consideratione*, a work on perfection and the knowledge of God that included a program for the restoration of ecclesiastical discipline, to guide him and his successors.

Eugene III organized the Second Crusade (1146–48), and at his urging Bernard made a fervent call for the crusade in a sermon at Vezelay. It is indicative both of the spirit of the times and the contradictions in human character that a person who taught so eloquently about love and practiced such a deep piety could also promote a crusade. For his part, Bernard saw the invasions of the Saracens as unjust and hoped to rescue the Eastern churches while also diverting the energies of Western knights from domestic violence to a just war. The failure of the armies of Kings Louis VII of France and Conrad III of Germany to cooperate doomed the effort to failure.

Bernard, the last great representative of the older style of Christian education, lived in the theology of the church fathers and was distrustful of human learning. In contrast to both Anselm and Abelard, he could have said, "I believe in order that I may experience." Impatient with Abelard's rationalism and contention that there were contradictions in the fathers, he became a prime mover in securing the latter's condemnation at the Council of Sens (1140) and by Pope Innocent II (1141).

Bernard reminded the dialecticians of the need for traditional theology. He appealed to the book of religious experience in addition to the books of nature and of Scripture. Bernard suggested four possible reasons for acquiring knowledge: to make a name for oneself out of vanity; to sell the information out of a base desire for gain; to help others out of charity; and to learn for oneself out of prudence.

Among Bernard's early writings are *On Humility*, based on Benedict's rule and discussing three degrees of humility and twelve of pride (human beings always find more fascination in the different ways to sin than in the different ways to be virtuous). Another is *On the Love of God*, based on what Bernard thought was an expression by Augustine: "The measure of the love of God is to love him beyond all measure." He describes the four degrees of love: the love of self for the sake of self (selfish love); the love of God for what he gives (mercenary love); love of God for what he is (filial love that is true, pure, and just); love even of self only for God's sake (divine love).

Bernard's greatest work was his *Sermons on the Song of Songs*, drawing on a long history of Christian spiritual interpretation that allegorized the book as the love between Jesus Christ and the church and between Christ and the human soul. In it he taught that love for the human nature of Christ leads to spiritual love. Important in the quest for the divine is desire; like the love offered to one's chosen lady in courtly poetry, love for God was to be pure, disinterested, and perfect. Christians should learn from the example of Christ to love him tenderly, wisely, and strongly.

The Cistercian influence brought a reform at Cluny under the abbot Peter the Venerable, yet the latter retained a broader view of the place of the arts in the religious life than Bernard allowed. Bernard's writings on the arts were not part of a controversy simply between Citeaux and Cluny, for some early Cistericians promoted sumptuous religious art and there were Cluniac houses interested in monastic reform. Nor was the controversy over the place of the arts a repetition of the Iconoclastic Controversy, for both sides accepted art but differed over how much, what kind, and to what purpose it was put.

Bernard objected to the excessive use of art to attract donations from the wealthy and from pilgrims, to the saturation of sensory experience it stimulated, to its expense that took away from relief of the poor, and to its distraction from spiritual meditation by the monks.

Defenders justified the sumptuous artworks as aids to devotion, as being for the honor of God and the saints, as having Old Testament precedents, and as expressing an association between beauty and holiness.

Bernard feared that beautiful pictures and carvings of saints would cause "more admiration for the beauty of the statues than for the virtues of the saints."

Two temperaments clashed—one appreciative of the arts and delighting in beauty, the other (without rejecting a place for religious art) austere and fearful that the delights of beauty could distract the soul from the things of the spirit. On a personal level, however, Peter and Bernard were reconciled.

According to Bernard, hymn singing is the highest form of prayer. His own poetry falls below the quality of his prose: He sacrificed meter to the sense. The hymns "Jesus, the Very Thought of Thee" and "Jesus, Thou Joy of Loving Hearts" were due to his influence rather than written by him, for he inspired a school of hymnody.

Bernard's continuing influence is due to his unique combination of an ascetic and mystical holiness with literary genius. He taught people to deny their inclinations toward the creaturely and sensual and to cultivate a devotional, penitential, and Christ-centered experience of piety.

His spirituality is characterized by an emphasis on progress (the lack of desire to advance in the spiritual life is already a retrogression), on humility, on the love of God, and on devotion to Mary (although he denied the immaculate conception of Mary).

"O vanity of vanities.... Every part of the church shines, but the poor man is hungry. The church walls are clothed in gold, while the children of the church remain naked.... What is gold doing in the holy place? To speak plainly, greed is the root of all evil,... for the sight of these sumptuous and amazing vanities encourages man to give rather than to pray. So riches attract riches, money attracts money.... The more the abundance of riches, the more willingly men give" (Bernard of Clairvaux, *Apologia*).

Bernard's mystical piety often employed physical imagery: He was said to have received spiritual substance from the breast of Mary. Aside from the Marian piety, Bernard's spirituality is not distinctively Roman Catholic and belongs to the highest in Christian devotion. He is a reminder that piety unites, whereas other things divide.

III. OTHER IMPORTANT THINKERS OF THE TWELFTH CENTURY

Education before the late eleventh century was more oral than text based. It became more centered on texts in the twelfth century, and this is reflected in a great increase in literary productions.

Important twelfth-century Christian thinkers included Hugh of St. Victor, Otto of Freising, John Gratian, John of Salisbury, Peter Lombard, and Hildegard of Bingen.

A. Hugh of St. Victor (d. 1142)

In the early twelfth century two schools opened in Paris in addition to the old cathedral school: St. Genevieve (a collegiate church), set up by Abelard; and St. Victor (a house of Augustinian canons), founded in 1108 by William of Champeaux (d. 1121), an extreme Realist, after he was bested in dialectics at the cathedral school by Abelard.

St. Victor's preserved an emphasis on training in virtues, but entered into the new intellectual foment of the age. Hugh arrived at St. Victor's about 1115 and became director of studies in 1133. He was said to have come from Saxony, but this may not be correct; the cultural unity of the Middle Ages often makes the place of one's origin irrelevant.

Bernard and the Victorines represented the continuation of a "monastic" theology primarily interested in the spiritual life, but the latter were also engaged with the new "scholastic" theology that addressed logical and theoretical issues.

Moreover, Hugh and Bernard reflected two different approaches to the cultivation of virtue. Whereas Bernard began with the conscience, the inner state that from beauty of soul leads to outward grace, Hugh emphasized disciplining outward conduct in order to teach the virtuous life. Hugh attempted to render theology scientific while keeping its monastic character.

Bonaventure would later call Hugh a preacher, a mystic, and a scholar. Unprepared to distinguish between *scientia* (knowledge) and *sapientia* (wisdom), Hugh did not want there to be a wall between the intellectual and the devotional lives. In this regard he preserves the spirit of earlier medieval educational ideals. Hugh promoted a well-rounded education, because the liberal arts "paved the way for the mind to penetrate to the full knowledge of philosophical truth."

Breathing a personal spirit and beauty into his work that is often absent from later Scholastics, Hugh has been called "the heart of God." His spiritual teachings emphasized prayer and the interior life. He spoke of meditation as the active quest in prayer for the divine love, and spoke of contemplation as the possession of a deep peace that comes from the union in love with God.

Taking account of the views of both Bernard and Abelard, Hugh (1) modified the spirituality of Bernard by giving an express place to the understanding in his mysticism, and (2) rescued the dialectical method of Abelard from the discredit brought on it by respecting tradition and uniting faith and reason. (Hugh's successors at St. Victor continued his spirituality. They are known as the Victorines, most notable of whom was Richard.)

Hugh described "three eyes" with which human beings were created and the effect of original sin on them. The eye of the intellect that sees God and spiritual reality was totally blinded by the fall. The eye of reason was partly blinded. The eye of the flesh was unblinded, but is deceptive in that it sees only the external world.

Hugh also described four stages, each involving three degrees, by which the soul returns to God: awakening that involves fear, sorrow, and love; purgation that includes patience, mercy, and compunction; illumination that covers thinking, meditation, and contemplation; and union that requires temperance, prudence, and fortitude.

Out of Hugh's numerous and wide-ranging works, special attention belongs to his *De sacramentis christianae fidei* ("On the Sacraments of the Christian Faith"). It is the first medieval synthesis of theology, and it is Christocentric, being arranged according to dispensations—before and after Christ. Book I is preparation for the incarnation, and Book 2 is the incarnation with its consequences. Originally written for the monks at St. Victor and not intended for beginners, it nevertheless circulated more widely.

In *De sacramentis christianae fidei*, Hugh taught the importance of the historical sense of Scripture, but he emphasized the allegorical sense as going beyond the literal. The historical and the theoretical (or contemplative) methods are followed throughout the work. For instance, he emphasizes that the account of creation in Genesis is allegorical. A follower of Augustine, he quotes him almost as much as the Bible.

For Hugh, all the Christian life is sacramental, so the sacraments are innumerable, but he prepared the way for a distinction between sacramental rites and major sacraments, and he expressed the view that

"Learn everything, and then you will see there is nothing useless" (Hugh of St. Victor).

sacraments are efficacious signs, not only signifying but also transmitting grace. Every creature is a sensible expression of a divine thought. One moves from the study of the world as well as of the Scriptures to a meditation on the divine.

In the second book of *De sacramentis christianae fidei*, Hugh gave much attention to the church, insisting on the oneness of the body of Christ.

B. Otto of Freising (c. 1114–58)

Otto studied under Abelard and Hugh of St. Victor. After being abbot of the Cistercian house of Morimond, he became bishop of Freising in 1138. He helped introduce the study of Aristotle into Germany and participated in the Second Crusade (1147–48).

Otto is notable as a philosopher of history. He dedicated his *Chronicon, or History of the Two Cities* to his nephew Frederick Barbarossa. In this work he contemplates the failure of the Second Crusade undertaken under such great spiritual leadership. He modifies Augustine's "Two Cities" by understanding their union in the Catholic Church as the continuation of the Roman Empire.

Otto also wrote a history of the early part of Frederick Barbarossa's reign.

C. John Gratian (d. c. 1160)

Little of the life of John Gratian is known, but it is thought that he was a teacher of law at Bologna and possibly a member of the order of Camaldolese. His fame rests on his *Concordantia discordantium canonum* ("Reconciliation of Discordant Canons," c. 1141), later known as the *Decretum Gratiani*, in which he brought together the strands of canon law—patristic texts, conciliar decisions, and papal pronouncements.

In the study of civil law, Irnerius (late eleventh century) of Bologna had earlier recovered the *Corpus Iuris Civilis* of Justinian. Gratian had predecessors also in the compilation of legal authorities for the canon law, notably Ivo, bishop of Chartres (d. 1116). By pointing out apparent conflicts in the authorities and laying down principles by which these could be reconciled, Ivo inspired the methodology of Abelard (chapter 20) and anticipated Gratian.

The importance of legal study is reflected in the fact that most of the popes of the twelfth and thirteenth centuries were trained in canon law.

Gratian began the *Decretum* by distinguishing natural law (which is divine) from usage (which is human), moral law from human ordinance, customs from written ordinances, natural law from civil laws

"The human race is ruled by two things: natural law and usages. The law of nature is that which is contained in the Law and the Gospel, by which each person is ordered to do to another what he wishes to be done to himself and by which he is forbidden to inflict on another what he does not wish to be done to himself" (Gratian, *Decretum* 1).

and the laws recognized by almost all nations, and civil enactments from ecclesiastical canons.

Gratian made another distinction between the moral laws and the symbolic precepts in the law of Moses. The latter have been changed. An example is the prohibition in the law of Moses of a woman after childbirth or in menstruation from entering the temple, but she now may enter church and take communion immediately after childbirth or while in menstruation.

According to Gratian, ecclesiastical enactments are superior to secular authorities. The written law of the church, in decreasing order of authority, is in Scripture, papal decretals, decisions of ecumenical councils, decisions of provincial and diocesan councils, and writings of the church fathers.

Former collections of canon law were private, but Gratian's work—although never receiving formal approval—became (as a sourcebook) the universal basis for the study and practice of canon law. His collection was the first to systematize the material, for his work was not only a collection but also a treatise on canonical science. Thus Gratian sought to give ecclesiastical law the same systematic presentation that civil law had in Justinian's compilation.

Gratian followed the method of Abelard in arranging the authorities, but he went further in reconciling discrepancies and offering solutions to difficulties (his title is a key to his approach). The *Decretum* was a counterpart in canon law to Peter Lombard's *Sentences* in theology (see below) in systematizing the tradition, but the *Decretum* established itself sooner as a standard text.

Later Gratian's work was amplified and glossed: about 1215–18 Johannes Teutonicus and others prepared the *Ordinary Gloss*. The name *Corpus Iuris Canonici* was given to the whole work in the sixteenth century. With subsequent modifications and revisions (the latest in 1983), it still serves as the basis of the canon law of the Roman Catholic church.

D. John of Salisbury (c. 1115–80)

John went from his native Salisbury in England to study at Chartres and at Paris under Abelard. As secretary to Thomas Becket and later as his biographer, he shared the archbishop's exile and was present in Canterbury cathedral when Thomas was murdered during a dispute with Henry II.

In 1176 John of Salisbury became bishop of Chartres and encouraged its school. John was the first important medieval writer acquainted with all of Aristotle's logical writings. More of a moralist and Christian

Bernard of Chartres, a master of its school, likened the moderns in relation to the classics to dwarfs "who have alighted on the shoulders of giants" and so "see more numerous and distant things not by virtue of their own keen vision or their own stature but because they are raised aloft by the giants' magnitude" (quoted by John of Salisbury—the analogy is itself classical, attributed to the first-century Latin author Lucan).

humanist than a theologian, he defended—in his *Metralogicon*—the place of reason and dialectics from their critics, who were motivated by love of orthodoxy, exaggerated mysticism, and the excesses of dialecticians.

John was also important as a political theorist, especially his *Policraticus*. Well acquainted with the Latin classics, he shows the confidence of the Schoolmen in the learning of the past.

E. Peter Lombard (c. 1100–1160)

Born of humble parents in Lombardy, Peter studied at Rheims and at St. Victor in Paris before becoming a teacher of theology at the cathedral school of Notre Dame in Paris. He was named bishop of Paris in 1159. Peter was first a Scripture exegete and then a theologian. His glosses on the Psalms and Paul's letters, the *Magna Glosatura*, replaced the *Glossa ordinaria* on those books and became the most frequently cited work of biblical exegesis in the later Middle Ages.

As with other medieval theologians, Peter was most indebted to Augustine, but he also used John of Damascus, whose work had recently become available in Latin. Peter authored the textbook of scholasticism, *Four Books of Sentences*, from which he is known as the "Master of the Sentences." He combined the dialectic of Abelard's *Sic et Non* and the mysticism of Hugh's *De sacramentis*. Through him the best of Abelard became a part of the medieval church's heritage.

Peter Lombard, Master of Sentences, chapter 69 (Museum of Notre Dame, Paris).

Peter was not an original thinker, but because of his position as bishop and as head of the school that became the University of Paris, his work had a kind of authority with many. The *Sentences* was popular also because of its logical order, its clarity and systematic arrangement, its comprehensiveness, and its fairness on controversial issues while stating the contemporary consensus.

Peter accomplished for theology what John Gratian did for canon law. In spite of some initial opposition, the book was accepted as orthodox by the Fourth Lateran Council in 1215. It came to displace other *Summae* of theology, and all theologians had to study it for two years. The work continued to be commented on for centuries until replaced in the sixteenth century as a textbook by Thomas Aquinas's *Summa Theologiae*. Luther, for example, as part of his studies wrote a commentary on the *Sentences*.

Peter himself had a more modest estimate of his work, comparing himself to the widow offering her two mites at the temple. With rare humility for a theologian, he realized that knowledge of his work was not necessary for salvation.

Book I of the *Sentences* treats the Trinity and the knowledge and will of God. Book II covers creation, angels, the six days of Genesis 1, the fall, and grace. Book III discusses the incarnation, virtues, sins, and the commandments. Book IV presents the sacraments and eschatology.

The distinction in the fourth book between sacramentals (symbolic actions) and sacraments proper contributed to establishing the number of sacraments as seven.

According to Peter, the union of words (*verba*) and matter or the thing (*res*) makes a sacrament. The outward act, the sign of the sacrament, was itself effective and the cause of the result of the sacrament, its grace. He fixed the number of sacraments as: (1) baptism, (2) confirmation, (3) canons (penance), (4) altar (eucharist), and (5) last altar (extreme unction) — all Christians partake of these five — plus (6) marriage, and (7) ordination.

Important in fixing the number at seven was the list of the sevenfold gifts of the Holy Spirit going back to the Greek and Latin versions of Isaiah 11:2–3. Peter Lombard identified the Holy Spirit with love, so there are seven conduits through which love flows to human beings.

It was also traditional to allegorize the seven peoples with whom the Israelites had to fight after their deliverance from Egypt as the vices that Christians have to fight, so there were seven sacraments to meet the exigences of life.

F. Hildegard of Bingen (1098–1179)

Born of a noble family, Hildegard was placed from the age of eight in a convent near Bingen, over which community she became abbess in 1136. Later she built her own convent nearby. From an early age she received religious visions that gave her a sense of being a divinely appointed prophetess. Her prophecies did not offer predictions of the future, but revealed the depths of meaning in the Scriptures.

Hildegard combined mystical contemplation and an active itinerant ministry, going on preaching tours and opposing heresies. Her ministry was accepted by Bernard and Pope Eugene III. She was doctrinally orthodox. Her Trinitarian understanding of nature, for instance, is shown in her frequent analyses of things into three components or aspects.

Hildegard's writings include *Scivias domini* ("Know the Ways of God"), an early theological work relating twenty-six visions; *Liber vitae meritorum* ("Book of Life's Merits"), another visionary work discussing the virtues and vices and their resultant joys and punishments in the afterlife; and *Liber divinorum operum* ("Book of Divine Works"), an impressive mature work recounting visions of the world and created things. Her visions especially centered on the process of salvation and the last judgment. She accompanied her writings with remarkable drawings.

The letters include correspondence with Frederick Barbarossa, kings, and churchmen. She had diverse interests, writing songs and also writing on natural history and medical texts, notable for their scientific observations.

G. Non-Christian Thinkers

The twelfth century was a time of intellectual revival not only in Christianity but also in Islam and Judaism, whose thinkers appropriated the full corpus of Aristotle a century before Christian thinkers did in the thirteenth century.

Moses Maimonides (ca. 1135–1204), who lived in Spain and then Egypt, in his *Guide to the Perplexed* created a synthesis of Jewish theology and Aristotelianism that was much admired by Christian thinkers, who undertook a comparable task in the thirteenth century.

The differences between the Arabic philosophers Ibn Sina (Avicenna, 980–1037), who followed Plato, and Ibn Rushd (Averroës, 1126–98), who followed Aristotle, paralleled the change in Christian theology that began in the thirteenth century from dependence on Platonism to dependence on Aristotelianism.

Averroës, who represented the peak of rationalism in Islam, became a disturbing influence on Christian intellectual life in the thirteenth century because he developed a philosophical world view independent of theology.

IV. THE CHURCH AND THE ARTS

A. Romanesque Architecture

Apart from the Carolingian and Ottonian ages, the period from the late fifth to the eleventh century did not see much building activity in western Europe. Some art historians have applied the term "Romanesque" broadly to developments from the Carolingian age to the twelfth century, but others limit the term to the architecture and decorative arts of the late eleventh and the twelfth centuries.

The time between 1050 and 1350, when the outstanding works of Romanesque and Gothic (treated in the next chapter) architecture were produced, has been called a "cathedral crusade." Eighty cathedrals, not to mention thousands of parish and monastery churches, were built in France alone.

The construction boom was made possible by the return of relative peace and order to western Europe, increased trade that brought greater wealth to cities, and new developments in architectural skills.

Early Romanesque churches were basilicas, some on an enormous scale, with the addition of towers (usually twin, but sometimes one) on the west end and an ambulatory with radiating chapels around the choir on the east end.

Later Romanesque buildings differed from basilicas in using stone vaulted ceilings instead of flat wood ceilings. The stone vaults and greater size required stronger and thicker columns and walls.

Whereas an ancient basilica carried the view forward to the altar and the apse without interruption, the vaults, subdivided into bays of equal size, gave the interior of the Romanesque churches the appearance of a series of visually distinct but repeated spatial units, each following the other in monumental rhythm. Rounded arches were used not only for the vaulting, but also for upper walls (supported by columns) and for the framework of windows.

Benedictine church at Chapaize, France (built about 1000 and later rebuilt), typical of moderate-sized Romanesque churches in Burgundy.

Some elements of the Romanesque style continued in use even after Gothic became fashionable in the late twelfth and thirteenth centuries.

The great abbey at Cluny at the beginning of the twelfth century could house 400 monks and 2,000 visitors. Its church, built between 1080 and 1230—the largest in Christendom before the construction of St. Peter's in the sixteenth century—influenced many smaller Romanesque churches.

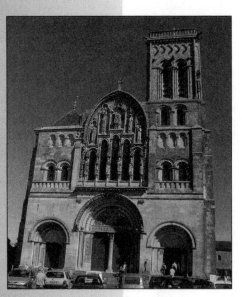

The abbey church of Vezelay, France, an outstanding example of Romanesque architecture.

One of the enduring monuments of Romanesque is the abbey church of Vézelay, Sainte Madeleine (dedicated to Mary Magdalene) in Burgundy, an object of pilgrimage because of the alleged remains of Mary Magdalene, and a major gathering place on the pilgrim road to Santiago Compostela in northern Spain.

The Norman structures in England, such as Durham cathedral, also represent the Romanesque style. Large Romanesque buildings were required by the large numbers of clergy and monks at certain centers, by the huge crowds on festivals, and by the needs of liturgical processions. Churches provided a spatial framework for the liturgy but also made an artistic statement.

The characteristics of Romanesque buildings are solidity, simplicity, and a sense of permanence.

B. Sculpture and Painting

The facades of Romanesque churches proclaimed the building as "the house of God and the gate of heaven." Richly sculptured large portals at the entrance became a Romanesque characteristic.

Cluny promoted the theme of Jesus Christ in glory, and this scene became ubiquitous over the door (the tympanum) of Romanesque churches, where Christ is shown seated in majesty (and/or in judgment) accompanied by figures from the book of Revelation—often the twenty-four elders and usually the four living creatures (symbols of the four evangelists). Like a feudal lord, Christ is attended by his senior vassals, the twelve apostles, below him. Indeed, Christ in majesty was the best known artistic theme in the period from 800 to 1200.

For the first thousand years of her existence the Christian church made little use of three-dimensional art, although it is found on rings, lamps, and other objects for personal use, some small pieces of sculpture for household decoration, and the bas-reliefs of sarcophagi.

Portal of the church of St. Trophimus in Arles, France, with Christ in glory surrounded by symbols of the Four Evangelists.

The Eastern church, while making extensive use of two-dimensional paintings and mosaics, has never, even in later years, favored sculpture, finding it too close to pagan idolatry.

But from the twelfth century in the West, when skill had been achieved in the various arts, sculpture was used profusely not only on the outside at the portals of churches, but also inside to ornament column capitals, baptismal fonts, choir screens, and pulpits.

The nature of Gothic architecture (chapter 23) allowed for copious use of sculpture to decorate both the exterior and interior of buildings—the Duomo in Milan contains 4,400 statues on the outside and inside. Some of the finest Romanesque sculpture adorned the capitals of columns inside churches and monasteries. The principal Gothic sculptures are statues on the outside of buildings.

Romanesque paintings on the walls of churches and especially in manuscript illuminations reached their height in the twelfth century. Romanesque art was abstract, solemn, and majestic. It discounted everyday life as ephemeral and directed attention to the abiding matters of the spirit. The proportions of bodies were distorted to enhance the massiveness of the depictions. Most figures are short and heavy, and the facial features and folds of garments are indicated by only a few lines.

Pictorial art was largely religious, even that produced by secular artists and that intended for royal or aristocratic patrons. Paintings decorated especially churches and monasteries or illustrated Bibles and writings of the church fathers.

The second half of the eleventh century and the twelfth century saw an unprecedented production of illuminated Bibles throughout Europe. The iconographic repertoire of Romanesque art was quite comprehensive, representing many more biblical scenes than were included in earlier periods.

The most widely copied work in the illuminated manuscripts of tenth-to-twelfth-century Spain was the commentary on Revelation by Beatus (c. 786), one of the opponents of Adoptianism in the Carolingian period, who gave a spiritual interpretation of the ages of human history and of the millennium.

This medieval art continued (as did early Christian art) to borrow models from classical art, but invested the forms with a Christian and contemporary significance.

C. Poetry and Music

As the Carolingian renaissance of the eighth and ninth centuries saw the development of a new style of handwriting, so in the mid-twelfth century emerged Gothic script.

Two original artistic creations were products of the twelfth century: Gothic architecture and vernacular poetry. The former will be discussed in the next chapter, for its most notable representatives were achieved in the thirteenth century.

Lyric poetry was produced from the eleventh and twelfth centuries in southern France by the troubadours, who wrote and sang in the Occitan or Provençal language. This romance and adventure literature spread to northern Europe in the twelfth and thirteenth centuries with the trouvères of northern France and poets in Germany.

Lintel of the temptation of Eve, by Giselburtus (1130), from the church of St. Lazarus in Autun, France — one of the earliest expressions of the revival of sculpted human form in Western art (Rolin Museun, Autun).

Vernacular literature could be used for religious purposes (chapter 24), but some of its earliest representatives were primarily secular, although raising religious questions and indeed reflecting the religious spirit of the age by expressing even secular themes in religious language.

The romantic literature made feminine qualities virtues and enhanced the dignity and value of women, but it also reinforced the double standard of sexual morality for men and women.

The poetry of "courtly love" was characterized by the abject humility of the lover toward the beloved, the conventions of courtesy, love for a married person, and love described in religious terms. The theme involved two paradoxes—the worship of love in terms of the Christian cult of the saints (the bed is an altar) that was almost a parody of Christian faith, and the portrayal of a man's subservience to a woman that reversed society's conventions of male dominance. Although the presence of adulterous love has caught the greatest attention of readers, more striking is the emphasis on conjugal love.

At the height of the medieval development of vernacular poetry stand Chrétien of Troyes (fl. 1165–91) from northern France and the German Gottfried von Strasbourg (fl. 1210). Chrétien wrote two famous works. *Lancelot* approves the hero's adulterous love for Guinivere but upholds the lady's moral and social superiority. *Perceval* (*Le conte du grail*) features a celibate hero and is important in the development of the motif of the search for the holy grail, a dish for serving rich food, but in other versions a chalice. Gottfried wrote *Tristan and Isolde*, which shows how adulterous passion destroys the lovers psychologically.

Wolfram von Eschenbach (fl. early thirteenth century) in his *Willehalm* and *Parzival* (in which the search for the grail becomes the education of the hero) also subverts the theme of courtly love from within the literary genre of romance. He contrasts the enduring joys of marital love with the passing pleasure of extramarital affairs. He celebrates chivalry's ideal of loyalty, but also offers a Christian criticism of chivalry. He shows sympathy for the heathen by suggesting that God does not punish a person for ignorance and that the good pagan merits God's grace.

In the early Middle Ages, church music continued to be homophonic (monophonic). Polyphony developed principally in the eleventh and twelfth centuries, although it is attested as early as the ninth century. Manuscripts from the thirteenth century began to denote in addition to the

Virgin and Child in ivory (before 1279), from Sainte Chapelle, Paris (Louvre, Paris).

Romanesque depiction of Christ's crucifixion, in the church of St. Sernin, Toulouse, France.

tones the durations (measure) of the notes. Two types of polyphony may be distinguished: descant, in which one or more voices were added note on note to a plain chant melody; and organum, in which one or more voices embellished with many notes each note of the plain chant. In both types the same text was sung.

The organ was the only instrument accepted into liturgical usage, and it was rarely used, being heard mainly at Pentecost and Christmas. Only in the thirteenth century is there clear evidence of the organ being used regularly; it replaced the singing of some liturgical texts in the late fourteenth century.

V. ACTS OF PIETY

Prayer and penance had provided the religious inspiration for the Crusades. Some aspects of their expression may be commented on here. The Psalms remained the basic standard of prayer. The goal of imitating God led to a greater emphasis on internalizing of devotion. The monastic disciplines of reading (*lectio*), meditation (*meditatio*), and prayer (*oratio*) set the pattern for devotions. These stages of listening to the Word of God, open dialogue with God, and intimate experience of conversation with him became identified in mysticism with the stages of purification, enlightenment, and union.

The cult of the saints continued to be central in popular piety. The annual saints' feast days were the occasion for local and regional fairs that combined trade, entertainment, and social gatherings with religious ceremonies and processions. Every illness had its own saint who specialized in its treatment.

Since the fifth century the word *sanctus* had not been used for all the devout dead—it was limited to official saints. In the age of the martyrs their recognition as saints was a spontaneous response by their fellow believers; then the acknowledgement of local saints became a decision by the bishop.

The first documented canonization by a pope was by John XV in 993 of Ulrich of Augsburg (d. 973). Canonization of saints by bishops and by the pope continued for some time until it became a papal prerogative in the twelfth century. Since possession of relics of saints had not only spiritual but also economic benefits (because of pilgrimage to their sites), the sale and theft of relics became common. Relics occupied the place in piety in the West that icons did in the East as the visual expression of spiritual presence.

Pilgrimage to shrines of the saints continued to be an important expression of piety and act of penitence (often imposed as part of the sacrament of penance), and it was now easier with the return of political stability and increased economic activity. An early version of a tourist's handbook is the *Pilgrim's Guide* from the twelfth century. In pointing out things to see, the book gives special attention to works of art, preeminently the reliquaries.

Nor is the souvenir trade something new: Pilgrims purchased pins with emblems associated with a saint to wear on their caps to show the site they had visited. Jerusalem held the highest place as an object of pilgrimage, even if fewer people were able to go there than to other sites. Santiago Compostela (St. James of Campus Stellae, the "field of stars," already a pilgrim site since the supposed discovery of the sepulcher of the apostle James in 813) in northwest Spain, the shrine of the Three Kings (the Magi, whose relics were moved from Milan by Frederick I) at Cologne, and the shrine of Thomas Becket at Canterbury joined Rome as popular goals of pilgrimage.

Many miracle stories circulated about the cures and interventions of the saints and their relics on behalf of the faithful. Ecclesiastical authorities made efforts to control the cults of the saints, but it remained true that popular attachment to relics counted for more than official authentication in establishing a cult.

The cult of Mary became prominent in the eleventh and twelfth centuries, especially under the influence of Bernard of Clairvaux. Evidences of the special devotion to Mary are the large number of miracles attributed to her intercession, the interest in relics (especially clothing) associated with her, the number of churches dedicated to her, and her prominence in liturgical, artistic, and theological developments.

The recitation of "Hail Mary, full of grace ..." (*Ave Maria*) came into use in the late twelfth century and joined the "Our Father" as the most common forms of prayer.

In popular piety, following the lead of Bernard and Francis of Assisi, Mary as a tender and merciful figure concerned with ordinary human needs, with which she was more identified than was the exalted Jesus Christ, found expression in prayers, hymns, and works of art.

Increasingly, however, the theological accent shifted from the earthly mother of Jesus to the virgin mother of God and queen of heaven, evident in the prominence of this theme in later medieval art. From the twelfth century the thought that Mary had been preserved from original sin (the immaculate conception) gained ground, although it was opposed by all the leading theologians before Duns Scotus at the end of the thirteenth century.

Pious activities such as the sacrifice of the mass, veneration of saints and relics, and confession and works of satisfaction in the sacrament of penance, came in the twelfth century to be related to a more concrete understanding of purgatory.

Apse mosaic in the church of Santa Maria in Trastevere, Rome (1140): Christ and the Virgin enthroned, flanked by popes and/or saints Innocent II, Lawrence, and Callistus on the left and Peter, Cornelius, Julius, and Calepodius on the right.

The notion of an intermediate place of purging of lesser sins before entrance into heavenly bliss had been around for centuries, popularized by Gregory the Great, but the scholastic theologians of the twelfth century—in developing the theology of penance—formulated the view that in purgatory were completed the punishments for sins not satisfied by penitential acts in this life.

The doctrine of purgatory was then given classical formulation by Thomas Aquinas, officially defined at the Council of Lyons (1274), and received imaginative expression in Dante's *Divine Comedy*.

Medieval teaching on good works, in keeping with the love of grouping things in sevens, resulted in classifying seven spiritual works of mercy: converting the sinner, instructing the ignorant, counseling the doubtful, comforting the sorrowful, bearing wrongs patiently, forgiving injuries, and praying for the living and the dead.

These were matched by seven corporal works of mercy (based on Matthew 25:35–36): feeding the hungry, giving drink to the thirsty, clothing the naked, giving shelter to the stranger, caring for the sick, caring for prisoners, and burying the dead. Welfare was done by the church, not the government, which historically has only recently assumed this responsibility.

Since the priests, monks, and canons were the models of the religious life, there occurred to an extent the "monasticising" or "clericalization" of the laity, as the more devout among the laity imitated the monks and canons in observing the hours of prayer.

VI. CHURCH AND STATE IN THE TWELFTH CENTURY

One of the successful Norman kingdoms developed in Sicily and southern Italy, united in the eleventh century by the victories of Roger I over the eastern empire in southern Italy and over the Saracens in Sicily. The kingdom reached its height under Roger II, who assumed the title of "king" in 1130, and under William II (1166–89). At the meeting place of the Latin West, the Byzantine East, and the Islamic South and East, this kingdom came to have great cultural significance (along with Spain) in the transmission of new learning to western Europe. The Norman kings were patrons of the arts, still visible in the cathedrals of Sicily.

The second half of the twelfth century was dominated politically by two notable kings—Henry II of England (1154–89) and Frederick I Barbarossa of Germany (1152–90). The period is conveniently bracketed by the dates of accession to office and death of some of the leading figures of the time (1152–53 to 1197–98). Frederick I Barbarossa became king of Germany in 1152 (emperor in 1155), and Bernard of

Clairvaux died in 1153. Frederick's son, Henry VI, died in 1197, and Innocent III became pope in 1198.

Two popes during this half century are particularly notable. Hadrian IV (1154–59) is the only English pope. He was abbot of an Augustinian monastery near Avignon before he became a cardinal bishop of Albano under Eugene III. One of his first acts as pope was to secure the expulsion from Rome of Arnold of Brescia, who was captured by Frederick I Barbarossa (1152–90) and condemned to death. Hadrian required full homage from Frederick before agreeing to crown him emperor (1155).

Frederick I Barbarossa was one of the most notable rulers of the Hohenstaufen dynasty, which had come to power with Conrad III in 1138. Hadrian interpreted the coronation as bestowing a *beneficium*. The imperial court was enraged, and Hadrian had to explain that he meant "kindnesses," not "benefices." In 1157 Frederick added the epithet "holy" (*sacrum*) to the empire in order to compete with the church's claim, setting the *sacrum imperium* alongside the *sancta ecclesia* and preparing the way for the title "Holy Roman Empire" to be applied to the territories ruled by the emperor.

Alexander III (1159–81) was elected by a majority of the cardinals but was able to defend himself only with the greatest difficulty against an antipope set up by imperial authority. Frederick I Barbarossa took

Reliquary of Thomas Becket made at Limoges, France (c. 1180), with gilt copper and enamel on a wood core, and showing (lower part) martyrdom and haloed soul being carried to heaven and (upper part) burial and ascent to heaven (Victoria and Albert Museum, London).

Private collection/The Bridgeman Art Library

Charlemagne as a model and practically controlled the appointment of bishops, but there was Italian opposition to him. An expedition to Italy in 1166 was unsuccessful due to an epidemic, and the Lombard League of Italian cities defeated him in 1176. By the Peace of Venice, 1177, he recognized Alexander III as pope.

Under Alexander III occurred the Third Lateran Council (the Eleventh Ecumenical, 1179) that modified the provisions for papal election by requiring a two-thirds vote of *all* the cardinals to elect a pope.

In England church-state tensions were reflected in the conflict between King Henry II (1154–89) and Thomas Becket, archbishop of Canterbury (1162–70). Thomas had been an intimate friend of the king as his Chancellor and tutor of his son before being elected archbishop at the instigation of the king. Once in office, however, Becket upheld ecclesiastical claims in a dispute over whether accused churchmen were to be tried in royal or ecclesiastical courts.

After continuing conflict the anger of the king led him to utter words taken by four of his knights as authorization to kill the cleric. Thomas was assassinated in his cathedral, the spot still marked in Canterbury cathedral. He was immediately regarded as a martyr and was canonized within two years. Pilgrimages to the site became common and provided the setting for Chaucer's *Canterbury Tales* (written c. 1387).

Toward the end of the century, the Third Crusade (1187–92) was prompted by the Christian defeat at Hattin in Galilee in 1187 by Saladin, who moved on to capture Jerusalem and left Christians holding only a narrow strip of land along the eastern Mediterranean coast.

The main routes of the third and fourth Crusades.

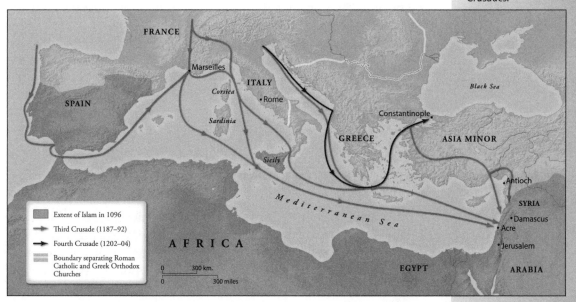

The Third Crusade involved the most famous names in the crusading enterprise, around whom gathered many popular tales. Frederick I Barbarossa led a large army across Hungary and the Balkans, but he was drowned crossing a river in Cilicia. Philip II Augustus, king of France (1180–1223), by founding a centralized bureaucratic state became the architect of the French monarchy. The reign of Richard I the Lion-Hearted, king of England (1189–99), provided the background for the Robin Hood legend.

Philip and Richard's armies started out from Vezelay. Their enterprise was hampered by their quarrels, whereas Saladin (1171–93), himself a Kurd, who often comes across as more noble than his Christian counterparts, was able to unite the Muslims. The armistice of 1192 left Jerusalem in Muslim hands but assured Christian pilgrims free access to the city.

The former Crusader states were reduced to a narrow coastal strip from Beirut to Ascalon, known as the Kingdom of Acre, and often administered from Cyprus, which had been conquered by Richard on his way to the Holy Land.

VII. INSTITUTIONAL LIFE OF THE CHURCH

The basic organizational unit of the church continued to be the diocese, headed by a bishop. The location of his chair (*cathedra*) identified his church as the cathedral. Under monastic influence, the clergy of the cathedral, known as canons, formed a chapter. Endowments provided their income and gave them considerable independence from the bishop. They, rather than the bishop, had responsibility for the cathedral buildings and their upkeep.

A dean headed the chapter and supervised the material affairs of the church. The chapter included a chancellor, who was its secretary, in charge of seals, and overseer of the school and library; a treasurer, who was responsible for the relics and other treasures and looked after endowments; and a cantor, who arranged religious services and directed the choir.

VIII. SOME DEVELOPMENTS IN THE EASTERN CHURCHES

The twelfth century saw some significant developments affecting the Greek Orthodox church. The study of canon law was advanced, and two of the most influential commentators on the canons of the Greek church were active: Johannes Zonaras (twelfth century), who also wrote a universal history, and Theodore Balsamon (c. 1140–after 1195).

In monastic history, Christodulus obtained—through the influence of the mother of emperor Alexius Comnenus—possession of the island of Patmos. There in 1088 he established the monastery of St. John that still exists. The monastery of the Pantokrator, notable for its associated infirmary and home for the aged, was founded in 1136 in Constantinople. At the close of the twelfth century Savas established the first Serbian house on Mount Athos.

The Serbs, who had been converted between 867 and 874, were caught between pressures from Roman Catholicism in Hungary and Croatia and from Greek Orthodoxy in Bulgaria. The Orthodox form of Christianity became firmly established in the late twelfth century, especially through the influence of the monk Rastko (Sava).

If the fifth century was the golden age of Armenian literature (chapter 12), with a revival in the tenth century, then the twelfth century (in the wake of the Crusades) was its silver age. The end of the twelfth century saw the re-creation of an Armenian kingdom in Cilicia, outside the territory of ancient Armenia. This last Armenian kingdom fell in 1375 to the Mamelukes of Egypt.

The Cilician period was a high point of Armenian culture, evidenced by the illuminated manuscripts, the principal surviving representatives of Armenian art, produced during this period. An outstanding example is the Freer Gallery Gospel codex in Washington, D.C.

Medieval Georgia reached its height in the twelfth century. Fittingly for a country converted by a woman and whose first royal convert was a woman, the climax of Georgia's golden age was under Queen Tamar (1178–1213) of the Bagratid dynasty, which claimed descent from David and Solomon and ruled in Georgia from the eighth to the beginning of the nineteenth century.

A distinctive Georgian church architecture emerged and achieved its greatest monuments in the eleventh and twelfth centuries. From the tenth to the thirteenth centuries Georgia excelled in cloisonné enamel and in gold and silver crafts generally for ecclesiastical objects. Georgian church music had long been polyphonic even though Latin and Greek music was still monophonic.

A painting of St. Savas by Zdenka Zivkovic (thirteenth century) on a limestone pilaster in the nave of the church of St. Saba in Geroso, Serbia.

IX. SUMMARY

The twelfth century was characterized by a "renaissance" involving many notable achievements in monastic reform, theology, literary productivity, piety, art, and architecture. All in all, the influence of the church advanced in many areas of life—religious, political, and artistic.

Looking back from a later perspective, however, one could say that these accomplishments but prepared the way for even greater accomplishments in the thirteenth century.

FOR FURTHER STUDY

Armi, C. Edson. *Masons and Sculptors in Romanesque Burgundy: The New Aesthetic of Cluny III.* 2 vols. University Park: Pennsylvania State University Press, 1983.

Barlow, F. *Thomas Becket.* Berkeley: University of California Press, 1986.

Berman, C. H. *The Cistercian Evolution: The Invention of a Religious Order in Twelfth-Century Europe.* Philadelphia: University of Pennsylvania Press, 2000.

Burton, Janet, and Julie Kerr. *The Cistercians in the Middle Ages.* Rochester, NY: Boydell, 2011.

Colish, Marcia L. *Peter Lombard.* 2 vols. Leiden: Brill, 1993.

Evans, G. R. *Bernard of Clairvaux.* New York: Oxford University Press, 2000.

Knowles, David. *Thomas Becket.* London: A. & C. Black, 1970.

Kuttner, Stephan. *Gratian and the Schools of Law 1140–1234.* London: Variorum, 1983.

Lekai, Louis J. *The Cistercians: Ideals and Reality.* Kent, OH: Kent State University Press, 1977.

Pranger, M. Burcht. *Bernard of Clairvaux and the Shape of Monastic Thought: Broken Dreams.* Leiden: Brill, 1994.

Rosenmann, Philipp W. *The Story of the Great Medieval Book: Peter Lombard's "Sentences."* Toronto: University of Toronto Press, 2007.

Stoddard, Whitney S. *Art and Architecture in Medieval France.* New York: Harper & Row, 1972.

Toman, Rolf, and Achim Bednorz. *Romanesque: Architecture, Sculpture, Painting.* Cologne, Ger.: Könemann, 1997.

23

The Glory of the Western Medieval Church

The Thirteenth Century

The thirteenth century has often been considered, justly so, the golden age of medieval Catholicism.

Among the achievements of that century were the influence of the papacy on civil affairs and society, the effectiveness of the new mendicant religious orders in taking the Christian message to the people, the organization of universities, the great intellectual achievements in creating summaries of theology, and the construction of soaring Gothic cathedrals.

In Scholasticism and in architecture it seemed that all of reality had been encompassed in grand syntheses, all at the service of the church under the leadership of the pope. The thirteenth century began with Innocent III as pope, the one who most nearly realized the ideals and goals of the medieval papacy.

I. INNOCENT III (1198–1216)

Innocent III was born Lothair of Segni to a noble family in 1160. He had the best of academic credentials, studying theology at Paris and law at Bologna. As a student he wrote in almost disgusting detail *On the Misery of the Human Condition*. His other early works were *On the Mysteries of the Mass* and *On the Four Marriages*.

A. View of the Papacy

Rising rapidly in the papal service, Lothair became a cardinal deacon in 1189 and was elected pope in 1198 while not yet in priest's orders. He proved himself an able administrator. Less a canonist than a theologian, Innocent demonstrated considerable pastoral concern, but this was subordinate to his goal of papal authority.

The Glory of the Western Medieval Church

On his consecration, Innocent III preached on the text, "See, today I appoint you over nations and kingdoms to uproot and tear down, to destroy and overthrow, to build and to plant" (Jeremiah 1:10), and applied to himself the words, "Who is the faithful servant? I will put him in charge of my household" (cf. Matthew 25:21).

Innocent spoke not in the papal "we," but as "I"—he meant business. Instead of "vicar of Peter" (the previous papal title), he preferred "vicar of Christ" (previously used for any bishop or priest but now employed for the first time, it seems, by the pope of himself) as more indicative of his authority, and he based his policies on the powers this title gave. (His successor, Innocent IV, called himself "vicar of God," indicating authority even over unbelievers.)

Innocent also applied the words of God to Moses, "I have made you like God to Pharaoh" (Exodus 7:1), to himself as the pope in relation to civil rulers. Innocent saw himself (as he put it at his coronation) as the intermediary "between God and man, under God and over man, less than God but greater than man, judge over all and judged by no one (save the Lord)." He interpreted the papal miter (a tall cap) as the sign of his religious office and the papal tiara (a triple crown) as representing terrestrial dominion.

In a dispute between the kings of England and France, Innocent justified his examining the case on the grounds that "We do not intend to judge concerning the feudal obligation, but concerning the sin." As Roland Bainton has observed, "Since sin is quite prevalent, this gave him a wide area of jurisdiction."

Innocent might be the "servant of the servants of God," but he also considered himself the *verus imperator* (the true emperor). When the crusaders brought back the supposed seamless robe of Christ, Innocent placed it on his shoulders.

Innocent called himself "Melchizedek," a priest-king (cf. Hebrews 7:1–4), who would bring a centralized Christian society into being. To this end he worked for reform of the church: advocating celibacy of the clergy, opposing simony, combating bribery by the curia and usury in society, enforcing canon law, insisting that bishops be irreproachable and that priests be resident in their parishes. Religious concerns and not ambition as a world ruler apparently motivated his efforts to secure the freedom of the church, promote Crusades, and achieve peace among nations.

The centralization of the government of the church progressed under Innocent III and his successors in the thirteenth century. During the thirteenth century the practice of the pope providing (appointing) bishops and other high ecclesiastical officials on his own authority, a practice that began in the twelfth century, accelerated greatly.

The papal court during the twelfth century had become the court of appeal in a wide variety of cases (marriage and divorce, wills, vows, patronage, elections), and papal delegates and legates carried papal justice and authority throughout western Europe.

The papal states provided the temporal base for the papal monarchy. Innocent III continued the policy of regaining the boundaries of the original papal territories, and he effectively established the papal states as they existed for the rest of the medieval period. In order to be spiritually free, he felt he must also be politically free, but he was uncomfortable in the narrowing vice about the papal states that resulted from the empire controlling southern as well as northern Italy.

B. Relations with the Empire and Frederick II

In the bull *Venerabilem Fratrum* (1202) Innocent affirmed the right of the Roman church to transfer the empire from one dynasty to another, as had been done in transferring it from the Greeks to the Germans in the person of Charlemagne. The bull did not dispute the right of electors to choose the ruler, but it affirmed the right of the pope to examine the qualifications of the candidate, decide disputed elections, and settle moral issues involved.

After the death of Henry VI, Innocent initially sided with Otto IV, but then backed Philip of Swabia. On the latter's death, Otto received the imperial crown from Innocent, but when Otto pursued his own policy in regard to Sicily, the pope excommunicated him. Innocent now put forward his ward Frederick II, son of Henry VI, but he did not prove the kind of ruler Innocent would have wanted.

With a certain messianic aura, Frederick II moved north. The confused state of affairs in Germany is reflected by his election as king in 1211 being confirmed in 1212 and his being crowned king twice, in 1213 at Mainz and again in 1215 at Aachen. The empire was secured for him when the French defeated Otto IV and his English allies at Bouvines in 1214.

Frederick II was crowned emperor in 1220 by Pope Honorius III (1216–27) in St. Peter's basilica after he agreed to make laws against heresy a part of imperial legislation, to uphold the rights of the church, and to go on a Crusade. Frederick then proceeded to exalt his imperial rule as comparable to that of ancient Rome alongside the papal authority.

His Crusade, the sixth, was the only one that turned out to be cursed and not blessed by the papacy. To the consternation of many, Frederick II negotiated rather than won by force of arms a peace with the Muslims that allowed Christian control of Jerusalem (except for the mosque of Omar), Bethlehem, Nazareth, and pilgrim routes from the coast, but new Turkish rulers soon reoccupied the areas.

An accomplished linguist and learned in the sciences, Frederick II was a religious skeptic. He had stormy relations with the papacy, being twice excommunicated by Gregory IX—in 1227 and in 1239—and declared deposed by Innocent IV at the Council of Lyons in 1245, the Thirteenth Ecumenical Council and the first case of the implementation of Gregory VII's *Dictatus Papae* 12.

Death came in 1250. The ambivalent reactions to Frederick II are captured by the opposing evaluations of him: *stupor mundi* ("wonder of the world") by his admirers for his great learning and abilities, and "Antichrist" or the forerunner of the Antichrist by supporters of the papacy.

C. Relations with England

A disputed election of the archbishop of Canterbury drew Innocent III into the internal affairs of England. The monks claimed the right to elect their own prior, and the suffragan bishops claimed their right, supported by the king. Innocent set aside both candidates and installed Stephen Langton, who is credited in the history of biblical studies with the division of the Bible into chapters.

When King John (brother of Richard the Lion-Hearted) refused Stephen Langton, Innocent placed England under the interdict, which meant that no sacraments could be performed (a punishment that had originated as an archepiscopal power but extended to a papal one), and excommunicated John. Philip II of France threatened to depose John, who then acquiesced and issued a charter of ecclesiastical liberties in 1213 granting free clerical elections, but reserving some rights for himself. He then went further and placed his realms under papal protection as a papal fief and gave an oath of fealty to Innocent.

Because of the king's debacle at Bouvines, the barons extracted from King John at Runnymeade in 1215 the *Magna Carta*, a basic document restricting the crown's feudal and sovereign rights and so preparing for the development of the liberties of the English people. It established the principle that, as an English lawyer of the thirteenth century said, "In England law rules and not will [of the king]." Stephen Langton was involved in the affair and may have been the author of the document. The pope put himself on the wrong side of history when he declared that, since John was now a papal vassal, what happened at Runnymeade was also rebellion against the pope.

D. Fourth Crusade

The Fourth Crusade (1202–4) was a joint papal and Venetian venture. The Doge (Duke) of Venice promised to outfit the crusaders if they would capture the rival commercial city of Zara on the Balkan coast on their way to the Holy Land.

Then the crusaders were persuaded to restore the deposed emperor Alexius IV by capturing Constantinople (1203–4). In the outcome, the city was pillaged and burned by the crusaders, many of its treasures were carried to Venice, and its relics were eventually dispersed over western Europe. A contemporary chronicler lamented, "Even the Muslims would have been more merciful."

A Latin patriarch and Latin emperor were chosen. The division between the Latin and Greek churches was completed only at this time, when the hatred for Western Christendom by the people and clergy of the Greek Church began. The excommunications of 1054 did not have the popular impact that the damage wreaked on Constantinople in 1204 had.

The Fourth Crusade failed to help the Latin states in the East, greatly weakened the Byzantine empire, and further alienated the Greek Church from the Latin West. It was in this context that the Byzantine emperor, needing all the allies he could muster, recognized the Serbian church as autonomous and in 1219 appointed Sava, a monk from Mount Athos, its archbishop. Memories are long in the East, and Orthodox Christians in the twentieth century affirmed that they had more religious liberty under the Marxists than they did under the crusaders.

The crusading idea was still alive, and in 1212 the tragic Children's Crusade took place. The crusade was joined by thousands of teenage boys from France and Germany—some sent back home, some perishing in a storm at sea, and some sold into slavery in North Africa and Egypt.

Innocent III then turned the crusading idea against the Albigensians in southern France (chapter 24). The idea of crusades was applied not only in southern France, but also to European political warfare in the Baltics and against Frederick II in southern Italy. Although Innocent III tried to keep the purposes of the church foremost and to restrain political crusades, later popes were even less successful.

E. Fourth Lateran Council

The Fourth Lateran Council (the twelfth of the ecumenical councils in Roman reckoning), the largest medieval council (400 bishops and 800 abbots and others), met in 1215. Among other things this important council condemned the Albigensians, made the Inquisition (already introduced by bishops) obligatory on the whole church, approved the language of transubstantiation (although apparently not excluding other interpretations of the Real Presence), and required that confession of sins to a priest and communion be observed at least once a year at Easter (communion had become even less frequent). The council is one of the principal sources of the canon law of the Catholic Church.

Prior to Innocent III the papal curia resisted representatives of the "apostolic poverty" movements, but he began a policy of accommodating their impulses to the church as long as orthodox doctrine and hierarchical authority were recognized. Thereby Innocent III opened the way for a significant new development in monastic history, the rise of the mendicant orders.

II. THE MENDICANT RELIGIOUS ORDERS

Poverty was one of the standard vows assumed by earlier monks, but this was understood of the individual, not of the community. Some monastic establishments in fact became quite well-to-do, such as Cluny and eventually some of the Cistercian houses. The more diligent and pious the monastic communities were, the more they flourished and the more outsiders wanted to assist the monks. With increasing ease of life, these successful communities became laxer in their religious life, so new reform movements arose in order to return to stricter ideals. The mendicant monks sought to impose poverty on their communities as well as on individual monks.

The mendicant religious orders should be seen as an expression of a wider enthusiasm in the late twelfth and early thirteenth centuries for evangelical poverty as forming the essence of the spiritual life. Various groups sought to imitate the life of the apostles in poverty and wandering evangelism outside of traditional religious communities, but not all who were impressed with these qualities were part of religious communities.

The lay men and women who were officially recognized as saints in the twelfth and thirteenth centuries had in common charity work in imitation of Jesus Christ. They often combined preaching and criticism of Catholic priests with loyalty to the church. Their elevation to sainthood was due to promotion by the secular clergy, and their recognition was limited to their local diocese.

In common with Francis of Assisi, they had a penitential spirituality, a desire to conform their lives to the example of Christ, an emphasis on humility and poverty, and attention to the needs of the marginal-

A Cistercian monk described the cycle in monastic life: "Discipline begets abundance, and abundance, unless we take the utmost care, destroys discipline; discipline in its fall pulls down abundance" (Caesarius of Heisterbach, c. 1180–1240).

ized in society by almsgiving and encouragement. They differed from Francis in choosing to remain strictly in the lay state.

The mendicant friars thus emerged as a third type of medieval religious order alongside the monks living in monasteries and the canons, who served cathedral and sometimes parish churches. They differed from earlier religious communities in seeking to impose poverty on the order itself and not just on the individual members. They formed a counterpart within the church to the enthusiasm for "apostolic poverty" manifest in heretical and schismatic movements of the late twelfth century (chapter 24).

These orders also departed from the practice of a cloistered life in order to engage in preaching to the people. A medieval Latin verse expressed the difference in the locations favored by monks: "Bernard loved the valleys, Benedict the mountains, Francis the towns, Dominic the populous cities." Although the Franciscans began first, the Dominicans received official papal approval first.

A. Dominic (c. 1170–1221) and the Dominicans

Dominic was born in the region of Castile (northern Spain). Zealous and with good theological training, he assisted his bishop Diego at Osma in working among heretics and from him developed a style of itinerant, mendicant preaching on the example of the apostles.

In 1215 Dominic established in the diocese of Toulouse a society of preachers who were to prepare themselves by theological studies and a life of asceticism for the care of souls and instruction in the faith. This *Ordo Fratrum Praedicatorum* ("Order of Preaching Brothers," abbreviated O.P.) was the first religious community dedicated to preaching. Innocent III recommended that the preachers follow the Augustinian Rule, and in 1216 Pope Honorius III gave official confirmation to the new order.

The order in 1220 renounced property and fixed incomes, but it maintained closer connections with the older orders and interpreted the obligation to poverty less strictly than the Franciscans. The order was to own only its actual houses and churches and be supported by alms—not by fixed revenues and income from properties. Instead of manual labor, the members were to occupy themselves with study, preaching, and pastoral work. Dominic also took steps leading to the establishment of an order of Dominican nuns.

Dominic's own practices set the pattern for the order: strict life, poverty, fasting and other abstinences, prayer, penitence, and enthusiasm for intellectually informed preaching. Under the next general of the order, Jordan, the activities that became characteristic of Dominicans were further developed: preaching, care of souls, missions, combating heresy (Pope Gregory IX entrusted the Inquisition almost exclusively to the order), and training in theology (especially in the universities). The order grew rapidly in the thirteenth century, gaining about 15,000 members in 557 houses by the end of the century. In the fourteenth century the Dominicans actively cultivated mysticism in Germany.

A story told about Dominic illustrates the contrast between Dominic and Francis: Interrupted in his studies by the chirping of a sparrow, Dominic caught the bird and plucked it. The incident surely did not happen, but one may be equally confident that the tale would not have been told about Francis. For one thing, Francis would not have been studying, and he would not have harmed any creature.

While Dominic lacked the warmth of religious feeling and the personality of Francis, he surpassed him in keenness of intellect, training, and practicality. Dominic was austere, systematic in his approach, a disciplinarian, and possessed of the qualities of an ecclesiastical statesman—in each respect the opposite of Francis.

B. Francis of Assisi (1182–1226) and the Franciscans

Francis, unpretentious and gentle, has been the best-loved (even by Protestants) of the medieval saints. This outstanding representative of medieval piety had an unpromising beginning as a dissolute youth, the son of a wealthy cloth merchant in Assisi (central Italy) whose affections for things French prompted the name for his son.

Francis of Assisi and scenes from his life and miracles, by an anonymous thirteenth-century artist (Museo Civico, Pistoia, Italy).

A lengthy illness led to the conversion of the high spirited, gallant youth and Francis's decision to marry "Lady Poverty" (he had a penchant for personifying objects and qualities). Notable steps in the redirection of his life included exchanging his clothes with those of a beggar whom he met while on pilgrimage in Rome, breaking with his father over his charity to the poor, devoting himself to the repair of the church of San Damiano, and responding to the reading of Matthew 10:5–16 in the little church of the Portiuncula by adopting its directions literally for his life.

Francis gave himself to bringing the message of the gospel in popular preaching to the masses. Interested also in preaching to non-Christians, Francis joined the Fifth Crusade in 1219 and gained permission to preach in Muslim lands before returning to Italy in 1220.

A Prayer of Francis of Assisi

"O Lord, our Christ, may we have your mind and your spirit; make us instruments of your peace; where there is hatred, let us sow love; where there is injury, pardon; where there is discord, union; where there is doubt, faith; where there is despair, hope; where there is darkness, light; and where there is sadness, joy."

"O divine Master, grant that we may not so much seek to be consoled as to console; to be understood, as to understand; to be loved, as to love; for it is in giving that we receive; it is in pardoning that we are pardoned; and it is in dying that we are born to eternal life. Amen." (Francis of Assisi)

Francis was conspicuous for his humility, and as like-minded men joined him he named them the *Ordo Fratrum Minorum* ("Order of Little Brothers" or "Friars Minor," abbreviated O.F.M). His first rule (*Regula primitiva*) for them, now lost, was written in 1209. In 1210 Pope Innocent III gave oral permission for the group to continue, with the condition that Francis and his companions receive tonsure and that Francis swear obedience to the pope and his companions swear obedience to Francis.

Not given to administration, Francis resigned as the group's head in 1220, but he participated in the drawing up of a new rule in 1221 (*Regula non bullata* or *Regula prima*) in order to adapt the contents to the needs of a growing order. The Scripture citations and pious, edifying outpourings of the heart from the first rule were included, but more definite regulations were added.

The third rule of 1223 (*Regula bullata*), when Honorius III gave papal approval, was still less Francis's work and provided for a more carefully arranged life to replace the freedom of the old wandering life of apostolic poverty and simple-hearted devotion.

Francis brought a new feeling for nature, expressed in his "Canticle of the Sun," addressing "brother sun," "sister moon," "brother earth," and "sister sea." One of the charming anecdotes, remembered in art as well as literature, was of Francis preaching in the woods to the birds, who flapped their wings in joy and listened so attentively that Francis chided himself for not having thought to preach to them before.

Such a story illustrates his other striking attitudes: constant joyousness, sincerity, and artless simplicity. The concern for nature and animals also found expression in his making a Christmas crib in 1223, beginning the still popular custom of manger scenes at Christmas.

Early on Francis was associated with Clare (c. 1193–1253), and in 1212 he invested her with the Franciscan habit and so instituted the "Poor Clares," the "Second Order" of Franciscan nuns. Clare settled at the church of San Damiano outside Assisi, where she was joined by other young noble women, forming the only women's house "founded" by Francis. She was the first woman to write a rule approved by the papacy (in 1253), and Innocent III exempted her community from the decree of the Fourth Lateran Council (1215) that required new religious houses to follow one of the old monastic rules.

Like Francis, Clare refused to accept possessions and regular income for her community, resolving that they would live on alms and earnings from their own work. Such dependence on divine providence for day-to-day needs was especially daring for a group of women dedicated to the religious life. Whereas for Francis and Dominic asceticism was a means of attaining inner freedom, Clare (and after her other female Franciscans and Dominicans) valued extreme abstinence as fundamental to Christian perfection. She was canonized in 1255, two years after her death.

Francis founded in 1221 the Third Order, "The Brothers and Sisters of Penance," a lay community that tried to carry out the fundamental principles of the Franciscan life while continuing married life in the world.

The most unusual incident in Francis's life was his receiving the stigmata on September 14, 1224. After a period of forty days of fasting, prayer, and contemplation on Mount La Verna, he had a vision in which a seraph flew toward him and filled him with unutterable pleasure. At the center of the vision was a cross with the seraph nailed to it. When the vision disappeared, Francis felt sharp pains in his body and then saw the signs of the wounds of the crucifixion of Christ on his own body. His closest disciple, brother Leo, is the principal source for the story of the stigmata, but other contemporaries indicate they had seen the wounds. Debate has surrounded the genuineness of the experience and whether such can be explained on psychological grounds from intense meditation or only as a miracle.

Exhausted from his sojourn on the mountain, Francis had to be carried back to Assisi, and he remained in ill health until his death on October 3, 1226. He was canonized two years later by Gregory IX. In 1230 his remains were transferred to the new double basilica at Assisi built in his honor (Romanesque lower basilica, 1230–32; Gothic upper basilica, 1232–39), adorned with works by several artists, including twenty-eight frescoes (painted 1296–98) depicting scenes from his life

Statue of St. Claire outside St. Francis of Assisi Church, Ranchos de Taos, New Mexico.

by Giotto, who marked the transition from Medieval to Renaissance painting.

Characteristic features of Francis and the Franciscan movement were poverty, humility, and simplicity. The Franciscans united an austere renunciation of the world with an evangelical mission to it. This combination introduced a basic tension into the movement. After Francis's death different tendencies among his followers came more into the open.

Some wanted the literal observance of the rule in the spirit of Francis's original intentions, reaffirmed in his *Testament* toward the end of his life; they became the Spirituals (see chapter 24). Others wanted more accommodation to traditional monastic orders according to the practice of the Dominicans, a position promoted by Elias of Cortona (Minister General 1232–39); these became the Conventuals.

A middle party represented by the popular miracle-worker Anthony of Padua and the Minister General Bonaventure (see below) held the movement together for a time. By 1300 the number of Franciscans was estimated at between 30,000 and 40,000, but the tensions over the interpretation of apostolic poverty produced sharp conflict in the fourteenth century.

C. New Features of the Mendicant Orders

1. Mendicancy, or corporate poverty

With the return of a money economy to western Europe, poverty was exalted as a great virtue. Previously, the monks had opposed pride and gluttony by exalting obedience and chastity. Now with new wealth by commercial classes in the cities, existing alongside great poverty of the masses, the mendicants emphasized again the virtue of poverty, in part in response to the "apostolic poverty" advocated by heretical movements and critics of the church.

The Franciscans saw poverty as an end within itself and so were plagued with controversy over the subject, whereas the Dominicans viewed it (as they did learning) as a means to effective preaching and fighting against heretics.

2. Popular preaching

Another new feature of the mendicant orders was preaching to the common people by Francis, and to others by Dominic. At this first crisis presented by urbanization to the Western church, the friars responded with a pastoral concern for all strata of society, primarily in the cities, attempting to reach people by the example of virtuous lives and by communication of the gospel on the people's level.

3. Education, especially university teaching

The rise of universities presented new challenges, and the mendicant orders had greater freedom to move into these new centers of learning. The Franciscans were not far behind the Dominicans in responding to the opportunities.

4. Third orders, or lay brotherhoods

The mendicant orders promoted a renewal of piety among the laity who responded to their preaching and were encouraged to translate their ideals into everyday life.

5. Immediate subjection to the Roman see

Several monasteries already enjoyed this status, but now the whole order was placed in this relationship. The centralized organization of each order with the relative autonomy of the provinces of each gave the papacy an efficient instrument to meet challenges facing the church.

6. Mobility

The friars were not bound to the old requirement of "stability," staying in one's "monastic place." In the days of Benedict of Nursia "stability" was necessary in order to bring order and discipline to the monastic life. Now it was necessary to go to where the people were to bring the Christian message to them.

7. An order of friars

This was anticipated in some respects by the Cistercians, but now was developed more fully. The organizational structure instituted by the mendicants and their itinerant preaching meant that new recruits, unlike earlier monks, entered an order rather than an individual monastery and professed obedience to the order's superior rather than to the head of a local house.

Other mendicant orders include the Carmelites (the "Order of the Brothers of Our Lady of Mount Carmel," begun as hermits in the Holy Land in the twelfth century before they became mendicants and were recognized by Innocent IV in 1247), the Hermits of St. Augustine (recognized by Alexander IV in 1256), and the Servites (beginning as a lay brotherhood but adopting the Augustinian Rule in 1240 and recognized as a mendicant order by Martin V in 1424).

III. THE ORGANIZATION OF UNIVERSITIES

The roots of the development of universities belong in the intellectual revival of the eleventh and twelfth centuries, but the decisive period for their formation came in the latter half of the twelfth century, and their institutional organization was not defined until the thirteenth century.

Factors contributing to the emergence of universities as separate organizations were the increase in scholarly literature, the specialization in subject matter at certain places, the increase in the number of students, and the internationalization of students and teachers.

Traditional settings for education could no longer accommodate the situation. Students went to places where the subjects they wanted were taught. Outstanding teachers, such as Abelard, attracted large numbers of students to certain cities, and students would move as the teachers did or as a new name gained fame. In education the teacher always matters more than the place, however famous its name.

Although the intellectual ferment out of which universities arose was most evident in cathedral schools, sometimes neither the teachers nor students were formally attached to either the cathedral, collegiate, or monastic schools—unlike the earlier situation. The chancellor of the cathedral chapter (as, for example, at Notre Dame in Paris) or the archdeacon (as at Bologna), however, did give teachers a license to teach.

"The Italians have the papacy, the Germans the empire, and the French the university."

In addition to the chancellor's supervision, the teachers began to unite in order to control admission to their membership. They took as their model the craft and trade guilds, whose initiation ceremonies influenced the academic ceremonies. At Bologna the students also formed a guild with strict regulations of the teaching by the professors (the Italian students were often in their thirties and forties and so were more mature). The teachers at the schools in Paris formed a corporation to secure their rights and privileges. That corporation became a model for many northern universities.

The universities became a third force in Christendom alongside the *imperium* (empire) and the *sacerdotium* (priesthood).

At first the term *studium generale* was used for schools of higher learning with a faculty of arts and a faculty of at least one of the advanced subjects (medicine, law, or theology) that taught students from all over Europe.

The word *universitas* first meant a legal corporation, in this case an organization of teachers and students. It was used this way for a gathering of teachers, of students, or of both, first attested in 1215. Its modern institutional sense of "university," the whole community of students and masters, came into use at the end of the fourteenth century. "College" referred to the group of those persons who lived together; only later did it refer to the house itself.

Although the traditional seven liberal arts continued to be taught, a threefold classification prevailed: rational philosophy (grammar, rhetoric, logic), natural philosophy (metaphysics, mathematics, and physics), and moral philosophy (ethics). By the twelfth century the study of medicine was concentrated at Salerno (where there was already a long-standing fame in this field) and at Montpellier, the study of law was concentrated at Bologna, and by the end of the century philosophy and theology were the focus at Paris and Oxford.

The principal forms of teaching were by lecture and disputation (chapter 21). "Ordinary" lectures were on the fixed syllabus for the course of study and were compulsory. "Extraordinary" or "cursory" lectures were given by less prominent teachers and older students on less important subjects. Copies of the textbooks had to be made by hand or their contents obtained by notes on the teacher's lectures. University cities became centers of a thriving book business.

Supervised by the church and administered by the professors, the early universities had a certain independence. The Third Lateran Council (1179) under Pope Alexander III decreed that each cathedral church was to provide a benefice to support a teacher, who was forbidden to collect fees from poor boys, and whose license to teach was to be granted without charge and was to be granted to any qualified candidate. In

Tomb of a professor
with scenes of stu-
dents (fourteenth cen-
tury) (Museo Civico
Medievale, Bologna).

Bologna the teachers depended for support on students' fees. Students enjoyed the status of a cleric (clerk), receiving the tonsure (shaved head) to distinguish them from the laity but without receiving clerical orders (although in Italy laymen as well as clerics went to school).

Agreements with communal, ecclesiastical, or royal authorities gave a legal basis that was regularized from about 1200. Often these regulations were a codification of earlier customs. In cases of disputes with local authorities, the universities could generally count on the support of the papacy to ensure their independence. The typical patterns in the organization of universities may be illustrated from Paris, Bologna, and Oxford.

At Paris the professors and students were exempted from civil jurisdiction by King Philip II Augustus in 1200 and within the next two decades from the jurisdiction of the bishop. The papacy issued a statute in 1215 maintaining its supervision of the "university," which by 1222 had its essential organization in place.

There were four faculties in Paris—theology (the first to attain autonomy, 1219), medicine, liberal arts, and canon law—and the professors and students were grouped according to four nations (French, Picard, Norman, and English, which included Germans and Scandinavians). The arts faculty was the largest and took the lead in disciplines other than theology, and its rector became the true head of the university. It moved increasingly to become a faculty of philosophy. In 1245 the pope gave the university its own seal and thus full legal existence.

Even as ancient Rome's great contribution to Western civilization was its system of law, so it was in Bologna that the study of law flourished. The origins are obscure, but in the eleventh and twelfth centuries the study of law at Bologna experienced a growth in scope and importance.

Three systems of law contributed to the formation of western legal codes—Roman, Germanic, and ecclesiastical law—but before the eleventh century Germanic practices had been integrated into Roman law so that the two branches of study were based on Justinian's compilation of civil law (but containing much pertaining to religion) and on the church's canon law.

At Bologna the students were organized as guilds (*universitates*) according to their region of origin ("nations"). The Holy See established its control of the university from 1224 by subordinating professors and students, whether clerical or lay, to the local bishop, who appointed the chancellor. Each *universitas* of students elected its own rector, to whom was given the oath of obedience that incorporated the student into the university.

At Oxford the papal legate in 1214 granted privileges to the *studium*, which was placed under the bishop of Lincoln, who selected the chancellor from the professors of theology. The bishop of Lincoln, Robert Grosseteste, himself a former chancellor, gave the statutes to the university in 1252–53.

In the early centuries of the church most theological thought was produced by bishops (apart from some outstanding teachers like Justin and Origen). In the early Middle Ages it came especially from monks (who in some cases were also bishops, as Anselm and Peter Lombard). From the twelfth century onwards theology came from the professors in the universities.

In modern times when higher education has seemed to many, in church and society alike (although for different reasons), as inimical to religion, it is well to be reminded that universities had much of their impetus from theology and their origin within the framework of the church.

The peak of medieval intellectual culture attained in the thirteenth century, then, was due to three factors:

1. The development of universities

As "iron sharpens iron" (Proverbs 27:17), the proximity and contact of keen minds stimulates learning and remains the basic component of university intellectual life.

2. The presence of the mendicant orders

The friars, not bound by the limitations of traditional monastic orders, were available to move their best minds into new situations and immediately saw the opportunities that universities provided for their preaching mission. Dominicans were at Paris by 1217, and Franciscans two years later. There were sharp conflicts between representatives of the older orders and the friars over teaching prerogatives at the universities, but the mendicants established themselves as permanent and formidable participants in intellectual life.

3. The availability of the entire corpus of Aristotle

Some of Aristotle's writings on logic had been available throughout the Middle Ages, but the complete corpus became available to western Europe in the thirteenth century. Some became known by a circuitous route—translated from Greek into Syriac in the early Christian centuries, then into Arabic after the Muslim conquests of the Near East, and then introduced to Latin scholars in southern Italy and Spain where there was direct contact with Arabic learning.

Translations from Arabic into Latin, as well as contacts between Western Christians and Muslims, had begun well before the Crusades, but these accelerated in the twelfth and thirteenth centuries. The philosophy of Arabic thinkers like Avicenna and Averroës and Jewish thinkers like Maimonides (chapter 22), all of whom sought to interpret faith in revealed religion in relation to the philosophy of Aristotle, had a significant influence on Christian intellectual life. The works of Aristotle were also translated directly from Greek into Latin.

The presence of a formidable non-Christian system of thought, especially as it was incorporated into Muslim philosophy, stimulated the thinking of Scholastic theologians.

IV. THOMAS AQUINAS (1225–74)

Other thinkers produced *summae* in the thirteenth century, but this enterprise reached its summit in the work of Albert the Great and his greater student Thomas Aquinas, who produced a synthesis of faith and reason, of science and sanctity, that still today in principle, if not in details, has its appeal.

Thomas was the youngest son of the count of Aquino. At five he was sent to school at nearby Monte Cassino. When Frederick II expelled its monks in 1239, Thomas went to Naples, which had the first university independent of the church (founded by Frederick II in 1224) to finish his arts course. There he resolved to pursue an intellectual career and enter the Dominican order, which he did in 1244. His family, strongly opposed to this, held him prisoner for fifteen months before relenting.

Thomas went to Paris, where he came under the influence of Albert the Great (Albertus Magnus). Albert's gifts were more in natural science

The Glory of the Western Medieval Church

than philosophy and theology, but he introduced Thomas to Aristotle and to a program of reconciling Aristotelian philosophy with Christian theology. Thomas accompanied Albert to Cologne in 1248; he then returned to Paris as a lecturer (1252–59) and received his Master of Theology in 1256. Pope Alexander IV's letter of recommendation to the Chancellor of Notre Dame in Paris contains a classic understatement, "Thomas Aquinas [is] ... a man of noble descent, distinguished by high moral standards and learning."

As a theologian to the papal court in Italy (1259–68), Thomas studied Aristotle especially, and then he returned to Paris (1268–72).

The Augustinians who defended the old methods in theology and enemies of the mendicant orders both opposed Thomas, who was caught up in the controversy over the adoption of Arabic philosophy by some professors in the arts faculty. Attacks on various teachings by Thomas both before and after his death evidence both a confusion of faith with its traditional defense and "guilt by association." Still, Thomas is a striking example of how a teaching once regarded by some with suspicion may become the chief basis of apologetics in a later day.

While teaching in Naples (1272–74), Thomas was sent as a theologian to the Council of Lyons (chapter 24), but died on the way.

Thomas's powers of memory and concentration were legendary, for it was reported that he could dictate different works at once to several secretaries without losing continuity of thought on any. The extent of Thomas's writings is immense. His philosophy is expounded in a series of commentaries on Aristotle and others. Much of Thomas's theology and spirituality is contained in exegetical commentaries on the Bible, which for him was the only source of revelation. (Because of the silence of many secondary works, it is easy to forget how central the Bible was to the Schoolmen.)

Thomas compiled the *Catena aurea*, a continuous commentary on the Gospels taken from patristic sources, both Latin and Greek. Among his many other works, note may be taken of the liturgy he composed (1264) for the newly instituted feast of Corpus Christi, some hymns for which continue in use in the Roman Catholic Church.

Thomas is another example of the combination of spirituality and Scholasticism in the Middle Ages. Indeed Thomas near the end of his life had a mystical experience that he described in this way: "Everything I have written seems like straw by comparison with what I have seen and what has been revealed to me."

Modern students tend to put the scholastic theologians and the mystical theologians—that is, those who emphasized reason and those who emphasized an affective spirituality—in separate boxes. The approaches may have differed. One begins with Christian beliefs and

A story told of Thomas reports Jesus saying to him, "You have written well of me, Thomas, what reward will you receive?" His reply was, "None but yourself."

uses them to reflect on religious experiences and practices, the other begins from experience and reports on it in a way to induce a similar experience in others. But in the Middle Ages these approaches were seen as complementary, each informing the other.

The culmination of Thomas's literary work came in his *Summa contra Gentiles*, an apologetic work synthesizing Christian arguments against non-Christian views, and his *Summa Theologiae*, a systematic theology left unfinished at his death but completed by his students from his other works.

Thomas wrote his *Summae* in the form of the Scholastic *quaestio*, a written dialogue (chapter 21). The four parts of his *Summa Theologiae* are divided into articles (statements of a question), and the discussion of each article has five segments: the statement of the issue in a "yes" or "no" form, a list of objections to the position he will adopt, a statement of Thomas's own viewpoint, arguments for this position, and an answer to each of the objections raised to his position.

Thomas's great achievement was to place Aristotle at the service of the church, completing a task begun by Albert. Christian theology from the patristic period had been built up in a Platonic (specifically Neoplatonic) philosophical framework. It was the achievement of Thomas to reconstruct Christian theology according to Aristotle, although there is a lot of Plato in him as well. He aimed at a philosophical and theological synthesis of his inherited Christian ideas with the new Greek, Jewish, and Arabic sources now available to him in Latin translations.

The church of Jacobins in Toulouse, the first house of the Dominicans and the site of the tomb of Thomas Aquinas.

As one historian expressed it, "[Thomas] believed not only that there was all truth Somewhere but also that there was some truth everywhere." Yet Thomas acknowledged, "No human being can attain a perfect knowledge of the truth."

Central to Thomas's use of theological language was his principle of the analogy of being. Words used of God that are also used of human beings do not have the same meaning (univocity), nor do they have different meanings (equivocity). Rather they have similar meanings, because they have something in common; they are analogous.

The basic approach of Thomas was to make a clear distinction but not a separation between reason and faith, between nature and grace, and between the corresponding natural theology and revealed theology.

Impressed with how much the pre-Christian thinker Aristotle had learned without benefit of revelation, Thomas allowed a large area of truths that could be discerned by human reason alone. "Faith presupposes reason as grace presupposes nature," something Luther and Calvin would not say. Some truths, the "preambles of faith," can in principle be demonstrated by reason.

Still, there were some things that can be known only by revelation—these are articles of faith necessary for salvation (such as the incarnation). These revealed truths rested on those truths that could be learned by reason, did not contradict them, but went well beyond them.

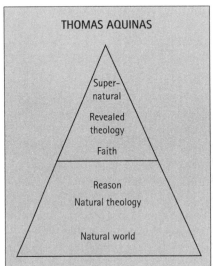

The Thomist triangle. Revealed theology rests on natural theology. There is a continuity and point of contact between nature and the supernatural so that the former provides analogies with the latter.

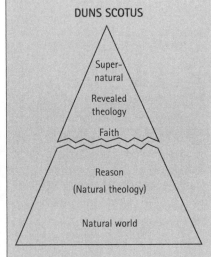

The Duns Scotus triangle. There is a break between the natural world and the supernatural, so there is no analogy between one and the other.

Thomas said reason could demonstrate the existence of God. He formulated five proofs for the existence of God, building on Aristotle's Unmoved Mover. These "five ways" are different formulations of the cosmological argument, reasoning from observable effects back to a First Cause. For example, motion (or change) requires a Mover, since an infinite regress of one thing after another causing the movement or change of another thing does not explain motion itself.

Thomas rejected Anselm's ontological argument as only applicable for a purely intelligent being; but human beings as both body and mind must begin with sense perception. Here he follows Aristotle's epistemology, that the basis of knowledge is information received through the senses that the mind then organizes and generalizes.

One can learn of the existence of God by the use of the reason, but the Trinity, in contrast, is a matter of revelation. Revelation is necessary even for truths that can be learned by reason, for such truths otherwise "would be known only by a few, and that after a long time, and with an admixture of error."

This principle was applied in various areas. In ethics, the four virtues of classical antiquity—prudence, courage, moderation, and justice—are supplemented and completed by the three revealed virtues of Christian teaching—faith, hope, and charity—to give the seven cardinal virtues.

In the field of law, there is a natural law that can be discerned by reason to which all human beings are subject. Human governments establish positive laws in addition to this for their subjects. There is also a revealed law (the Mosaic and the gospel) that applies to believers. Natural law serves as a standard for evaluating positive laws. Throughout, Thomas reasoned on the principle that "Grace does not nullify nature, but completes it."

Thomas's theology shows a special interest in the incarnation and the sacraments. He noted that the incarnation would not have occurred without the fall. The incarnation came about through the Blessed Virgin Mary, who was not herself, however, immaculately conceived.

Thomas also set forth the basic doctrine of the sacraments, but this part of his *Summa* was incomplete at his death. The sacraments are channels of God's grace, which is thought of—in Roman Catholic theology generally in contrast to Protestantism—not so much as God's attitude toward human beings, but as a kind of substance that can be infused into human beings.

Thomas employed the Aristotelian distinction between substance (what something really is) and accidents (outwardly perceived qualities) to explain transubstantiation and argued from the presence of the whole Christ in each of the elements of the eucharist to justify communion in one kind (the bread) by the laity.

"Since grace does not nullify nature, but completes it, reason should be the servant of faith, just as the natural inclination of the will is the servant of love.... Sacred doctrine uses [the authority of philosophers] as supporting and probable arguments. It uses the canonical Scriptures as the proper authority from which it is bound to argue, and uses other teachers of the church as authorities from which one may indeed argue with propriety, yet only with probability" (Thomas Aquinas, *Summa Theologiae* 1.1.8).

Thomas also set forth the basic doctrine of the pope as the successor of Peter who personifies the church, defines what the faith is, and has fullness of authority that must be obeyed in order to receive salvation.

The Dominicans officially imposed Thomas's teachings on the order in 1278. The Church of Rome canonized him in 1323, declared him a "doctor of the Church" in 1567, enjoined his study on all students of theology in 1879, and made him the patron of all Catholic universities in 1880. Only in recent years has the dominance in Catholic theology and philosophy of Thomas Aquinas, the "Doctor Angelicus," weakened.

In recent times the question has been raised whether the influence of Thomas's distinction between reason and faith, and between philosophy and theology, led to secularization. If so, it was far from his intention and was a long time in coming.

V. FRANCISCAN ALTERNATIVES TO THOMAS AQUINAS

The Franciscan counterpart to Thomas Aquinas was Bonaventure (c. 1217–74), born Giovanni di Fidanza and known as the "Doctor Seraphicus." After joining the Franciscan order in 1243, Bonaventure studied theology under Alexander of Hales in Paris and received his doctorate (1253–54). He was a professor in Paris until 1257 when he was elected Minister General of his order. He took an active part in the Council of Lyons, dying shortly after the reunion with the Greek church was proclaimed (chapter 24).

A theologian, a mystic, and a philosopher, Bonaventure showed himself a great systematic mind with clarity and comprehensiveness of analysis. One of his major theological writings is the *Breviloquium* (1256–57).

Faithful to the Augustinian tradition, Bonaventure made the love of God rather than the truth or knowledge of God the goal. Although the contrast may be exaggerated, the Dominicans sought to enlighten the mind whereas the Franciscans aimed at changing the heart.

Bonaventure gave priority to the study of the Scriptures as the foundation of theology: "The whole of Scripture is the heart of God, the mouth of God, the tongue of God, the pen of God" (*Collationes in Hexaemeron* 12.17). The councils of the church, the writings of the fathers, and the teachings of more recent masters, in this order, are to guide the interpretation of the Scriptures.

Bonaventure's greatest work of mystical theology, the *Mind's Journey to God*, was written as a guide to contemplation and sets forth his

"The purpose of theology is that we become virtuous and attain salvation. This is accomplished by an inclination of the will rather than bare speculation" (Bonaventure, *Breviloquium* prologue 5.2).

view that all learning is directed toward the love of God. He warns against one who believes "that it suffices to read without unction, speculate without devotion, investigate without wonder, examine without exultation, work without piety, know without love, understand without humility, be zealous without divine grace, see without wisdom divinely inspired" (Prologue 4).

Bonaventure's doctrine of divine illumination provides the foundation of his philosophy. The simplest act of knowing requires something more than a knowable object and a knowing mind; there must be light by which the perceiver perceives what is perceived. As natural light makes possible sense perception, so the interior light of reason makes possible the grasping of philosophical truths, and the light of grace makes possible the reception of the revealed truths of faith.

There is a continuity between natural knowledge and "supernatural" illumination, but the difference in degree between human reason and faith becomes a difference of kind. The cosmological argument is valid only in virtue of the actual presence of God to the human mind as the light of its understanding; the ontological argument is not really an argument at all but an interpretation of God's immediate presence in the soul. The existence of God really needs no demonstration, being self-evident as a matter of direct observation. Religious knowledge is not a mere inference but the interpretation of experience. Given to describing things in threes, he analyzed the object of faith as threefold: God, who can be known directly; what is revealed by the authority of Scripture; and what is investigated in theological inquiry.

Every object in the universe, according to Bonaventure, speaks to us of God (the doctrine of exemplarism). He may be seen in his resemblances, or expressions, in the world. Some objects are only a shadow of God's existence; others, having a more distinct resemblance, are a trace of the divine; yet others, as in the case of the soul, are an image of God. When we seek God within, we turn towards him, for there is a small spark (*scintilla*) of pure divine light within the soul. The ordinary person of good will, as easily as the learned scholar, can see God clearly.

Roger Bacon (c. 1220–c. 1292) was an Englishman, a Franciscan, and a student and teacher at Oxford (where he came under the influence of Grosseteste) and Paris. He could be sharply critical of those with whom he disagreed, including Thomas Aquinas, but he never constructed an alternative philosophical system. Oxford's foremost scholar in the medieval period and widely learned, Bacon advocated changes in the educational system so as to emphasize the biblical languages (he wrote grammars for Greek and Hebrew), mathematics, natural sciences, and moral philosophy. He complained of the practice of the faculty of theology at Paris in giving preference to lectures on the *Sentences* of Peter Lombard over lectures on the Scriptures. His interests in nature and in the wider world scene (especially Islam, with an emphasis on the need to learn Arabic), so that he conceived a plan for evangelizing the world, were reflective of the broader intellectual interests possible by the thirteenth century, but the extent of his influence at the time appears to have been minimal.

John Duns Scotus (c. 1265–1308), called the "Doctor Subtilis" as the sharpest thinker of the Middle Ages, represents the climax of Franciscan Augustinism. He was born in Scotland and joined the Franciscans there, studied and taught in Oxford, completed his doctorate in Paris, and died in Cologne—such was the international character of scholarship in the Latin West. Duns Scotus became the master theologian of the Franciscan school. Continuing the work of Bonaventure, he differed from the latter in being primarily a philosopher without his predecessor's mysticism.

Quaestiones Quodlibetales of Duns Scotus that he debated in Paris in 1302–3 (printed in 1477).

In the philosophical issues of the day Duns took a mediating position between the Aristotelianism of Thomas and the Augustinism of Henry of Ghent, holding against the former that the intellect can have an intuitive knowledge in addition to the knowledge of universal ideas abstracted from sense experience and against the latter that necessary principles can be known by natural knowledge and are not limited to the certitude that only divine illumination can bring. He rejected both negative theology (humans can only affirm what God is not, since language about God and humanity is equivocal) and Thomas's philosophy of analogy and instead affirmed univocity, arguing that analogy indeed implies (if only in a limited way) univocity.

Duns Scotus emphasized the radical contingency of all created beings (only God exists necessarily) and of God's actions. The existence of God is shown by the existence of contingent beings; since they have been caused, an infinite series of causes is impossible and there must be some being that exists necessarily. God has complete freedom with regard to all his actions, so he is bound neither by external nor internal constraints in his dealings with creatures. Duns continued the Franciscan position that everything must be considered from the point of view of love. Love rules and orders his whole thought, for love lies at the beginning of God's being and work and effects the consummation of the union of the elect with God.

One of Duns's characteristic emphases is voluntarism, the thesis that the will is primary and independent with regard to the intelligence. God is primarily will, not the union of will and intellect that he is in Thomas. For example, the death of Christ is an atonement because God chose that way; another way could have provided a sufficient satisfaction if God had so willed it. Humans have genuine freedom of the will, which means that one can will what one does not in fact choose to will. The intellect may offer guidance to the will, but the will is able to go against the suggestion of reason.

Christ's coming, as the supreme manifestation of God's love, is not made dependent on the fall. Duns was the first major theologian to defend the immaculate conception of Mary.

Like other Scholastic theologians of the twelfth and thirteenth centuries, Duns Scotus saw a harmony of reason and faith but he separated them more than Thomas Aquinas did. Whereas Thomas rested theology on philosophy, Duns placed a gap between them. His criticisms of Thomas's system provided a basis for the distinct Franciscan theological tradition into the eighteenth century. Although himself still functioning within the medieval Scholastic framework, Duns's voluntarism pointed the way to Ockham's remodeling of this framework in the fourteenth century. It was more the implications that later thinkers saw in his arguments than Duns's own position that occasioned the later skepticism of rational proofs for Christian theology.

The play on his name, "dunce," was a result of the reaction of Humanists against the subtleties of Scholastic philosophy.

VI. POPULAR PIETY

The spirit of the age that produced the great syntheses in theology found expression in an encyclopedic collection of saints' lives designed to encourage devotion to the saints by the laity. As Aquinas's *Catena aurea* compiled a commentary on the Gospels from patristic comments, James of Voragine about the same time (in the 1260s) collected saints' lives in the *Legenda aurea* (*Golden Legend*). James was a Dominican and later (1292–98) archbishop of Genoa. Arranging his accounts according to the dates of saints' days in the liturgical calendar, he employed simple language and added miracle stories. His popularizing work was successful, for his compilation became the most copied text of the Middle Ages, surviving in more than 1,000 manuscripts and translated into nearly all the vernacular languages of western Europe.

"Books of Hours," giving devotions for the daily hours of prayer, began in the thirteenth century. These were often beautifully decorated with miniature paintings.

VII. GOTHIC ARCHITECTURE AND ART

The extensive building programs of the twelfth and thirteenth centuries are indicative of the devotion of the people as well as of the increasing prosperity of those times. Churchmen and cities vied for the prestige of building the tallest and largest buildings. One means of encouraging financial support was the granting of indulgences to those who contributed, so that money that once went to support crusades went to the construction of religious buildings.

Gothic cathedrals have been compared to the Scholastic summas of theology as syntheses of reality aiming to depict its totality and as expressions of the human aspiration to reach up to God. They and their art offered a "model" of the cosmos, a summary of history, a mirror of the moral life, and an image of the heavenly city. Reflective of all reality, many of the Gothic churches included sculptures of kings, common people, and even demons in addition to saints. Romanesque churches looked like fortresses for refuge in troubled times; Gothic churches, on the other hand, were characterized by openness and harmony, corresponding to Scholasticism's emphasis on rationality and the reconcili-

Left to right:

Choir of the church of St. Denis, Paris (twelfth century).

Notre Dame, Paris, an example of Gothic architecture.

Purity and Splendor

Mindful of Bernard's criticisms of wealth, Abbot Suger defended the use of lavish decoration:

"Let every one be convinced in his own mind. As for myself, I declare that it has always seemed right to me that everything that is most precious should above all add to the celebration of the Holy Eucharist.... Golden vessels, precious stones, and all that creation holds most valuable must be set forth.... Those who criticize us claim that this celebration needs only a holy mind, a pure soul, and faithful intention. We are certainly in complete agreement that these are what matter above all else. But we believe that outward ornaments and sacred chalices should serve nowhere so much as in our holy sacrifice, and this with all inward purity and all outward splendor" (Suger, *On his Administration* 33).

---

ation of opposites. As indicative of the prominence of the cult of Mary in the later Middle Ages, most Gothic cathedrals were dedicated to her.

The first example of the new style was the abbey church at St. Denis. The burial site of French kings, it was founded on the north side of Paris in the seventh century and rebuilt by Abbot Suger in the twelfth century (the choir consecrated in 1144). From this beginning, Gothic produced its greatest works in the thirteenth century: Chartres, Rheims, and Amiens. It spread to England—notably Salisbury, but influencing many other cathedrals—and to Germany, where the most splendid is Cologne. Gothic remained the prevailing form of architecture north of the Alps until the end of the fifteenth century, and buildings were still being built in this style in the twentieth century.

St. Denis set the norm for the west facade of French Gothic cathedrals with two towers, three sculptured portals, and a round window above the central entrance. Three other external characteristics of the developed Gothic style are easily observed in contrast to its Romanesque predecessor: pointed instead of rounded arches, cross-ribbed instead of groin vaults, and flying buttresses (first used in a Gothic cathedral at Notre Dame, Paris). All had been used before, and such stylistic and technical features, although characteristic, are less important than the overall conception of architectural space. Gothic represented an integrated, unified design in contrast to the modular design of a combination of parts in Romanesque. Two aspects of this coordinated effect that were without precedent are their proportions and their luminosity. The characteristic elements of Gothic were brought together in order to achieve soaring height and to open up space.

The Glory of the Western Medieval Church

The proportions may be seen both in horizontal and vertical dimensions. As in Romanesque architecture, the use of transepts gave to Western Gothic churches the shape of a T, the Latin cross. They were constructed in segments of three, each unit of equal size.

The choir on the east end was three units in length, the third unit intersected by the transepts, each one unit in length. The nave was six units long, ending at the west entrance. If "massive" is the word for Romanesque, "verticality" is the word for Gothic architecture, which seems to defy, or even reverse, gravity. The flying buttresses made possible higher and thinner walls. The verticality was emphasized by the use of spires instead of the squat towers of Romanesque buildings.

Since the walls were higher and thinner, much greater use became possible of windows, which had the appearance of transparent walls. Earlier architects had been concerned to protect interiors from sunlight, but Gothic architects opened up their buildings not only in space but also to light. Stained glass came into its own and after the mid-twelfth century replaced frescoes in the decoration of wall surfaces. Window glass with colored figures was a development of the medieval West.

Left to right:

Floor plan of the church of St. Sernin, Toulouse, Romanesque Pilgrimage Church, c. 1080 – 1120.

Floor plan of the Chartres cathedral in France, begun in 1145.

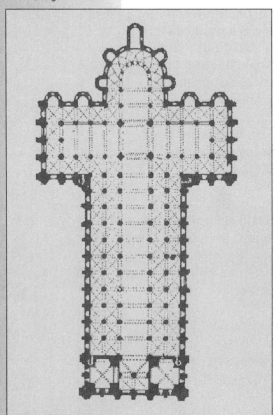

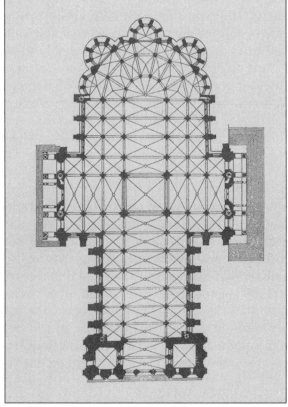

Stained glass refers to molten glass colored by the addition of metallic oxides, then hardened, cut into pieces, painted, and set into a design. Known by literary references from the ninth century, the craft was well established by the twelfth century. Subjects depicted in stained glass included Christological scenes, biblical history, and saints' lives. Glass was expensive, ranking with gold and silver in preciousness. Economic prosperity, therefore, and not a new interest in the theology of light, which was always present in the Christian tradition, made possible the stained-glass triumphs of the twelfth and thirteenth centuries, but the theology of light was invoked to justify the luminosity that stained glass made possible. As the glory of Christian art in the late antique and Byzantine periods was walls and domes covered with mosaics and in the Romanesque period was illuminated manuscripts, its glory in the high Middle Ages was stained glass. Stained glass achieved by the transmission of light the brightness and richness of color that mosaics did by reflection of light.

As Romanesque churches provided visual lessons in their wall paintings and column capitals depicting biblical and other historical scenes, so Gothic churches by their stained glass on the inside and sculpture on the outside provided narrative programs for instruction in the Christian faith. The sculptural decoration of the portals of the churches was designed to present coherent doctrinal messages. Under the arches of the church doorway the statues of apostles standing above statues of the prophets represented the church standing on the foundation of the Old Testament, and Christ in glory over the entrance way proclaimed that all must come under his authority before entering his house.

The Christ in glory or in judgment shown in the tympanum of Romanesque churches continued to be present in Gothic churches, but instead of an emphasis on the threat of damnation more space was given to the hope of salvation. The program was much enlarged: angels holding instruments of the passion, the Virgin Mary and St. John as intercessors, the angel Michael weighing souls, and the resurrection of the dead. The Lord in majesty began to be replaced or supplemented in French Gothic cathedrals of the late twelfth century by the coronation of the Virgin (seated beside Christ and receiving a crown from him) or the last judgment (with the saved and the lost separated on his right hand and left hand respectively). Indeed, Mary took an increasing prominence in sculpture, not only adorning portals, but also appearing in a huge number of statues of the Virgin and Child both inside and outside of churches. This supplementing of Christ as judge with scenes of Mary as queen of heaven and virgin mother has been interpreted as a shift from the potentially frightening concern with eschatological themes to an expression of a more forgiving aspect of the Virgin as intercessor. Other frequently appearing subjects in medieval sculpture are the apostles, prophets, angels, the wise and foolish virgins, and personifications of virtues and vices.

Besides the stone carving on the outside and occasionally on the inside of churches, wood carving found expression on the inside on choir screens, choir stalls, crucifixes, and free-standing statues of the Virgin. Churches were used for burial of prominent people. By the beginning of the thirteenth century the shallow effigies set into the floor of churches began to be replaced by figures in high relief resting on free standing tombs or recessed into niches.

The theme of the suffering Jesus had appeared in art as early as the eleventh century, but it now became more pronounced. The devotion to the humanity of Jesus found expression in the feast of Corpus Christi and in the elevation of the host (the bread as Christ the victim) at the eucharist, in new hymns to the Sacred Heart of Jesus, in devotion to the cross and the wounds of Jesus, and most clearly in art. This cult of the human Jesus has been related to the crusaders' interest in Jesus' homeland, but the attention to the body of the dying Christ was especially promoted by the concerns of the Franciscan Order.

This shift in the artistic and devotional tradition is evident in the way the crucifix began to change in the thirteenth century. Christ on the cross was no longer the draped and passionless figure "ruling from the cross" but was now shown more realistically as naked except for a

Two French ivories depicting Gothic representations of the crucifixion (early fourteenth and late fourteenth century respectively) (British Museum, London).

Stained-glass windows in Chartres cathedral, France.

loin cloth, legs crossed, in a twisted pose showing the writhing agony. The Romanesque royal Christ was being replaced by the Gothic "Man of Sorrows."

The relic preserved in Chartres cathedral was supposedly the tunic worn by Mary when she conceived Jesus. It was saved when the cathedral burned in 1194. Some of the twelfth-century stained glass was saved and incorporated into the new Gothic cathedral, which offers some of the finest of surviving medieval stained glass. The interior architecture remains uncluttered in contrast to many medieval churches so that it serves as a frame for the stained glass. The sculpture in the west facade of Chartres is also significant, having the same significance for Gothic sculpture as the choir of St. Denis had for Gothic architecture. Gothic sculpture began to move away from the stiff, frontal appearance of Romanesque sculpture to a refined naturalism with more nearly three-dimensional figures, the shape of whose bodies show under the drapery and whose head types are more individualized.

A striking example of proportion and luminosity on a smaller scale than the great cathedrals is the French royal chapel, Sainte-Chapelle, built between 1242 and 1248 by King Louis IX (chapter 24), who brought a building boom to Paris. Built to house Jesus' crown of thorns and a portion of the true cross that Louis IX obtained from the Latin emperor of Constantinople in 1204, Sainte-Chapelle is the quintessence of Gothic—in architecture, sculpture, and stained glass. Its upper chapel combines color, light, and perspective in a brilliant and spectacular way. The walls seem to disappear before the huge expanse of stained glass whose panels depict biblical scenes from Genesis to Revelation.

As soaring monuments to religious devotion, Gothic cathedrals still lift the spirits of visitors. On the other hand, they have the disadvantage of not being made for fellowship in worship.

VIII. SUMMARY

The thirteenth century witnessed some of the greatest accomplishments of medieval Western Christianity: the influence of the papacy, the growth of the friars as a new expression of monasticism, the development of universities as independent intellectual centers, great systems of thought in philosophy and theology, and splendid Gothic cathedrals as triumphs of piety and technical skill. Not all was a story of success, however, and there were at work other forces and movements that would bring about the dissolution of the medieval synthesis in the fourteenth and fifteenth centuries. To those other currents we now turn.

FOR FURTHER STUDY

Cross, R. *Duns Scotus*. New York: Oxford University Press, 1999.

Davies, Brian. *The Thought of Thomas Aquinas*. Oxford: Clarendon, 1992.

Erlande-Brandenburg, Alain. *Gothic Art*. New York: Abrams, 1989.

Hayes, Zachary. *The Hidden Center: Spirituality and Speculative Christology in St. Bonaventure*. New York: Paulist, 1981.

Kretzmann, N., and E. Stump, eds. *The Cambridge Companion to Aquinas*. Cambridge: Cambridge University Press, 1995.

Moorman, John. *A History of the Franciscan Order from Its Origins to the Year 1517*. Oxford: Clarendon, 1968.

Morris, Colin. *The Papal Monarchy: The Western Church from 1050 to 1250*. Oxford: Clarendon, 1989.

Pederson, Olaf. *The First Universities*. Cambridge: Cambridge University Press, 1997

Powell, James M., ed. *Innocent III: Vicar of Christ or Lord of the World*. 2nd ed. Washington: Catholic University of America Press, 1994.

Wilson, Christopher. *The Gothic Cathedral*. London: Thames and Hudson, 1990.

Wolf, K. B. *The Poverty of Riches: St. Francis of Assisi Reconsidered*. Oxford: Oxford University Press, 2003.

Portents of Decline

A ll periods of human history are marked by achievements and failures, and this was no less true of the thirteenth century. Although
the twelfth and thirteenth centuries registered many of the greatest
achievements of medieval Western Christianity, there were areas
where its goals were not achieved. Eight areas may be mentioned in
which there were serious deficiencies in the medieval synthesis.

I. LATE MEDIEVAL DISSENT: THE PROBLEM OF DIVISION

Reforms within the church had in a measure failed. The Cluniac
reform had imposed celibacy, and the result was widespread concubinage. Cluny had sponsored the Truce of God and the Peace of God, but
then came a holy war and disillusionment whether God had willed it.
The papal reform gave the church's direction to civil affairs, and the
outcome was crusades to drive the Normans out of Sicily and against
the Greek church.

Many thought that the time had come for reform from outside the
church. The church came to apply the reproach of "heresy" not only
to those doctrinally deviant, but also to those who did not conform or
submit to the hierarchical church. The Waldenses began as an effort
at reform from within, became schismatic, and were finally counted
as heretical. The Cathari or Albigensians continued (or revived) the
ancient heresy of dualism.

The church responded by turning the crusade against internal heretics and developing the Inquisition in order to identify and root out
heretics. These major movements had their predecessors and contemporaries, some of which found a place within the church and some
did not.

None of the eleventh-and-early-twelfth-century heresies included
someone of strong intellectual ability and academic training, and this
fact no doubt limited their chances of survival.

A. Samples of Earlier Heretical Teachers

Individual heretical teachers arose from time to time in the Middle Ages. Most of these are inadequately known from the reports of enemies and did not gain many followers.

An example is Henry the Monk in the early twelfth century. He started as a preacher of repentance and became a reformer of marriage, insisting that it was not a sacrament and that consent of the partners alone made a marriage. Under pressure from opposition and as a result of a fervent acceptance of the New Testament, Henry rejected the clergy, their sacraments, and the externals of religion. He denied the sacrifice of the mass, confession to priests, prayers for the dead, original sin (hence also infant baptism, which was to be replaced by baptism on personal responsibility), and the need for church buildings.

Peter de Bruys (of Bruis—d. c. 1140), active especially in southern France, was expelled from the priesthood. He too objected to the excessive materialization of religion: church buildings, the Mass as a sacrifice, prayers for the dead, veneration of crucifixes, the authority of the church, the Old Testament, the church fathers and traditions of the church, and infant baptism. He died when opponents threw him into a fire his supporters had built to burn crucifixes.

Different from these in his political involvements was Arnold of Brescia (d. 1155). He studied under Abelard and shared the latter's condemnation at Sens in 1140. Coming to Rome, he became incensed at the temporal involvements of the papacy and took a leading part in trying to set up a democratic republic. He advocated poverty for the church and denied the validity of sacraments administered by unworthy priests.

Arnold's rejection of the Donation of Constantine and belief that the emperor should receive his crown from the citizens of Rome, and not the pope, brought him for a time into the favor of the imperial party in the city. His program of reducing the church to purely spiritual matters ultimately did not fit the plans of either emperors or popes. Eugene III excommunicated Arnold in 1148. A treaty between Frederick Barbarossa and Pope Eugenius III in 1153 led to his arrest, his eventual hanging, and the suppression of his republic in 1155.

B. Poverty and Penitential Movements

The Gregorian reform had emphasized the importance of worthy priests to carry out religious functions. Recognizing that worthiness and office often did not coincide, some began to regard the instructions of the Gospels and apostles as more important than ecclesiastical office in authorizing a person to preach and minister.

A new spirituality, based not on contemplative withdrawal as in traditional monasticism, but instead based on conformity to the earthly ministry of Jesus Christ, arose. The emphasis in this new spirituality was on the humanity of Jesus rather than on the divine King of heaven. The two concepts of voluntary Christian poverty and itinerant evangelical preaching came to be regarded as the essence of Christianity. This ideal of the "apostolic life" (*vita apostolica*) gave rise to movements in addition to the Mendicant religious orders (chapter 23).

The leaders of these movements—Humiliati, Waldensians, Beguines—as well as of the Mendicants, did not come from the lower economic orders but represented a religious response to new social, economic, and cultural conditions.

The Humiliati emerged in Lombardy, northern Italy, in the late twelfth century. They aimed at a purer moral life and wore clothing of undyed wool to express their humility. They were included in condemnations of all unlicensed preaching at the Third Lateran Council under Pope Alexander III (1179) and more comprehensively at the Council of Verona under Pope Lucius III (1184).

The condemnations at Verona concerned not heretical dogmas but secret meetings, opposition to taking oaths, and preaching without permission. Three types of Humiliati are recognizable: those who followed a religious life while living in their own homes; celibate laity (men and women) living in community; and clerics (canons and canonesses) living in double monasteries.

In 1201 the papacy of Innocent III approved a rule for the Humiliati that included permission for preaching on moral and penitential subjects in their communities, but not on articles of faith, thus making a distinction between private exhortation and public preaching.

Confraternities of devotion, notably those promoting devotion to the Virgin and made up of lay men and women, preceded the Third Orders of the Mendicants. These lay confraternities emphasized charitable activities, whereas the Mendicants increasingly gave attention to the spiritual and mystical aspects of the religious life.

Indicative of the religious spirit of the times was the Order of Penitents, who borrowed from the Humiliati and Beguines. Their manner of life, which appeared in the late twelfth century, is described in a document of about 1215: They wore a robe made out of poor and undyed fabric, fasted more frequently than others, recited the seven canonical prayers daily, made confession and took communion three times a year, and refused the shedding of blood and taking of oaths.

The penitential spirit found its most extreme expression in the Flagellants. They emerged in the later thirteenth century under the influence of the eschatological excitement associated with the teachings of

Joachim of Fiore, but became better known in the fourteenth century. Taking public a form of private penitence sometimes practiced in the monasteries, the Flagellants beat themselves until the blood flowed in the belief that physical suffering was redemptive.

The penitential ideal was exemplified in Margaret of Cortona (d. 1297), who placed herself under the spiritual direction of the Franciscans. Her extreme mortifications included fasting, flagellating herself, and sleeping on the bare ground with a stone for a pillow. Her Franciscan spiritual director wrote her biography, attributing her ecstasies and visions concerning the Passion of Jesus Christ to the merits she acquired through penitence.

The "Brothers and Sisters of the Free Spirit" apparently drew on the philosophical teachings of John Scotus Eriugena and the mysticism of Beguines and Beghards. Their monistic pantheism led to the conclusion of a direct identification with God that released them from the moral law. Charges of sexual immorality inevitably followed these premises. They likely did not form an organized sect, and the little that is known of them comes from opponents. Indeed, there are grounds for the suspicion that such a movement did not really exist, but was invented by heresy hunters to characterize certain individual mystics.

Women took a prominent place in promoting a life of voluntary poverty and penitential asceticism centering on the sufferings of Christ, and some of these were condemned for heresy.

C. Waldenses

Peter Waldo (better Valdes) was a rich merchant in Lyons. About 1173 he provided an income for his wife and separated from her, placed his daughters in a convent, and distributed his property among the poor in order to begin an itinerant life of preaching.

His movement came to emphasize three principal points: a life of voluntary poverty, access to the Bible in the vernacular, and public preaching. He and his followers sought recognition at the Third Lateran Council (1179). Their way of life was approved, but they were forbidden to preach except by invitation of the clergy.

Valdes and his "Poor Men of Lyons" disregarded this restriction and preached against the worldliness of the clergy. Hence, a council at Verona in 1184 included them with the Cathari in an excommunication. Some returned to the church as the "Catholic Poor," pursuing the same activities as before. Others, although doctrinally orthodox and even (especially in France) attending Mass and keeping a formal connection with the Roman Catholic church, organized themselves apart from the church and appointed their own ministers.

Waldenses in Lombardy came to the Donatist position of doubting the validity of sacraments administered by unworthy priests and so took a position of greater separation from the Catholic church than did the French branch of the movement. A split between them occurred in 1205, and a conference at Bergamo in 1218 failed to heal it.

Valdes was a generation ahead of the Mendicants, who began with a similar program of poverty and itinerant preaching. If the treatment had been reversed, Valdes might now be the saint and Francis the heretic. The difference was that Francis remained submissive to the church, receiving ordination as a deacon, whereas Valdes championed lay preaching as a mandate of the gospel, even without church authorization. Valdes died in the early thirteenth century, but his movement grew.

The Waldenses had the Gospels translated into the vernacular. Rejecting only the practices they saw as clearly against Scripture, they opposed especially prayers for the dead, purgatory, images, and veneration of saints and relics. Their concern to live by the Sermon on the Mount led them to refuse oaths and any form of killing. Catholic sources attributed to them asceticism, millennialism, and spirit-possession, but such may have been less generally held.

The Waldenses survived sometimes severe persecution in less accessible Alpine valleys and in 1532 began an accommodation with the Genevan reformers. They are the only Medieval sect to have a documented continuity to the present.

D. Cathari or Albigensians

The Cathari, or Cathars ("the pure ones"), were known in France as Albigensians or Albigenses from the town of Albi in Languedoc, a center of their strength. They continued the dualism that reached back to the Manichaeans (the Cathari were regularly called "Manichees") and was transmitted to Europe by the Bogomils (named for a Bulgarian priest), active in the Balkans from the eighth century.

Traces of dualist teaching appeared again in the Balkans and Turkey in the eleventh century, and it found a receptive hearing from some devoted to a rigorist morality in France and northern Italy by the twelfth century. The organized sect of the Cathari became particularly vigorous in the twelfth and thirteenth centuries with some original documents surviving from the thirteenth century. Catharism was the strongest heresy faced by the Catholic church in the thirteenth century, but it disappeared in the fourteenth.

The charge of dualism was leveled against many to whom it did not apply, so it is difficult now to disentangle all the different threads of "heresy." Not all the Cathari gave prominence to this philosophical view, some adhering to a moderate and others a more radical dualism, and their popular appeal came more from a good manner of life than from their explanation of the origin of evil.

Nevertheless, the charge of dualism was correct in regard to the basic position of the Cathari. According to their dualism of spirit and matter, the Cathari condemned the flesh and material creation as evil. This entailed a rejection of marriage and procreation, of animal products for food, and of anything material in worship.

The *perfecti* ("perfect" members) lived up to the rigid asceticism and from them the clergy were drawn. The one sacrament of the group, which made a person one of the perfect, was the *consolamentum*, a baptism of the Holy Spirit conferred by the laying on of hands. The *credentes* ("believers") lived ordinary lives but could receive the *consolamentum* as they approached death.

The austerity of the lives of the Cathari contrasted with the laxity of the Catholic clergy and commended them to the people. Their rejection of doctrines like hell and purgatory and practices like infant baptism led to the confusion of other protest movements with them and the application of the term Cathari to all regarded by the Catholic church as heretics.

Catharism failed before Catholicism because it could not give an adequate explanation of the whole of Scripture, and its assurance of salvation was to an exclusive few.

Other factors in the triumph of Catholicism included the attractiveness of a human Jesus Christ and of a positive view of creation and nature, increased education, the effectiveness of the friars as preachers and confessors, the higher level of orthodox piety, and the development of the third orders and lay confraternities as outlets for lay piety.

Principally, however, the challenge of Catharism was put down by coercion—the force of arms and threat of punishment.

E. Crusade and Inquisition

Innocent III's first efforts at converting the heretics by preaching and debates met with little success. He then approved a crusade against the Albigenses that lasted from 1209 to 1229. The crusade, led first by Simon de Montfort and then King Louis VIII of France, soon turned political. The counts of Toulouse (Raymond VI and then VII) were targeted, and the struggle resulted in the incorporation of Languedoc into the kingdom of France. The crusade crushed the heresy but also devastated southern France.

The Inquisition was an ecclesiastical institution to search out heretics and bring them to punishment. Punishment was based on the

Exterior of the Roman-
esque church of St.
Sernin in Toulouse.

laws of Christian emperors in antiquity who—in spite of the church's general teaching against the use of physical force—sometimes punished heretics with death, since heresy was considered the equivalent of witchcraft. Innocent III issued a decretal in 1199 that for the first time equated heresy with the crime of treason under Roman law.

In the late twelfth century bishops were expected to make legal inquiry of heretics in their dioceses and hand these over to the secular authorities for punishment. The Fourth Lateran Council (1215) confirmed these regulations and threatened excommunication of temporal rulers who failed to rid their territory of heresy.

The Council of Toulouse in 1229 at the close of the Albigensian War drew up the procedures to be followed in seeking out and punishing heresy. The inquisitorial procedure replaced the accusatorial in seeking out heretics. The essence of the *inquisitio* procedure was that instead of an accuser bringing a public accusation, the judge himself made an inquiry by presenting the charges against a defendant. The action was intended to be started by public opinion.

Pope Gregory IX in 1231 approved Emperor Frederick II's introduction of the penalty of burning to death, on the basis that heresy was equivalent to treason. In 1233 he appointed papal inquisitors, primarily Dominicans, to work in southern France. The papal inquisition made the episcopal inquisition of secondary significance. Inquisitorial handbooks were written to guide inquisitors in their questioning of suspects.

Pope Innocent IV in 1252 gave approval to use of the rack in the examination as a way of securing confessions. It was now accepted as

> ### A Two-Edged Sword
>
> When the city of Beziers was being besieged, Arnold, abbot of Cite-aux and leader of the crusade, was asked by the soldiers how they could tell the Catholics from the heretics. He replied, "Kill them all, for God will know his own."

official policy that force had precedence over preaching and peaceful persuasion in dealing with heresy.

The defects in the Inquisition are obvious from a modern legal standpoint. The charges and the names of accusers and witnesses were kept secret. Wide powers of arrest and imprisonment were granted. No witnesses were called for the defense, nor was there counsel for the defense. Torture was used. The death penalty was brutally applied.

Zealous interrogation backed by force gained evidence to support accusations. The coercion implicit in a penal system blurred, if it did not overwhelm, the goal of healing and saving souls. However, according to legal practices of the time, the abuses were more with individuals and the way the Inquisition was carried out than with the system itself.

The popular religious movements of the twelfth and early thirteenth centuries and the rise of a vernacular religious literature (below) provide the context in which the regional Council of Toulouse in 1229 banned all use of biblical texts by the laity, even in Latin.

F. Philosophical Error

The concern about heresy also posed a problem in intellectual circles. In 1277 the bishop of Paris, Stephen Tempier, issued a condemnation of 219 philosophical and theological propositions that he associated with some masters in the faculty of arts at the university.

The preface to the condemned propositions accused certain teachers with holding to a theory of "double truth," by which some ideas were said to be "true according to philosophy, but not according to the Catholic faith." The position and its description is probably a conclusion drawn by the bishop and other opponents of the censured faculty members rather than something explicitly held by anyone.

Sixty-eight of the 219 propositions cannot be found in any contemporary author. The problem was that certain teachers opted to expound Aristotle by his own internal logic rather than to seek an integration of his views with the Christian faith. It is common to argue with the implications one sees in a rejected viewpoint rather than with what its defenders actually say.

II. WOMEN'S SPIRITUALITY: THE PROBLEM OF COMPREHENSIVENESS

The percentage of women canonized or considered for canonization as saints increased significantly in the thirteenth to fifteen centuries, but most of the lay women who achieved sainthood came from royalty or the aristocracy.

A notable example is Elizabeth of Hungary and Thuringia (1207–31), who married Ludwig IV, Landgrave of Thuringia, in 1221. After her husband's death in 1227, she settled in Marburg and took the robe of a penitent. Always characterized by a keen sense of justice and a refusal to compromise with manifestations of evil, she gave herself in humility to charitable service to the sick and poor.

The new religious orders of the twelfth and thirteenth centuries developed female branches, such as the Cistercian and Carthusian nuns, Premonstratensian canonesses, and the second orders of the Dominicans and Franciscans. Large numbers of these female houses came into existence. The male religious orders initially resisted assuming their oversight on the grounds that this responsibility took them away from their primary calling, but with the help of the papal curia these female houses were incorporated into the Mendicant orders.

The religious experiences of many women, both those inside and those outside the church, shared certain features: asceticism, paranormal phenomena, and visionary experiences. These features gave to women, however much some were dependent on male associates for guidance, a religious authority normally denied to them in medieval culture. The institutional church, however, had difficulty coming to terms with these experiences and with finding ways to incorporate women's spirituality into its corporate life. For all the comprehensiveness of Scholastic theology and mysticism, there were limits that some mystics, especially women, transgressed.

The Beguines, who were centered in the Low Countries, may be taken as representative of the women who sought new expressions in their religious life. Beginning in the twelfth century, they made their presence most felt in the thirteenth and fourteenth centuries. For them, women took the lead in practicing an "apostolic" lifestyle. Their male counterparts, the Beghards (both terms, however, were sometimes loosely used of both men and women), were not so numerous.

The Beguines formed an intermediate style of religious life — adopting celibacy but not taking a lifetime vow and retaining the use of private property. Some lived in communities and supported themselves by handicrafts, but some wandered about and lived off alms, giving the way of life a bad reputation.

In several instances, free associations of women living in the "beguine style" evolved into independent religious houses that were then incorporated into the Dominican order, which after 1245 more readily received women's communities under its umbrella.

Condemnations of the Beguines and Beghards at the Council of Vienne, 1311–14, marked a turn of official attitude against lay women and men who sought to live a religious life while remaining in the world.

In the thirteenth century there became evident a third form of medieval theology: in addition to monastic theology (as represented, for instance, by Bernard of Clairvaux) and Scholastic theology (as in Thomas Aquinas and Duns Scotus), there emerged a vernacular theology. All would have agreed that the goal of theology is the love of God, but in the vernacular theology the relationship shifts away from the intellect to experience. This would climax in fourteenth-century mysticism.

Of special importance for vernacular theology were accounts of visions, and the distinctive contribution of vernacular theology was in the area of mysticism. Earlier Western mystical authors had described the union with God as a loving union of wills. In the thirteenth century, and first among the women vernacular theologians, the mystical union was described as a "union without difference," in which there is an annihilation of the will so that one can "live without a why." This formulation was quite problematic for orthodox theologians.

Vernacular theological literature—in the form of tracts, poetry, reports of experiences, and letters—had among its first representatives women spiritual writers. Among the new religious movements, and especially among women in the Dominican order that placed such a stress on theological training, there arose persons who wanted to read and write religious works, but who did not know Latin.

Beguine spirituality produced some of the earliest theological writing in the emerging vernacular tongues of Europe. Writers included Hadewijch from Flanders (thirteenth century but dates uncertain), whose writings, drawing on the rhetoric of courtly love, focus on bridal mysticism; Mechthild of Magdeburg (c. 1207–1282); and Margaret Porette, whose *Mirror of Simple Souls* is now recognized as a profound work of speculative mysticism. They represent the mystical context in which Meister Eckhart (c. 1260–c. 1328) developed his teaching. The organized church never quite knew how to treat these women, both because of their being women and because their teaching was questionable. Margaret of Porette was burned at the stake for heresy in 1310.

One of the learned women visionaries was Gertrude the Great (1256–1301/2) of the convent at Helfta. Never formally canonized, she was popularly regarded as a saint. Gertrude composed prayers (*Spiritual Exercises*) to guide the devotions of her sister nuns. She also recorded her visions of Jesus Christ and Mary, collected after her death in the *Herald of Divine Love*. She often had visions of the heart of Christ, making her an early advocate of devotion to the Sacred Heart of Jesus.

Of special interest at a time when devotion to Mary was so strong is Gertrude's concern that veneration was being given to Mary that properly belonged to Jesus Christ, who, possessing maternal as well as masculine characteristics, left no need for a feminine expression of deity. However, Gertrude viewed Mary, the Virgin Mother, as seated beside Christ, and she even asked Christ to intercede for her with Mary, whom she felt was displeased with her for directing devotion to Christ alone.

III. THE JEWS: A PROBLEM OF TOLERATION

Jews in western Europe had been subject to various restrictions since the conversion of the empire, especially in regard to proselytizing by them, but their situation greatly worsened in the eleventh century, and negative attitudes toward Jews were intensified by sentiments associated with the crusading movement.

The atmosphere was shown by extensive violence against Jews in western Europe already in 1010, apparently related to rumors that Jews had conspired with the caliph Al-Hakim, who destroyed the Holy Sepulcher in Jerusalem in 1009. The Crusades themselves marked a turn from co-existence to active animosity in attitudes of Christians toward Jews, with the result that pogroms against the Jews occurred in several places in connection with the Crusades.

Many slanders against the Jews circulated. For instance, some believed that Jews ritually commemorated the crucifixion of Jesus by kidnapping Christian children and killing them. Others accepted the charge that the Talmud and other Jewish literature were full of blasphemies against the Christian religion.

Various official actions were taken against the Jews. The French king Philip II Augustus expelled Jews from his royal domains in 1182, but in 1198 allowed them to return. They were expelled from France again by Philip IV in 1306. The Fourth Lateran Council (1215) under Pope Innocent III required Jews and Muslims to wear distinctive clothing, forbade Jews to be seen in public on Christian fast days and to charge excessive interest on loans (but allowed them to continue as moneylenders, a practice forbidden to Christians), and renewed prohibitions on their holding public office, blaspheming Christ, and making converts. Pope Innocent IV in 1244 wrote to the king of France in support of the doctors of theology in Paris, who ordered the burning of the Hebrew Talmud.

Nevertheless, not all attitudes were negative. An interest in Jewish exegesis of the Bible was shown in various periods—by Alcuin, Stephen Harding, the Victorines, and Nicholas Lyra. The popes fairly consistently resisted severe persecution of the Jews.

IV. THE COUNCIL OF LYONS (1274): THE PROBLEM OF RELATIONS WITH THE EAST

A. Leading Figures of the Time

In the background of subsequent events was the figure of King Louis IX of France (1226–70), the embodiment of the highest ideas of medieval kingship and the last crusading king. Louis IX captured the Egyptian port of Damietta in 1249, but lost it the following year and had to pay ransom for the release of himself and his men. Proceeding to Syria, he strengthened the fortifications still in Christian hands before returning to France.

Pious in his personal life, Louis IX worked for justice in the administration of France. He is responsible for one of the great triumphs of medieval art and architecture, the royal chapel of Sainte-Chapelle in Paris (chapter 23). Having embarked on a further crusade, Louis IX died in Tunis.

Louis IX's brother, Charles of Anjou (1226–85), who may be considered the first modern "imperialist," attempted to use the crusading impulse for his own political ends. An ambitious and sometimes cruel but able ruler, he came to govern Anjou, Provence, and the Kingdom of Naples and Sicily.

Moreover, as a direct vassal of the pope and overlord of Albania, Charles of Anjou converted the idea of empire into imperialism. The Byzantine idea of empire involved a definite boundary in succession to the old Roman Empire. In the West the empire was as much a theory, indeed a theological-legal concept, as it was a geographical entity. Indeed it had no embodiment from 1250 to 1273, for there was no emperor in Germany. The papacy initially favored Charles as a counter to the German empire and maintained support for him against opponents to his rule in Sicily at the end of his career.

Charles of Anjou had a claim to the Latin kingdom in the East, and to forestall his ambitions, the eastern emperor Michael Palaeologus favored a general council and reunion of the Greek church with the papacy. Michael had retaken Constantinople for the Greeks in 1261 and founded the dynasty of the Palaeologi that ruled over the now small Byzantine empire (mainly the region around Constantinople and the Peloponnesus) until 1453. He entered into negotiations with the West as early as 1263.

Michael stressed spiritual motives for union: He was willing to accept the *filioque* clause, but asked that the Greeks not have to alter the creed so as not to destroy the rhythm when it was sung. He was also willing to accept the supremacy of the pope by having his name first in the liturgy and by recognizing his appellate jurisdiction. Michael hoped that by winning the support of the papacy, he could hold back Charles of Anjou.

Pope Gregory X (1271–76) had accompanied Prince Edward of England (soon to become King Edward I) on crusade in connection with Louis IX's Seventh Crusade after the sultan of Egypt had taken much of Palestine. He was elected pope while he was in Palestine after a three-year vacancy in the papal office. Gregory X was interested in church reform (problems were concubinage and the holding of multiple church offices with the consequent absenteeism), in the deliverance of Jerusalem, in union with the Greeks, and in settlement of the question of the German emperor. These concerns came together in the Second Council of Lyons, 1274.

Exterior of the cathedral in Lyons, site of the Fourteenth Ecumenical Council.

B. Proceedings at the Council

The council that met in 1274 at Lyons, a free city of the western empire, is counted by the West as the Fourteenth Ecumenical Council (the second at Lyons). The prime movers in the gathering of the council were Pope Gregory X (acting against the interests of his vassal Charles of Anjou) and Michael Palaeologus (acting against the deepest instincts of his people).

Indeed, what Gregory seemed not to realize was that attitudes in the East toward the West were too hardened for the eastern emperor to be in a position to impose a union in matters of faith on his church, although he was able to persuade a significant delegation to attend the council. Thomas Aquinas wrote *Against the Errors of the Greeks* to be used as a basis of theological discussion at the council. On Thomas's death, Bonaventure took his place at the council and was made a cardinal by Gregory X.

Among the noteworthy events associated with the council was the papal approval of Rudolf of Hapsburg over Alfonso of Castile as German emperor. Rudolf founded the Hapsburg dynasty that ruled until 1918 (in Austria), succeeding the Hohenstaufen dynasty of German emperors that ruled from 1138 to 1254.

The high point of the council was the reunion with the Greek church, already agreed to in principle, celebrated by the singing of the creed in Greek and in Latin. Significant for the future was that Avignon was ceded to the papacy.

Among the decrees of the council was the requirement that a pope be elected by the cardinals locked in one room and put on dwindling rations after three days and deprived of their revenues until a decision was reached. These stern conditions were to prevent another three-year vacancy in the papacy.

C. Aftermath of the Council

Plans for a crusade occupied much attention at the council, but it never materialized, the idea dying with Gregory X. With the fall of Acre in 1291 to the Mameluke Turks, who ruled in Egypt, the last Christian holding in the Holy Land was back in the possession of the Muslims. People in western Europe continued to talk about crusades to the Holy Land for over two hundred more years, but nothing came of the talk. The union of the Latin and Greek churches did not last. Indeed it died before Michael Palaeologus did, for he was excommunicated by the pope in 1281. The "Sicilian Vespers," a revolt in 1282 against Charles of Anjou's rule in Sicily, ended his political ambitions.

The council that seemed to promise so much in reforming and reuniting the church and reinvigorating the Crusades failed to realize these goals and ultimately had little effect on the course of events.

V. CHRISTIANITY ON THE FRONTIERS: PROBLEMS OF MISSIONS

Syriac Christianity declined in the tenth to twelfth centuries. As one writer lamented, "The monks were no longer missionaries." Education increased among the Muslims so that they were less dependent on their educated Christian subjects, and under the influence of non-Arab elements in the government Muslim rulers became less tolerant.

The use of Syriac, except in the liturgy, declined among the east Syrians (Church of the East) in the tenth century and virtually ceased in the thirteenth. A revival of Syriac Christian literature occurred in the twelfth and thirteenth centuries among the west Syrian Jacobites.

Illustrious names of authors who preserved much of previous history and learning included Dionysius bar Salibi (d. 1171), who wrote a massive commentary on the entire Bible; Michael the Syrian (1126–99), whose *Chronicle* recorded world history to 1195; and Bar Hebraeus (1226–86), greatest of all with a synthesis of Jacobite theology, notes on the Bible, histories, and a summary of canon law. Thereafter Syriac waned before Arabic until it became mainly a liturgical language.

Meanwhile, during the thirteenth century the Church of the East experienced another period of geographical expansion into central Asia, positioning itself for political influence at a crucial period for Asian and world history.

During the thirteenth century another wave of invaders (after the Turks) from central Asia made their presence felt—the Mongols (or Tartars) led by Genghis Khan (1167–1227) and his successors. Their sweep west reached Poland and Hungary temporarily (1241), but Russia fell under control of the Mongols until the fifteenth century. Only the region around Novgorod maintained a semblance of independence and became a center of renewal in the Russian church.

Alexander Nevsky became a national hero by defeating Swedish and other western invaders and negotiating lower tribute payments to the Mongols. The Mongol rule meant Russia developed in isolation from the West and was responsible for moving the center of Russian government and civilization from Kiev north to Moscow. The Orthodox church gave a sense of national unity to the Russian people during this time of foreign rule, as it did later to the Greeks under Turkish rule.

History is the story not only of accomplishments and failures, but also of missed opportunities. Marco Polo's account of his travels to the East (late thirteenth century) makes frequent reference to encountering Jacobite and Nestorian Christians along the way. They had already made the Turkic and Mongol rulers familiar with the Christian faith. Nestorian merchants had begun the conversion of the Keraits, a Turko-Mongol tribe, in the eleventh century. After overrunning them, Genghis Khan took the Christian princess Sorkaktani as the wife for one of his sons.

Sorkaktani became the mother of three emperors: Mongke, Great Khan of Mongolia; Hülegü, Ilkhan of Persia; and Kublai Khan, emperor of China. Hülegü married a daughter of the East Roman emperor, favored the Dyophysite ("Nestorian") Christians, and sought an alliance with the West, sending representatives to the Council of Lyons in 1274. His successors, however, brought Persia back into the Muslim fold by the end of the century.

Kublai Khan, a shamanist who favored Buddhism (contrary to Marco Polo's wishful thinking) but tolerant of all religions, moved his capital to the city now known as Beijing. When Nicolo and Maffeo Polo (father and uncle of Marco Polo) returned from Kublai's capital in 1269, they carried a message from him asking the pope to send a hundred teachers of the Christian religion.

In response to Kublai's request, Pope Gregory X sent two Dominicans, who turned back when they met warfare in Armenia. A Franciscan, John of Montecorvino in Italy, arrived in China in 1294, the year of Kublai Khan's death, and later a few other Franciscans followed him; but they were too little too late, and besides they failed to reach the native Chinese.

The death of Kublai Khan in 1294 and the conversion of the Ilkhan Ghazan of Persia to Islam in 1295 signaled the beginning of the collapse of the Church of the East after the great promise of the thirteenth century. By the mid-fourteenth century all the Mongol khanates had converted to Islam.

Tamerlane (1336–1405), another descendant of Ghengis Khan, led a new wave of invasions by the Mongol Turks that overran central and western Asia. Although a Muslim, he spared neither Muslims nor Christians. His conquests virtually obliterated the missions of the east Syrians and began the long decline of the Church of the East.

Military suppression alone did not explain the ultimate disappearance of this church from central Asia. The use of Syriac in the liturgy gave a sense of being a foreign religion. Education declined. Evangelistic fervor was lost. The members and their leaders accommodated to their rulers' standards of worldly success.

The story was more favorable in some other countries. Ethiopia in the thirteenth century emerged from a period of some six centuries for which there exists virtually no Ethiopian documentation. During that time a synthesis formed of the early Axumite and biblical traditions with the native African traditions. The establishment (or restoration in Ethiopian terms) of the Solomonic dynasty in 1270 coincided with the beginning of a golden age of Ethiopian literature and art, brought to an end by a destructive Turkish invasion in the sixteenth century.

In the Ethiopian church imitation was the process by which sites and buildings were endowed with a special sanctity. For instance, a consecrated altar was considered a symbol of the Old Testament ark of the covenant. Church and state in Ethiopia were closely intertwined, for the monarch (a presumed descendant of Solomon and so related to Jesus Christ) provided the church with large grants of land and other resources and was himself virtually the head of the church in many of its affairs.

During the twelfth and thirteenth centuries there circulated in western Europe the legend of Prester John, a powerful Christian ruler in Asia, given some credence by the presence of Christians among the Mongols. Failure to locate such a ruler led to the conclusion that this imaginary ruler was none other than the Christian emperor of Ethiopia, whose existence was well attested.

An important western proponent of missions to Muslims and Jews was Raymond Lull (Ramon Llull—c. 1233–c. 1315). Born in Majorca off the coast of Spain not long after it was freed from Muslim rule, he became a mystic and a poet in Latin and his native Catalan.

Having studied Arabic and joined the Third Order of Franciscans, Raymond advocated converting Muslims by preaching and martyrdom rather than by force of arms. He promoted the study of eastern languages in universities and the use of rational arguments to convert non-Christians. Missionaries should learn the languages of unbelievers and should also bring some of them to the West to learn Latin.

His mission trips to North Africa and elsewhere were unsuccessful, but his efforts did encourage the study of Arabic and other eastern languages by Western Christians.

VI. WORSHIP AND PASTORAL CARE: A PROBLEM IN THE RELIGIOUS LIFE

The traditional methods of the church were ineffectively utilized to communicate the Christian gospel and Scriptures and to include the people in worship. There was a general failure of catechetical and pastoral care that became more pronounced in the later Middle Ages.

The success of the Mendicants was in part a response to the failures of the secular clergy. The liturgy continued in Latin, which by the high Middle Ages was less and less understood by the ordinary people as the vernacular languages of Europe were developing into their modern European counterparts. Hence the religious expressions of the people were primarily ritual acts and gestures.

Attendance at the celebration of the Mass did not involve communion—the requirement by the Fourth Lateran Council (1215) of confession and communion once a year was intended as an improvement. The Mass was a ritual celebrated for the people rather than with the people. Those who could afford to do so set up endowments to support a priest to say frequent Masses for the benefit of their souls. The sacrifice of the Mass was an objective event that "took place"—it was effective whether anyone other than the priest was present or not.

One can tell much about concerns of an age by its hortatory literature: in the third century, exhortations to martyrdom; in the fourth century, exhortations to baptism for those delaying its reception; in the thirteenth century most of the sermons that survive, many delivered during Lent, are exhortations to make confession. Little preaching in fact had come to be done in church, so the Mendicant orders' preaching activity was a refreshing revival of preaching.

The merit of St. Yves (1253–1303) in Brittany, the only parish priest to be canonized in the Middle Ages, was his foregoing the opportunity for ecclesiastical advancement in order to care for the souls of the peasants of Brittany. (His compassion was the exception. A thirteenth-century chronicler recorded that the peasants in Alsace did not object to their priests having concubines, for in such circumstances there was less concern for the virtue of their daughters.)

Other efforts were made both inside and outside the liturgy to teach Christian lessons to the people. There are examples of dramatized liturgy, a forerunner of liturgical drama, as early as the tenth century. Christian drama began in a liturgical context with the elaboration of the Easter and Christmas stories. Manuscripts of developed musical liturgical dramas exist from the thirteenth century.

The main use of drama occurred in a non-liturgical context. Miracle plays became especially popular in the thirteenth and fourteenth centuries. Two main types of dramatization were of miracles performed by Mary in response to prayers and of episodes from the life of a saint involving a miracle. Morality plays involving allegorical depictions of personified virtues and vices belong to the fourteenth and fifteenth centuries. The term "mystery plays" (for reenactments of biblical history or lives of the saints) was in use in the fifteenth and sixteenth centuries. The earliest complete Passion play comes from the end of the thirteenth century.

The interest in the saints as models of the Christian life remained high, and on the positive side, many people honored their virtues (chapter 23 on the *Golden Legend*).

VII. ESCHATOLOGY AND FANATICISM: A PROBLEM OF HOPE

In spite of modern presumptions that "millennarian" thought would have been strong around the year 1000, it is noteworthy that it was stronger in the thirteenth than in the eleventh or twelfth centuries.

Joachim of Fiore (d. 1202), abbot of a Cistercian monastery in Calabria (southern Italy), found his Trinitarian views condemned at the Fourth Lateran council, but he submitted to the papacy. Of more consequence was his Trinitarian periodization of history, which fueled eschatological expectations.

The first age, the age of the Father, was the period of marriage under the Law of Moses; the second age, the age of the Son, was the period of the clergy under grace that was to last 1,260 years; the third age, the age of the Spirit, will be the age of the monks, who having the mind of the Spirit would live in liberty without the mediation of the church.

Joachim himself was not so much concerned with chronology as his later followers were. He described the three periods by a word, *status*, that did not have temporal connotations, but rather meant "condition" or "constitutional order." Hence, there was an overlapping in time of the three divine arrangements. Joachim's three conditions or circumstances of God's regimen for human society reflected three central concerns: the interpretation of Scripture, the mystery of the Trinity, and the meaning of history. The last age would see the rise of new religious orders that would convert the world and usher in the church of the Spirit.

Such a scheme could be seen as a note of optimism—a perfect age was dawning—or as pessimism about the existing institutional church. The latter was the interpretation given his thought by the spiritual Franciscans (chapter 23), who saw themselves as such a new order and Francis as the herald of the new age. One of these rigorist Franciscans, Peter John Olivi (c. 1248–98), used these ideas in his commentary on Revelation, condemned in 1326 by Pope John XXII. Although Olivi never identified the carnal church—the whore of Babylon—with the Roman church, others did.

Olivi is significant for another reason, for he advocated the doctrine of papal infallibility. There was a tradition of affirming inerrancy in regard to faith and morals for the universal church and in particular the Roman church. The canon lawyers of the twelfth century who championed the sovereignty of the pope, however, had not drawn the conclusion of personal infallibility, because, if the decrees of previous popes were not reformable, this would limit the absolute authority and freedom of the present pope. But this was precisely what Olivi wanted to do.

Pope Nicholas III in 1279 decreed the observance of the rule of evangelical poverty for the Franciscan order, allowing the use but not ownership of property. Olivi did not want this ruling reversed, although he himself went further in arguing that the use should be that by a pauper. He personalized and gave a polemical edge to the claim of inerrancy for the pope.

For some time the doctrine of papal inerrancy was promoted only by the radical Franciscans and the papacy took no interest in it (Pope John XXII even condemned it as a "pernicious novelty"). Guido Terreni integrated the idea into medieval ecclesiology: The universal church required a supreme teaching authority (the papacy), and such teaching authority required the counsel and consent of the universal church.

The leader of the Spiritual Franciscans after Olivi's death, Ubertino da Casale, branded Pope Boniface VIII as the beast of Revelation, the "mystical Antichrist." The identification of the pope with the Antichrist has its origin in the thirteenth century. On the other hand, there were expectations of an "Angelic Pope" who would come to restore the church to its pristine condition before the end of time.

In circles influenced by Joachim, Olivi, and the Spiritual Franciscans, as well as by the Waldensians, there emerged during the twelfth to fourteenth centuries the idea that the church had fallen into corruption and that there was a need to restore apostolic faith and practice. Such a conviction was to become a significant ingredient in the reformatory movements of the fifteenth and sixteenth centuries.

VIII. BONIFACE VIII (1294–1303): THE PROBLEM OF THE NATIONAL MONARCHIES

The success of Innocent III's successors was not so much due to the papacy winning acceptance for its theory of the empire as its ability to enlist the support of national monarchies outside the empire. These kingdoms, especially of France and England, used the conflict of the empire and the papacy to bring about a shift in the balance of power detrimental to both, especially in the second half of the thirteenth century.

The paradox of the late thirteenth and early fourteenth century is that the papacy's opposition to the "universal" empire led to the decline of the "universal" papacy. The papacy favored the French monarchy at the expense of the German empire, but with the result that it fell itself under the influence of the French crown. The principal political antagonists of the papacy became the new national monarchies. Those monarchies, having more internal cohesiveness and greater loyalty of their citizens, achieved a success in their struggles with the papacy that the empire seldom enjoyed.

A. Boniface's Predecessor, Celestine V

Celestine had been a Benedictine monk, but he retired into solitude. Many disciples of his ascetic life gathered around him, and he pled the cause of his mendicants before the Council of Lyons (1274). They were called Celestines from his papal name after his election as pope.

The Colonna and Orsini factions in the college of cardinals produced a stalemate in the papal election of 1294. In a pious move, Celestine was chosen as a compromise dark horse. He was about eighty, a spiritual man of no education and crude language. Celestine was hailed as the "Angel Pope," and there were great hopes that he would lead a spiritual reform of the church, bringing on the new spiritual age expected by the Spiritual Franciscans.

Charles II of Anjou now ruled only at Naples, but inherited some of his father's ambitions. He prevailed on Celestine to live at Naples and secured a controlling influence on the pope, who readily granted Charles's nominations for administrative posts. Celestine rapidly lost supporters and resigned before the end of the year. Dante would later put Celestine in the Inferno for his "great withdrawal," the refusal of piety to express itself in power.

B. Boniface VIII (1294–1303): "Pride Goes before a Fall"

Benedict of Gaetani had risen through service in the curia until he was elected pope. The very opposite of his predecessor, Boniface was strong-willed, shrewd, ambitious, an authority in canon law, but also not free of avarice and nepotism.

Two events associated with the year 1300 are notable for the future. Boniface VIII proclaimed the year a Jubilee, providing a plenary (full) indulgence for those who confessed their sins and made a pilgrimage to a basilica in Rome in that year or any succeeding one hundredth year.

Boniface VIII, gold-plated copper on wood by Manio Bandini of Sienna (early fourteenth century) (Museo Civico Medievale, Bologna, Italy).

One of the pilgrims in that year was Dante Aligheri (1265–1321), a magistrate from Florence, who became indignant at the pope and at the bazaar in spiritual goods he observed. Dante saw the Jubilee traffic as the worst form of simony, now extended in meaning to include all sale of spiritual goods.

As a result of his visit to Rome, Dante became anti-papal, and the events of 1300 became the basis of his views expressed in two books. The first book, *On Monarchy*, argued for a universal political rule to balance the papacy's spiritual rule. The second book, the *Divine Comedy*, is the most significant literary expression of the medieval Christian world view.

The theological basis of the *Divine Comedy* is mostly that of Thomas Aquinas, but Dante offers a poetic synthesis comparable to the scholastic and architectural syntheses of the thirteenth century. In the work, Virgil, the poet of the pagan Roman Empire, conducts Dante, poet and theorist of a Holy Roman Empire, through the *Inferno*. Dante became the publicist of Europe, and he applied the imagery of Revelation now not to persecuting pagan Rome but to the secularized Roman Church.

It was Boniface's political struggles, however, that held the immediate attention of his pontificate. National monarchs had now replaced the emperor as the principal antagonists of the church, and the national states succeeded where the empire had failed in asserting secular power over the church.

In England and France, the clergy were being taxed and often fleeced to support the wars of these monarchs. Boniface in 1296 issued the bull *Clericis laicos*, directed against Edward I of England (1272–1307) and Philip IV the Fair of France (1285–1314). Boniface distinguished clergy and laity, but in the haste of the situation did not do so tactfully. He forbade the clergy to pay taxes without papal assent. Philip replied by forbidding all transport of valuables to Rome. The pope had to back down and even sought a reconciliation by canonizing Philip's grandfather, Louis IX (and so we have St. Louis).

The contest between Boniface and Philip was renewed in 1301 when the papal legate was brought to trial. Boniface issued in 1302 the bull *Unam sanctam*, influenced by the political theology of Giles of Rome and James of Viterbo. A noble document if one leaves polemical considerations aside, *Unam sanctam* summarizes the papal theory of the twelfth and thirteenth centuries, but, like a building often, it was the symbol of an age gone by.

Much of the content of *Unam sanctam* is a synthesis of earlier teaching: There is one, holy, catholic, and apostolic church outside of which there is no salvation; there is one body and one Head, whose representative is the pope; there are two swords, one (spiritual) to be used by the church by the hand of the priest and the other (temporal) by the hand of the king under the direction of the priest for the church; no one may judge the pope, and the spiritual power has the right to guide the secular power and judge it when it does not act rightly; and this relationship is ordained by God.

Then at the end of *Unam sanctam* comes the famous conclusion:

> Furthermore, we declare, state, and define that it is altogether necessary to salvation for every human creature to be subject to the Roman pontiff.

Students of the document have differed whether it claims a direct control of secular power. The concluding words, derived from Thomas Aquinas (who was speaking of spiritual powers) and offensive to Protestants, have become an embarrassment in a more ecumenical age and are now explained as applying to the controversy at hand and not having the universal sweep they appear to pronounce.

John of Paris spoke to the conflict between the French king and the pope in *On the Royal and the Papal Power*, setting forth a political theology that would limit the papacy's jurisdiction in temporal affairs. The king took a more direct approach to limiting the pope's actions. In alliance with the Colonna faction in Rome, he had Boniface kidnapped. The people of Anagni rescued the pope after three days, but he died in Rome a month later.

Boniface's claims for the papacy placed him in the succession of Gregory VII and Innocent III, but his failure foreshadowed the diminishing political power of the papacy.

C. Aftermath

Boniface's second successor, Clement V, in 1305 transferred the papal residence to Avignon (1309), a principality ceded to the pope at the Council of Lyons but under French influence. Clement did not consider this move unusual, for other popes had lived elsewhere to avoid the political machinations at Rome, but the popes stayed in Avignon so long (until 1377) and were under such French influence that this nearly seventy-year period came to be known as the Babylonian Captivity of the Papacy.

IX. SUMMARY

With its mixture of triumphs and failures the church history of the thirteenth century is no different from other centuries, distinguished only by being more spectacular in its successes and shortcomings.

On the threshold of the fourteenth century an observer would have been uncertain whether the glories or the challenges of the thirteenth century would predominate in the years ahead. The fourteenth and fifteenth centuries in historical hindsight are referred to as the late Middle Ages, the Renaissance, or pre-Reformation — or all of these. Whatever the preferred designation, the events of that period developed out of the thoughts and institutions that had preceded it. Strands from the early and medieval church encountered new impetuses in the fourteenth and fifteenth centuries that would lead to new alignments in the sixteenth and seventeenth centuries.

This narrative, like the ship of the church that is its subject, has traversed many currents of institutional ebb and flow and intellectual torrent. The church was buffeted by winds of doctrine and sea changes of civilization: from early theological discussion of its fundamental beliefs to impressive summas of philosophical theology, from Semitic to Greco-Roman to Germanic and Slavic cultures.

The church developed from an insignificant group of disciples to a persecuted minority to a triumphant state church to an embattled institution to a world ruling power to an authority under challenge. Forces of vitality and renewal always had arisen among the followers of Jesus, and they would again in the trying times to follow.

FOR FURTHER STUDY

Grundmann, Herbert. *Religious Movements in the Middle Ages.* Notre Dame, IN: University of Notre Dame Press, 1995.

Lambert, Malcolm D. *Medieval Heresy: Popular Movements from the Gregorian Reform to the Reformation.* Oxford: Blackwell, 2002.

McGinn, Bernard. *The Calabrian Abbott: Joachim of Fiore in the History of Western Thought.* New York: Macmillan, 1985.

Moore, R. I. *The War on Heresy.* Cambridge, MA: Belknap Press, 2012.

Peters, Edward. *Inquisition.* Berkeley: University of California Press, 1989.

Sackville, L. J. *Heresy and Heretics in the Thirteenth Century: The Textual Representations.* York, UK: York Medieval Press, 2011.

General Bibliography

REFERENCE WORKS

Atlas of the Christian Church. Edited by Henry Chadwick and G. R. Evans. New York: Facts on File, 1987.

Atlas of the Early Christian World. Edited by F. van der Meer and Christine Mohrmann. London: Nelson, 1958.

Atlas of Medieval Europe. Edited by Angus Mackay with David Ditchburn. London: Routledge, 1997.

Augustine through the Ages: An Encyclopedia. Edited by Allan D. Fitzgerald. Grand Rapids: Eerdmans, 1999.

Dictionary of Early Christian Literature. Edited by Siegmar Doupp and Wilhelm Geerlings. New York: Crossroad, 2000.

Dictionary of the Middle Ages. Edited by Joseph Reese Strayer. 13 vols. New York: Scribner, 1982–1989.

Encyclopedia of Early Christianity. Edited by Everett Ferguson. 2nd ed. 2 vols. New York: Garland/Taylor and Francis, 1997.

Encyclopedia of the Early Church. Edited by Angelo DiBerardino. 2 vols. Cambridge: James Clarke, 1992.

The Fathers of the Church: A Comprehensive Introduction. Hubertus Drobner. Peabody, MA: Hendrickson, 2005.

History of Theology. Vol. 1: *The Patristic Period.* Edited by Angelo Di Berardino and Basil Studer. Vol. 2: *The Middle Ages.* Edited by Giulio D'Onofrio. Collegeville, MN: Liturgical Press, 1997, 2008.

Medieval France: An Encyclopedia. Edited by William W. Kibler and Grover A. Zinn. New York: Garland, 1995.

The Oxford Dictionary of Byzantium. Edited by Alexander P. Kazhdan. 3 vols. Oxford: Oxford University Press, 1991.

The Oxford Dictionary of the Christian Church. 3rd ed. revised. Edited by F. L. Cross and E. A. Livingstone. Oxford: Oxford University Press, 2005.

OTHER WORKS

Atiya, Aziz S. *A History of Eastern Christianity.* London: Methuen, 1968.

Bainton, Roland H. *Early Christianity.* Princeton, NJ: Van Nostrand, 1960.

Idem. *The Medieval Church.* Princeton, NJ: Van Nostrand, 1962.

Chadwick, Henry. *The Church in Ancient Society: From Galilee to Gregory the Great.* Oxford: Clarendon, 2001.

Cook, William A., and Ronald B. Herzman. *The Medieval World View: An Introduction.* New York: Oxford University Press, 2013.

Copleston, F. C. *A History of Medieval Philosophy.* New York: Harper & Row, 1972.

Cross, R. *Duns Scotus.* New York: Oxford University Press, 1999.

Deanesly, Margaret. *A History of the Medieval Church, 590–1500.* 9th ed. London: Methuen, 1972.

Evans, G. R. *The Medieval Theologians.* Oxford: Blackwell, 2001.

Ferguson, Everett, ed. *Studies in Early Christianity.* 18 vols. New York: Garland, 1993.

Idem. *Recent Studies in Early Christianity.* 6 vols. New York: Garland, 1999.

Frend, W. H. C. *The Rise of Christianity.* Philadelphia: Fortress, 1984.

Gregory, Timothy E. *A History of Byzantium.* Oxford: Wiley-Blackwell, 2010.

Hussey, J. M. *The Orthodox Church in the Byzantine Empire.* Oxford: Clarendon, 1986.

Jedin, Hubert, and John Dolan, eds. *Handbook of Church History.*
> Vol. 1: Karl Baus, *From the Apostolic Community to Constantine.* London: Burns & Oates, 1965.
> Vol. 2: Karl Baus, Hans-Georg Beck, Eugen Ewig, and Hermann Josef Vogt, *The Imperial Church from Constantine to the Early Middle Ages.* New York: Seabury, 1980.
> Vol. 3: Friedrich Kempf, Hans-Georg Beck, Eugen Ewig, and Josef Andreas Jungmann, *The Church in the Age of Feudalism.* New York: Herder and Herder, 1969.
> Vol. 4: Hans-Georg Beck, Karl August Fink, Josef Glazik, Erwin Iserloh, and Hans Wolter, *From the High Middle Ages to the Eve of the Reformation.* New York: Seabury, 1980.

Logan, F. Donald. *A History of the Church in the Middle Ages.* London: Routledge, 2012.

Nieuwenhove, Rik. *An Introduction to Medieval Theology.* Cambridge: Cambridge University Press, 2012.

Pelikan, Jaroslav. *The Christian Tradition.* Chicago: University of Chicago Press.
> Vol. 1: The Emergence of the Catholic Tradition (100–600) (1971).
> Vol. 2: The Spirit of Eastern Christendom (600–1700) (1974).
> Vol. 3: The Growth of Medieval Theology (600–1300) (1978).

Southern, R. W. *Western Society and the Church in the Middle Ages.* Harmondsworth, UK: Penguin, 1970.

Thomson, John A. F. *The Western Church in the Middle Ages.* New York: Oxford University Press, 1998.

Ware, Timothy Kallistos. *The Orthodox Church.* Baltimore: Penguin, 1969.

Wilken, Robert L. *The First Thousand Years: A Global History of Christianity.* New Haven: Yale University Press, 2012.

Young, Frances, Lewis Ayres, and Andrew Louth, eds. *The Cambridge History of Early Christian Literature.* Cambridge: Cambridge University Press, 2004.

Timeline from Christ to Pre-Reformation

(c. = circa, "about"; fl = flourit, "flourished")

Dates	Political Rulers	Writers/Thinkers	Bishops	Events
30/33				Death of Jesus
54–68	Nero			Deaths of James, Peter, Paul
70				Destruction of Jerusalem
81–96	Domitian			
98–117	Trajan	Pliny Younger		
c. 100–156		Apostolic Fathers		
117–38	Hadrian			
117–211		Apologists		
c. 135–c. 165		Valentinus		
144				Marcion disfellowshipped
c. 160				Montanist movement begins
c. 160–215		Clement Alexandria		
161–80	Marcus Aurelius			Martyrs of Lyons
c. 180	Irenaeus, fl.			
185–251	Origen			
189–99			Victor	Paschal controversy
190–230				Monarchian controversy
193–211	Septimius Severus			
197–222		Tertullian, fl.		
200–258		Cyprian		
203				Martyrdom of Perpetua
217–22			Callistus	
249–51	Decius			Persecution
251–53			Cornelius	Novatian schism
253–58	Valerian			Persecution
254–57			Stephen	
c. 260–c. 339		Eusebius Caesarea		
c. 271				Anthony adopts ascetic life
284–305	Diocletian			Great Persecution
c. 300–336		Arius, fl.		
c. 300–373		Athanasius		
c. 301				Armenia adopts Christianity
306–37	Constantine			
c. 306–73		Ephraem		
311				Donatist schism begins
313				"Edict of Milan"
323				Pachomius adopts cenobite life
325				Council of Nicaea
329–390		Gregory Nazianzus		

Dates	Political Rulers	Writers/Thinkers	Bishops	Events
330				Byzantium becomes capital
330–79		Basil the Great		
331–95		Gregory Nyssa		
337–52			Julius	
337–61	Constantius II			
339–97		Ambrose		
341				Ulfilas' mission to Goths
347–407		John Chrysostom		
347–420		Jerome		
c. 350				King of Ethiopia baptized
350–428		Theodore Mopsuestia		
c. 350–425		Pelagius		
354–430		Augustine		
361–63	Julian			
365–433		John Cassian		
366–84			Damasus	
c. 375–444		Cyril Alexandria		
379–95	Theodosius I			
381				Council of Constantinople
401–7			Innocent I	
410				Alaric sacks Rome
428–31			Nestorius	
431				Council of Ephesus
432				Patrick's mission to Ireland
439				Vandals take Carthage
440–61			Leo I	
444–451			Dioscorus	
451				Council of Chalcedon
451				Attila defeated
455				Vandals sack Rome
476				Last Roman emperor deposed
481–511	Clovis			
492–96			Gelasius	
493–525	Theodoric			
c. 500		Pseudo-Dionysius, fl.		
512–38			Severus Antioch	
527–65	Justinian			
529				Council of Orange
529				Benedict founds Monte Cassino
553				Council of Constantinople II
c. 580–662		Maximus Confessor		
586–601	Reccared			
589				Third council of Toledo
590–604			Gregory I	
596				Augustine's mission to England

CHURCH HISTORY

Dates	Political Rulers	Writers/Thinkers	Bishops	Events
610–641	Heraclius			
622				Hegira of Muhammad
636				Muslims take Jerusalem
c. 650–c. 750		John of Damascus		
664				Council of Whitby
673–735		Venerable Bede		
680–81				Council of Constantinople III
697				Muslims take Carthage
712				Muslims take Toledo
716–54				Mission of Boniface to Germany
717–41	Leo III Isaurian			
732				Charles Martel defeats Muslims
754				Stephen II anoints Pippin
768–814	Charlemagne			
c. 780–856		Rabanus Maurus		
787				Council of Nicaea II
800				Charlemagne crowned by Leo III
831–68				First Eucharistic controversy
843				Division of Charlemagne's realm
845–82			Hincmar	
858–67			Nicholas I	
858–67, 878–68			Photius	
864				Mission of Cyril and Methodius
871–99	Alfred of Wessex			
910				Cluny founded
910–29	Duke Wenceslas			
936–73	Otto I			
965				Conversion of Harald Buetooth
966				Baptism of Prince Mieczyslaw
988				Baptism of Vladimir
997–1038	Stephen I Hungary			
c. 1000–c. 1100				Middle Byzantine art fl.
1016–30	Olaf Haraldsson			
1033–1109		Anselm		
1039–56	Henry III			
1043–58			Michael Cerularius	
1049–54			Leo IX	
1049–79				Second Eucharistic controversy
c. 1050–c. 1250				Romanesque architecture, fl.
1054				Schism between East and West
1056–1106	Henry IV			
1073–85			Gregory VII	
1074–1122				Investiture controversy
1079–1142		Abelard		
1090–1153		Bernard of Clairvaux		

Dates	Political Rulers	Writers/Thinkers	Bishops	Events
1096–99				First Crusade
1098				Monastery at Cîteaux founded
1098–1160		Hildegard of Bingen		
1100–1160		Peter Lombard		
1118				Knights Templar founded
1122				Concordat of Worms
1123				First Lateran Council
c. 1135–1202		Joachim of Fiore		
c. 1140–c. 1300				Gothic architecture, fl.
c. 1141				Gratian's Decretal
1147–49				Second Crusade
1152–97	Frederick Barbarossa			
1154–89	Henry II England			
1162–70			Thomas Becket	
1173				Waldensian movement begins
1187–92				Third Crusade
1198–1216			Innocent III	
c. 1200				Organization of universities
1202–4				Fourth Crusade
1209–29				Crusade against Albigensians
1210				Papal approval of Franciscans
1211–50	Frederick II			
1215				*Magna Carta*
1215				Fourth Lateran Council
1215				Dominicans founded
1217–74		Bonaventure		
c. 1220–c. 1292		Roger Bacon		
1225–74		Thomas Aquinas		
1226	Louis IX France			
1226–85	Charles of Anjou			
1229				Rules for Inquisition
c. 1248–98		Peter John Olivi		
c. 1265–1308		Duns Scotus		
1274				Council of Lyons
1291				Fall of Acre to Muslims
1294–1303			Boniface VIII	

Index

CHURCH HISTORY